COLLECTOR'S EDITION

Fruits Basket

NATSUKI TAKAYA

2

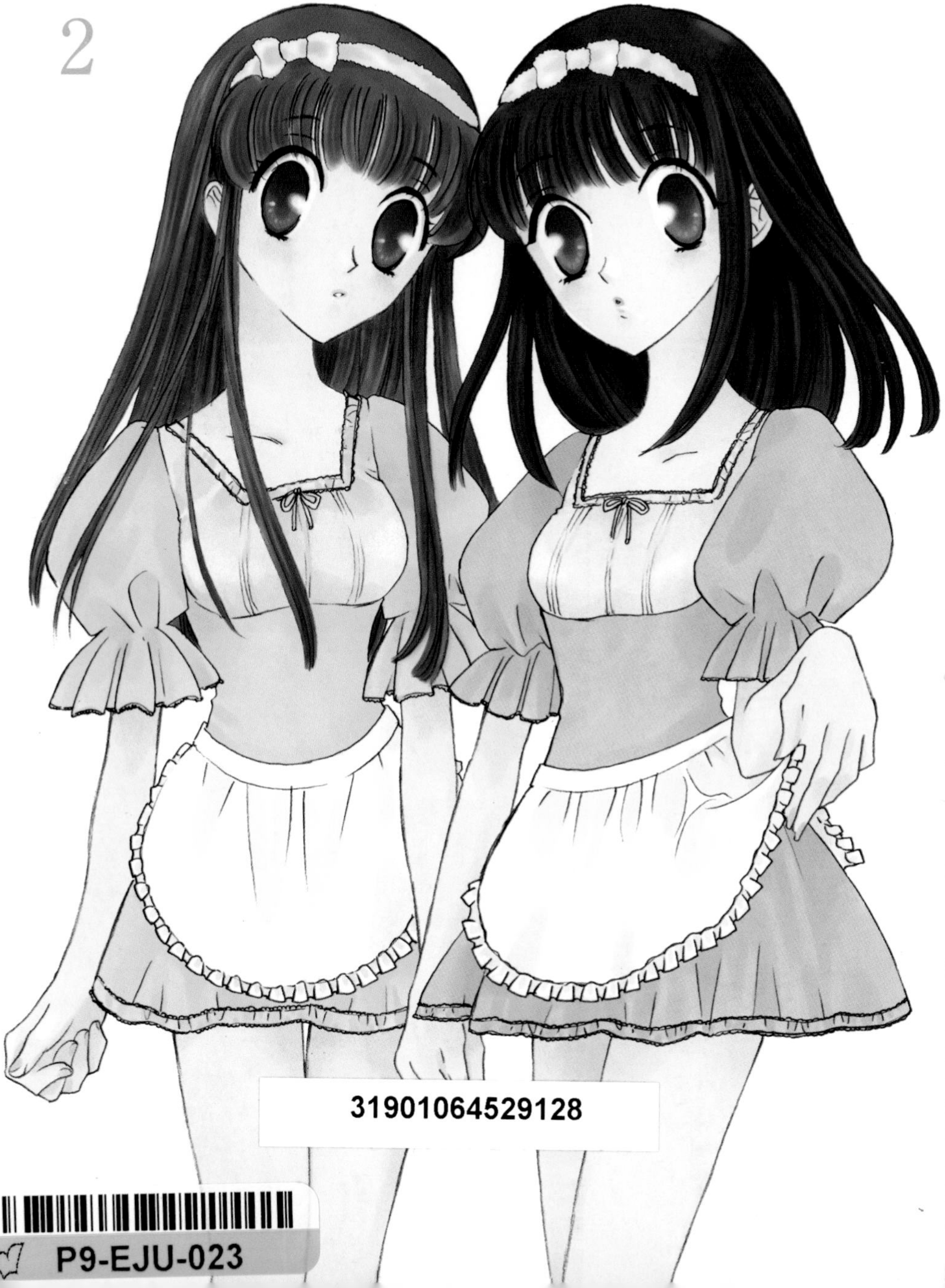

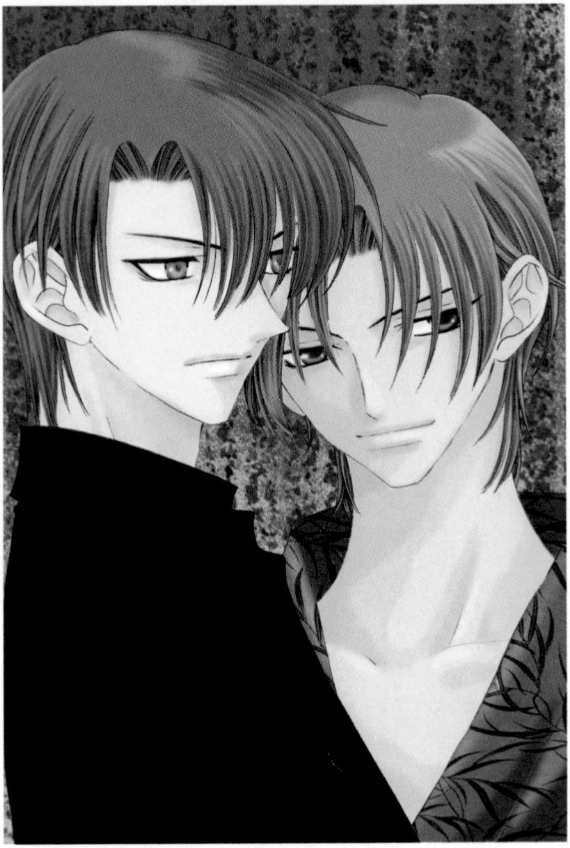
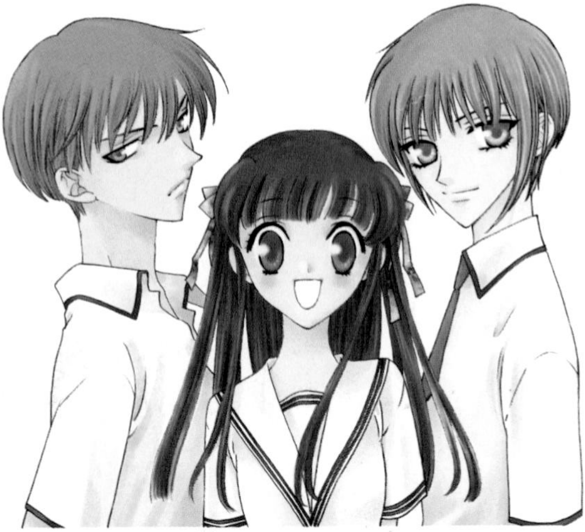
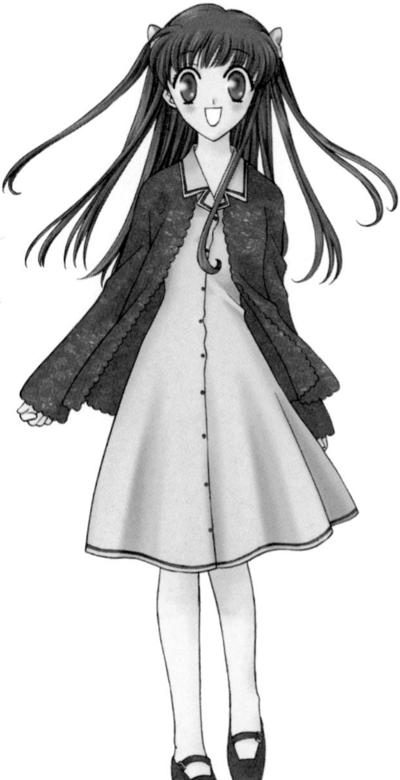

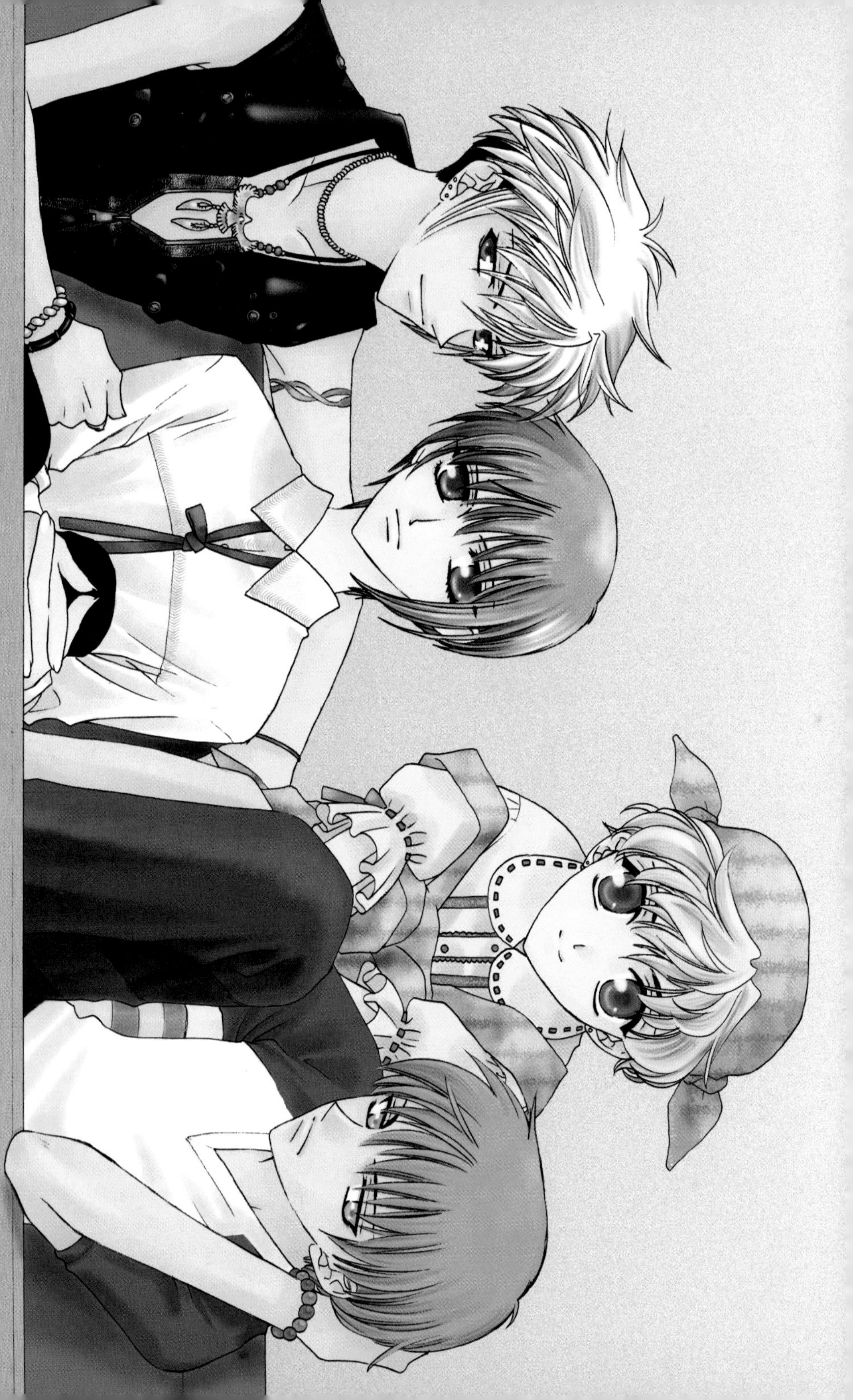

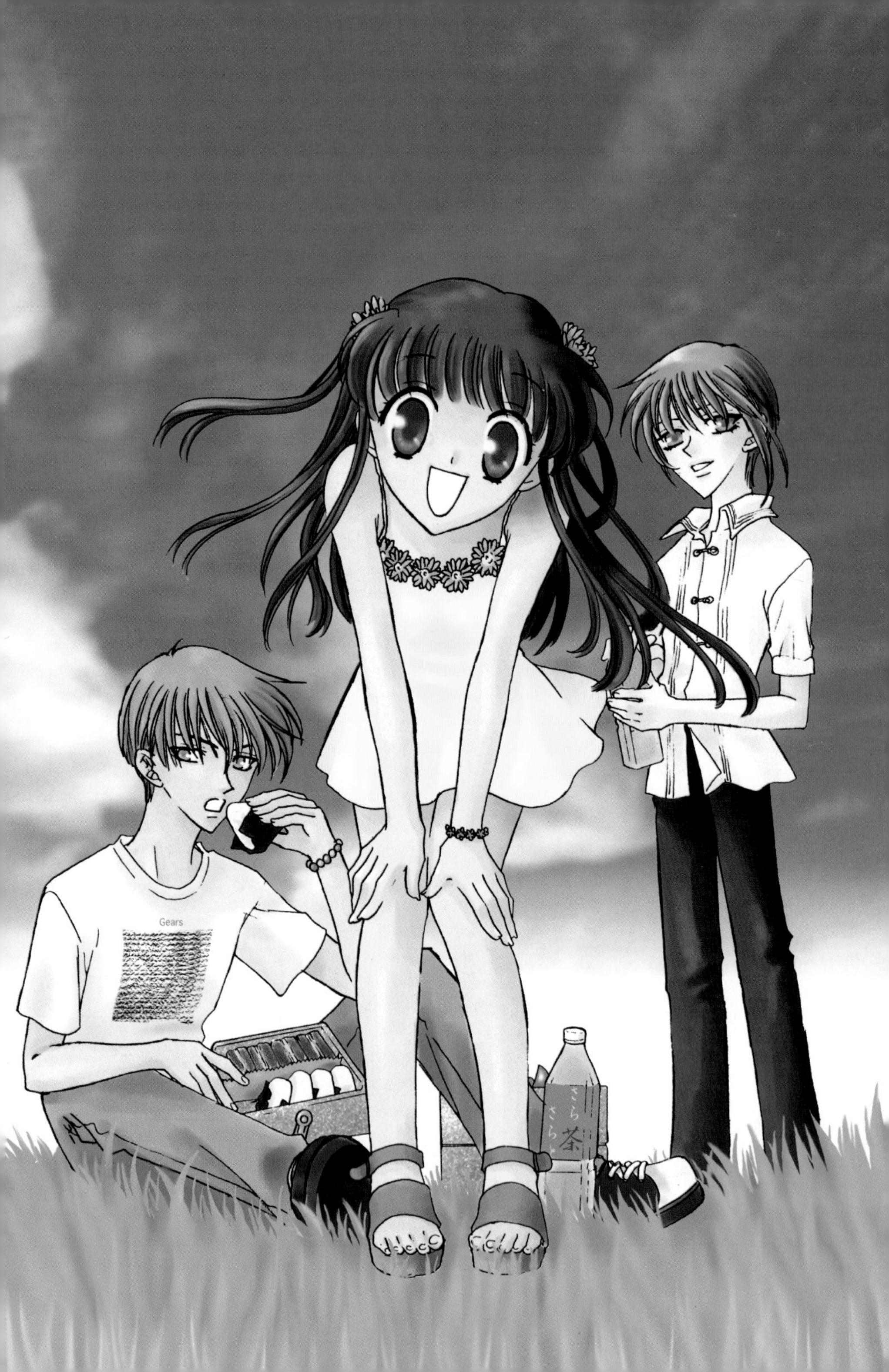
Gears

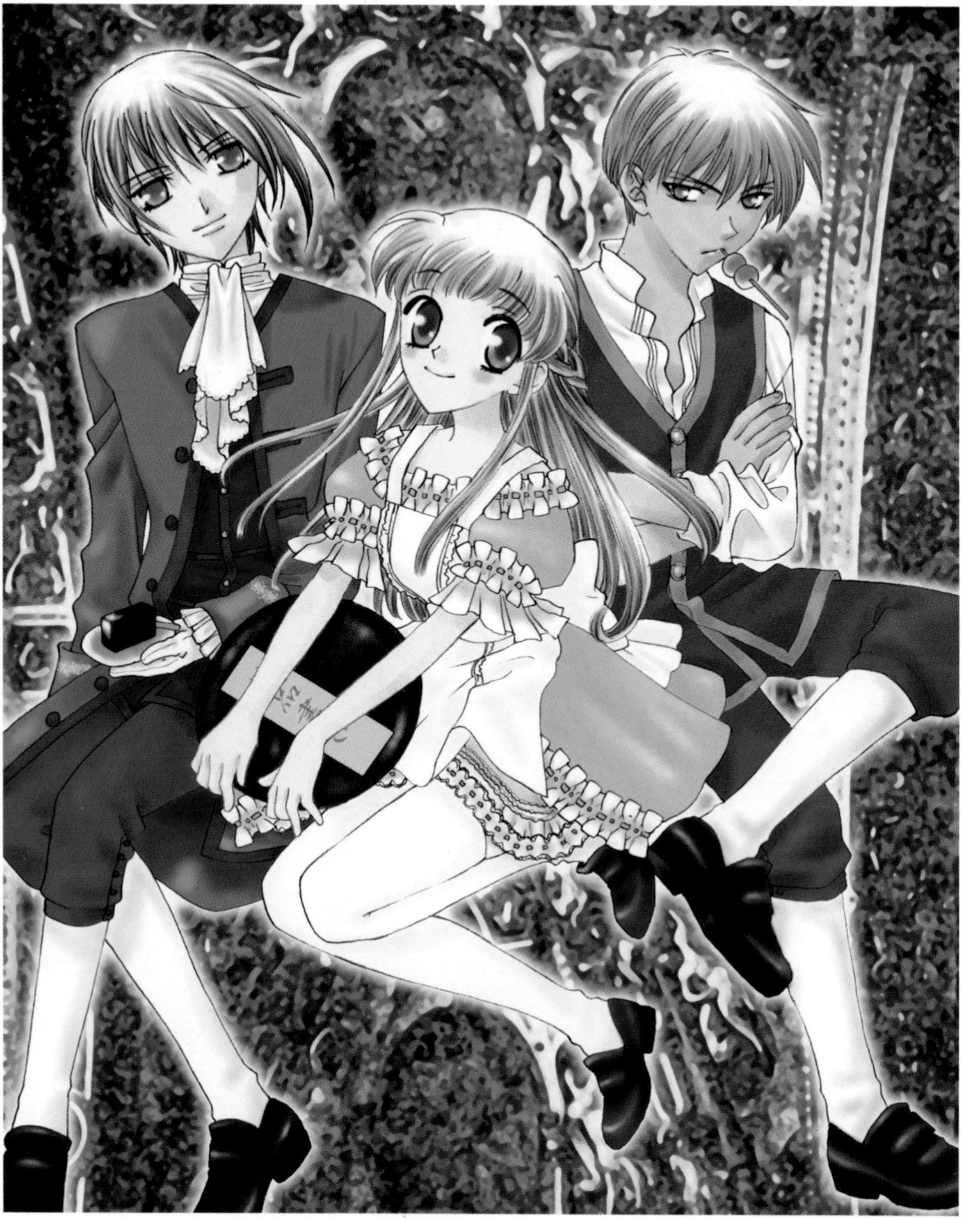

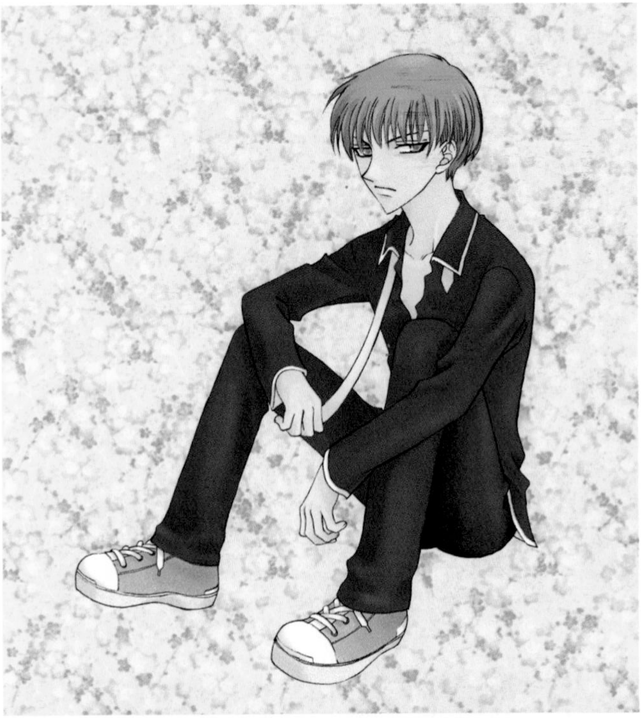
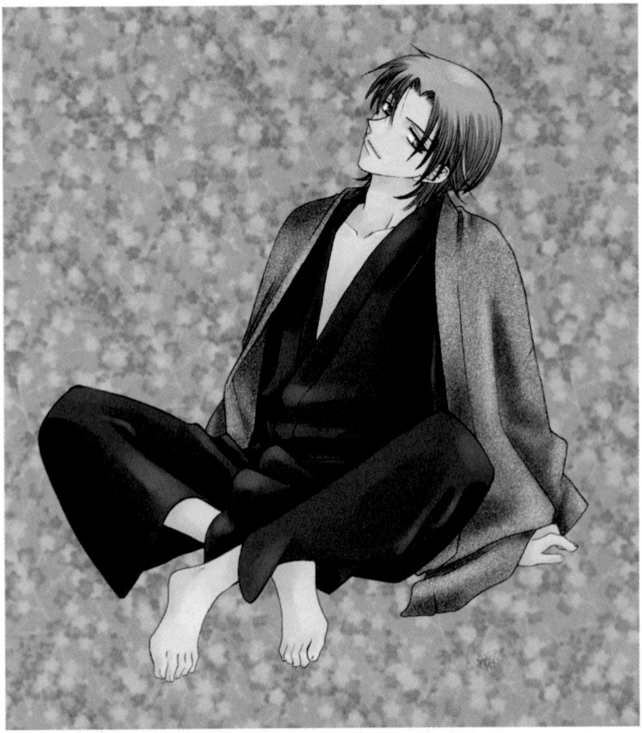

Fruits Basket

Chapter 13

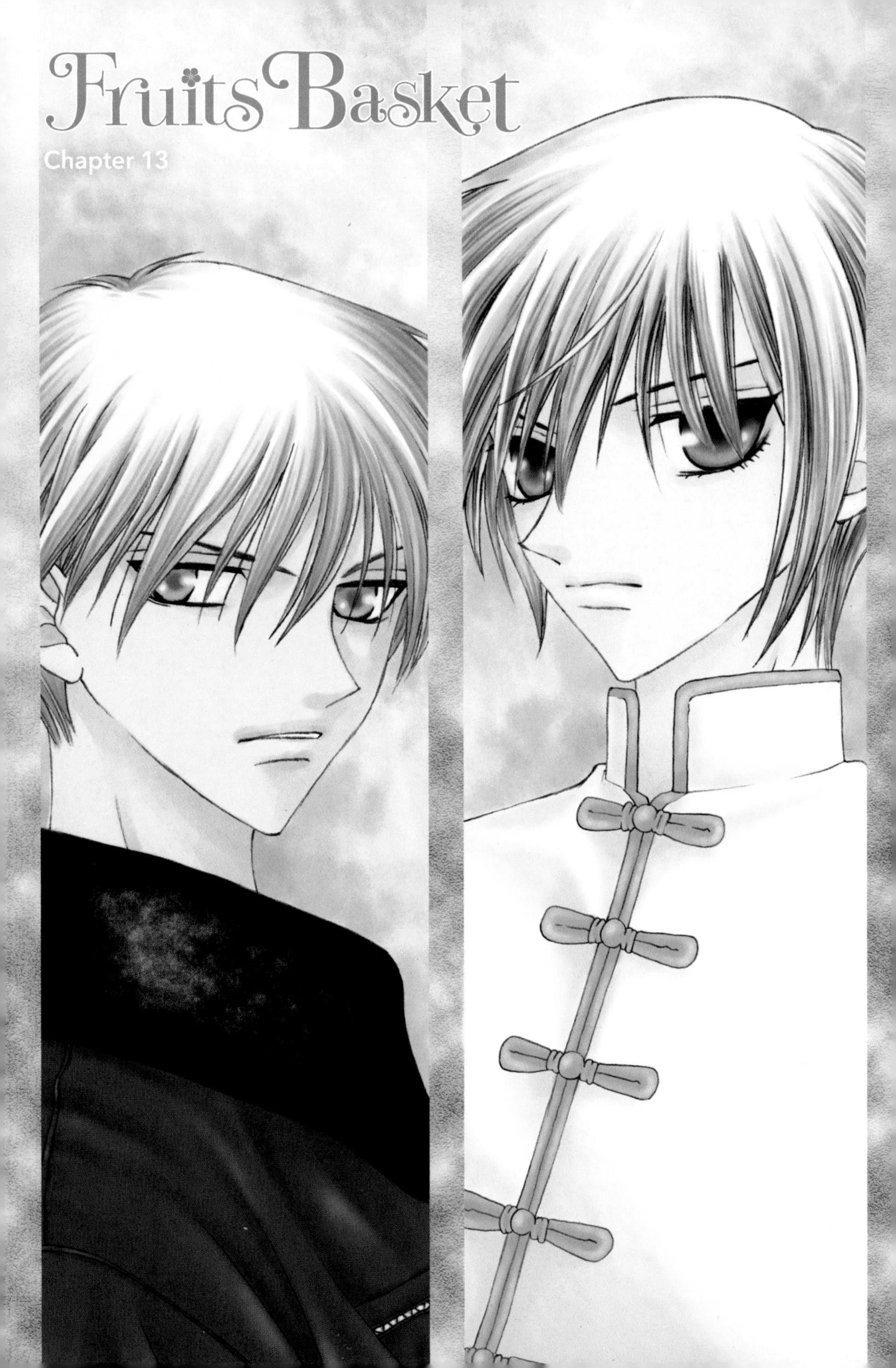

TABLE OF CONTENTS

COLLECTOR'S EDITION

Fruits Basket 2

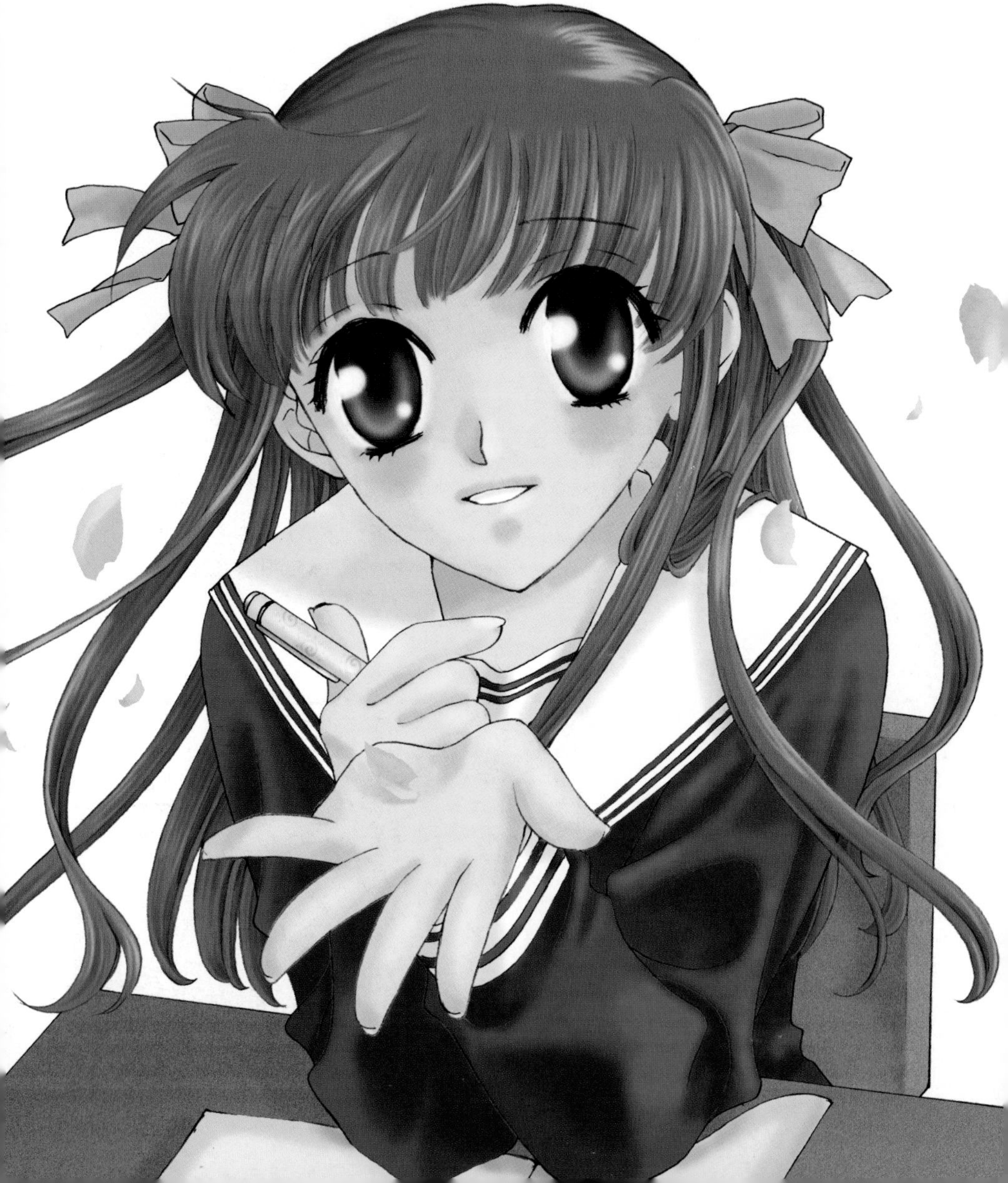

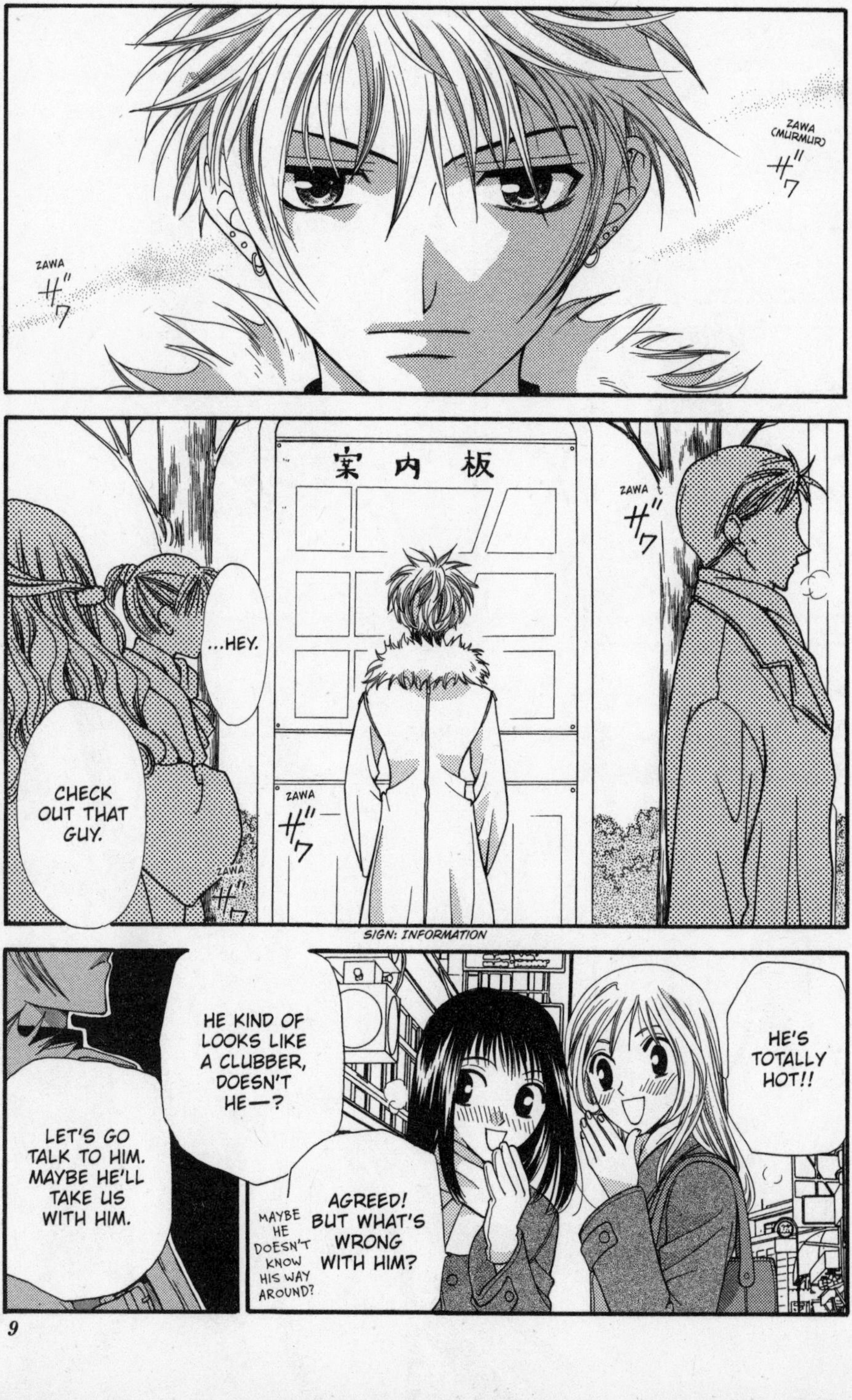
ZAWA (MURMUR)
ザワ
ZAWA
ザワ
案内板
ZAWA
ザワ
...HEY.
CHECK OUT THAT GUY.
ZAWA
ザワ
ZAWA
ザワ
SIGN: INFORMATION
HE'S TOTALLY HOT!!
HE KIND OF LOOKS LIKE A CLUBBER, DOESN'T HE—?
AGREED! BUT WHAT'S WRONG WITH HIM?
MAYBE HE DOESN'T KNOW HIS WAY AROUND?
LET'S GO TALK TO HIM. MAYBE HE'LL TAKE US WITH HIM.

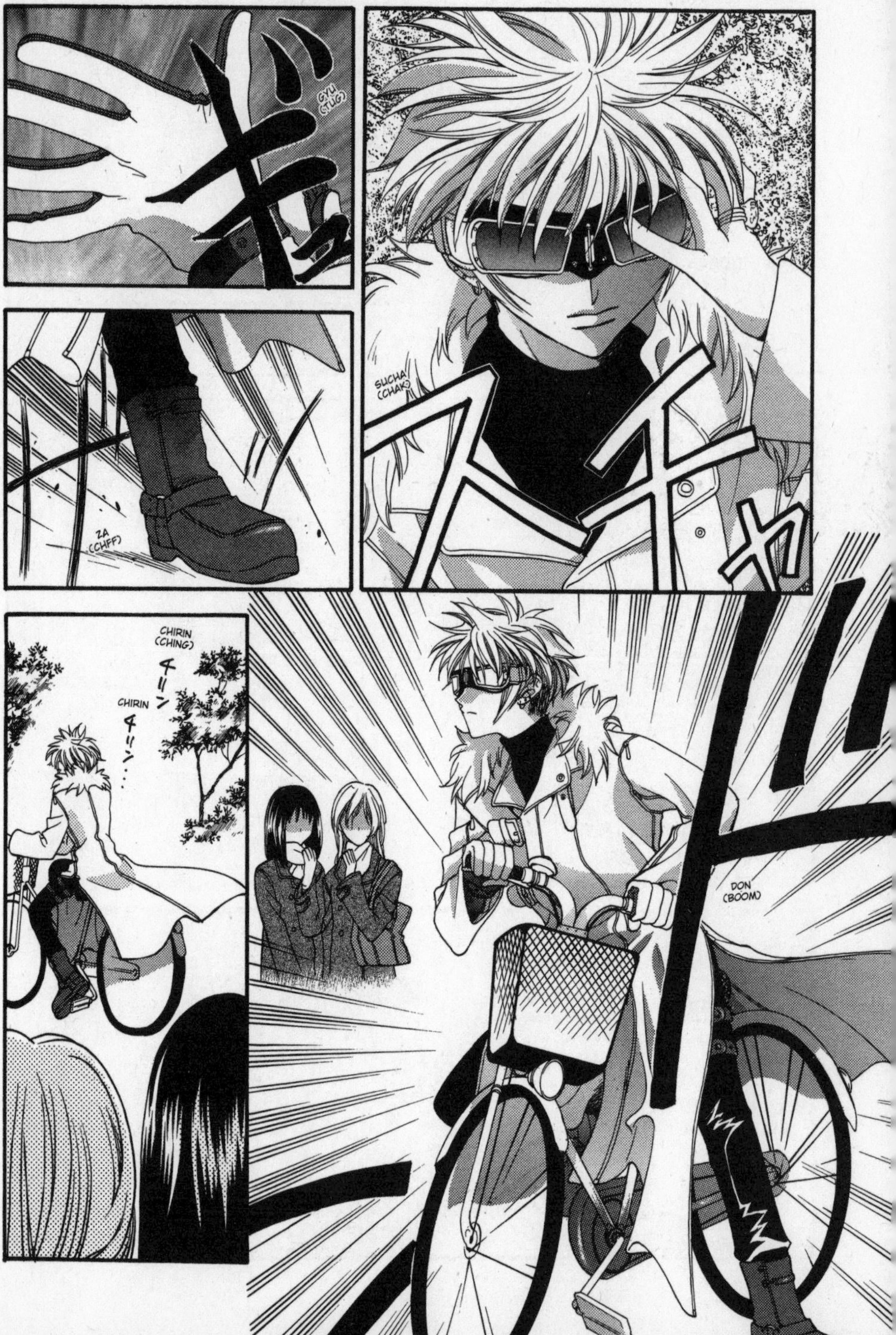
SUCHA (CHAK)
GYU (TUG)
ZA (CHFF)
DON (BOOM)
CHIRIN (CHING)
CHIRIN

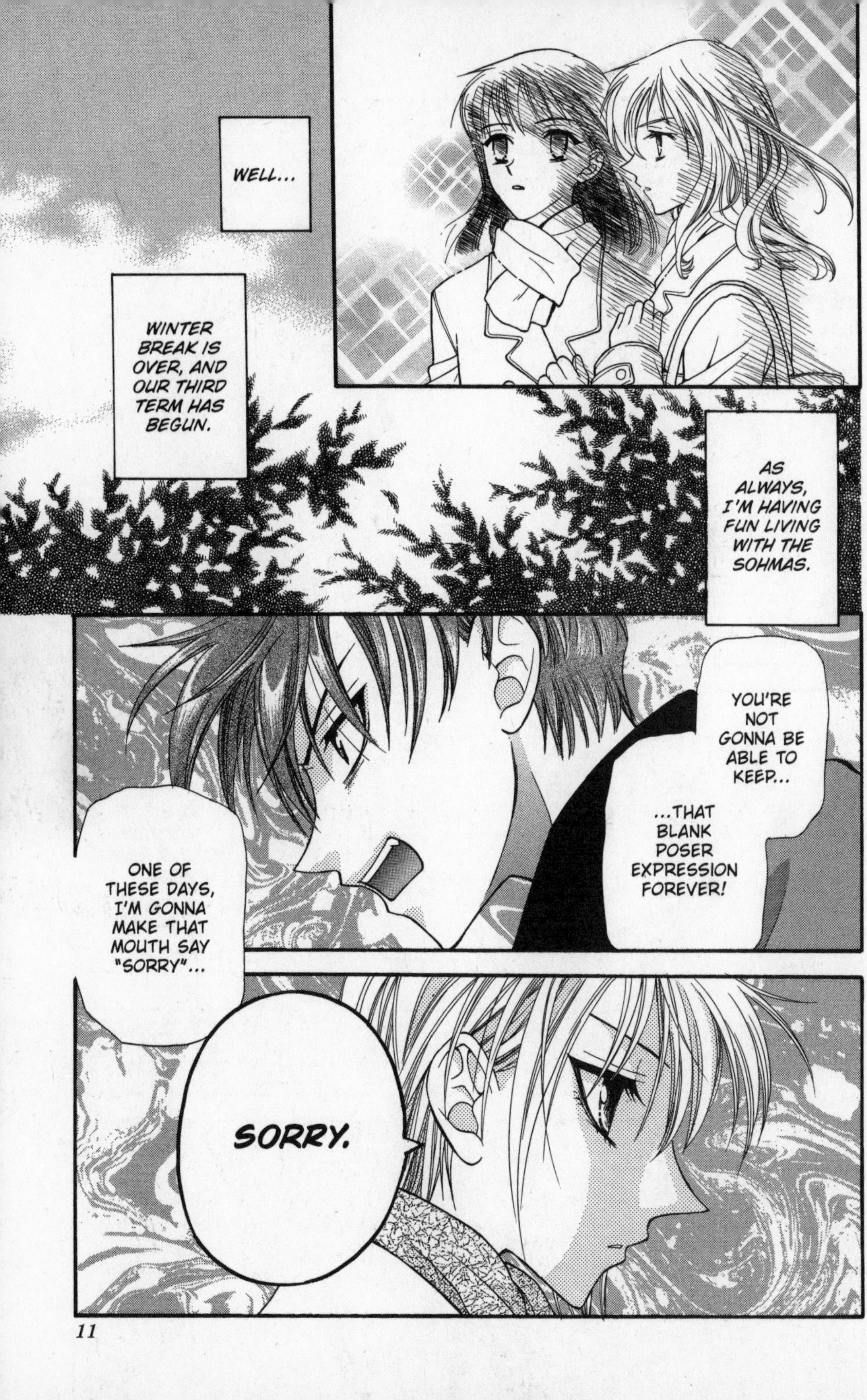
WELL...
WINTER BREAK IS OVER, AND OUR THIRD TERM HAS BEGUN.
AS ALWAYS, I'M HAVING FUN LIVING WITH THE SOHMAS.
YOU'RE NOT GONNA BE ABLE TO KEEP...
...THAT BLANK POSER EXPRESSION FOREVER!
ONE OF THESE DAYS, I'M GONNA MAKE THAT MOUTH SAY "SORRY"...
SORRY.

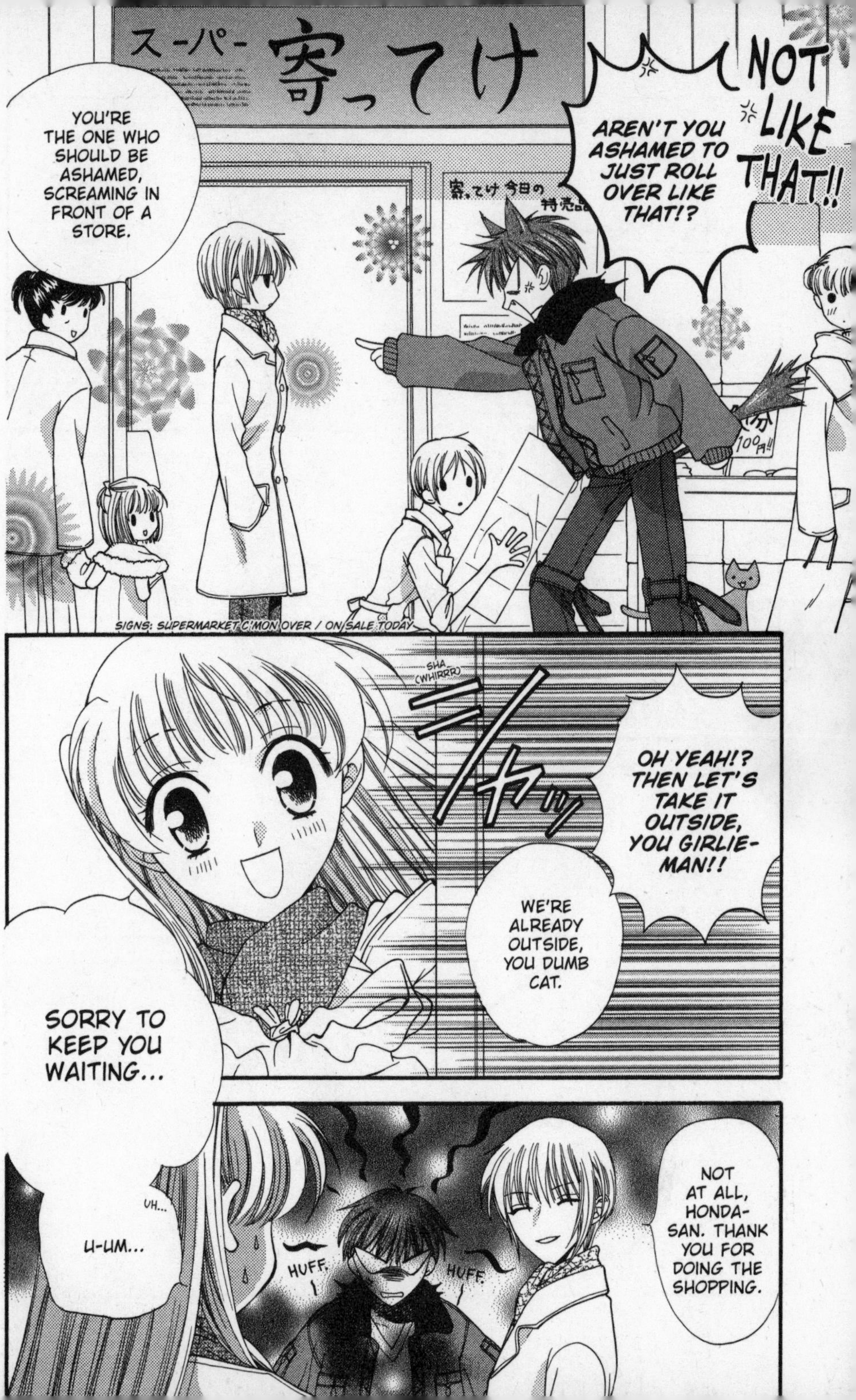
NOT LIKE THAT!!
AREN'T YOU ASHAMED TO JUST ROLL OVER LIKE THAT!?
スーパー 寄ってけ
寄ってけ 今日の 特売品
YOU'RE THE ONE WHO SHOULD BE ASHAMED, SCREAMING IN FRONT OF A STORE.
SIGNS: SUPERMARKET C'MON OVER / ON SALE TODAY
OH YEAH!? THEN LET'S TAKE IT OUTSIDE, YOU GIRLIE-MAN!!
WE'RE ALREADY OUTSIDE, YOU DUMB CAT.
SHA (WHIRRR)
SORRY TO KEEP YOU WAITING...
NOT AT ALL, HONDA-SAN. THANK YOU FOR DOING THE SHOPPING.
HUFF
HUFF
UH...
U-UM...

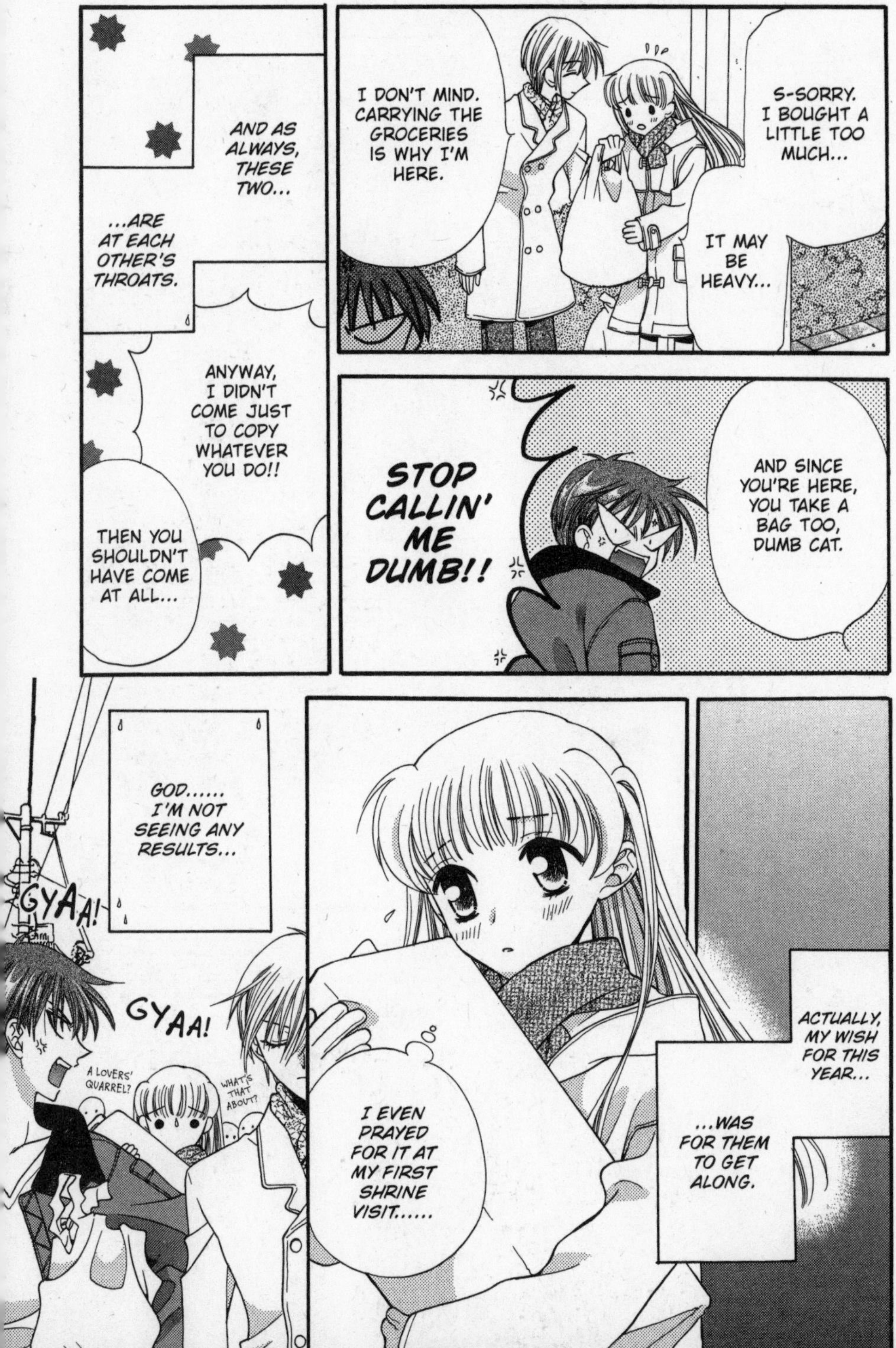
S-SORRY. I BOUGHT A LITTLE TOO MUCH...
IT MAY BE HEAVY...
I DON'T MIND. CARRYING THE GROCERIES IS WHY I'M HERE.
AND SINCE YOU'RE HERE, YOU TAKE A BAG TOO, DUMB CAT.
STOP CALLIN' ME DUMB!!
AND AS ALWAYS, THESE TWO...
...ARE AT EACH OTHER'S THROATS.
ANYWAY, I DIDN'T COME JUST TO COPY WHATEVER YOU DO!!
THEN YOU SHOULDN'T HAVE COME AT ALL...
ACTUALLY, MY WISH FOR THIS YEAR...
...WAS FOR THEM TO GET ALONG.
I EVEN PRAYED FOR IT AT MY FIRST SHRINE VISIT......
GOD...... I'M NOT SEEING ANY RESULTS...
GYAA!
GYAA!
WHAT'S THAT ABOUT?
A LOVERS' QUARREL?

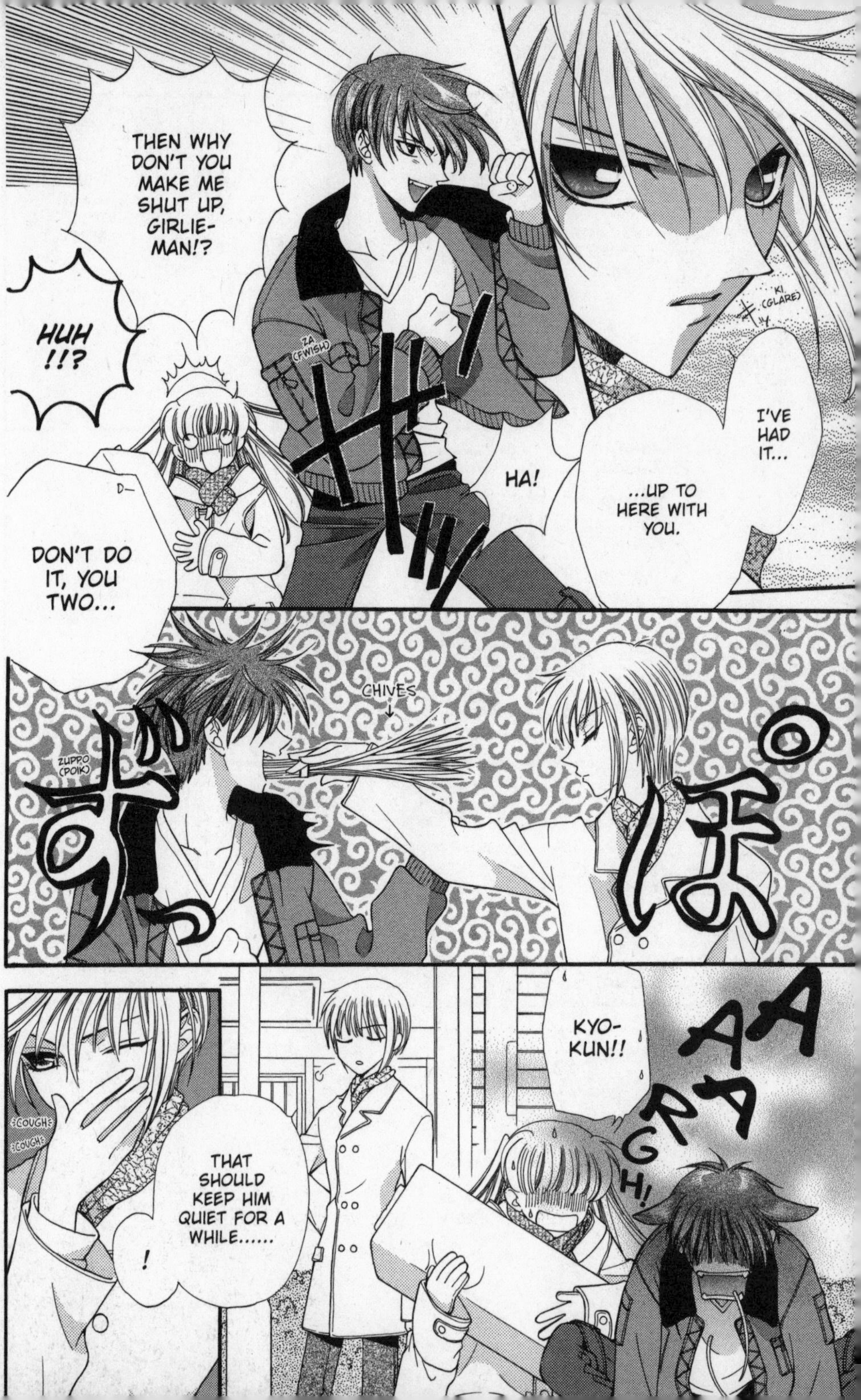
KI (GLARE)
I'VE HAD IT...
...UP TO HERE WITH YOU.
THEN WHY DON'T YOU MAKE ME SHUT UP, GIRLIE-MAN!?
HA!
ZA (FWISH)
HUH!!?
D—
DON'T DO IT, YOU TWO...
CHIVES
ZUPPO (POIK)
KYO-KUN!!
AAARGH!
THAT SHOULD KEEP HIM QUIET FOR A WHILE......
!
COUGH
COUGH

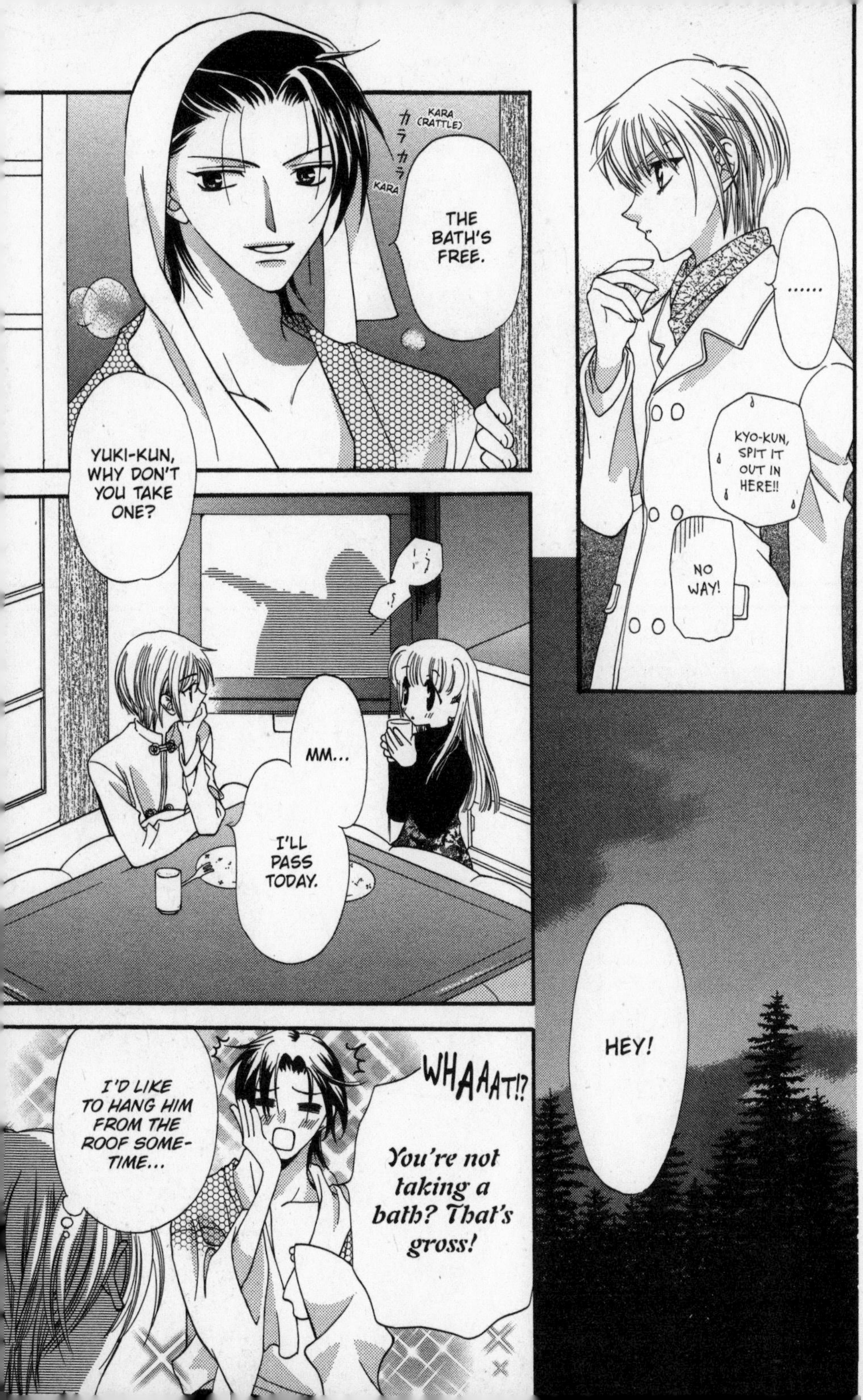
......
KYO-KUN, SPIT IT OUT IN HERE!!
NO WAY!
HEY!
カラ
KARA (RATTLE)
カラ
KARA
THE BATH'S FREE.
YUKI-KUN, WHY DON'T YOU TAKE ONE?
MM...
I'LL PASS TODAY.
WHAAAT!?
You're not taking a bath? That's gross!
I'D LIKE TO HANG HIM FROM THE ROOF SOME-TIME...

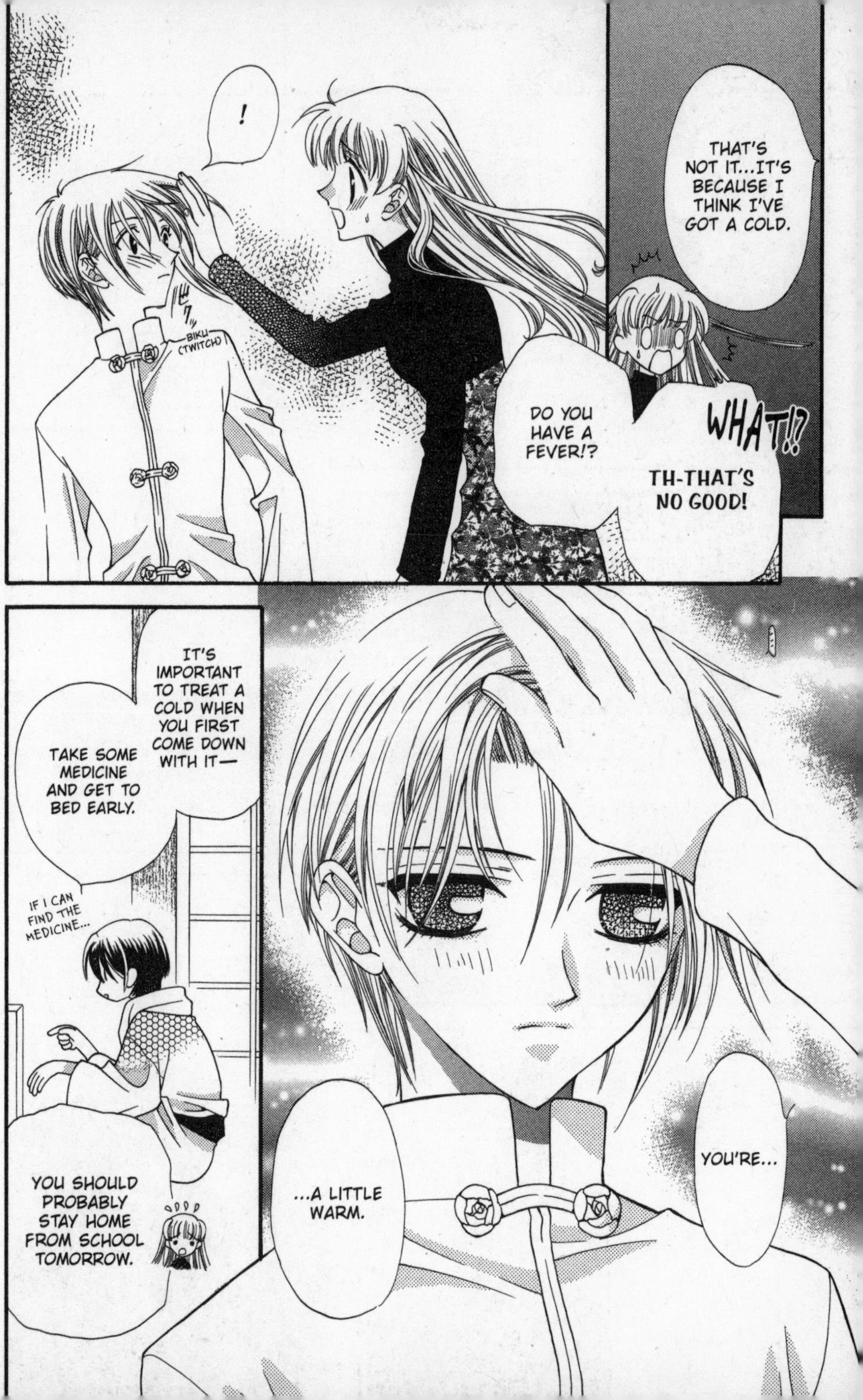
THAT'S NOT IT...IT'S BECAUSE I THINK I'VE GOT A COLD.
WHAT!?
TH-THAT'S NO GOOD!
DO YOU HAVE A FEVER!?
!
BIKU (TWITCH)
...
YOU'RE...
...A LITTLE WARM.
IT'S IMPORTANT TO TREAT A COLD WHEN YOU FIRST COME DOWN WITH IT—
TAKE SOME MEDICINE AND GET TO BED EARLY.
IF I CAN FIND THE MEDICINE...
YOU SHOULD PROBABLY STAY HOME FROM SCHOOL TOMORROW.

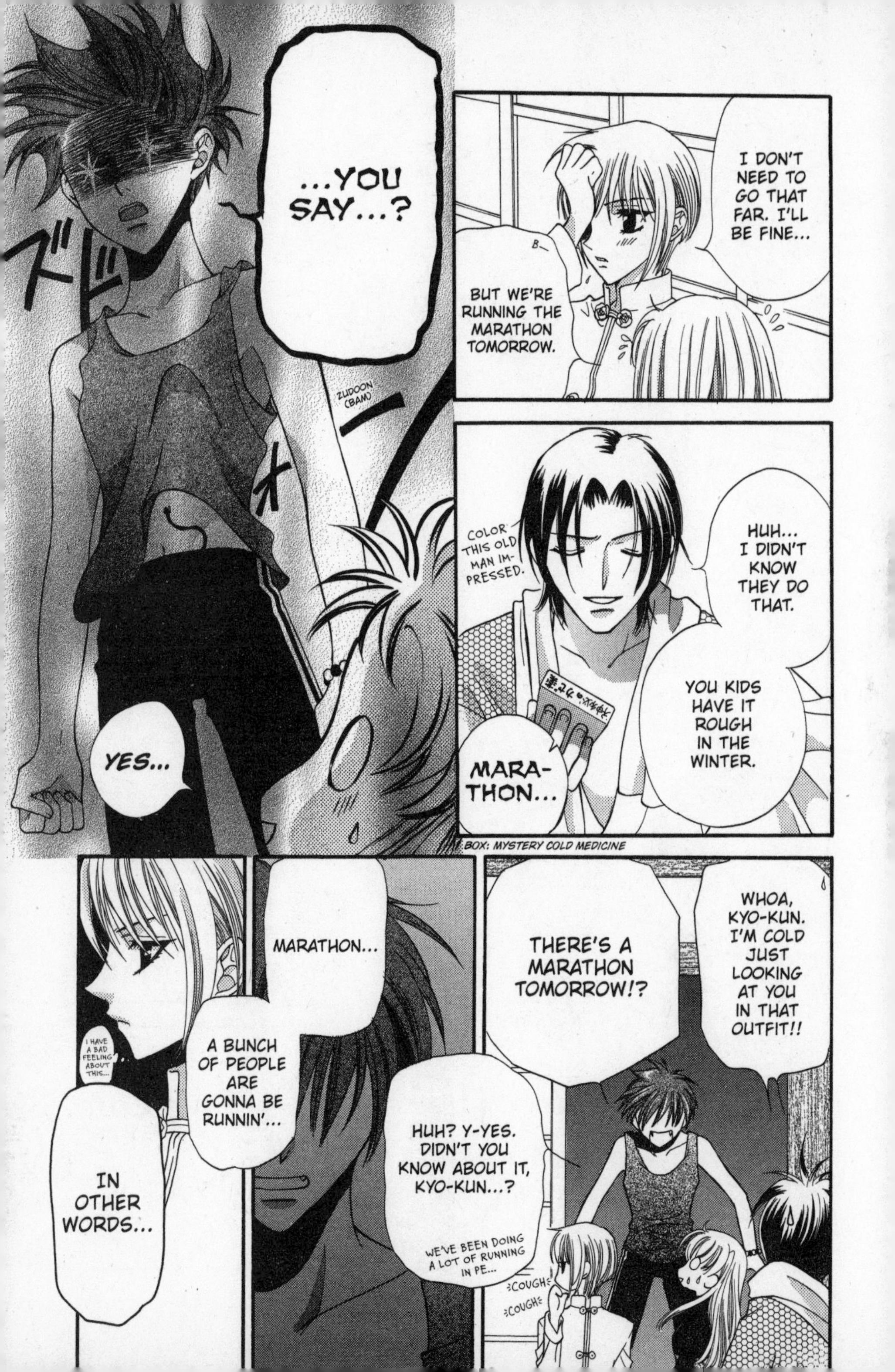
I DON'T NEED TO GO THAT FAR. I'LL BE FINE...
B-
BUT WE'RE RUNNING THE MARATHON TOMORROW.
HUH... I DIDN'T KNOW THEY DO THAT.
YOU KIDS HAVE IT ROUGH IN THE WINTER.
COLOR THIS OLD MAN IMPRESSED.
MARA-THON...
BOX: MYSTERY COLD MEDICINE
...YOU SAY...?
ZUDOON (BAM)
YES...
WHOA, KYO-KUN. I'M COLD JUST LOOKING AT YOU IN THAT OUTFIT!!
THERE'S A MARATHON TOMORROW!?
HUH? Y-YES. DIDN'T YOU KNOW ABOUT IT, KYO-KUN...?
WE'VE BEEN DOING A LOT OF RUNNING IN PE...
COUGH
COUGH
MARATHON...
A BUNCH OF PEOPLE ARE GONNA BE RUNNIN'...
I HAVE A BAD FEELING ABOUT THIS...
IN OTHER WORDS...

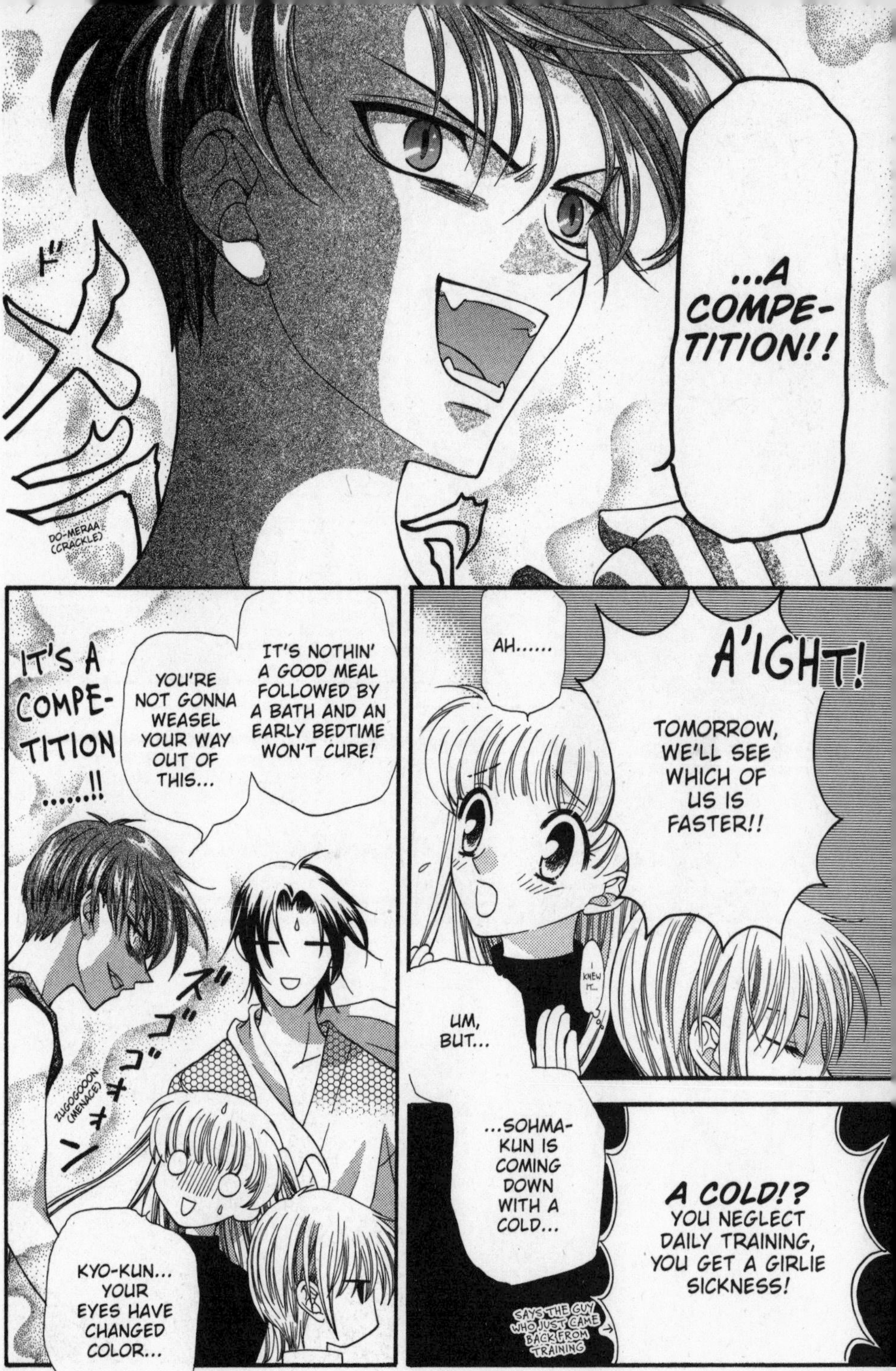
...A COMPETITION!!
DO-MERAA (CRACKLE)
AH......
A'IGHT!
TOMORROW, WE'LL SEE WHICH OF US IS FASTER!!
I KNEW IT...
UM, BUT...
...SOHMA-KUN IS COMING DOWN WITH A COLD...
A COLD!? YOU NEGLECT DAILY TRAINING, YOU GET A GIRLIE SICKNESS!
SAYS THE GUY WHO JUST CAME BACK FROM TRAINING
IT'S NOTHIN' A GOOD MEAL FOLLOWED BY A BATH AND AN EARLY BEDTIME WON'T CURE!
YOU'RE NOT GONNA WEASEL YOUR WAY OUT OF THIS...
IT'S A COMPETITION......!!
ZUGOGOOON (MENACE)
KYO-KUN... YOUR EYES HAVE CHANGED COLOR...

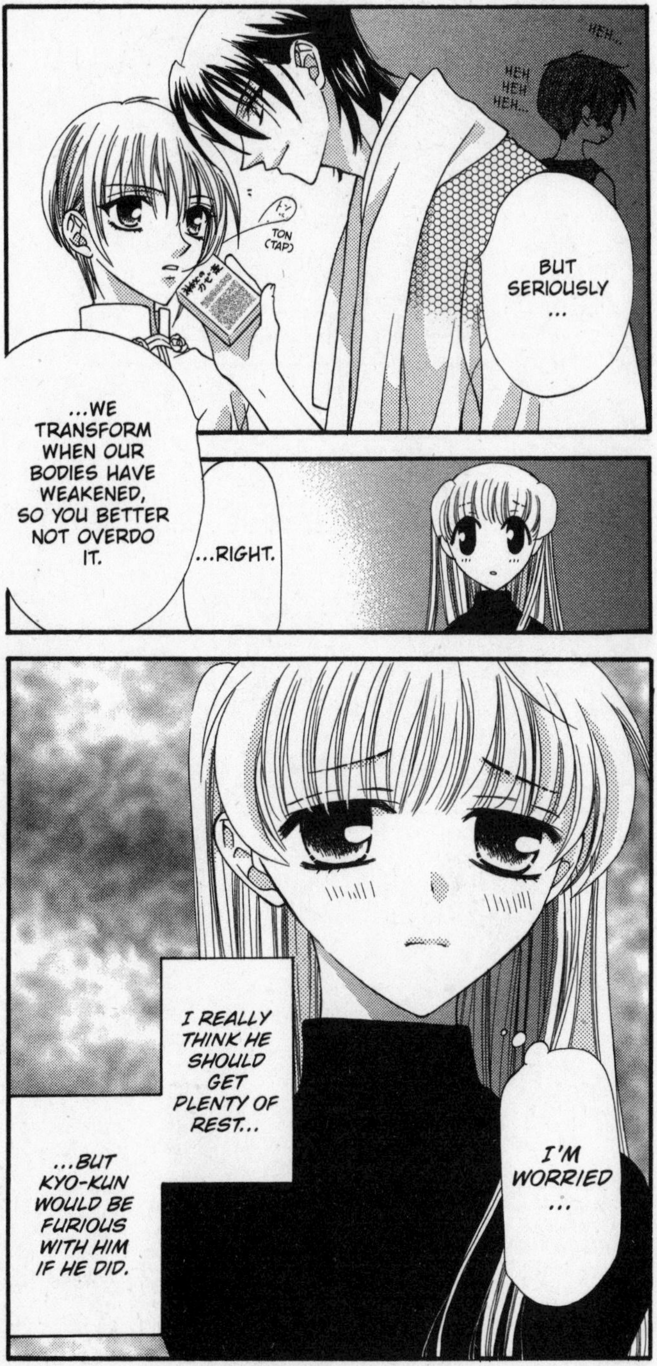
HEH...
HEH HEH HEH...
BUT SERIOUSLY ...
TON (TAP)
...WE TRANSFORM WHEN OUR BODIES HAVE WEAKENED, SO YOU BETTER NOT OVERDO IT.
...RIGHT.
I'M WORRIED ...
I REALLY THINK HE SHOULD GET PLENTY OF REST...
...BUT KYO-KUN WOULD BE FURIOUS WITH HIM IF HE DID.

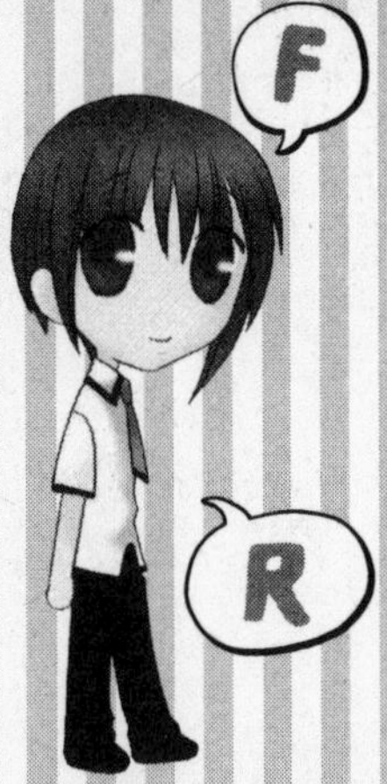
F
R

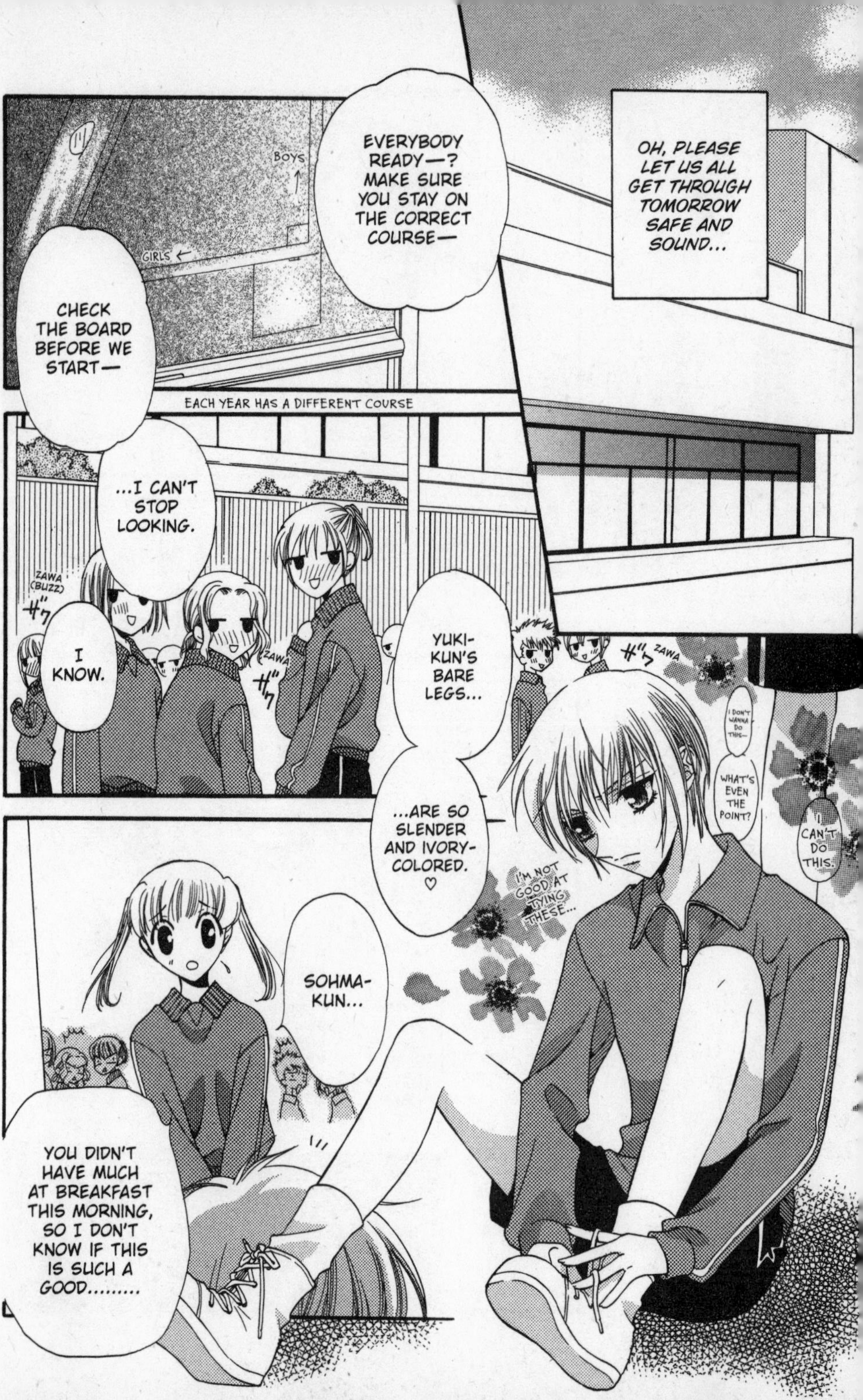
OH, PLEASE LET US ALL GET THROUGH TOMORROW SAFE AND SOUND...
EVERYBODY READY—? MAKE SURE YOU STAY ON THE CORRECT COURSE—
BOYS ↑
GIRLS ←
CHECK THE BOARD BEFORE WE START—
EACH YEAR HAS A DIFFERENT COURSE
ZAWA
...I CAN'T STOP LOOKING.
ZAWA (BUZZ)
I KNOW.
ZAWA
YUKI-KUN'S BARE LEGS...
...ARE SO SLENDER AND IVORY-COLORED. ♡
I DON'T WANNA DO THIS—
WHAT'S EVEN THE POINT?
I CAN'T DO THIS.
I'M NOT GOOD AT TYING THESE...
SOHMA-KUN...
YOU DIDN'T HAVE MUCH AT BREAKFAST THIS MORNING, SO I DON'T KNOW IF THIS IS SUCH A GOOD.........

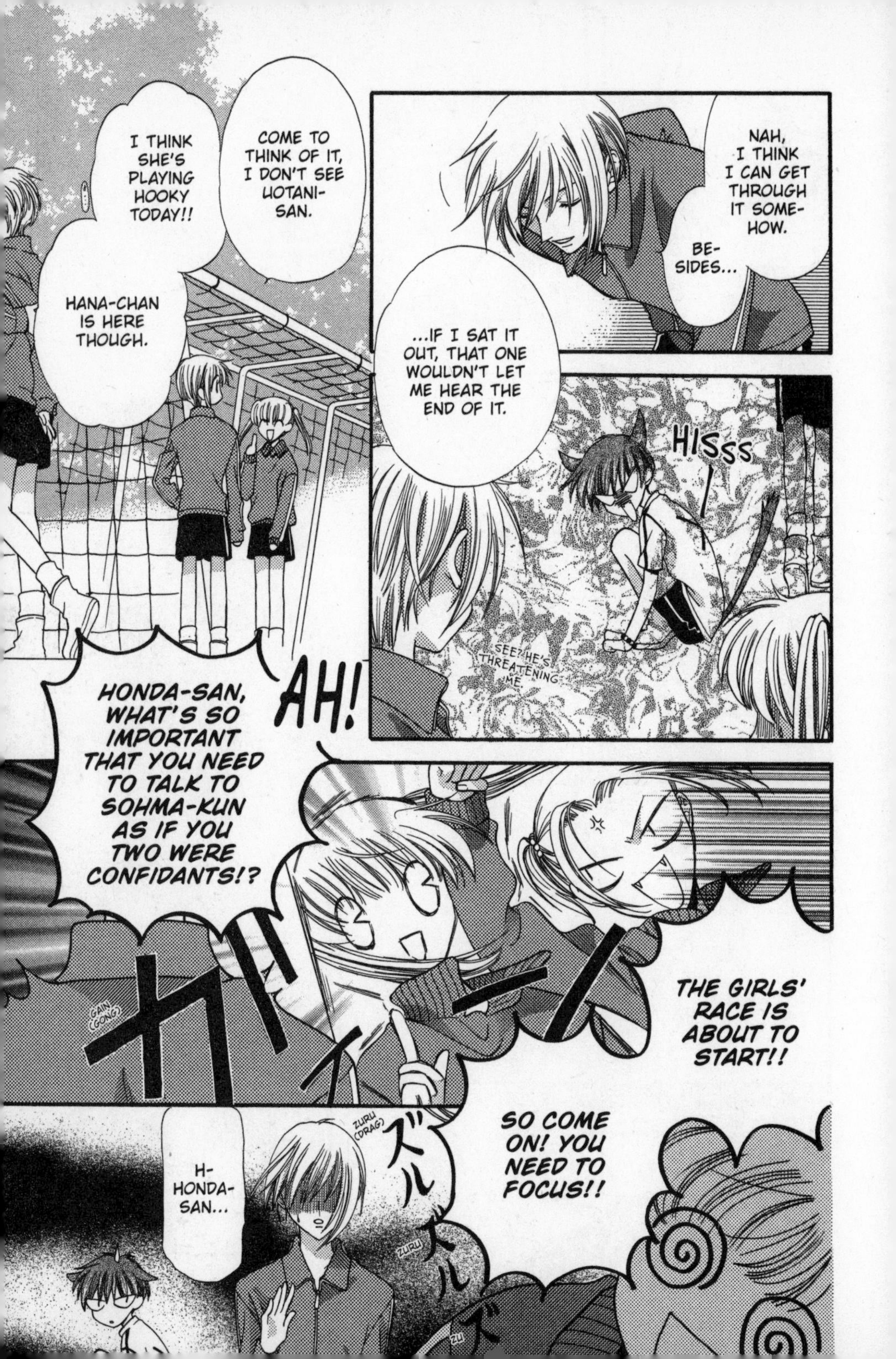
NAH, I THINK I CAN GET THROUGH IT SOME-HOW.
BE-SIDES...
...IF I SAT IT OUT, THAT ONE WOULDN'T LET ME HEAR THE END OF IT.
HISSS
SEE? HE'S THREATENING ME.
COME TO THINK OF IT, I DON'T SEE UOTANI-SAN.
I THINK SHE'S PLAYING HOOKY TODAY!!
HANA-CHAN IS HERE THOUGH.
AH!
HONDA-SAN, WHAT'S SO IMPORTANT THAT YOU NEED TO TALK TO SOHMA-KUN AS IF YOU TWO WERE CONFIDANTS!?
THE GIRLS' RACE IS ABOUT TO START!!
GAIN (GONG)
SO COME ON! YOU NEED TO FOCUS!!
ZURU (DRAG)
ZURU
ZU
H-HONDA-SAN...

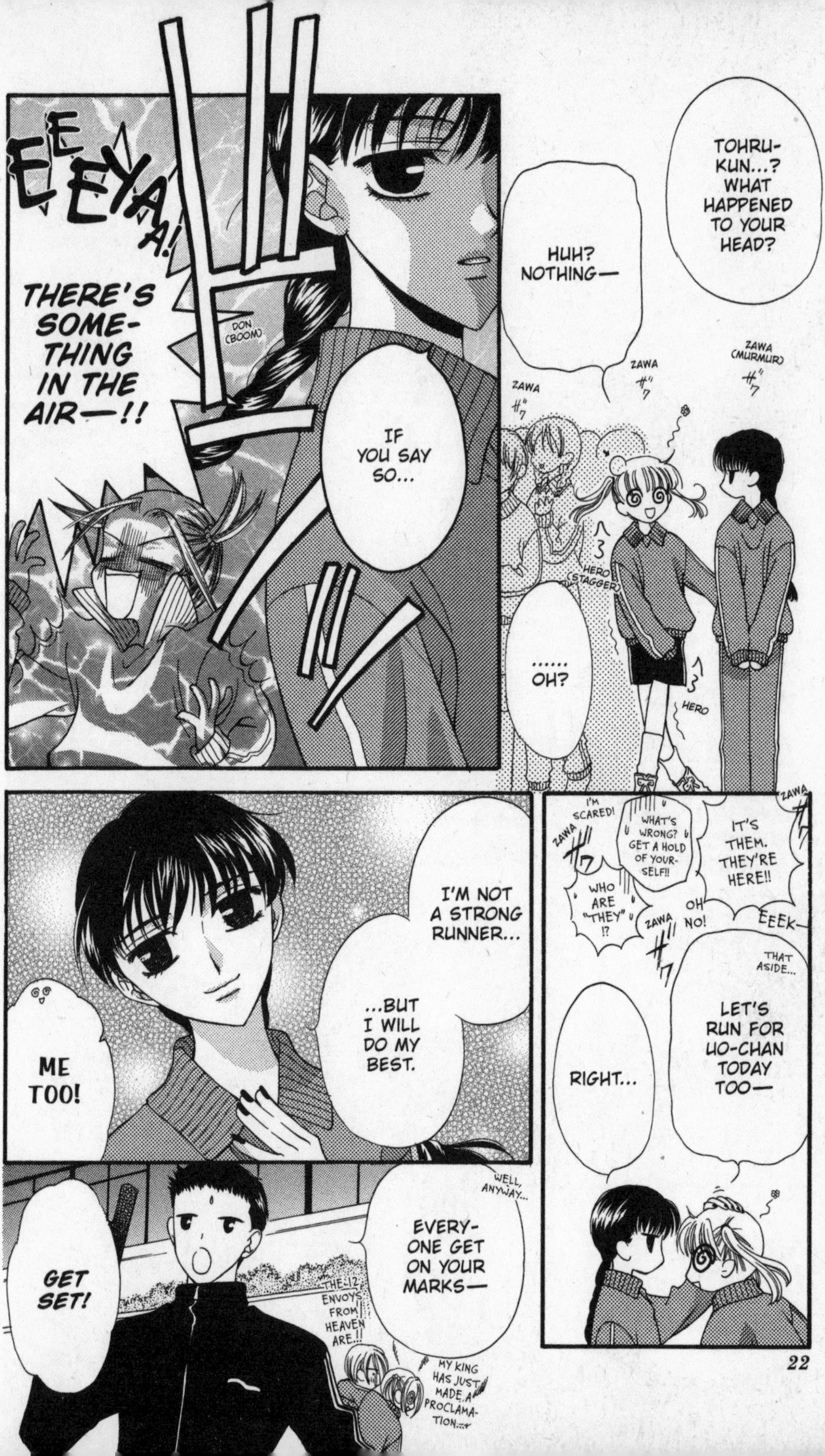

TOHRU-KUN...? WHAT HAPPENED TO YOUR HEAD?
HUH? NOTHING—
ZAWA (MURMUR)
ZAWA
ZAWA
HERO (STAGGER)
HERO
......OH?
EEEYAAA!
THERE'S SOME-THING IN THE AIR—!!
DON (BOOM)
IF YOU SAY SO...
ZAWA
IT'S THEM. THEY'RE HERE!!
WHAT'S WRONG? GET A HOLD OF YOUR-SELF!!
I'M SCARED!
ZAWA
WHO ARE "THEY" !?
ZAWA
OH NO!
EEEK—
THAT ASIDE...
LET'S RUN FOR UO-CHAN TODAY TOO—
RIGHT...
I'M NOT A STRONG RUNNER...
...BUT I WILL DO MY BEST.
ME TOO!
WELL, ANYWAY...
EVERY-ONE GET ON YOUR MARKS—
GET SET!
THE 12 ENVOYS FROM HEAVEN ARE..!!
MY KING HAS JUST MADE A PROCLAMA-TION..!

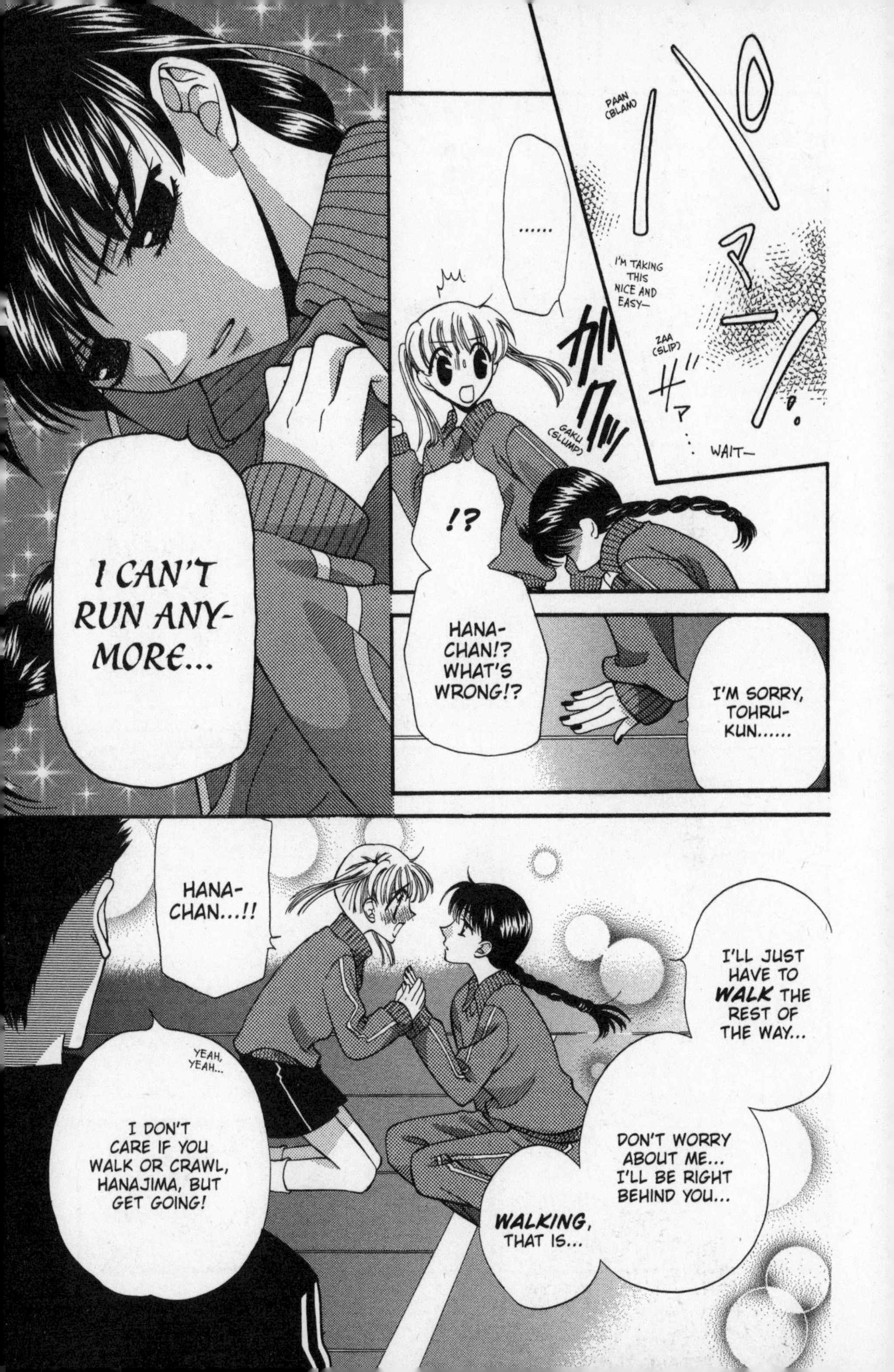
PAAN (BLAM)
I'M TAKING THIS NICE AND EASY—
ZAA (SLIP)
WAIT—
......
GAKU (SLUMP)
!?
HANA-CHAN!? WHAT'S WRONG!?
I'M SORRY, TOHRU-KUN......
I CAN'T RUN ANYMORE...
I'LL JUST HAVE TO WALK THE REST OF THE WAY...
HANA-CHAN...!!
DON'T WORRY ABOUT ME... I'LL BE RIGHT BEHIND YOU...
WALKING, THAT IS...
YEAH, YEAH...
I DON'T CARE IF YOU WALK OR CRAWL, HANAJIMA, BUT GET GOING!

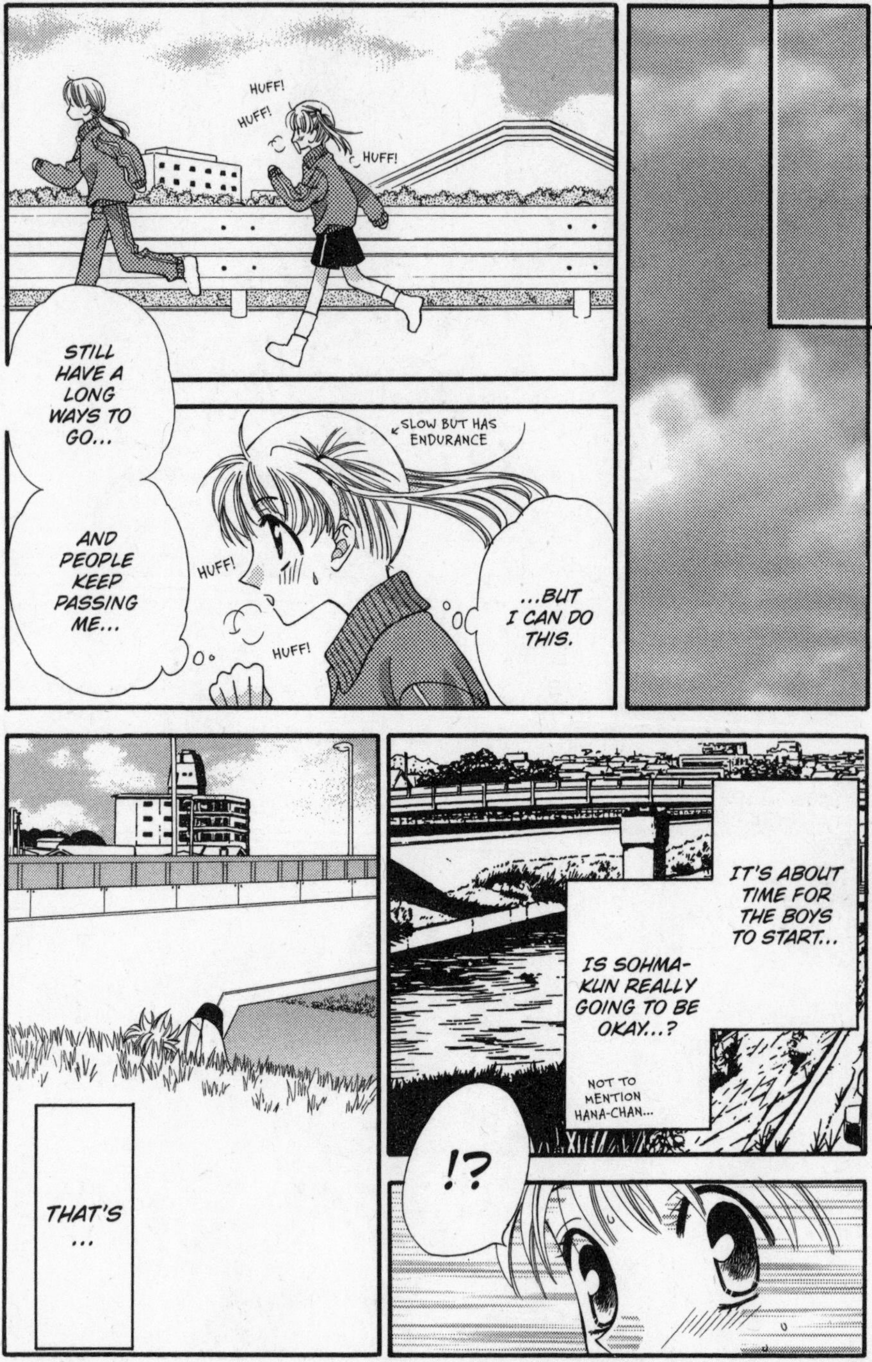
HUFF!
HUFF!
HUFF!
SLOW BUT HAS ENDURANCE
STILL HAVE A LONG WAYS TO GO...
AND PEOPLE KEEP PASSING ME...
HUFF!
HUFF!
...BUT I CAN DO THIS.
IT'S ABOUT TIME FOR THE BOYS TO START...
IS SOHMA-KUN REALLY GOING TO BE OKAY...?
NOT TO MENTION HANA-CHAN...
!?
THAT'S ...

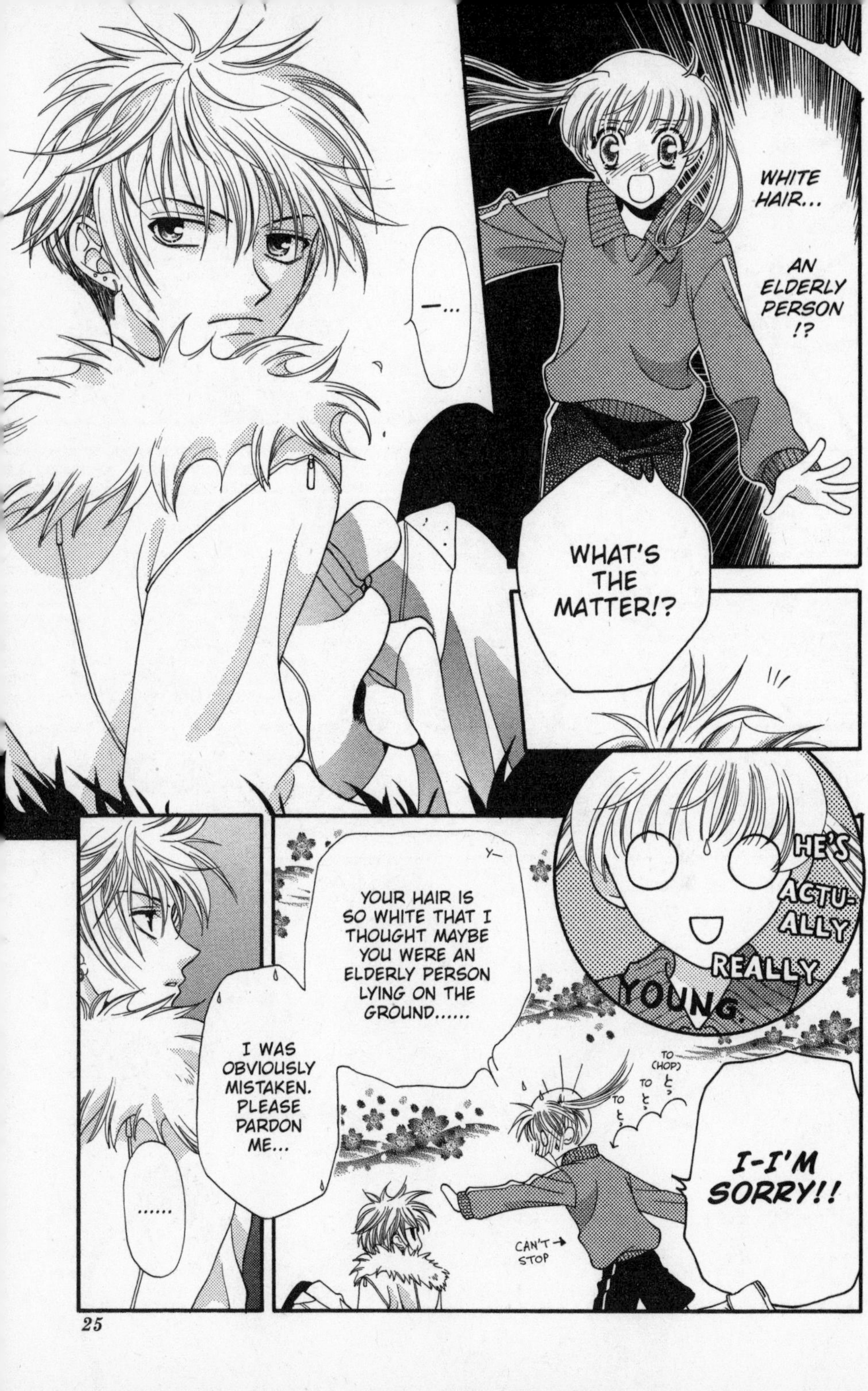
WHITE HAIR...
AN ELDERLY PERSON !?
WHAT'S THE MATTER!?
HE'S ACTU-ALLY REALLY YOUNG.
—...
I-I'M SORRY!!
TO TO TO (HOP)
CAN'T STOP
Y—
YOUR HAIR IS SO WHITE THAT I THOUGHT MAYBE YOU WERE AN ELDERLY PERSON LYING ON THE GROUND......
I WAS OBVIOUSLY MISTAKEN. PLEASE PARDON ME...
......

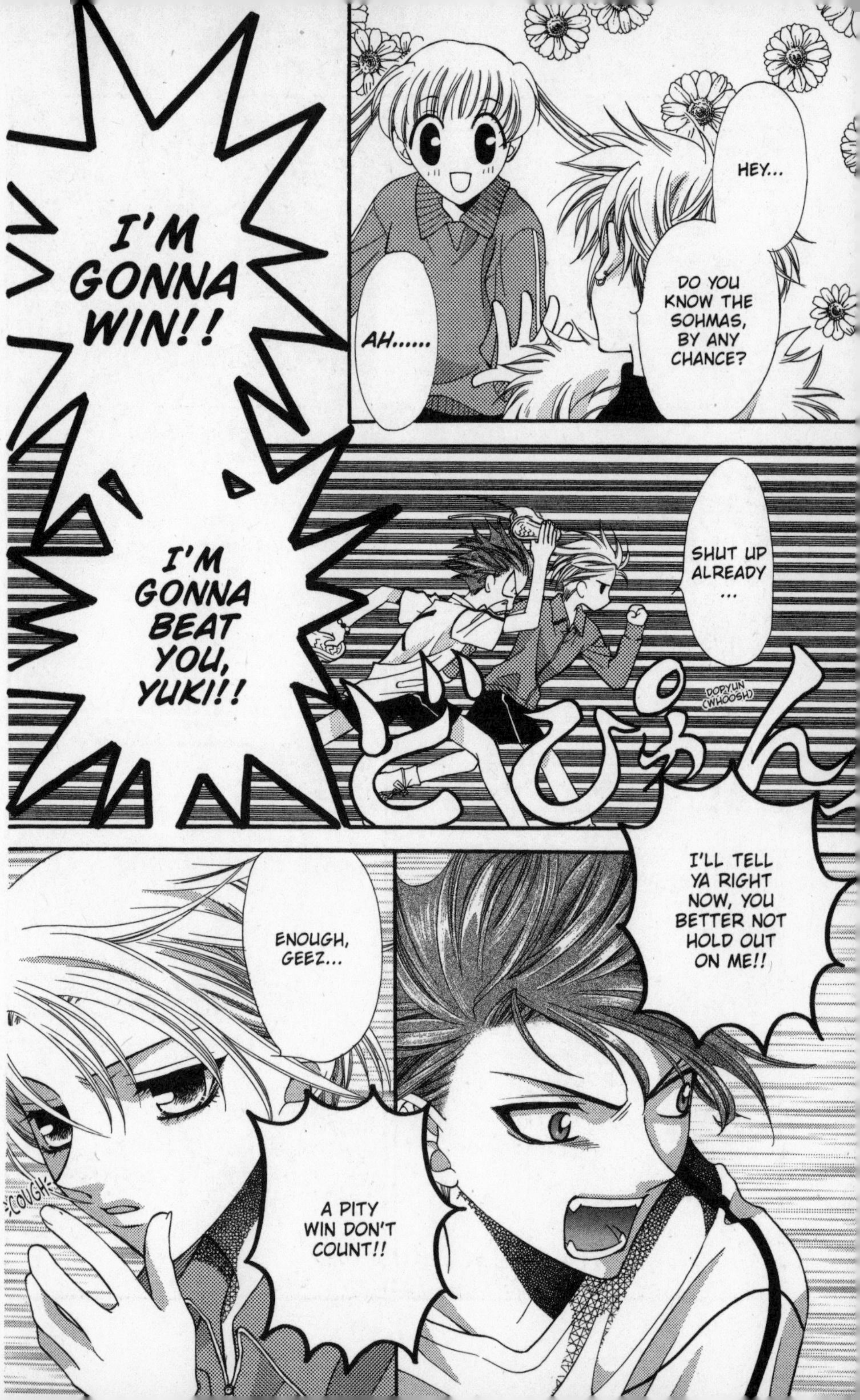
HEY...
DO YOU KNOW THE SOHMAS, BY ANY CHANCE?
AH......
SHUT UP ALREADY ...
どぴゅん
DOPYUN (WHOOSH)
I'M GONNA WIN!!
I'M GONNA BEAT YOU, YUKI!!
I'LL TELL YA RIGHT NOW, YOU BETTER NOT HOLD OUT ON ME!!
A PITY WIN DON'T COUNT!!
ENOUGH, GEEZ...
COUGH

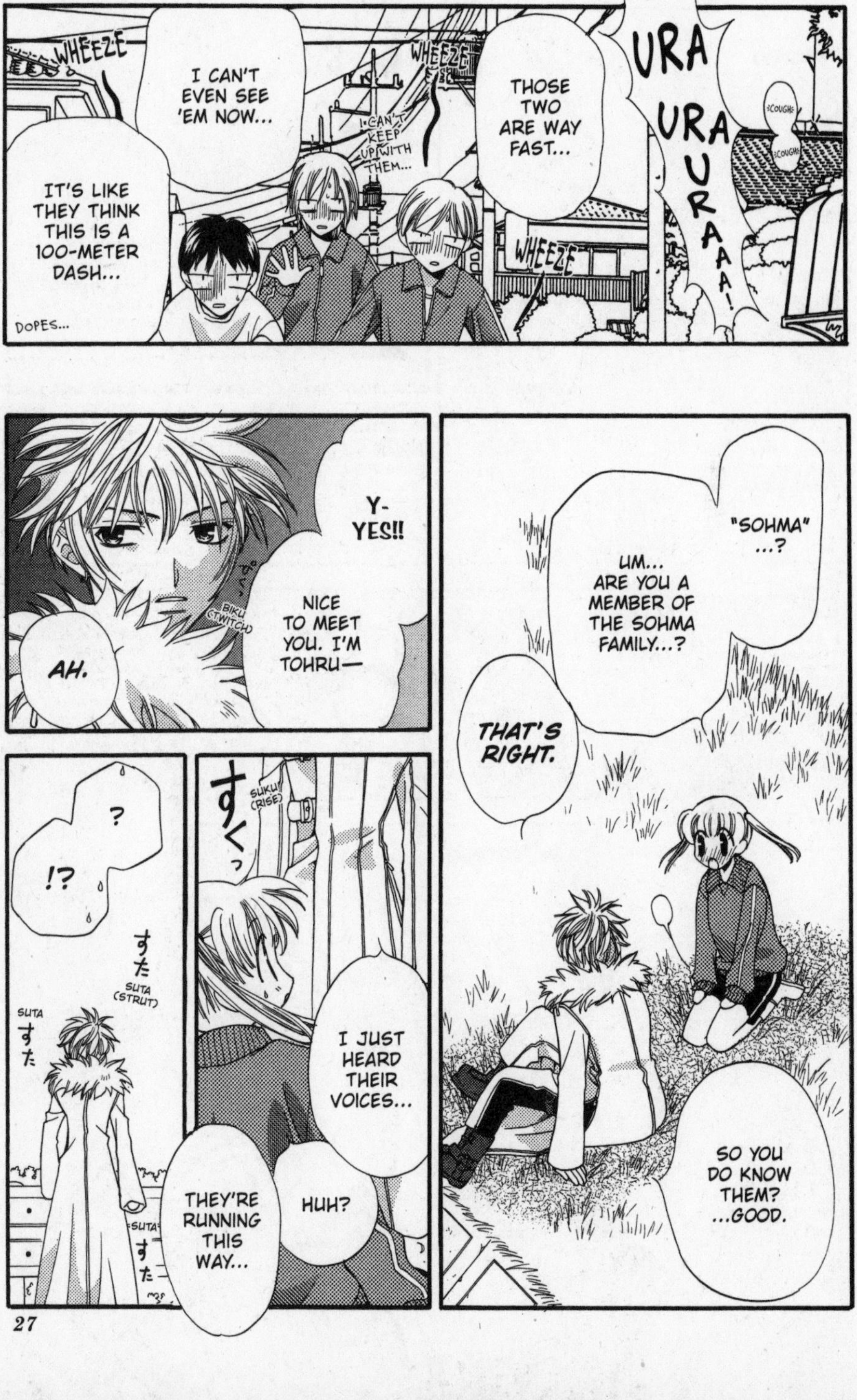
URA
URA
URAAAA!
COUGH
COUGH
THOSE TWO ARE WAY FAST...
WHEEZE
I CAN'T KEEP UP WITH THEM...
WHEEZE
I CAN'T EVEN SEE 'EM NOW...
WHEEZE
IT'S LIKE THEY THINK THIS IS A 100-METER DASH...
DOPES...
"SOHMA" ...?
UM... ARE YOU A MEMBER OF THE SOHMA FAMILY...?
THAT'S RIGHT.
SO YOU DO KNOW THEM? ...GOOD.
Y-YES!!
NICE TO MEET YOU. I'M TOHRU—
BIKU (TWITCH)
AH.
すくっ
SUKU (RISE)
I JUST HEARD THEIR VOICES...
HUH?
THEY'RE RUNNING THIS WAY...
?
!?
すた
SUTA (STRUT)
SUTA
すた
SUTA
すた

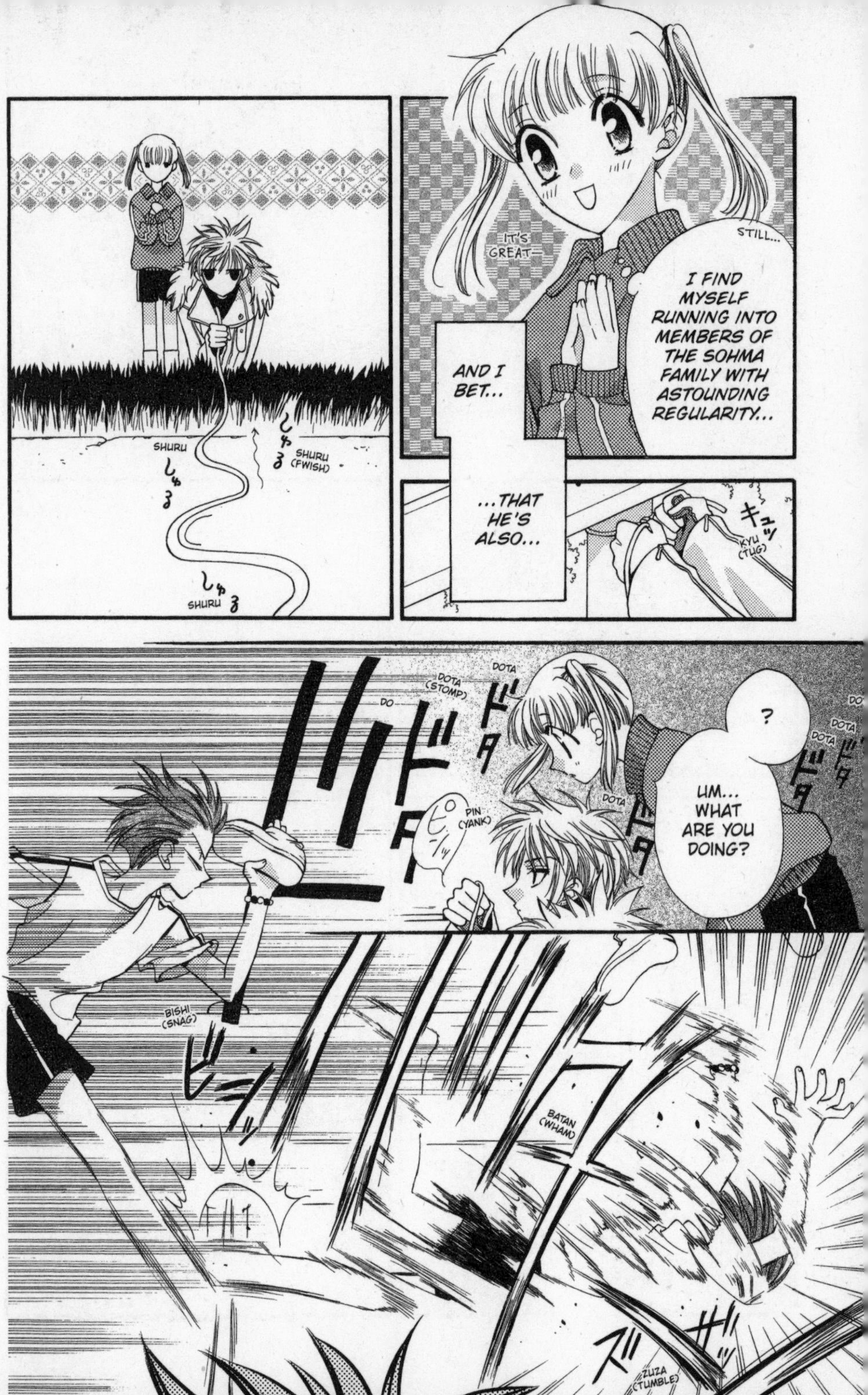
STILL...
IT'S GREAT—
I FIND MYSELF RUNNING INTO MEMBERS OF THE SOHMA FAMILY WITH ASTOUNDING REGULARITY...
AND I BET...
...THAT HE'S ALSO...
キュッ
KYU (TUG)
しゅる
SHURU (FWISH)
しゅる
SHURU
しゅる
SHURU
DOTA
DOTA
DOTA
DOTA
UM... WHAT ARE YOU DOING?
?
DOTA
DOTA (STOMP)
DO
PIN (YANK)
BISHI (SNAG)
BATAN (WHAM)
ZUZA (TUMBLE)

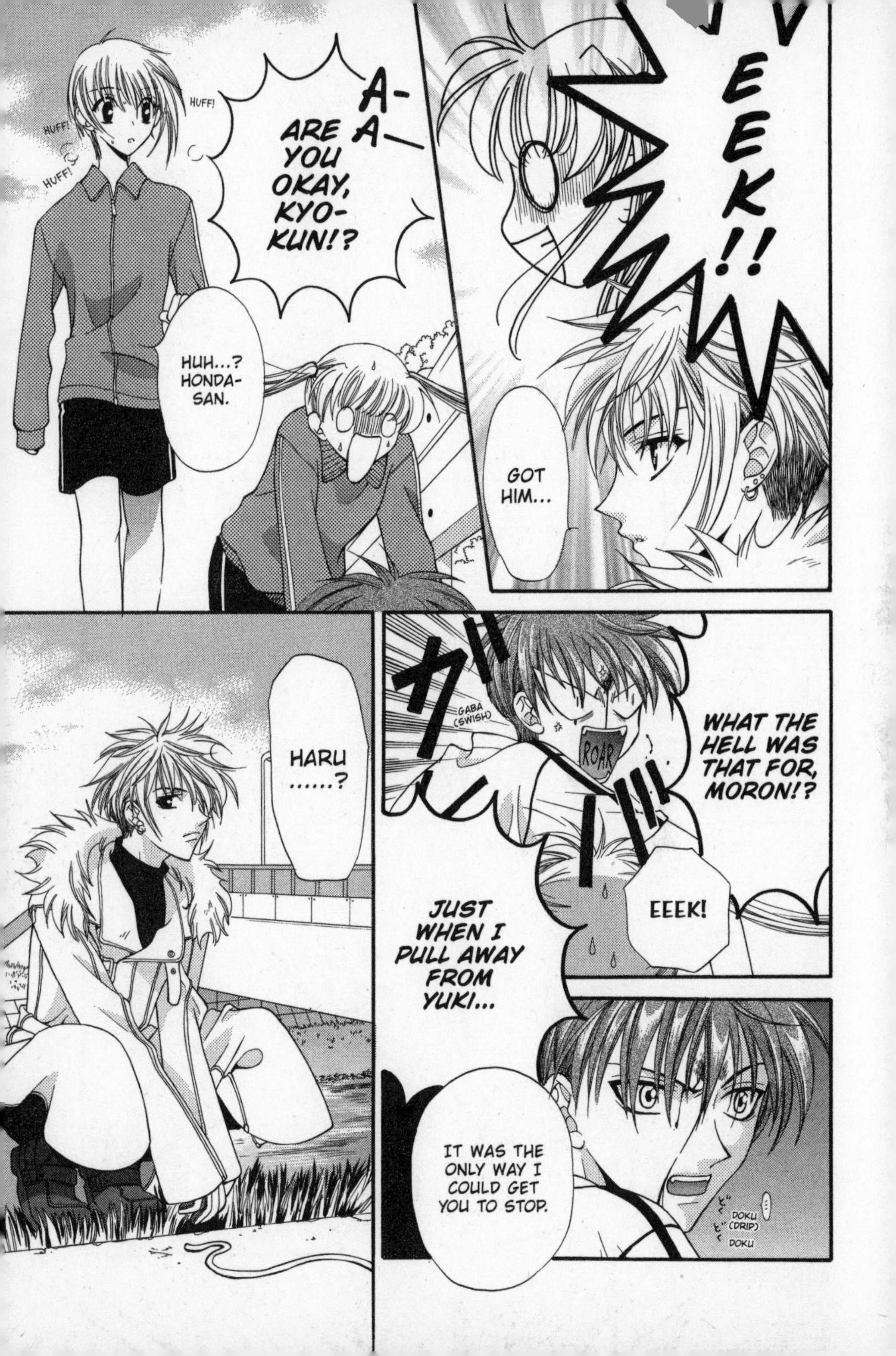
EEK!!
GOT HIM...
A-A—
ARE YOU OKAY, KYO-KUN!?
HUFF!
HUFF!
HUFF!
HUH...? HONDA-SAN.
GABA (SWISH)
ROAR
WHAT THE HELL WAS THAT FOR, MORON!?
EEEK!
JUST WHEN I PULL AWAY FROM YUKI...
DOKU (DRIP) DOKU
IT WAS THE ONLY WAY I COULD GET YOU TO STOP.
HARU ......?

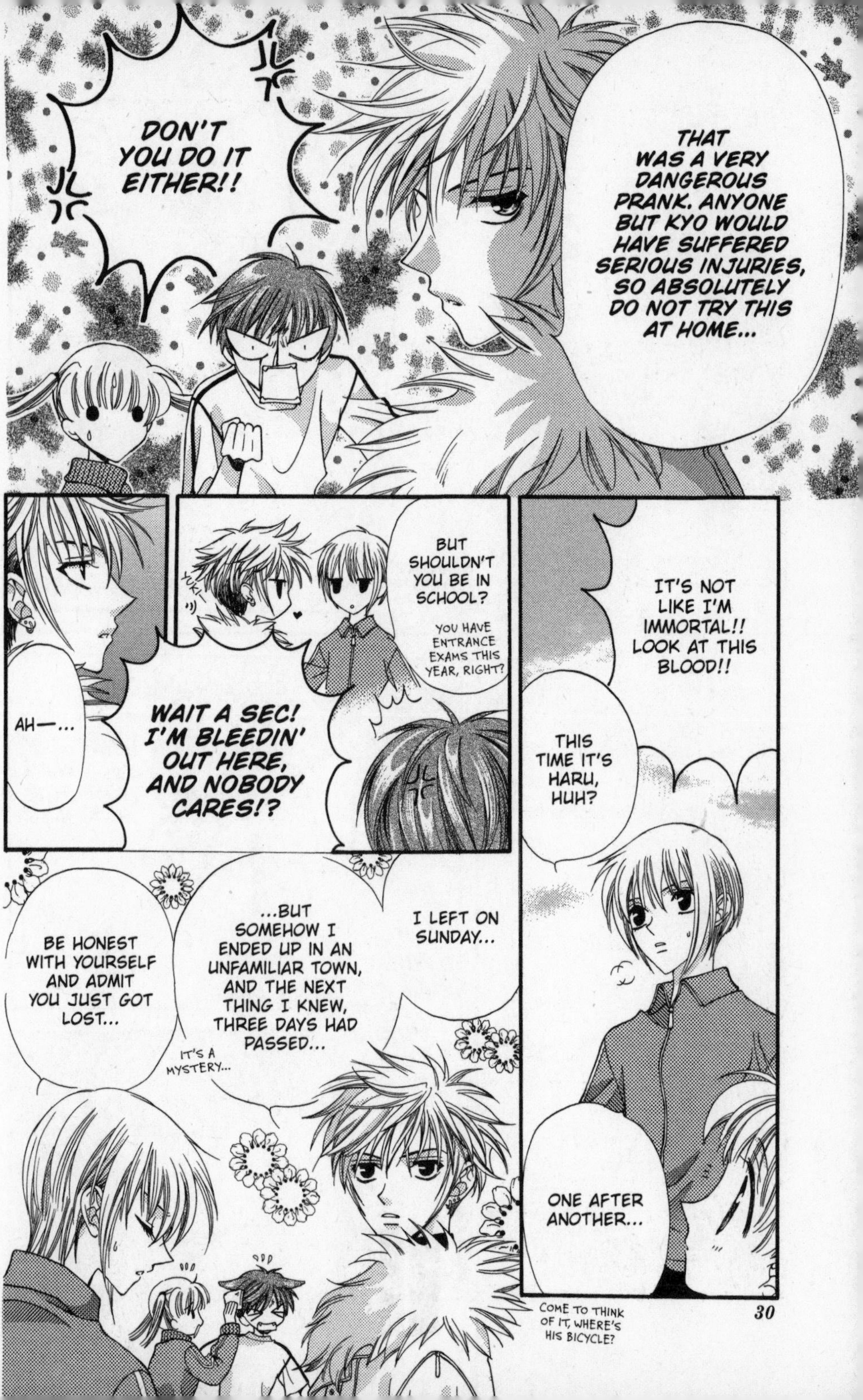
THAT WAS A VERY DANGEROUS PRANK. ANYONE BUT KYO WOULD HAVE SUFFERED SERIOUS INJURIES, SO ABSOLUTELY DO NOT TRY THIS AT HOME...
DON'T YOU DO IT EITHER!!
IT'S NOT LIKE I'M IMMORTAL!! LOOK AT THIS BLOOD!!
THIS TIME IT'S HARU, HUH?
ONE AFTER ANOTHER...
YUKI—
BUT SHOULDN'T YOU BE IN SCHOOL?
YOU HAVE ENTRANCE EXAMS THIS YEAR, RIGHT?
AH—...
WAIT A SEC! I'M BLEEDIN' OUT HERE, AND NOBODY CARES!?
I LEFT ON SUNDAY...
...BUT SOMEHOW I ENDED UP IN AN UNFAMILIAR TOWN, AND THE NEXT THING I KNEW, THREE DAYS HAD PASSED...
IT'S A MYSTERY...
BE HONEST WITH YOURSELF AND ADMIT YOU JUST GOT LOST...
COME TO THINK OF IT, WHERE'S HIS BICYCLE?

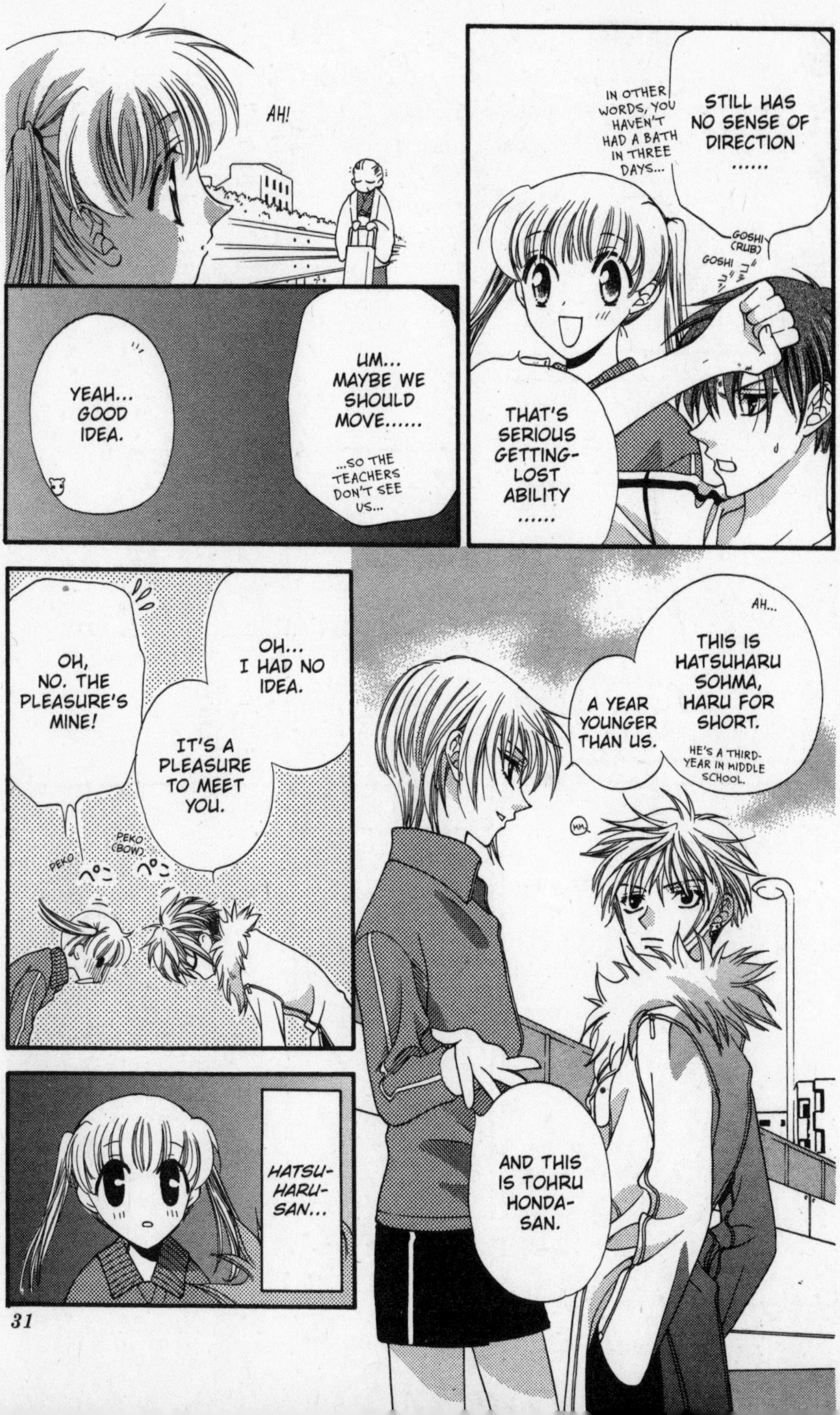
STILL HAS NO SENSE OF DIRECTION ......
IN OTHER WORDS, YOU HAVEN'T HAD A BATH IN THREE DAYS...
GOSHI (RUB)
GOSHI
THAT'S SERIOUS GETTING-LOST ABILITY ......
AH!
UM... MAYBE WE SHOULD MOVE......
...SO THE TEACHERS DON'T SEE US...
YEAH... GOOD IDEA.
AH...
THIS IS HATSUHARU SOHMA, HARU FOR SHORT.
HE'S A THIRD-YEAR IN MIDDLE SCHOOL.
A YEAR YOUNGER THAN US.
MM.
AND THIS IS TOHRU HONDA-SAN.
OH... I HAD NO IDEA.
IT'S A PLEASURE TO MEET YOU.
OH, NO. THE PLEASURE'S MINE!
PEKO (BOW)
PEKO
HATSU-HARU-SAN...

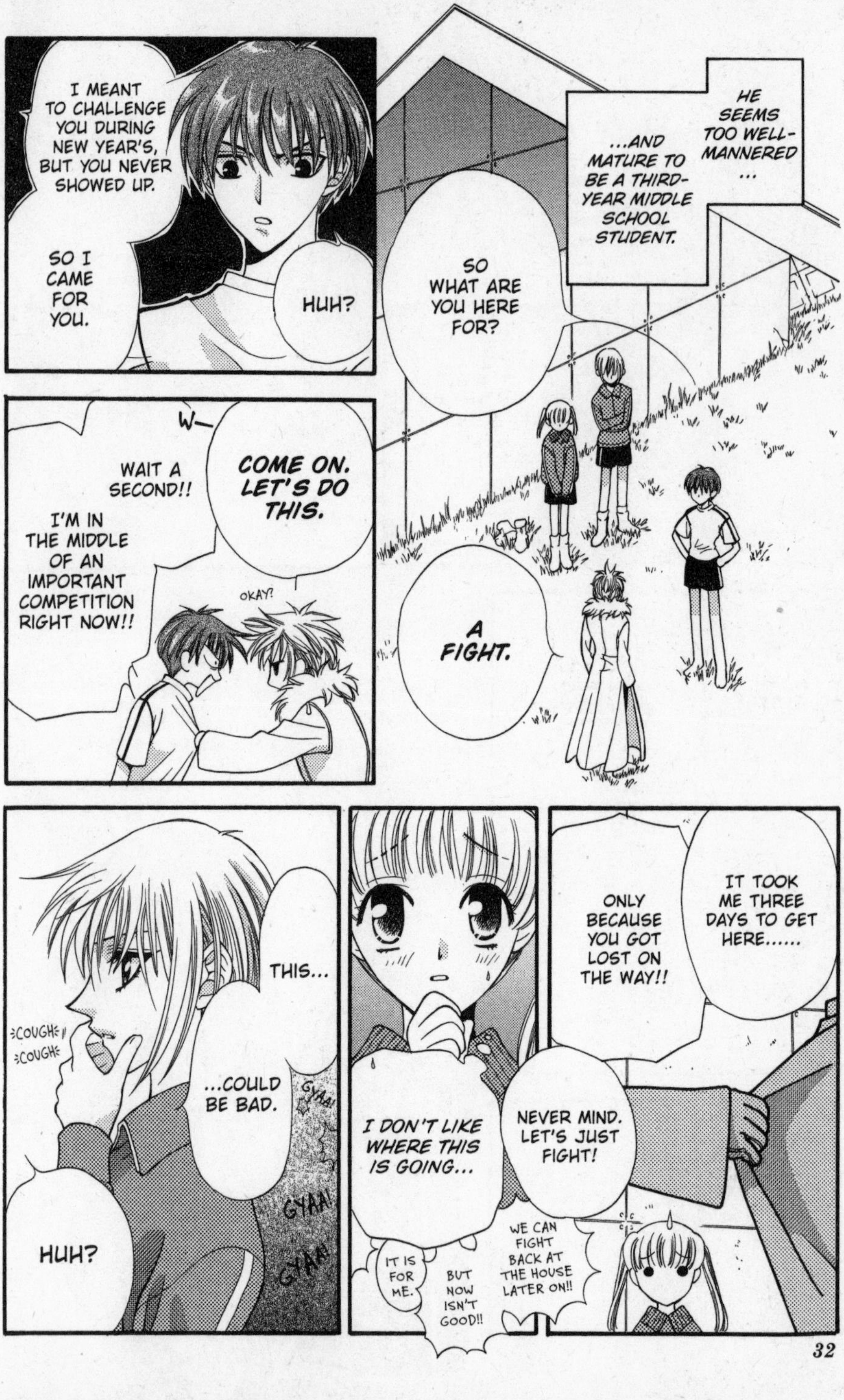
HE SEEMS TOO WELL-MANNERED...
...AND MATURE TO BE A THIRD-YEAR MIDDLE SCHOOL STUDENT.
SO WHAT ARE YOU HERE FOR?
A FIGHT.
HUH?
I MEANT TO CHALLENGE YOU DURING NEW YEAR'S, BUT YOU NEVER SHOWED UP.
SO I CAME FOR YOU.
COME ON. LET'S DO THIS.
W—
WAIT A SECOND!!
I'M IN THE MIDDLE OF AN IMPORTANT COMPETITION RIGHT NOW!!
OKAY?
IT TOOK ME THREE DAYS TO GET HERE......
ONLY BECAUSE YOU GOT LOST ON THE WAY!!
NEVER MIND. LET'S JUST FIGHT!
WE CAN FIGHT BACK AT THE HOUSE LATER ON!!
I DON'T LIKE WHERE THIS IS GOING...
BUT NOW ISN'T GOOD!!
IT IS FOR ME.
THIS...
...COULD BE BAD.
GYAA!
GYAA!
GYAA!
COUGH
COUGH
HUH?

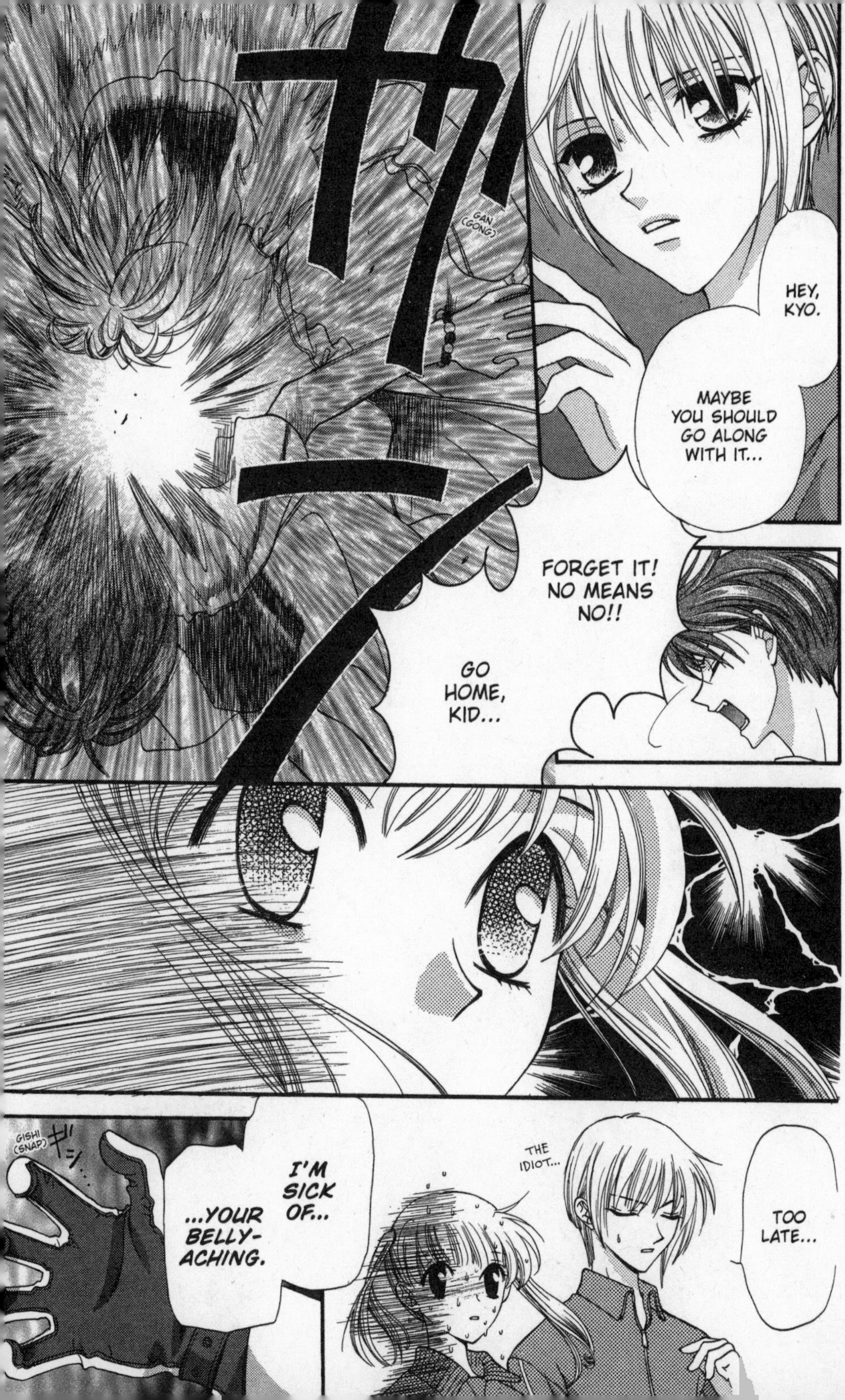
HEY, KYO.
MAYBE YOU SHOULD GO ALONG WITH IT...
FORGET IT! NO MEANS NO!!
GO HOME, KID...
GAN (GONG)
TOO LATE...
THE IDIOT...
I'M SICK OF...
...YOUR BELLY-ACHING.
GISHI (SNAP)

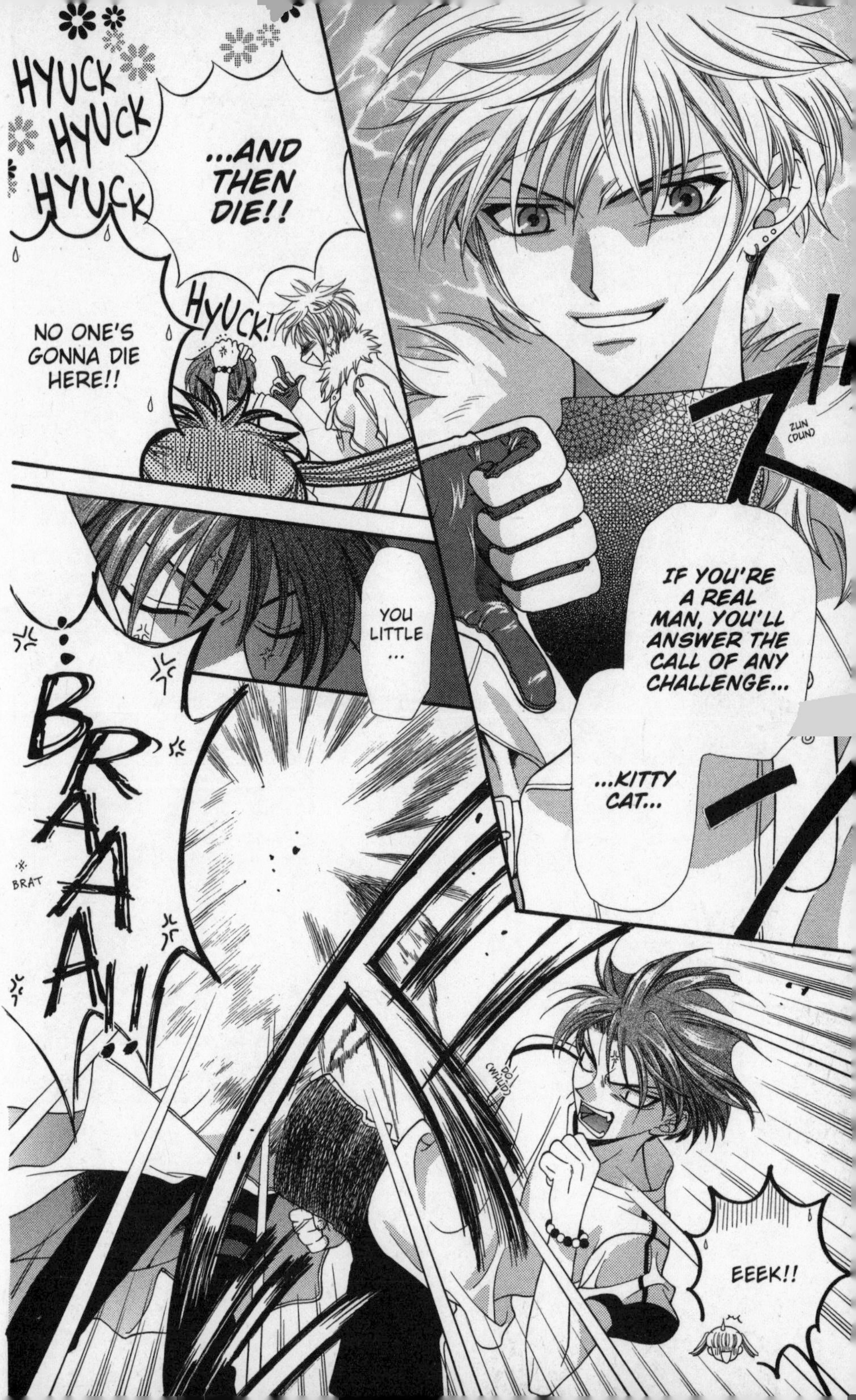
ZUN (DUN)
IF YOU'RE A REAL MAN, YOU'LL ANSWER THE CALL OF ANY CHALLENGE...
...KITTY CAT...
...AND THEN DIE!!
HYUCK HYUCK HYUCK
HYUCK!
NO ONE'S GONNA DIE HERE!!
YOU LITTLE ...
BRAAAA!!
*BRAT
DO! (WHUD)
EEEK!!

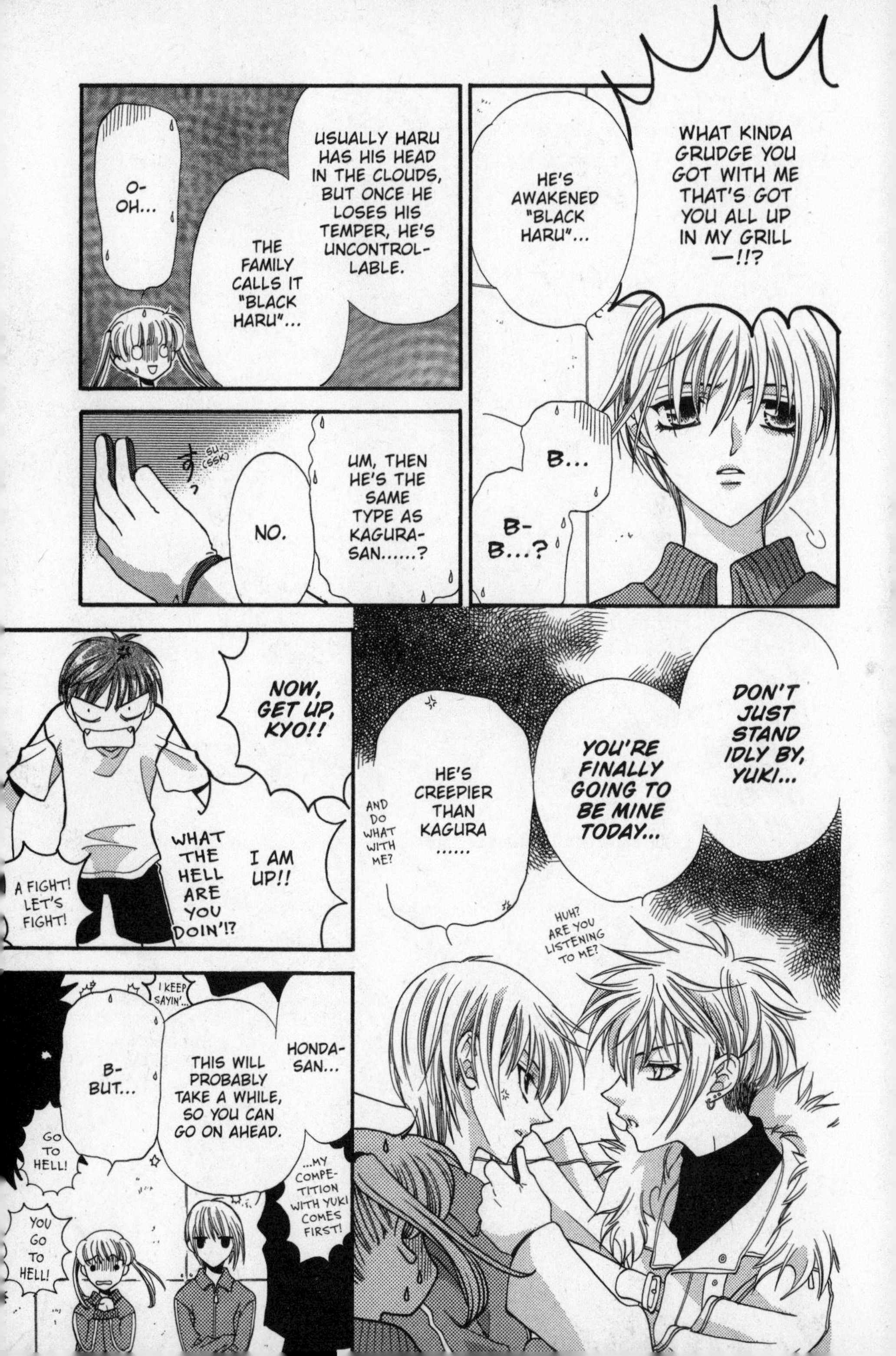
WHAT KINDA GRUDGE YOU GOT WITH ME THAT'S GOT YOU ALL UP IN MY GRILL—!!?
HE'S AWAKENED "BLACK HARU"...
B...
B-B...?
USUALLY HARU HAS HIS HEAD IN THE CLOUDS, BUT ONCE HE LOSES HIS TEMPER, HE'S UNCONTROL-LABLE.
THE FAMILY CALLS IT "BLACK HARU"...
O-OH...
UM, THEN HE'S THE SAME TYPE AS KAGURA-SAN......?
NO.
SU (SSK)
DON'T JUST STAND IDLY BY, YUKI...
YOU'RE FINALLY GOING TO BE MINE TODAY...
HE'S CREEPIER THAN KAGURA......
AND DO WHAT WITH ME?
HUH? ARE YOU LISTENING TO ME?
NOW, GET UP, KYO!!
I AM UP!!
WHAT THE HELL ARE YOU DOIN'!?
A FIGHT! LET'S FIGHT!
HONDA-SAN...
I KEEP SAYIN'...
THIS WILL PROBABLY TAKE A WHILE, SO YOU CAN GO ON AHEAD.
...MY COMPETITION WITH YUKI COMES FIRST!
B-BUT...
GO TO HELL!
YOU GO TO HELL!

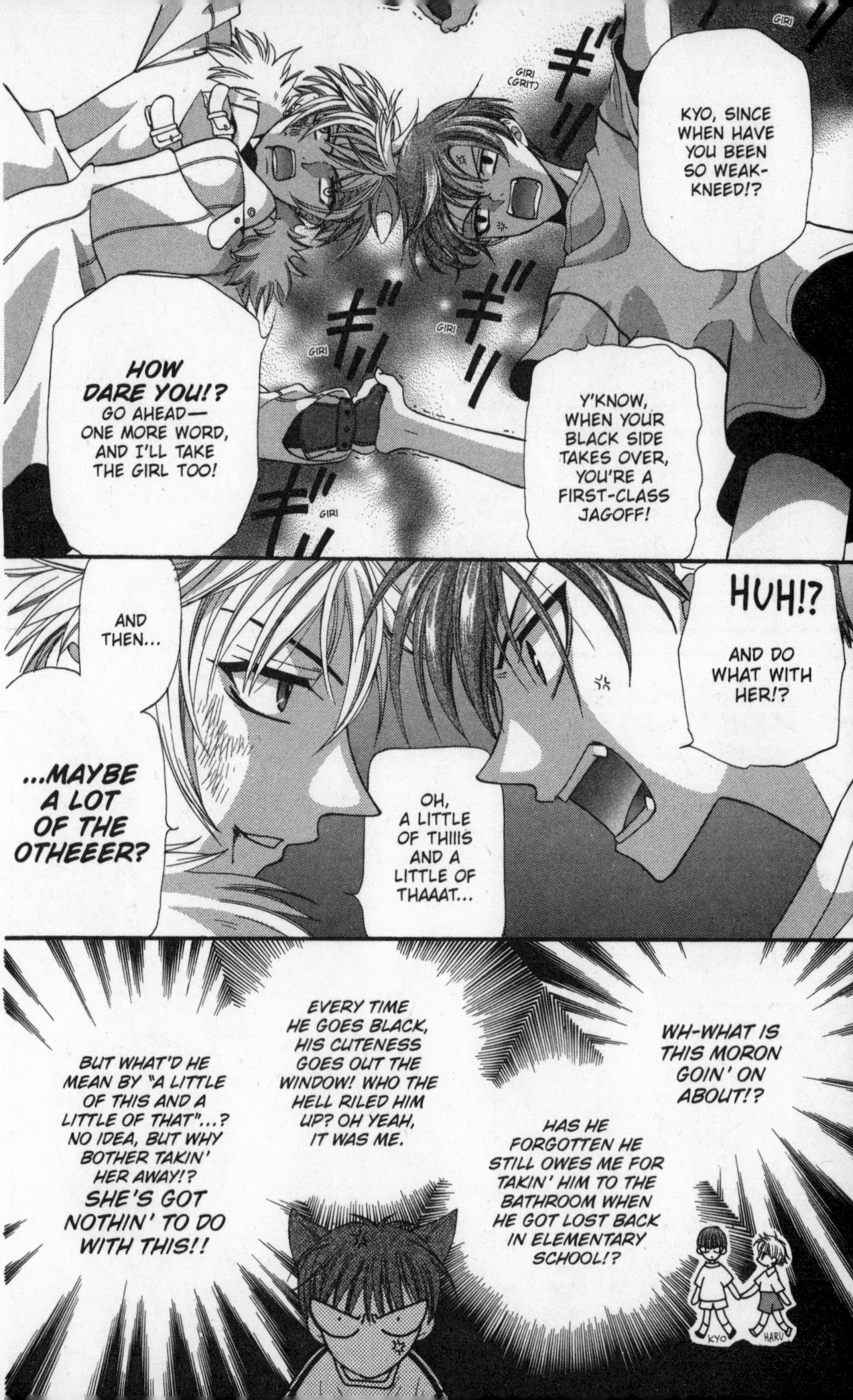
GIRI
KYO, SINCE WHEN HAVE YOU BEEN SO WEAK-KNEED!?
GIRI (GRIT)
Y'KNOW, WHEN YOUR BLACK SIDE TAKES OVER, YOU'RE A FIRST-CLASS JAGOFF!
GIRI
GIRI
HOW DARE YOU!? GO AHEAD—ONE MORE WORD, AND I'LL TAKE THE GIRL TOO!
GIRI
HUH!?
AND DO WHAT WITH HER!?
AND THEN...
OH, A LITTLE OF THIIIS AND A LITTLE OF THAAAT...
...MAYBE A LOT OF THE OTHEEER?
WH-WHAT IS THIS MORON GOIN' ON ABOUT!?
HAS HE FORGOTTEN HE STILL OWES ME FOR TAKIN' HIM TO THE BATHROOM WHEN HE GOT LOST BACK IN ELEMENTARY SCHOOL!?
KYO
HARU
EVERY TIME HE GOES BLACK, HIS CUTENESS GOES OUT THE WINDOW! WHO THE HELL RILED HIM UP? OH YEAH, IT WAS ME.
BUT WHAT'D HE MEAN BY "A LITTLE OF THIS AND A LITTLE OF THAT"...? NO IDEA, BUT WHY BOTHER TAKIN' HER AWAY!? SHE'S GOT NOTHIN' TO DO WITH THIS!!

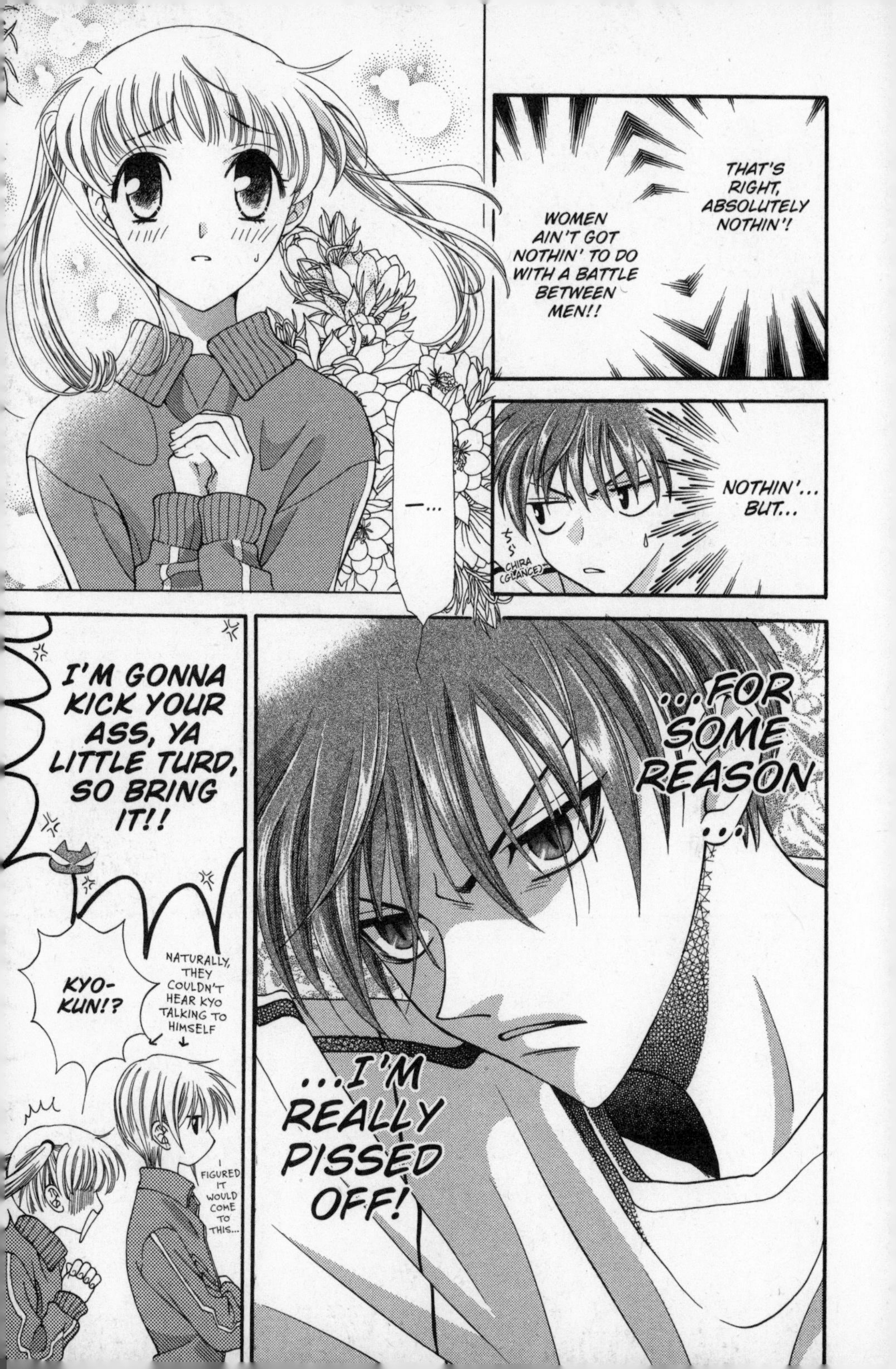

THAT'S RIGHT, ABSOLUTELY NOTHIN'!
WOMEN AIN'T GOT NOTHIN' TO DO WITH A BATTLE BETWEEN MEN!!
NOTHIN'... BUT...
CHIRA (GLANCE)
—...
...FOR SOME REASON...
...I'M REALLY PISSED OFF!
I'M GONNA KICK YOUR ASS, YA LITTLE TURD, SO BRING IT!!
NATURALLY, THEY COULDN'T HEAR KYO TALKING TO HIMSELF
KYO-KUN!?
I FIGURED IT WOULD COME TO THIS...

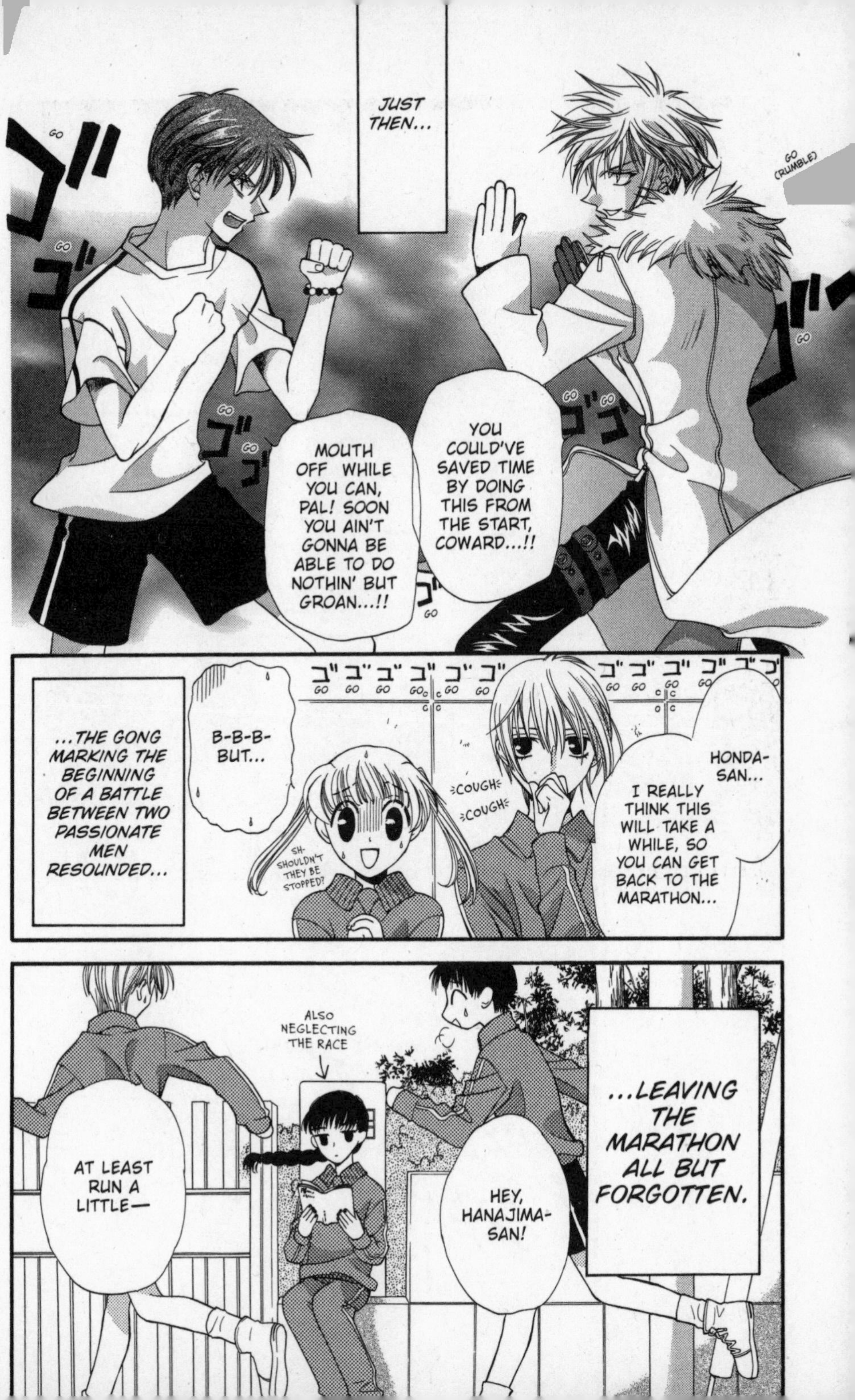
JUST THEN...
GO (RUMBLE)
GO
GO
YOU COULD'VE SAVED TIME BY DOING THIS FROM THE START, COWARD...!!
GO GO
MOUTH OFF WHILE YOU CAN, PAL! SOON YOU AIN'T GONNA BE ABLE TO DO NOTHIN' BUT GROAN...!!
GO
GO
GO
GO
GO GO GO GO GO GO
GO GO GO GO GO GO
HONDA-SAN... I REALLY THINK THIS WILL TAKE A WHILE, SO YOU CAN GET BACK TO THE MARATHON...
COUGH
COUGH
SH-SHOULDN'T THEY BE STOPPED?
B-B-B-BUT...
...THE GONG MARKING THE BEGINNING OF A BATTLE BETWEEN TWO PASSIONATE MEN RESOUNDED...
...LEAVING THE MARATHON ALL BUT FORGOTTEN.
HEY, HANAJIMA-SAN!
ALSO NEGLECTING THE RACE
AT LEAST RUN A LITTLE—

Chapter 14

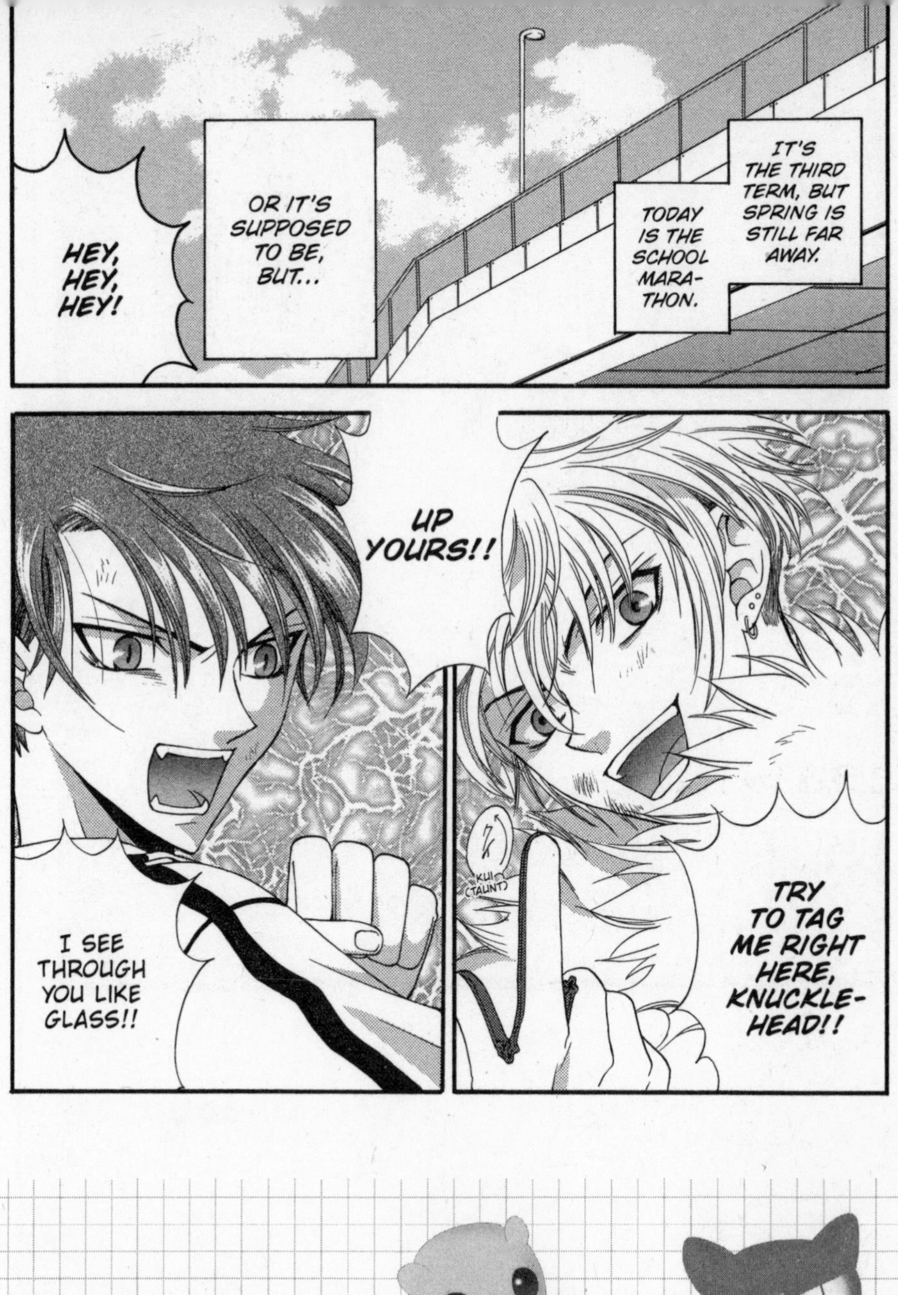
IT'S THE THIRD TERM, BUT SPRING IS STILL FAR AWAY.
TODAY IS THE SCHOOL MARA-THON.
OR IT'S SUPPOSED TO BE, BUT...
HEY, HEY, HEY!
TRY TO TAG ME RIGHT HERE, KNUCKLE-HEAD!!
KUI (TAUNT)
UP YOURS!!
I SEE THROUGH YOU LIKE GLASS!!

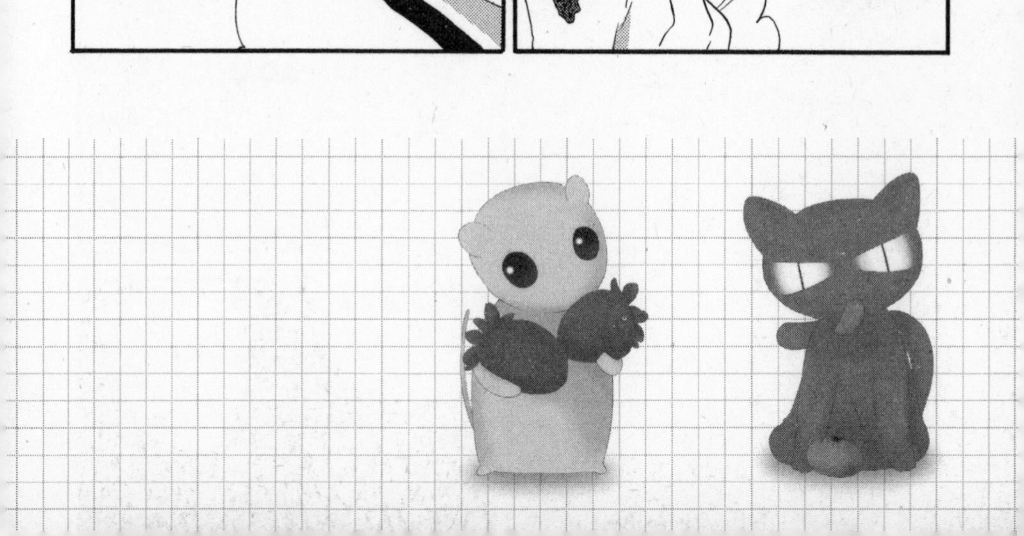

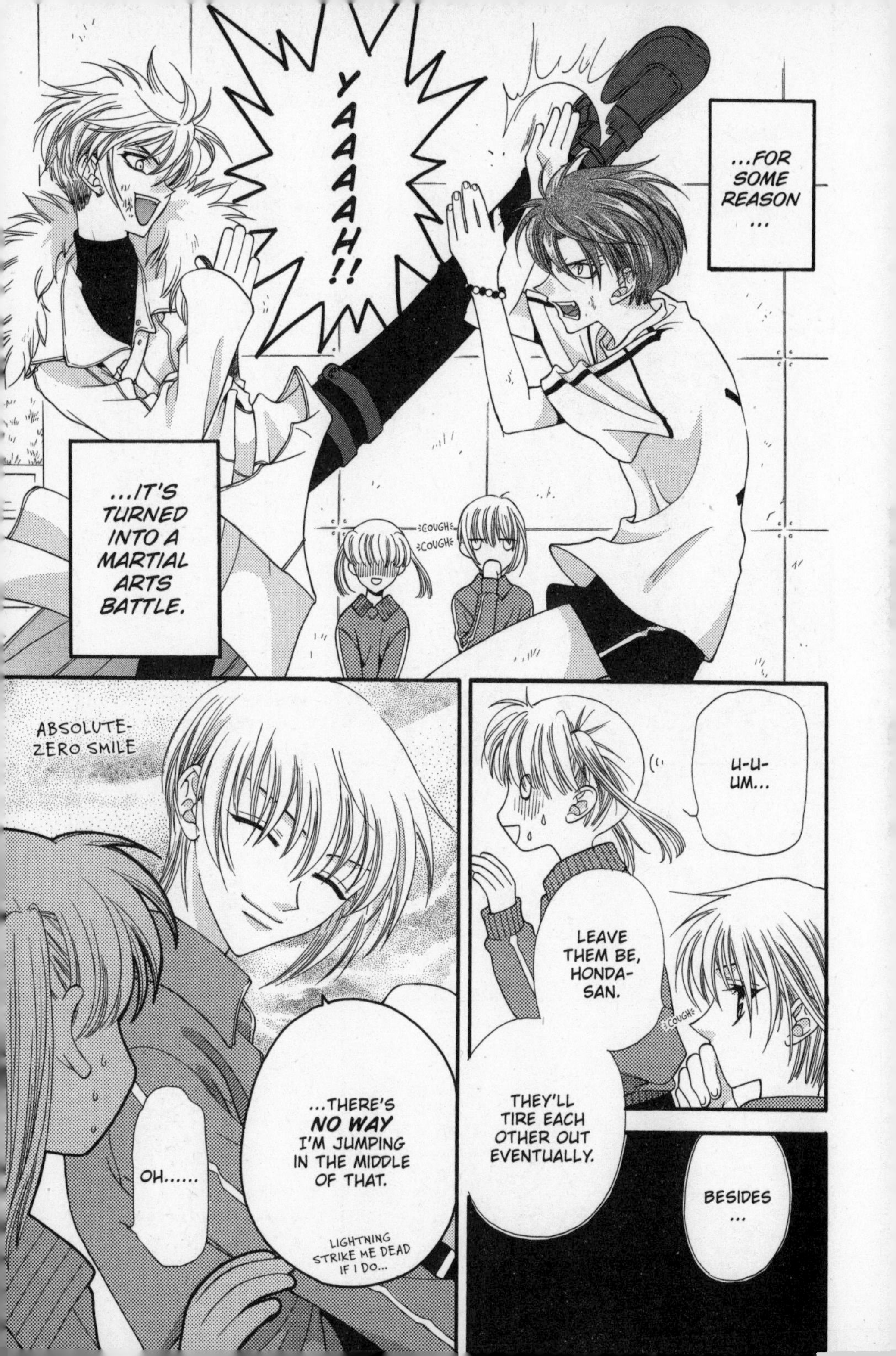
...FOR SOME REASON ...
YAAAAAH!!
COUGH
COUGH
...IT'S TURNED INTO A MARTIAL ARTS BATTLE.
U-U-UM...
LEAVE THEM BE, HONDA-SAN.
COUGH
THEY'LL TIRE EACH OTHER OUT EVENTUALLY.
BESIDES ...
ABSOLUTE-ZERO SMILE
...THERE'S NO WAY I'M JUMPING IN THE MIDDLE OF THAT.
LIGHTNING STRIKE ME DEAD IF I DO...
OH......

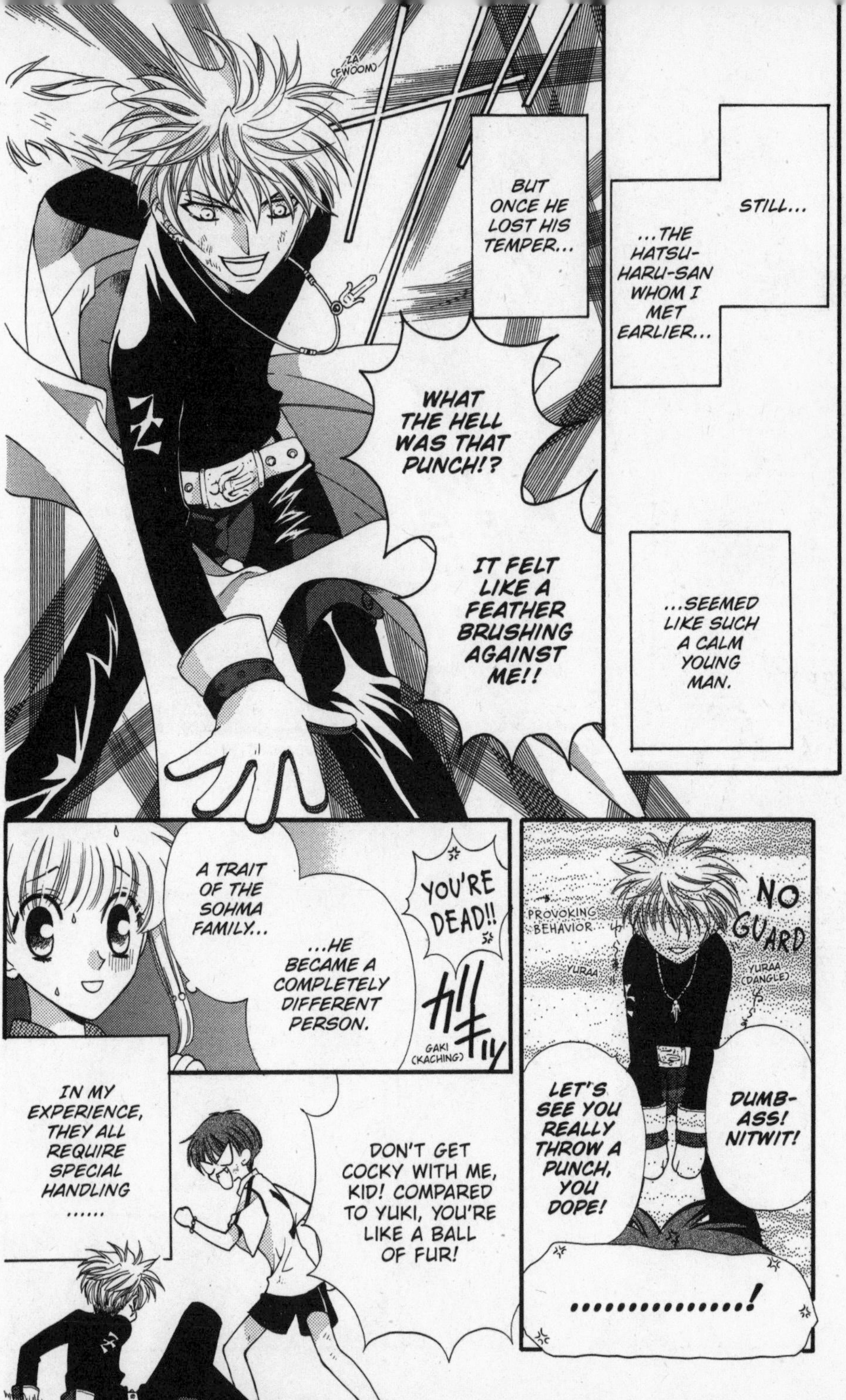
STILL...
...THE HATSU-HARU-SAN WHOM I MET EARLIER...
...SEEMED LIKE SUCH A CALM YOUNG MAN.
BUT ONCE HE LOST HIS TEMPER...
ZA (FWOOM)
WHAT THE HELL WAS THAT PUNCH!?
IT FELT LIKE A FEATHER BRUSHING AGAINST ME!!
NO GUARD
YURAA (DANGLE)
DUMB-ASS! NITWIT!
PROVOKING BEHAVIOR
YURAA
LET'S SEE YOU REALLY THROW A PUNCH, YOU DOPE!
................!
YOU'RE DEAD!!
GAKI (KACHING)
A TRAIT OF THE SOHMA FAMILY...
...HE BECAME A COMPLETELY DIFFERENT PERSON.
DON'T GET COCKY WITH ME, KID! COMPARED TO YUKI, YOU'RE LIKE A BALL OF FUR!
IN MY EXPERIENCE, THEY ALL REQUIRE SPECIAL HANDLING ......

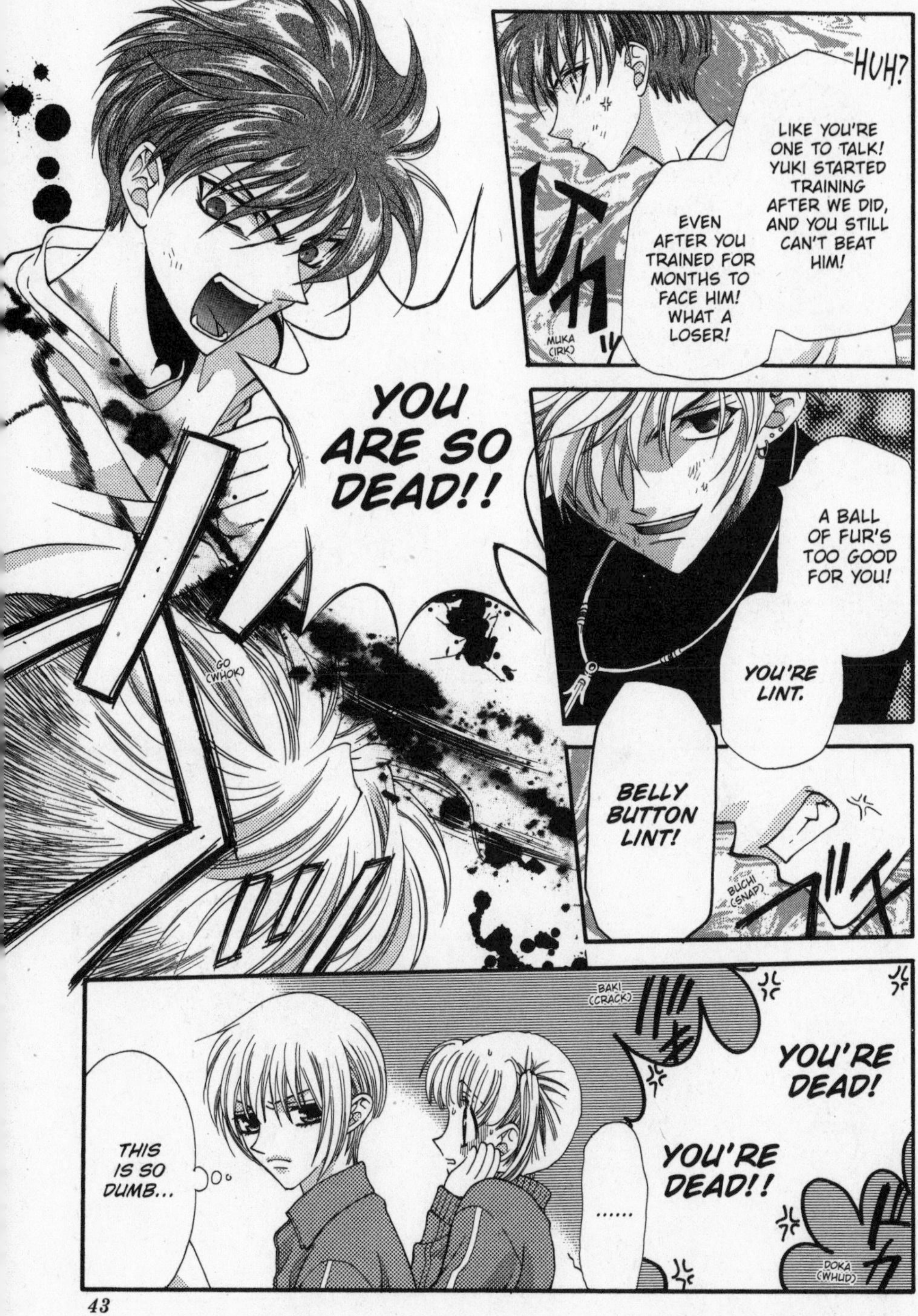
HUH?
LIKE YOU'RE ONE TO TALK! YUKI STARTED TRAINING AFTER WE DID, AND YOU STILL CAN'T BEAT HIM!
EVEN AFTER YOU TRAINED FOR MONTHS TO FACE HIM! WHAT A LOSER!
MUKA (IRK)
A BALL OF FUR'S TOO GOOD FOR YOU!
YOU'RE LINT.
BELLY BUTTON LINT!
BUCHI (SNAP)
YOU ARE SO DEAD!!
GO (WHOK)
BAKI (CRACK)
YOU'RE DEAD!
YOU'RE DEAD!!
......
THIS IS SO DUMB...
DOKA (WHUD)

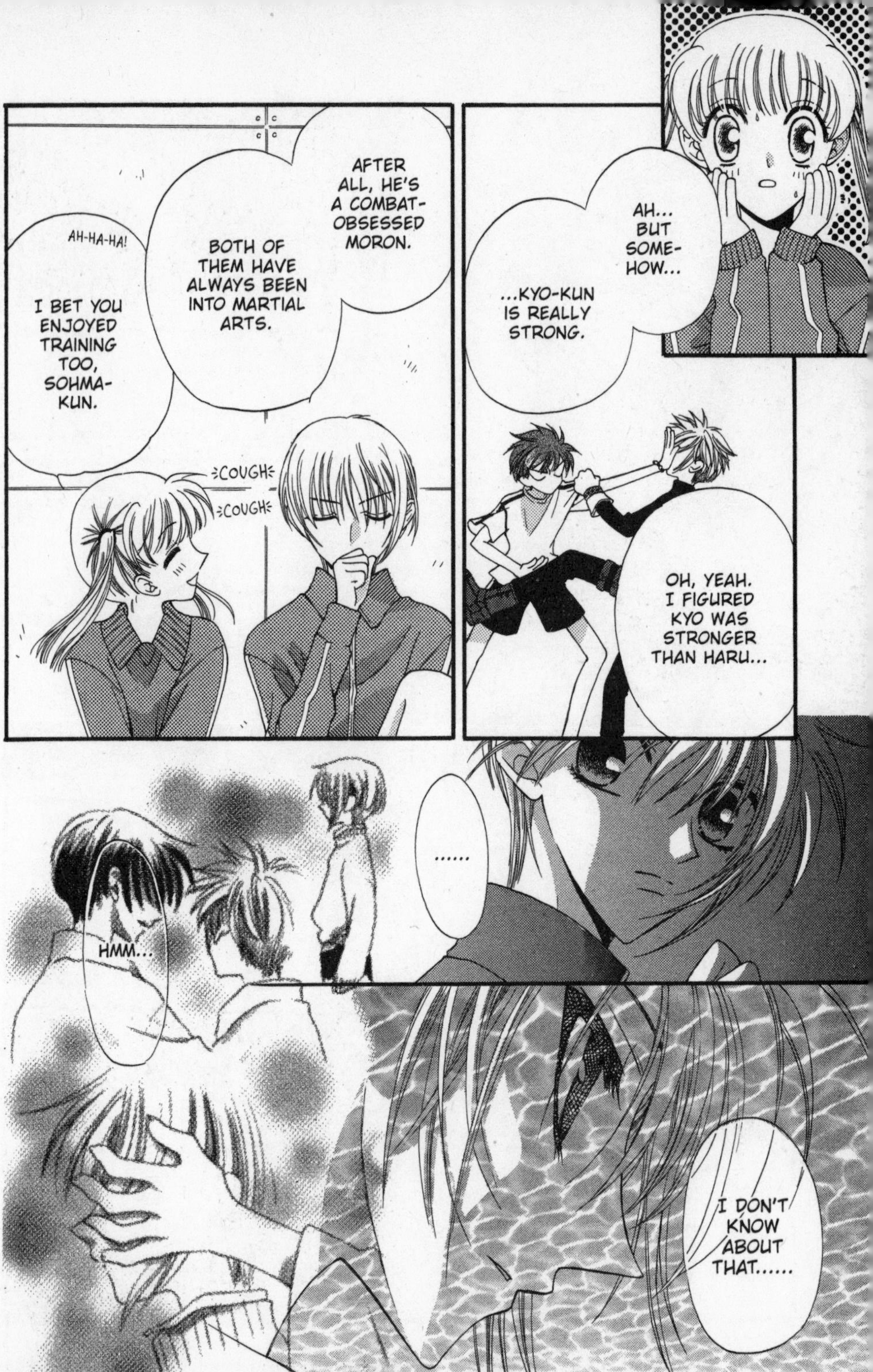
AH... BUT SOME-HOW...
...KYO-KUN IS REALLY STRONG.
OH, YEAH. I FIGURED KYO WAS STRONGER THAN HARU...
AFTER ALL, HE'S A COMBAT-OBSESSED MORON.
BOTH OF THEM HAVE ALWAYS BEEN INTO MARTIAL ARTS.
AH-HA-HA!
I BET YOU ENJOYED TRAINING TOO, SOHMA-KUN.
COUGH
COUGH
......
HMM...
I DON'T KNOW ABOUT THAT......

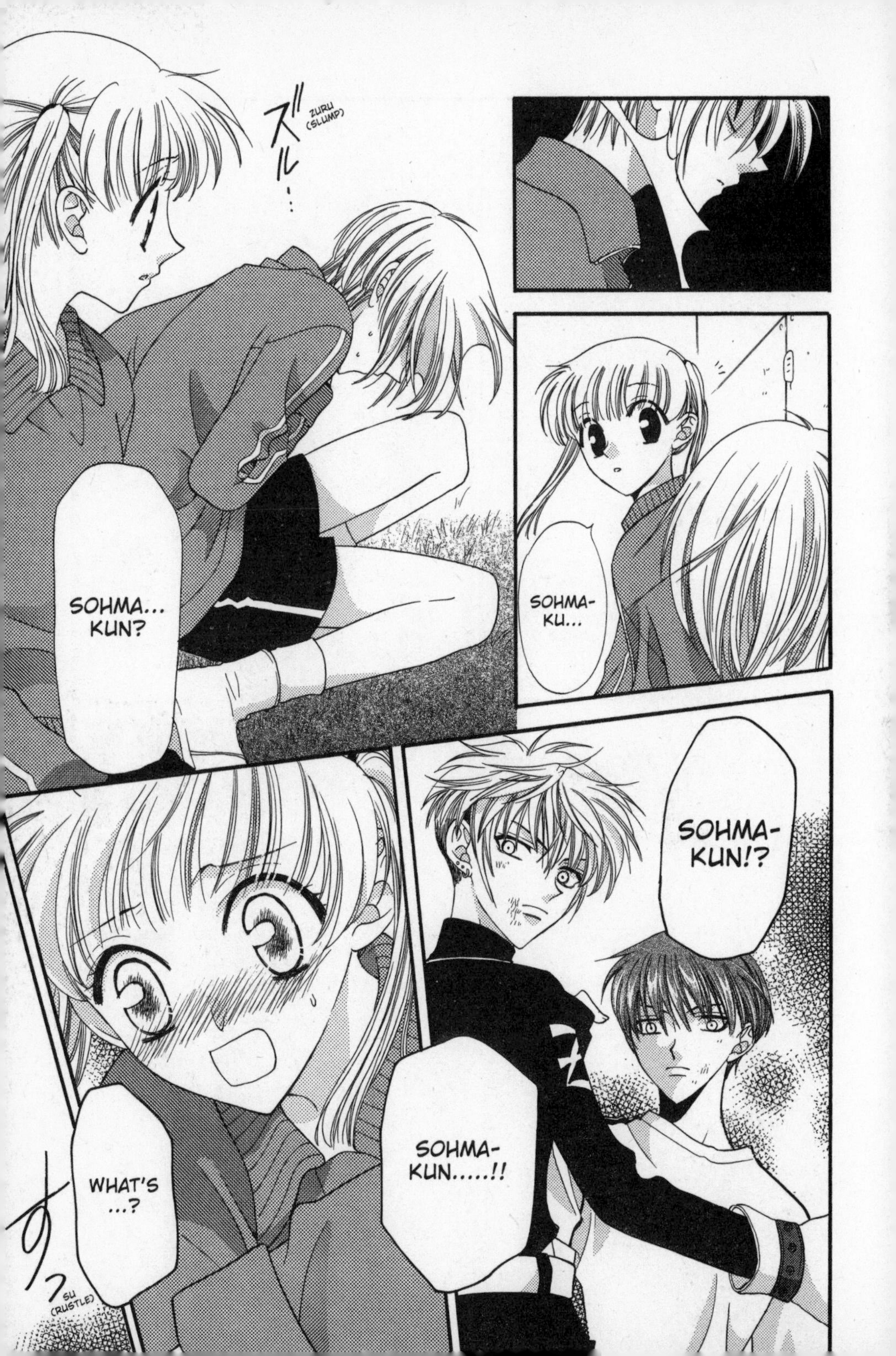
SOHMA-
KU...
ズル…
ZURU
(SLUMP)
SOHMA...
KUN?
SOHMA-
KUN!?
SOHMA-
KUN.....!!
WHAT'S
...?
すっ
SU
(RUSTLE)

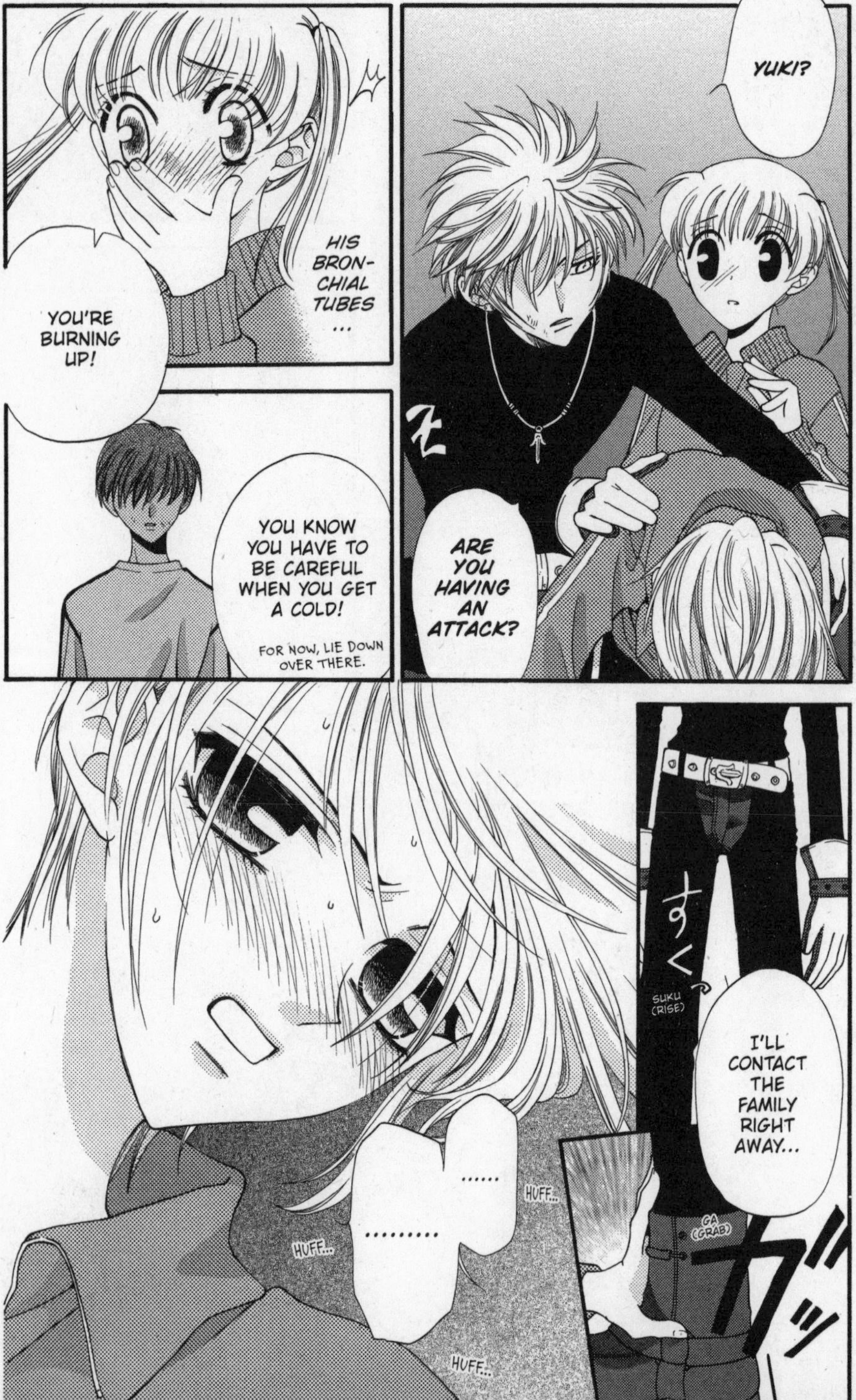
YUKI?
ARE YOU HAVING AN ATTACK?
HIS BRON-CHIAL TUBES ...
YOU'RE BURNING UP!
YOU KNOW YOU HAVE TO BE CAREFUL WHEN YOU GET A COLD!
FOR NOW, LIE DOWN OVER THERE.
すく
SUKU (RISE)
I'LL CONTACT THE FAMILY RIGHT AWAY...
GA (GRAB)
......
HUFF...
....
HUFF...
HUFF...

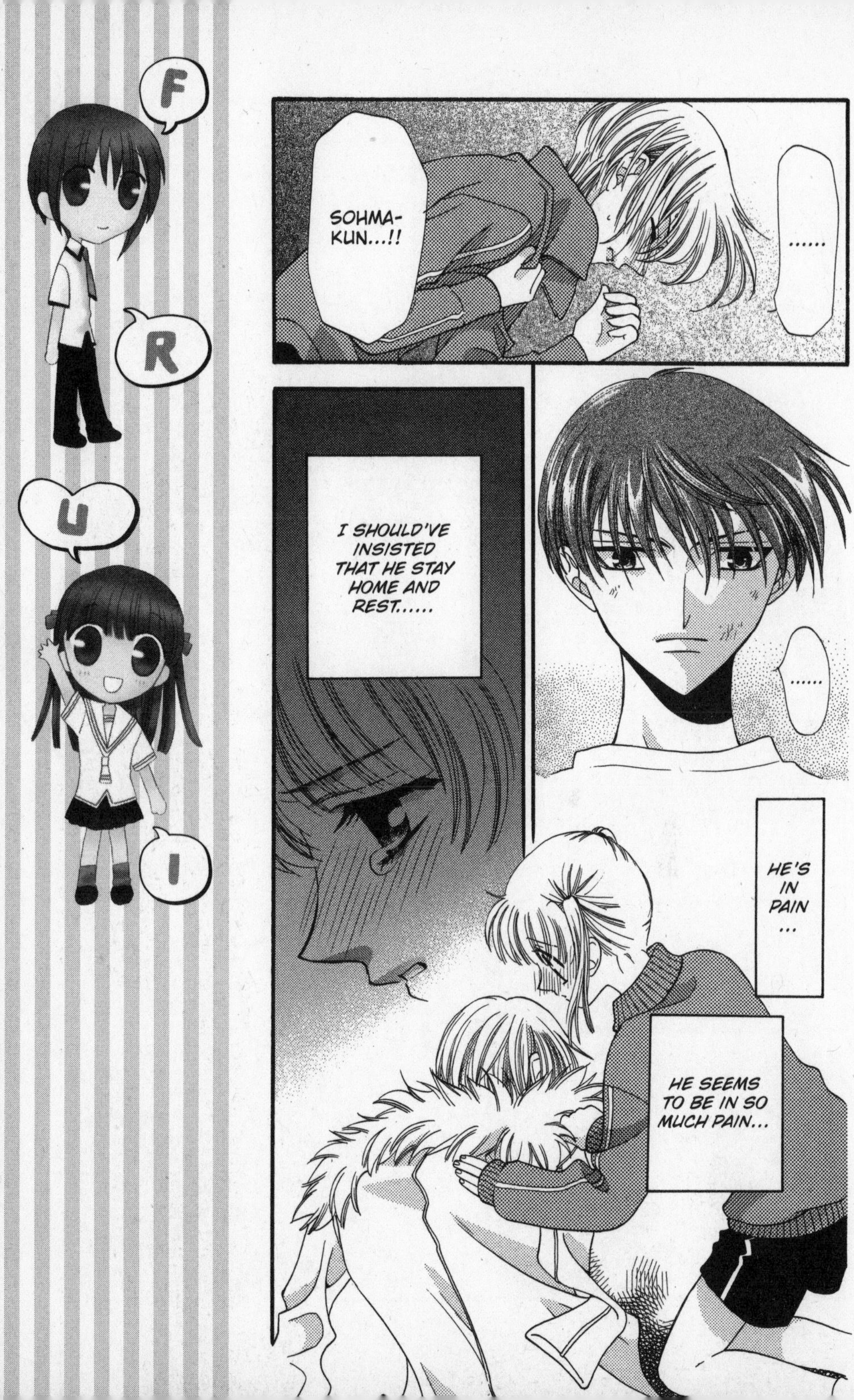
......
SOHMA-KUN...!!
......
HE'S IN PAIN...
HE SEEMS TO BE IN SO MUCH PAIN...
I SHOULD'VE INSISTED THAT HE STAY HOME AND REST......
F
R
U
I

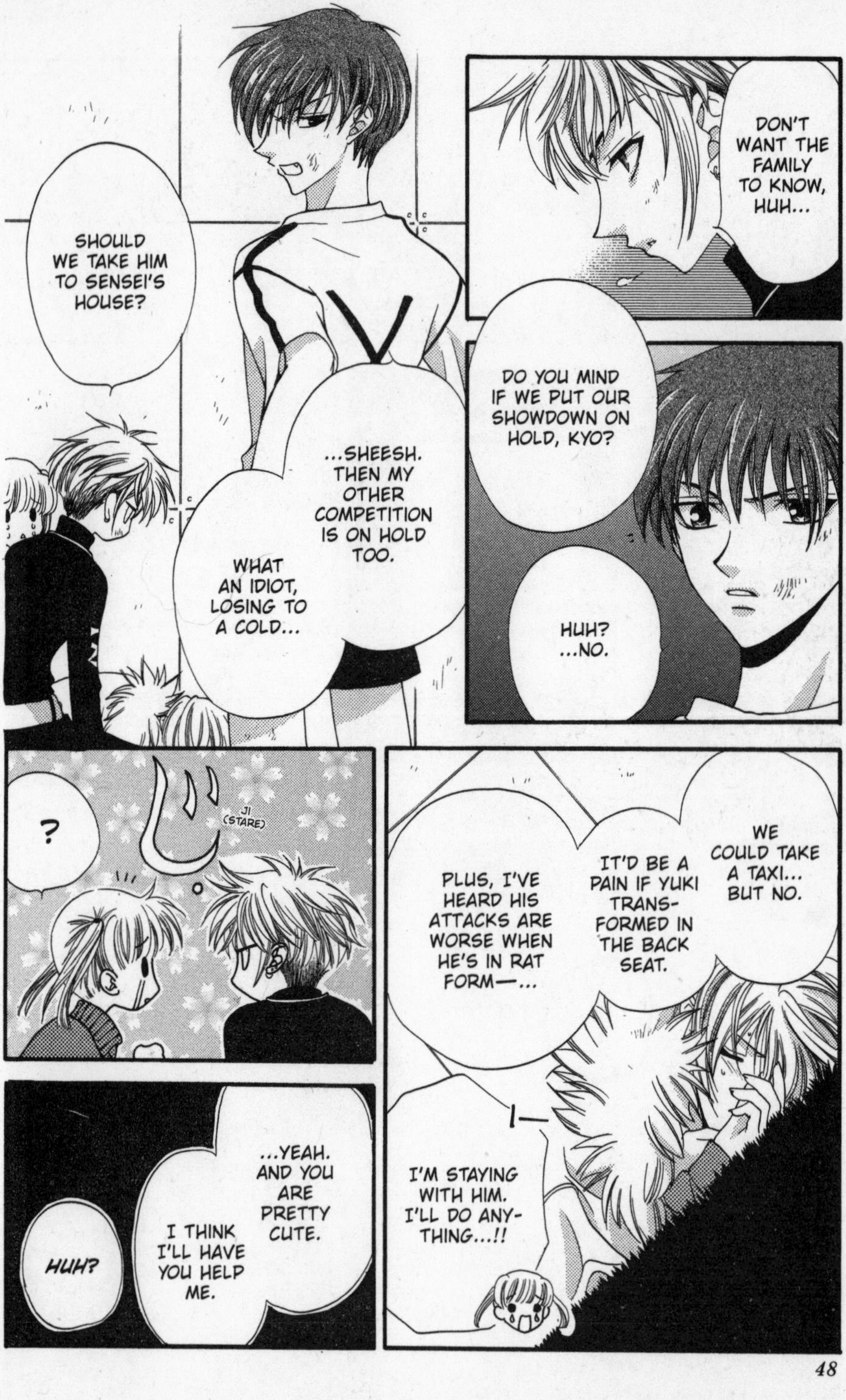
DON'T WANT THE FAMILY TO KNOW, HUH...
DO YOU MIND IF WE PUT OUR SHOWDOWN ON HOLD, KYO?
HUH? ...NO.
SHOULD WE TAKE HIM TO SENSEI'S HOUSE?
...SHEESH. THEN MY OTHER COMPETITION IS ON HOLD TOO.
WHAT AN IDIOT, LOSING TO A COLD...
WE COULD TAKE A TAXI... BUT NO.
IT'D BE A PAIN IF YUKI TRANS-FORMED IN THE BACK SEAT.
PLUS, I'VE HEARD HIS ATTACKS ARE WORSE WHEN HE'S IN RAT FORM—...
I—
I'M STAYING WITH HIM. I'LL DO ANY-THING...!!
JI (STARE)
?
...YEAH. AND YOU ARE PRETTY CUTE.
I THINK I'LL HAVE YOU HELP ME.
HUH?

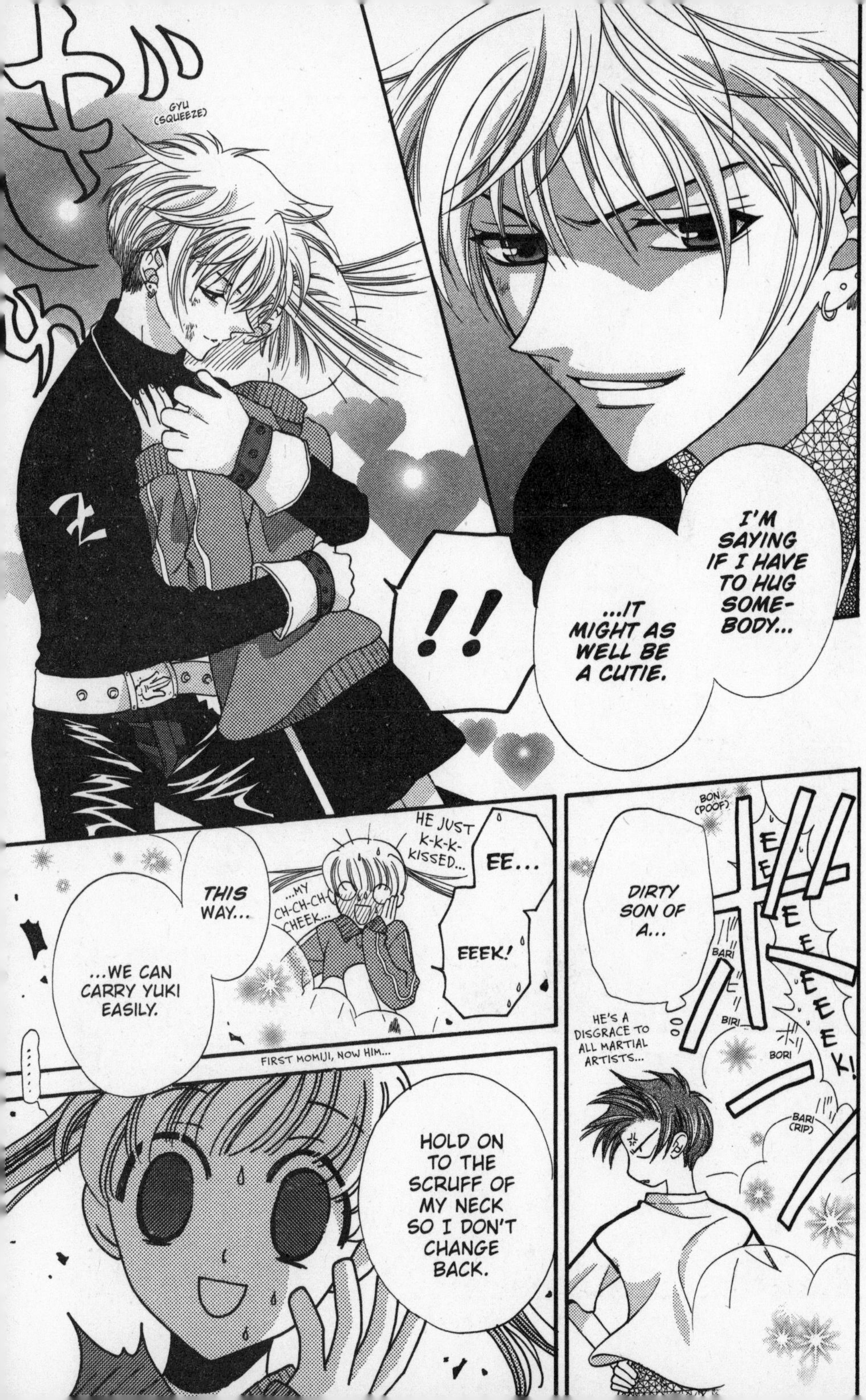
I'M SAYING IF I HAVE TO HUG SOME-BODY...
...IT MIGHT AS WELL BE A CUTIE.
!!
GYU (SQUEEZE)
BON (POOF)
DIRTY SON OF A...
EEEEEEEEK!
BARI
BIRI
BORI
BARI (RIP)
HE'S A DISGRACE TO ALL MARTIAL ARTISTS...
EE...
HE JUST K-K-K-KISSED...
...MY CH-CH-CH-CHEEK...
EEEK!
THIS WAY...
...WE CAN CARRY YUKI EASILY.
FIRST MOMIJI, NOW HIM...
HOLD ON TO THE SCRUFF OF MY NECK SO I DON'T CHANGE BACK.
...

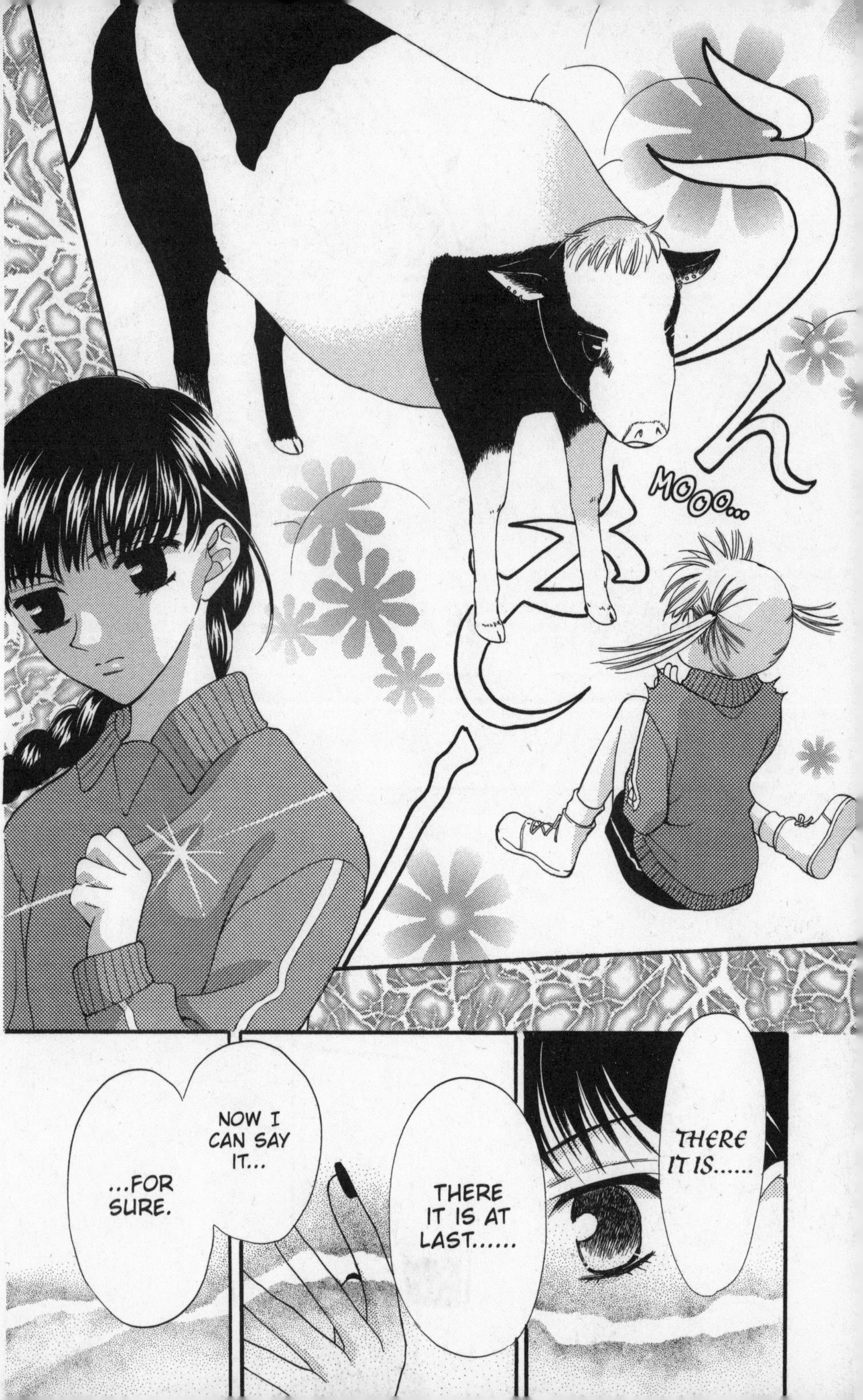
MOOO...
THERE IT IS......
THERE IT IS AT LAST......
NOW I CAN SAY IT...
...FOR SURE.

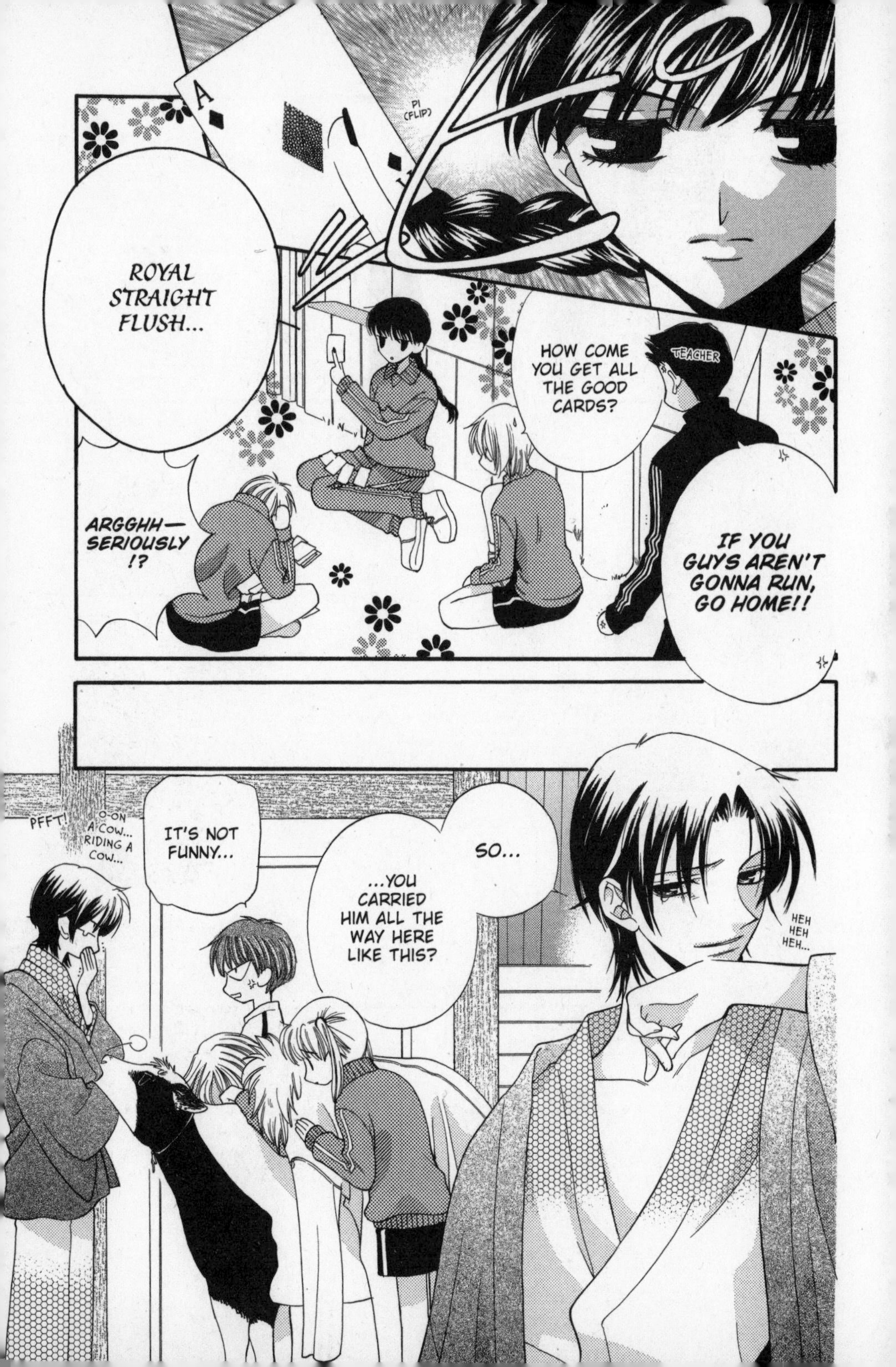
PI (FLIP)
ROYAL STRAIGHT FLUSH...
TEACHER
HOW COME YOU GET ALL THE GOOD CARDS?
IF YOU GUYS AREN'T GONNA RUN, GO HOME!!
ARGGHH—SERIOUSLY!?
HEH HEH HEH...
SO...
...YOU CARRIED HIM ALL THE WAY HERE LIKE THIS?
IT'S NOT FUNNY...
O-ON A COW... RIDING A COW...
PFFT!

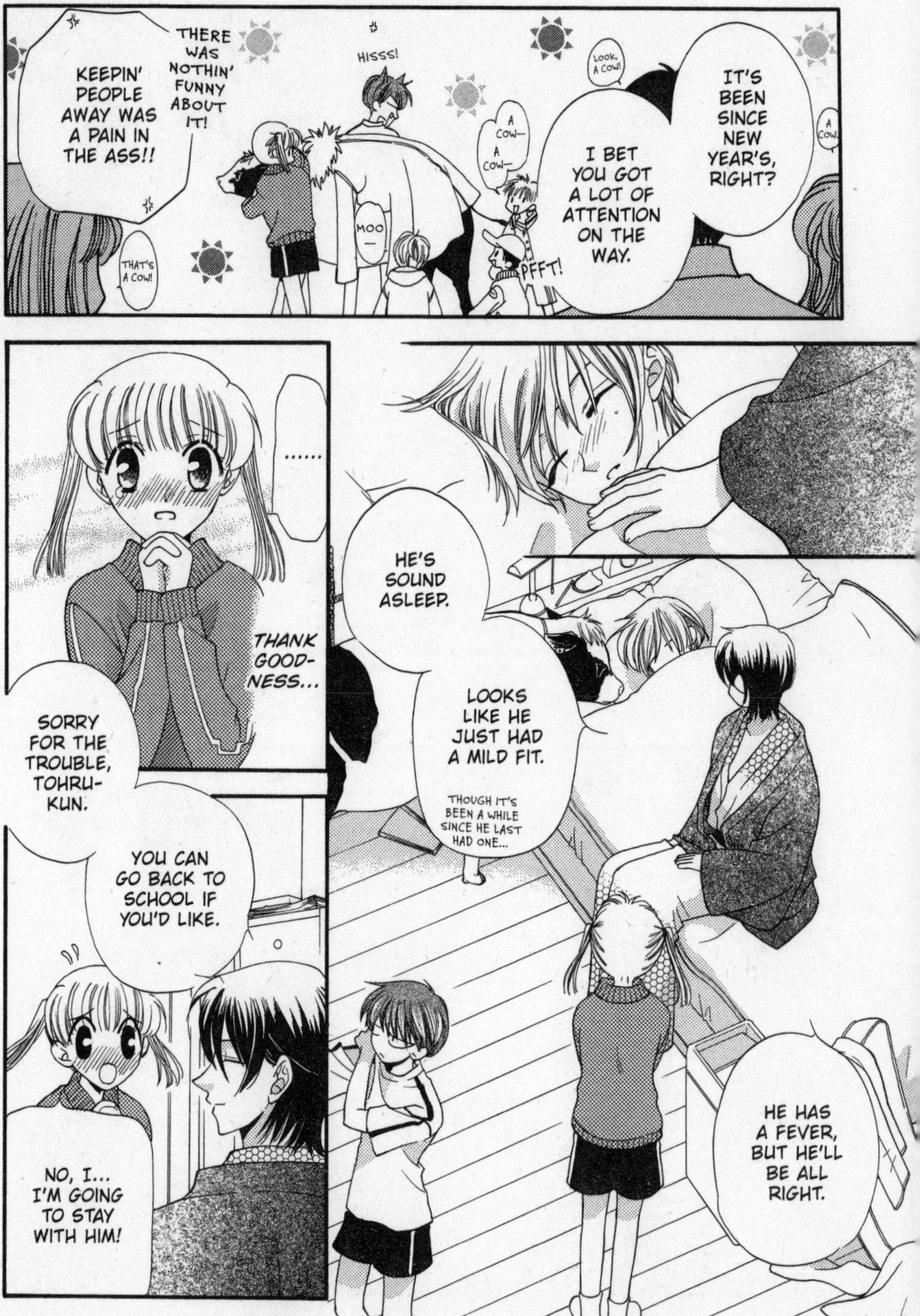
IT'S BEEN SINCE NEW YEAR'S, RIGHT?
A COW
LOOK, A COW!
I BET YOU GOT A LOT OF ATTENTION ON THE WAY.
PFFT!
A COW— A COW—
HISSS!
MOO
THERE WAS NOTHIN' FUNNY ABOUT IT!
KEEPIN' PEOPLE AWAY WAS A PAIN IN THE ASS!!
THAT'S A COW!
HE'S SOUND ASLEEP.
LOOKS LIKE HE JUST HAD A MILD FIT.
THOUGH IT'S BEEN A WHILE SINCE HE LAST HAD ONE...
HE HAS A FEVER, BUT HE'LL BE ALL RIGHT.
......
THANK GOODNESS...
SORRY FOR THE TROUBLE, TOHRU-KUN.
YOU CAN GO BACK TO SCHOOL IF YOU'D LIKE.
NO, I... I'M GOING TO STAY WITH HIM!

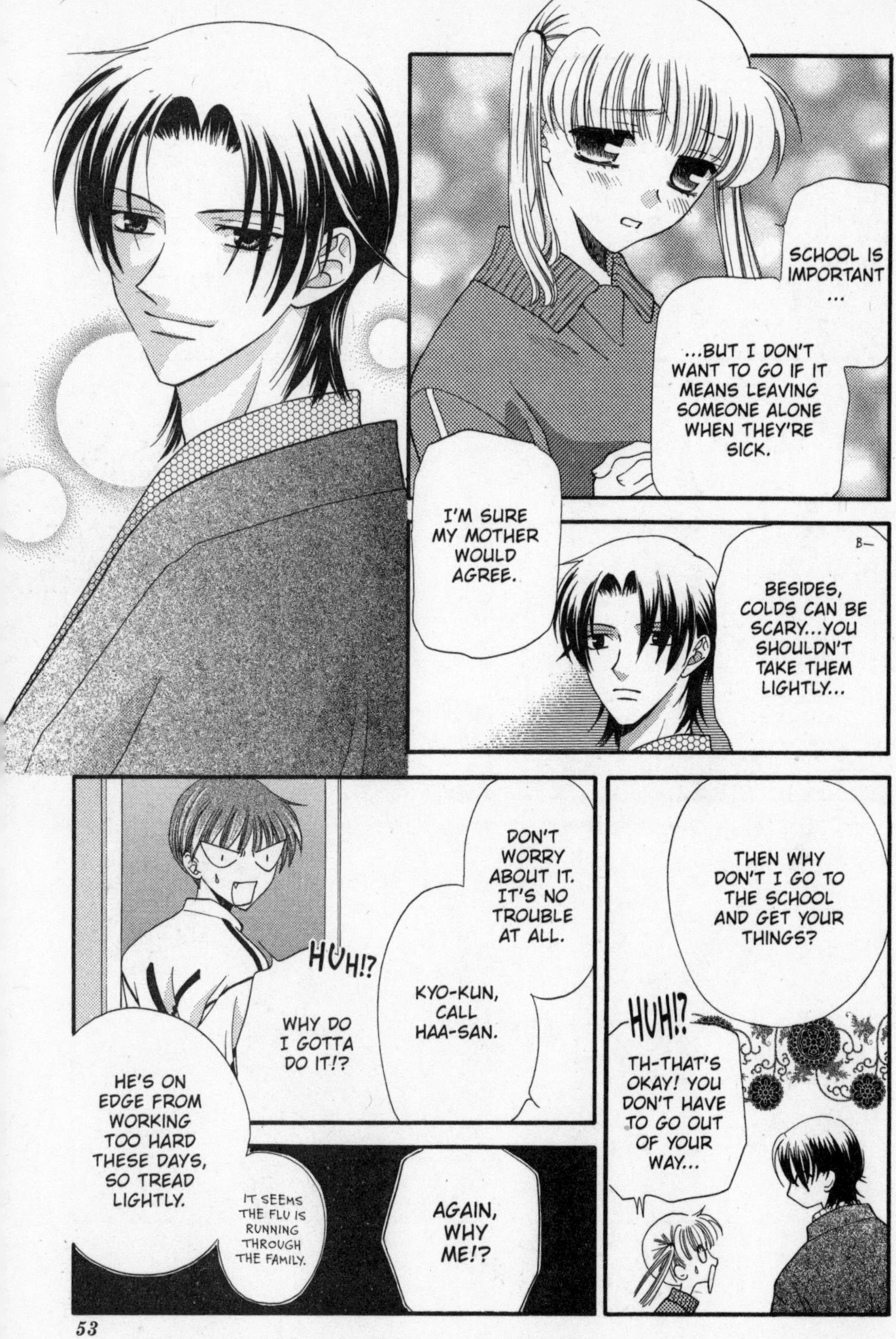
SCHOOL IS IMPORTANT ...
...BUT I DON'T WANT TO GO IF IT MEANS LEAVING SOMEONE ALONE WHEN THEY'RE SICK.
I'M SURE MY MOTHER WOULD AGREE.
B—
BESIDES, COLDS CAN BE SCARY...YOU SHOULDN'T TAKE THEM LIGHTLY...
THEN WHY DON'T I GO TO THE SCHOOL AND GET YOUR THINGS?
HUH!?
TH-THAT'S OKAY! YOU DON'T HAVE TO GO OUT OF YOUR WAY...
DON'T WORRY ABOUT IT. IT'S NO TROUBLE AT ALL.
KYO-KUN, CALL HAA-SAN.
HUH!?
WHY DO I GOTTA DO IT!?
HE'S ON EDGE FROM WORKING TOO HARD THESE DAYS, SO TREAD LIGHTLY.
AGAIN, WHY ME!?
IT SEEMS THE FLU IS RUNNING THROUGH THE FAMILY.

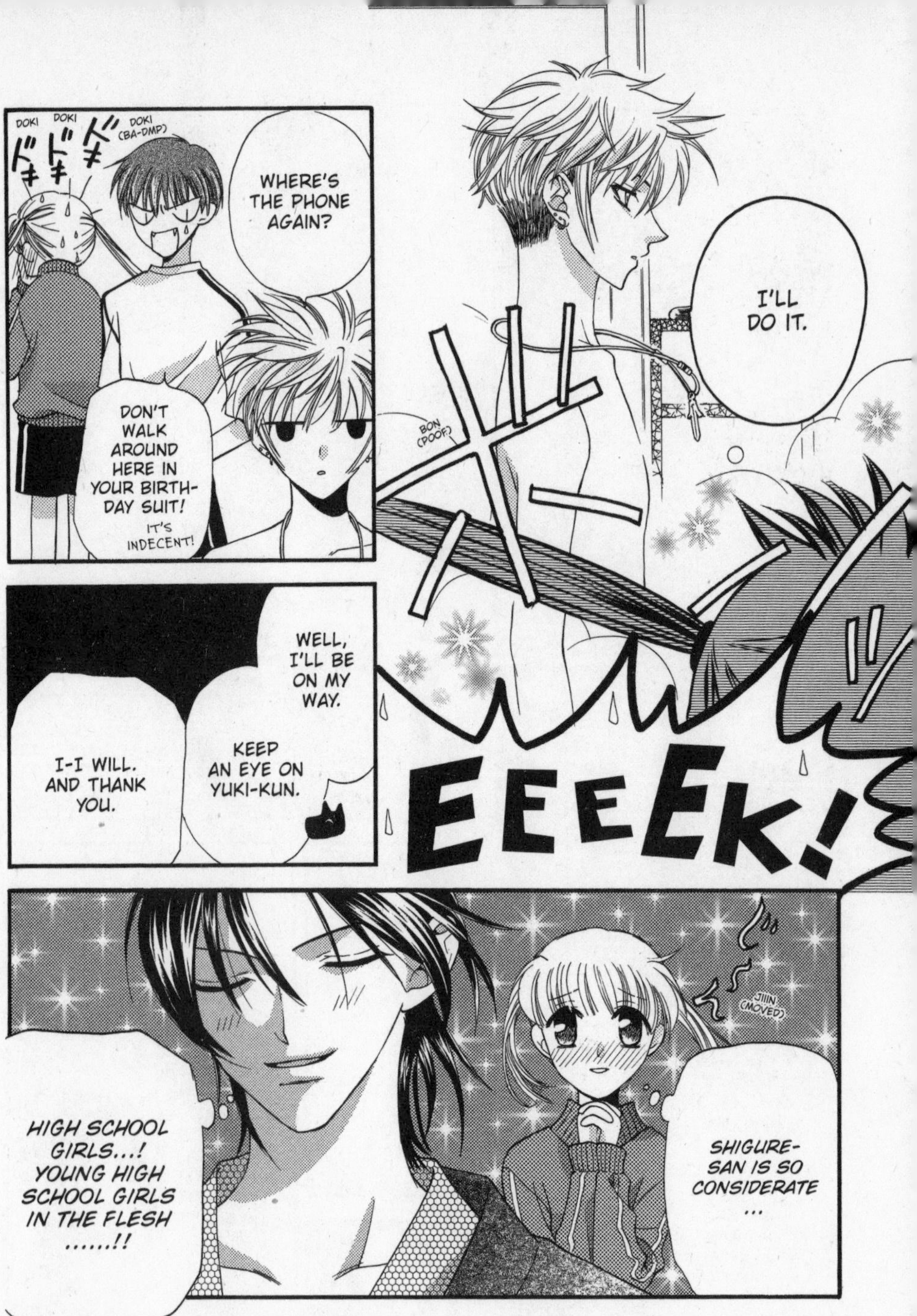
I'LL DO IT.
BON (POOF)
EEEEK!
WHERE'S THE PHONE AGAIN?
DOKI (BA-DMP)
DOKI
DOKI
DON'T WALK AROUND HERE IN YOUR BIRTH-DAY SUIT!
IT'S INDECENT!
WELL, I'LL BE ON MY WAY.
KEEP AN EYE ON YUKI-KUN.
I-I WILL. AND THANK YOU.
JIIN (MOVED)
SHIGURE-SAN IS SO CONSIDERATE ...
HIGH SCHOOL GIRLS...! YOUNG HIGH SCHOOL GIRLS IN THE FLESH ......!!

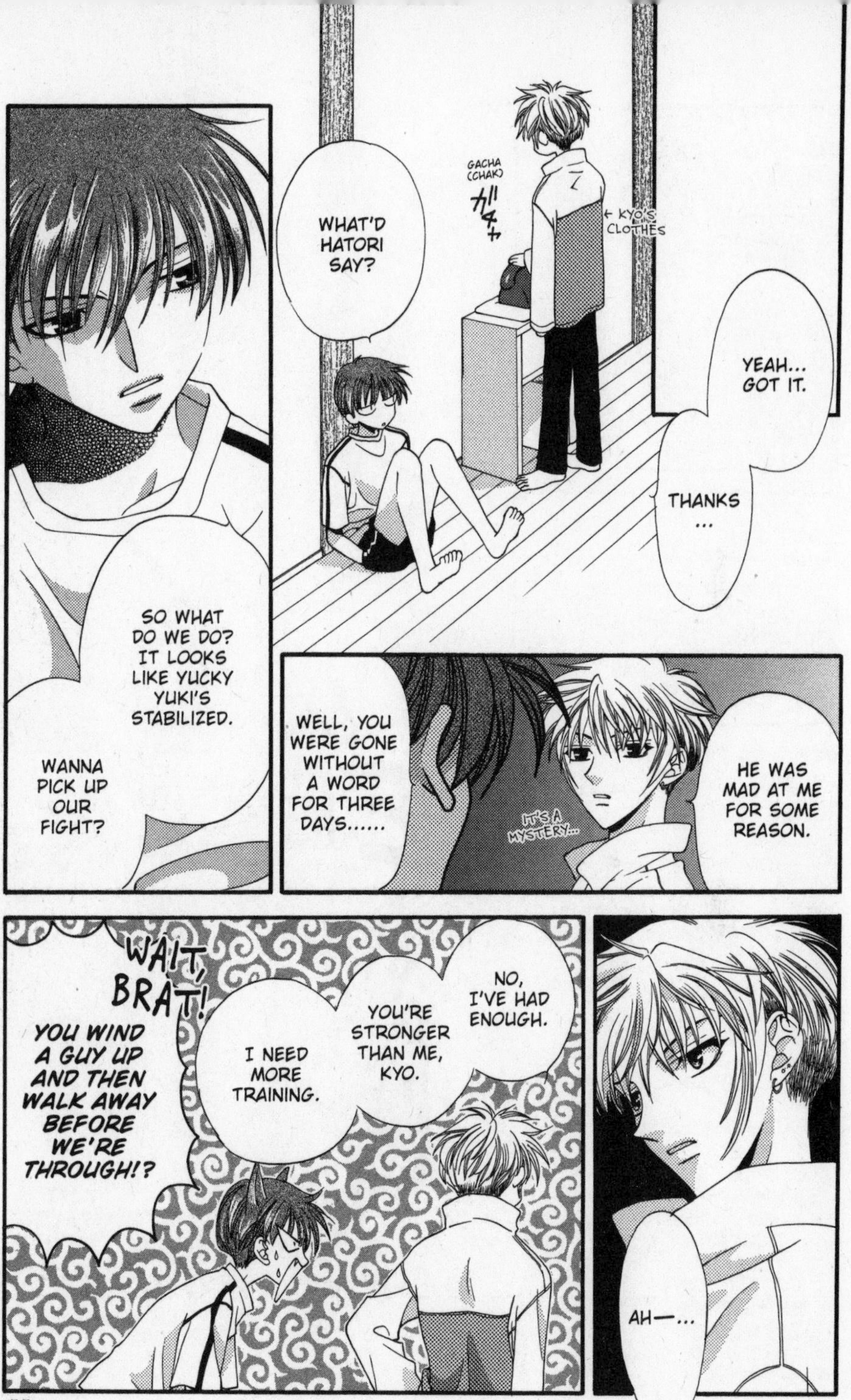
YEAH... GOT IT.
THANKS ...
GACHA (CHAK)
← KYO'S CLOTHES
WHAT'D HATORI SAY?
HE WAS MAD AT ME FOR SOME REASON.
IT'S A MYSTERY...
WELL, YOU WERE GONE WITHOUT A WORD FOR THREE DAYS......
SO WHAT DO WE DO? IT LOOKS LIKE YUCKY YUKI'S STABILIZED.
WANNA PICK UP OUR FIGHT?
AH—...
NO, I'VE HAD ENOUGH.
YOU'RE STRONGER THAN ME, KYO.
I NEED MORE TRAINING.
WAIT, BRAT!
YOU WIND A GUY UP AND THEN WALK AWAY BEFORE WE'RE THROUGH!?

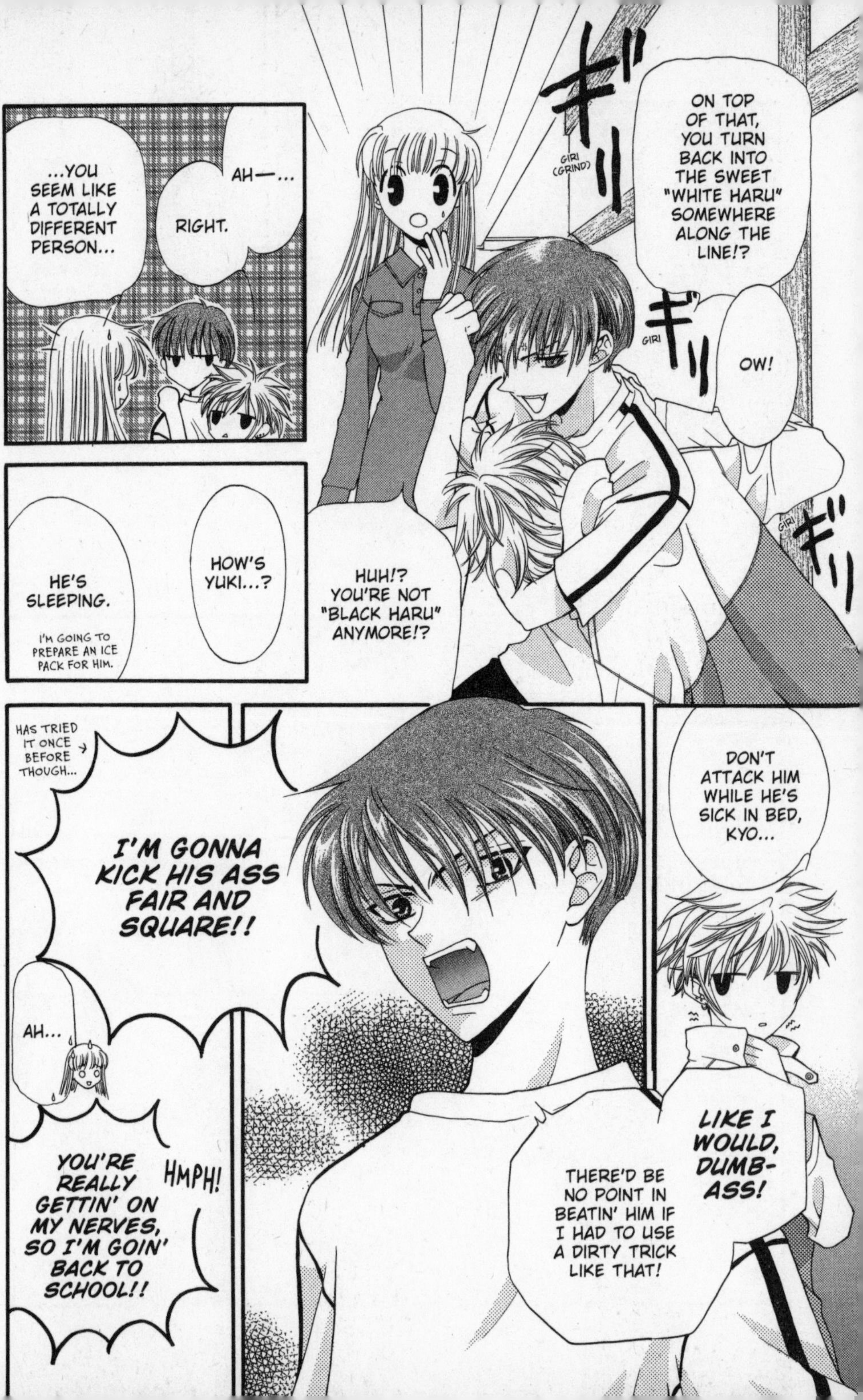
ギリ
GIRI (GRIND)
ON TOP OF THAT, YOU TURN BACK INTO THE SWEET "WHITE HARU" SOMEWHERE ALONG THE LINE!?
ギリ
GIRI
OW!
ギリ
GIRI
HUH!? YOU'RE NOT "BLACK HARU" ANYMORE!?
AH—... RIGHT.
...YOU SEEM LIKE A TOTALLY DIFFERENT PERSON...
HOW'S YUKI...?
HE'S SLEEPING.
I'M GOING TO PREPARE AN ICE PACK FOR HIM.
DON'T ATTACK HIM WHILE HE'S SICK IN BED, KYO...
LIKE I WOULD, DUMB-ASS!
THERE'D BE NO POINT IN BEATIN' HIM IF I HAD TO USE A DIRTY TRICK LIKE THAT!
I'M GONNA KICK HIS ASS FAIR AND SQUARE!!
HAS TRIED IT ONCE BEFORE THOUGH...
AH...
HMPH!
YOU'RE REALLY GETTIN' ON MY NERVES, SO I'M GOIN' BACK TO SCHOOL!!

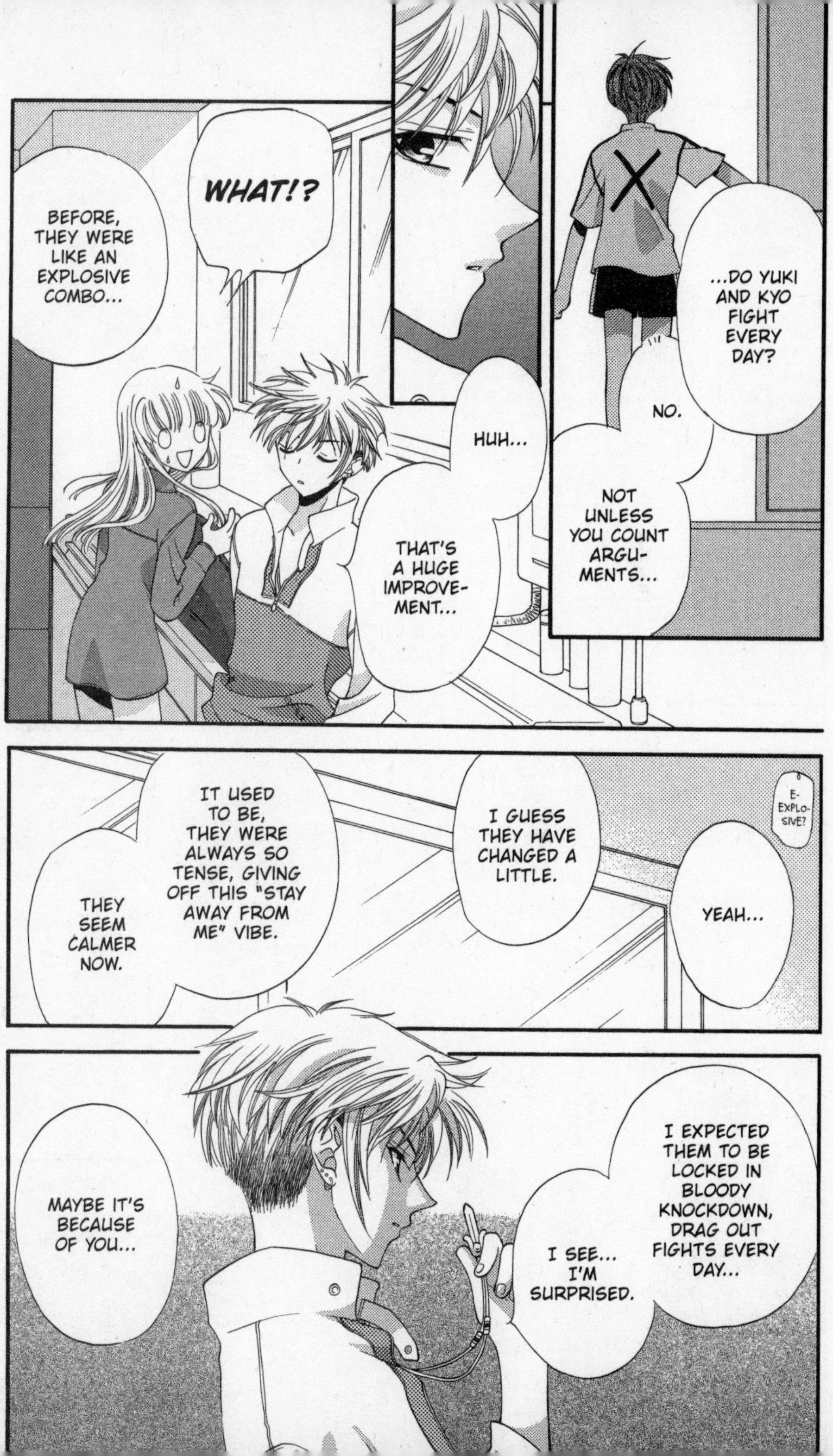
...DO YUKI AND KYO FIGHT EVERY DAY?
NO.
NOT UNLESS YOU COUNT ARGU-MENTS...
HUH...
THAT'S A HUGE IMPROVE-MENT...
WHAT!?
BEFORE, THEY WERE LIKE AN EXPLOSIVE COMBO...
E-EXPLO-SIVE?
YEAH...
I GUESS THEY HAVE CHANGED A LITTLE.
IT USED TO BE, THEY WERE ALWAYS SO TENSE, GIVING OFF THIS "STAY AWAY FROM ME" VIBE.
THEY SEEM CALMER NOW.
I EXPECTED THEM TO BE LOCKED IN BLOODY KNOCKDOWN, DRAG OUT FIGHTS EVERY DAY...
I SEE... I'M SURPRISED.
MAYBE IT'S BECAUSE OF YOU...

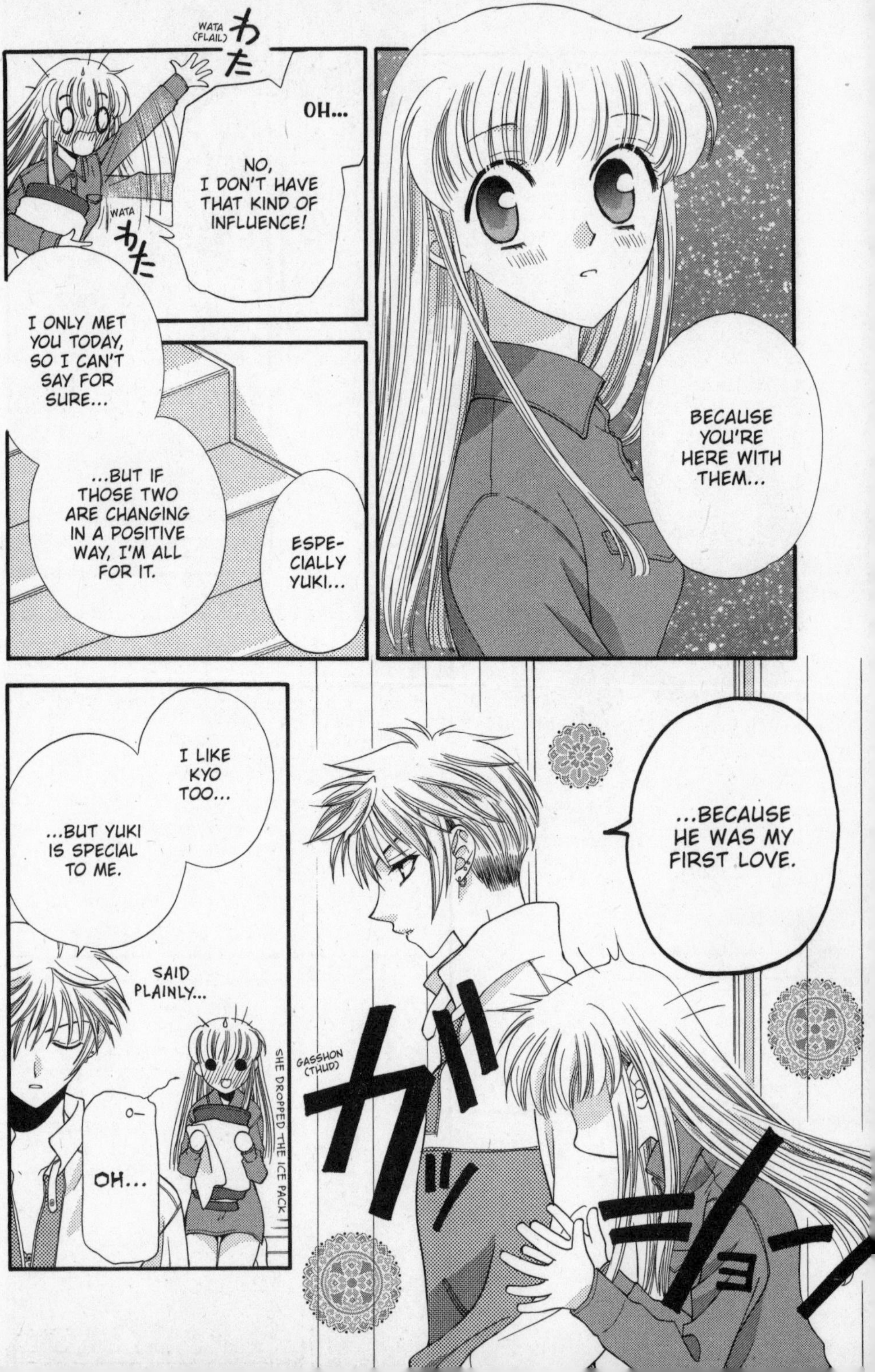
BECAUSE YOU'RE HERE WITH THEM...
WATA (FLAIL) わた
OH...
NO, I DON'T HAVE THAT KIND OF INFLUENCE!
WATA わた
I ONLY MET YOU TODAY, SO I CAN'T SAY FOR SURE...
...BUT IF THOSE TWO ARE CHANGING IN A POSITIVE WAY, I'M ALL FOR IT.
ESPE-CIALLY YUKI...
I LIKE KYO TOO...
...BUT YUKI IS SPECIAL TO ME.
SAID PLAINLY...
O—
OH...
SHE DROPPED THE ICE PACK
...BECAUSE HE WAS MY FIRST LOVE.
GASSHON (THUD)
ガシャーン

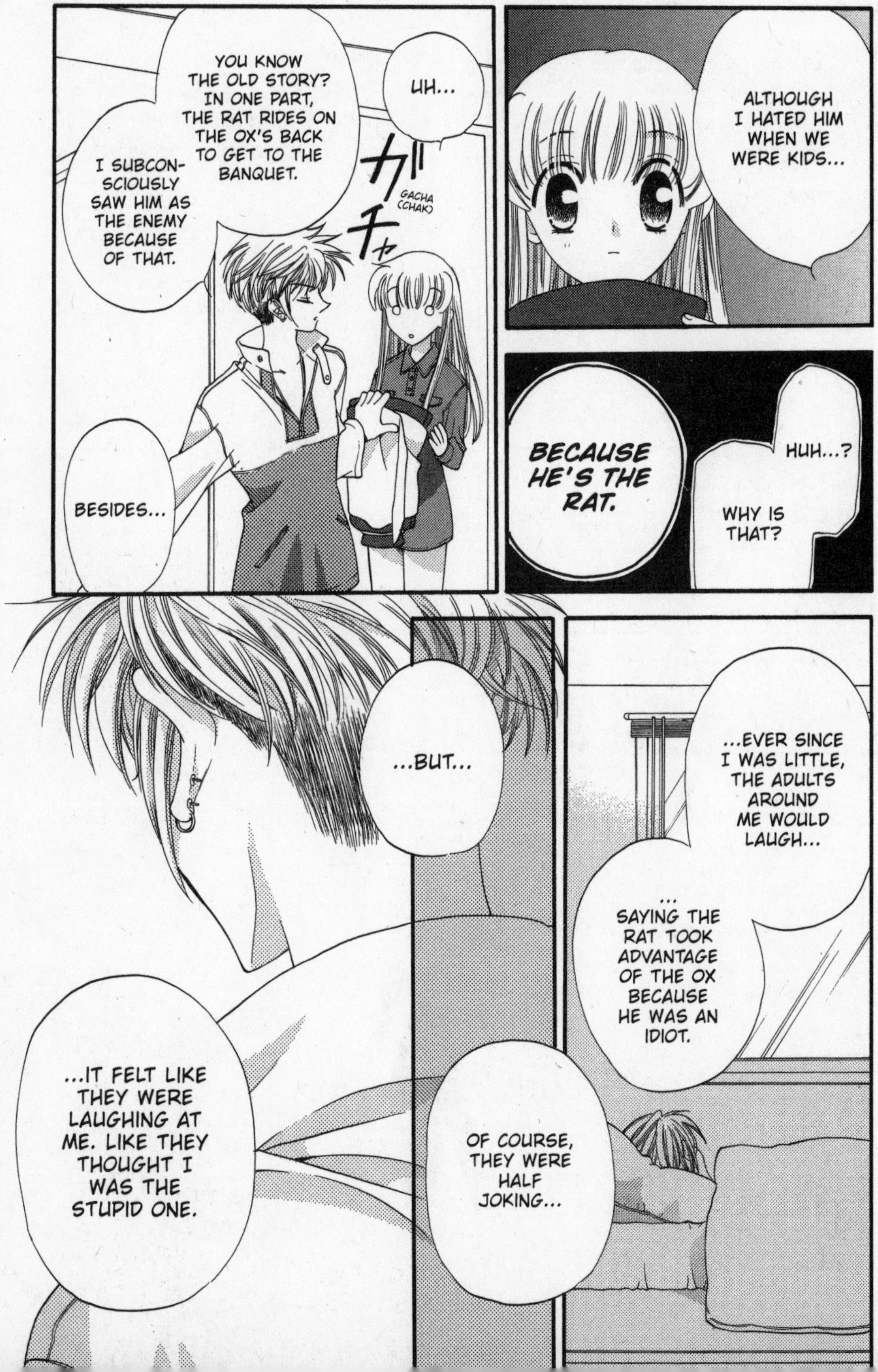
ALTHOUGH I HATED HIM WHEN WE WERE KIDS...
HUH...?
WHY IS THAT?
BECAUSE HE'S THE RAT.
UH...
ガチャ
GACHA (CHAK)
YOU KNOW THE OLD STORY? IN ONE PART, THE RAT RIDES ON THE OX'S BACK TO GET TO THE BANQUET.
I SUBCON-SCIOUSLY SAW HIM AS THE ENEMY BECAUSE OF THAT.
BESIDES...
...EVER SINCE I WAS LITTLE, THE ADULTS AROUND ME WOULD LAUGH...
...SAYING THE RAT TOOK ADVANTAGE OF THE OX BECAUSE HE WAS AN IDIOT.
OF COURSE, THEY WERE HALF JOKING...
...BUT...
...IT FELT LIKE THEY WERE LAUGHING AT ME. LIKE THEY THOUGHT I WAS THE STUPID ONE.

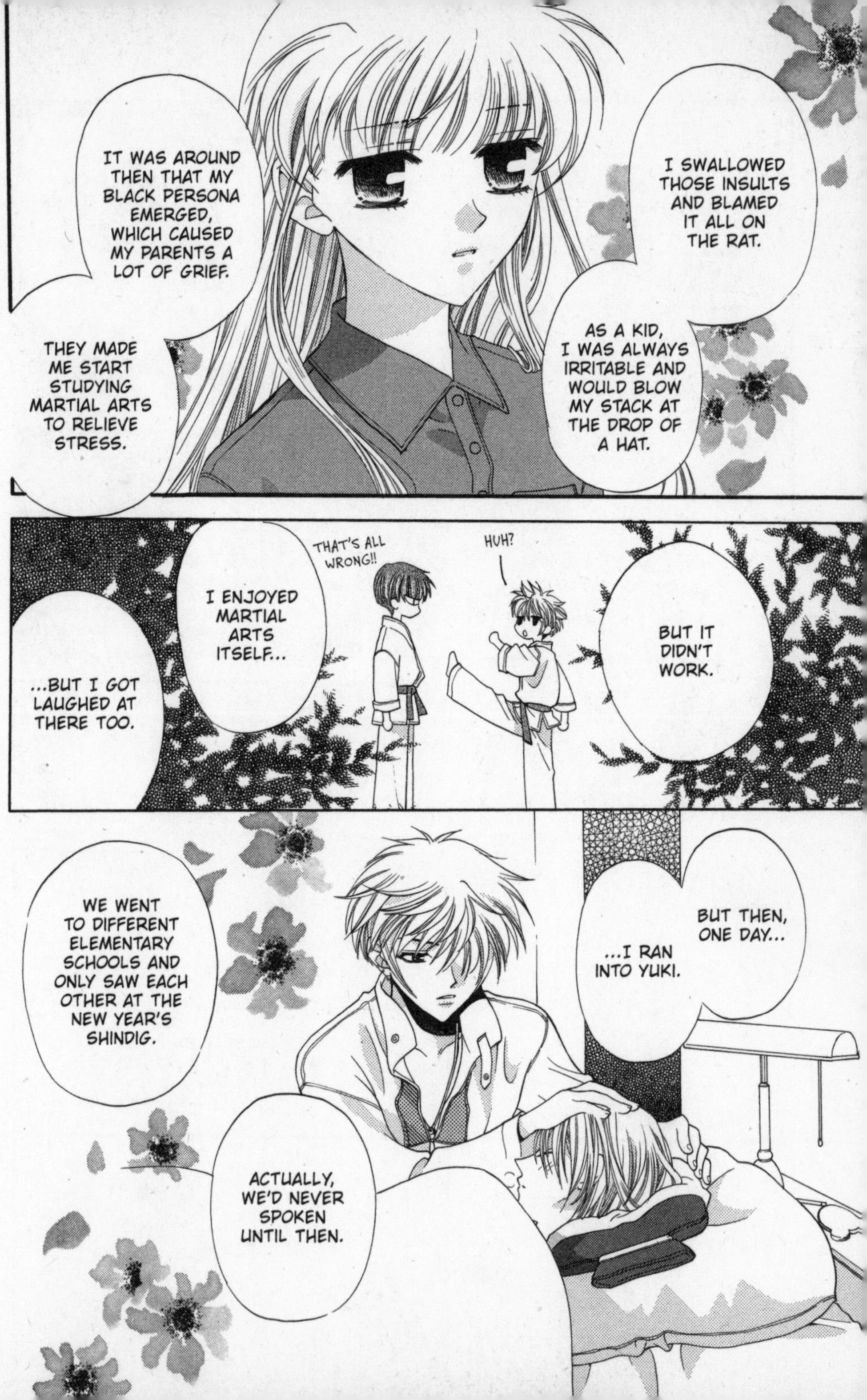
I SWALLOWED THOSE INSULTS AND BLAMED IT ALL ON THE RAT.
AS A KID, I WAS ALWAYS IRRITABLE AND WOULD BLOW MY STACK AT THE DROP OF A HAT.
IT WAS AROUND THEN THAT MY BLACK PERSONA EMERGED, WHICH CAUSED MY PARENTS A LOT OF GRIEF.
THEY MADE ME START STUDYING MARTIAL ARTS TO RELIEVE STRESS.
BUT IT DIDN'T WORK.
HUH?
THAT'S ALL WRONG!!
I ENJOYED MARTIAL ARTS ITSELF...
...BUT I GOT LAUGHED AT THERE TOO.
BUT THEN, ONE DAY...
...I RAN INTO YUKI.
WE WENT TO DIFFERENT ELEMENTARY SCHOOLS AND ONLY SAW EACH OTHER AT THE NEW YEAR'S SHINDIG.
ACTUALLY, WE'D NEVER SPOKEN UNTIL THEN.

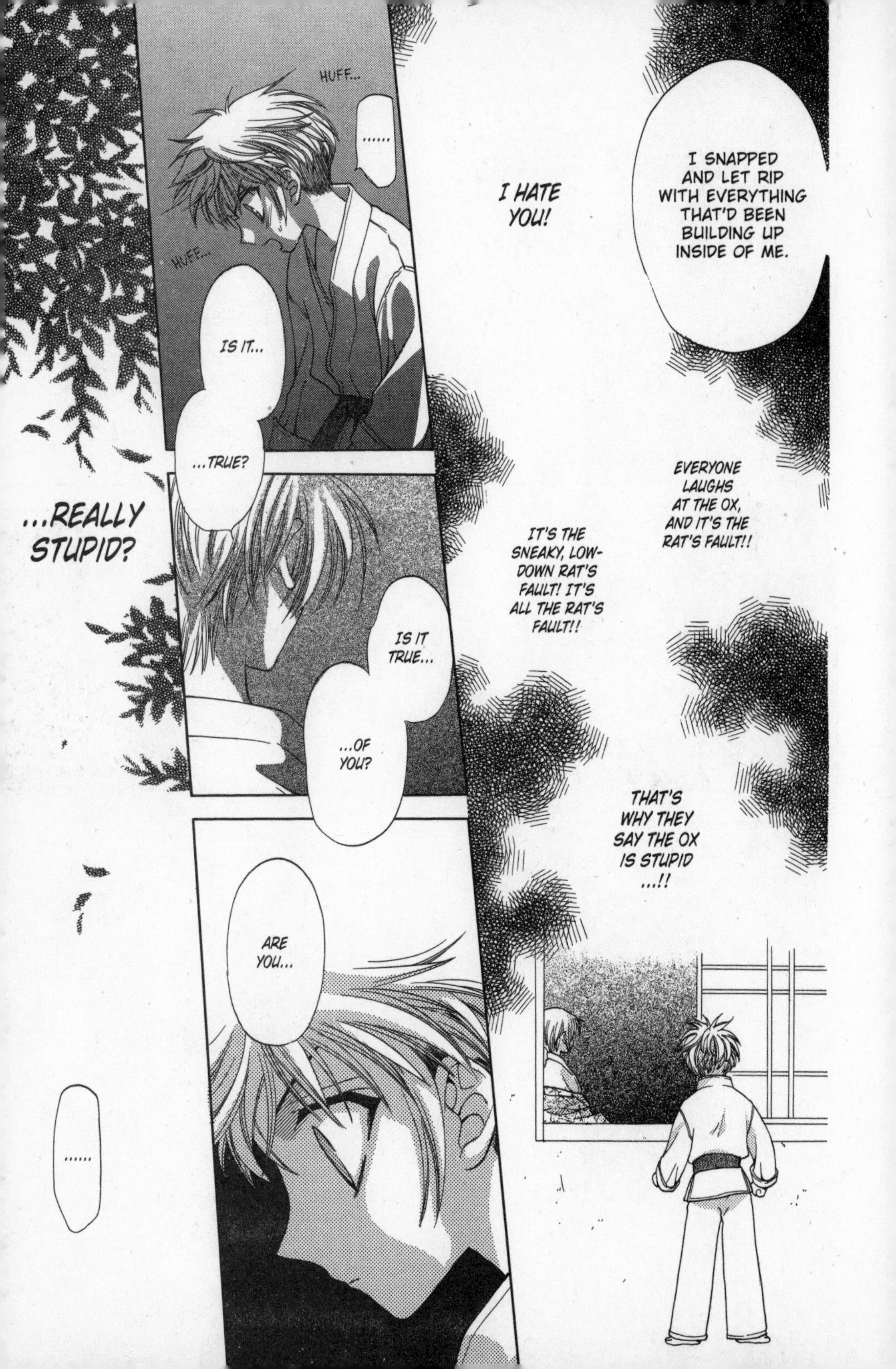
I SNAPPED AND LET RIP WITH EVERYTHING THAT'D BEEN BUILDING UP INSIDE OF ME.
I HATE YOU!
EVERYONE LAUGHS AT THE OX, AND IT'S THE RAT'S FAULT!!
IT'S THE SNEAKY, LOW-DOWN RAT'S FAULT! IT'S ALL THE RAT'S FAULT!!
THAT'S WHY THEY SAY THE OX IS STUPID ...!!
HUFF...
......
HUFF...
IS IT...
...TRUE?
...REALLY STUPID?
IS IT TRUE...
...OF YOU?
ARE YOU...
......

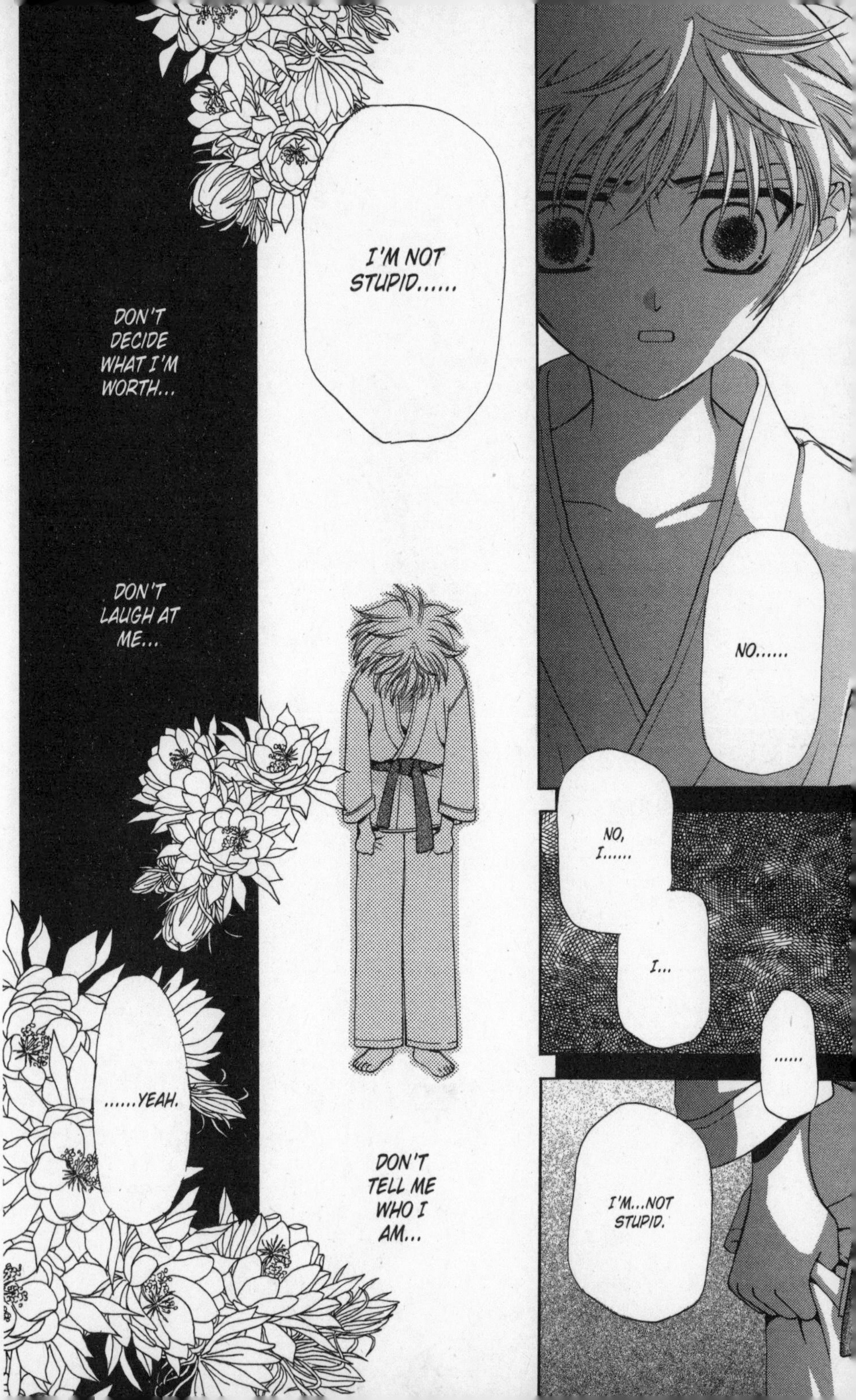
NO......
NO, I......
I...
......
I'M...NOT STUPID.
I'M NOT STUPID......
DON'T DECIDE WHAT I'M WORTH...
DON'T LAUGH AT ME...
DON'T TELL ME WHO I AM...
......YEAH.

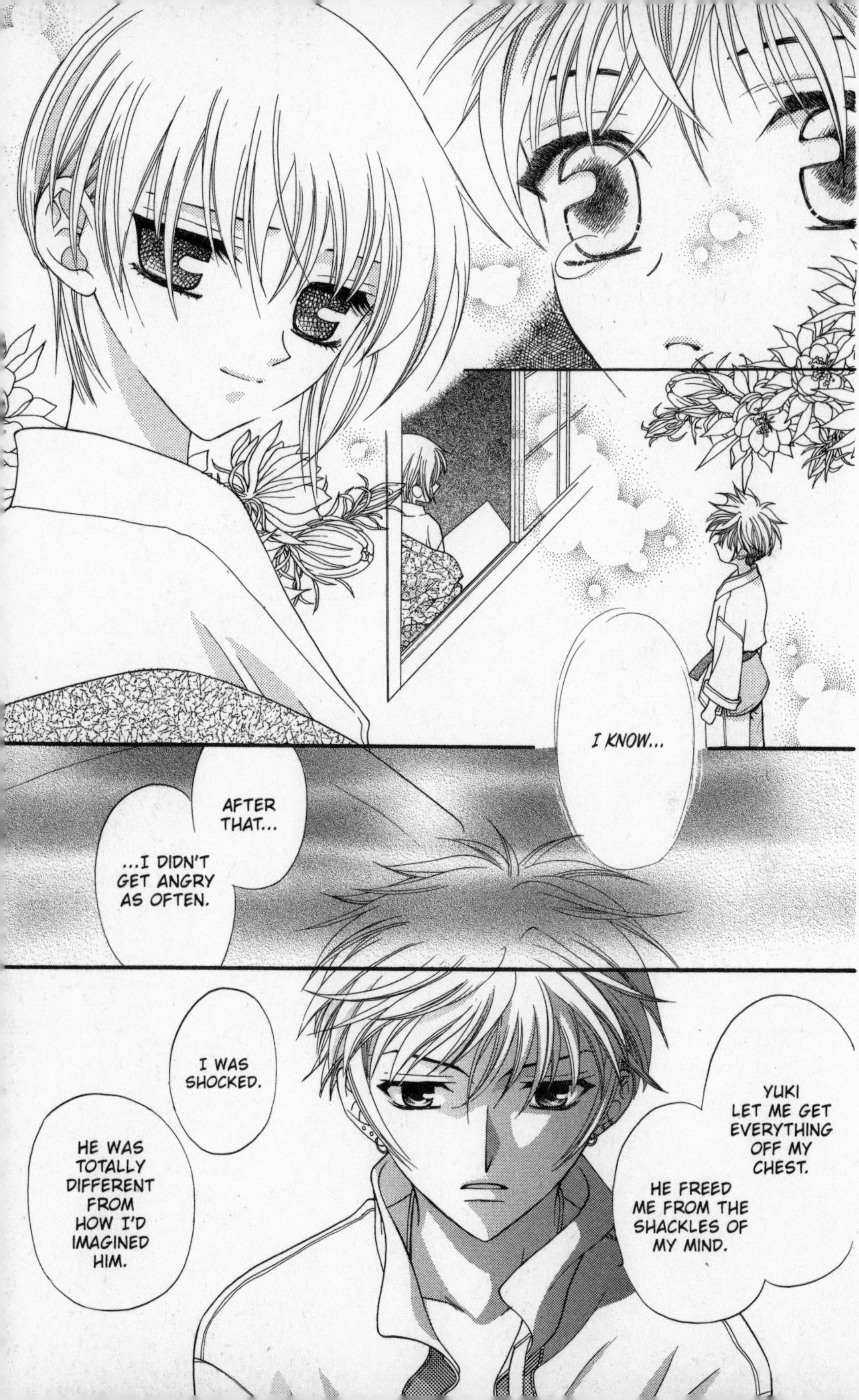
I KNOW...
AFTER THAT...
...I DIDN'T GET ANGRY AS OFTEN.
YUKI LET ME GET EVERYTHING OFF MY CHEST.
HE FREED ME FROM THE SHACKLES OF MY MIND.
I WAS SHOCKED.
HE WAS TOTALLY DIFFERENT FROM HOW I'D IMAGINED HIM.

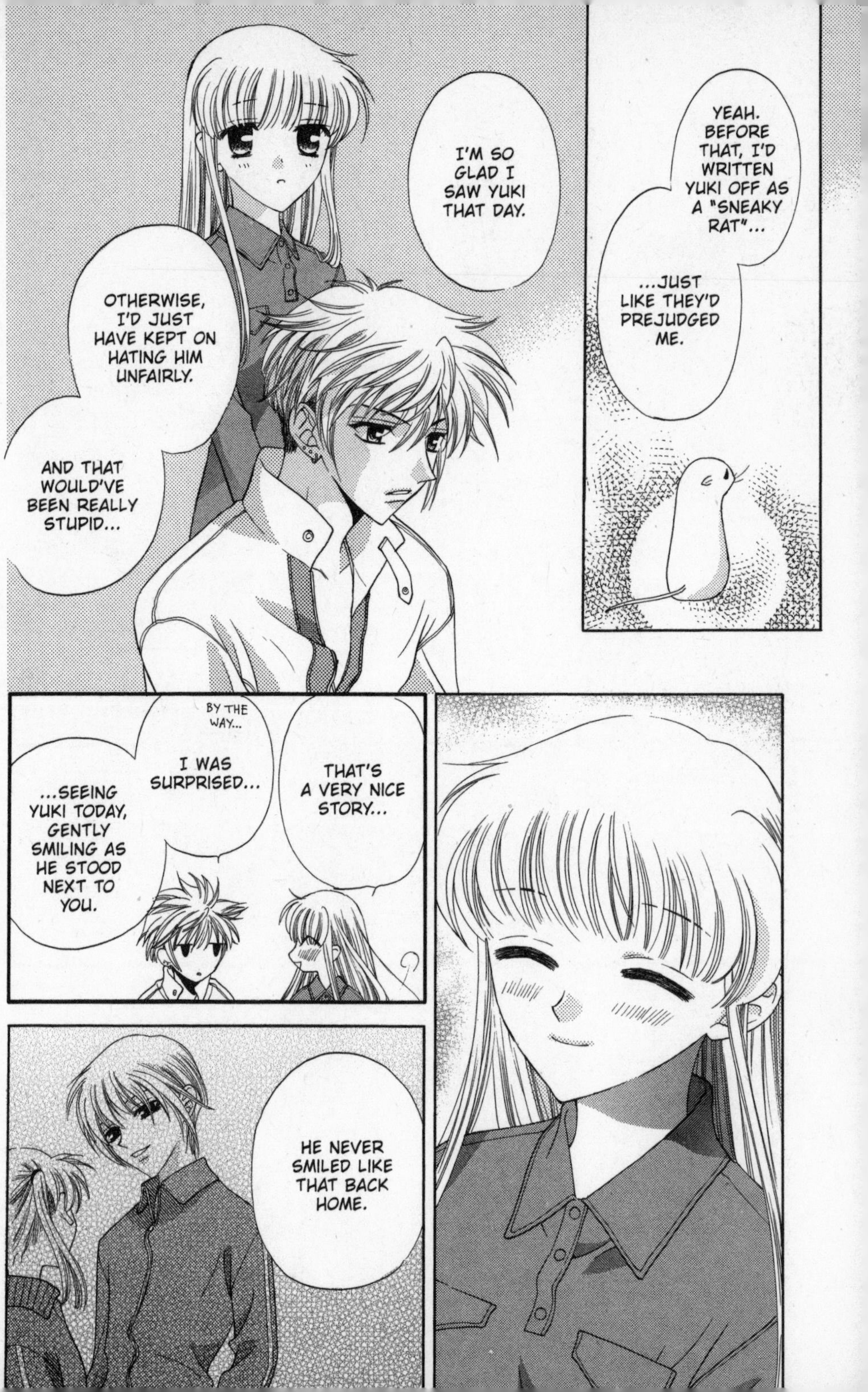
YEAH. BEFORE THAT, I'D WRITTEN YUKI OFF AS A "SNEAKY RAT"...
...JUST LIKE THEY'D PREJUDGED ME.
I'M SO GLAD I SAW YUKI THAT DAY.
OTHERWISE, I'D JUST HAVE KEPT ON HATING HIM UNFAIRLY.
AND THAT WOULD'VE BEEN REALLY STUPID...
THAT'S A VERY NICE STORY...
BY THE WAY...
I WAS SURPRISED...
...SEEING YUKI TODAY, GENTLY SMILING AS HE STOOD NEXT TO YOU.
HE NEVER SMILED LIKE THAT BACK HOME.

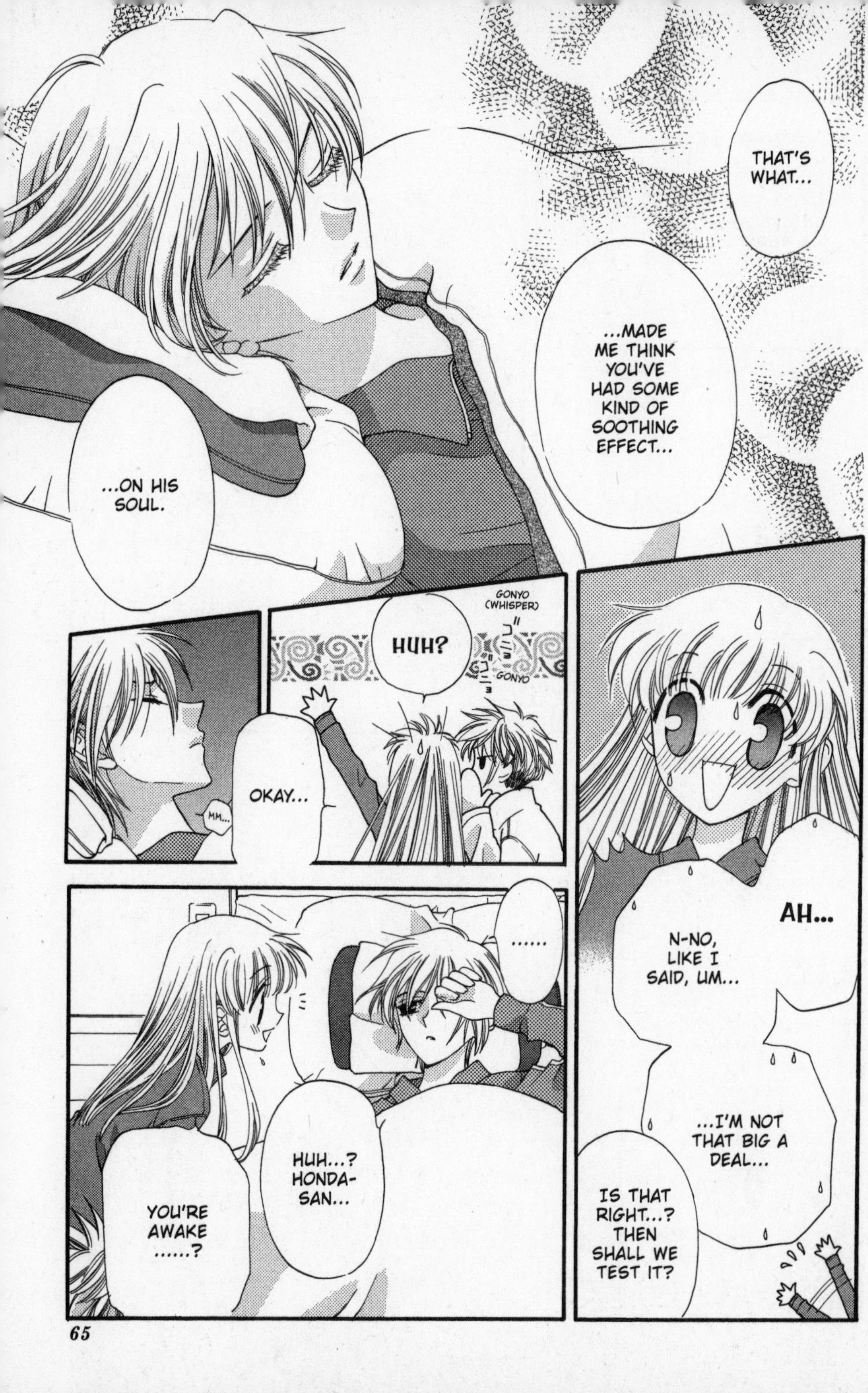
THAT'S WHAT...
...MADE ME THINK YOU'VE HAD SOME KIND OF SOOTHING EFFECT...
...ON HIS SOUL.
AH...
N-NO, LIKE I SAID, UM...
...I'M NOT THAT BIG A DEAL...
IS THAT RIGHT...? THEN SHALL WE TEST IT?
HUH?
GONYO (WHISPER)
GONYO
OKAY...
MM...
......
HUH...? HONDA-SAN...
YOU'RE AWAKE ......?

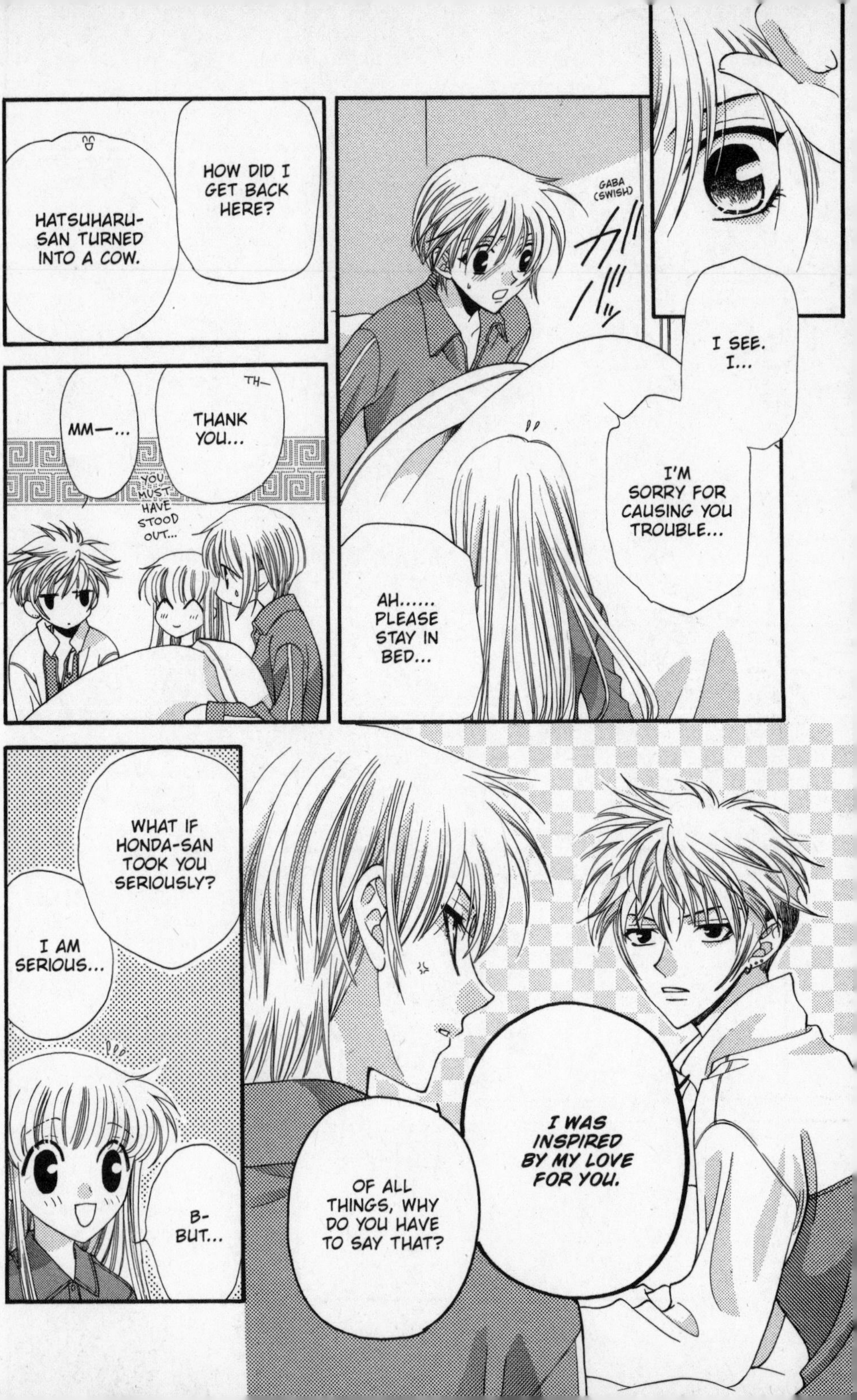
I SEE. I...
I'M SORRY FOR CAUSING YOU TROUBLE...
GABA (SWISH)
AH...... PLEASE STAY IN BED...
HOW DID I GET BACK HERE?
HATSUHARU-SAN TURNED INTO A COW.
TH— THANK YOU...
MM—...
YOU MUST HAVE STOOD OUT...
I WAS INSPIRED BY MY LOVE FOR YOU.
OF ALL THINGS, WHY DO YOU HAVE TO SAY THAT?
WHAT IF HONDA-SAN TOOK YOU SERIOUSLY?
I AM SERIOUS...
B-BUT...

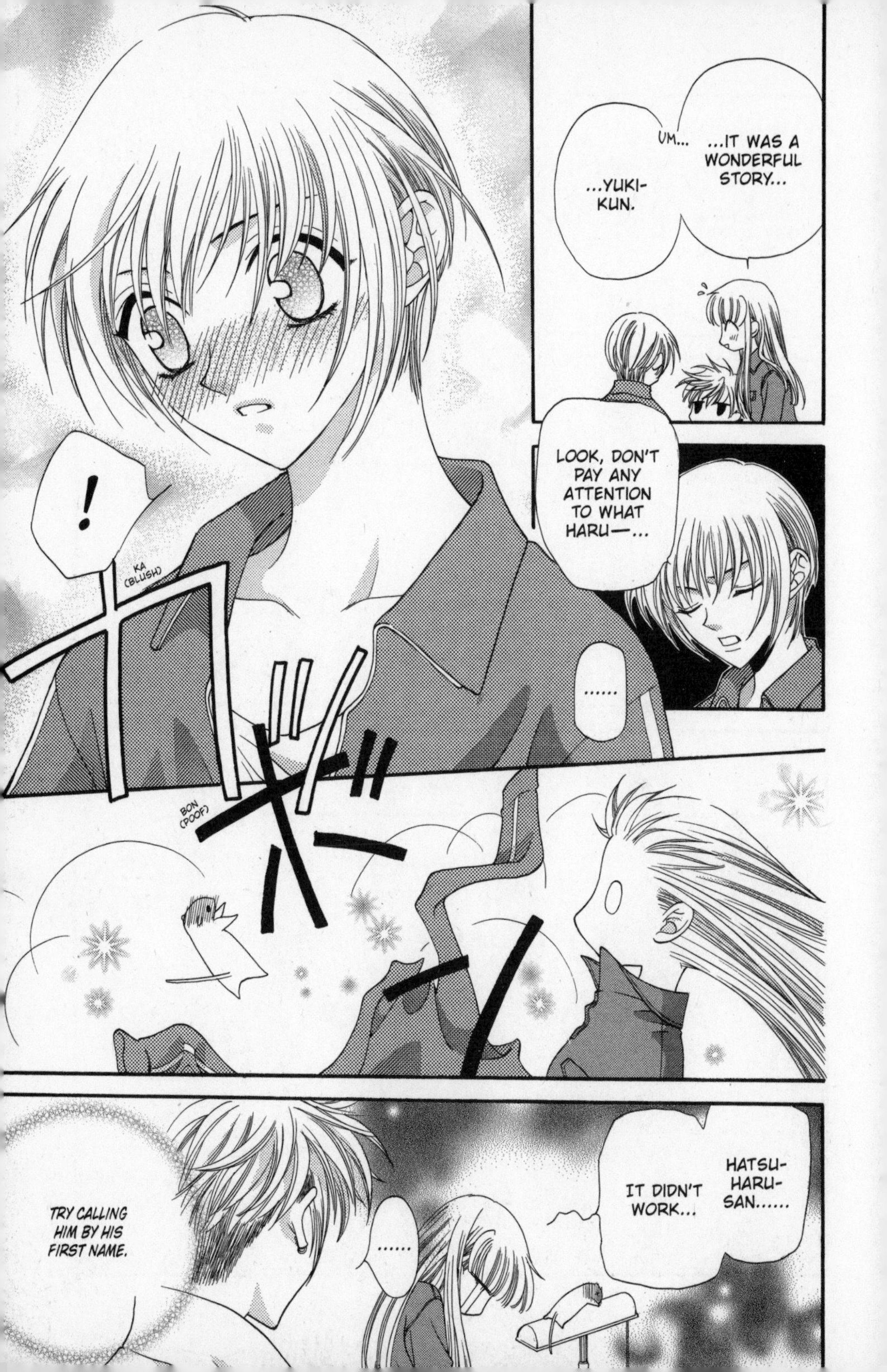
...IT WAS A WONDERFUL STORY...
UM...
...YUKI-KUN.
LOOK, DON'T PAY ANY ATTENTION TO WHAT HARU—...
......
!
KA (BLUSH)
BON (POOF)
HATSU-HARU-SAN......
IT DIDN'T WORK...
......
TRY CALLING HIM BY HIS FIRST NAME.

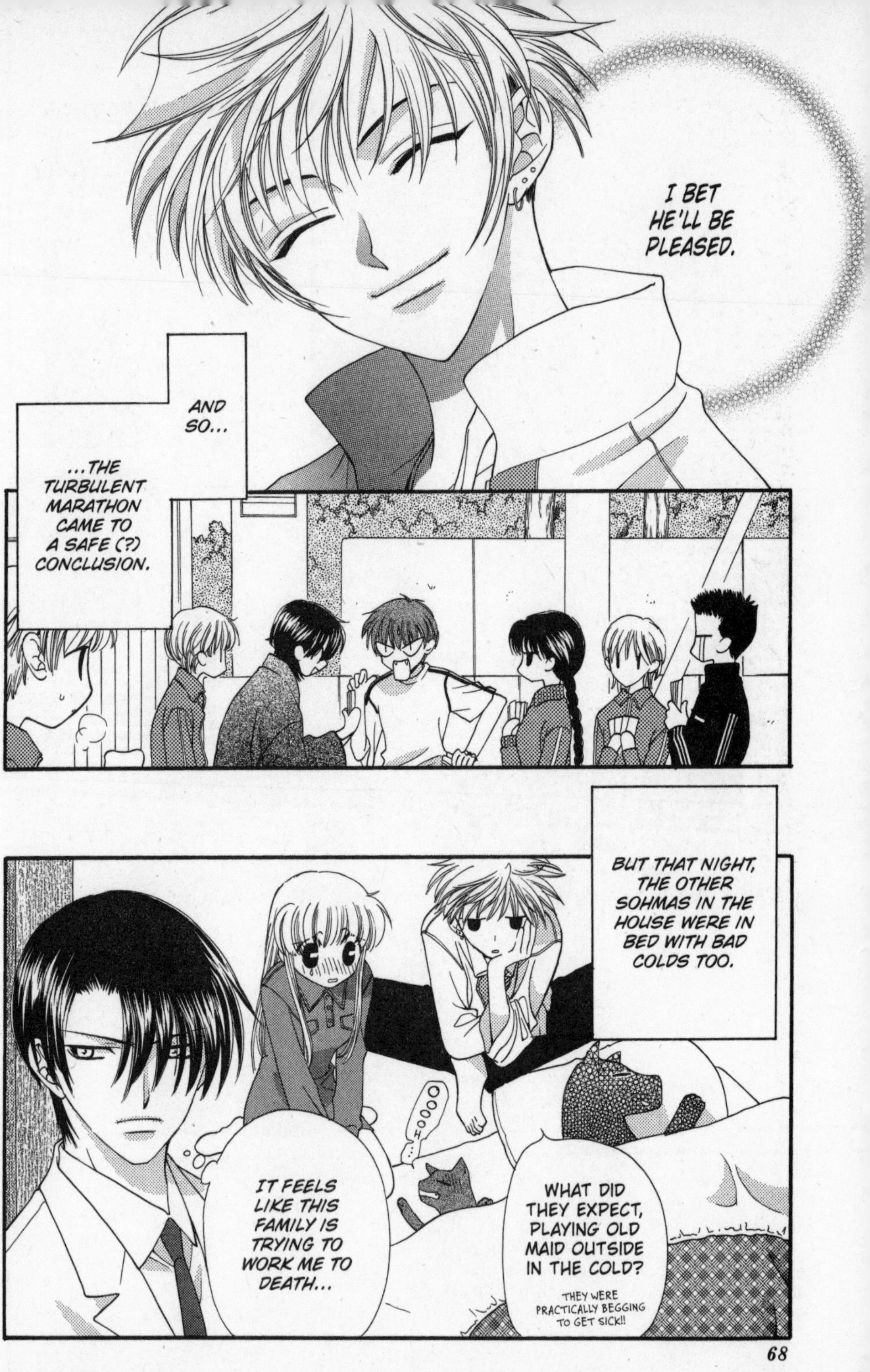
I BET HE'LL BE PLEASED.
AND SO...
...THE TURBULENT MARATHON CAME TO A SAFE (?) CONCLUSION.
BUT THAT NIGHT, THE OTHER SOHMAS IN THE HOUSE WERE IN BED WITH BAD COLDS TOO.
WHAT DID THEY EXPECT, PLAYING OLD MAID OUTSIDE IN THE COLD?
THEY WERE PRACTICALLY BEGGING TO GET SICK!!
OOOOH...
IT FEELS LIKE THIS FAMILY IS TRYING TO WORK ME TO DEATH...

Chapter 15

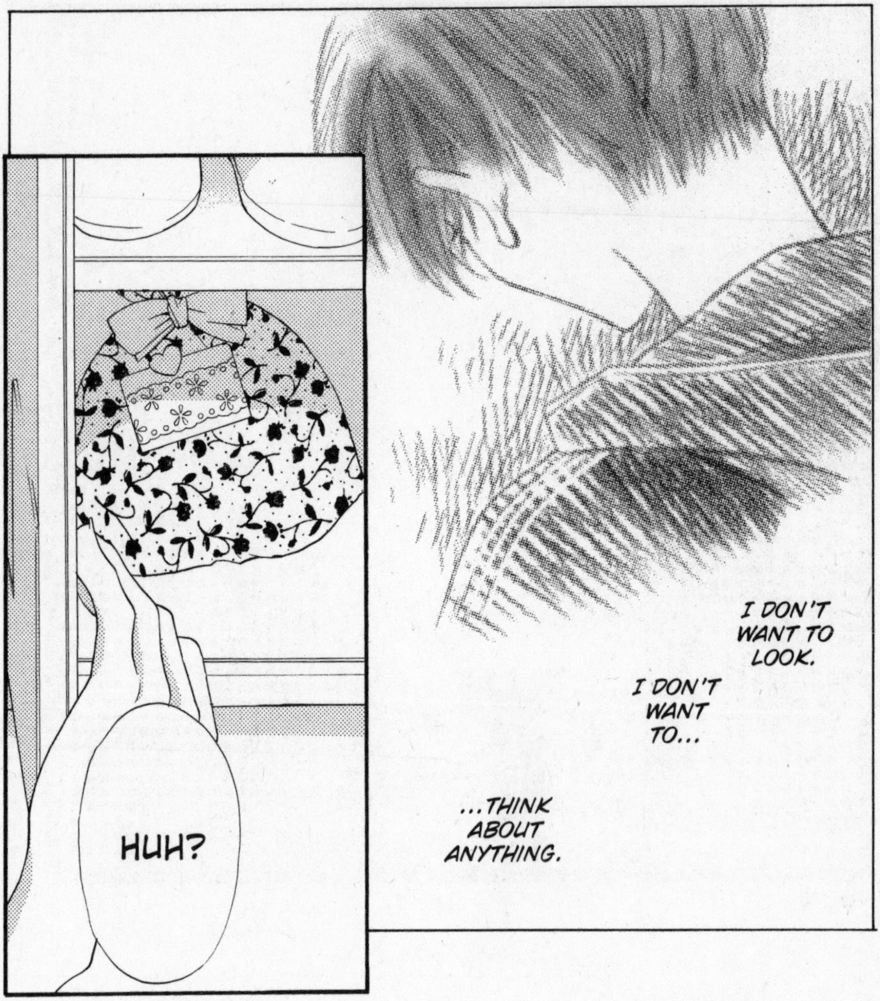
I DON'T WANT TO LOOK.
I DON'T WANT TO...
...THINK ABOUT ANYTHING.
HUH?

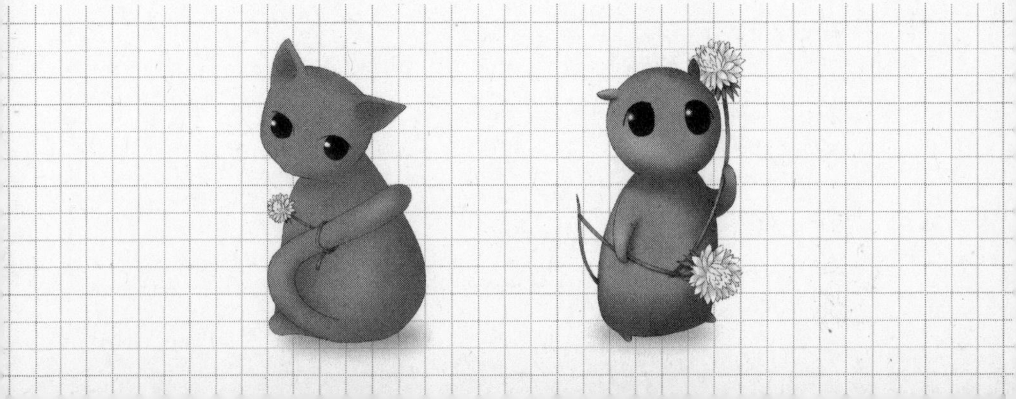

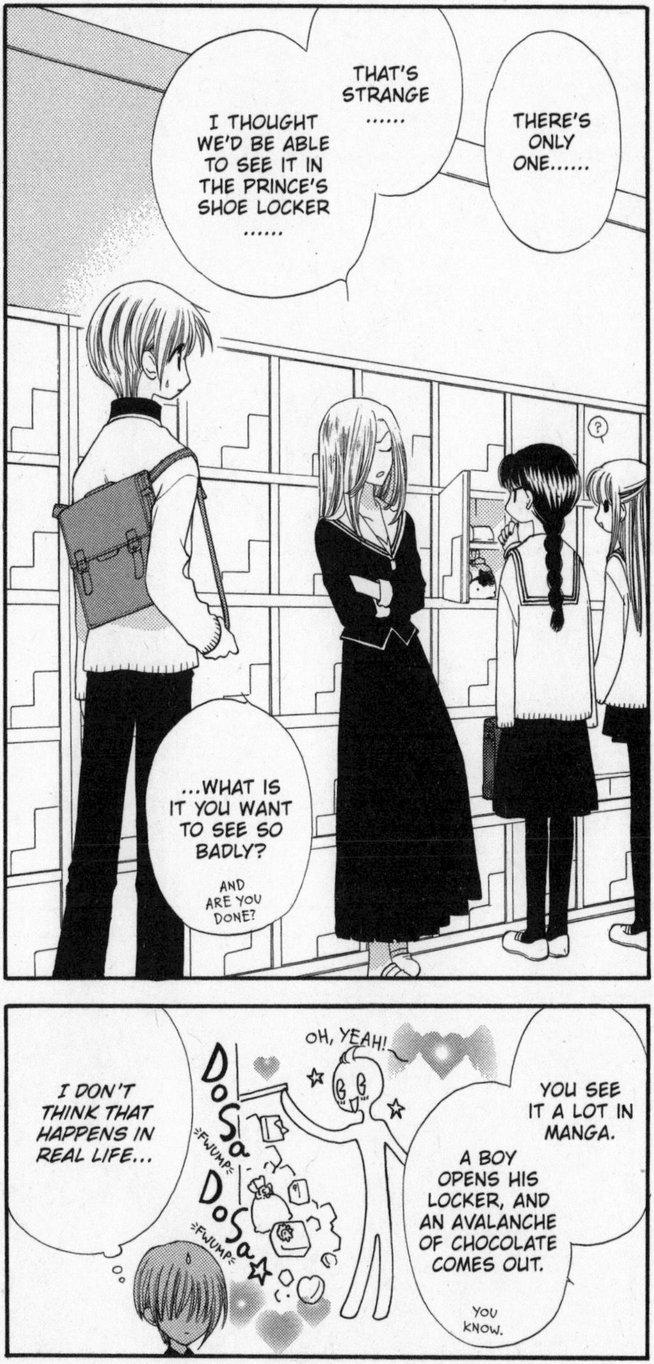
THERE'S ONLY ONE......
THAT'S STRANGE ......
I THOUGHT WE'D BE ABLE TO SEE IT IN THE PRINCE'S SHOE LOCKER ......
?
...WHAT IS IT YOU WANT TO SEE SO BADLY?
AND ARE YOU DONE?
YOU SEE IT A LOT IN MANGA.
A BOY OPENS HIS LOCKER, AND AN AVALANCHE OF CHOCOLATE COMES OUT.
YOU KNOW.
OH, YEAH!
DoSa
FWUMP
DoSa
FWUMP
I DON'T THINK THAT HAPPENS IN REAL LIFE...
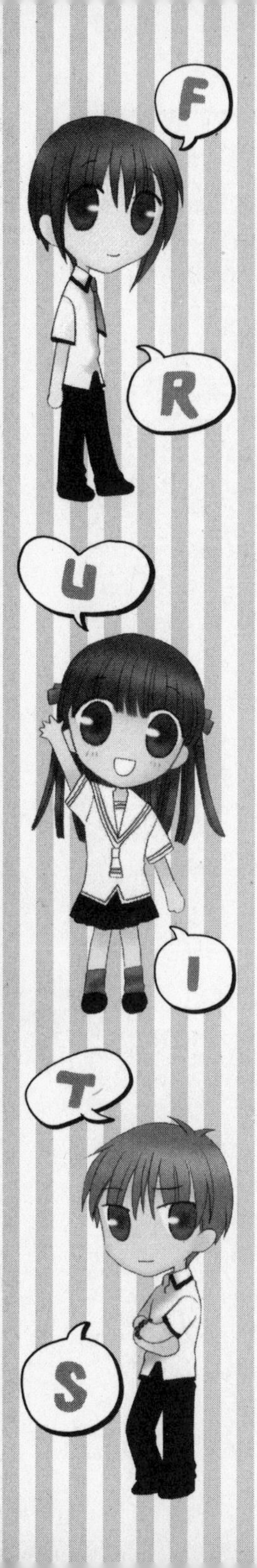
F
R
U
I
T
S

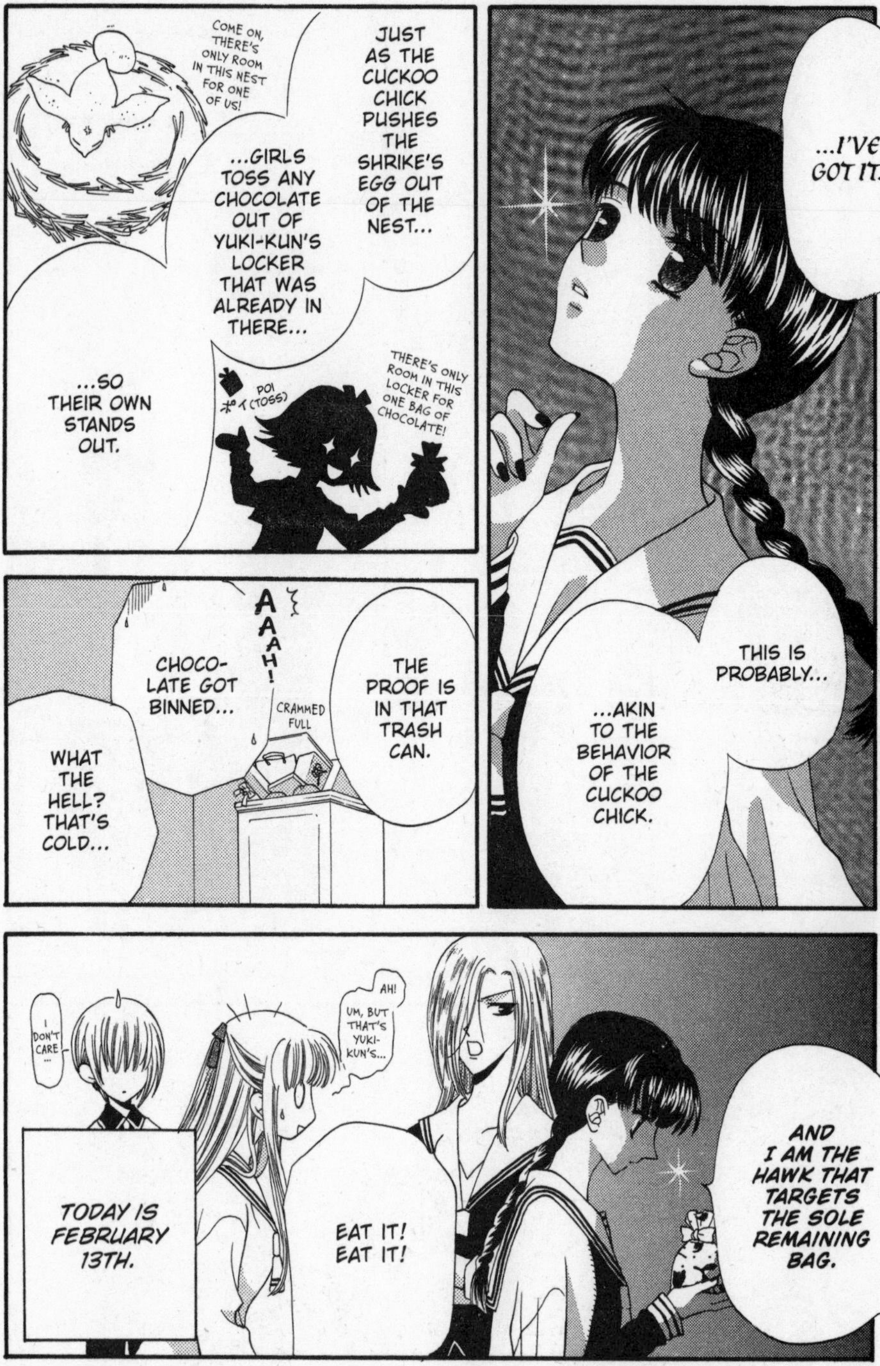
...I'VE GOT IT.
THIS IS PROBABLY...
...AKIN TO THE BEHAVIOR OF THE CUCKOO CHICK.
JUST AS THE CUCKOO CHICK PUSHES THE SHRIKE'S EGG OUT OF THE NEST...
COME ON, THERE'S ONLY ROOM IN THIS NEST FOR ONE OF US!
...GIRLS TOSS ANY CHOCOLATE OUT OF YUKI-KUN'S LOCKER THAT WAS ALREADY IN THERE...
THERE'S ONLY ROOM IN THIS LOCKER FOR ONE BAG OF CHOCOLATE!
ポイ POI (TOSS)
...SO THEIR OWN STANDS OUT.
THE PROOF IS IN THAT TRASH CAN.
AAAAH!
CHOCO-LATE GOT BINNED...
CRAMMED FULL
WHAT THE HELL? THAT'S COLD...
AND I AM THE HAWK THAT TARGETS THE SOLE REMAINING BAG.
AH!
UM, BUT THAT'S YUKI-KUN'S...
EAT IT! EAT IT!
I DON'T CARE...
TODAY IS FEBRUARY 13TH.

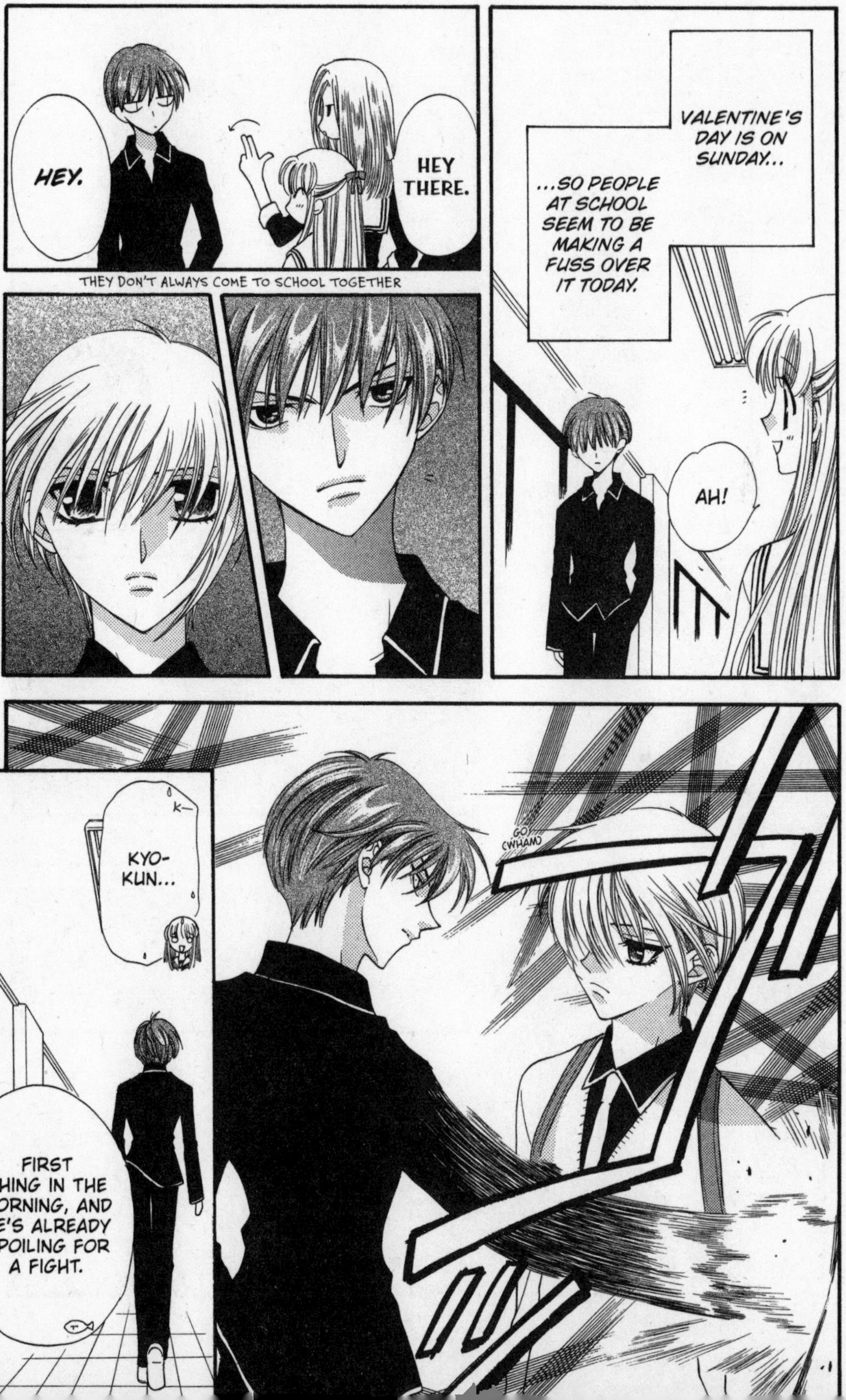
VALENTINE'S DAY IS ON SUNDAY...
...SO PEOPLE AT SCHOOL SEEM TO BE MAKING A FUSS OVER IT TODAY.
AH!
HEY THERE.
HEY.
THEY DON'T ALWAYS COME TO SCHOOL TOGETHER
GO (WHAM)
K—
KYO-KUN...
FIRST THING IN THE MORNING, AND HE'S ALREADY SPOILING FOR A FIGHT.

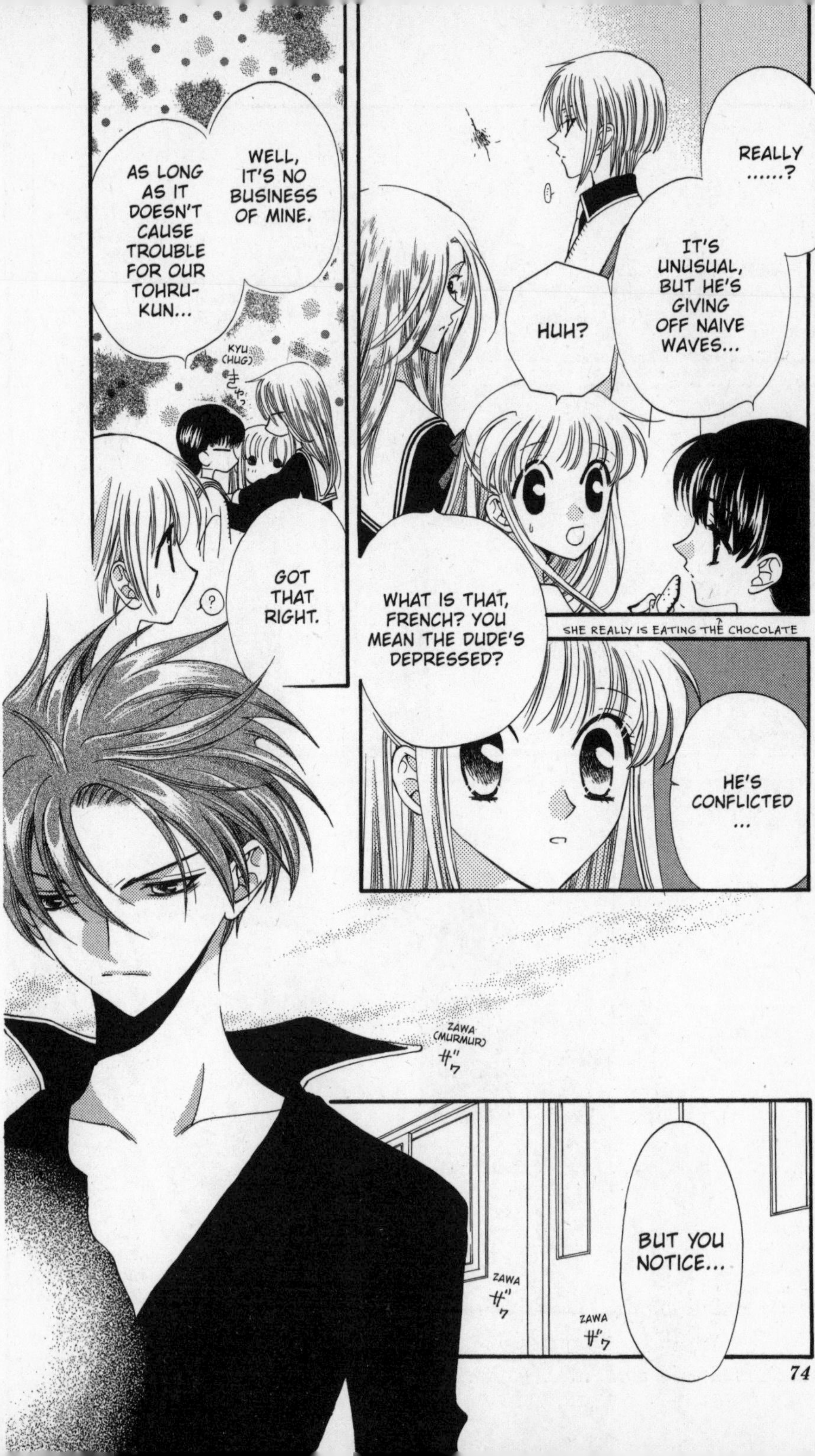

REALLY ......?
IT'S UNUSUAL, BUT HE'S GIVING OFF NAIVE WAVES...
HUH?
WHAT IS THAT, FRENCH? YOU MEAN THE DUDE'S DEPRESSED?
SHE REALLY IS EATING THE CHOCOLATE
HE'S CONFLICTED ...
WELL, IT'S NO BUSINESS OF MINE.
AS LONG AS IT DOESN'T CAUSE TROUBLE FOR OUR TOHRU-KUN...
KYU (HUG)
きゅっ
GOT THAT RIGHT.
BUT YOU NOTICE...
ZAWA (MURMUR)
ザワ
ZAWA
ザワ
ZAWA
ザワ

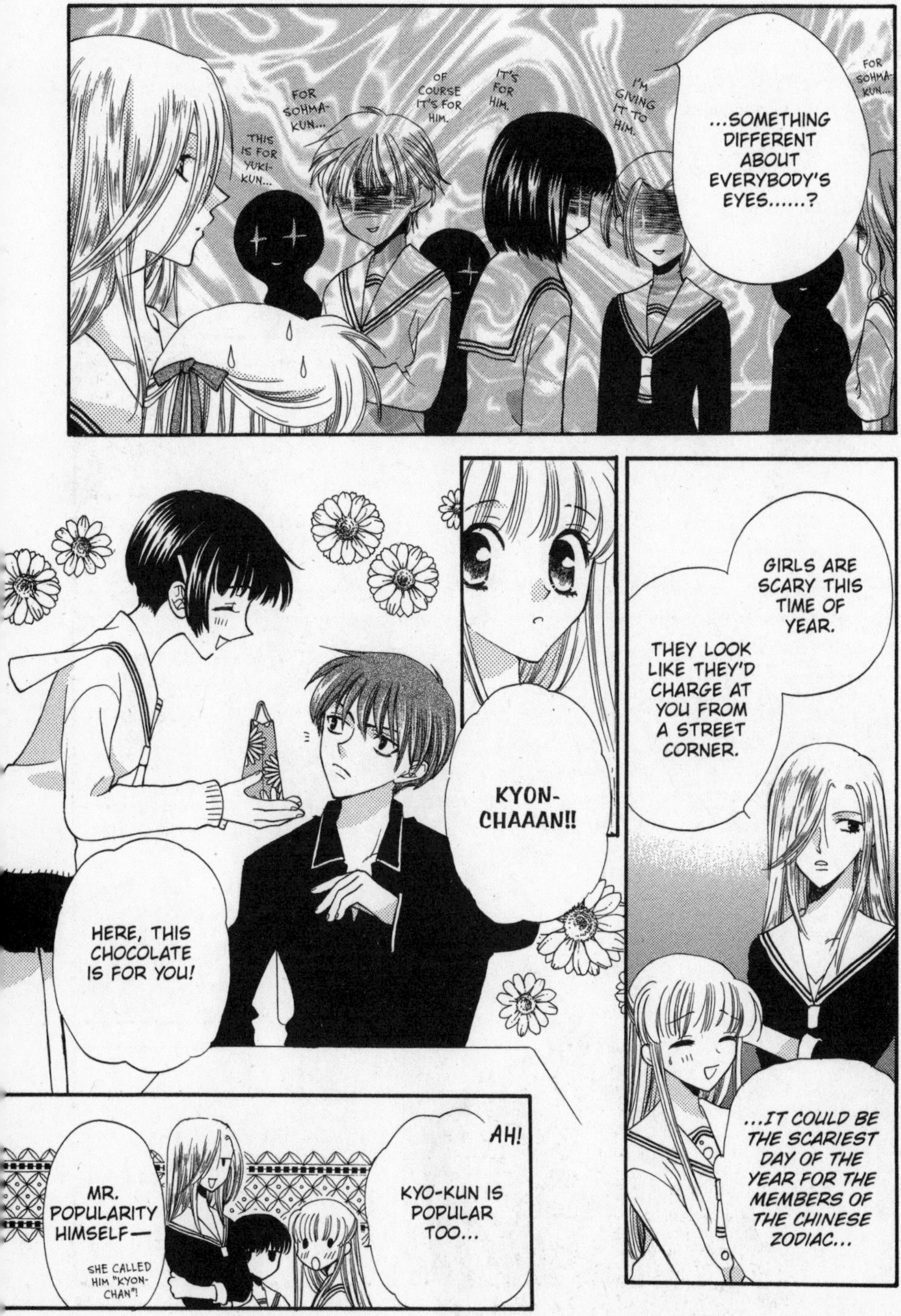
FOR SOHMA-KUN...
...SOMETHING DIFFERENT ABOUT EVERYBODY'S EYES......?
I'M GIVING IT TO HIM.
IT'S FOR HIM.
OF COURSE IT'S FOR HIM.
FOR SOHMA-KUN...
THIS IS FOR YUKI-KUN...
GIRLS ARE SCARY THIS TIME OF YEAR.
THEY LOOK LIKE THEY'D CHARGE AT YOU FROM A STREET CORNER.
...IT COULD BE THE SCARIEST DAY OF THE YEAR FOR THE MEMBERS OF THE CHINESE ZODIAC...
KYON-CHAAAN!!
HERE, THIS CHOCOLATE IS FOR YOU!
AH!
KYO-KUN IS POPULAR TOO...
MR. POPULARITY HIMSELF—
SHE CALLED HIM "KYON-CHAN"!

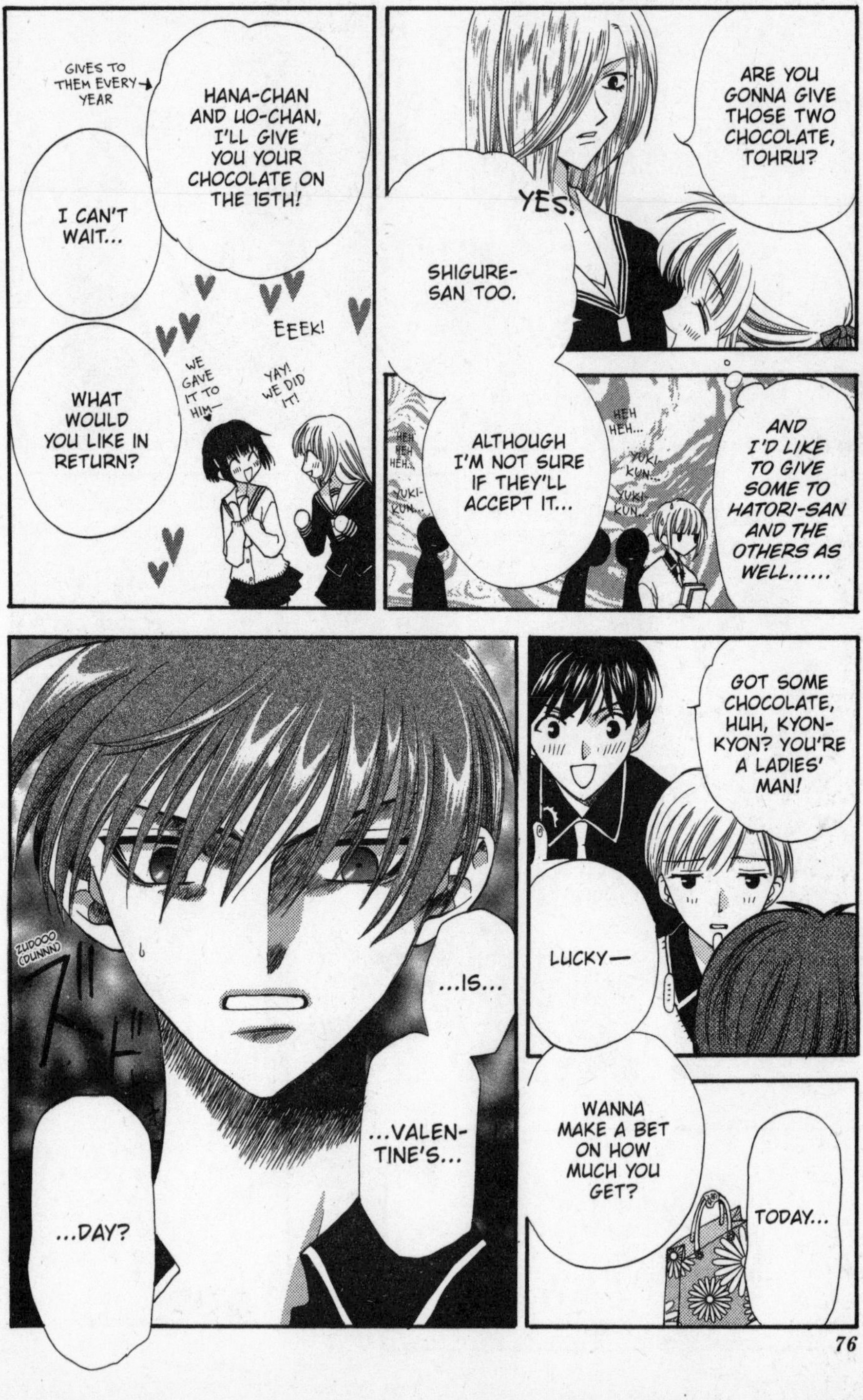
ARE YOU GONNA GIVE THOSE TWO CHOCOLATE, TOHRU?
YES.
SHIGURE-SAN TOO.
AND I'D LIKE TO GIVE SOME TO HATORI-SAN AND THE OTHERS AS WELL......
HEH HEH...
YUKI-KUN...
YUKI-KUN...
ALTHOUGH I'M NOT SURE IF THEY'LL ACCEPT IT...
HEH HEH HEH...
YUKI-KUN...
HANA-CHAN AND UO-CHAN, I'LL GIVE YOU YOUR CHOCOLATE ON THE 15TH!
GIVES TO THEM EVERY YEAR
I CAN'T WAIT...
EEEK!
YAY! WE DID IT!
WE GAVE IT TO HIM—
WHAT WOULD YOU LIKE IN RETURN?
GOT SOME CHOCOLATE, HUH, KYON-KYON? YOU'RE A LADIES' MAN!
LUCKY—
TODAY...
WANNA MAKE A BET ON HOW MUCH YOU GET?
...IS...
...VALEN-TINE'S...
...DAY?
ZUDOOO (DUNNN)

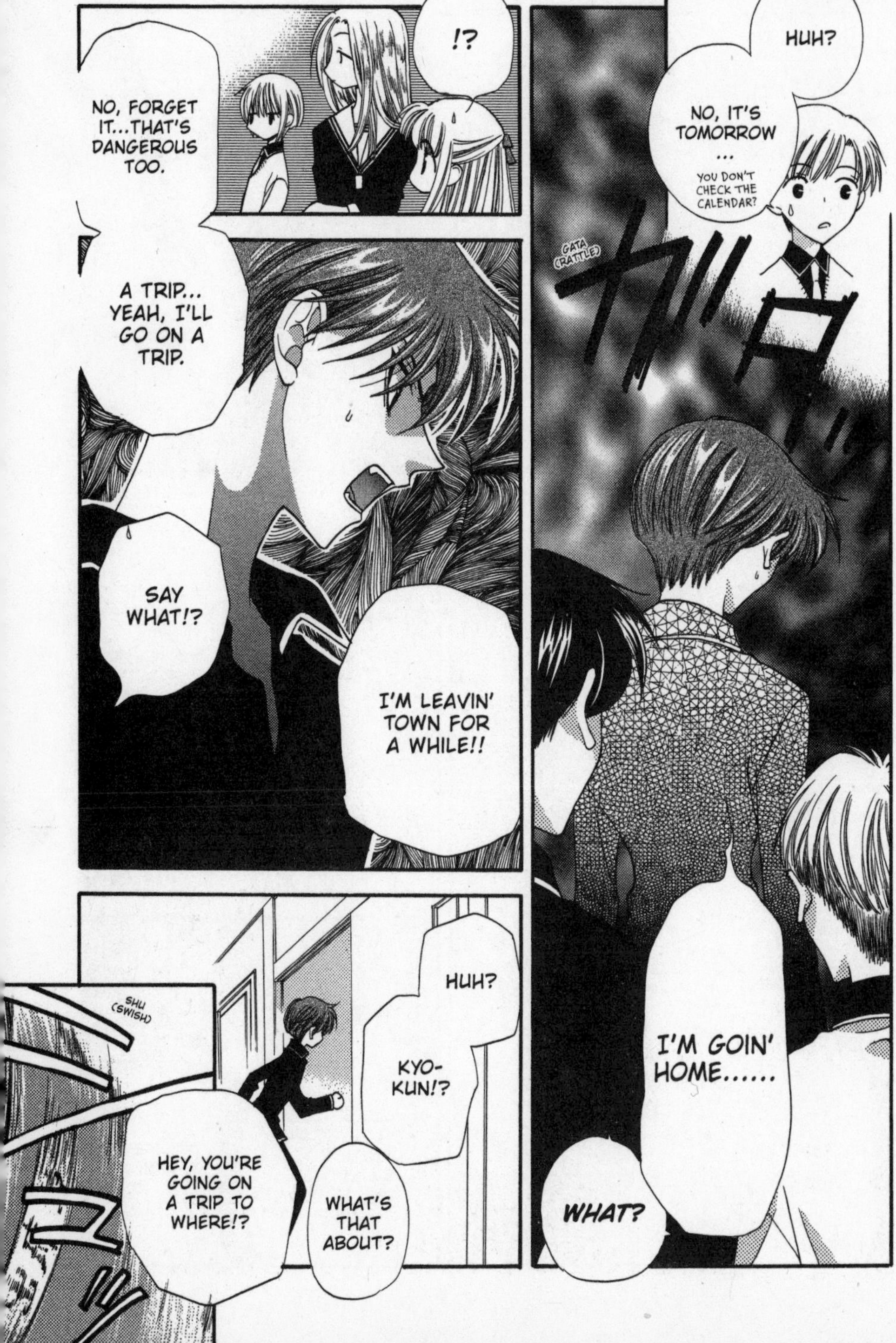
HUH?
NO, IT'S TOMORROW ...
YOU DON'T CHECK THE CALENDAR?
GATA (RATTLE)
I'M GOIN' HOME......
WHAT?
!?
NO, FORGET IT...THAT'S DANGEROUS TOO.
A TRIP... YEAH, I'LL GO ON A TRIP.
I'M LEAVIN' TOWN FOR A WHILE!!
SAY WHAT!?
HUH?
KYO-KUN!?
SHU (SWISH)
WHAT'S THAT ABOUT?
HEY, YOU'RE GOING ON A TRIP TO WHERE!?

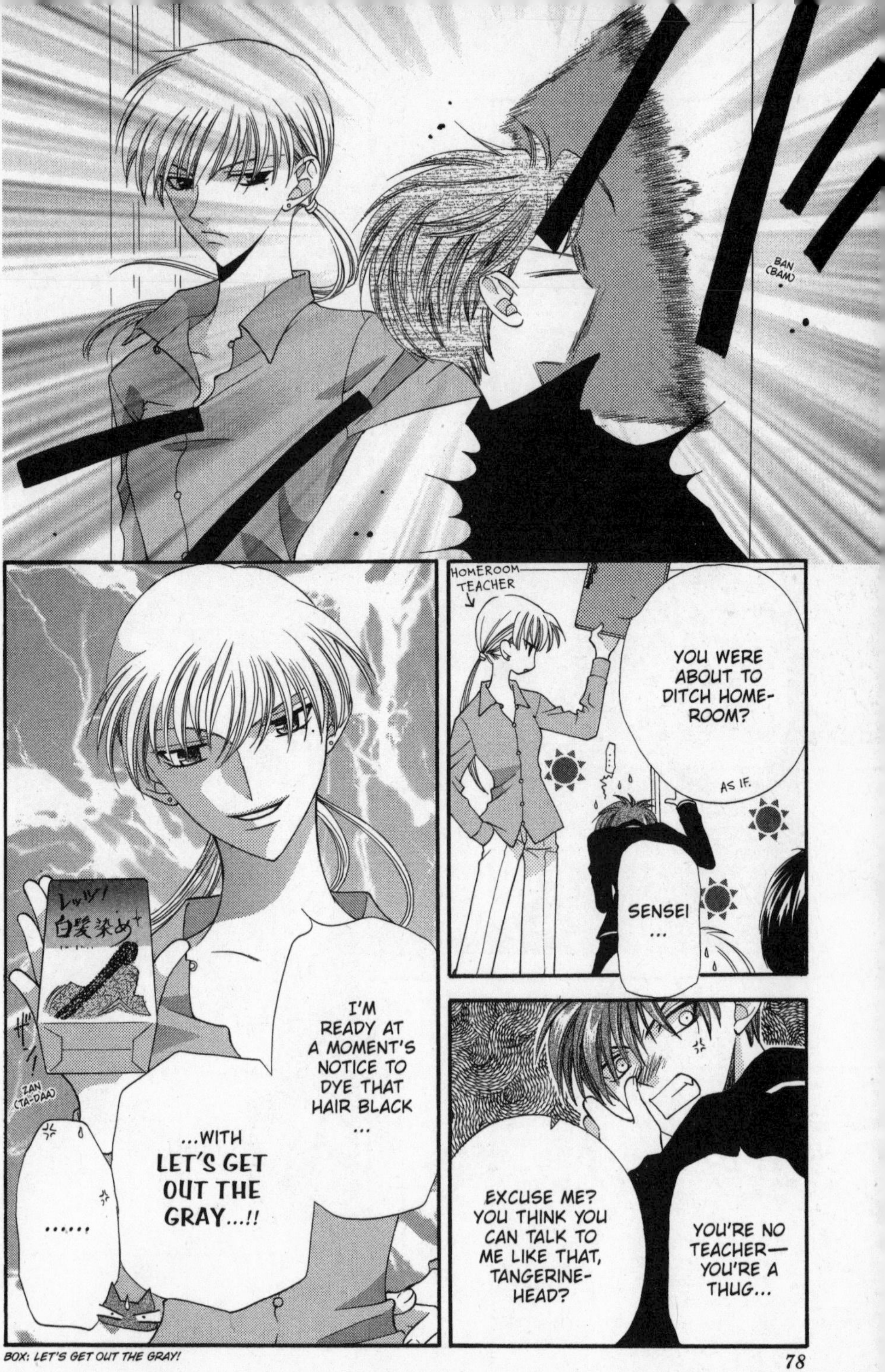
BAN (BAM)
HOMEROOM TEACHER
YOU WERE ABOUT TO DITCH HOME-ROOM?
AS IF.
SENSEI ...
YOU'RE NO TEACHER— YOU'RE A THUG...
EXCUSE ME? YOU THINK YOU CAN TALK TO ME LIKE THAT, TANGERINE-HEAD?
I'M READY AT A MOMENT'S NOTICE TO DYE THAT HAIR BLACK ...
レッツ!白髪染め
...WITH LET'S GET OUT THE GRAY...!!
ZAN (TA-DAA)
....

BOX: LET'S GET OUT THE GRAY!

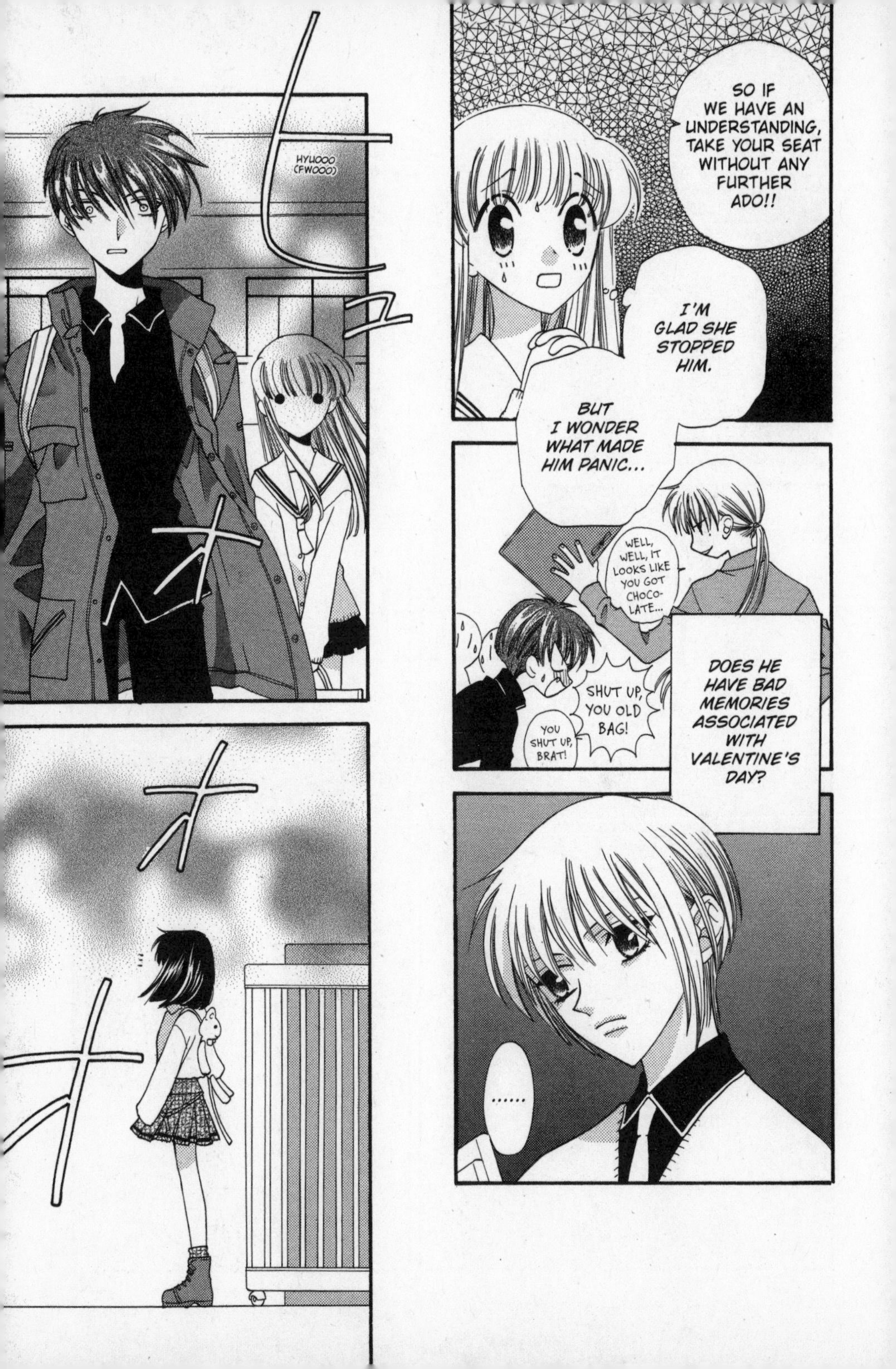
SO IF WE HAVE AN UNDERSTANDING, TAKE YOUR SEAT WITHOUT ANY FURTHER ADO!!
I'M GLAD SHE STOPPED HIM.
BUT I WONDER WHAT MADE HIM PANIC...
WELL, WELL, IT LOOKS LIKE YOU GOT CHOCO-LATE...
SHUT UP, YOU OLD BAG!
YOU SHUT UP, BRAT!
DOES HE HAVE BAD MEMORIES ASSOCIATED WITH VALENTINE'S DAY?
......
HYUOOO (FWOOO)

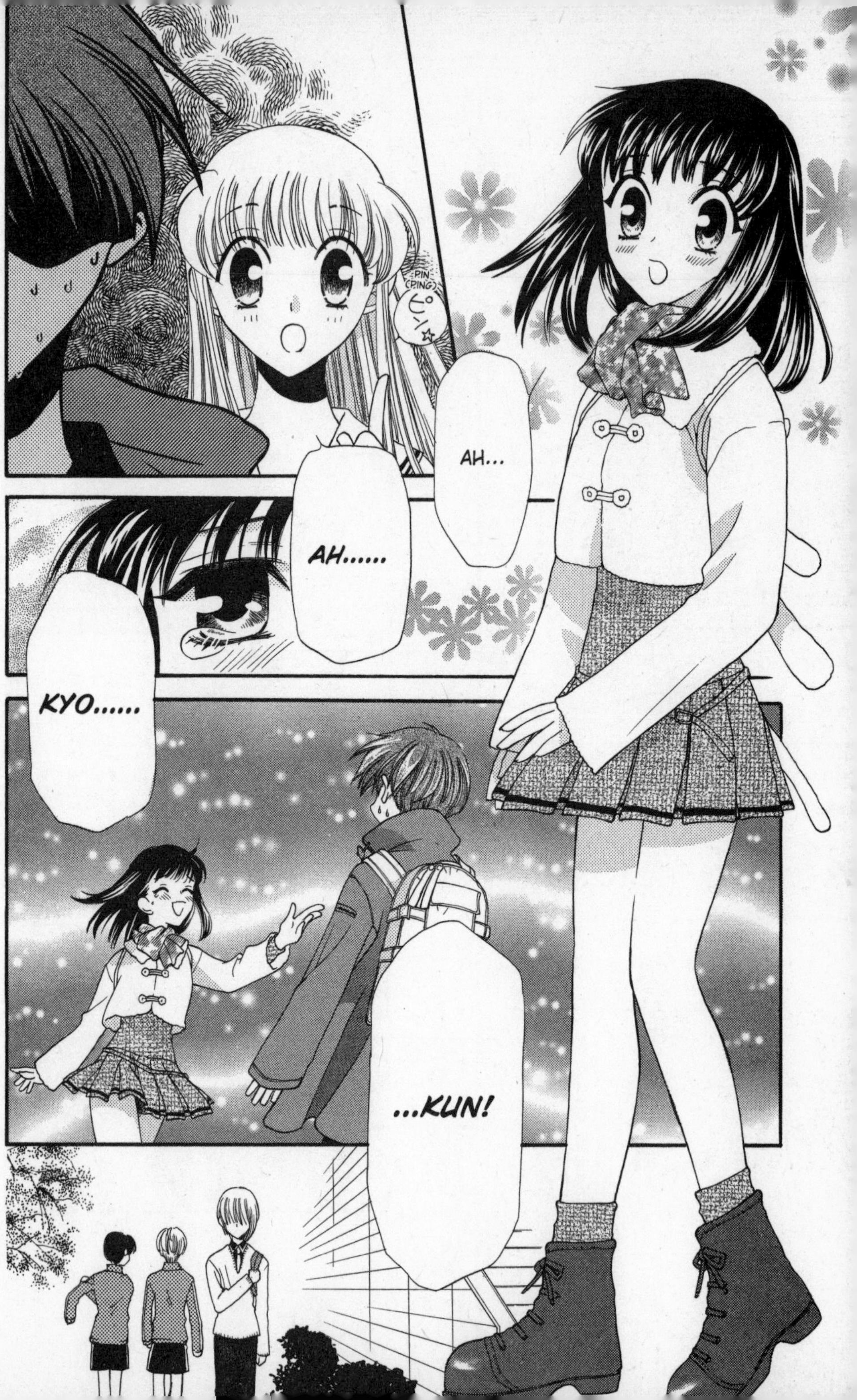

AH...
PIN (PING)
ピン☆
AH......
KYO......
...KUN!

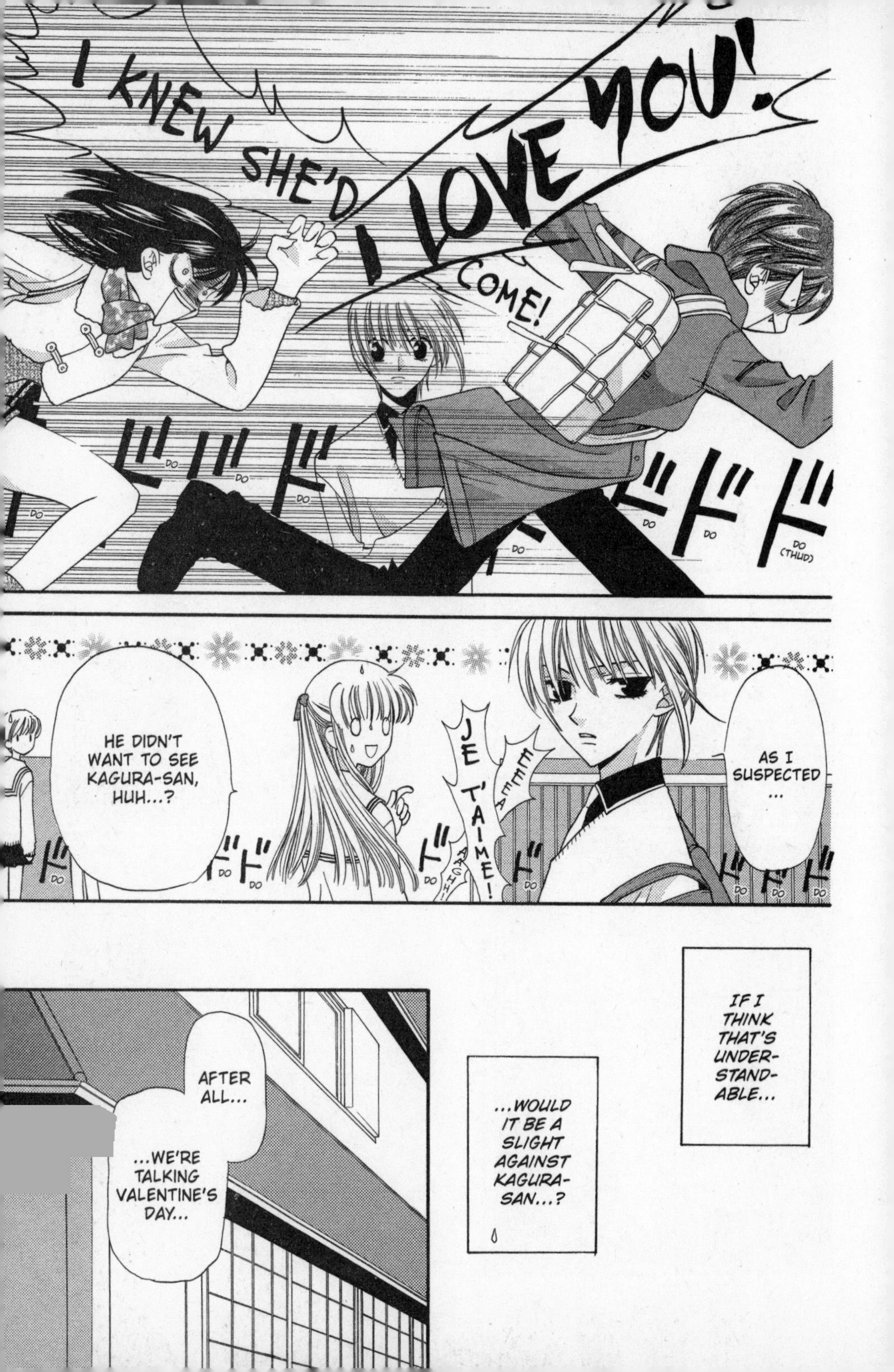
I LOVE YOU!
I KNEW SHE'D COME!
ドドド
DO DO DO (THUD)
ドドド
DO DO DO DO
AS I SUSPECTED...
JE T'AIME!
EEEEA
AAGH!
HE DIDN'T WANT TO SEE KAGURA-SAN, HUH...?
ドドド
DO DO DO DO DO DO DO
IF I THINK THAT'S UNDERSTANDABLE...
...WOULD IT BE A SLIGHT AGAINST KAGURA-SAN...?
AFTER ALL...
...WE'RE TALKING VALENTINE'S DAY...

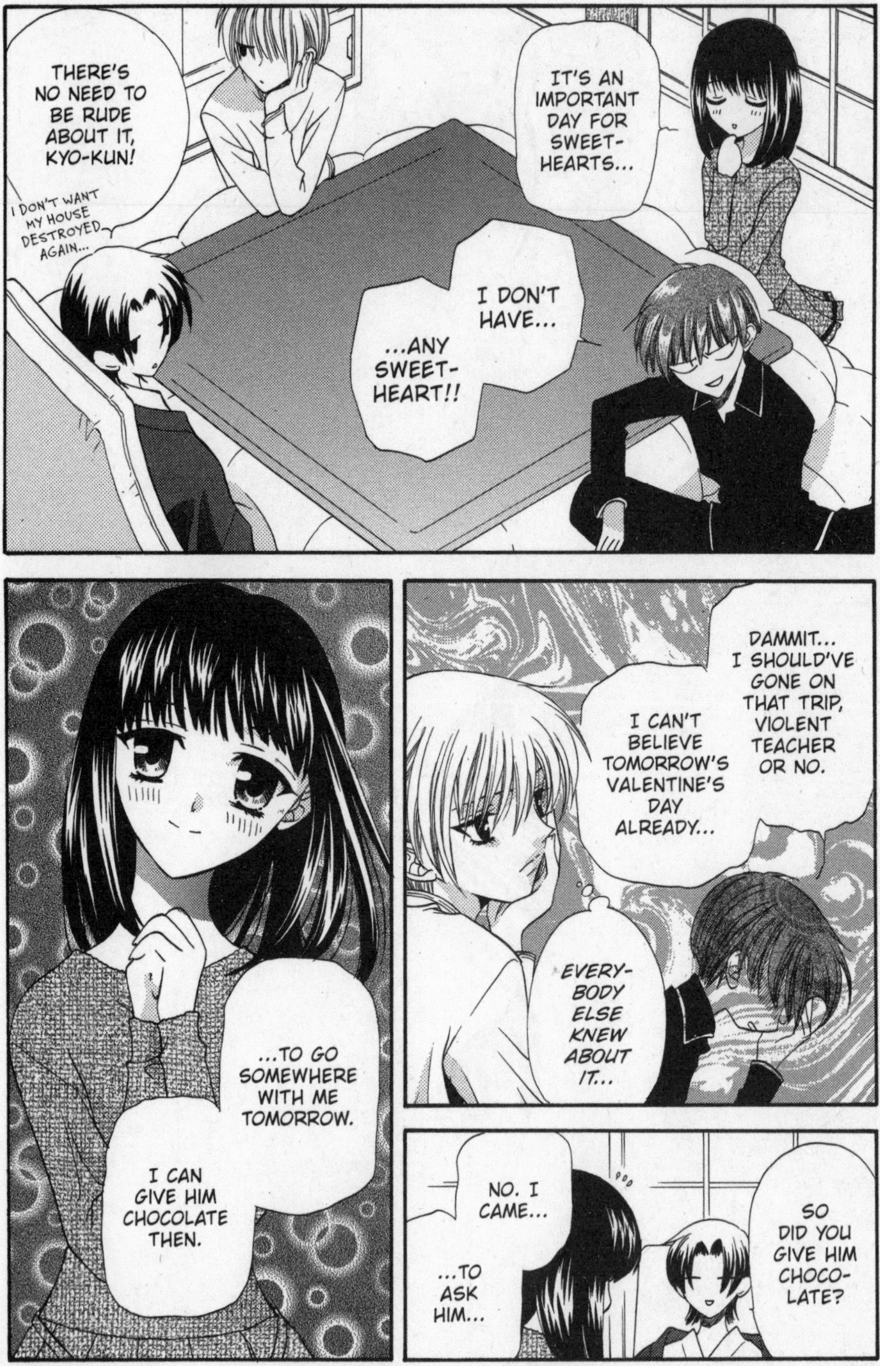
IT'S AN IMPORTANT DAY FOR SWEET-HEARTS...
I DON'T HAVE...
...ANY SWEET-HEART!!
THERE'S NO NEED TO BE RUDE ABOUT IT, KYO-KUN!
I DON'T WANT MY HOUSE DESTROYED AGAIN...
DAMMIT... I SHOULD'VE GONE ON THAT TRIP, VIOLENT TEACHER OR NO.
I CAN'T BELIEVE TOMORROW'S VALENTINE'S DAY ALREADY...
EVERY-BODY ELSE KNEW ABOUT IT...
SO DID YOU GIVE HIM CHOCO-LATE?
NO. I CAME...
...TO ASK HIM...
...TO GO SOMEWHERE WITH ME TOMORROW.
I CAN GIVE HIM CHOCOLATE THEN.

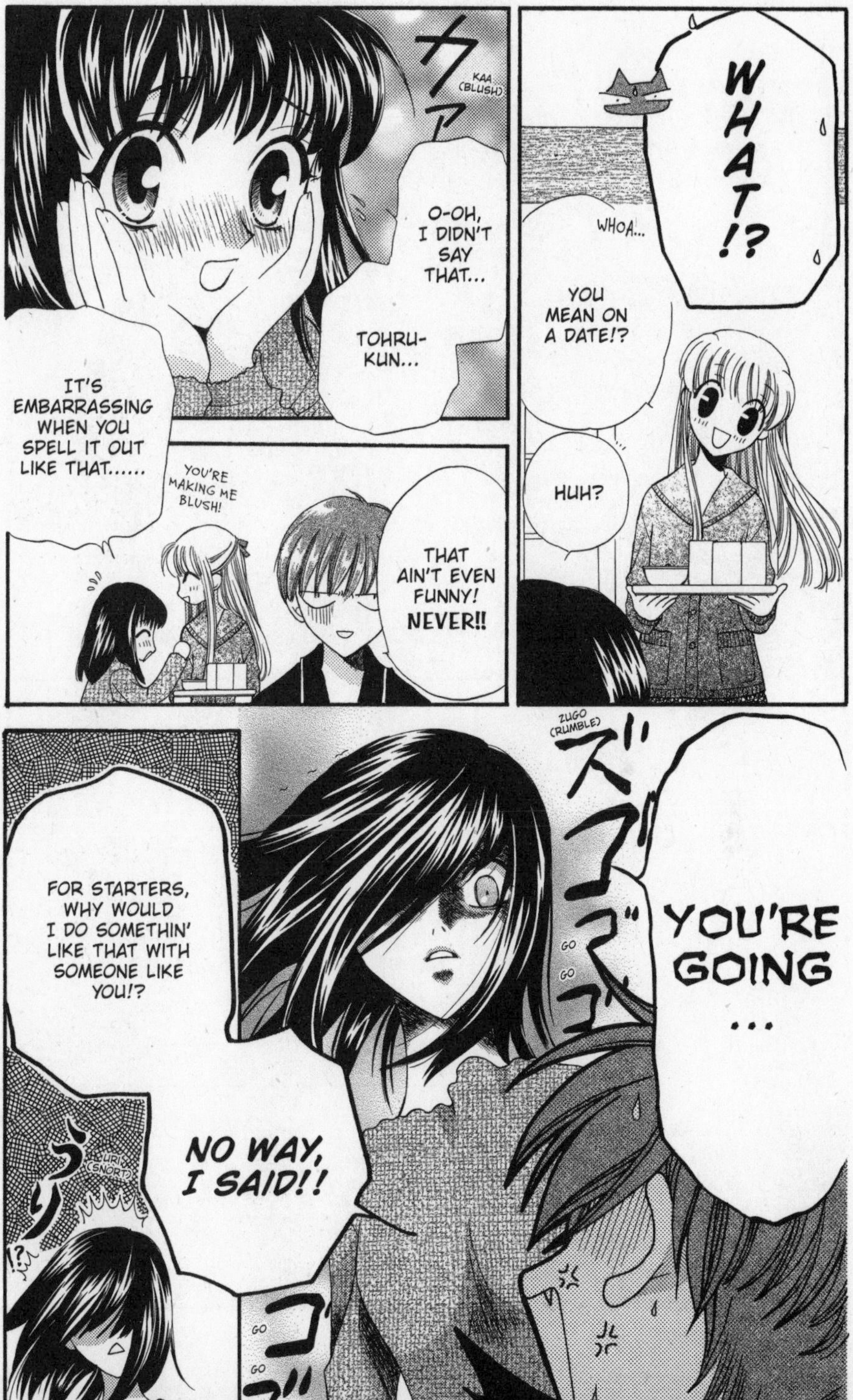
WHAT!?
WHOA...
YOU MEAN ON A DATE!?
HUH?
KAA (BLUSH)
O-OH, I DIDN'T SAY THAT...
TOHRU-KUN...
IT'S EMBARRASSING WHEN YOU SPELL IT OUT LIKE THAT......
YOU'RE MAKING ME BLUSH!
THAT AIN'T EVEN FUNNY! NEVER!!
ZUGO (RUMBLE)
YOU'RE GOING...
GO GO
FOR STARTERS, WHY WOULD I DO SOMETHIN' LIKE THAT WITH SOMEONE LIKE YOU!?
NO WAY, I SAID!!
URI (SNORT)
!?
GO GO

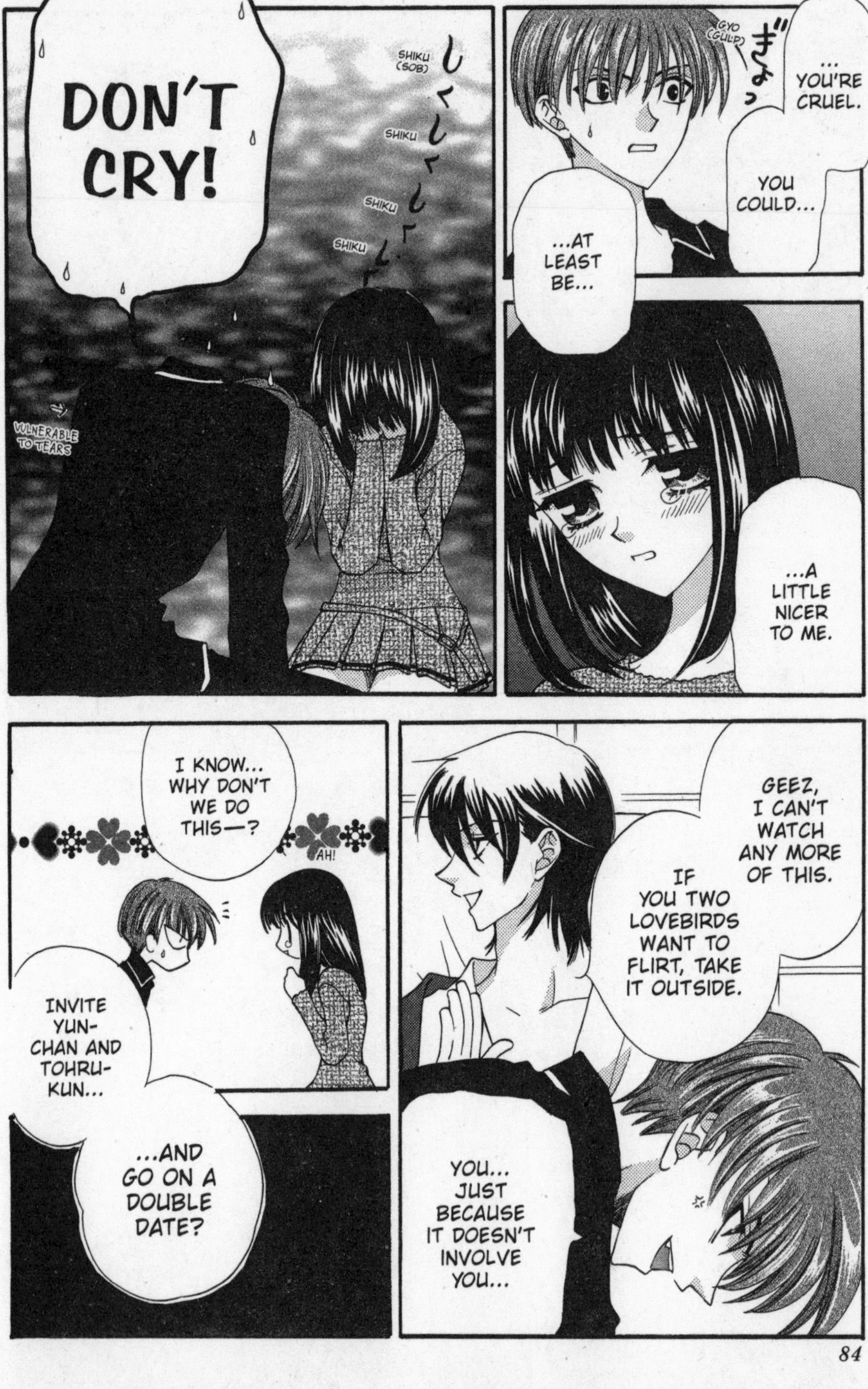

GYO (GULP)
... YOU'RE CRUEL.
YOU COULD...
...AT LEAST BE...
...A LITTLE NICER TO ME.
DON'T CRY!
SHIKU (SOB)
SHIKU
SHIKU
SHIKU
VULNERABLE TO TEARS
GEEZ, I CAN'T WATCH ANY MORE OF THIS.
IF YOU TWO LOVEBIRDS WANT TO FLIRT, TAKE IT OUTSIDE.
YOU... JUST BECAUSE IT DOESN'T INVOLVE YOU...
I KNOW... WHY DON'T WE DO THIS—?
AH!
INVITE YUN-CHAN AND TOHRU-KUN...
...AND GO ON A DOUBLE DATE?

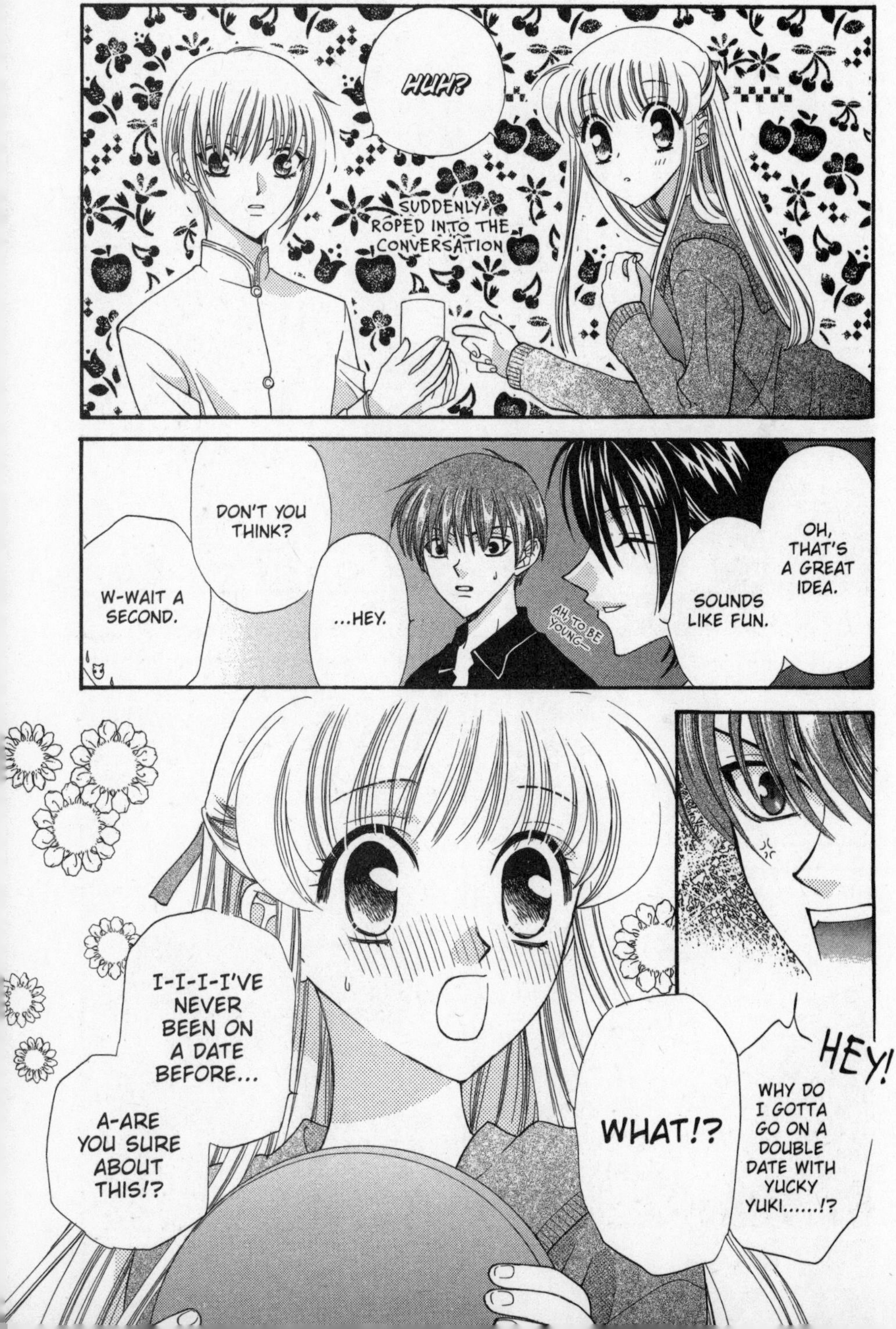
HUH?
SUDDENLY ROPED INTO THE CONVERSATION
OH, THAT'S A GREAT IDEA.
SOUNDS LIKE FUN.
AH, TO BE YOUNG—
...HEY.
DON'T YOU THINK?
W-WAIT A SECOND.
HEY!
WHY DO I GOTTA GO ON A DOUBLE DATE WITH YUCKY YUKI......!?
WHAT!?
I-I-I-I'VE NEVER BEEN ON A DATE BEFORE...
A-ARE YOU SURE ABOUT THIS!?

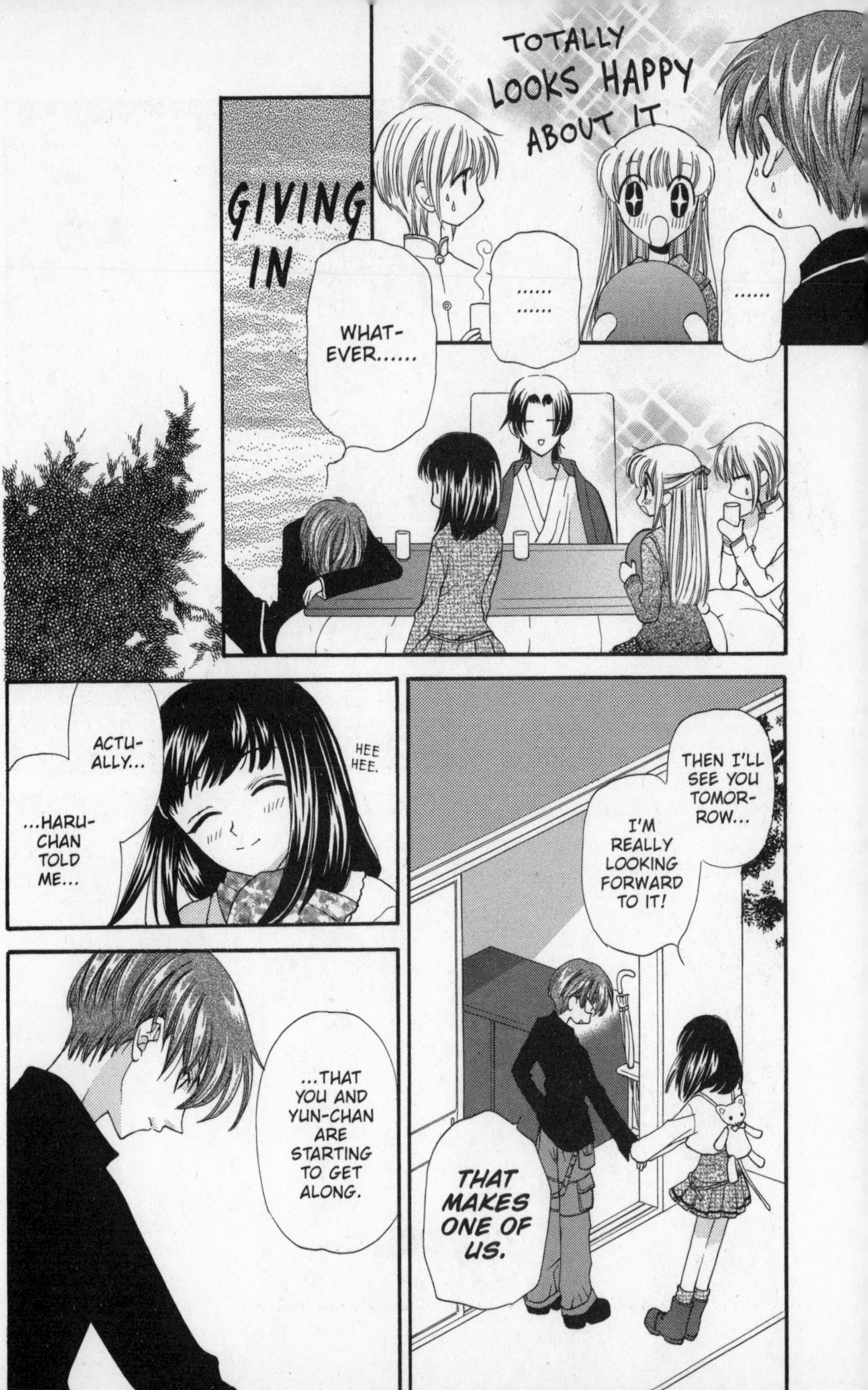
TOTALLY LOOKS HAPPY ABOUT IT
......
....
GIVING IN
WHAT-EVER......
THEN I'LL SEE YOU TOMOR-ROW...
I'M REALLY LOOKING FORWARD TO IT!
THAT MAKES ONE OF US.
ACTU-ALLY...
HEE HEE.
...HARU-CHAN TOLD ME...
...THAT YOU AND YUN-CHAN ARE STARTING TO GET ALONG.

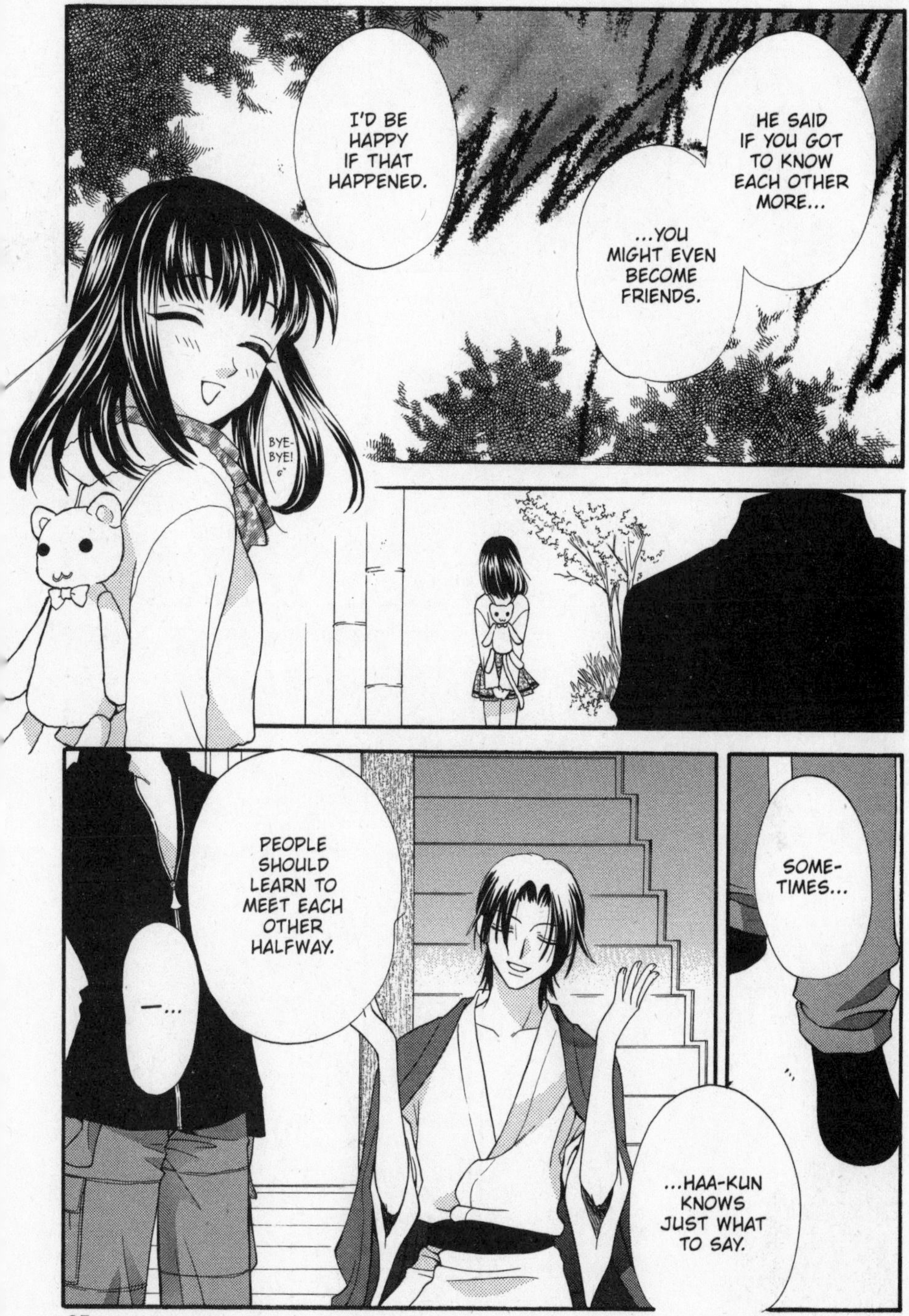
HE SAID IF YOU GOT TO KNOW EACH OTHER MORE...
...YOU MIGHT EVEN BECOME FRIENDS.
I'D BE HAPPY IF THAT HAPPENED.
BYE-BYE!
SOME-TIMES...
...HAA-KUN KNOWS JUST WHAT TO SAY.
PEOPLE SHOULD LEARN TO MEET EACH OTHER HALFWAY.
—...

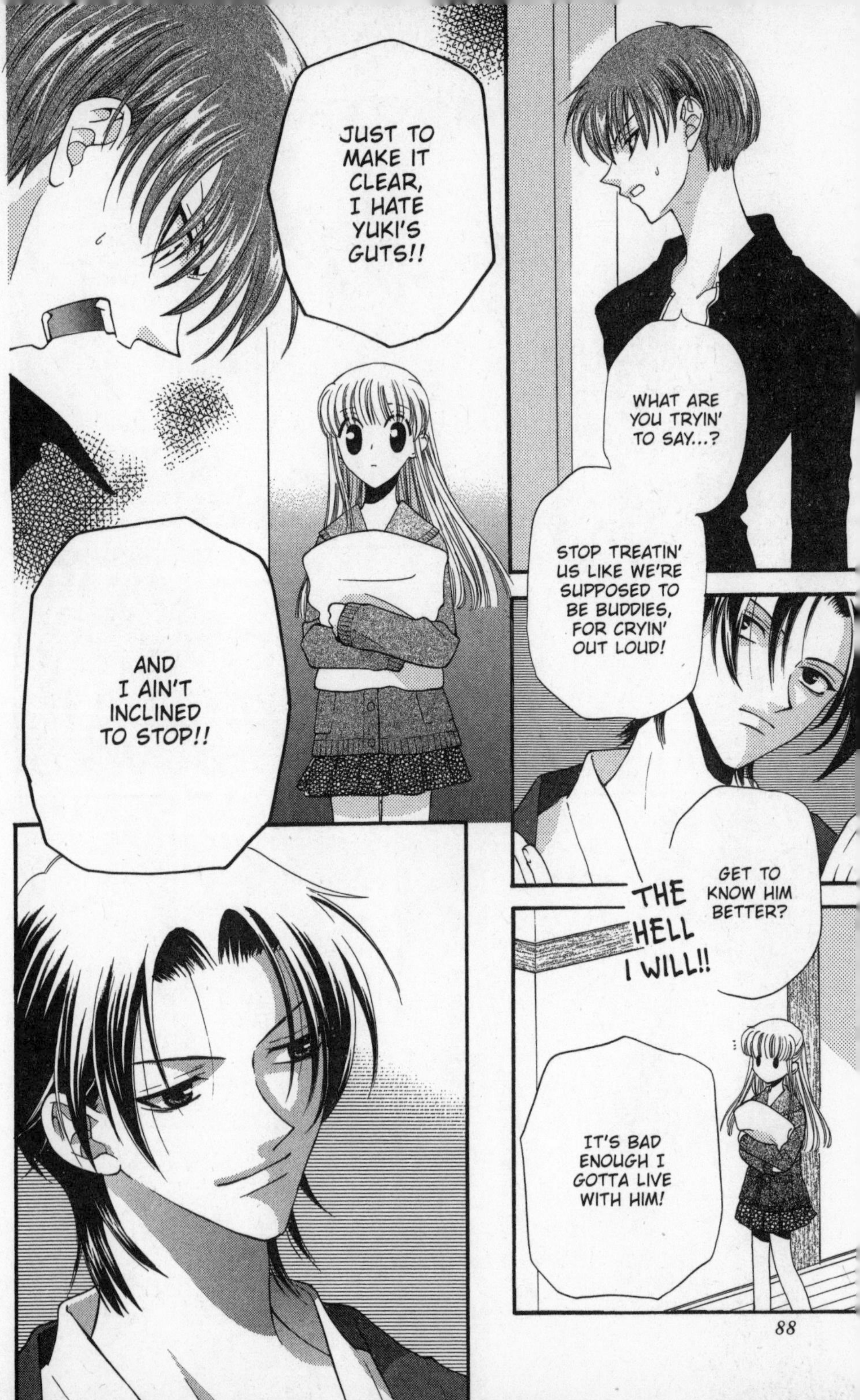
WHAT ARE YOU TRYIN' TO SAY...?
STOP TREATIN' US LIKE WE'RE SUPPOSED TO BE BUDDIES, FOR CRYIN' OUT LOUD!
GET TO KNOW HIM BETTER?
THE HELL I WILL!!
IT'S BAD ENOUGH I GOTTA LIVE WITH HIM!
JUST TO MAKE IT CLEAR, I HATE YUKI'S GUTS!!
AND I AIN'T INCLINED TO STOP!!

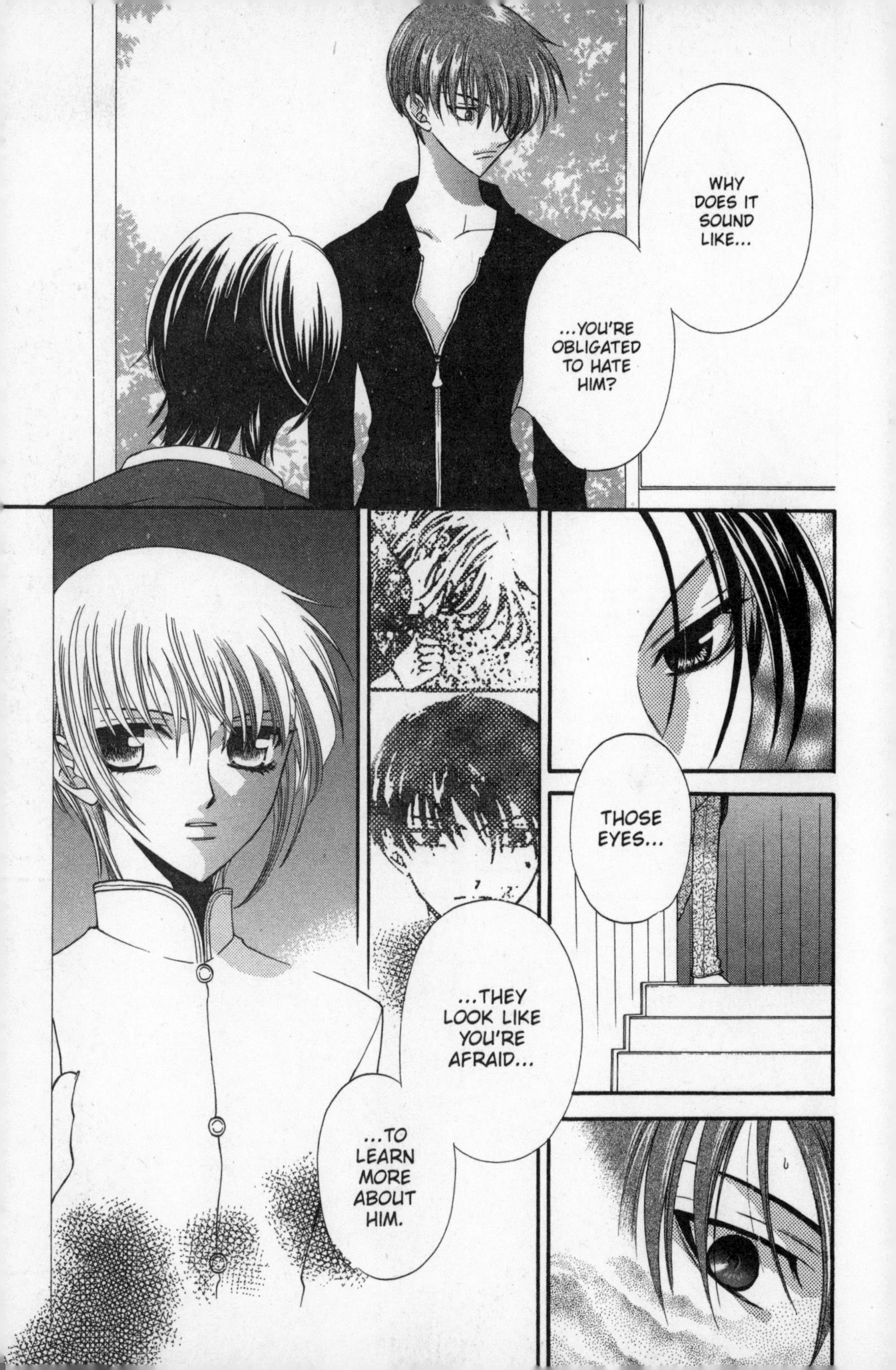
WHY DOES IT SOUND LIKE...
...YOU'RE OBLIGATED TO HATE HIM?
THOSE EYES...
...THEY LOOK LIKE YOU'RE AFRAID...
...TO LEARN MORE ABOUT HIM.

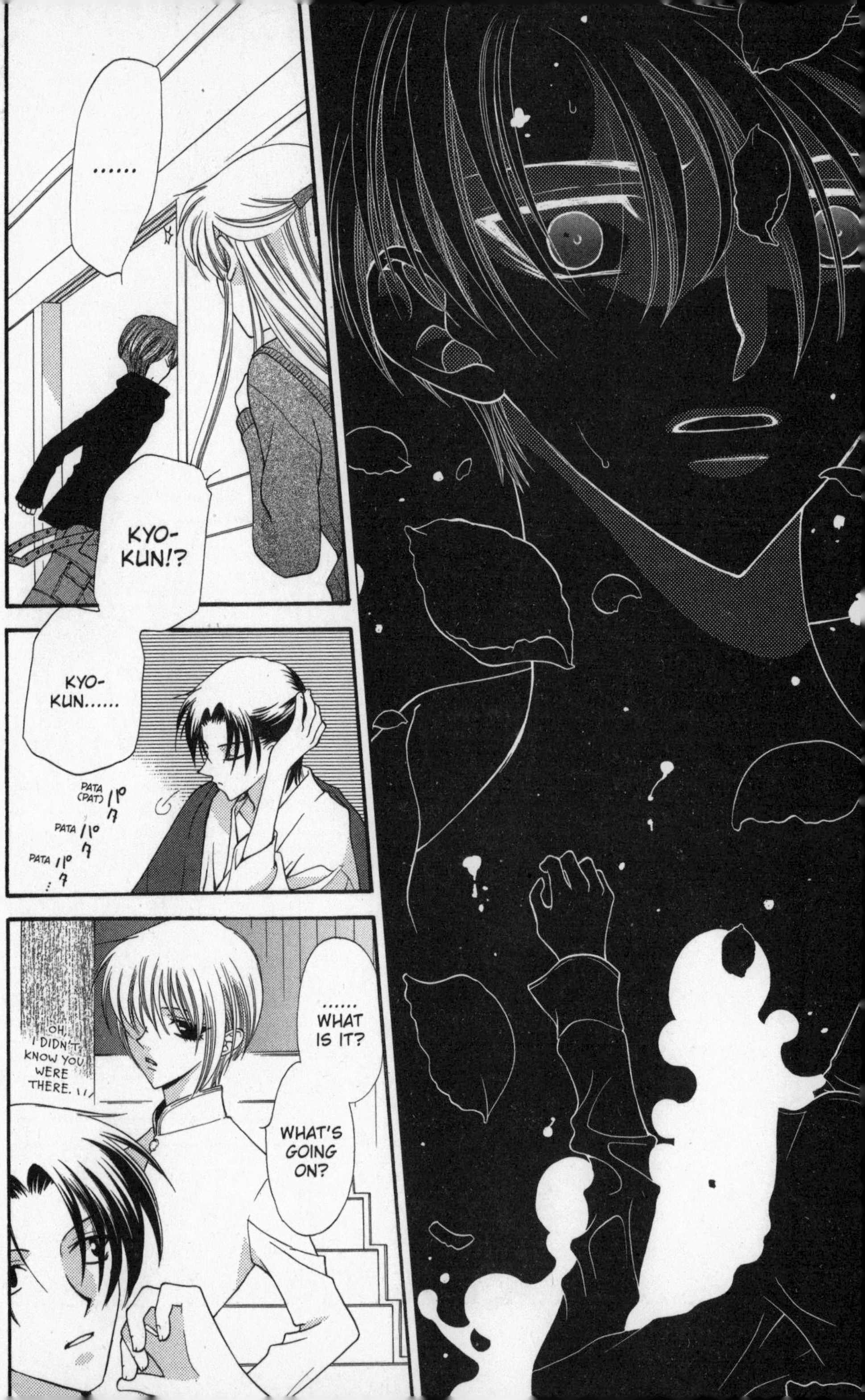
......
KYO-KUN!?
KYO-KUN......
PATA (PAT) パタ
PATA パタ
PATA パタ
...... WHAT IS IT?
WHAT'S GOING ON?
OH, I DIDN'T KNOW YOU WERE THERE.

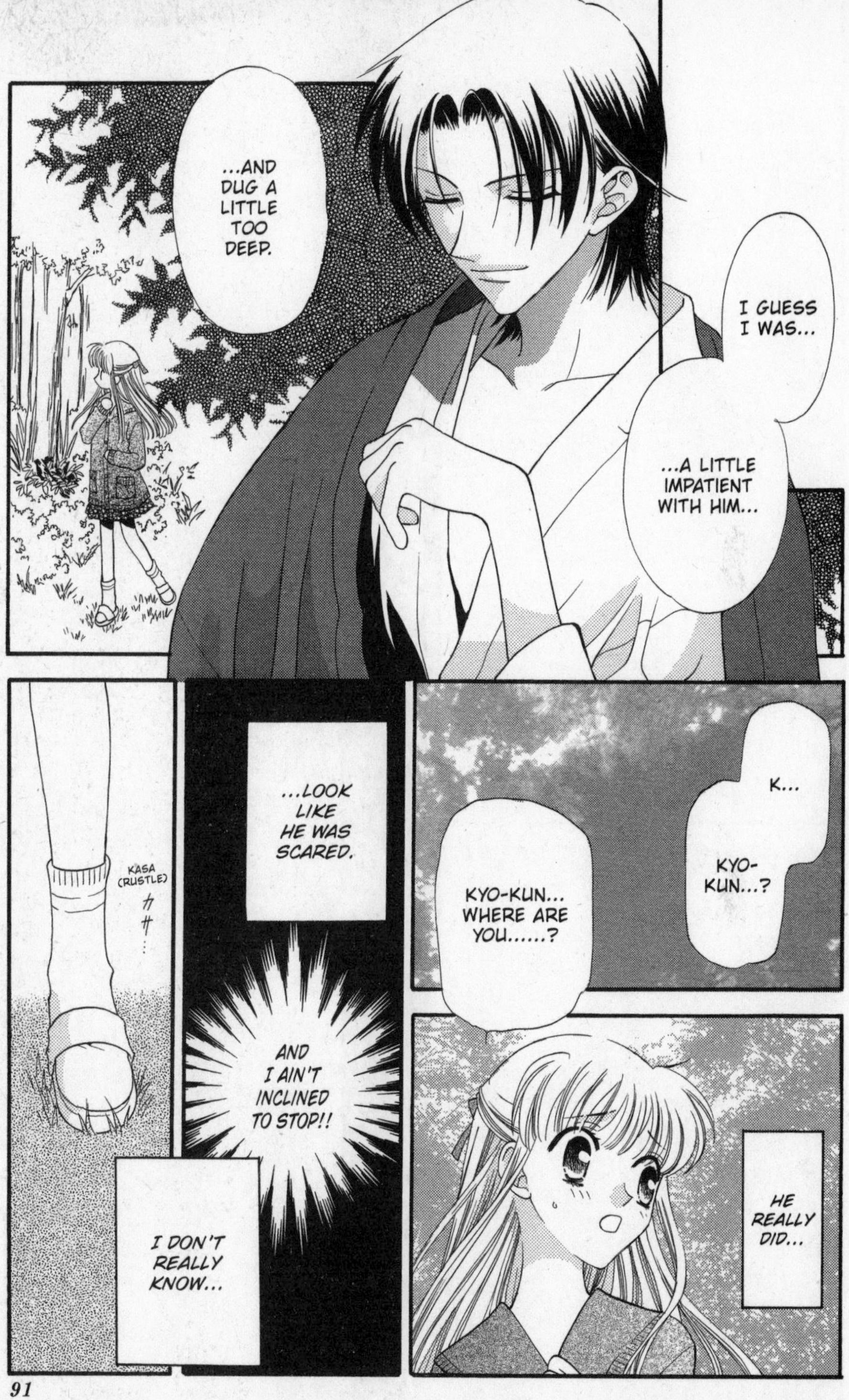
I GUESS I WAS...
...A LITTLE IMPATIENT WITH HIM...
...AND DUG A LITTLE TOO DEEP.
K...
KYO-KUN...?
KYO-KUN... WHERE ARE YOU......?
HE REALLY DID...
...LOOK LIKE HE WAS SCARED.
AND I AIN'T INCLINED TO STOP!!
KASA (RUSTLE)
カサ…
I DON'T REALLY KNOW...

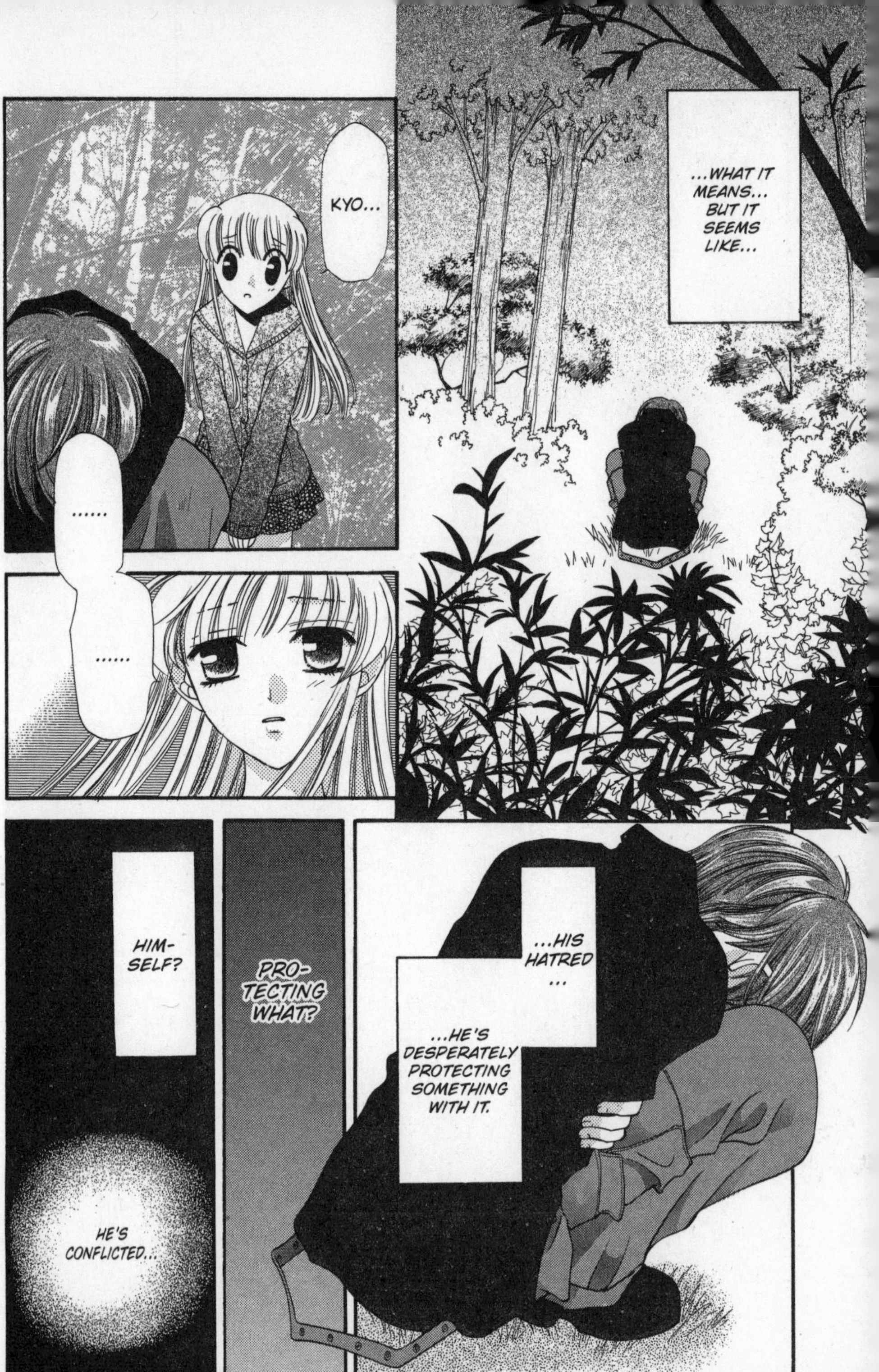
...WHAT IT MEANS... BUT IT SEEMS LIKE...
KYO...
......
......
...HIS HATRED ...
...HE'S DESPERATELY PROTECTING SOMETHING WITH IT.
PRO-TECTING WHAT?
HIM-SELF?
HE'S CONFLICTED...

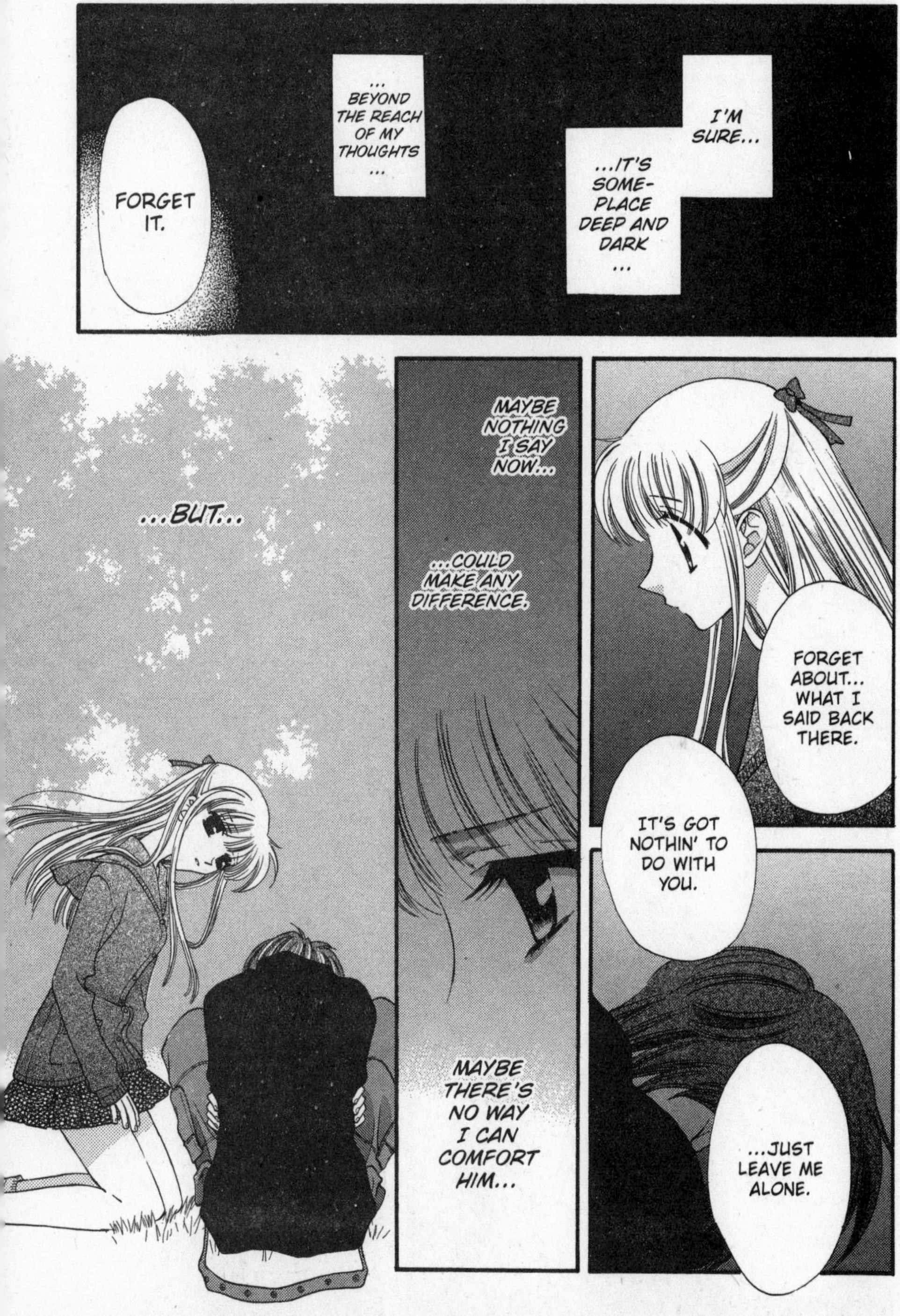
I'M SURE...
...IT'S SOME-PLACE DEEP AND DARK...
...BEYOND THE REACH OF MY THOUGHTS...
FORGET IT.
FORGET ABOUT... WHAT I SAID BACK THERE.
IT'S GOT NOTHIN' TO DO WITH YOU.
...JUST LEAVE ME ALONE.
MAYBE NOTHING I SAY NOW...
...COULD MAKE ANY DIFFERENCE.
MAYBE THERE'S NO WAY I CAN COMFORT HIM...
...BUT...

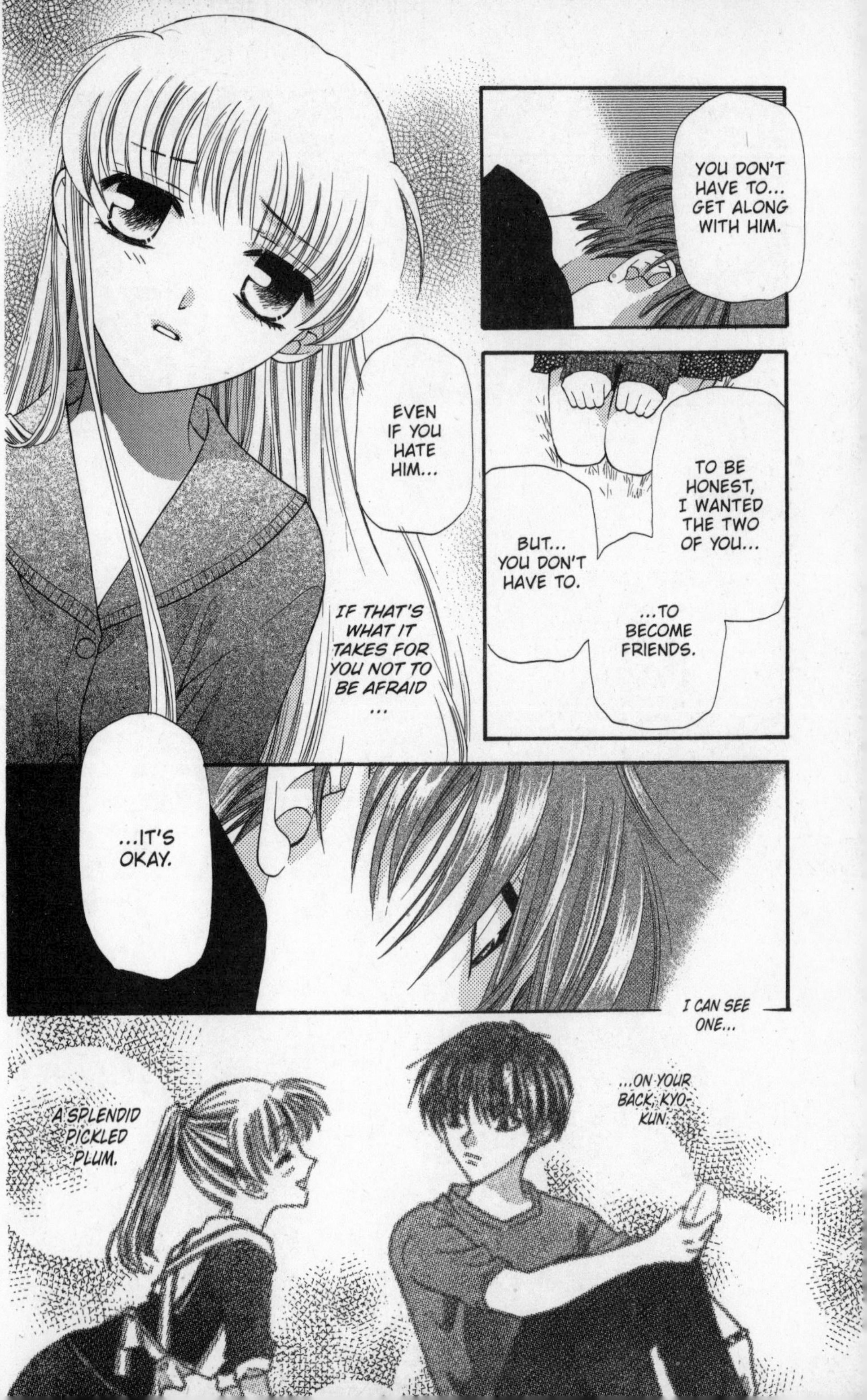

YOU DON'T HAVE TO... GET ALONG WITH HIM.
TO BE HONEST, I WANTED THE TWO OF YOU...
...TO BECOME FRIENDS.
BUT... YOU DON'T HAVE TO.
EVEN IF YOU HATE HIM...
IF THAT'S WHAT IT TAKES FOR YOU NOT TO BE AFRAID...
...IT'S OKAY.
I CAN SEE ONE...
...ON YOUR BACK, KYO-KUN.
A SPLENDID PICKLED PLUM.

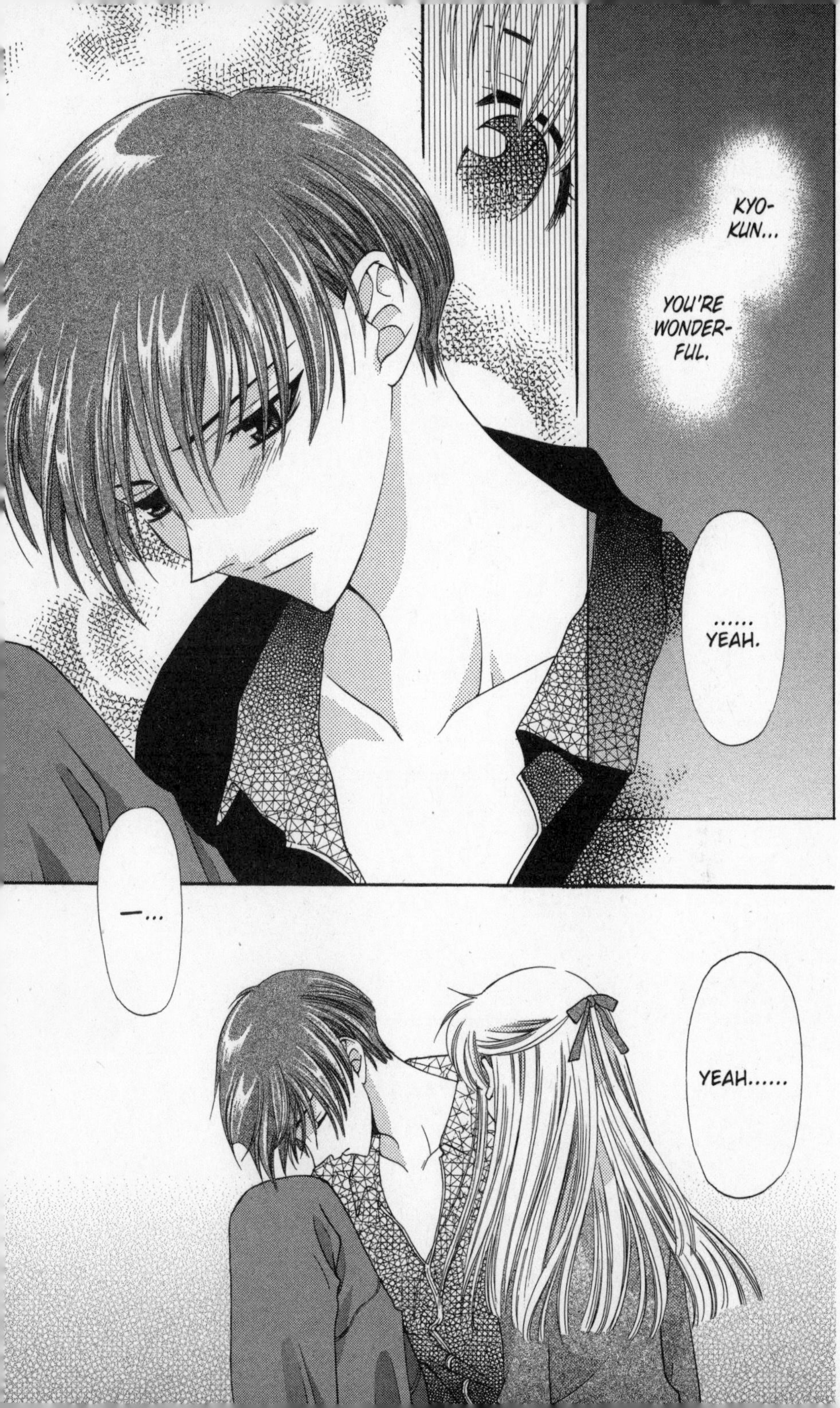
KYO-KUN...
YOU'RE WONDERFUL.
......YEAH.
YEAH......
—...

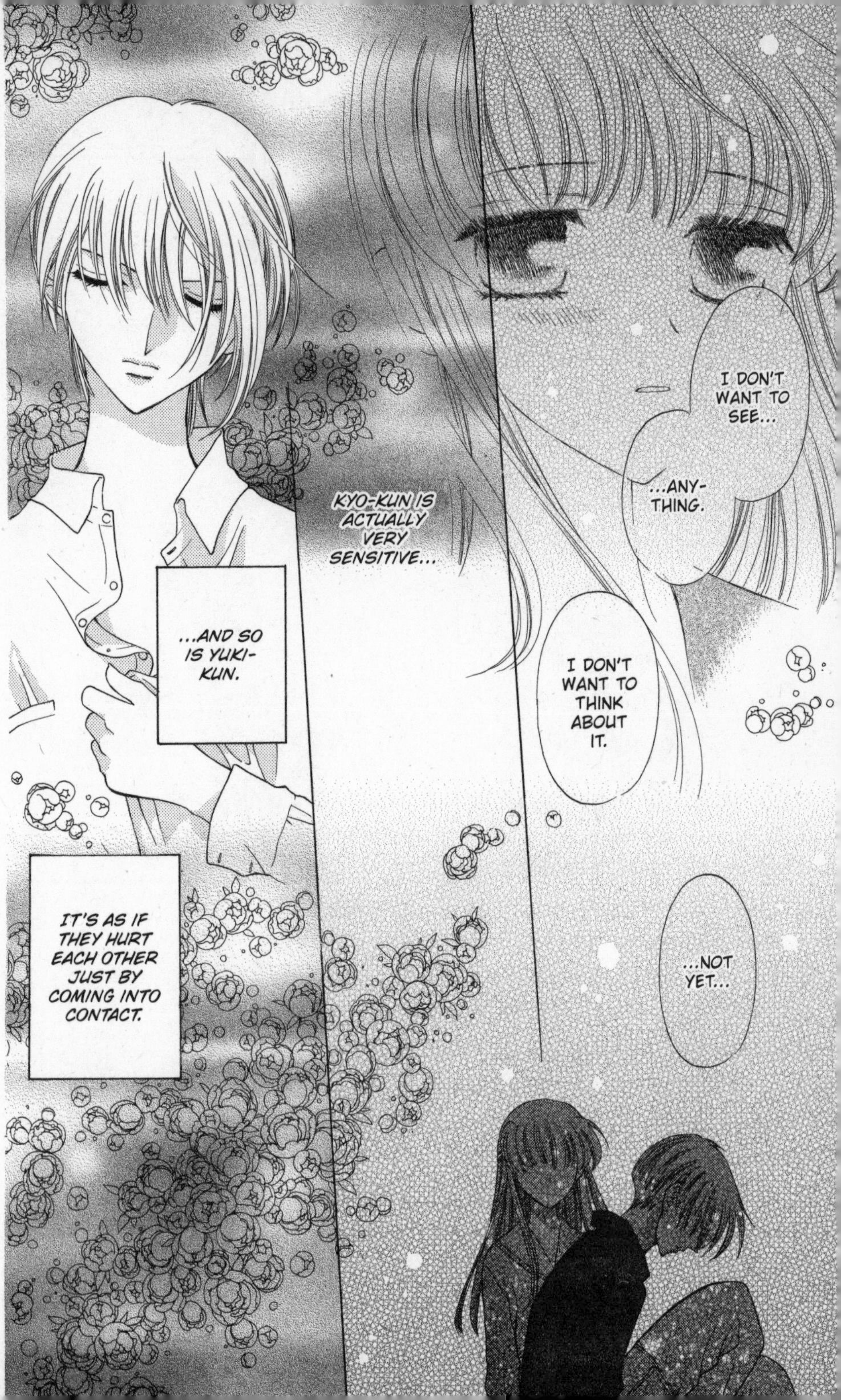
I DON'T WANT TO SEE...
...ANY-THING.
I DON'T WANT TO THINK ABOUT IT.
...NOT YET...
KYO-KUN IS ACTUALLY VERY SENSITIVE...
...AND SO IS YUKI-KUN.
IT'S AS IF THEY HURT EACH OTHER JUST BY COMING INTO CONTACT.

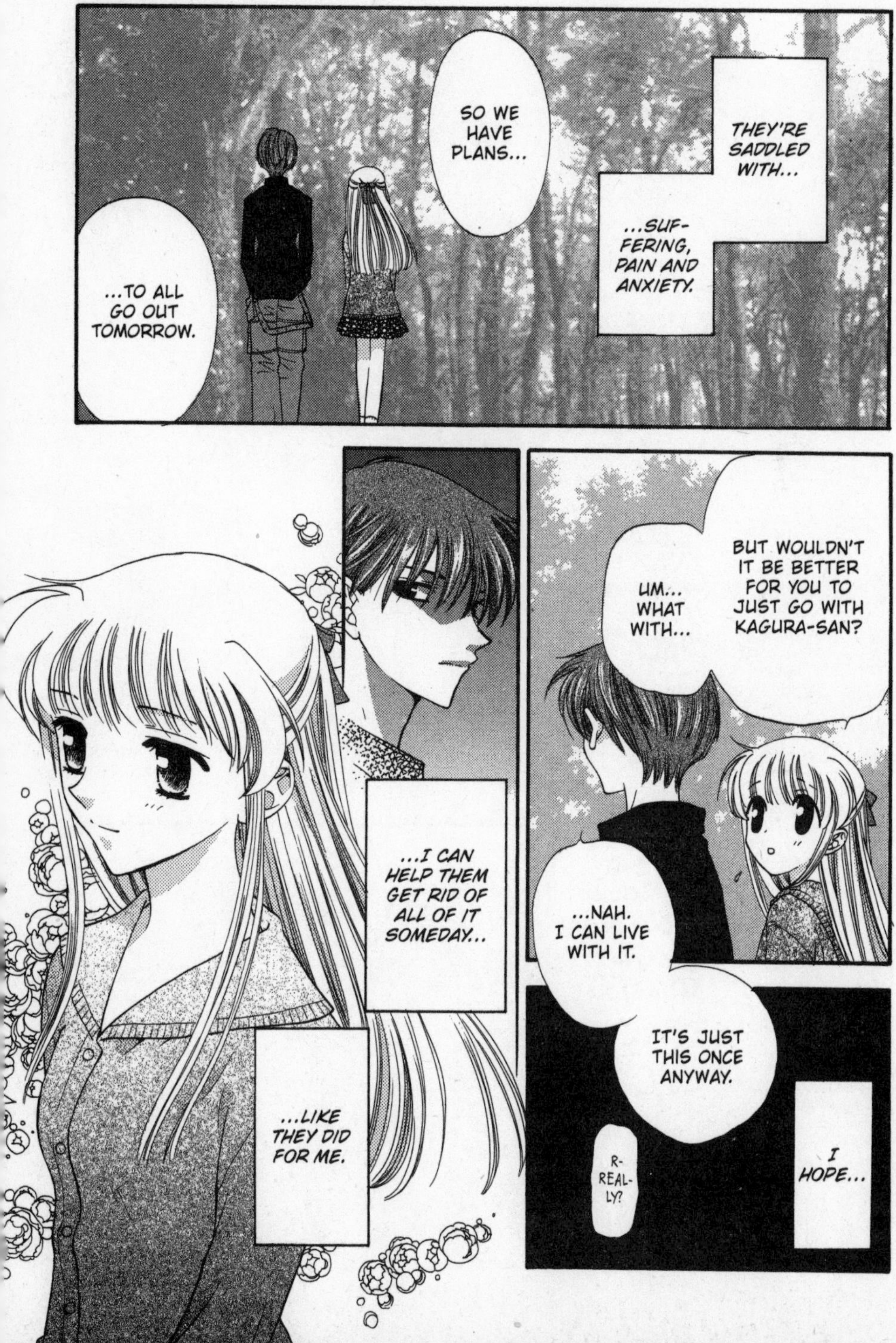
THEY'RE SADDLED WITH...
...SUF-FERING, PAIN AND ANXIETY.
SO WE HAVE PLANS...
...TO ALL GO OUT TOMORROW.
BUT WOULDN'T IT BE BETTER FOR YOU TO JUST GO WITH KAGURA-SAN?
UM... WHAT WITH...
...NAH. I CAN LIVE WITH IT.
IT'S JUST THIS ONCE ANYWAY.
I HOPE...
R-REAL-LY?
...I CAN HELP THEM GET RID OF ALL OF IT SOMEDAY...
...LIKE THEY DID FOR ME.

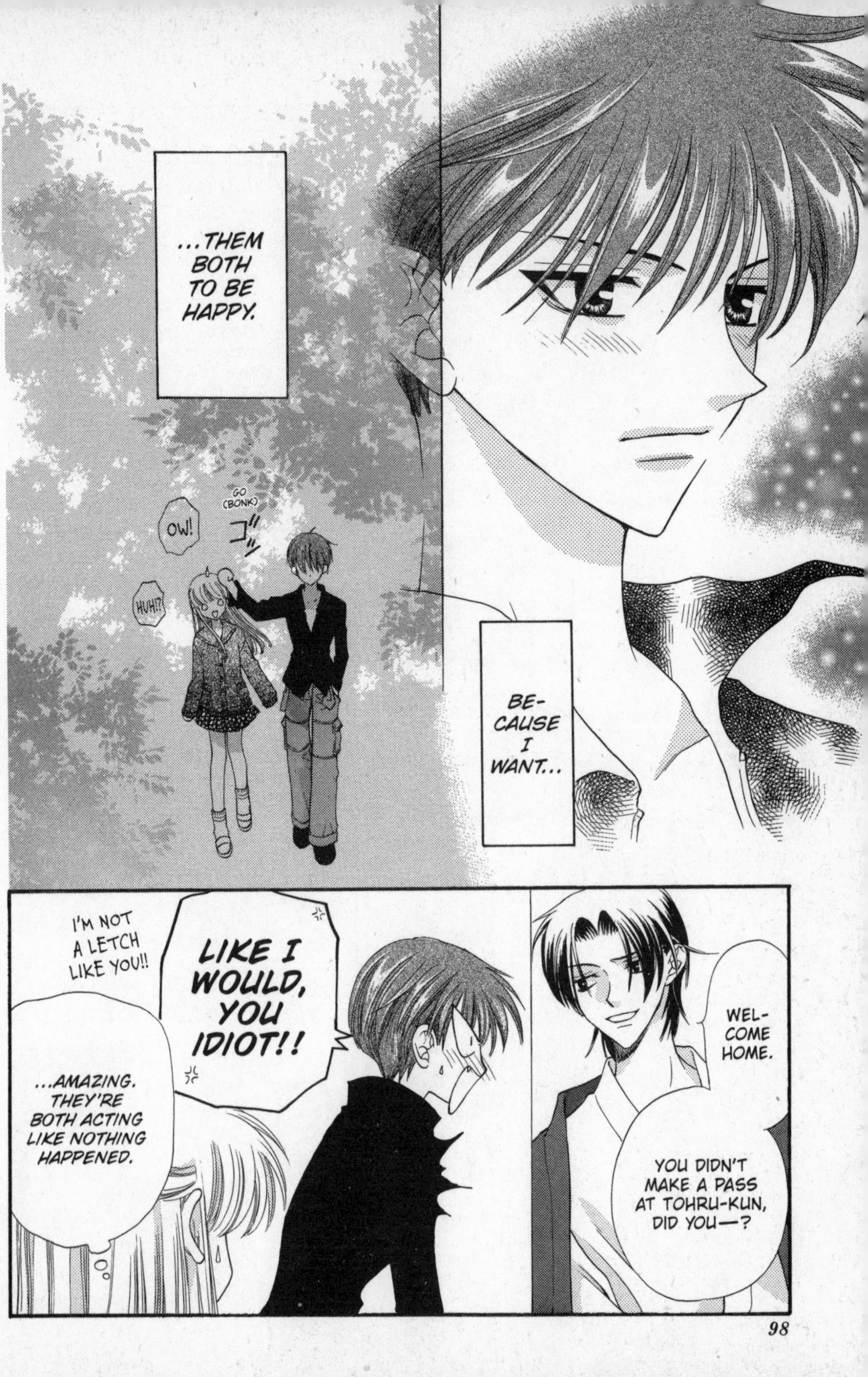
BE-CAUSE I WANT...
...THEM BOTH TO BE HAPPY.
GO (BONK)
ゴッ
OW!
HUH!?
WEL-COME HOME.
YOU DIDN'T MAKE A PASS AT TOHRU-KUN, DID YOU—?
LIKE I WOULD, YOU IDIOT!!
I'M NOT A LETCH LIKE YOU!!
...AMAZING. THEY'RE BOTH ACTING LIKE NOTHING HAPPENED.

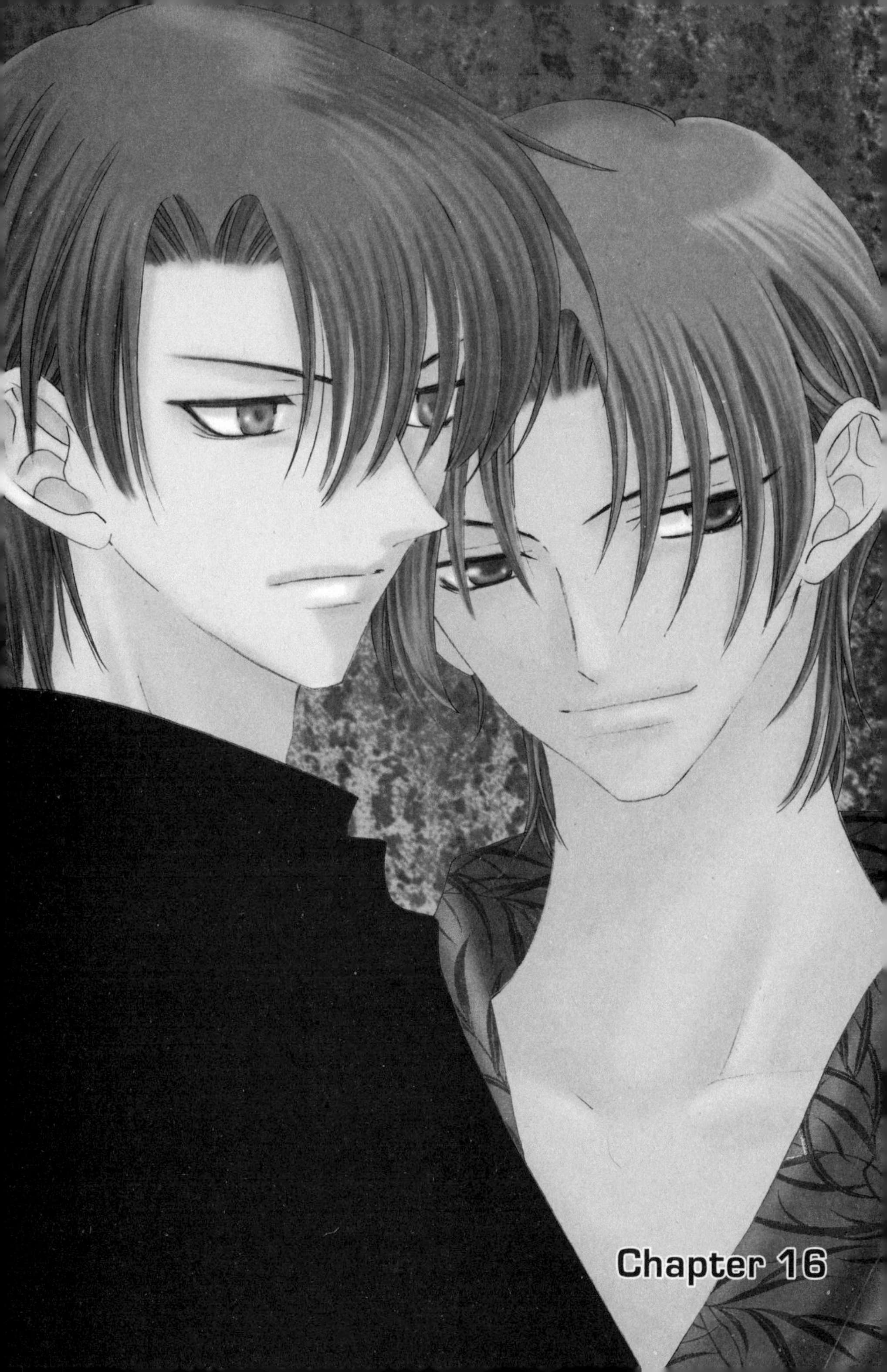
Chapter 16

COLLECTOR'S EDITION

Fruits Basket

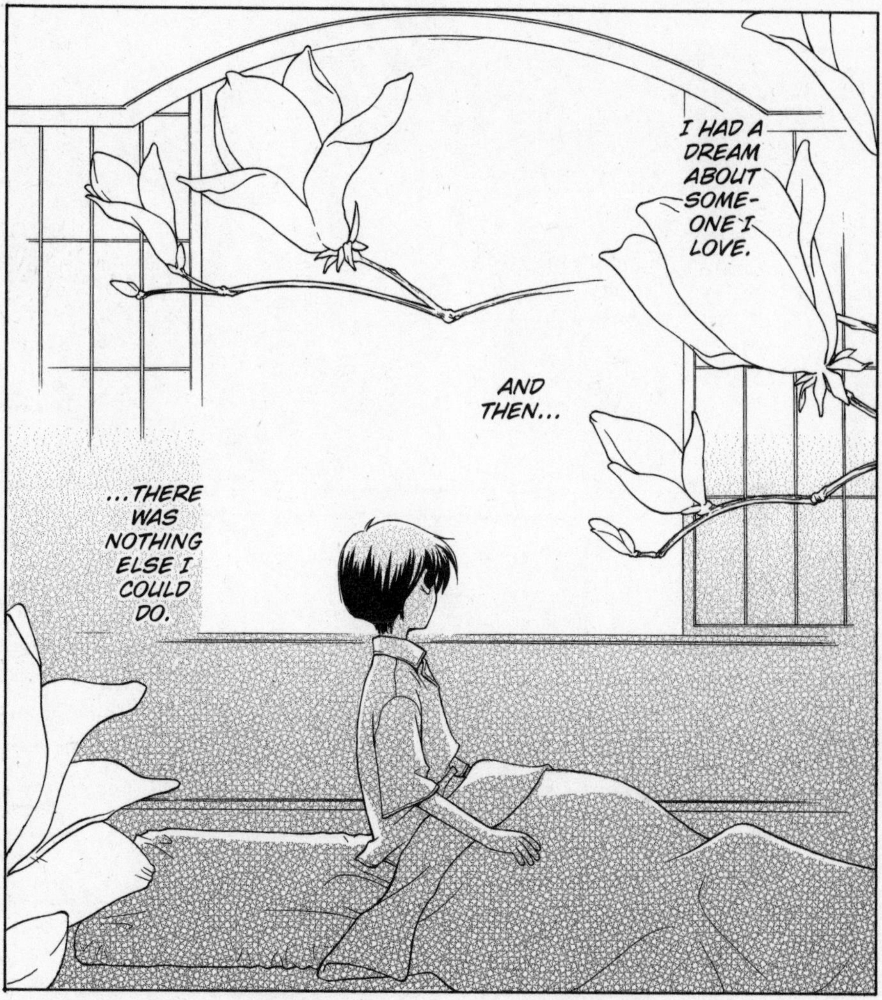
I HAD A DREAM ABOUT SOME-ONE I LOVE.
AND THEN...
...THERE WAS NOTHING ELSE I COULD DO.

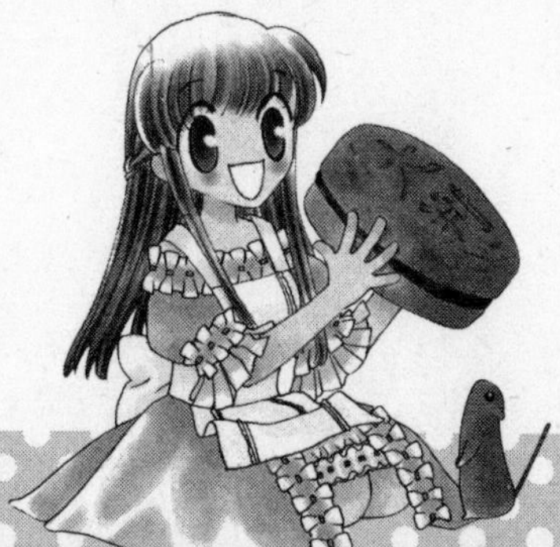

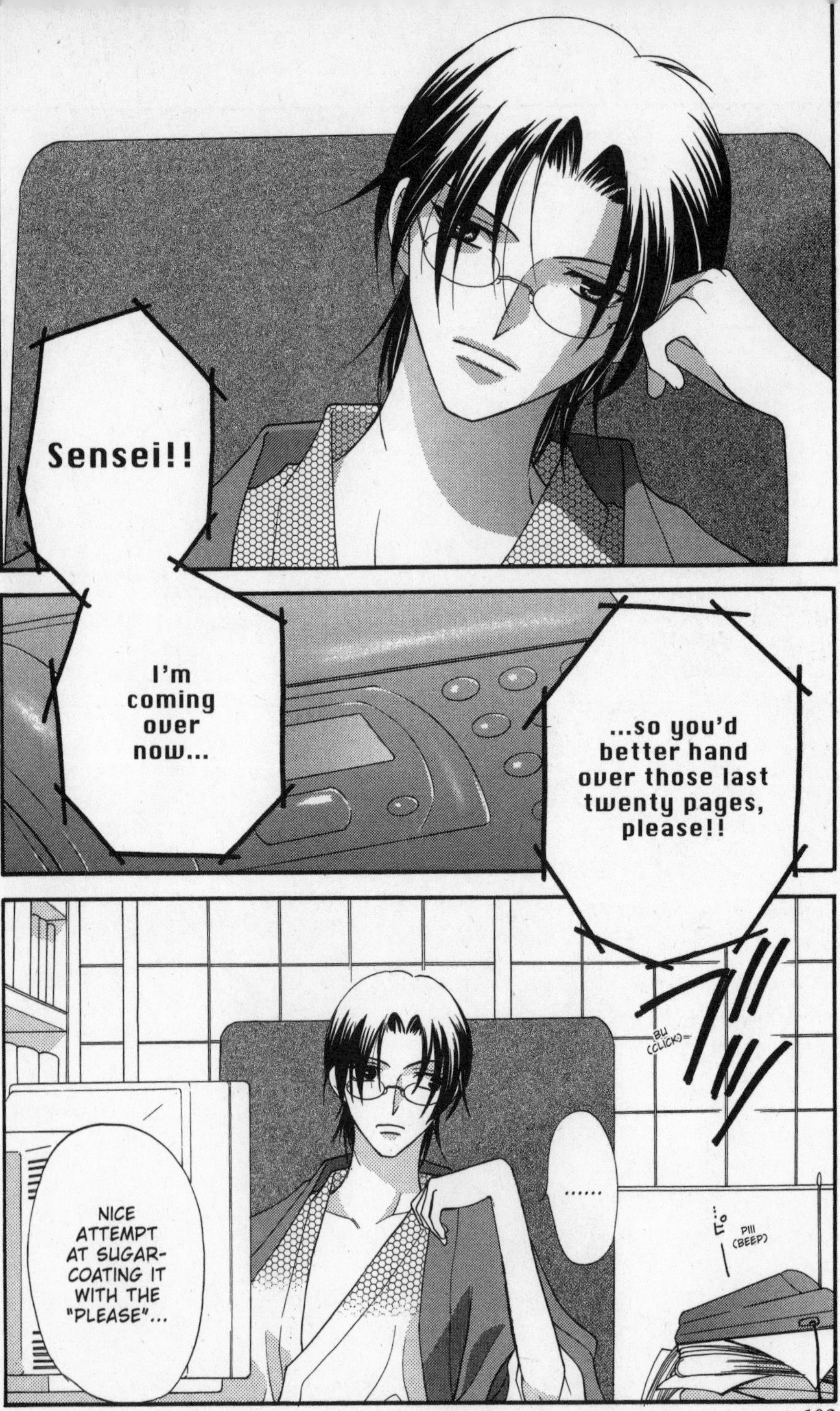
Sensei!!
I'm coming over now...
...so you'd better hand over those last twenty pages, please!!
BU (CLICK)
......
PIII (BEEP)
NICE ATTEMPT AT SUGAR-COATING IT WITH THE "PLEASE"...

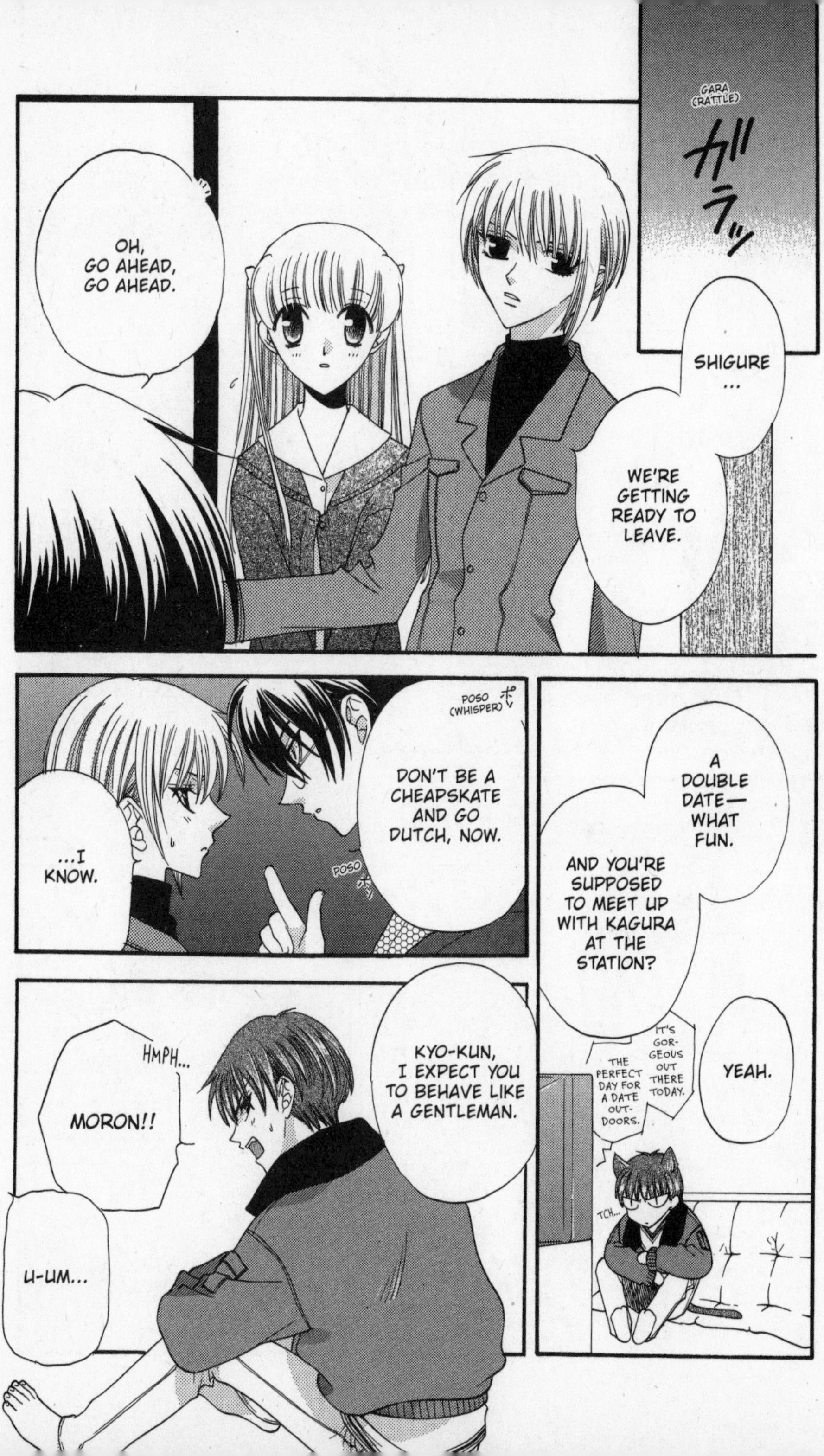
GARA (RATTLE)
SHIGURE...
WE'RE GETTING READY TO LEAVE.
OH, GO AHEAD, GO AHEAD.
A DOUBLE DATE—WHAT FUN.
AND YOU'RE SUPPOSED TO MEET UP WITH KAGURA AT THE STATION?
YEAH.
IT'S GORGEOUS OUT THERE TODAY.
THE PERFECT DAY FOR A DATE OUTDOORS.
TCH...
POSO (WHISPER)
DON'T BE A CHEAPSKATE AND GO DUTCH, NOW.
POSO
...I KNOW.
KYO-KUN, I EXPECT YOU TO BEHAVE LIKE A GENTLEMAN.
HMPH...
MORON!!
U-UM...

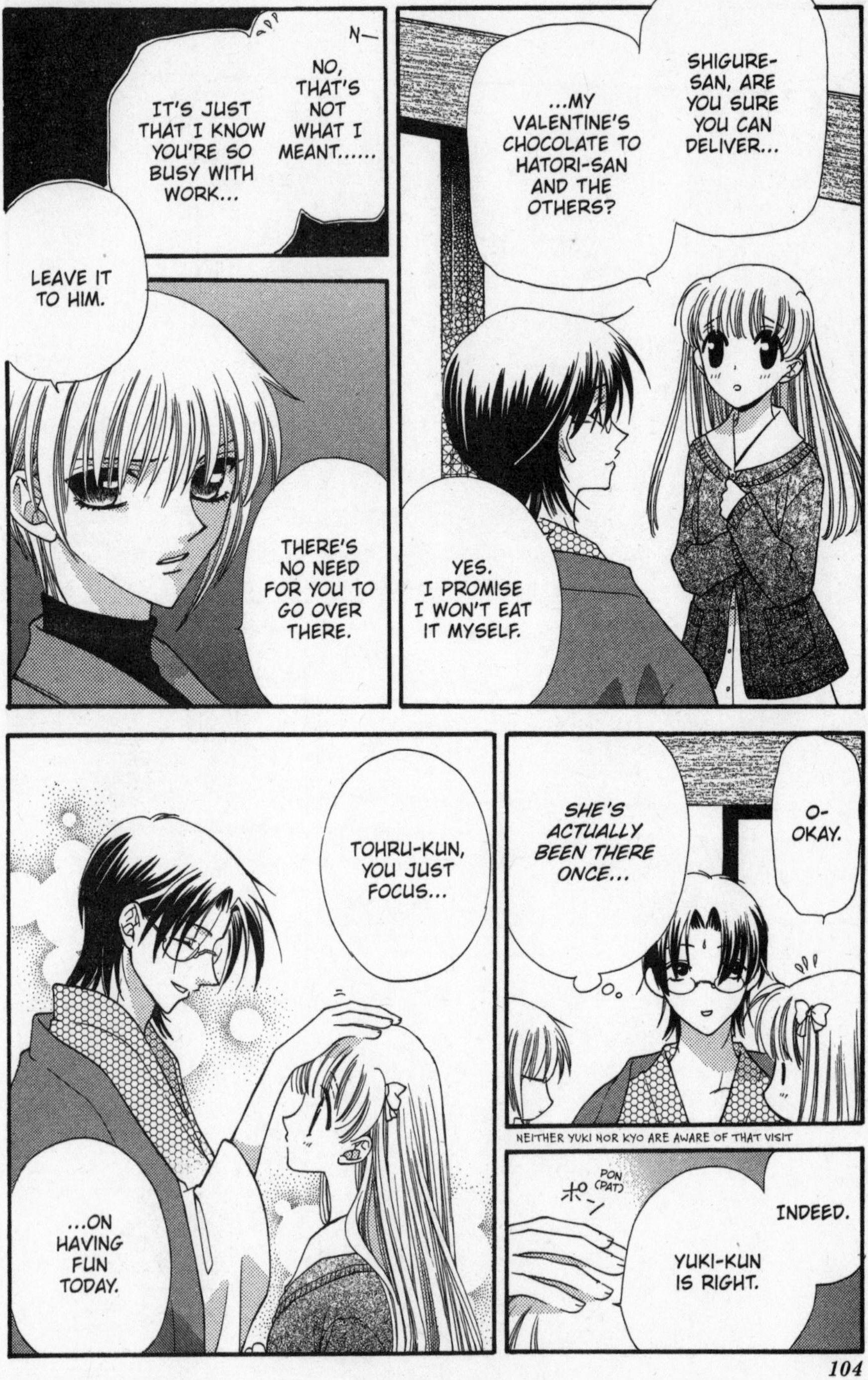
SHIGURE-SAN, ARE YOU SURE YOU CAN DELIVER...
...MY VALENTINE'S CHOCOLATE TO HATORI-SAN AND THE OTHERS?
YES. I PROMISE I WON'T EAT IT MYSELF.
N—
NO, THAT'S NOT WHAT I MEANT......
IT'S JUST THAT I KNOW YOU'RE SO BUSY WITH WORK...
THERE'S NO NEED FOR YOU TO GO OVER THERE.
LEAVE IT TO HIM.
O-OKAY.
SHE'S ACTUALLY BEEN THERE ONCE...
NEITHER YUKI NOR KYO ARE AWARE OF THAT VISIT
INDEED.
YUKI-KUN IS RIGHT.
PON (PAT)
TOHRU-KUN, YOU JUST FOCUS...
...ON HAVING FUN TODAY.

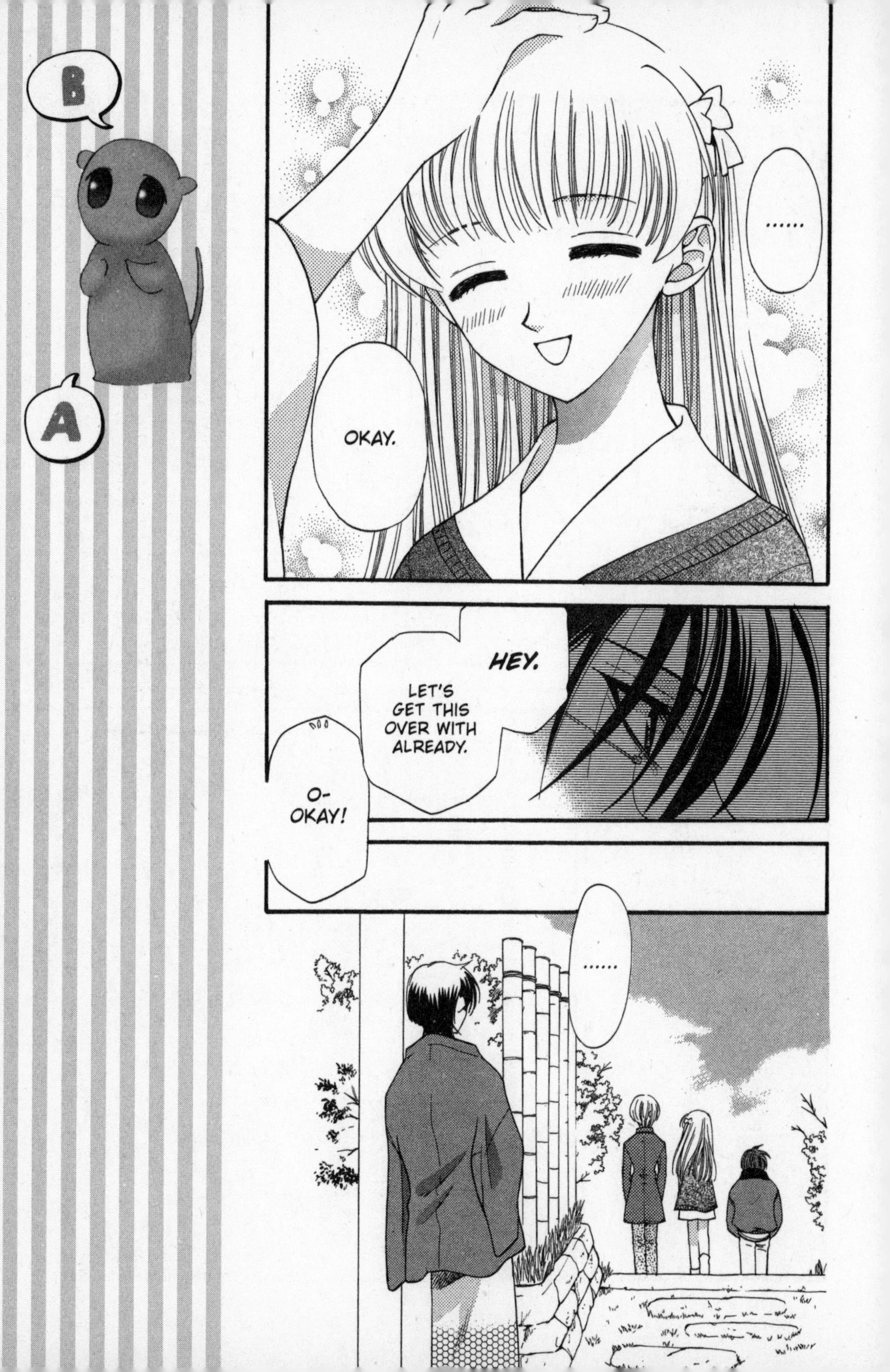
......
OKAY.
HEY.
LET'S GET THIS OVER WITH ALREADY.
O-OKAY!
......
B
A

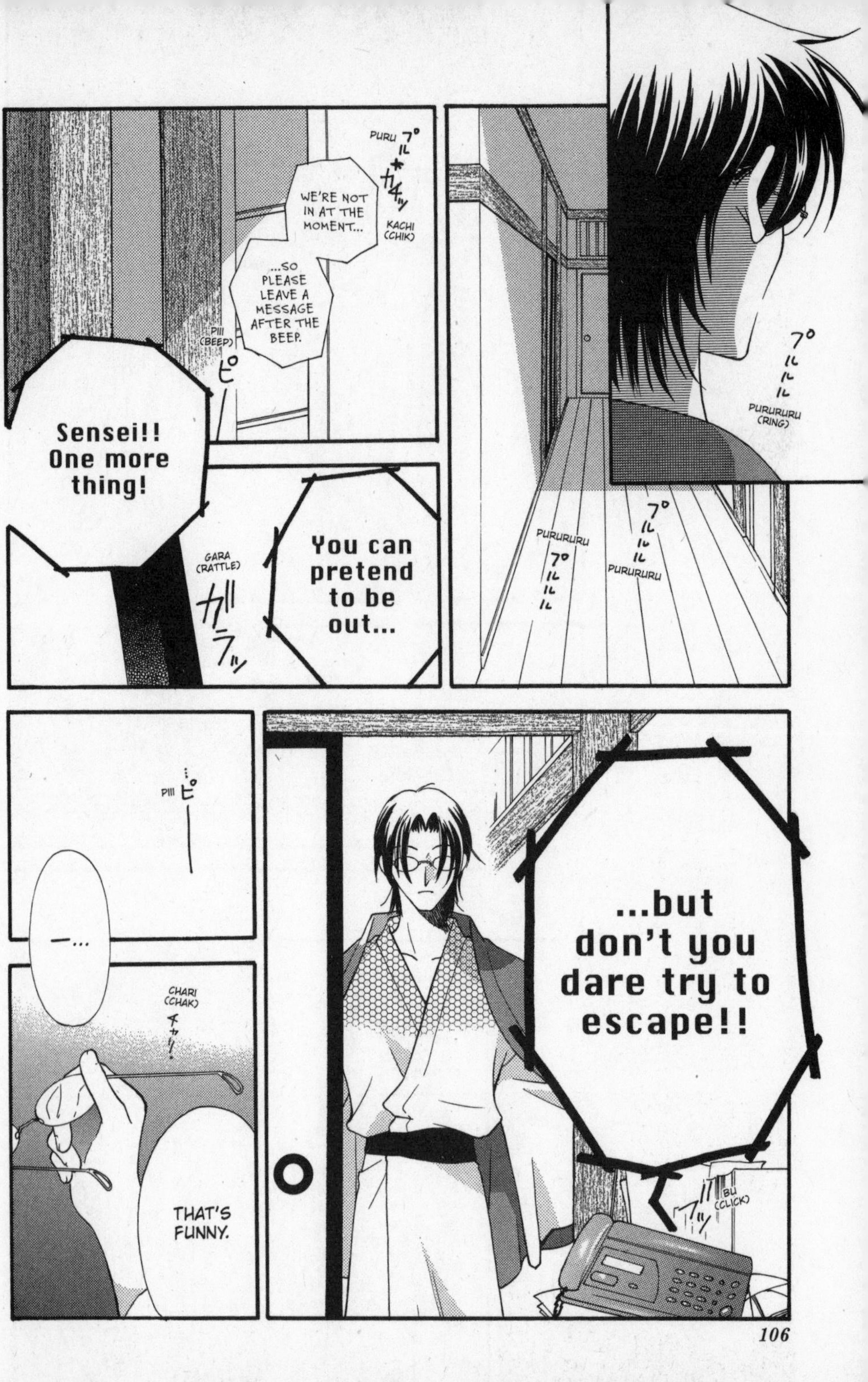
プルルル
PURURURU (RING)
プルルル
PURURURU
プルルル
PURURURU
PURU プル
ガチャッ
KACHI (CHIK)
WE'RE NOT IN AT THE MOMENT...
...SO PLEASE LEAVE A MESSAGE AFTER THE BEEP.
PIII (BEEP)
ピ
Sensei!! One more thing!
You can pretend to be out...
GARA (RATTLE)
ガラッ
...but don't you dare try to escape!!
BU (CLICK)
ブッ
PIII
...ピー
—...
CHARI (CHAK)
チャリ
THAT'S FUNNY.

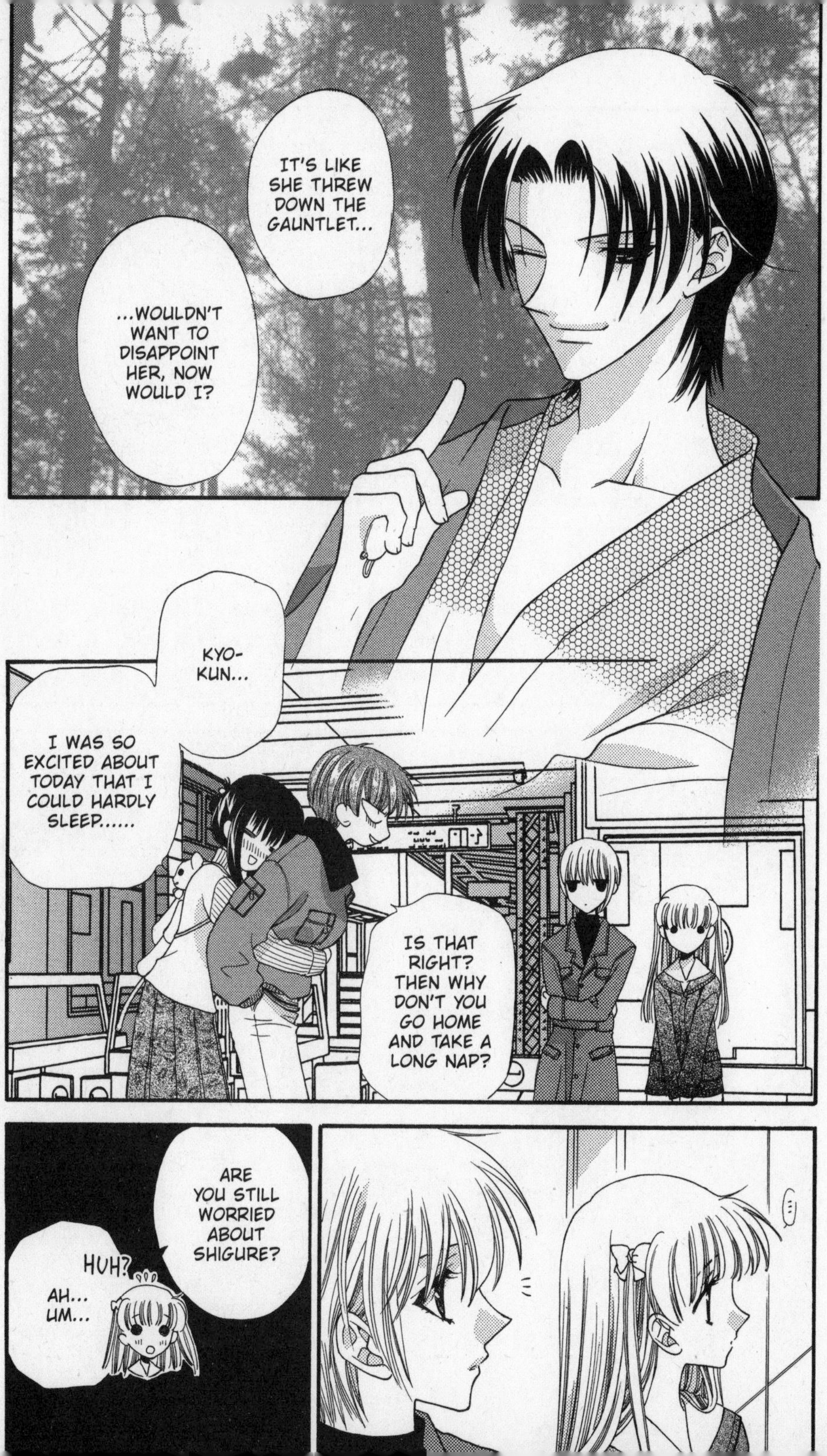
IT'S LIKE SHE THREW DOWN THE GAUNTLET...
...WOULDN'T WANT TO DISAPPOINT HER, NOW WOULD I?
KYO-KUN...
I WAS SO EXCITED ABOUT TODAY THAT I COULD HARDLY SLEEP......
IS THAT RIGHT? THEN WHY DON'T YOU GO HOME AND TAKE A LONG NAP?
ARE YOU STILL WORRIED ABOUT SHIGURE?
HUH?
AH... UM...

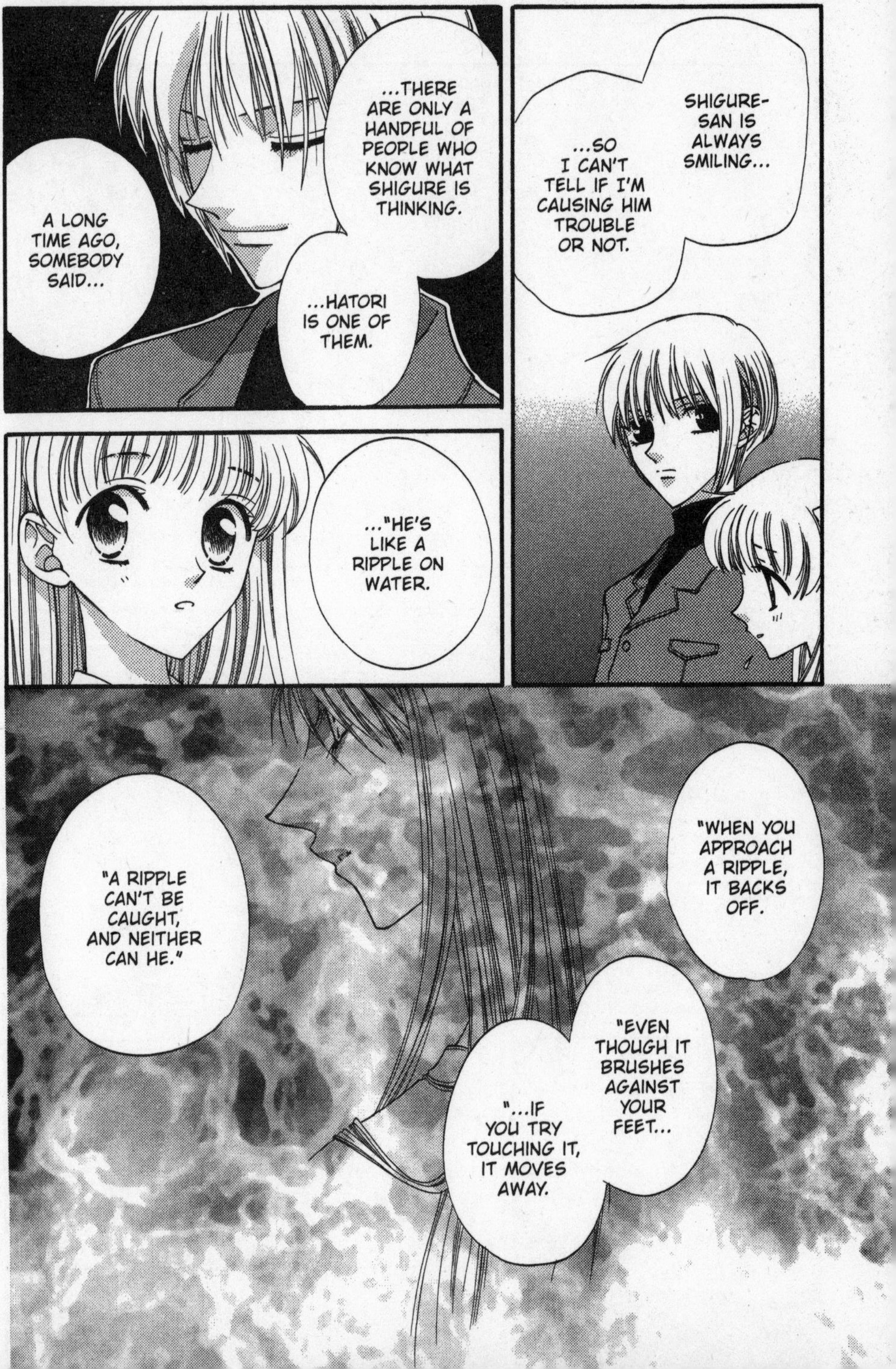
SHIGURE-SAN IS ALWAYS SMILING...
...SO I CAN'T TELL IF I'M CAUSING HIM TROUBLE OR NOT.
...THERE ARE ONLY A HANDFUL OF PEOPLE WHO KNOW WHAT SHIGURE IS THINKING.
...HATORI IS ONE OF THEM.
A LONG TIME AGO, SOMEBODY SAID...
..."HE'S LIKE A RIPPLE ON WATER.
"WHEN YOU APPROACH A RIPPLE, IT BACKS OFF.
"EVEN THOUGH IT BRUSHES AGAINST YOUR FEET...
"...IF YOU TRY TOUCHING IT, IT MOVES AWAY.
"A RIPPLE CAN'T BE CAUGHT, AND NEITHER CAN HE."

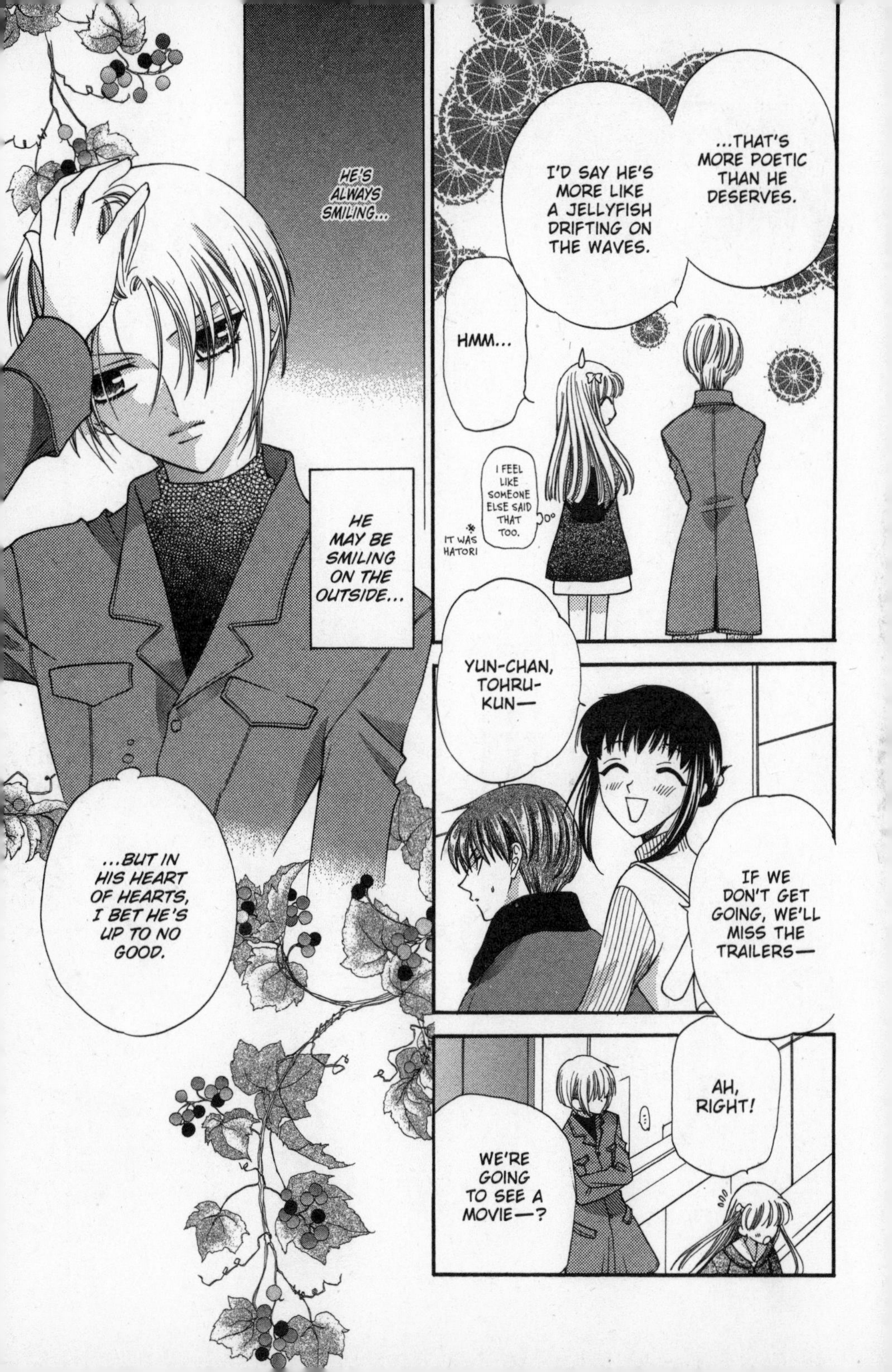
I'D SAY HE'S MORE LIKE A JELLYFISH DRIFTING ON THE WAVES.
...THAT'S MORE POETIC THAN HE DESERVES.
HMM...
I FEEL LIKE SOMEONE ELSE SAID THAT TOO.
※IT WAS HATORI
YUN-CHAN, TOHRU-KUN—
IF WE DON'T GET GOING, WE'LL MISS THE TRAILERS—
AH, RIGHT!
...
WE'RE GOING TO SEE A MOVIE—?
HE'S ALWAYS SMILING...
HE MAY BE SMILING ON THE OUTSIDE...
...BUT IN HIS HEART OF HEARTS, I BET HE'S UP TO NO GOOD.

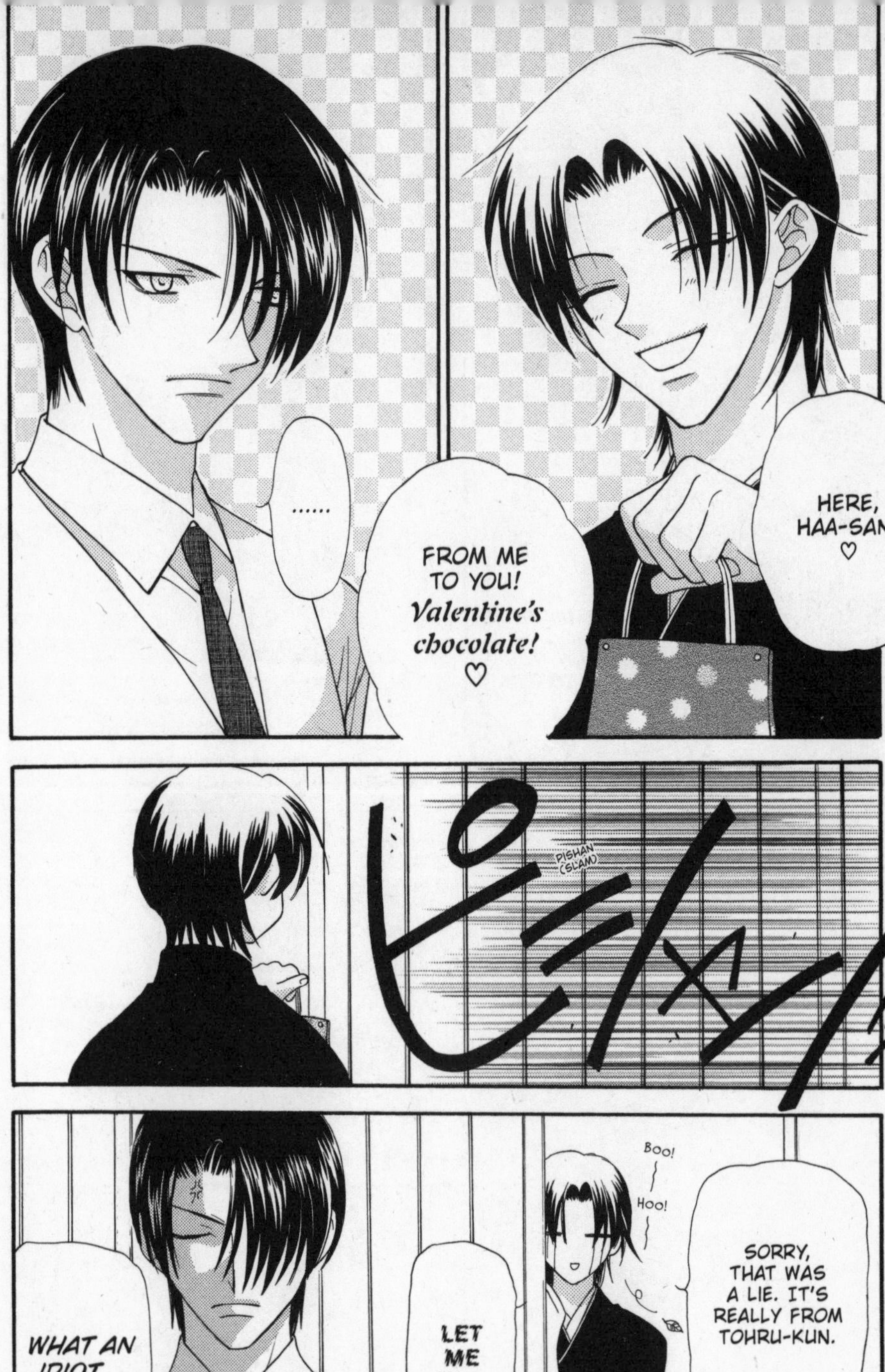
HERE, HAA-SAN! ♡
FROM ME TO YOU! Valentine's chocolate! ♡
......
PISHAN (SLAM)
BOO! HOO!
SORRY, THAT WAS A LIE. IT'S REALLY FROM TOHRU-KUN.
LET ME IN...
WHAT AN IDIOT...

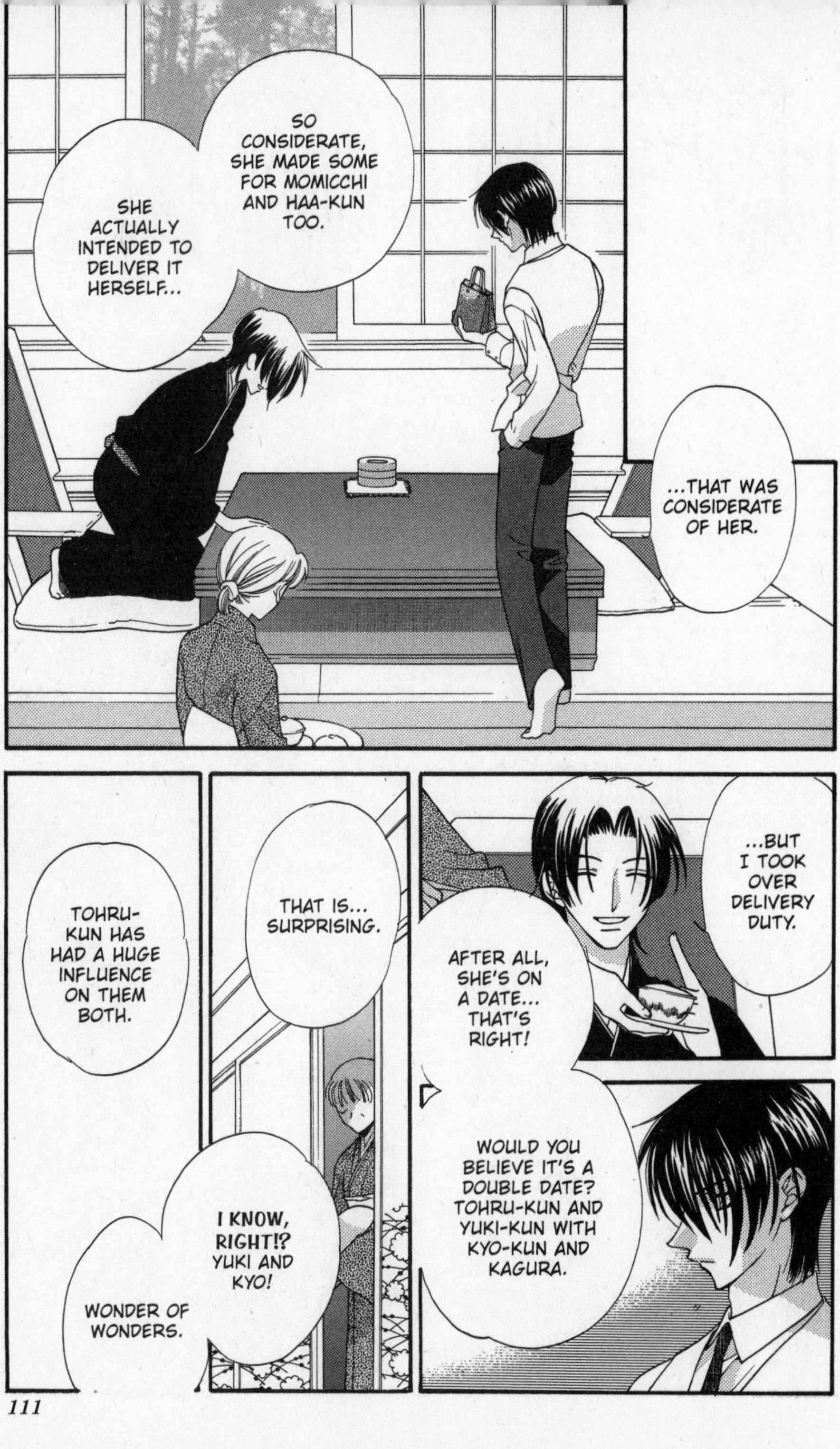
SO CONSIDERATE, SHE MADE SOME FOR MOMICCHI AND HAA-KUN TOO.
SHE ACTUALLY INTENDED TO DELIVER IT HERSELF...
...THAT WAS CONSIDERATE OF HER.
...BUT I TOOK OVER DELIVERY DUTY.
AFTER ALL, SHE'S ON A DATE... THAT'S RIGHT!
WOULD YOU BELIEVE IT'S A DOUBLE DATE? TOHRU-KUN AND YUKI-KUN WITH KYO-KUN AND KAGURA.
THAT IS... SURPRISING.
I KNOW, RIGHT!? YUKI AND KYO!
TOHRU-KUN HAS HAD A HUGE INFLUENCE ON THEM BOTH.
WONDER OF WONDERS.

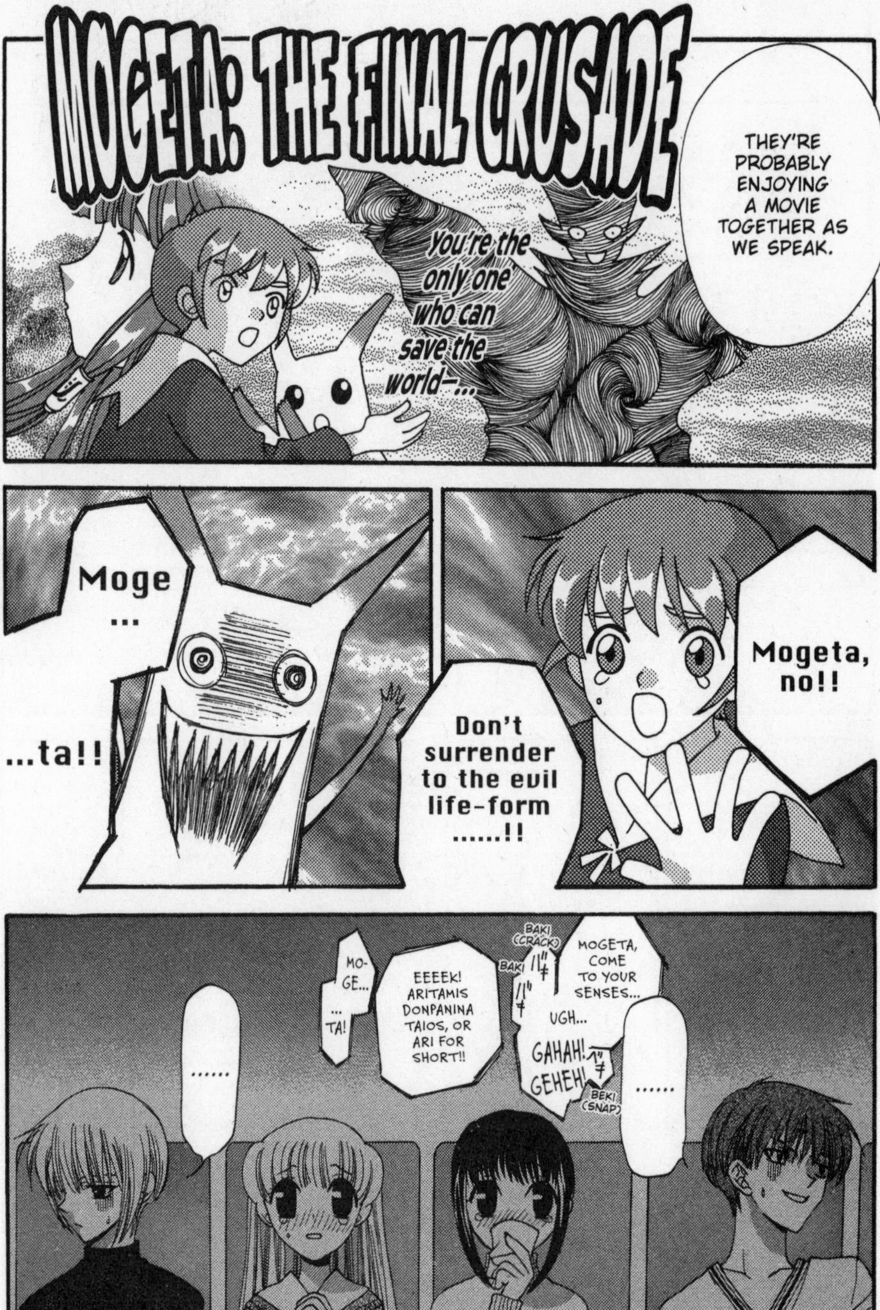
MOGETA: THE FINAL CRUSADE
THEY'RE PROBABLY ENJOYING A MOVIE TOGETHER AS WE SPEAK.
You're the only one who can save the world-...
Mogeta, no!!
Don't surrender to the evil life-form ......!!
Moge ...
...ta!!
......
MOGETA, COME TO YOUR SENSES...
BAKI (CRACK)
BAKI
UGH...
GAHAH! GEHEH!
BEKI (SNAP)
EEEEK! ARITAMIS DONPANINA TAIOS, OR ARI FOR SHORT!!
MO-GE... ... TA!
......

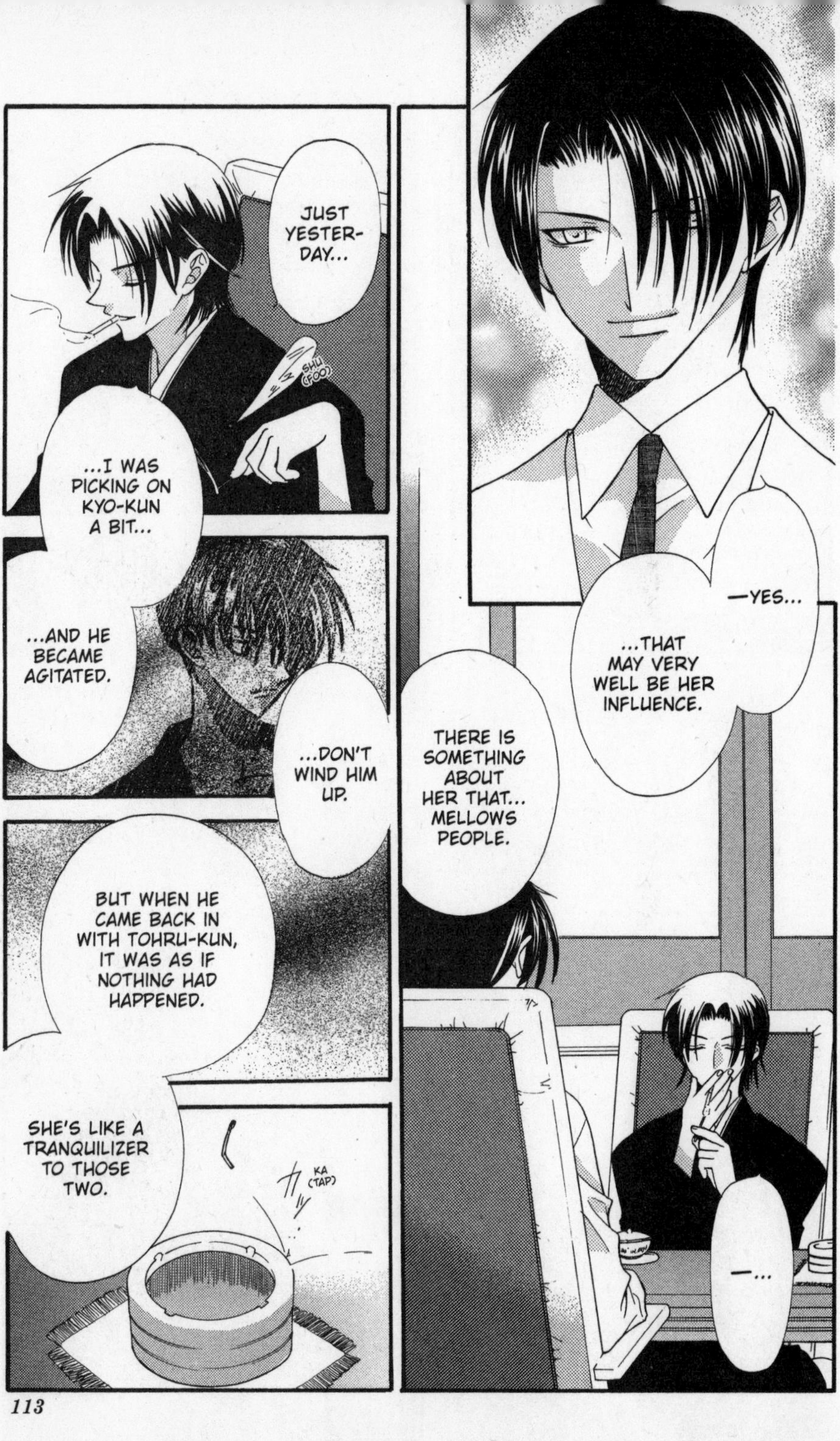
JUST YESTER-DAY...
SHU (FOO)
...I WAS PICKING ON KYO-KUN A BIT...
...AND HE BECAME AGITATED.
BUT WHEN HE CAME BACK IN WITH TOHRU-KUN, IT WAS AS IF NOTHING HAD HAPPENED.
SHE'S LIKE A TRANQUILIZER TO THOSE TWO.
KA (TAP)
—...
—YES...
...THAT MAY VERY WELL BE HER INFLUENCE.
THERE IS SOMETHING ABOUT HER THAT... MELLOWS PEOPLE.
...DON'T WIND HIM UP.

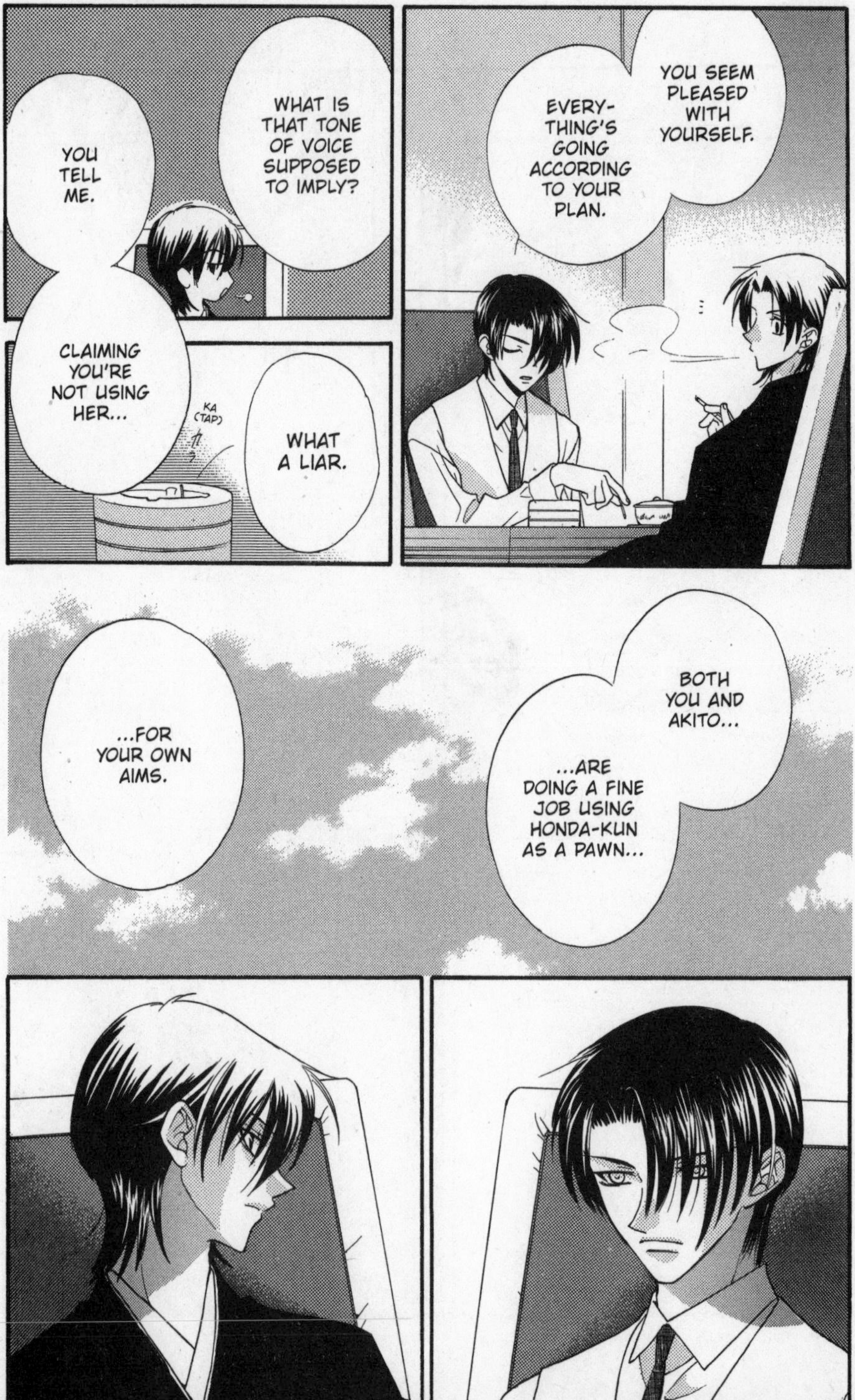
YOU SEEM PLEASED WITH YOURSELF.
EVERY-THING'S GOING ACCORDING TO YOUR PLAN.
...
WHAT IS THAT TONE OF VOICE SUPPOSED TO IMPLY?
YOU TELL ME.
CLAIMING YOU'RE NOT USING HER...
KA (TAP)
WHAT A LIAR.
BOTH YOU AND AKITO...
...ARE DOING A FINE JOB USING HONDA-KUN AS A PAWN...
...FOR YOUR OWN AIMS.

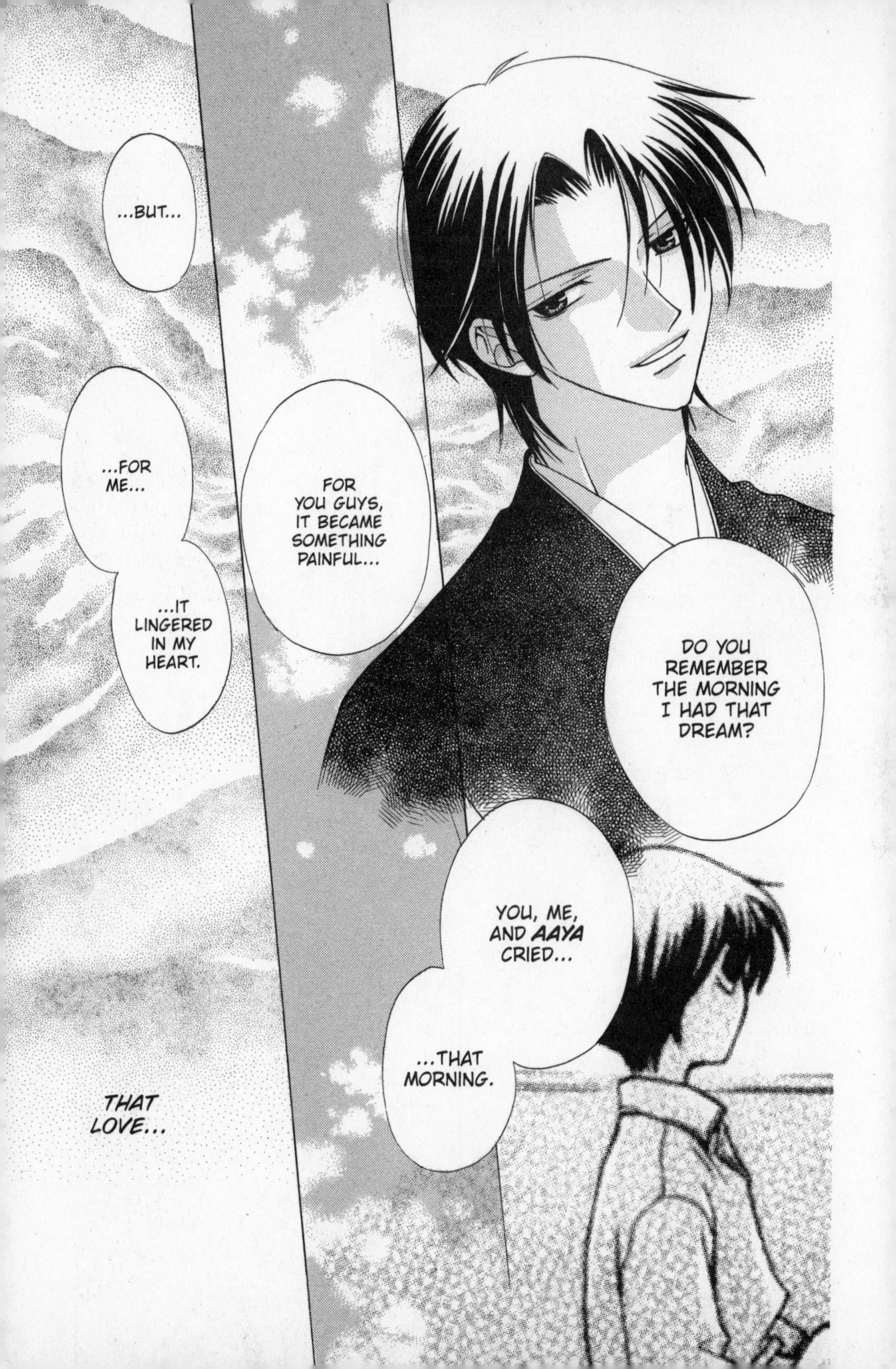
DO YOU REMEMBER THE MORNING I HAD THAT DREAM?
YOU, ME, AND AAYA CRIED...
...THAT MORNING.
FOR YOU GUYS, IT BECAME SOMETHING PAINFUL...
...BUT...
...FOR ME...
...IT LINGERED IN MY HEART.
THAT LOVE...

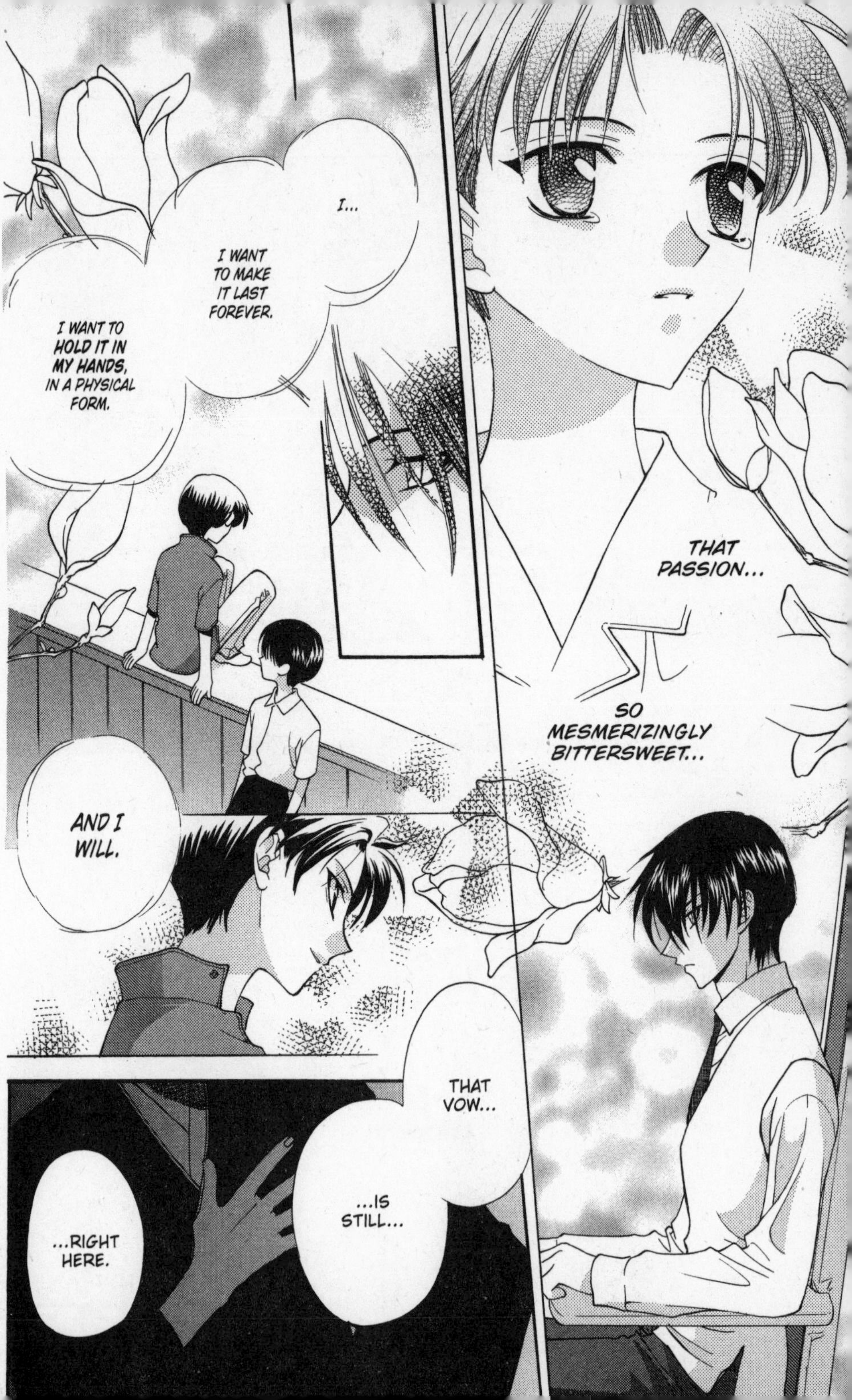
THAT PASSION...
SO MESMERIZINGLY BITTERSWEET...
I...
I WANT TO MAKE IT LAST FOREVER.
I WANT TO HOLD IT IN MY HANDS, IN A PHYSICAL FORM.
AND I WILL.
THAT VOW...
...IS STILL...
...RIGHT HERE.

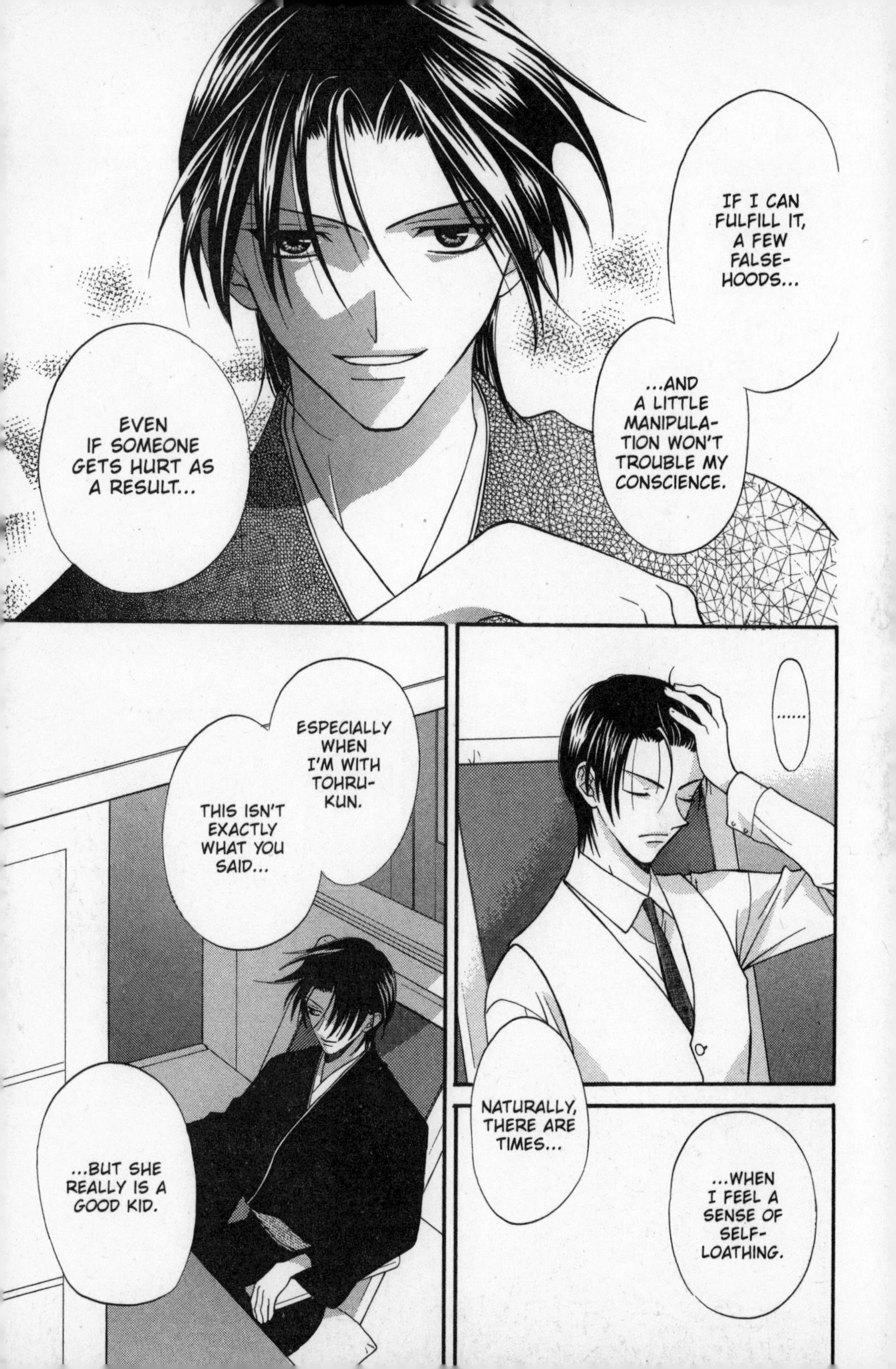
IF I CAN FULFILL IT, A FEW FALSE-HOODS...
...AND A LITTLE MANIPULA-TION WON'T TROUBLE MY CONSCIENCE.
EVEN IF SOMEONE GETS HURT AS A RESULT...
......
NATURALLY, THERE ARE TIMES...
...WHEN I FEEL A SENSE OF SELF-LOATHING.
ESPECIALLY WHEN I'M WITH TOHRU-KUN.
THIS ISN'T EXACTLY WHAT YOU SAID...
...BUT SHE REALLY IS A GOOD KID.

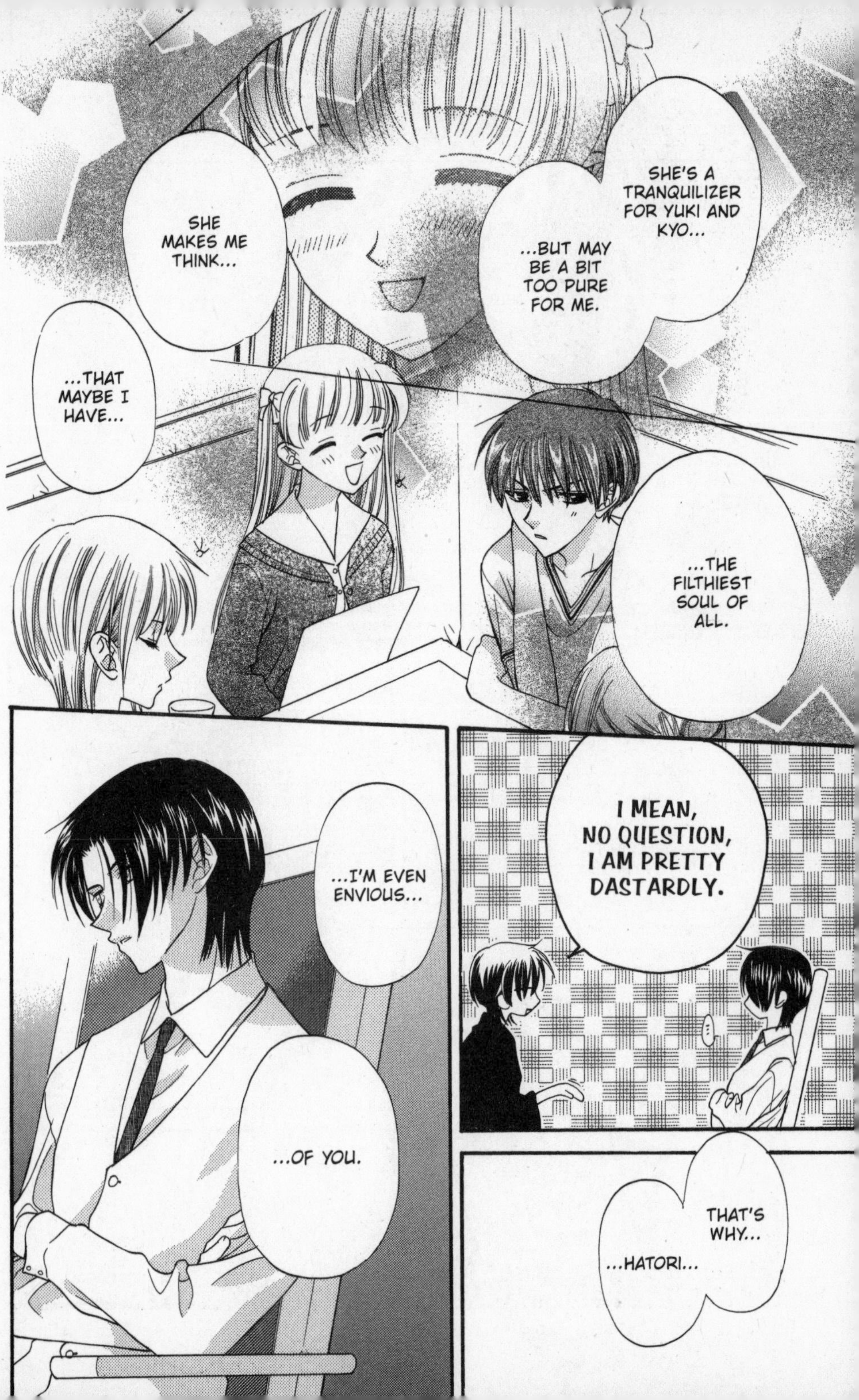
SHE'S A TRANQUILIZER FOR YUKI AND KYO...
...BUT MAY BE A BIT TOO PURE FOR ME.
SHE MAKES ME THINK...
...THAT MAYBE I HAVE...
...THE FILTHIEST SOUL OF ALL.
I MEAN, NO QUESTION, I AM PRETTY DASTARDLY.
THAT'S WHY...
...HATORI...
...I'M EVEN ENVIOUS...
...OF YOU.

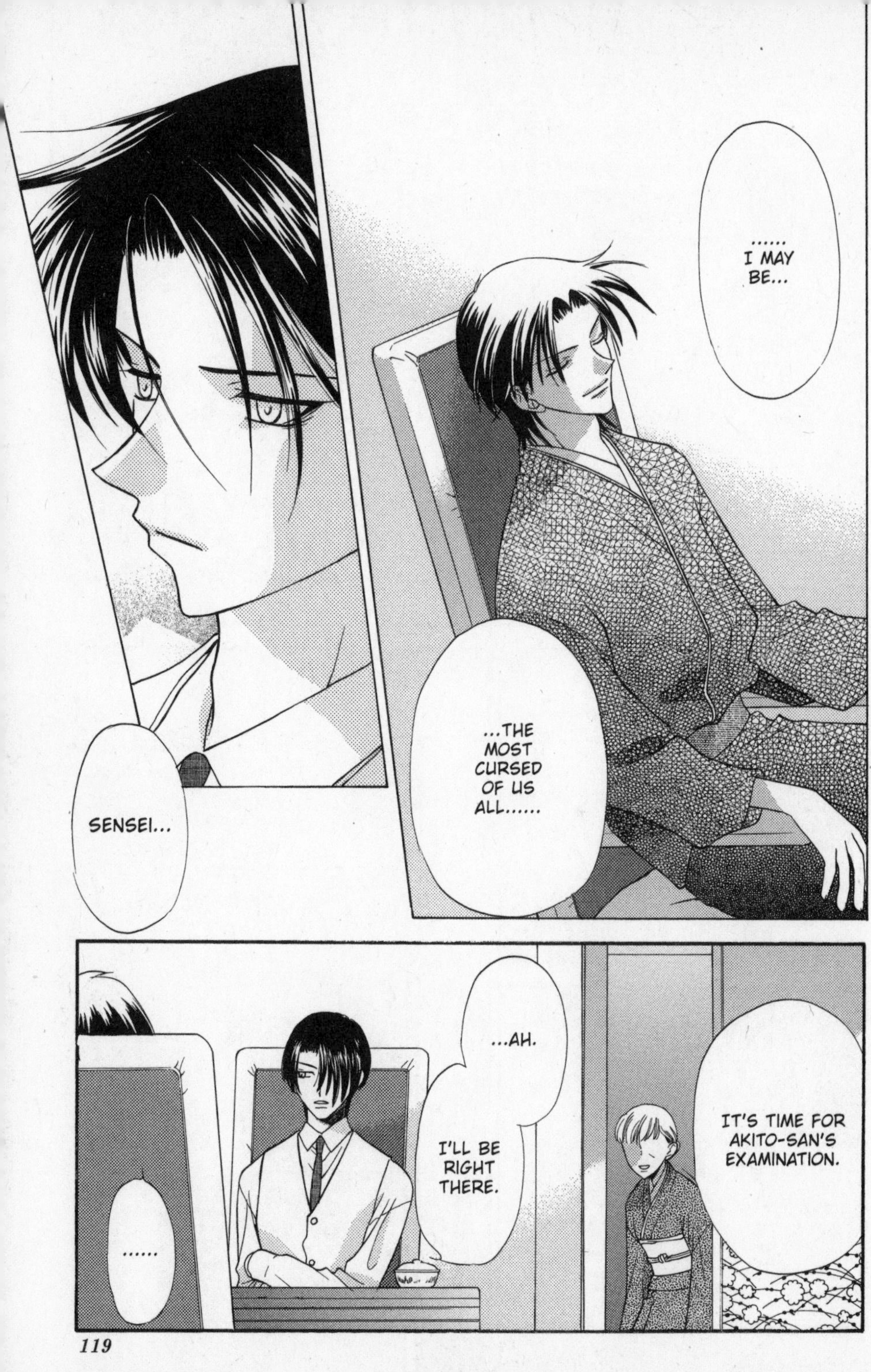
...... I MAY BE...
...THE MOST CURSED OF US ALL......
SENSEI...
IT'S TIME FOR AKITO-SAN'S EXAMINATION.
...AH.
I'LL BE RIGHT THERE.
......

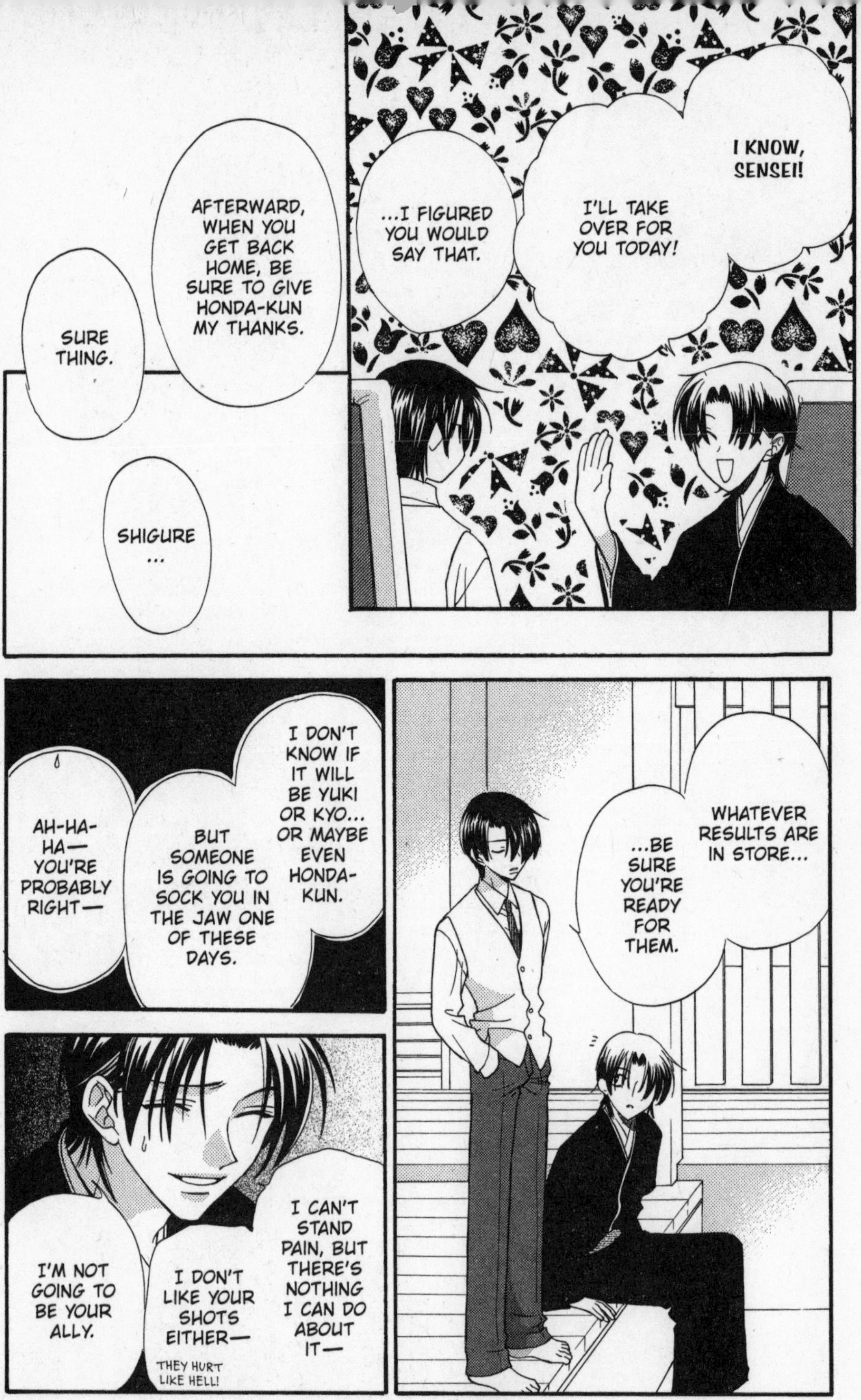

I KNOW, SENSEI!
I'LL TAKE OVER FOR YOU TODAY!
...I FIGURED YOU WOULD SAY THAT.
AFTERWARD, WHEN YOU GET BACK HOME, BE SURE TO GIVE HONDA-KUN MY THANKS.
SURE THING.
SHIGURE ...
WHATEVER RESULTS ARE IN STORE...
...BE SURE YOU'RE READY FOR THEM.
I DON'T KNOW IF IT WILL BE YUKI OR KYO... OR MAYBE EVEN HONDA-KUN.
BUT SOMEONE IS GOING TO SOCK YOU IN THE JAW ONE OF THESE DAYS.
AH-HA-HA— YOU'RE PROBABLY RIGHT—
I CAN'T STAND PAIN, BUT THERE'S NOTHING I CAN DO ABOUT IT—
I DON'T LIKE YOUR SHOTS EITHER—
THEY HURT LIKE HELL!
I'M NOT GOING TO BE YOUR ALLY.

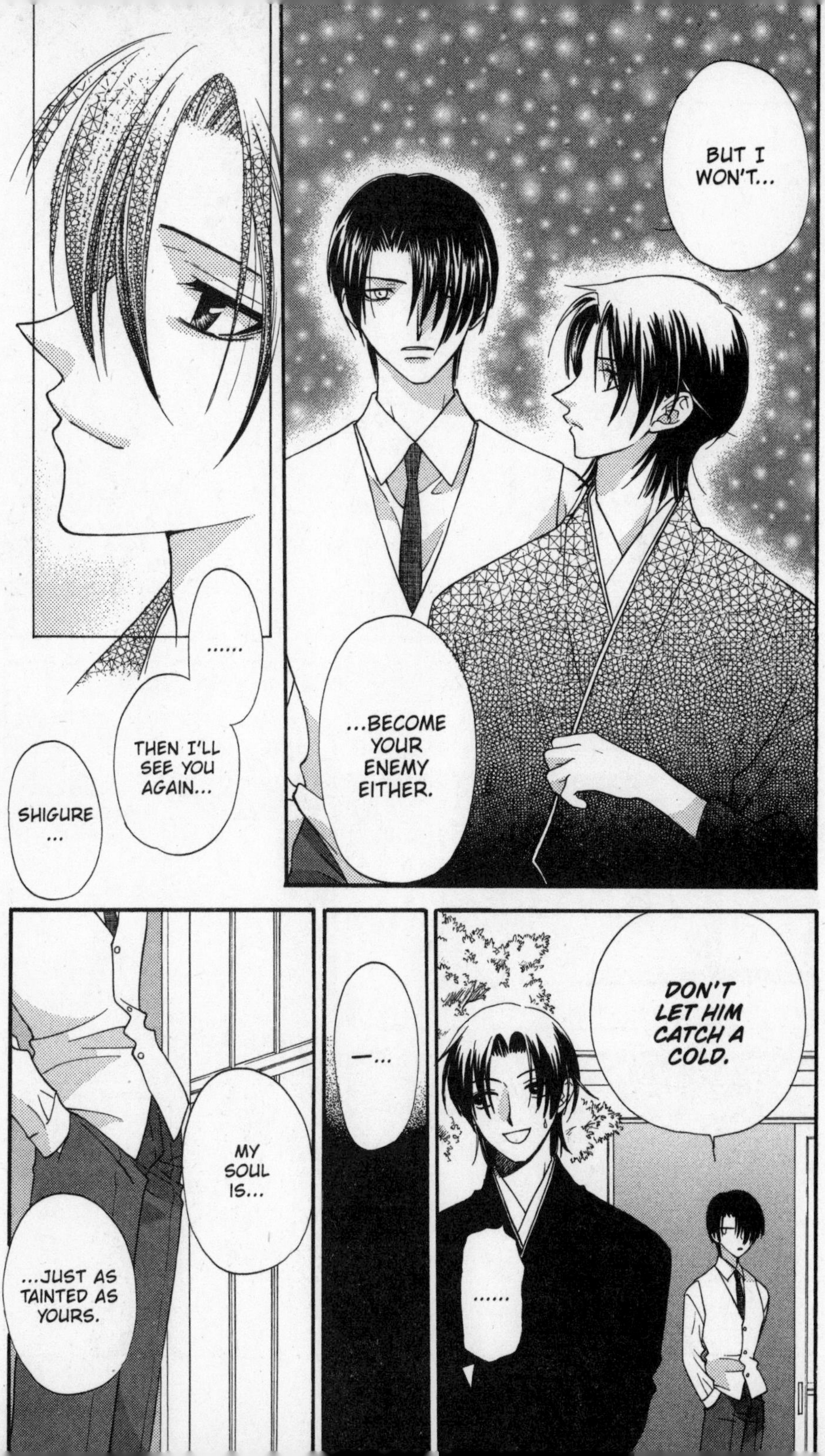
BUT I WON'T...
...BECOME YOUR ENEMY EITHER.
......
THEN I'LL SEE YOU AGAIN...
SHIGURE ...
DON'T LET HIM CATCH A COLD.
......
—...
MY SOUL IS...
...JUST AS TAINTED AS YOURS.

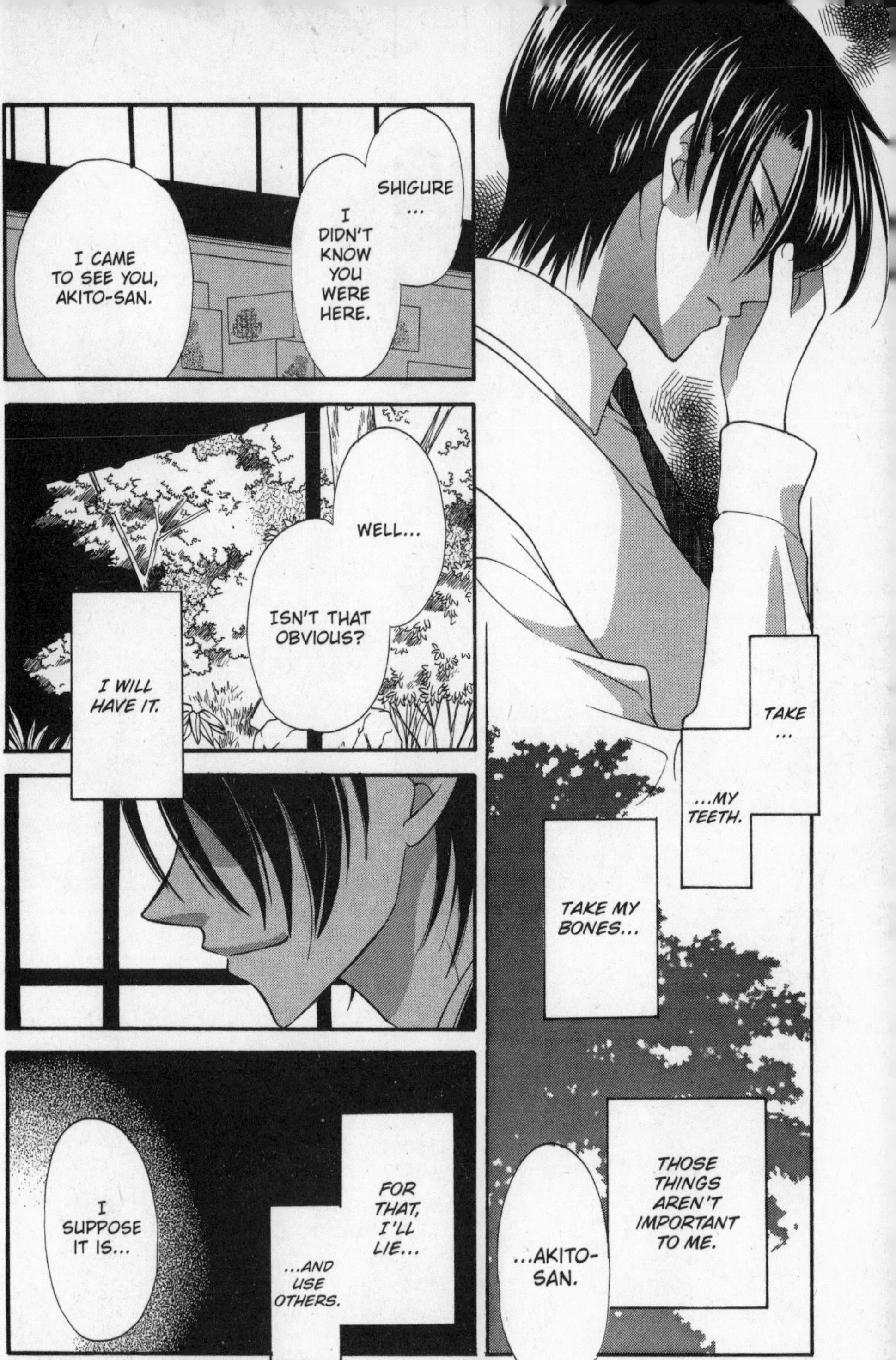
TAKE ...
...MY TEETH.
TAKE MY BONES...
THOSE THINGS AREN'T IMPORTANT TO ME.
...AKITO-SAN.
SHIGURE ...
I DIDN'T KNOW YOU WERE HERE.
I CAME TO SEE YOU, AKITO-SAN.
WELL...
ISN'T THAT OBVIOUS?
I WILL HAVE IT.
FOR THAT, I'LL LIE...
...AND USE OTHERS.
I SUPPOSE IT IS...

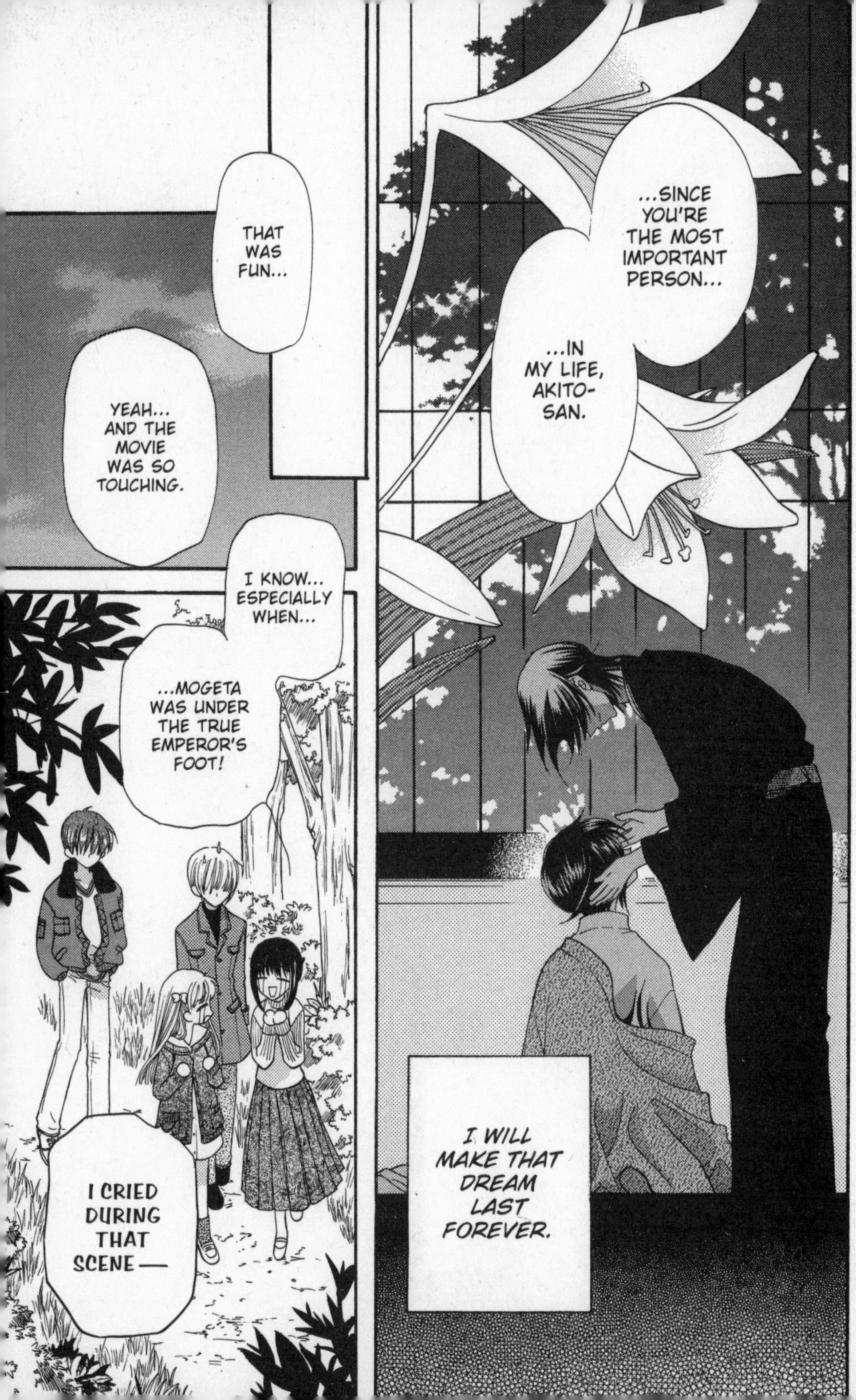
...SINCE YOU'RE THE MOST IMPORTANT PERSON...
...IN MY LIFE, AKITO-SAN.
I WILL MAKE THAT DREAM LAST FOREVER.
THAT WAS FUN...
YEAH... AND THE MOVIE WAS SO TOUCHING.
I KNOW... ESPECIALLY WHEN...
...MOGETA WAS UNDER THE TRUE EMPEROR'S FOOT!
I CRIED DURING THAT SCENE—

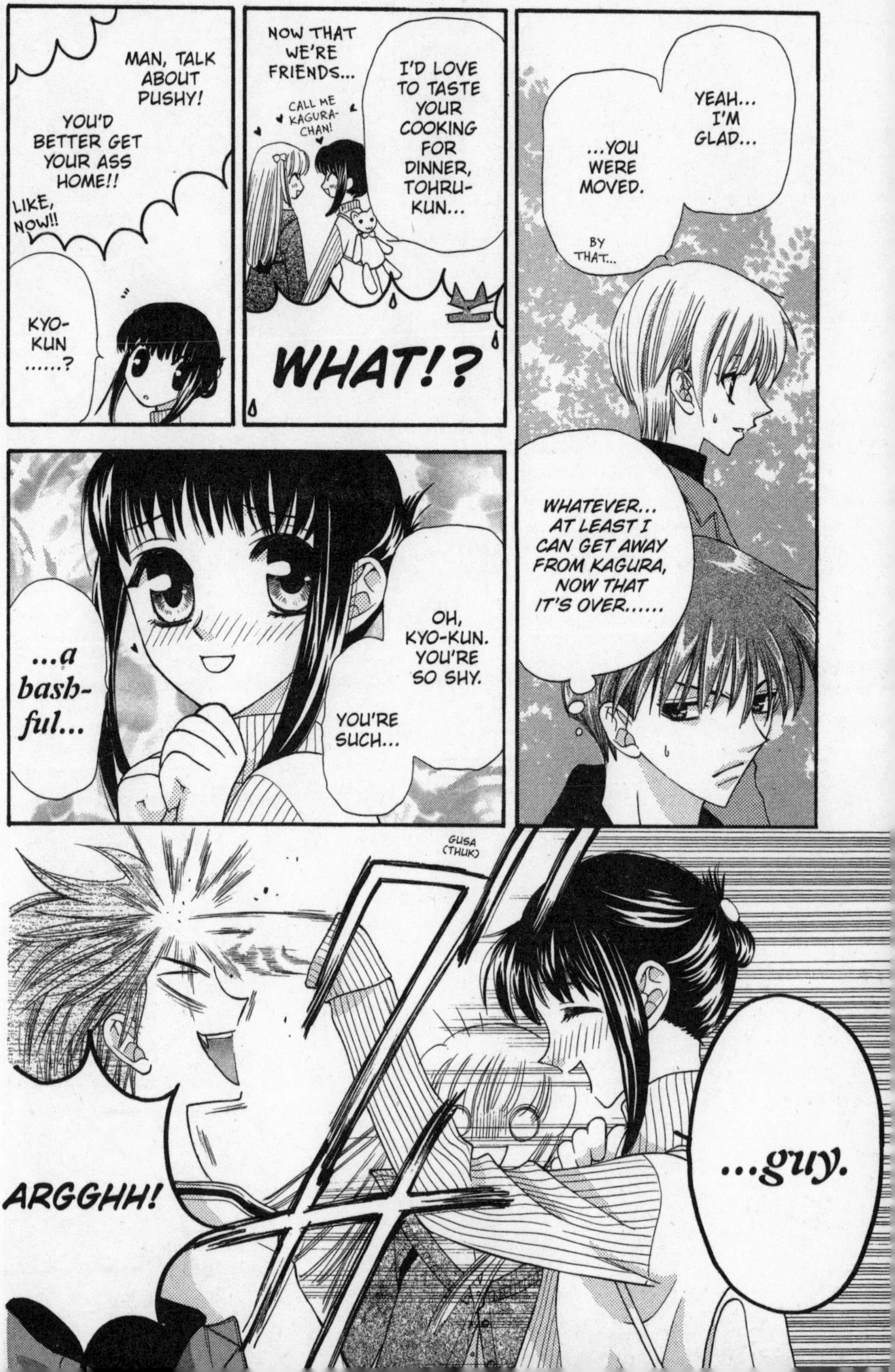
YEAH... I'M GLAD...
...YOU WERE MOVED.
BY THAT...
WHATEVER... AT LEAST I CAN GET AWAY FROM KAGURA, NOW THAT IT'S OVER......
NOW THAT WE'RE FRIENDS...
I'D LOVE TO TASTE YOUR COOKING FOR DINNER, TOHRU-KUN...
CALL ME KAGURA-CHAN!
WHAT!?
MAN, TALK ABOUT PUSHY!
YOU'D BETTER GET YOUR ASS HOME!!
LIKE, NOW!!
KYO-KUN ......?
OH, KYO-KUN. YOU'RE SO SHY.
YOU'RE SUCH...
...a bashful...
GUSA (THUK)
...guy.
ARGGHH!

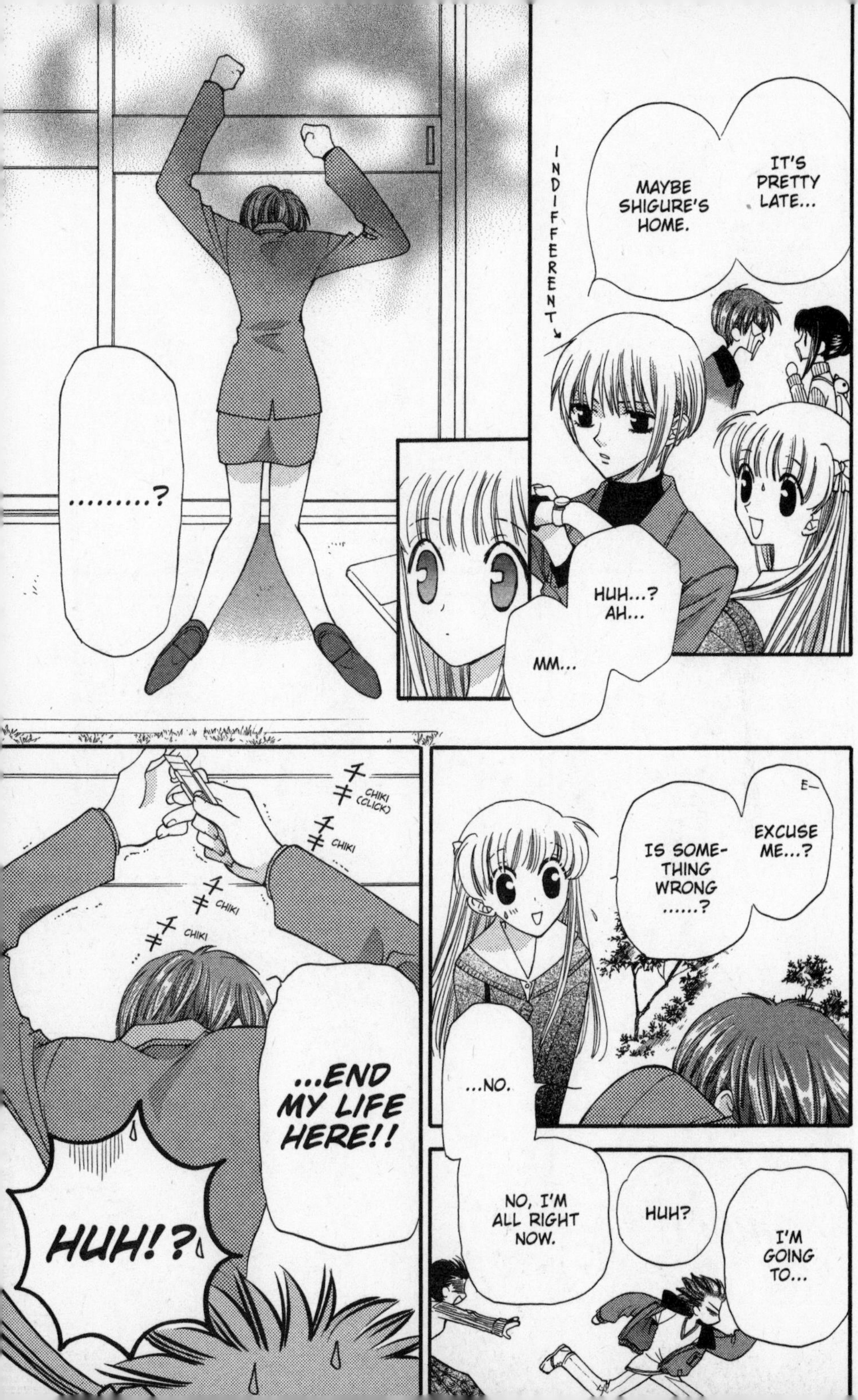
IT'S PRETTY LATE...
MAYBE SHIGURE'S HOME.
INDIFFERENT
HUH...? AH...
MM...
.........?
E—
EXCUSE ME...?
IS SOME-THING WRONG ......?
...NO.
I'M GOING TO...
HUH?
NO, I'M ALL RIGHT NOW.
チキ CHIKI (CLICK)
チキ CHIKI
チキ CHIKI
チキ CHIKI
...END MY LIFE HERE!!
HUH!?

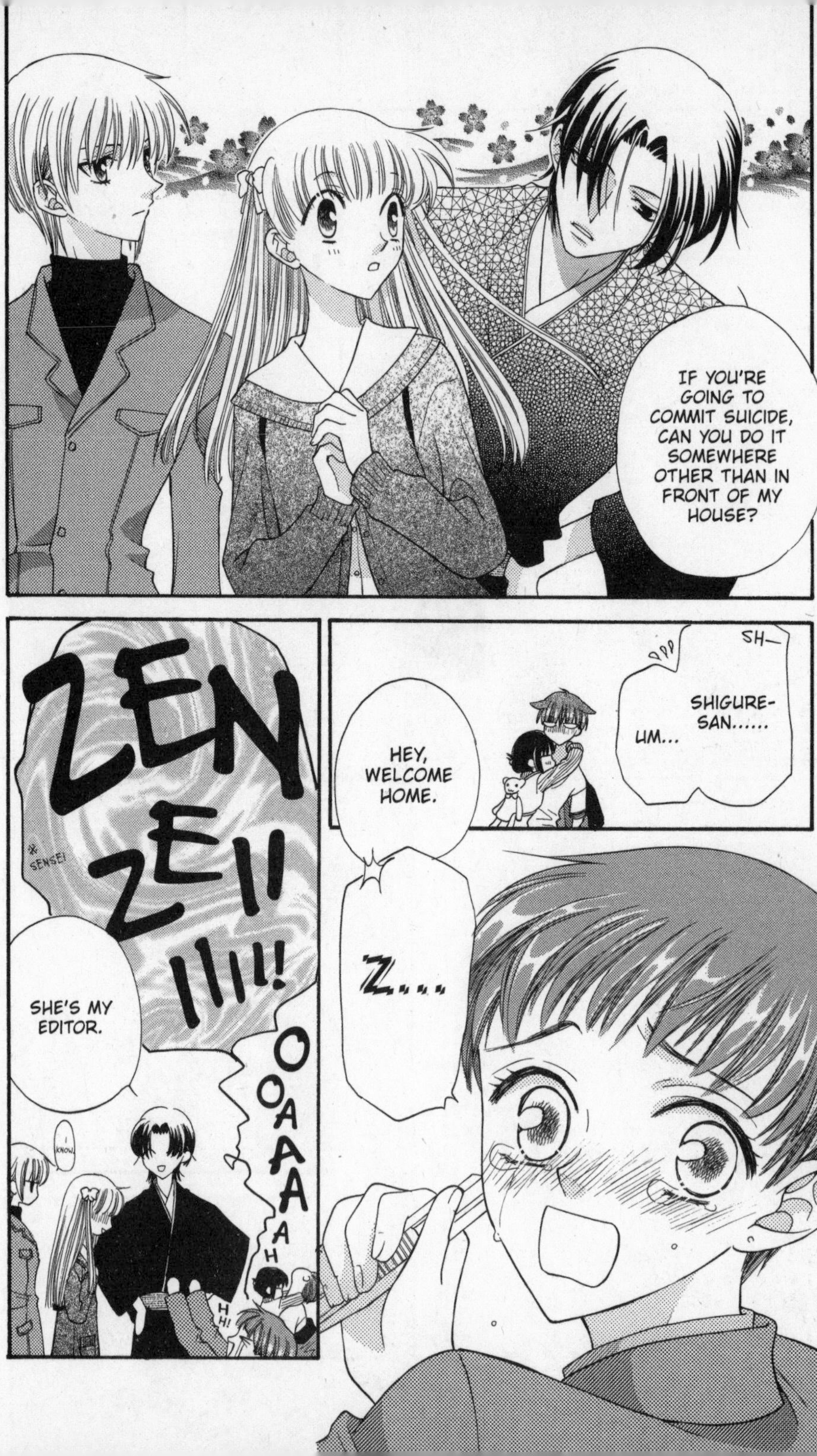
IF YOU'RE GOING TO COMMIT SUICIDE, CAN YOU DO IT SOMEWHERE OTHER THAN IN FRONT OF MY HOUSE?
SH—
SHIGURE-SAN......
UM...
HEY, WELCOME HOME.
Z....
ZEN ZEI!!!!!
※ SENSEI
OOAAAAAHH!
SHE'S MY EDITOR.
I KNOW.

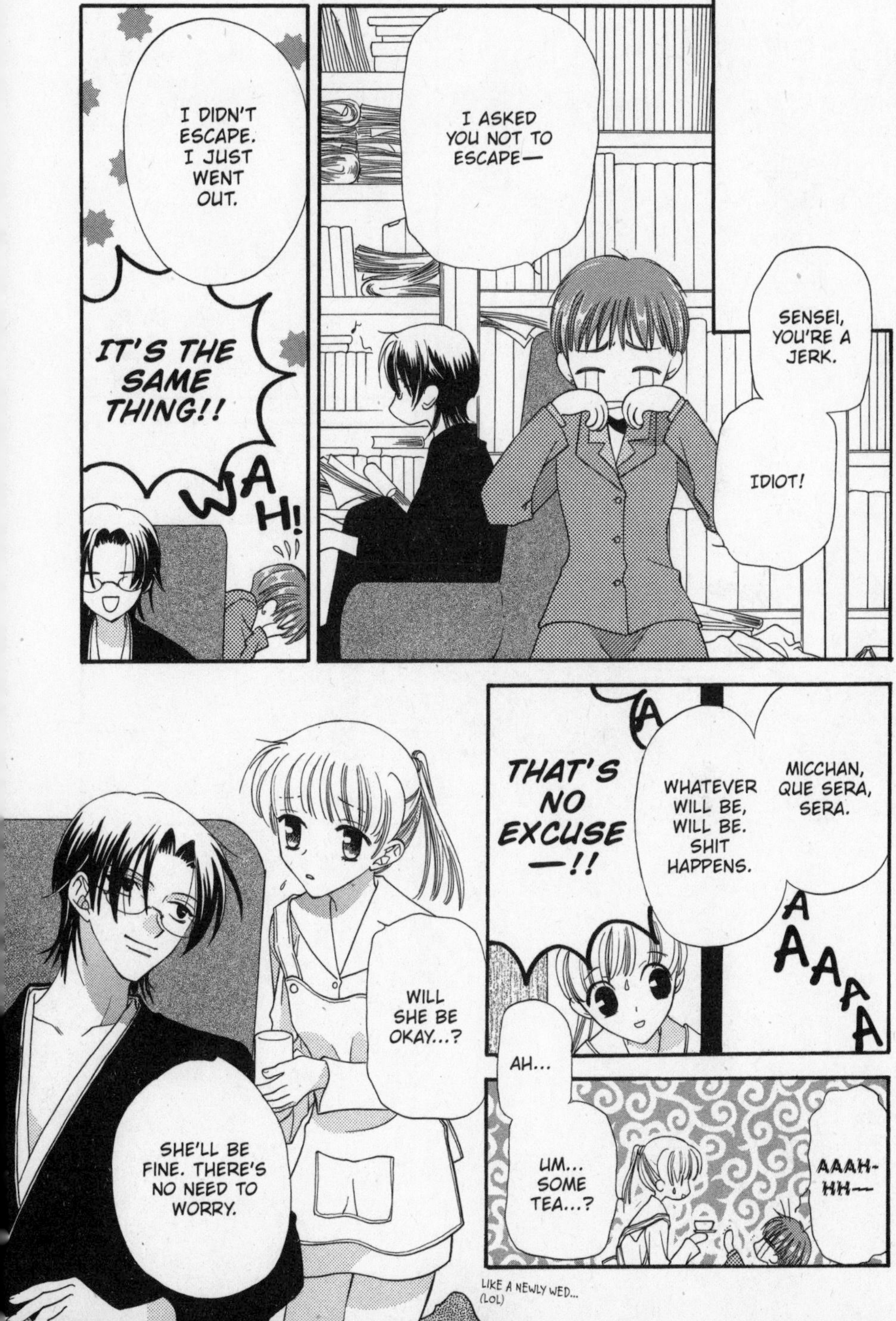
I ASKED YOU NOT TO ESCAPE—
SENSEI, YOU'RE A JERK.
IDIOT!
I DIDN'T ESCAPE. I JUST WENT OUT.
IT'S THE SAME THING!!
WAH!
MICCHAN, QUE SERA, SERA.
WHATEVER WILL BE, WILL BE. SHIT HAPPENS.
THAT'S NO EXCUSE—!!
AAAAAA
AAAH-HH—
UM... SOME TEA...?
AH...
WILL SHE BE OKAY...?
SHE'LL BE FINE. THERE'S NO NEED TO WORRY.
LIKE A NEWLY WED... (LOL)

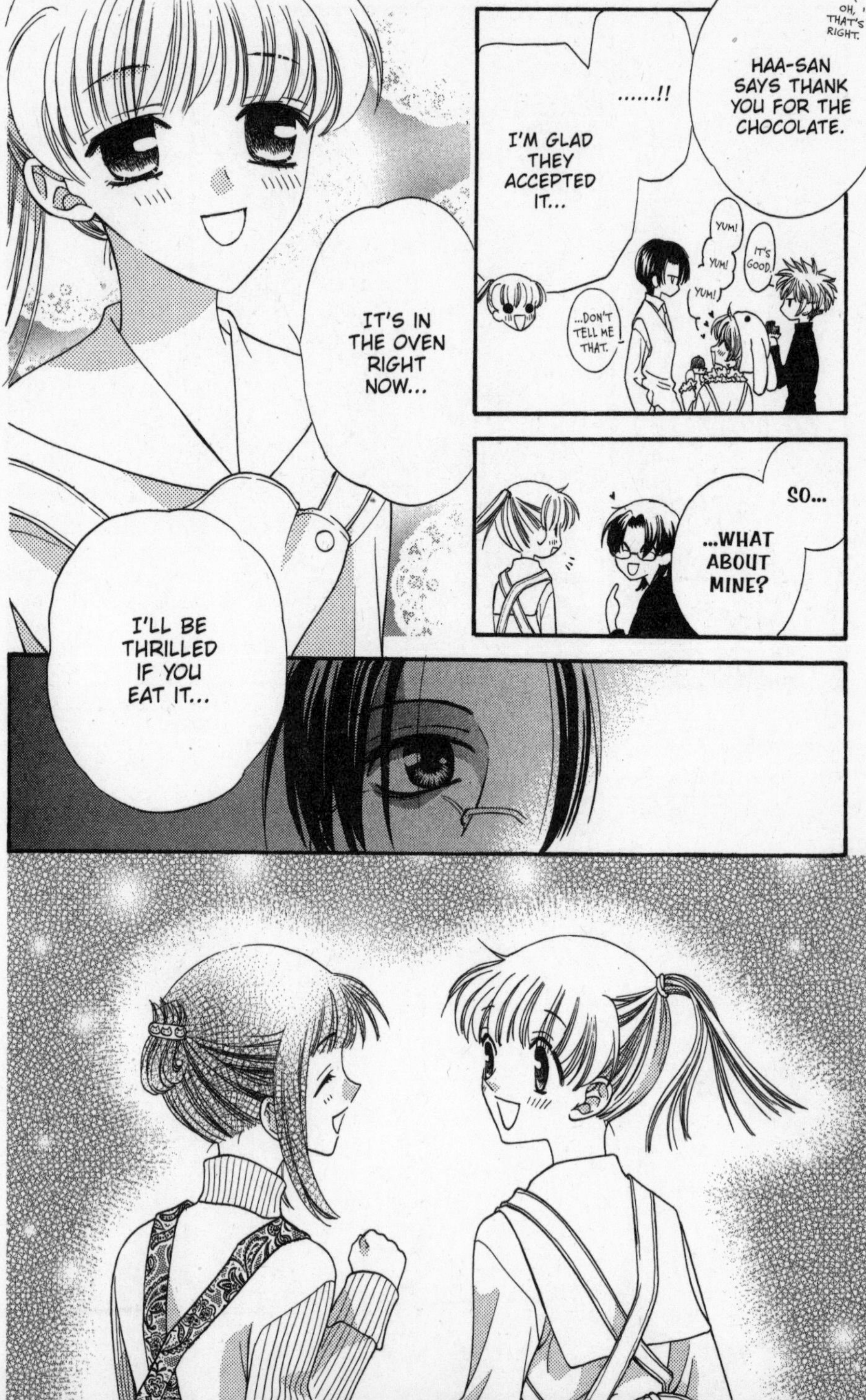
OH, THAT'S RIGHT.
HAA-SAN SAYS THANK YOU FOR THE CHOCOLATE.
......!!
I'M GLAD THEY ACCEPTED IT...
YUM!
YUM!
YUM!
IT'S GOOD.
...DON'T TELL ME THAT.
SO...
...WHAT ABOUT MINE?
IT'S IN THE OVEN RIGHT NOW...
I'LL BE THRILLED IF YOU EAT IT...

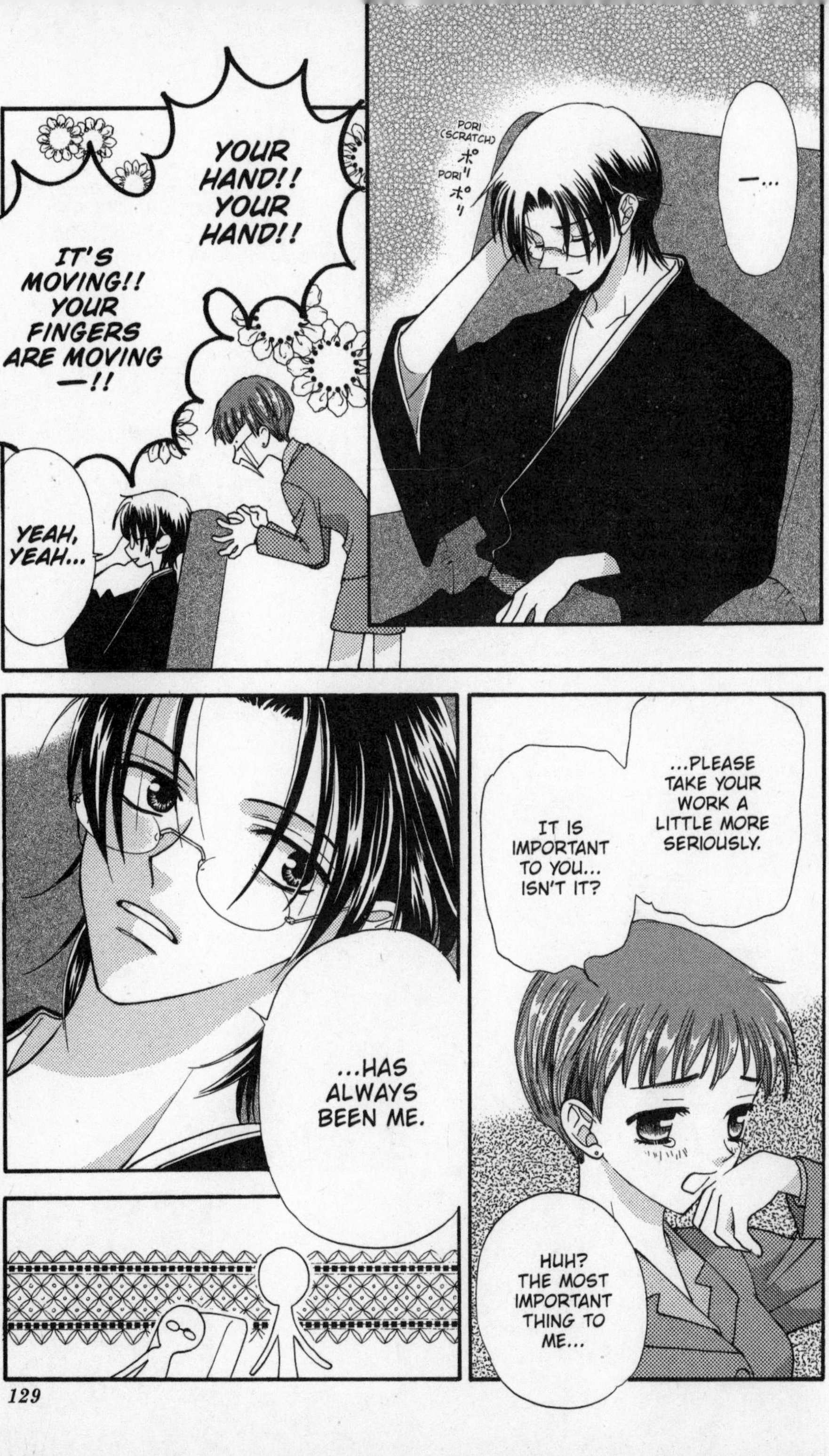
—...
PORI (SCRATCH) ポリ PORI ポリ
YOUR HAND!! YOUR HAND!!
IT'S MOVING!! YOUR FINGERS ARE MOVING—!!
YEAH, YEAH...
...PLEASE TAKE YOUR WORK A LITTLE MORE SERIOUSLY.
IT IS IMPORTANT TO YOU... ISN'T IT?
HUH? THE MOST IMPORTANT THING TO ME...
...HAS ALWAYS BEEN ME.

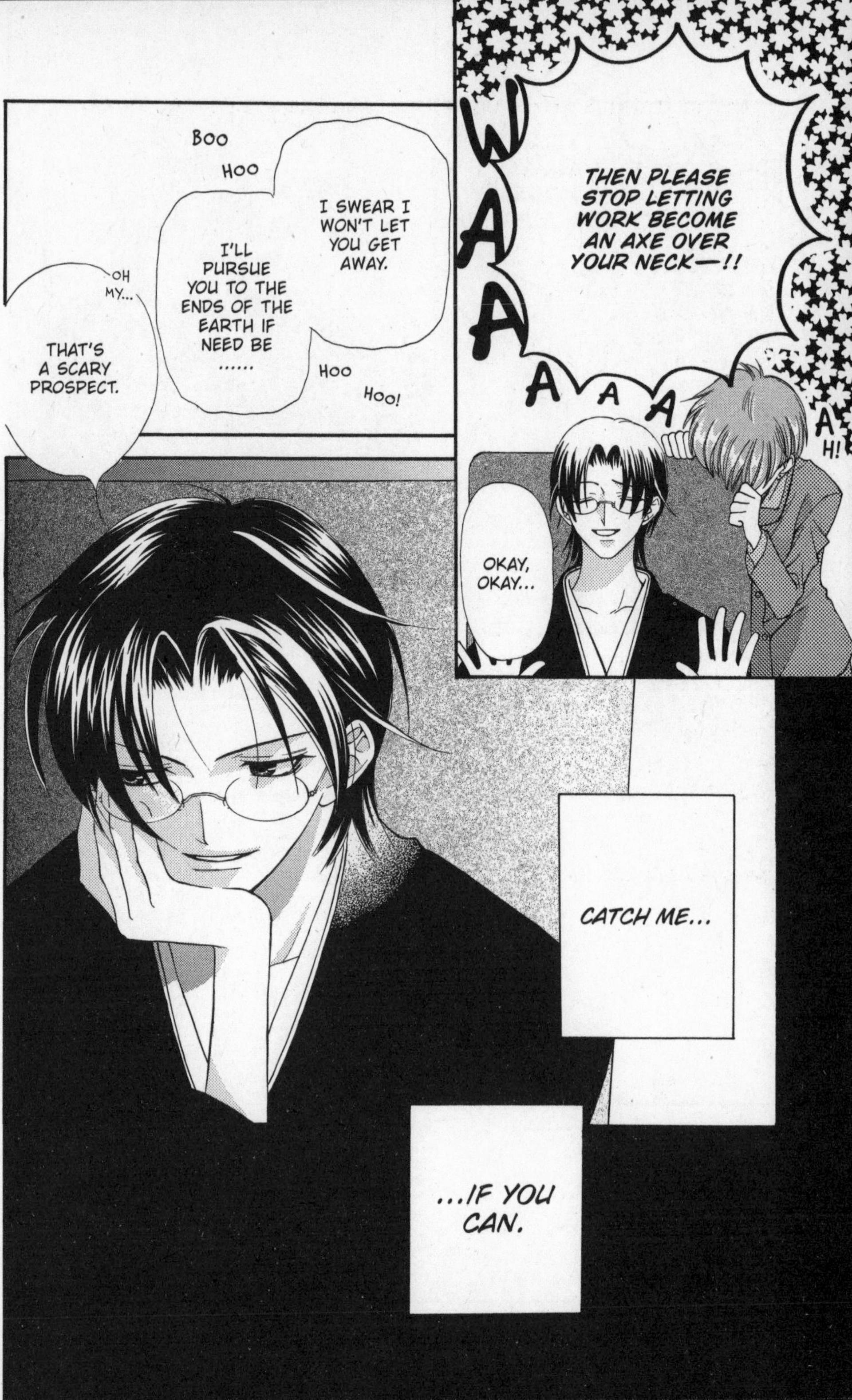
THEN PLEASE STOP LETTING WORK BECOME AN AXE OVER YOUR NECK—!!
WAAAAAAAH!
OKAY, OKAY...
I SWEAR I WON'T LET YOU GET AWAY.
I'LL PURSUE YOU TO THE ENDS OF THE EARTH IF NEED BE ......
BOO HOO
HOO HOO!
OH MY...
THAT'S A SCARY PROSPECT.
CATCH ME...
...IF YOU CAN.

Chapter 17

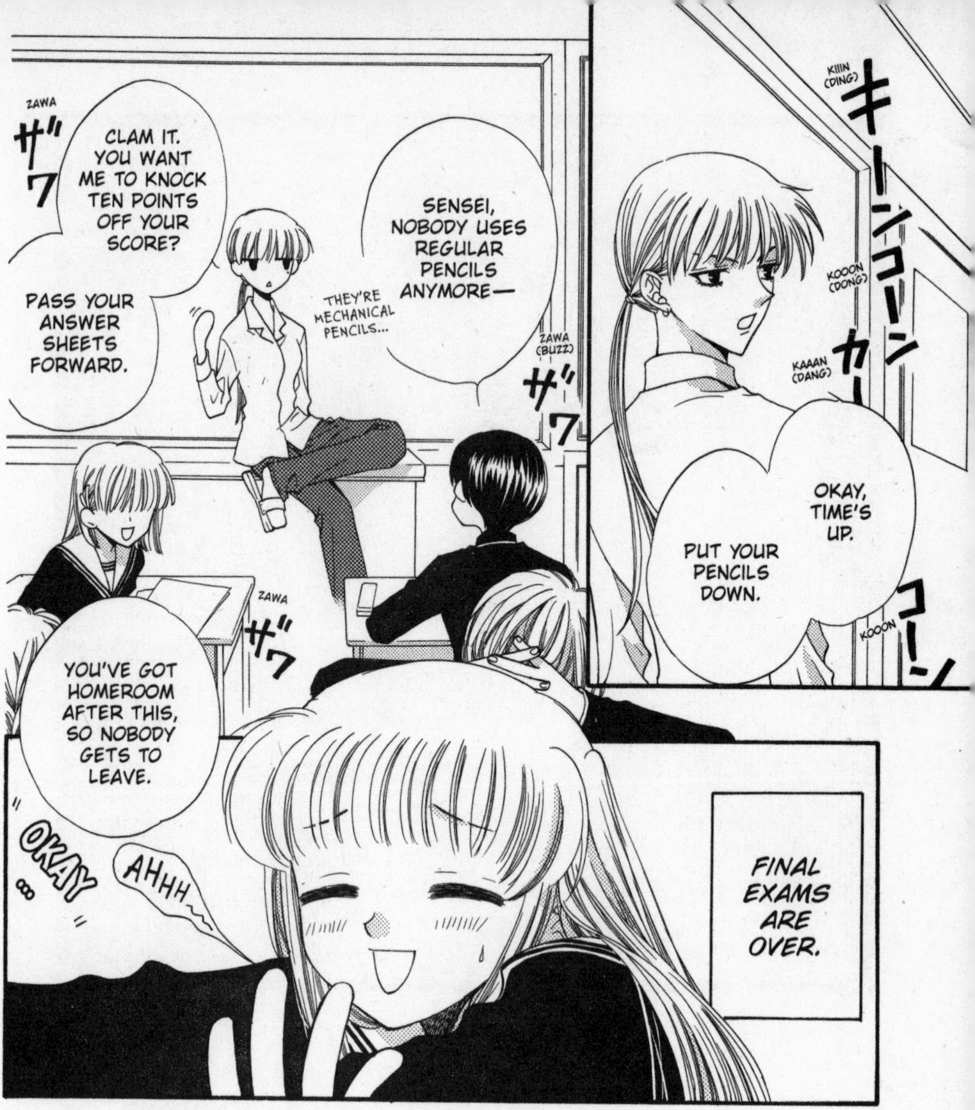
KIIIN (DING)
KOOON (DONG)
KAAAN (DANG)
KOOON
OKAY, TIME'S UP.
PUT YOUR PENCILS DOWN.
SENSEI, NOBODY USES REGULAR PENCILS ANYMORE—
THEY'RE MECHANICAL PENCILS...
ZAWA (BUZZ)
ZAWA
CLAM IT. YOU WANT ME TO KNOCK TEN POINTS OFF YOUR SCORE?
PASS YOUR ANSWER SHEETS FORWARD.
ZAWA
YOU'VE GOT HOMEROOM AFTER THIS, SO NOBODY GETS TO LEAVE.
FINAL EXAMS ARE OVER.
AHHH
"OKAY"

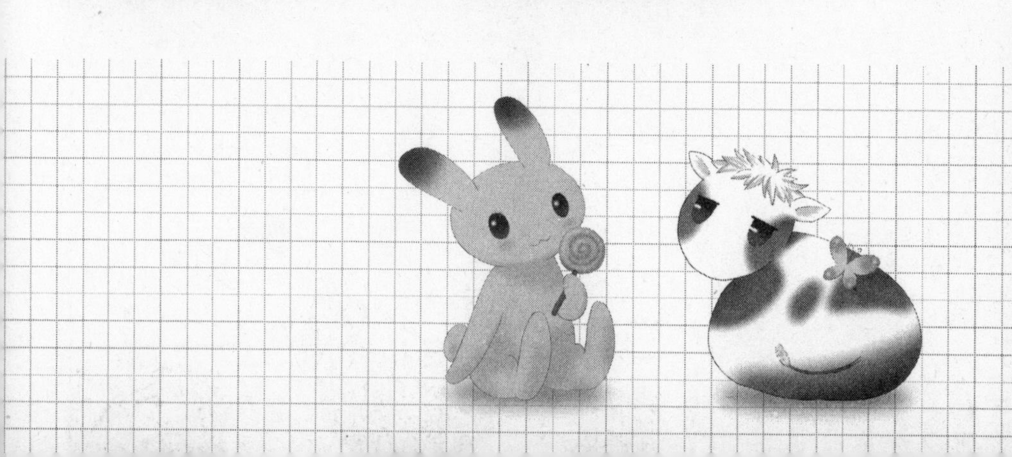

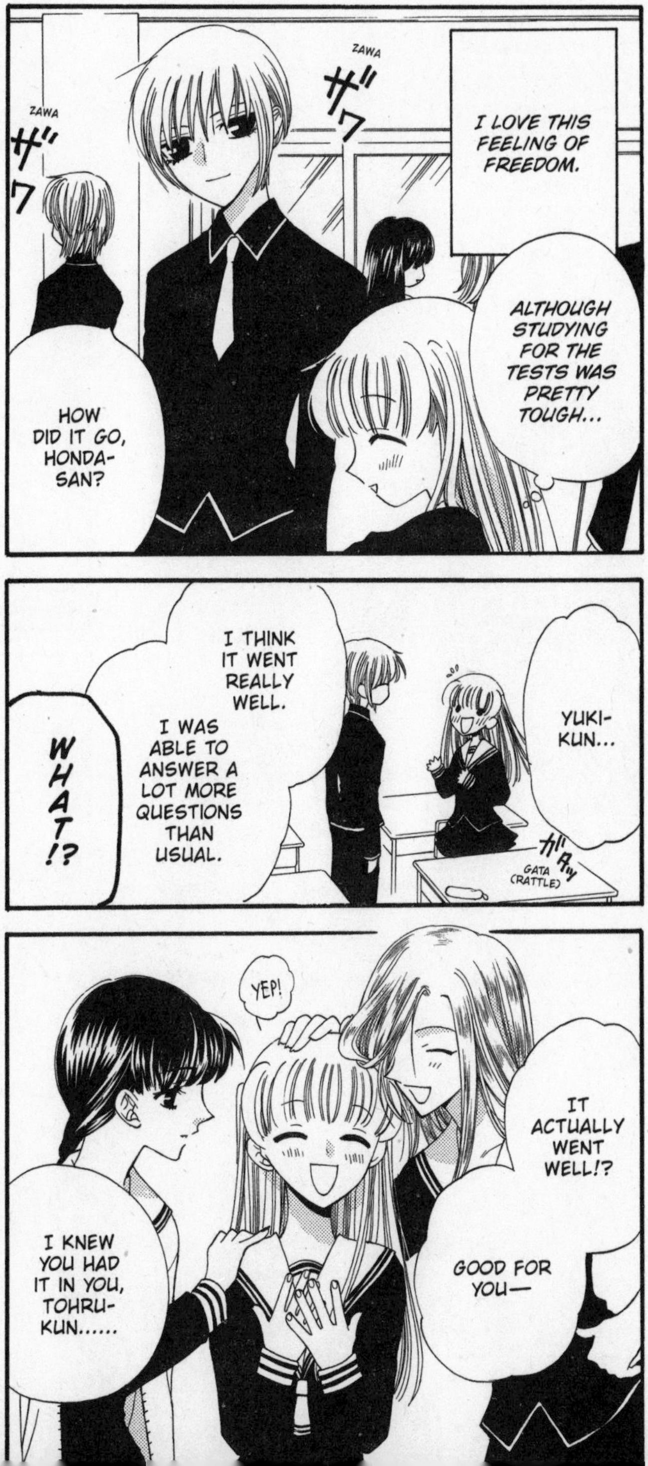
I LOVE THIS FEELING OF FREEDOM.
ALTHOUGH STUDYING FOR THE TESTS WAS PRETTY TOUGH...
ZAWA
ZAWA
HOW DID IT GO, HONDA-SAN?
YUKI-KUN...
I THINK IT WENT REALLY WELL.
I WAS ABLE TO ANSWER A LOT MORE QUESTIONS THAN USUAL.
GATA (RATTLE)
WHAT!?
YEP!
IT ACTUALLY WENT WELL!?
GOOD FOR YOU—
I KNEW YOU HAD IT IN YOU, TOHRU-KUN......
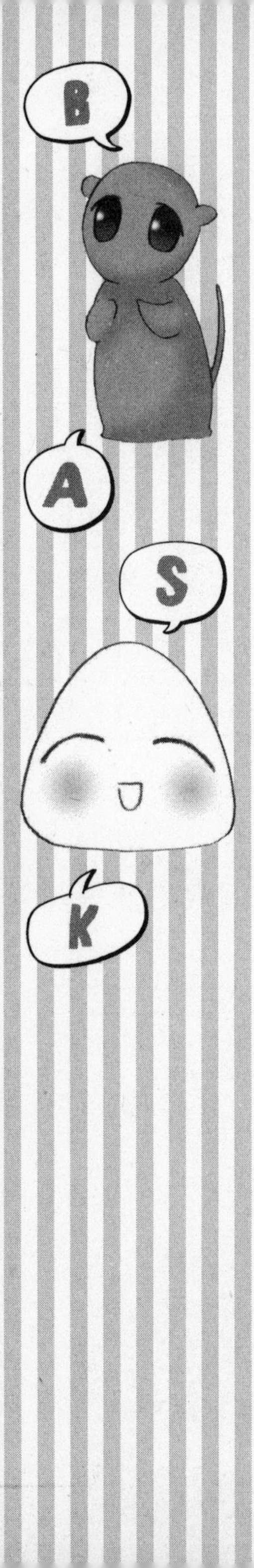
B
A
S
K

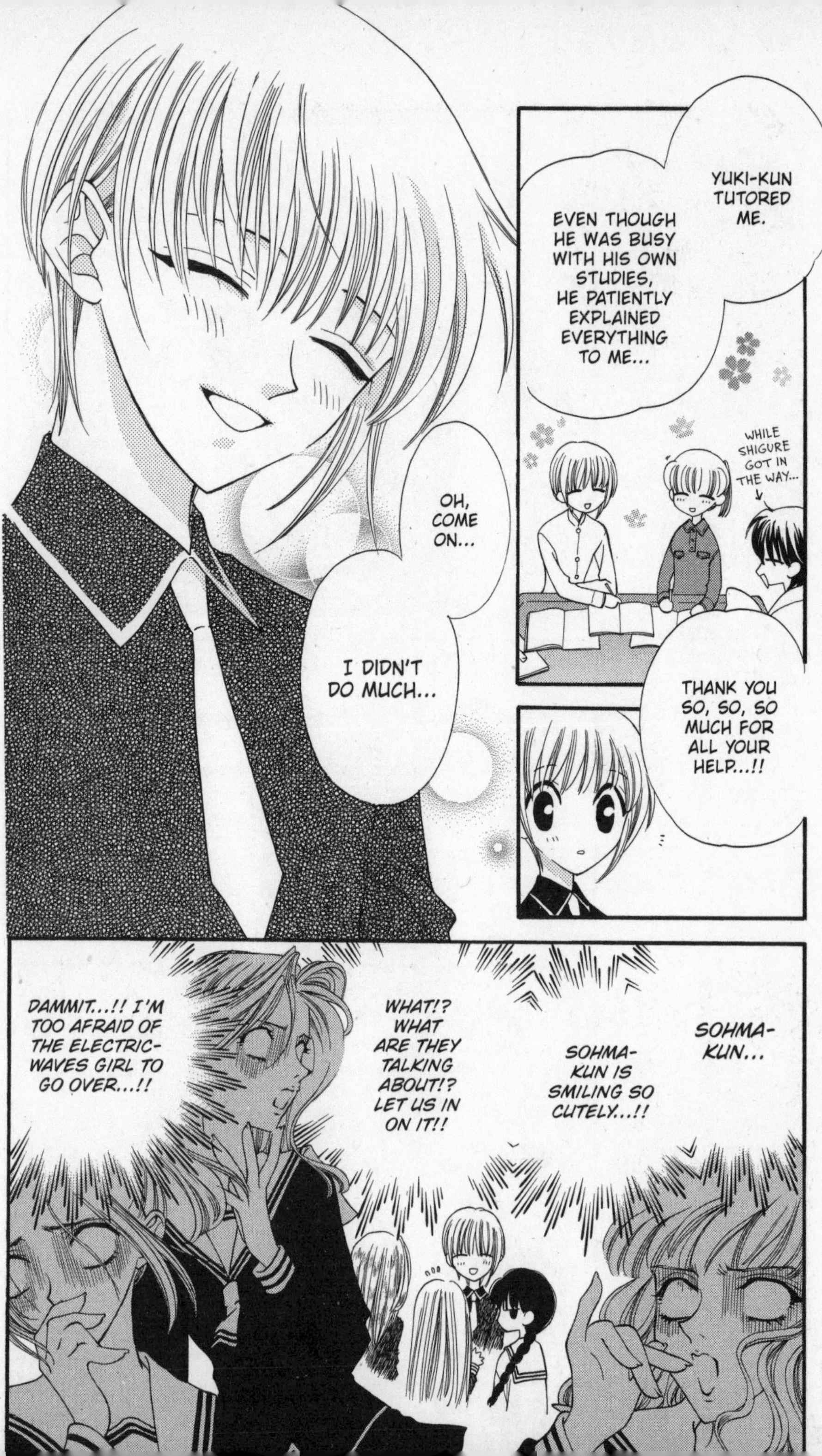
YUKI-KUN TUTORED ME.
EVEN THOUGH HE WAS BUSY WITH HIS OWN STUDIES, HE PATIENTLY EXPLAINED EVERYTHING TO ME...
WHILE SHIGURE GOT IN THE WAY...
THANK YOU SO, SO, SO MUCH FOR ALL YOUR HELP...!!
OH, COME ON...
I DIDN'T DO MUCH...
SOHMA-KUN...
SOHMA-KUN IS SMILING SO CUTELY...!!
WHAT!? WHAT ARE THEY TALKING ABOUT!? LET US IN ON IT!!
DAMMIT...!! I'M TOO AFRAID OF THE ELECTRIC-WAVES GIRL TO GO OVER...!!

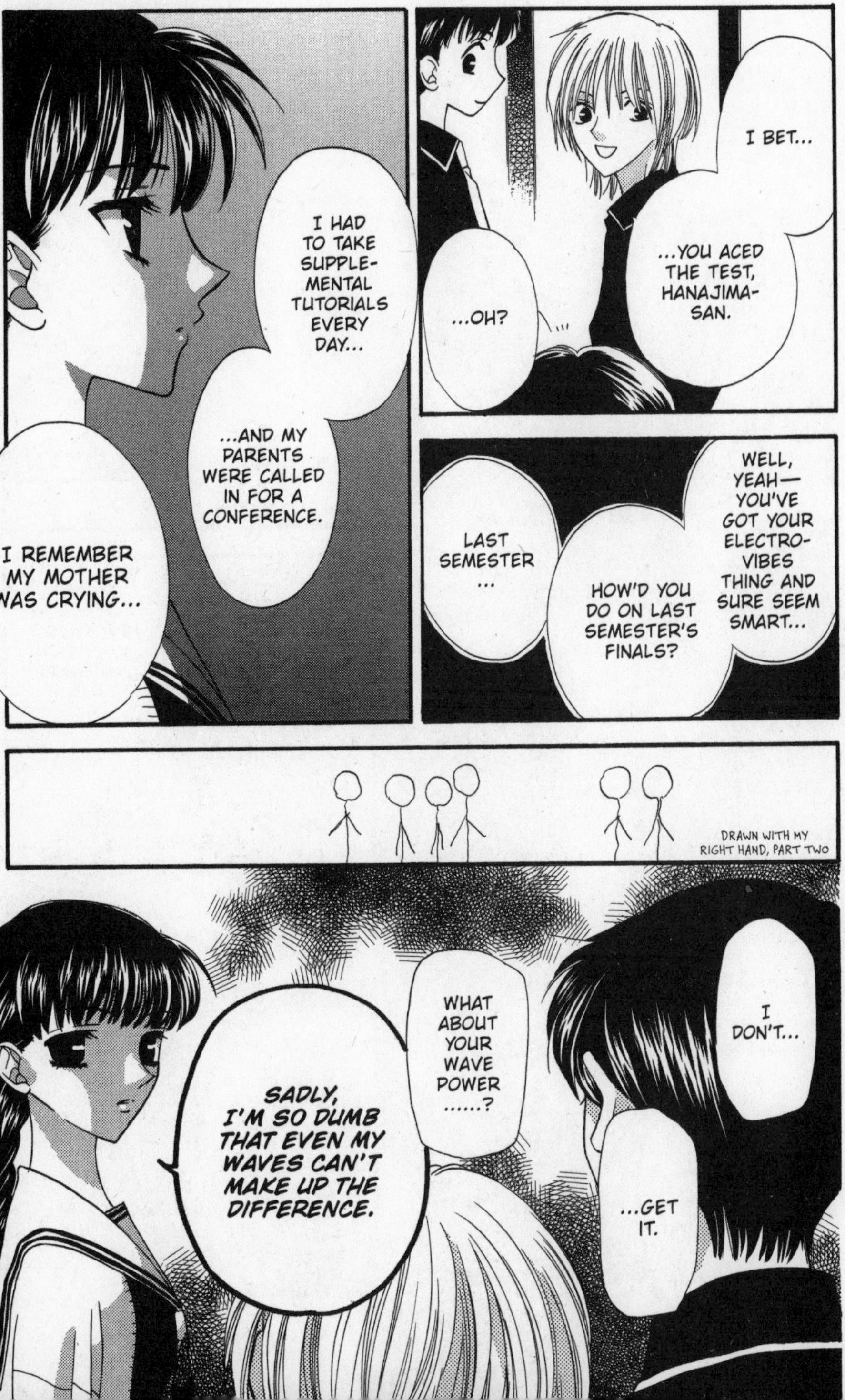
I BET...
...YOU ACED THE TEST, HANAJIMA-SAN.
...OH?
WELL, YEAH— YOU'VE GOT YOUR ELECTRO-VIBES THING AND SURE SEEM SMART...
HOW'D YOU DO ON LAST SEMESTER'S FINALS?
LAST SEMESTER ...
I HAD TO TAKE SUPPLE-MENTAL TUTORIALS EVERY DAY...
...AND MY PARENTS WERE CALLED IN FOR A CONFERENCE.
I REMEMBER MY MOTHER WAS CRYING...
DRAWN WITH MY RIGHT HAND, PART TWO
I DON'T...
...GET IT.
WHAT ABOUT YOUR WAVE POWER ......?
SADLY, I'M SO DUMB THAT EVEN MY WAVES CAN'T MAKE UP THE DIFFERENCE.

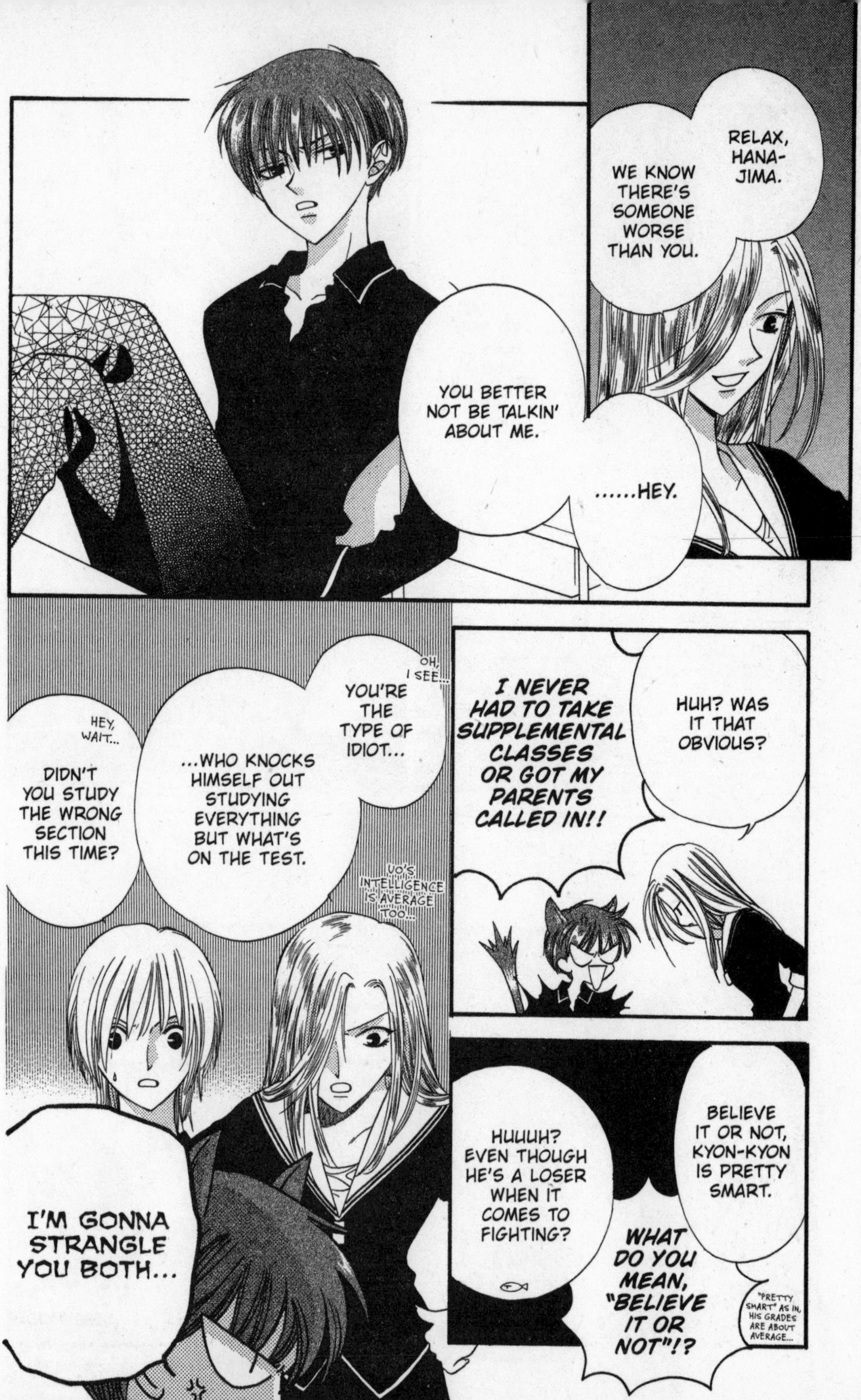
RELAX, HANAJIMA.
WE KNOW THERE'S SOMEONE WORSE THAN YOU.
......HEY.
YOU BETTER NOT BE TALKIN' ABOUT ME.
HUH? WAS IT THAT OBVIOUS?
I NEVER HAD TO TAKE SUPPLEMENTAL CLASSES OR GOT MY PARENTS CALLED IN!!
BELIEVE IT OR NOT, KYON-KYON IS PRETTY SMART.
HUUUH? EVEN THOUGH HE'S A LOSER WHEN IT COMES TO FIGHTING?
WHAT DO YOU MEAN, "BELIEVE IT OR NOT"!?
"PRETTY SMART" AS IN, HIS GRADES ARE ABOUT AVERAGE...
OH, I SEE...
YOU'RE THE TYPE OF IDIOT...
...WHO KNOCKS HIMSELF OUT STUDYING EVERYTHING BUT WHAT'S ON THE TEST.
HEY, WAIT...
DIDN'T YOU STUDY THE WRONG SECTION THIS TIME?
UO'S INTELLIGENCE IS AVERAGE TOO...
I'M GONNA STRANGLE YOU BOTH...

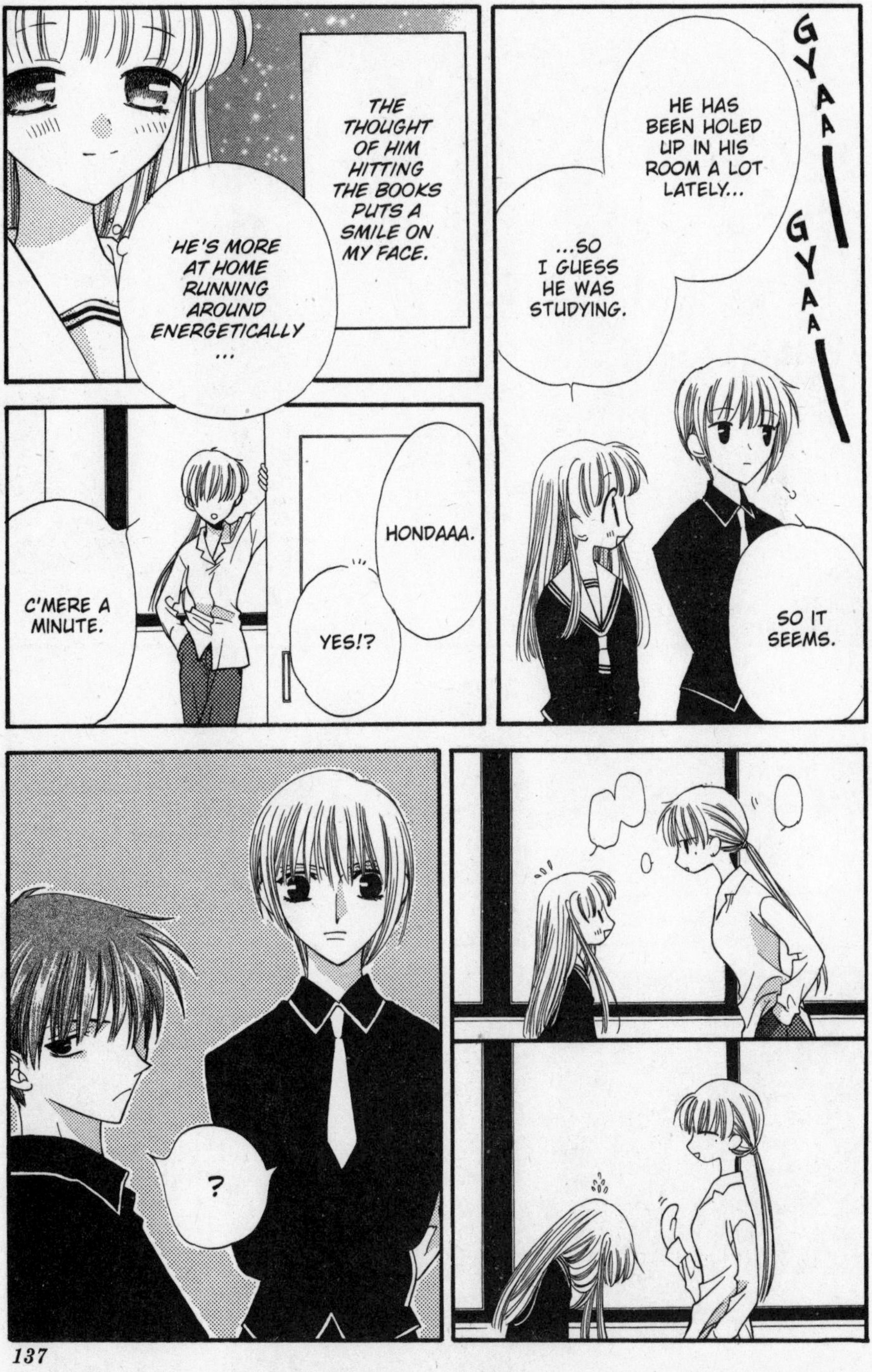
GYAA GYAA
HE HAS BEEN HOLED UP IN HIS ROOM A LOT LATELY...
...SO I GUESS HE WAS STUDYING.
SO IT SEEMS.
THE THOUGHT OF HIM HITTING THE BOOKS PUTS A SMILE ON MY FACE.
HE'S MORE AT HOME RUNNING AROUND ENERGETICALLY ...
HONDAAA.
YES!?
C'MERE A MINUTE.
?

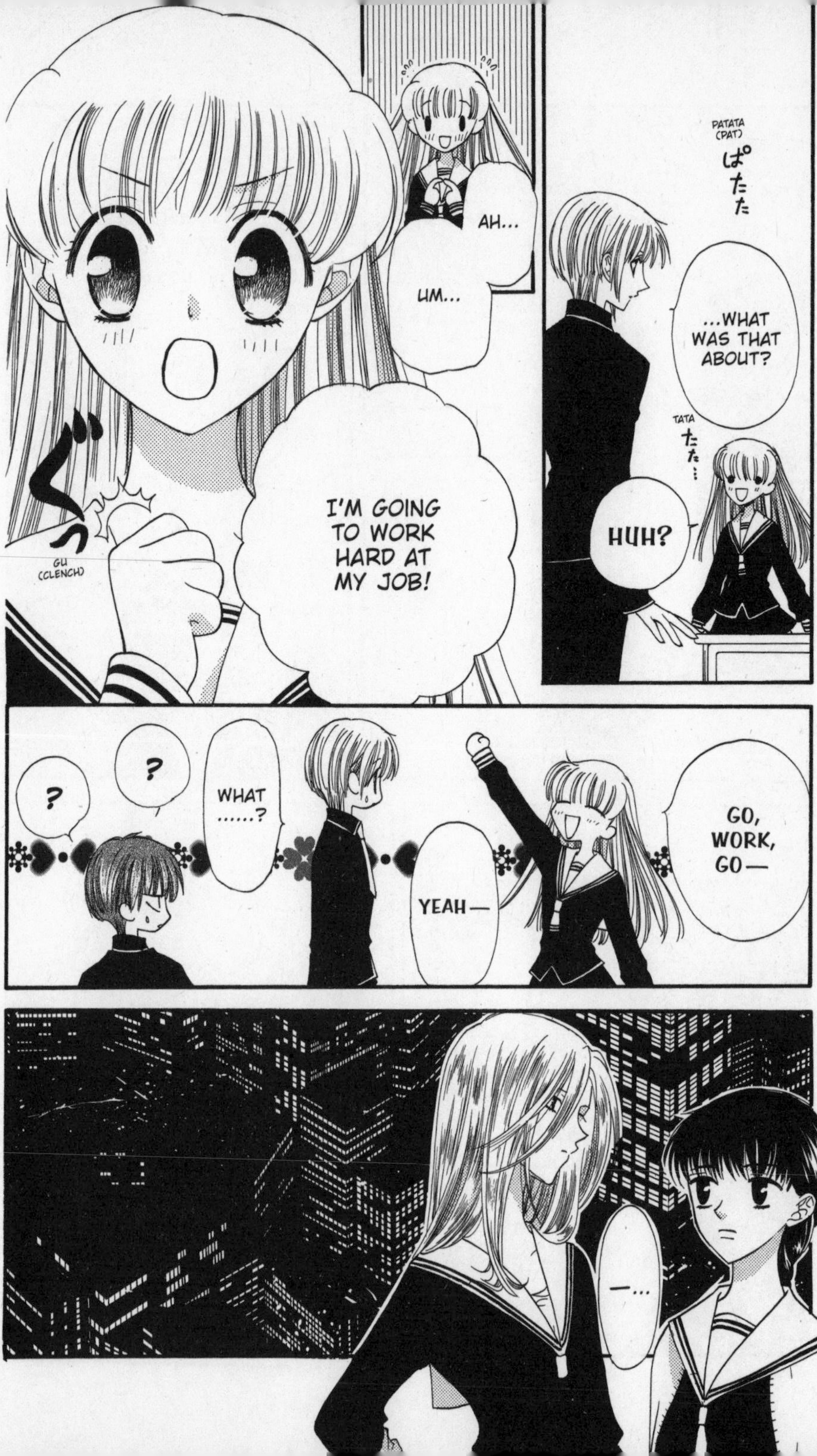
AH...
UM...
I'M GOING TO WORK HARD AT MY JOB!
ぐっ
GU (CLENCH)
ぱたた
PATATA (PAT)
...WHAT WAS THAT ABOUT?
たた…
TATA
HUH?
GO, WORK, GO—
YEAH—
WHAT ......?
?
?
—...

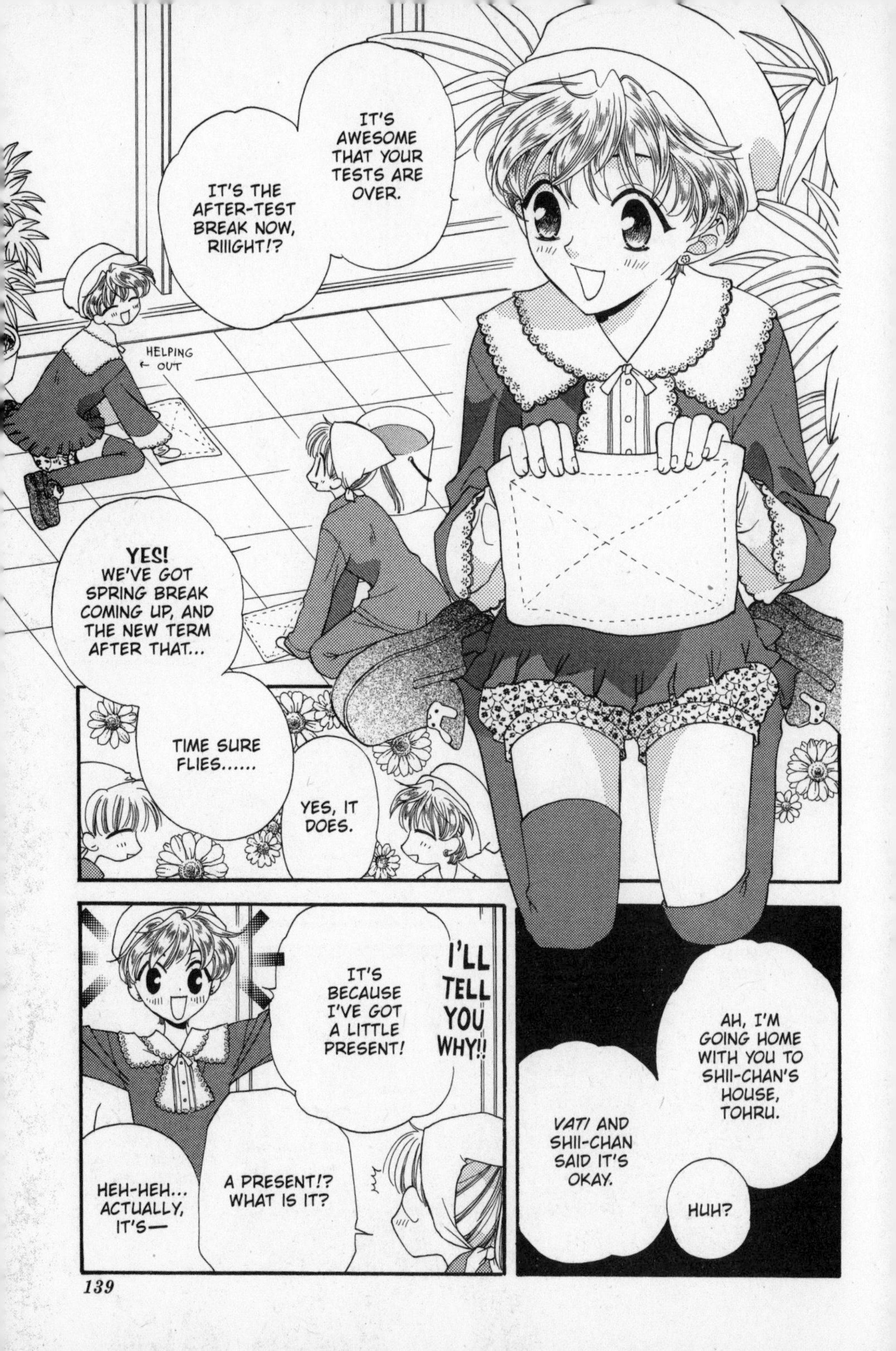
IT'S AWESOME THAT YOUR TESTS ARE OVER.
IT'S THE AFTER-TEST BREAK NOW, RIIIGHT!?
HELPING OUT
YES! WE'VE GOT SPRING BREAK COMING UP, AND THE NEW TERM AFTER THAT...
TIME SURE FLIES......
YES, IT DOES.
AH, I'M GOING HOME WITH YOU TO SHII-CHAN'S HOUSE, TOHRU.
VATI AND SHII-CHAN SAID IT'S OKAY.
HUH?
I'LL TELL YOU WHY!!
IT'S BECAUSE I'VE GOT A LITTLE PRESENT!
A PRESENT!? WHAT IS IT?
HEH-HEH... ACTUALLY, IT'S—

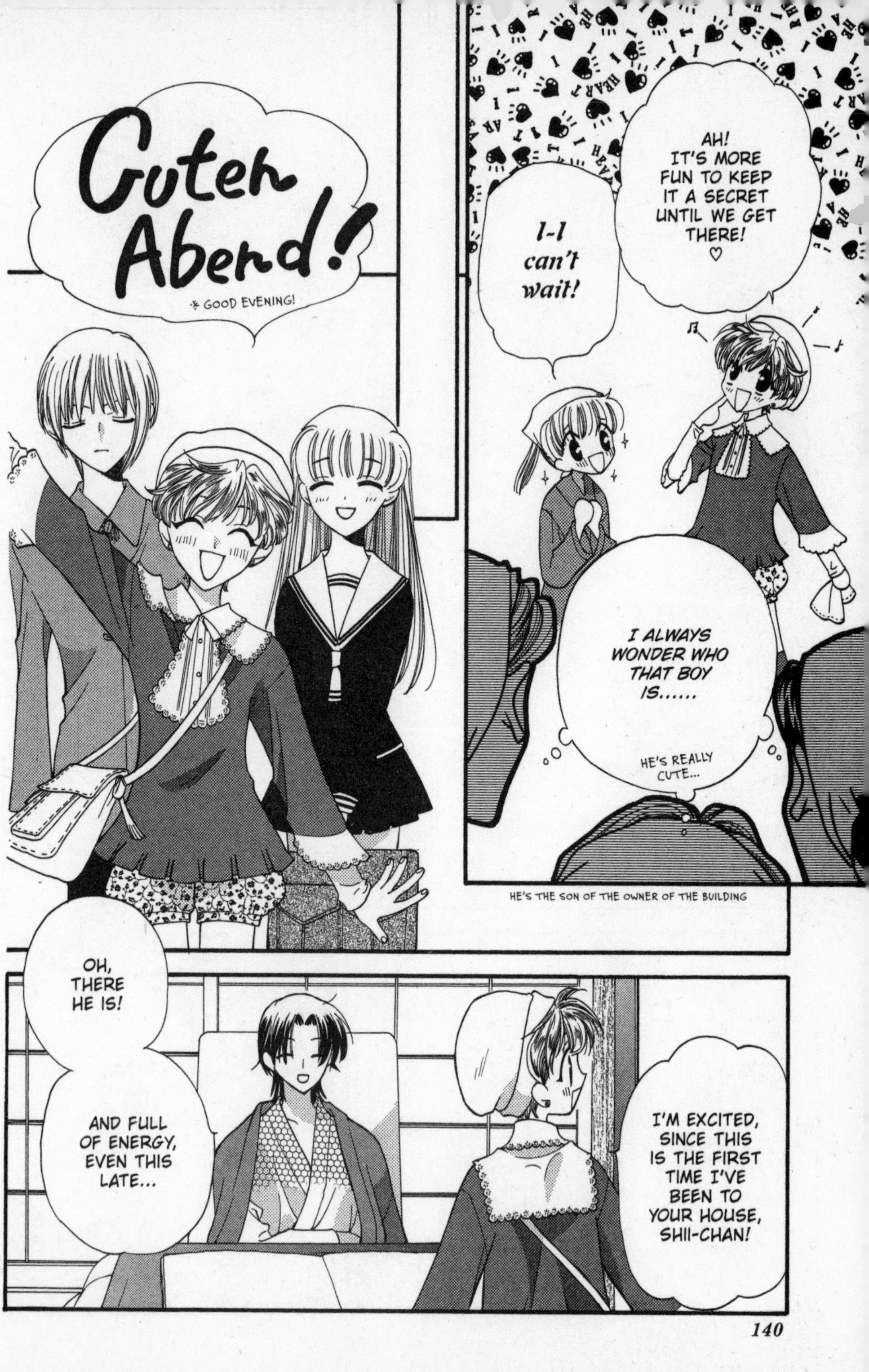
AH! IT'S MORE FUN TO KEEP IT A SECRET UNTIL WE GET THERE! ♡
I-I can't wait!
I ALWAYS WONDER WHO THAT BOY IS......
HE'S REALLY CUTE...
HE'S THE SON OF THE OWNER OF THE BUILDING
Guten Abend!
* GOOD EVENING!
I'M EXCITED, SINCE THIS IS THE FIRST TIME I'VE BEEN TO YOUR HOUSE, SHII-CHAN!
OH, THERE HE IS!
AND FULL OF ENERGY, EVEN THIS LATE...

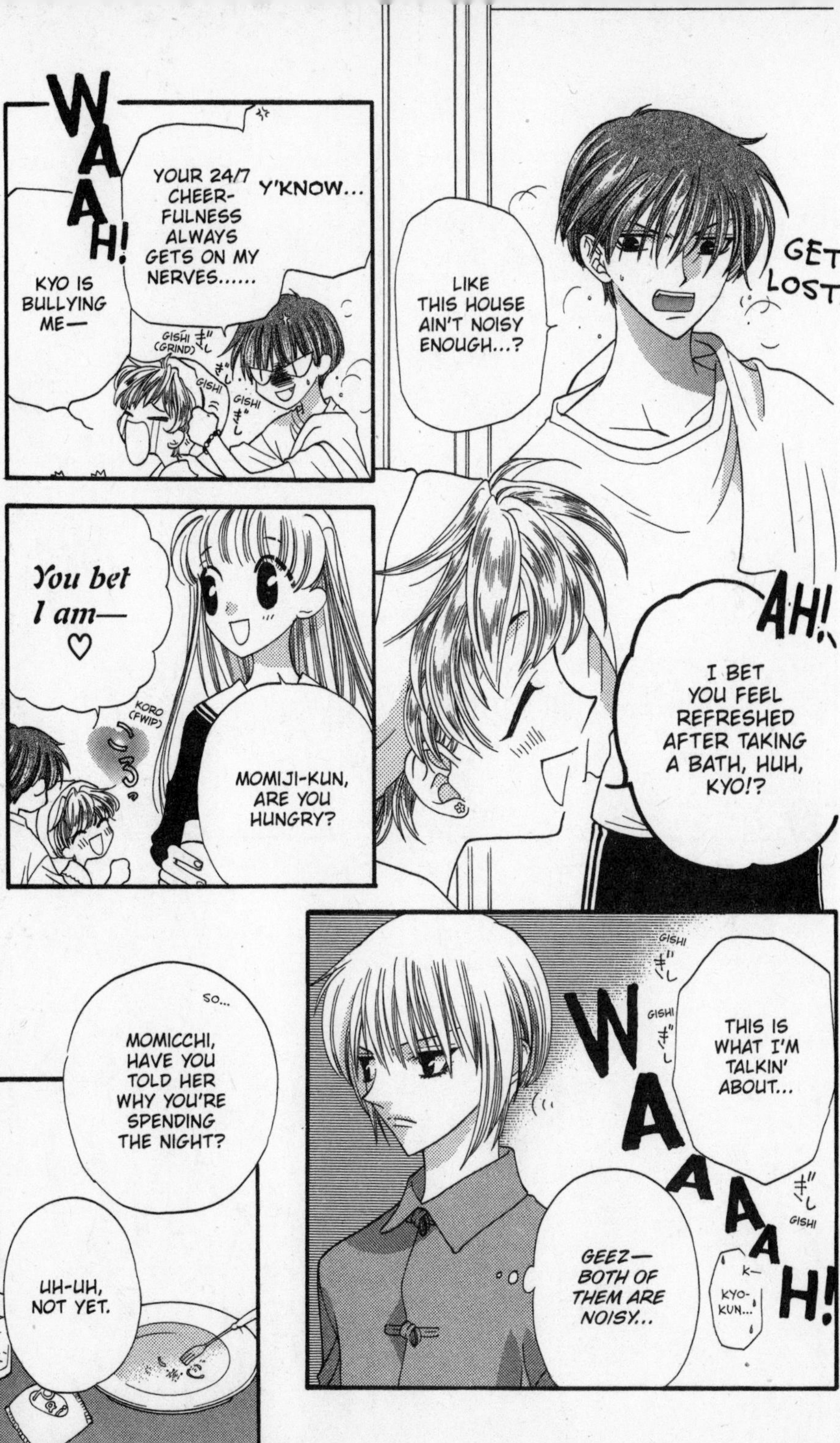
GET LOST!
LIKE THIS HOUSE AIN'T NOISY ENOUGH...?
AH!
I BET YOU FEEL REFRESHED AFTER TAKING A BATH, HUH, KYO!?
Y'KNOW...
YOUR 24/7 CHEER-FULNESS ALWAYS GETS ON MY NERVES......
WAAH!
KYO IS BULLYING ME—
GISHI (GRIND)
GISHI
GISHI
MOMIJI-KUN, ARE YOU HUNGRY?
You bet I am—♡
KORO (FWIP)
THIS IS WHAT I'M TALKIN' ABOUT...
GISHI
GISHI
WAAAAAH!
GISHI
GEEZ—BOTH OF THEM ARE NOISY...
K— KYO-KUN...
SO...
MOMICCHI, HAVE YOU TOLD HER WHY YOU'RE SPENDING THE NIGHT?
UH-UH, NOT YET.

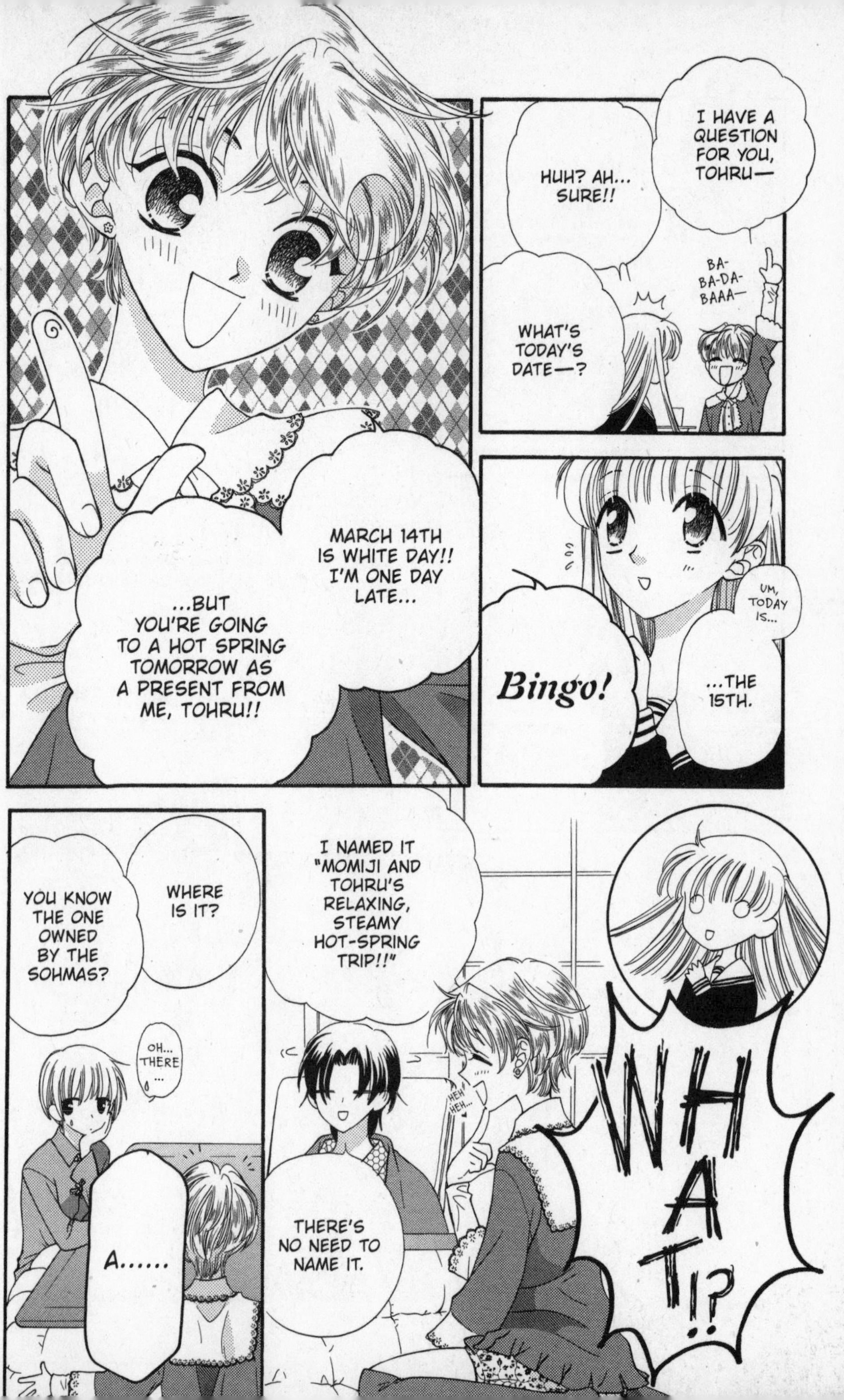
I HAVE A QUESTION FOR YOU, TOHRU—
BA-BA-DA-BAAA—
HUH? AH... SURE!!
WHAT'S TODAY'S DATE—?
UM, TODAY IS...
...THE 15TH.
Bingo!
MARCH 14TH IS WHITE DAY!! I'M ONE DAY LATE...
...BUT YOU'RE GOING TO A HOT SPRING TOMORROW AS A PRESENT FROM ME, TOHRU!!
WHAT!?
I NAMED IT "MOMIJI AND TOHRU'S RELAXING, STEAMY HOT-SPRING TRIP!!"
HEH HEH...
THERE'S NO NEED TO NAME IT.
WHERE IS IT?
YOU KNOW THE ONE OWNED BY THE SOHMAS?
OH... THERE...
A......

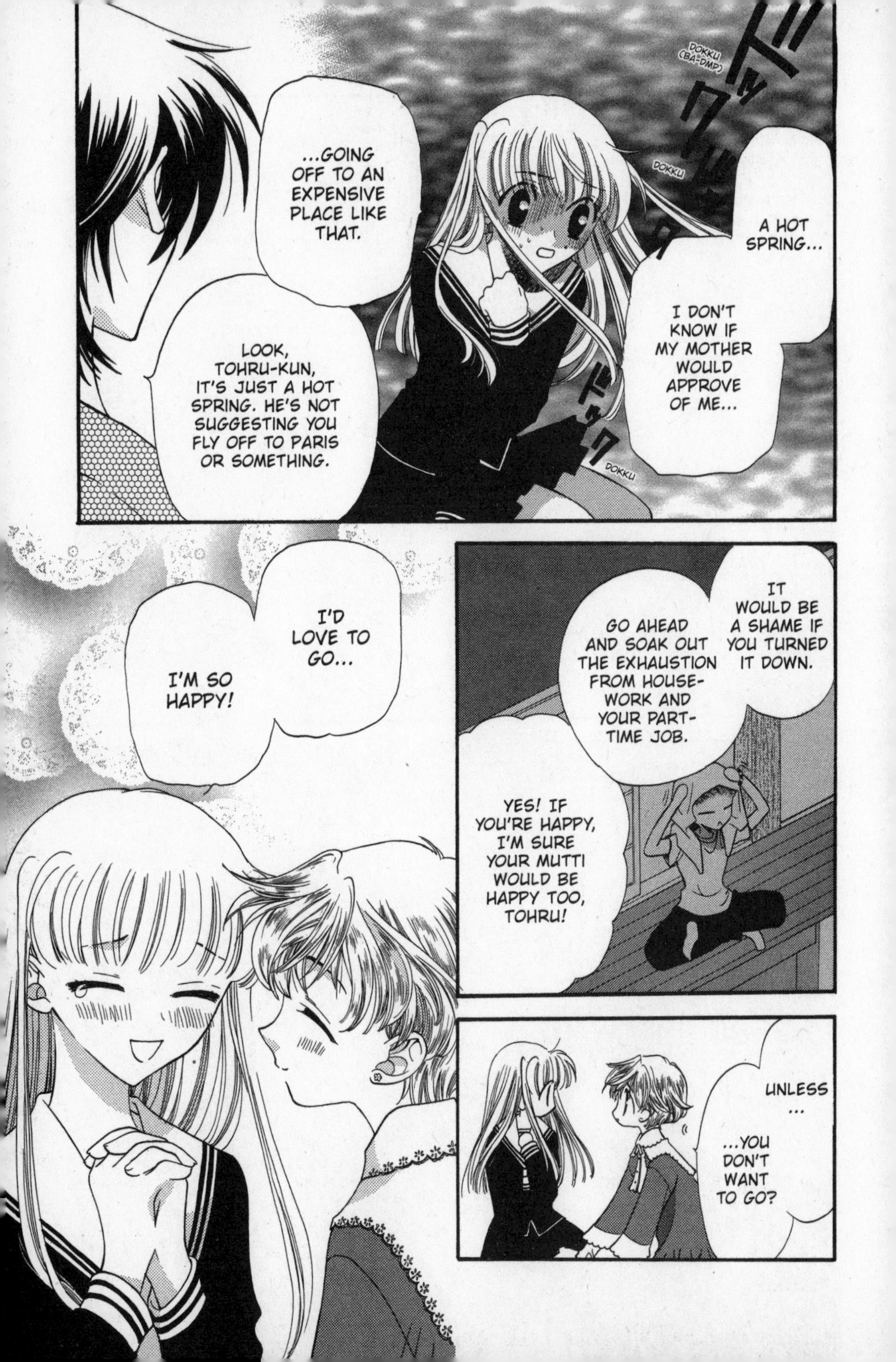
DOKKU (BA-DMP)
DOKKU
A HOT SPRING...
I DON'T KNOW IF MY MOTHER WOULD APPROVE OF ME...
DOKKU
...GOING OFF TO AN EXPENSIVE PLACE LIKE THAT.
LOOK, TOHRU-KUN, IT'S JUST A HOT SPRING. HE'S NOT SUGGESTING YOU FLY OFF TO PARIS OR SOMETHING.
IT WOULD BE A SHAME IF YOU TURNED IT DOWN.
GO AHEAD AND SOAK OUT THE EXHAUSTION FROM HOUSE-WORK AND YOUR PART-TIME JOB.
YES! IF YOU'RE HAPPY, I'M SURE YOUR MUTTI WOULD BE HAPPY TOO, TOHRU!
UNLESS ...
...YOU DON'T WANT TO GO?
I'D LOVE TO GO...
I'M SO HAPPY!

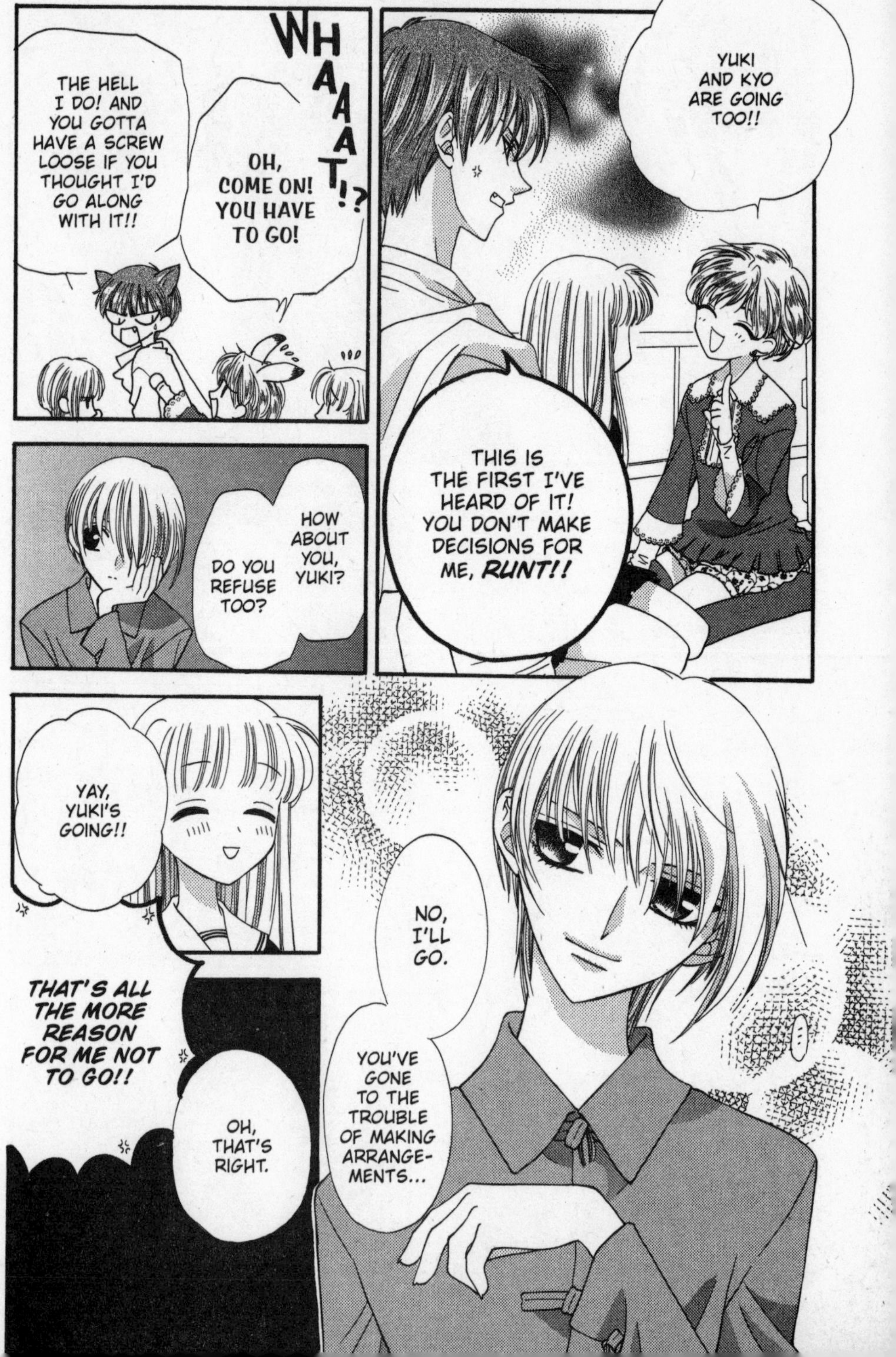
YUKI AND KYO ARE GOING TOO!!
THIS IS THE FIRST I'VE HEARD OF IT! YOU DON'T MAKE DECISIONS FOR ME, ***RUNT!!***
WHAAAT!?
OH, COME ON! YOU HAVE TO GO!
THE HELL I DO! AND YOU GOTTA HAVE A SCREW LOOSE IF YOU THOUGHT I'D GO ALONG WITH IT!!
HOW ABOUT YOU, YUKI?
DO YOU REFUSE TOO?
NO, I'LL GO.
YOU'VE GONE TO THE TROUBLE OF MAKING ARRANGE-MENTS...
...
YAY, YUKI'S GOING!!
THAT'S ALL THE MORE REASON FOR ME NOT TO GO!!
OH, THAT'S RIGHT.

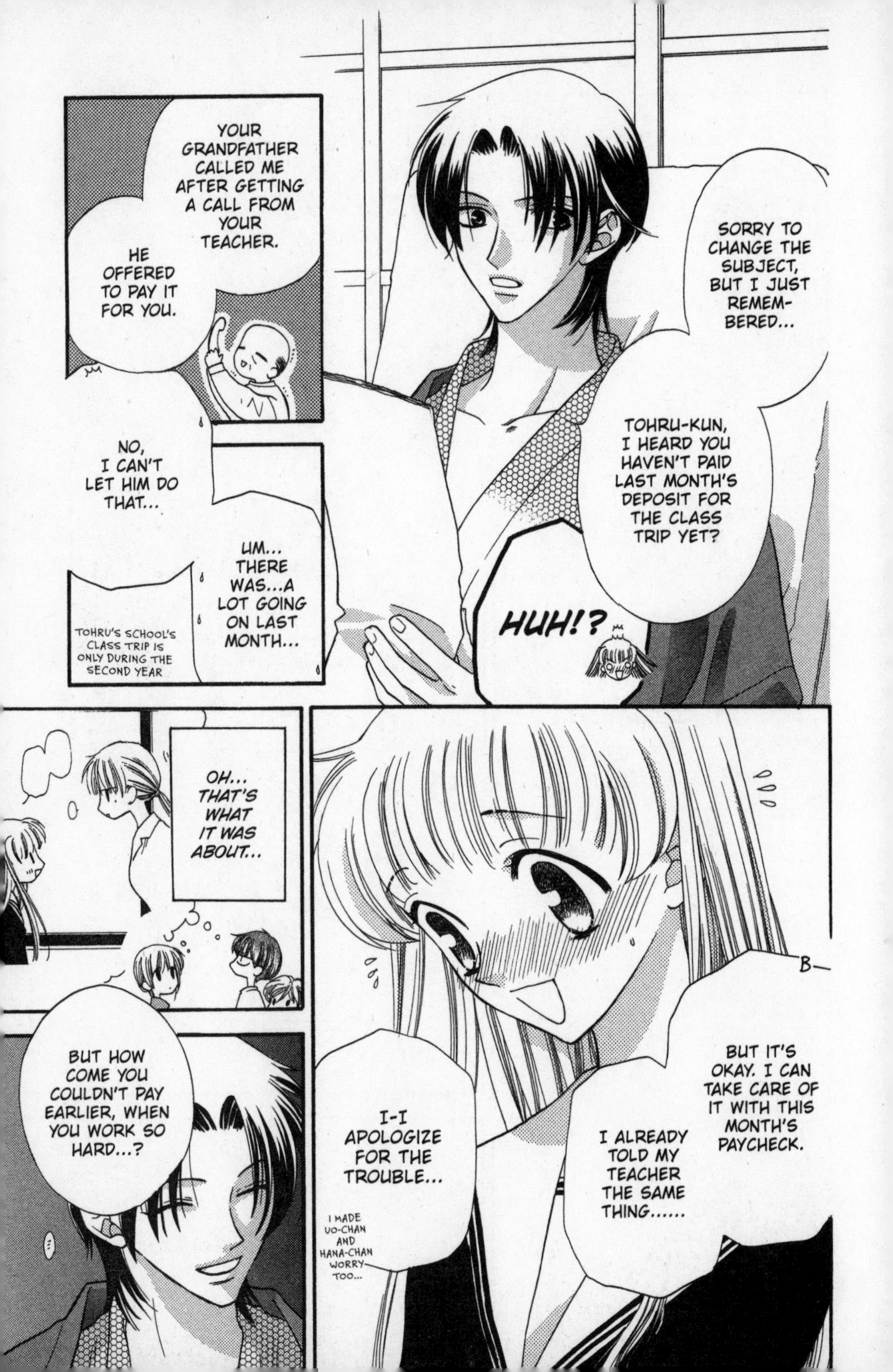
SORRY TO CHANGE THE SUBJECT, BUT I JUST REMEMBERED...
TOHRU-KUN, I HEARD YOU HAVEN'T PAID LAST MONTH'S DEPOSIT FOR THE CLASS TRIP YET?
HUH!?
YOUR GRANDFATHER CALLED ME AFTER GETTING A CALL FROM YOUR TEACHER.
HE OFFERED TO PAY IT FOR YOU.
NO, I CAN'T LET HIM DO THAT...
UM... THERE WAS...A LOT GOING ON LAST MONTH...
TOHRU'S SCHOOL'S CLASS TRIP IS ONLY DURING THE SECOND YEAR
B—
BUT IT'S OKAY. I CAN TAKE CARE OF IT WITH THIS MONTH'S PAYCHECK.
I ALREADY TOLD MY TEACHER THE SAME THING......
I-I APOLOGIZE FOR THE TROUBLE...
I MADE UO-CHAN AND HANA-CHAN WORRY TOO...
OH... THAT'S WHAT IT WAS ABOUT...
BUT HOW COME YOU COULDN'T PAY EARLIER, WHEN YOU WORK SO HARD...?

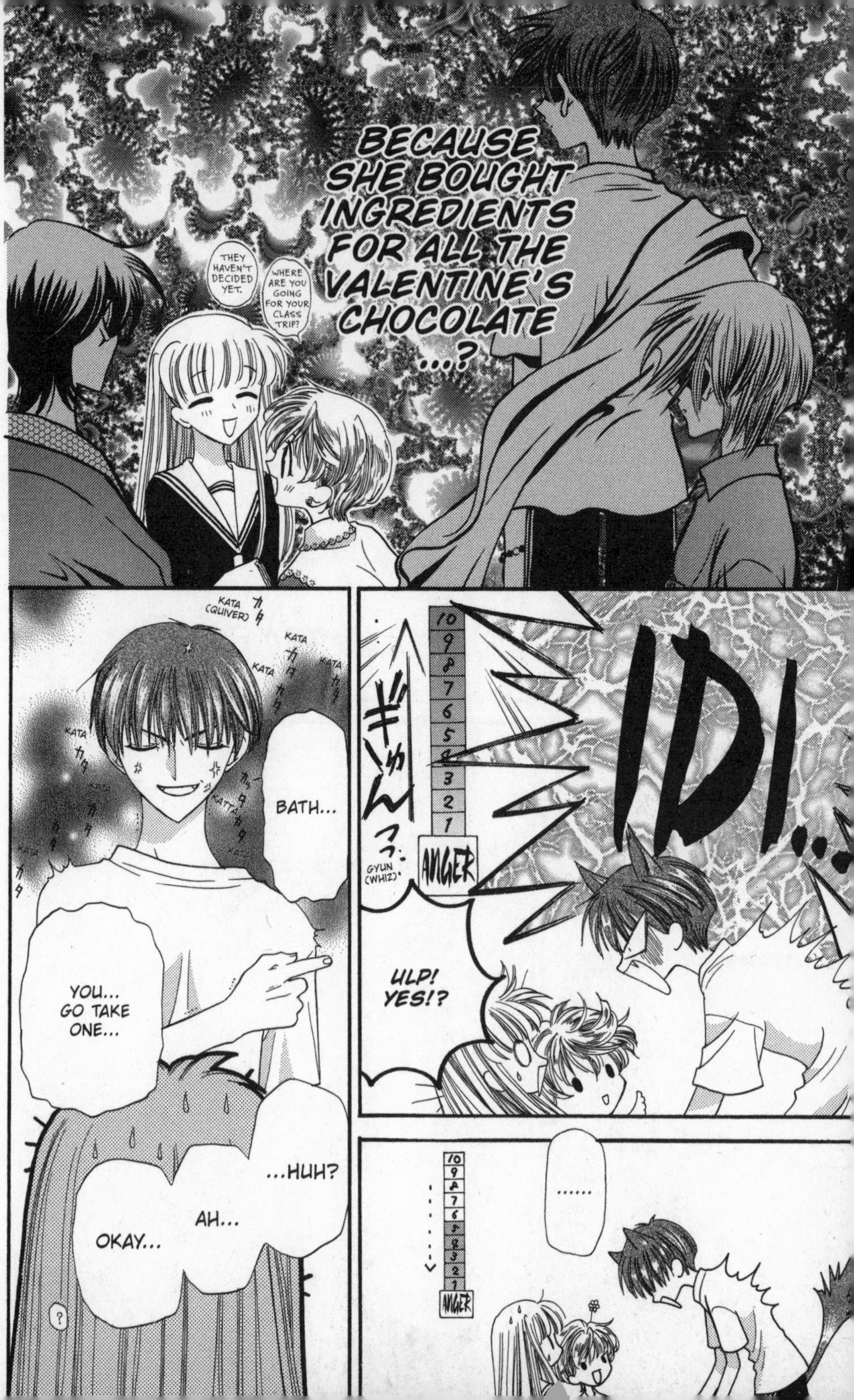
BECAUSE SHE BOUGHT INGREDIENTS FOR ALL THE VALENTINE'S CHOCOLATE ...?
WHERE ARE YOU GOING FOR YOUR CLASS TRIP?
THEY HAVEN'T DECIDED YET.
IDI...
10 9 8 7 6 5 4 3 2 1
ANGER
GYUN (WHIZ)
ULP! YES!?
10 9 8 7 6 5 4 3 2 1
ANGER
......
KATA (QUIVER)
KATA
KATA
KATA
KATA
KATA
KATTA
KATA
BATH...
YOU... GO TAKE ONE...
...HUH?
AH...
OKAY...
?

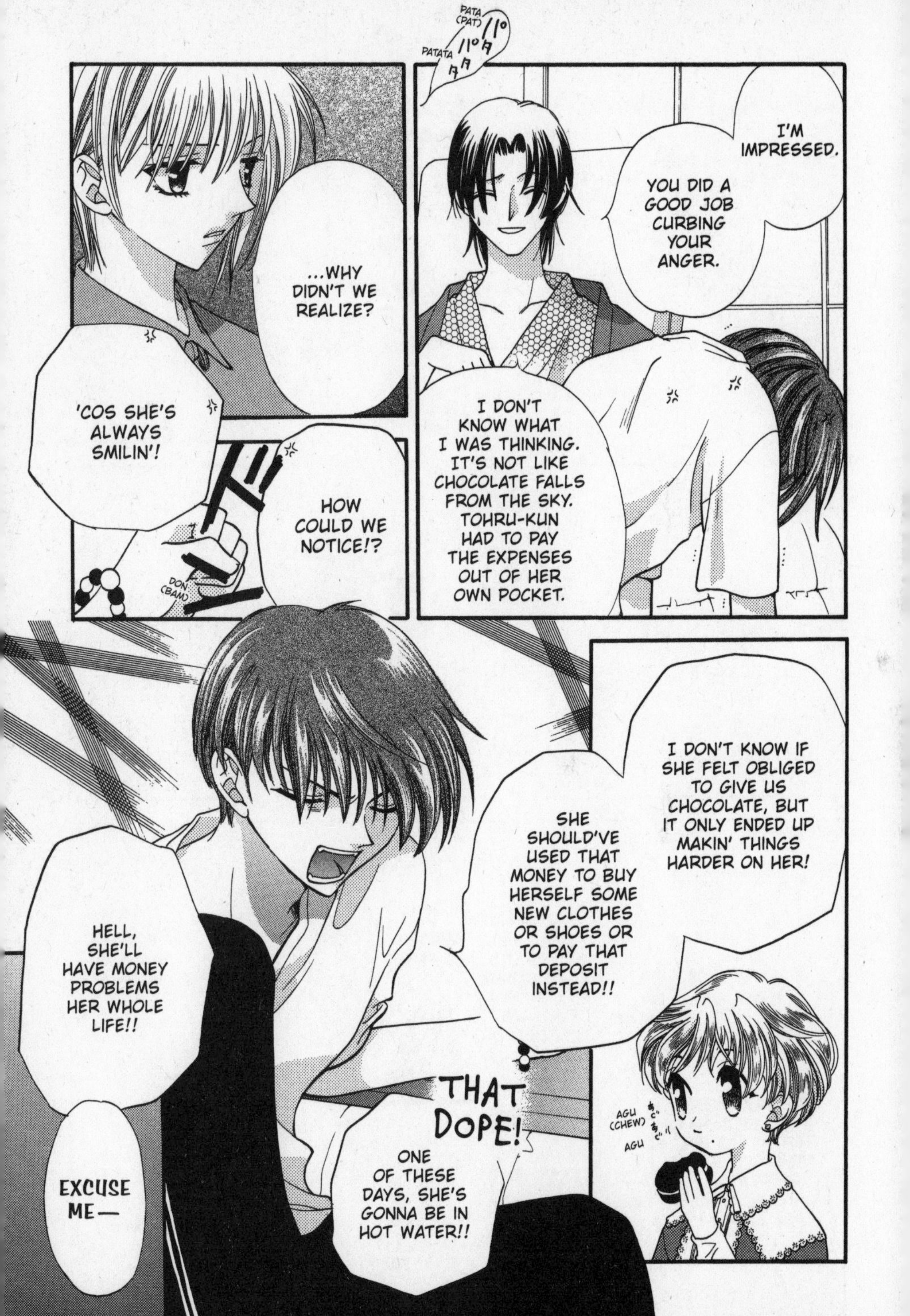
PATA (PAT) PATATA
I'M IMPRESSED.
YOU DID A GOOD JOB CURBING YOUR ANGER.
I DON'T KNOW WHAT I WAS THINKING. IT'S NOT LIKE CHOCOLATE FALLS FROM THE SKY. TOHRU-KUN HAD TO PAY THE EXPENSES OUT OF HER OWN POCKET.
...WHY DIDN'T WE REALIZE?
'COS SHE'S ALWAYS SMILIN'!
HOW COULD WE NOTICE!?
DON (BAM)
I DON'T KNOW IF SHE FELT OBLIGED TO GIVE US CHOCOLATE, BUT IT ONLY ENDED UP MAKIN' THINGS HARDER ON HER!
SHE SHOULD'VE USED THAT MONEY TO BUY HERSELF SOME NEW CLOTHES OR SHOES OR TO PAY THAT DEPOSIT INSTEAD!!
AGU (CHEW) AGU
THAT DOPE!
ONE OF THESE DAYS, SHE'S GONNA BE IN HOT WATER!!
HELL, SHE'LL HAVE MONEY PROBLEMS HER WHOLE LIFE!!
EXCUSE ME—

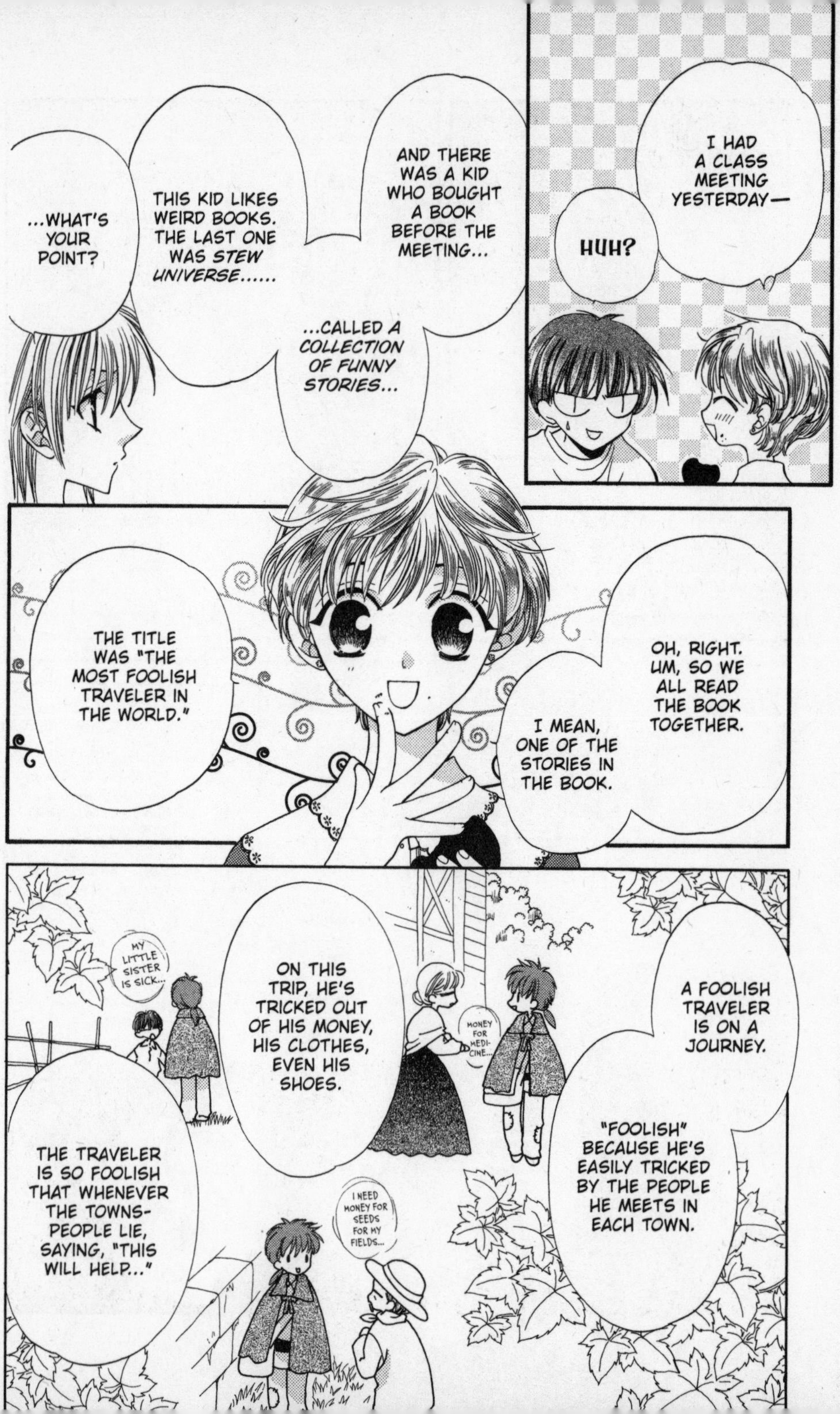
I HAD A CLASS MEETING YESTERDAY—
HUH?
AND THERE WAS A KID WHO BOUGHT A BOOK BEFORE THE MEETING...
...CALLED A *COLLECTION OF FUNNY STORIES*...
THIS KID LIKES WEIRD BOOKS. THE LAST ONE WAS *STEW UNIVERSE*......
...WHAT'S YOUR POINT?
OH, RIGHT. UM, SO WE ALL READ THE BOOK TOGETHER.
I MEAN, ONE OF THE STORIES IN THE BOOK.
THE TITLE WAS "THE MOST FOOLISH TRAVELER IN THE WORLD."
A FOOLISH TRAVELER IS ON A JOURNEY.
MONEY FOR MEDI-CINE...
ON THIS TRIP, HE'S TRICKED OUT OF HIS MONEY, HIS CLOTHES, EVEN HIS SHOES.
MY LITTLE SISTER IS SICK...
"FOOLISH" BECAUSE HE'S EASILY TRICKED BY THE PEOPLE HE MEETS IN EACH TOWN.
I NEED MONEY FOR SEEDS FOR MY FIELDS...
THE TRAVELER IS SO FOOLISH THAT WHENEVER THE TOWNS-PEOPLE LIE, SAYING, "THIS WILL HELP..."

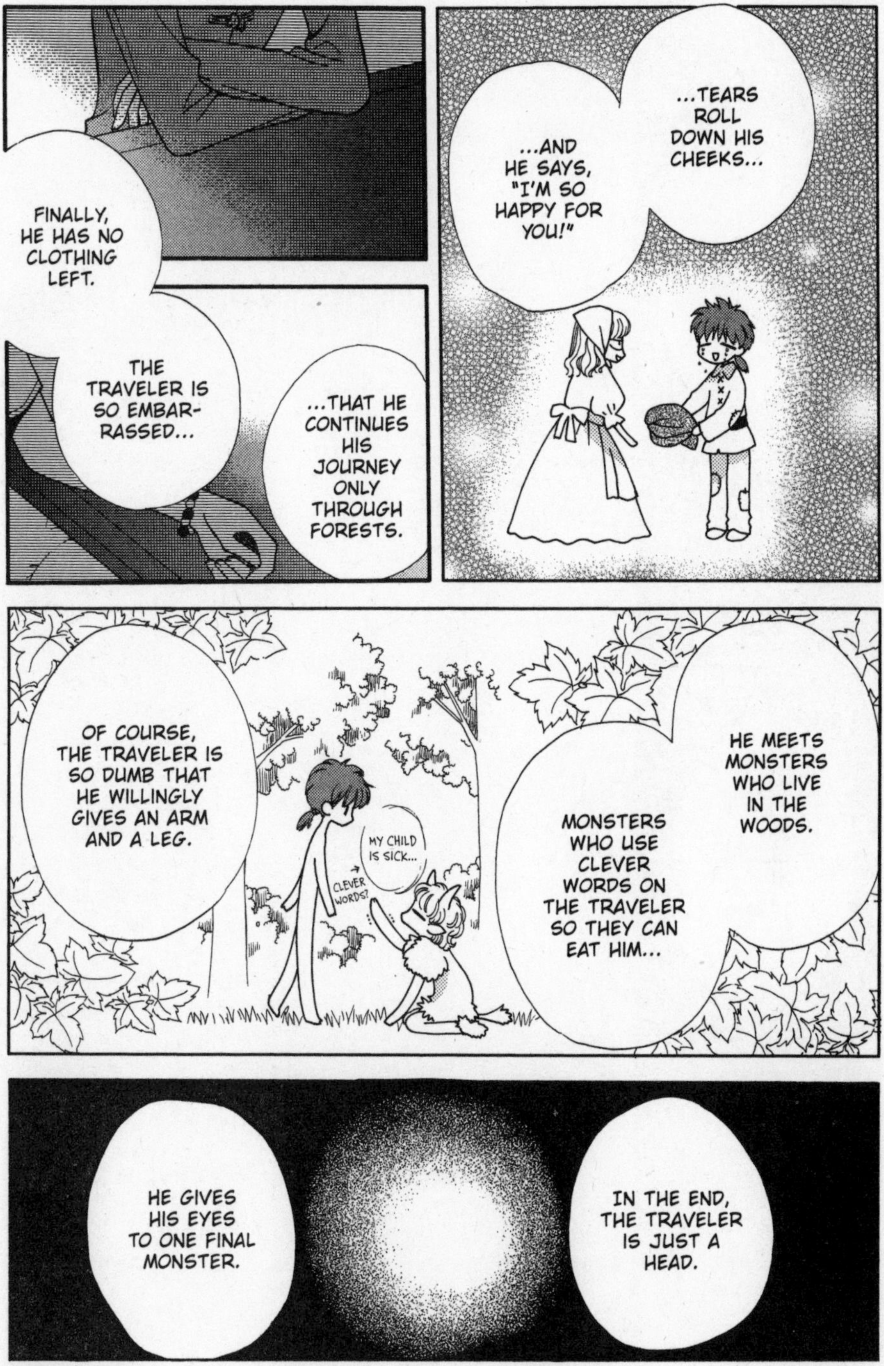

...TEARS ROLL DOWN HIS CHEEKS...
...AND HE SAYS, "I'M SO HAPPY FOR YOU!"
FINALLY, HE HAS NO CLOTHING LEFT.
THE TRAVELER IS SO EMBARRASSED...
...THAT HE CONTINUES HIS JOURNEY ONLY THROUGH FORESTS.
HE MEETS MONSTERS WHO LIVE IN THE WOODS.
MONSTERS WHO USE CLEVER WORDS ON THE TRAVELER SO THEY CAN EAT HIM...
MY CHILD IS SICK...
CLEVER WORDS?
OF COURSE, THE TRAVELER IS SO DUMB THAT HE WILLINGLY GIVES AN ARM AND A LEG.
IN THE END, THE TRAVELER IS JUST A HEAD.
HE GIVES HIS EYES TO ONE FINAL MONSTER.

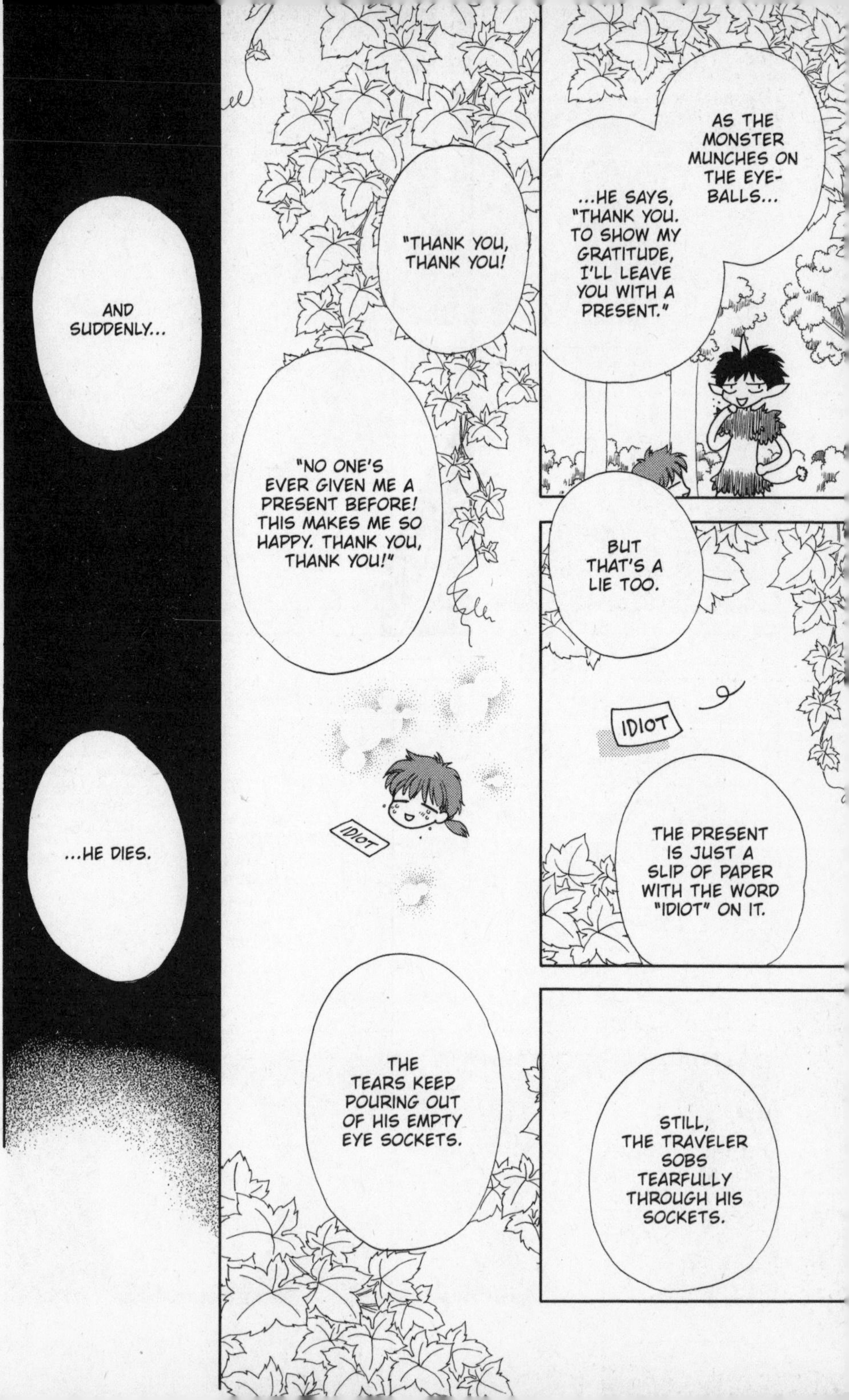
AS THE MONSTER MUNCHES ON THE EYE-BALLS...
...HE SAYS, "THANK YOU. TO SHOW MY GRATITUDE, I'LL LEAVE YOU WITH A PRESENT."
BUT THAT'S A LIE TOO.
IDIOT
THE PRESENT IS JUST A SLIP OF PAPER WITH THE WORD "IDIOT" ON IT.
STILL, THE TRAVELER SOBS TEARFULLY THROUGH HIS SOCKETS.
"THANK YOU, THANK YOU!
"NO ONE'S EVER GIVEN ME A PRESENT BEFORE! THIS MAKES ME SO HAPPY. THANK YOU, THANK YOU!"
IDIOT
THE TEARS KEEP POURING OUT OF HIS EMPTY EYE SOCKETS.
AND SUDDENLY...
...HE DIES.

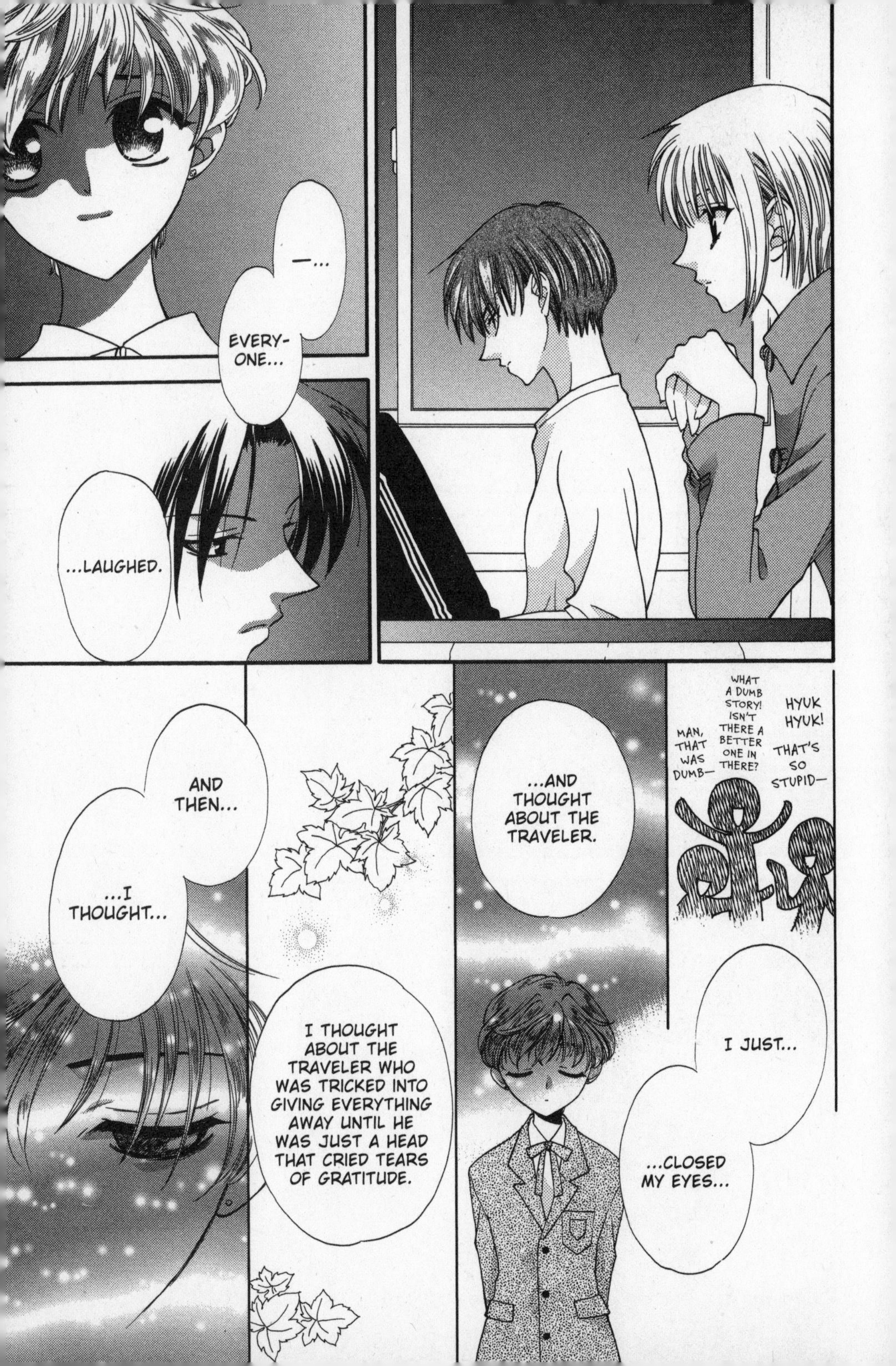
—...
EVERY-ONE...
...LAUGHED.
HYUK HYUK!
THAT'S SO STUPID—
WHAT A DUMB STORY! ISN'T THERE A BETTER ONE IN THERE?
MAN, THAT WAS DUMB—
I JUST...
...CLOSED MY EYES...
...AND THOUGHT ABOUT THE TRAVELER.
I THOUGHT ABOUT THE TRAVELER WHO WAS TRICKED INTO GIVING EVERYTHING AWAY UNTIL HE WAS JUST A HEAD THAT CRIED TEARS OF GRATITUDE.
AND THEN...
...I THOUGHT...

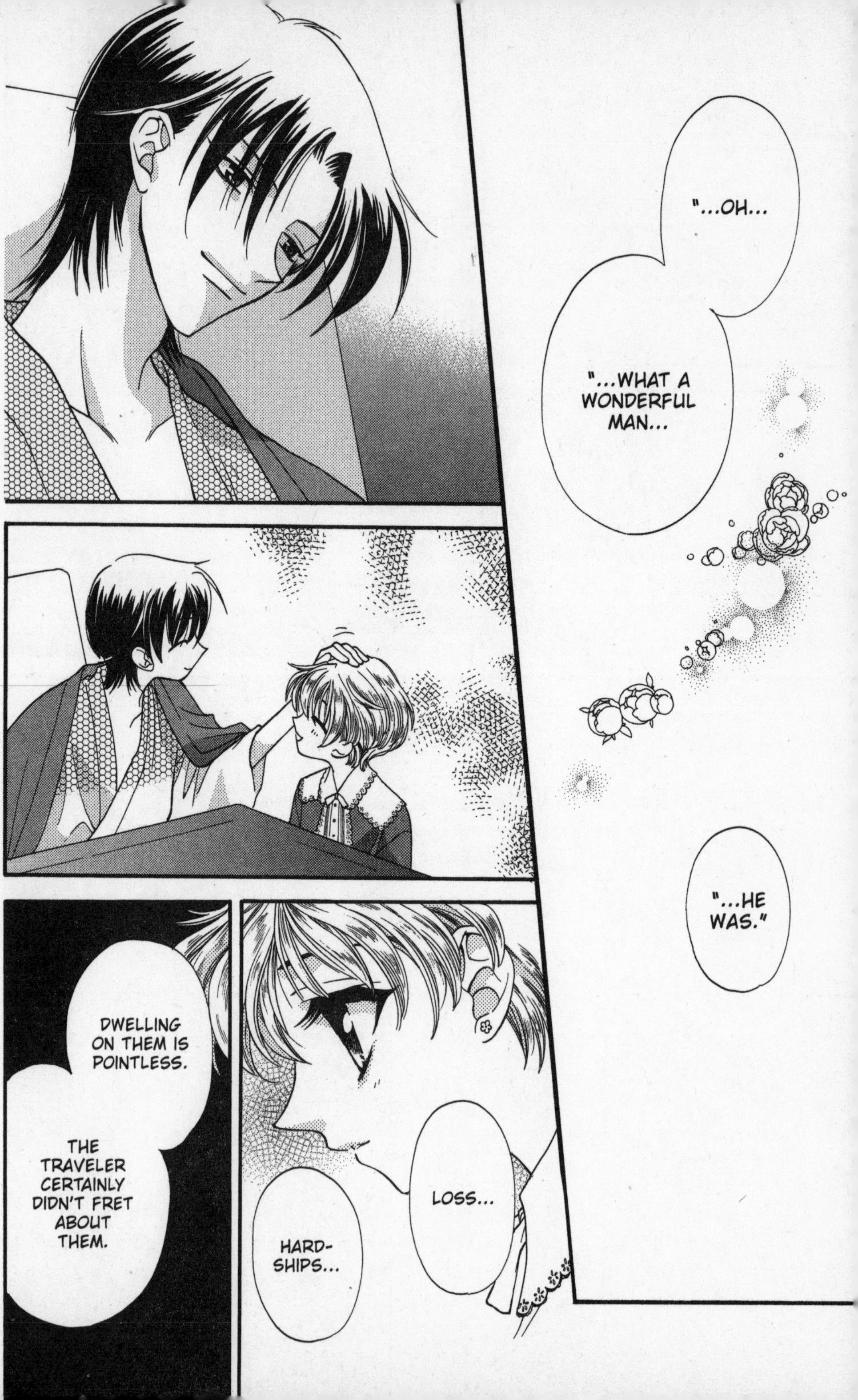
"...OH...
"...WHAT A WONDERFUL MAN...
"...HE WAS."
LOSS...
HARD-SHIPS...
DWELLING ON THEM IS POINTLESS.
THE TRAVELER CERTAINLY DIDN'T FRET ABOUT THEM.

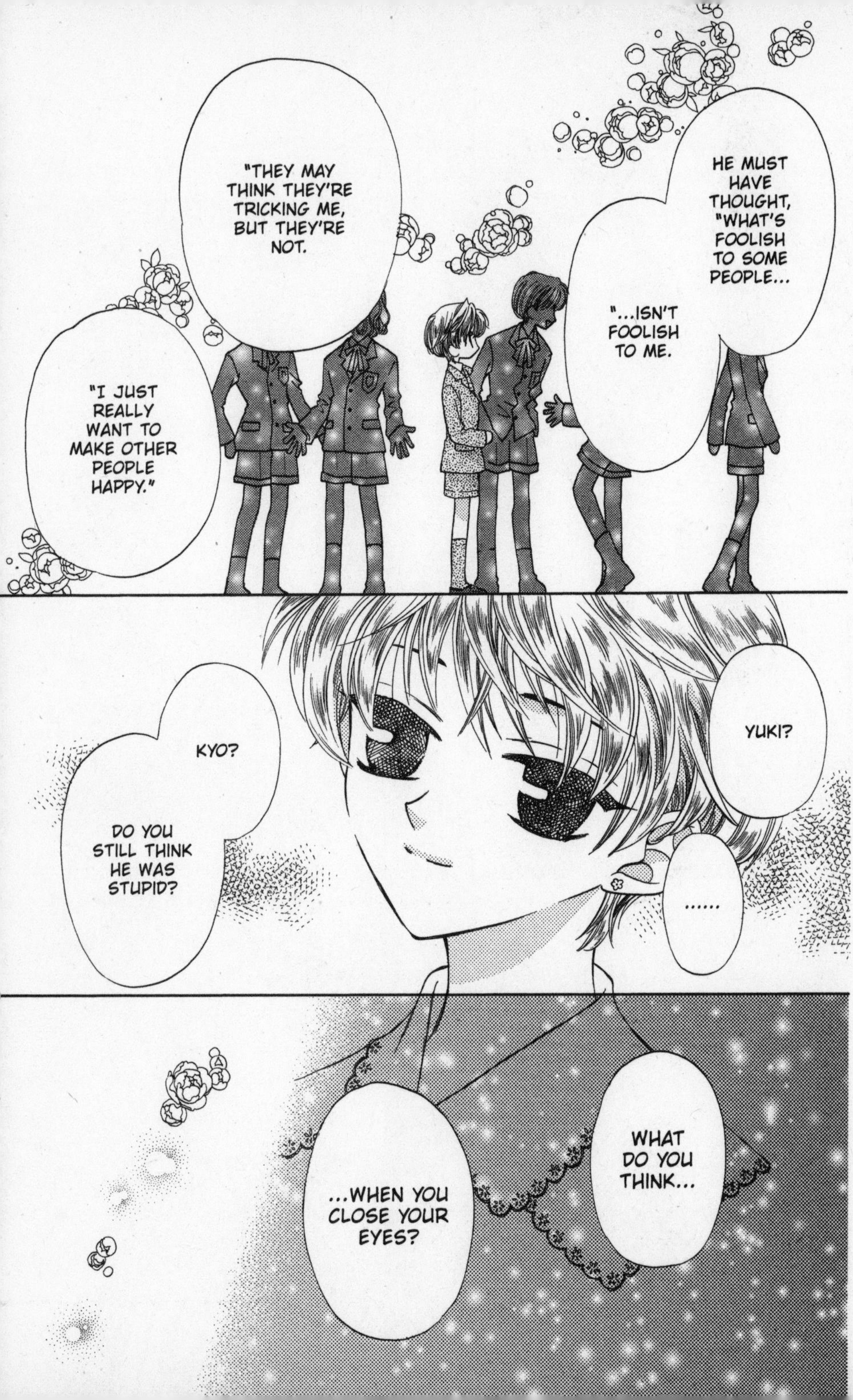
HE MUST HAVE THOUGHT, "WHAT'S FOOLISH TO SOME PEOPLE...
"...ISN'T FOOLISH TO ME.
"THEY MAY THINK THEY'RE TRICKING ME, BUT THEY'RE NOT.
"I JUST REALLY WANT TO MAKE OTHER PEOPLE HAPPY."
YUKI?
......
KYO?
DO YOU STILL THINK HE WAS STUPID?
WHAT DO YOU THINK...
...WHEN YOU CLOSE YOUR EYES?

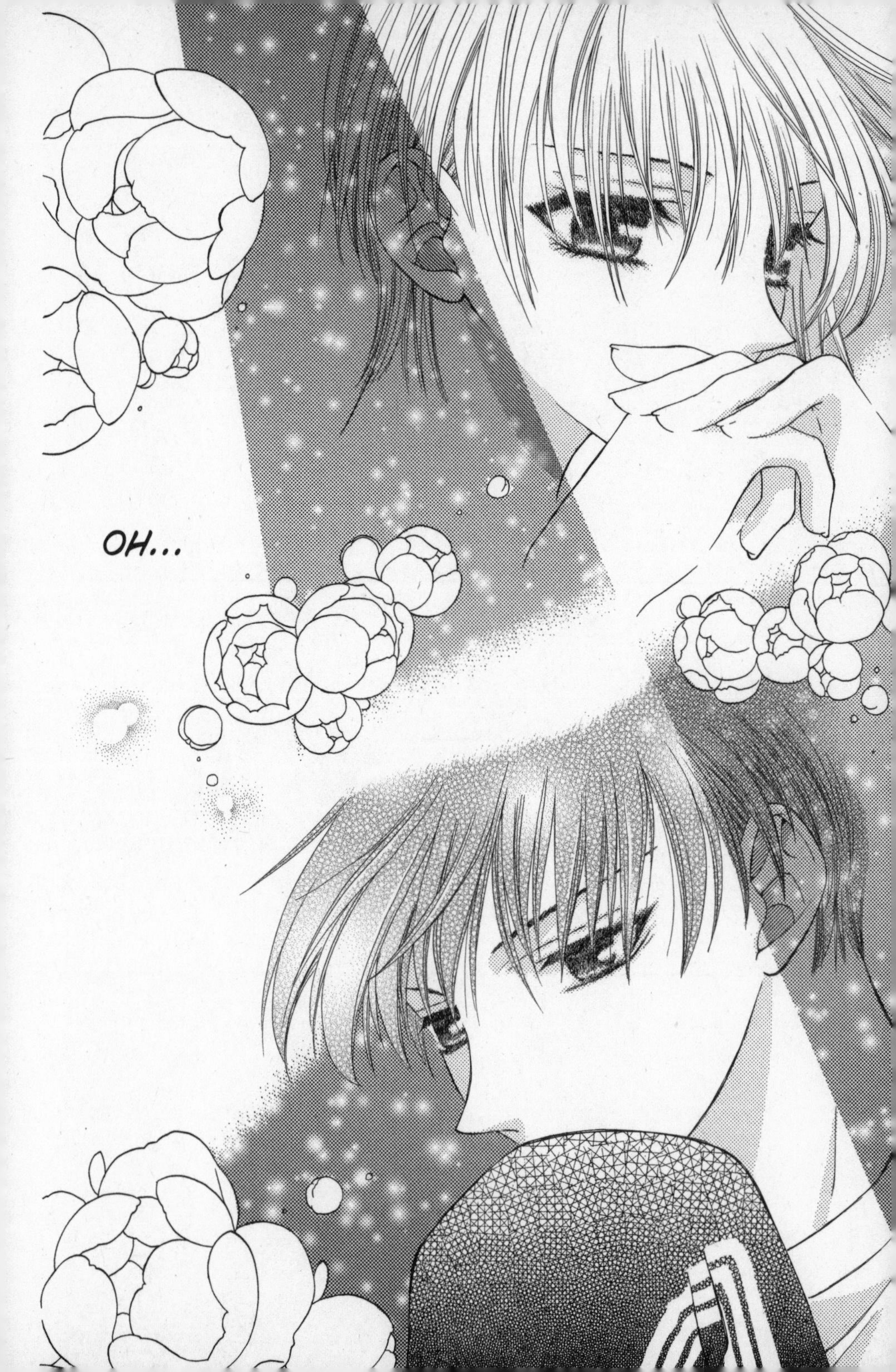
OH...

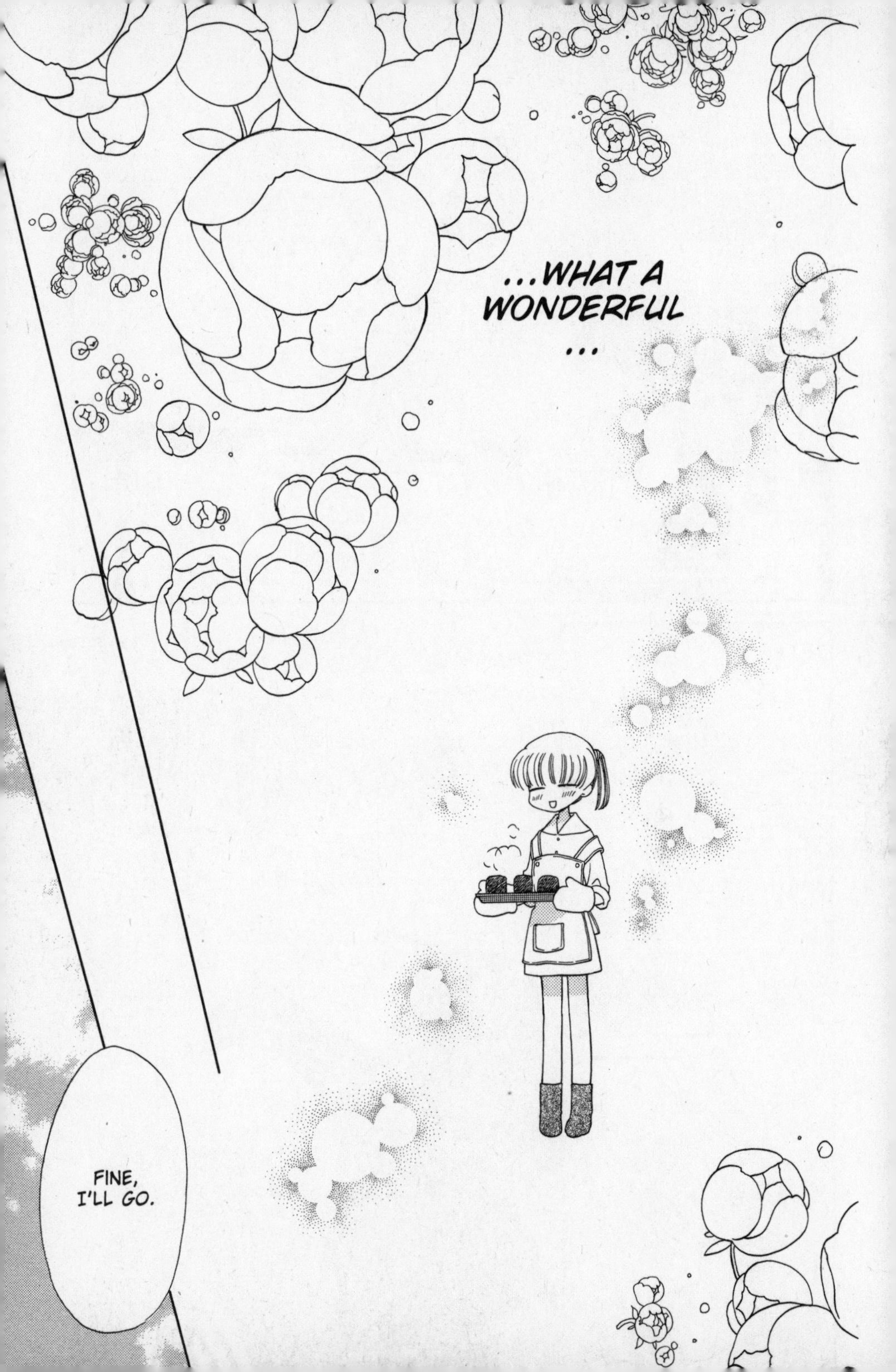
...WHAT A WONDERFUL ...
FINE, I'LL GO.

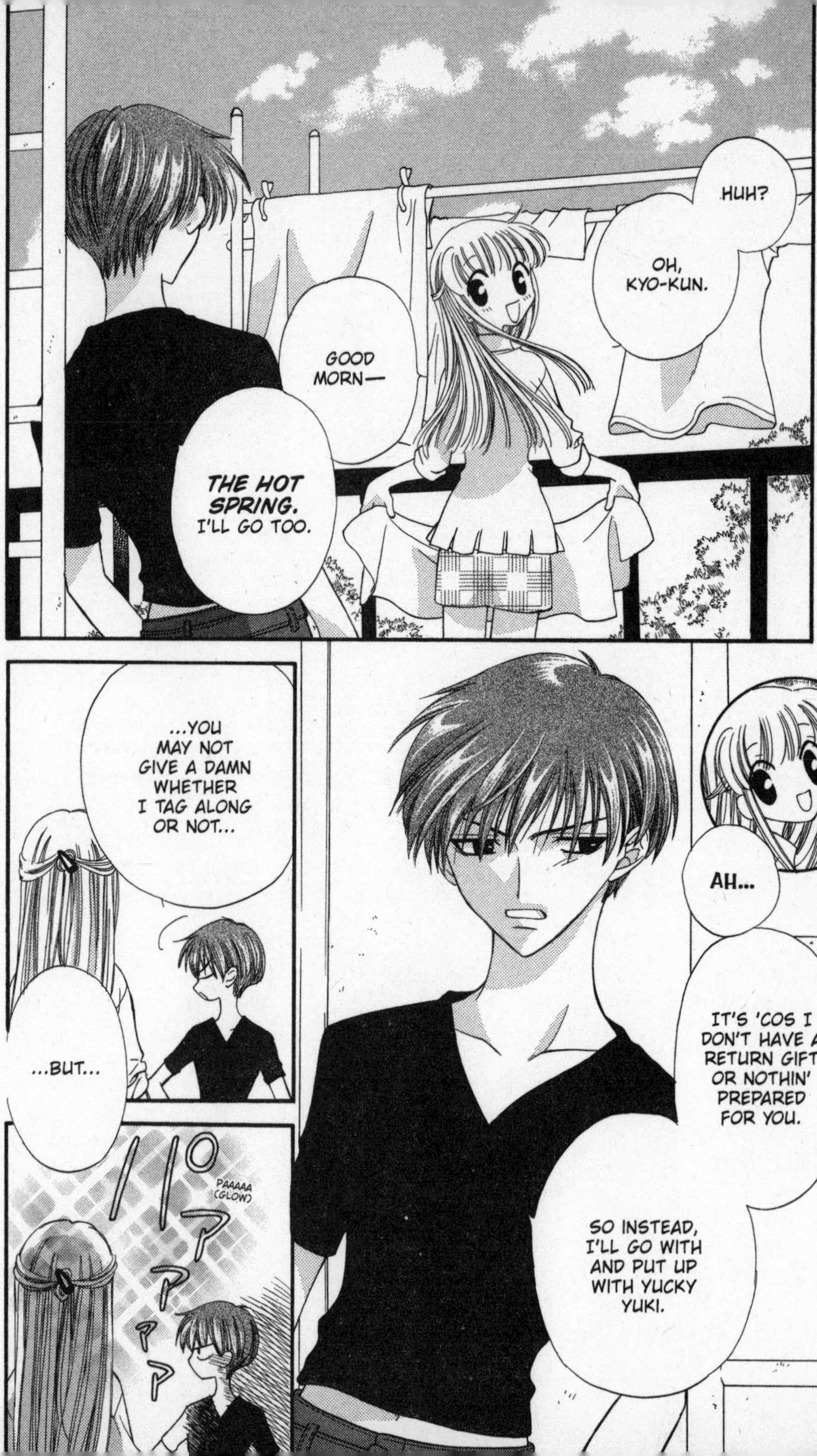
HUH?
OH, KYO-KUN.
GOOD MORN—
THE HOT SPRING. I'LL GO TOO.
AH...
...YOU MAY NOT GIVE A DAMN WHETHER I TAG ALONG OR NOT...
...BUT...
IT'S 'COS I DON'T HAVE A RETURN GIFT OR NOTHIN' PREPARED FOR YOU.
SO INSTEAD, I'LL GO WITH AND PUT UP WITH YUCKY YUKI.
PAAAAA (GLOW)

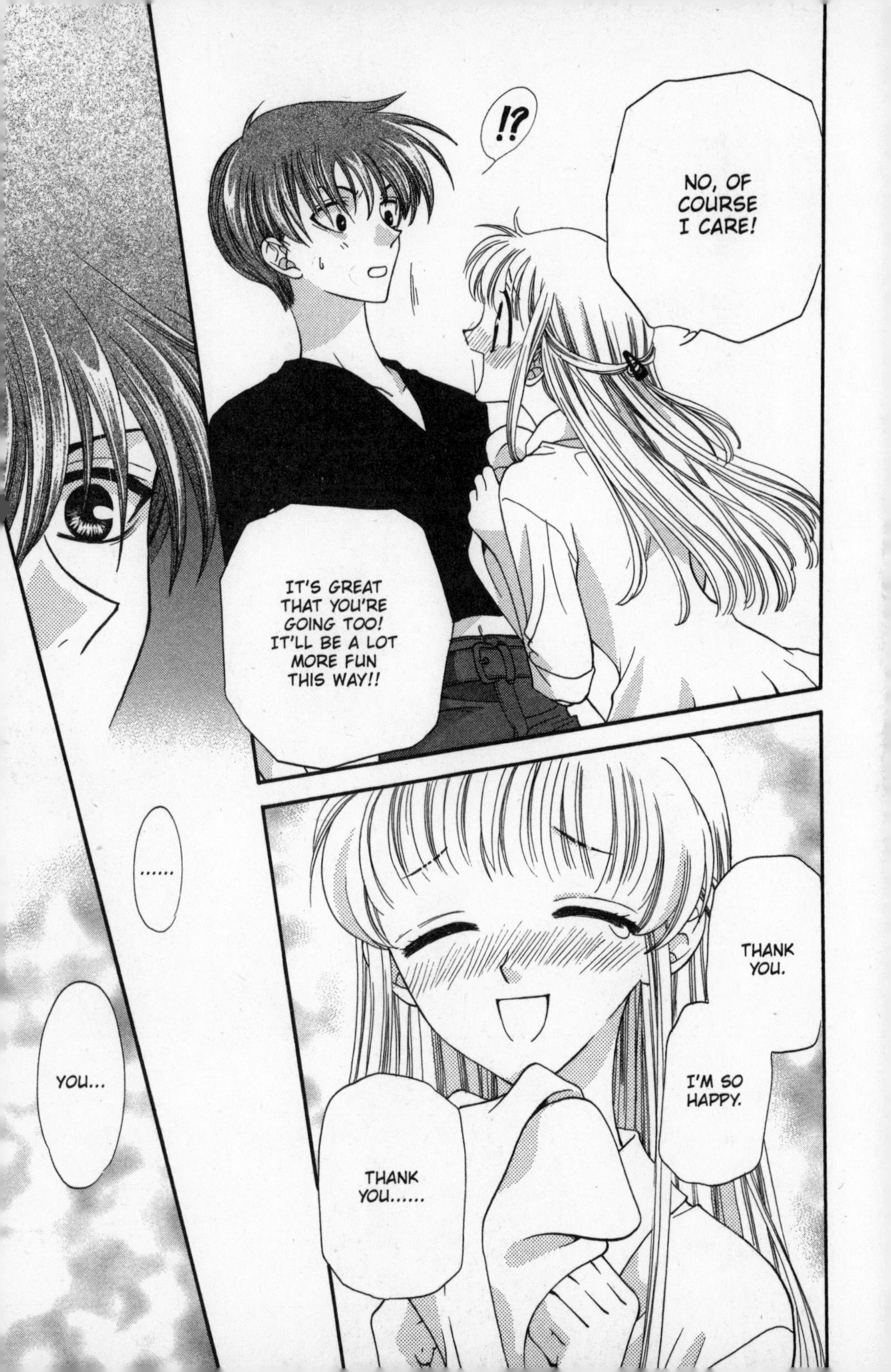
NO, OF COURSE I CARE!
!?
IT'S GREAT THAT YOU'RE GOING TOO! IT'LL BE A LOT MORE FUN THIS WAY!!
THANK YOU.
I'M SO HAPPY.
THANK YOU......
......
YOU...

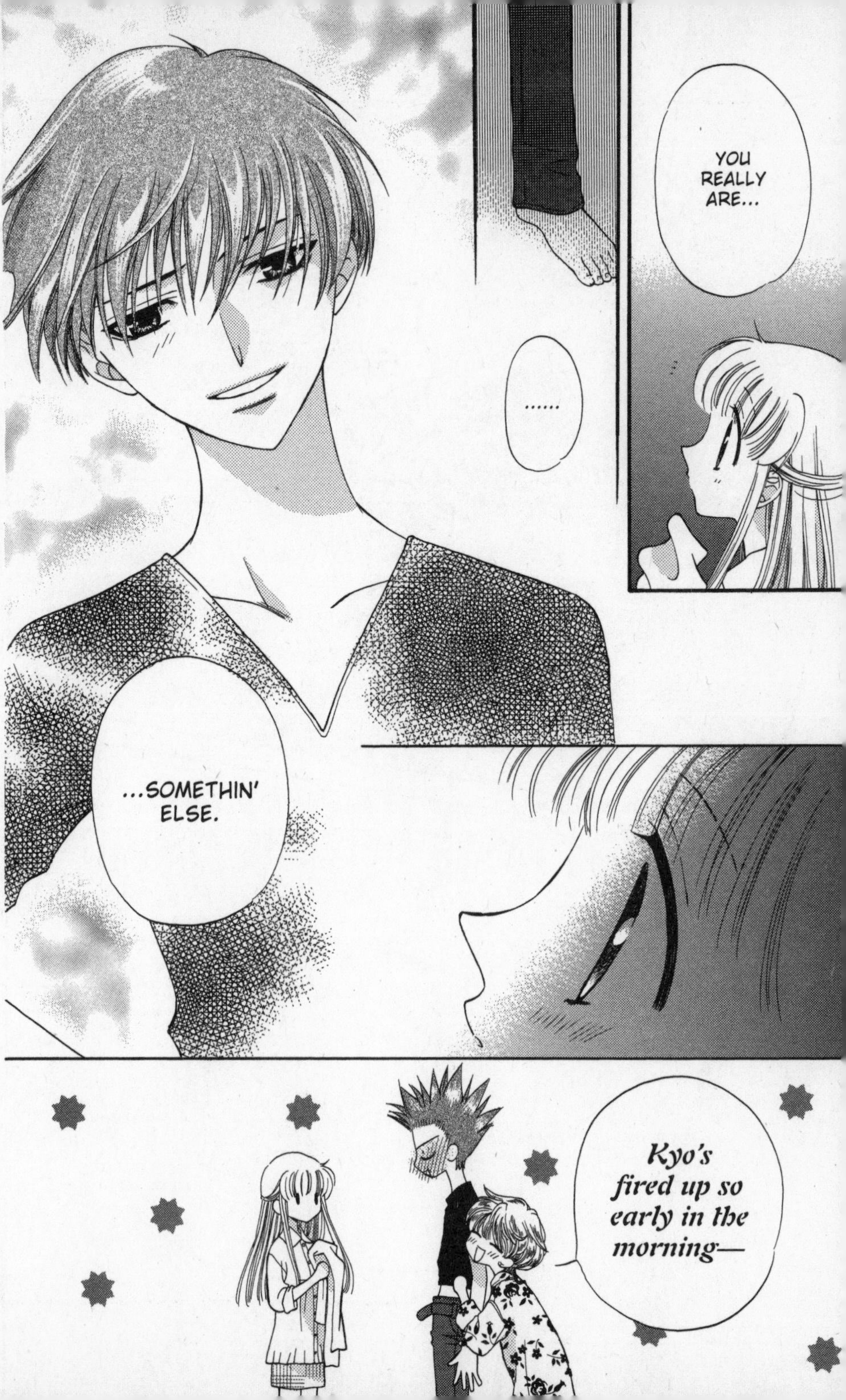
YOU REALLY ARE...
......
...SOMETHIN' ELSE.
Kyo's fired up so early in the morning—

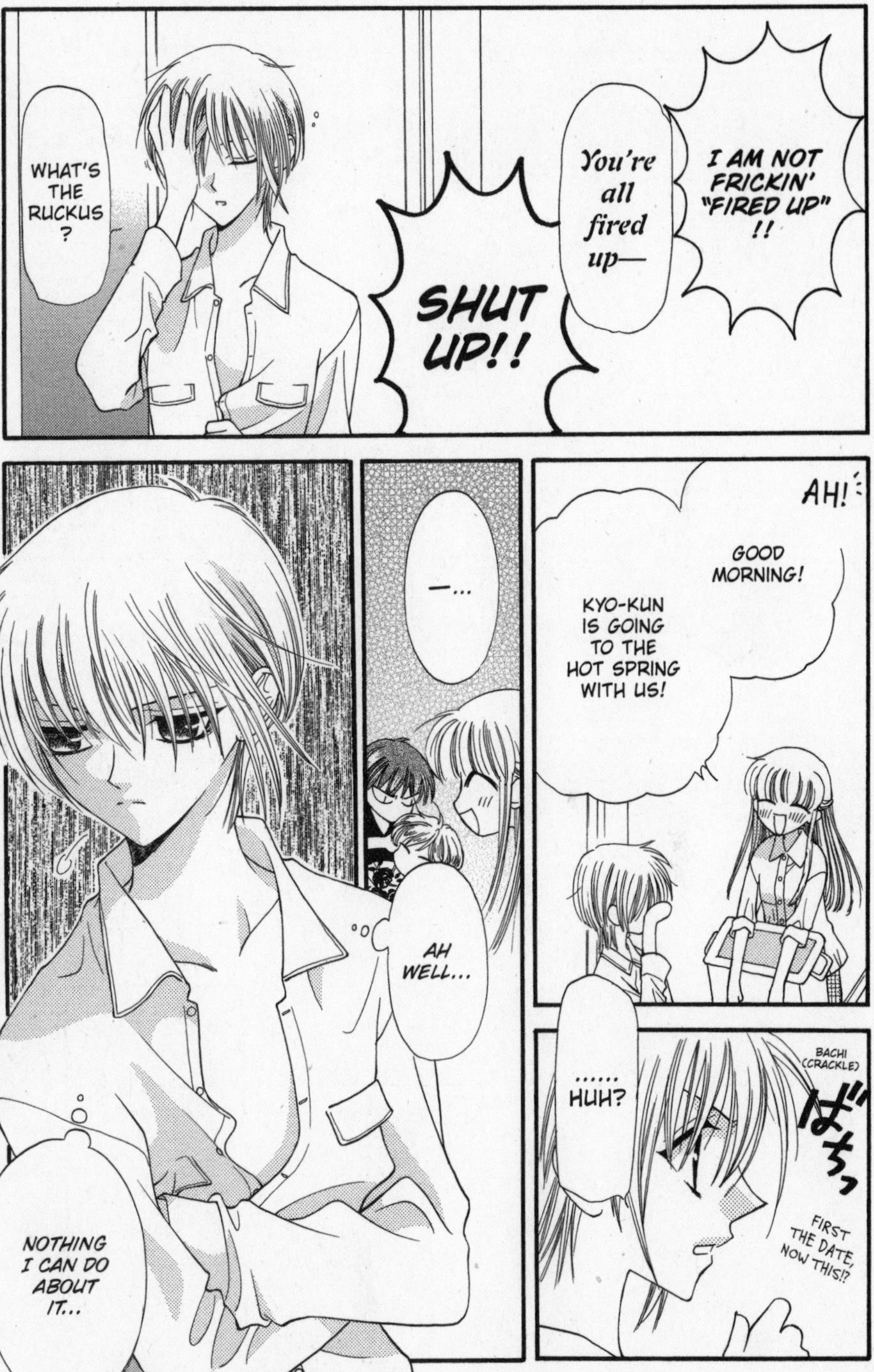

I AM NOT FRICKIN' "FIRED UP" !!
You're all fired up—
SHUT UP!!
WHAT'S THE RUCKUS?
AH!
GOOD MORNING!
KYO-KUN IS GOING TO THE HOT SPRING WITH US!
BACHI (CRACKLE)
ぱちっ
......HUH?
FIRST THE DATE, NOW THIS!?
—...
AH WELL...
NOTHING I CAN DO ABOUT IT...

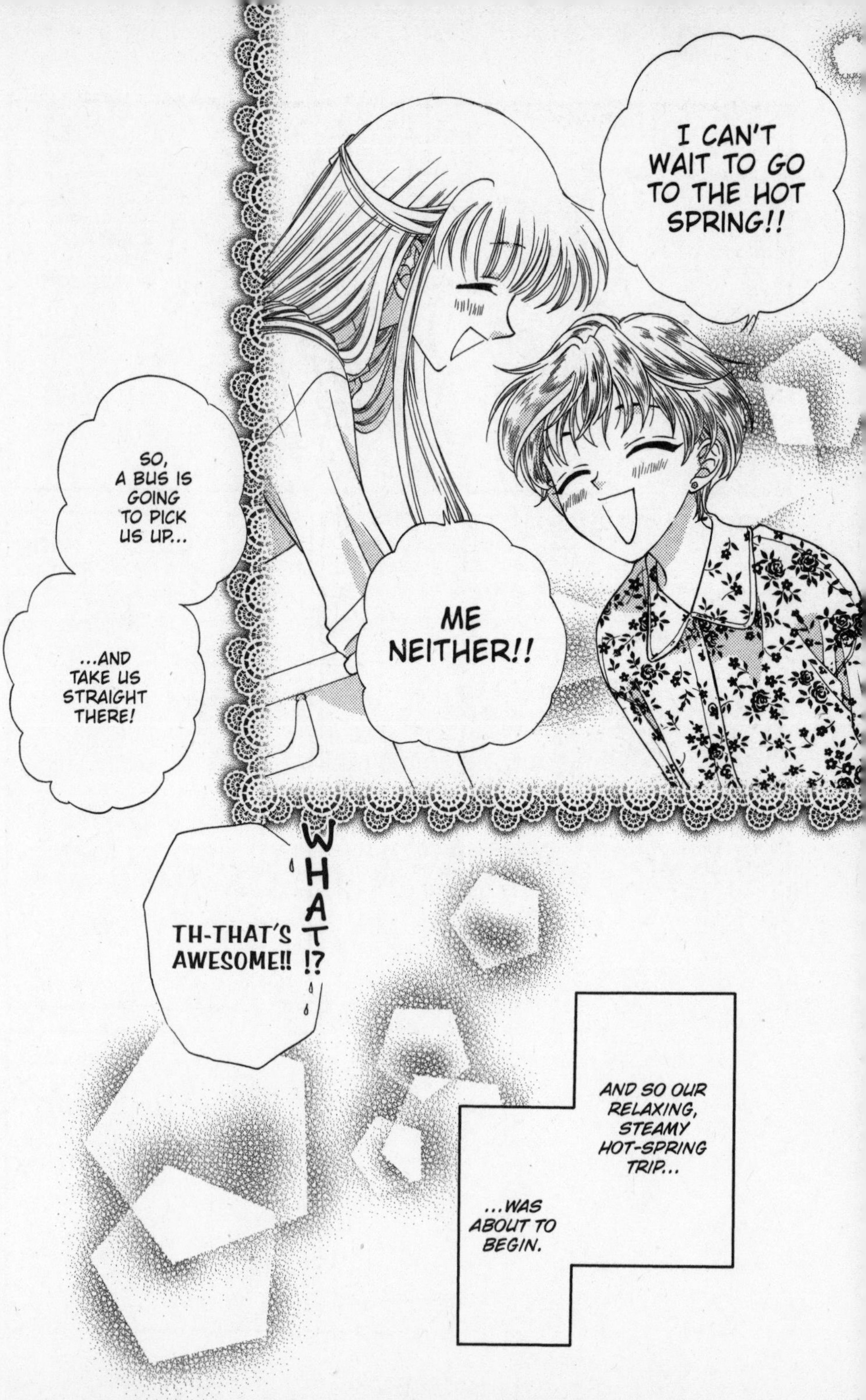
I CAN'T WAIT TO GO TO THE HOT SPRING!!
ME NEITHER!!
SO, A BUS IS GOING TO PICK US UP...
...AND TAKE US STRAIGHT THERE!
WHAT!?
TH-THAT'S AWESOME!!
AND SO OUR RELAXING, STEAMY HOT-SPRING TRIP...
...WAS ABOUT TO BEGIN.

Chapter 18

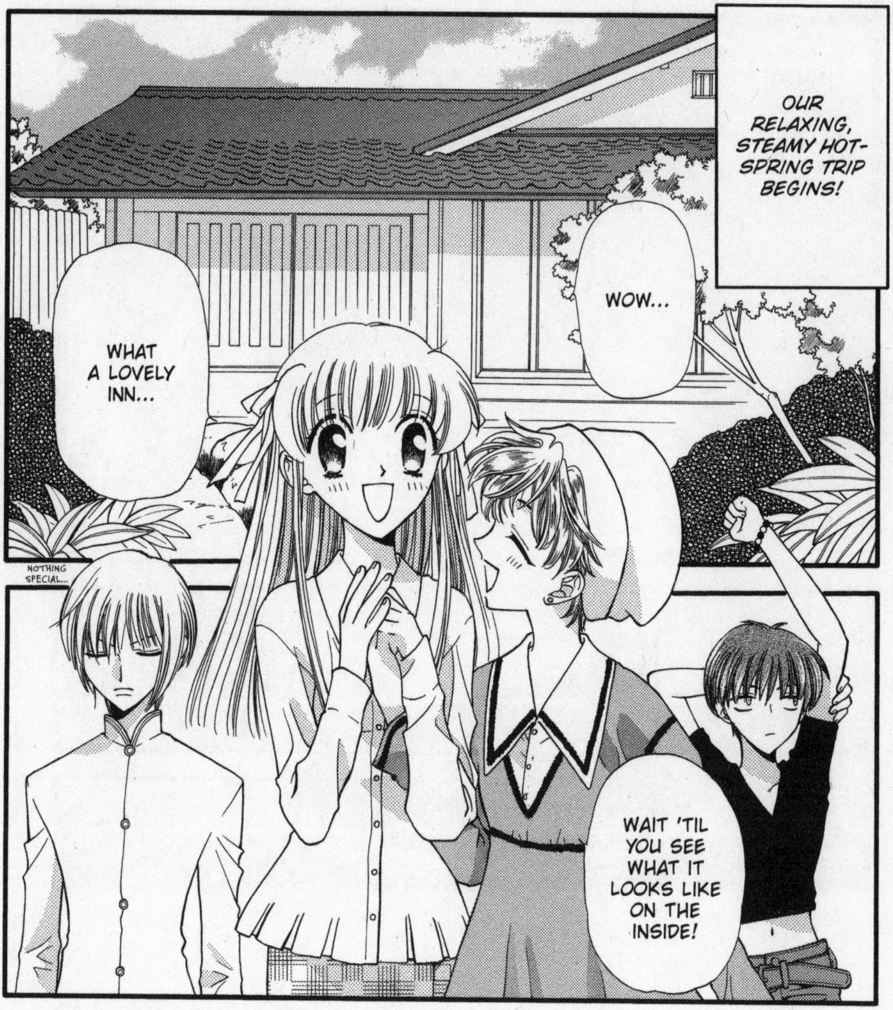
OUR RELAXING, STEAMY HOT-SPRING TRIP BEGINS!
WOW...
WHAT A LOVELY INN...
WAIT 'TIL YOU SEE WHAT IT LOOKS LIKE ON THE INSIDE!
NOTHING SPECIAL...

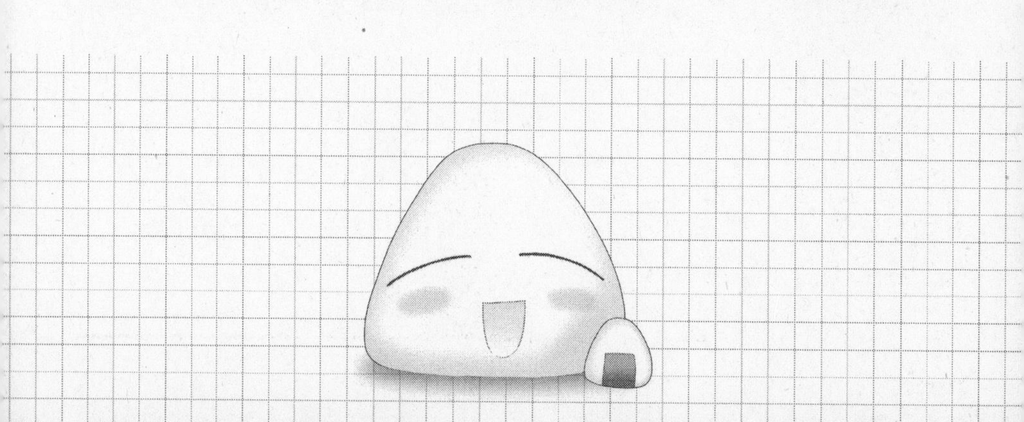

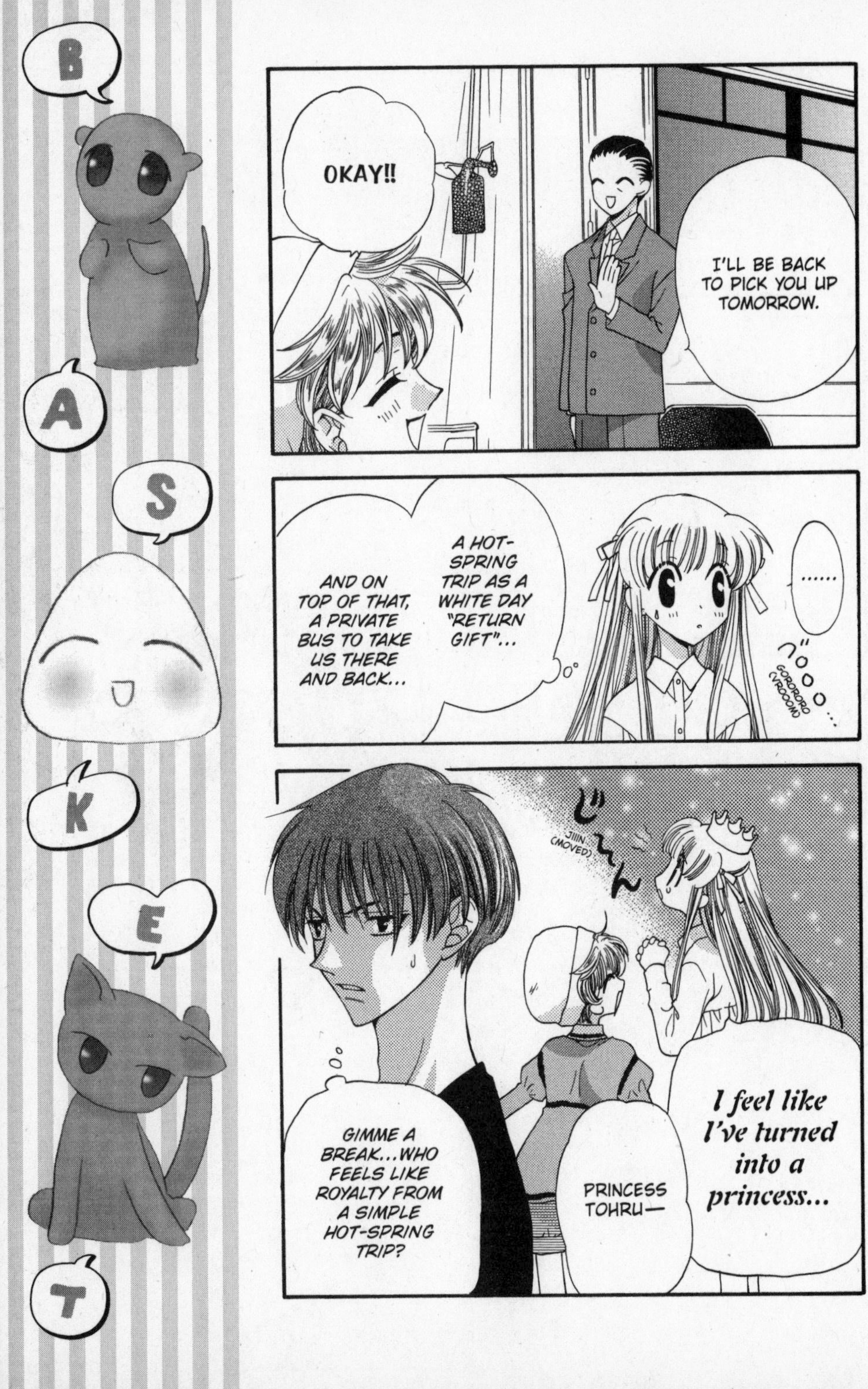
I'LL BE BACK TO PICK YOU UP TOMORROW.
OKAY!!
......
GOROROROO (VROOOM)
A HOT-SPRING TRIP AS A WHITE DAY "RETURN GIFT"...
AND ON TOP OF THAT, A PRIVATE BUS TO TAKE US THERE AND BACK...
JIIIN (MOVED)
I feel like I've turned into a princess...
PRINCESS TOHRU—
GIMME A BREAK...WHO FEELS LIKE ROYALTY FROM A SIMPLE HOT-SPRING TRIP?
B
A
S
K
E
T

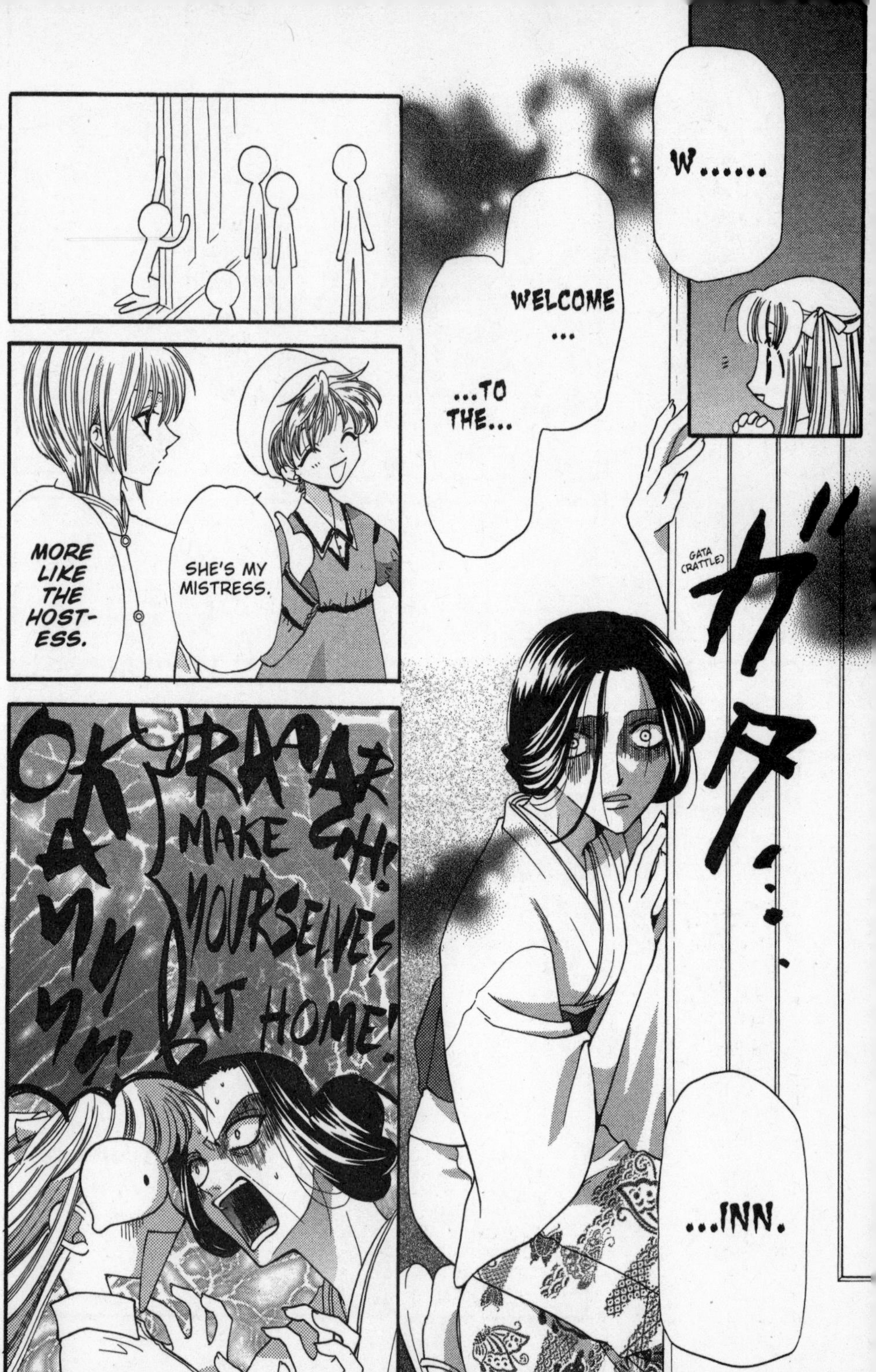
W......
WELCOME ...
...TO THE...
GATA (RATTLE)
...INN.
SHE'S MY MISTRESS.
MORE LIKE THE HOST-ESS.
MAKE YOURSELVES AT HOME!

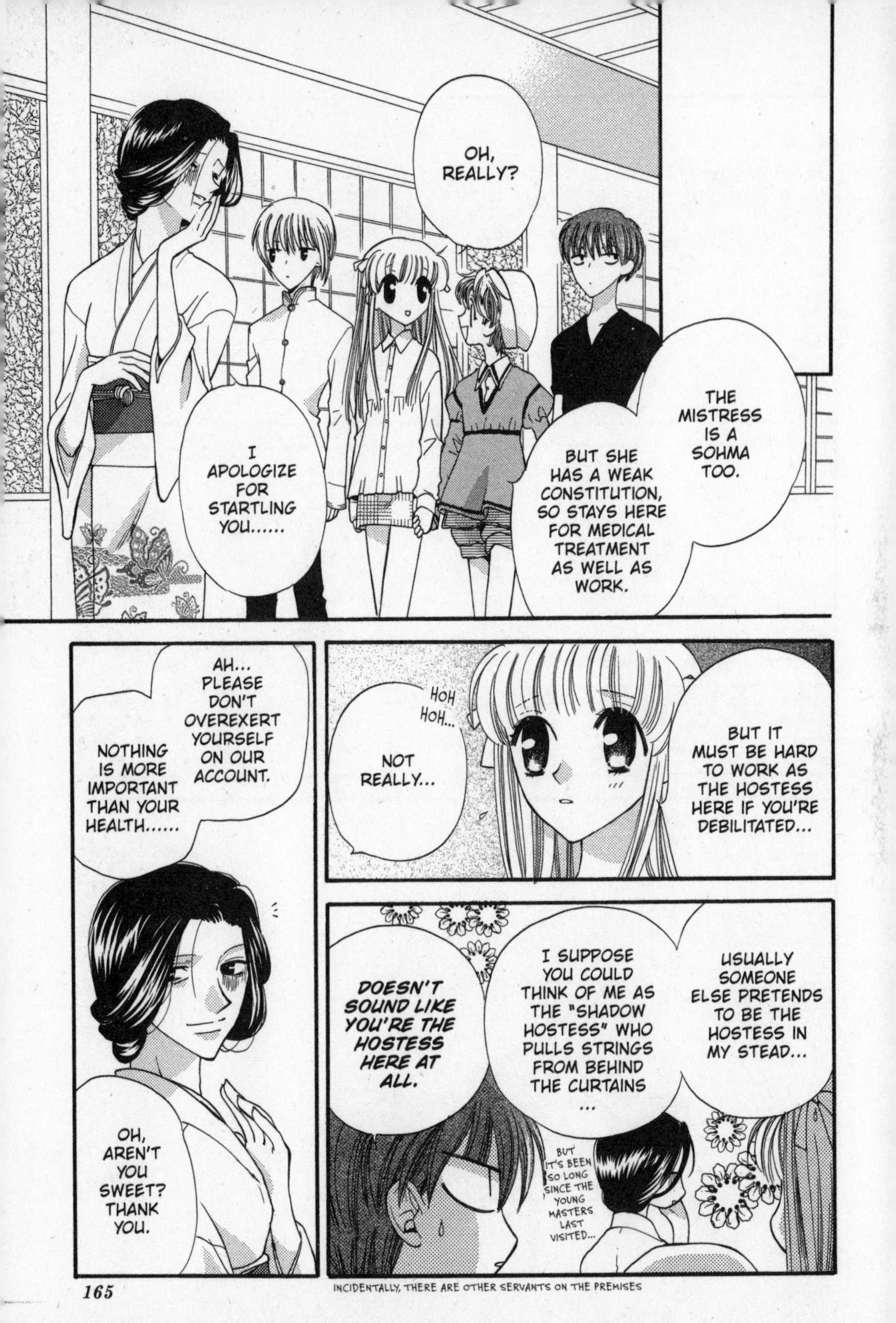
OH, REALLY?
THE MISTRESS IS A SOHMA TOO.
BUT SHE HAS A WEAK CONSTITUTION, SO STAYS HERE FOR MEDICAL TREATMENT AS WELL AS WORK.
I APOLOGIZE FOR STARTLING YOU......
BUT IT MUST BE HARD TO WORK AS THE HOSTESS HERE IF YOU'RE DEBILITATED...
HOH HOH...
NOT REALLY...
USUALLY SOMEONE ELSE PRETENDS TO BE THE HOSTESS IN MY STEAD...
I SUPPOSE YOU COULD THINK OF ME AS THE "SHADOW HOSTESS" WHO PULLS STRINGS FROM BEHIND THE CURTAINS ...
DOESN'T SOUND LIKE YOU'RE THE HOSTESS HERE AT ALL.
BUT IT'S BEEN SO LONG SINCE THE YOUNG MASTERS LAST VISITED...
AH... PLEASE DON'T OVEREXERT YOURSELF ON OUR ACCOUNT.
NOTHING IS MORE IMPORTANT THAN YOUR HEALTH......
OH, AREN'T YOU SWEET? THANK YOU.

INCIDENTALLY, THERE ARE OTHER SERVANTS ON THE PREMISES

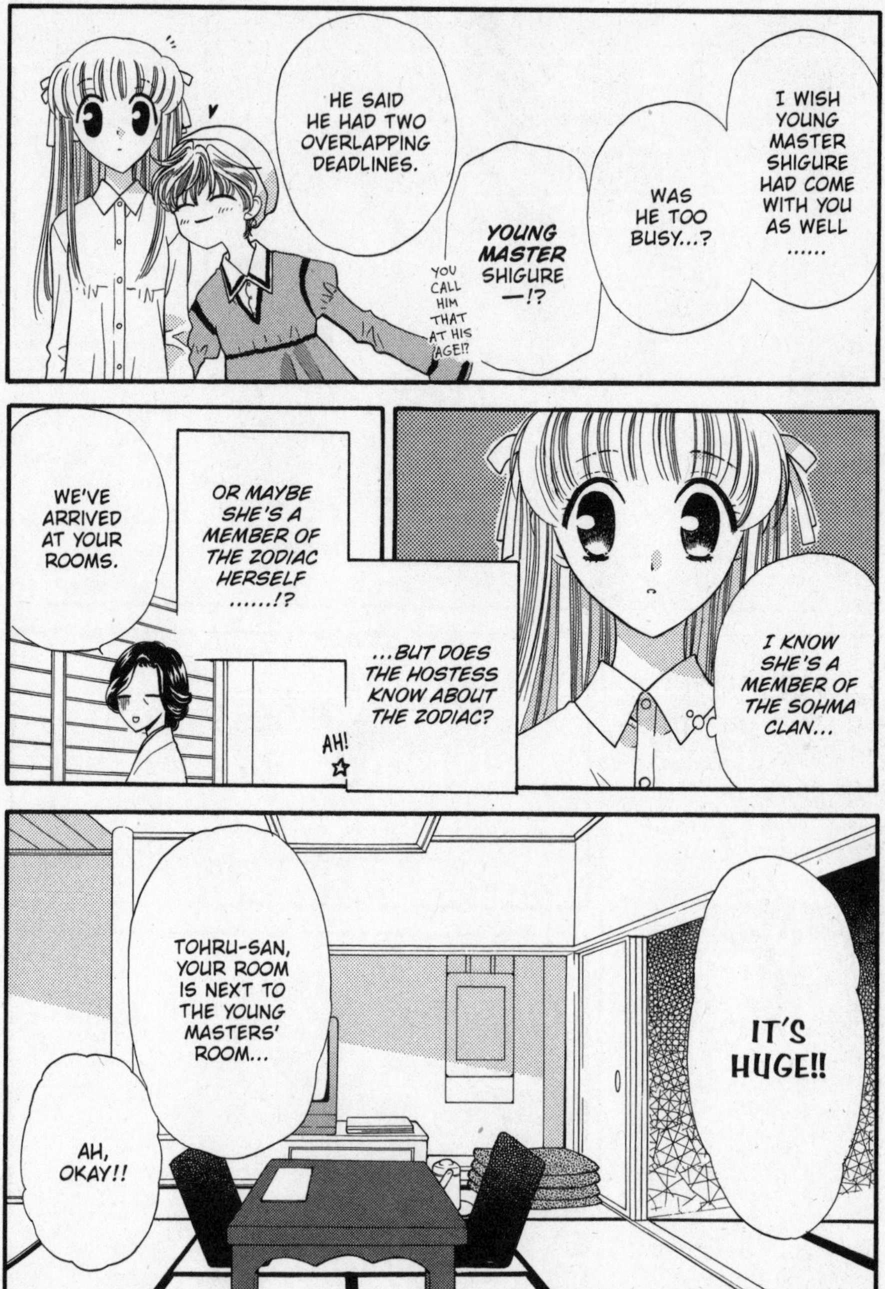
I WISH YOUNG MASTER SHIGURE HAD COME WITH YOU AS WELL ......
WAS HE TOO BUSY...?
YOUNG MASTER SHIGURE—!?
YOU CALL HIM THAT AT HIS AGE!?
HE SAID HE HAD TWO OVERLAPPING DEADLINES.
I KNOW SHE'S A MEMBER OF THE SOHMA CLAN...
...BUT DOES THE HOSTESS KNOW ABOUT THE ZODIAC?
OR MAYBE SHE'S A MEMBER OF THE ZODIAC HERSELF ......!?
AH! ☆
WE'VE ARRIVED AT YOUR ROOMS.
IT'S HUGE!!
TOHRU-SAN, YOUR ROOM IS NEXT TO THE YOUNG MASTERS' ROOM...
AH, OKAY!!

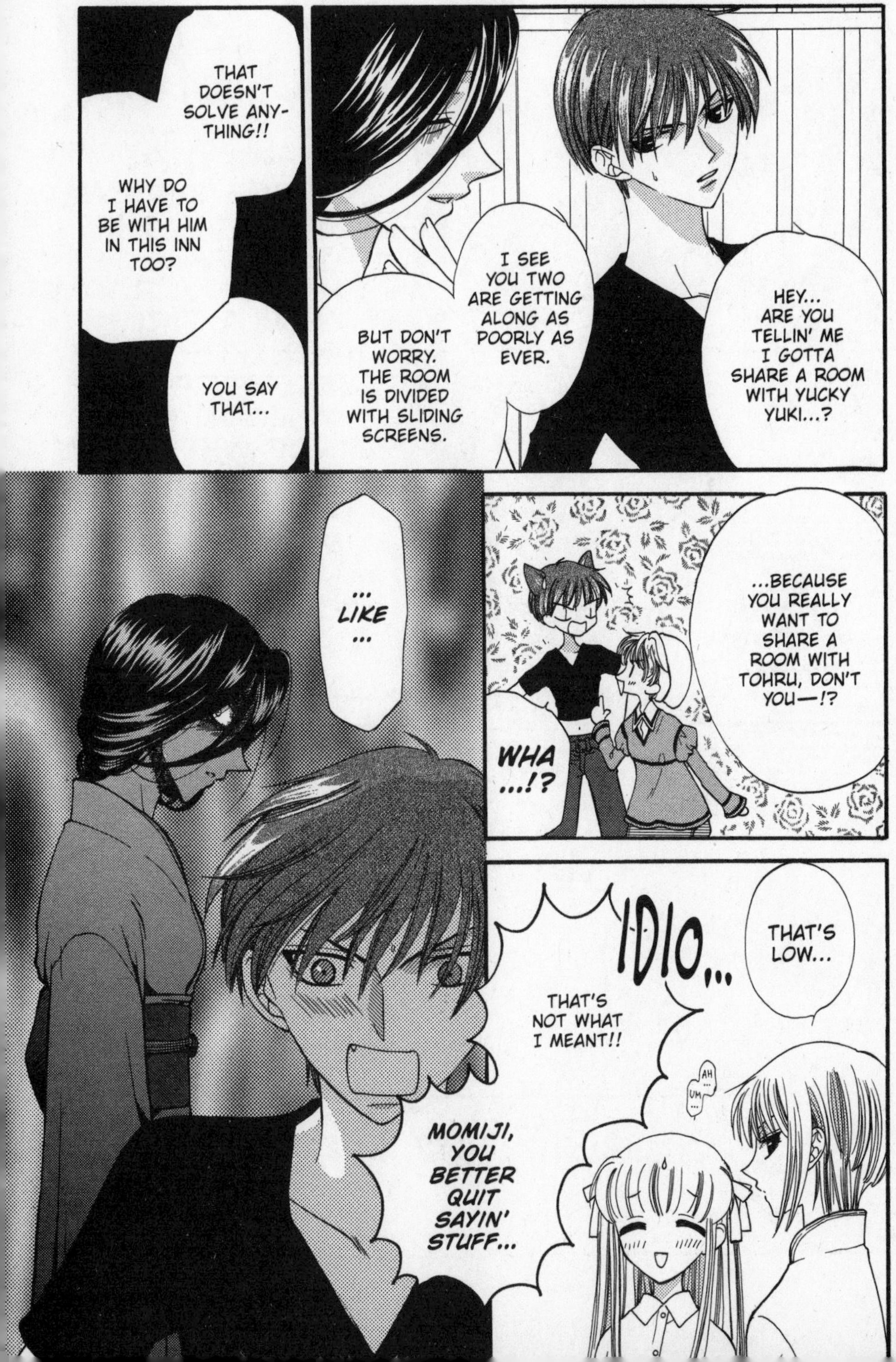
HEY... ARE YOU TELLIN' ME I GOTTA SHARE A ROOM WITH YUCKY YUKI...?
I SEE YOU TWO ARE GETTING ALONG AS POORLY AS EVER.
BUT DON'T WORRY. THE ROOM IS DIVIDED WITH SLIDING SCREENS.
THAT DOESN'T SOLVE ANY-THING!!
WHY DO I HAVE TO BE WITH HIM IN THIS INN TOO?
YOU SAY THAT...
... LIKE ...
...BECAUSE YOU REALLY WANT TO SHARE A ROOM WITH TOHRU, DON'T YOU—!?
WHA ...!?
THAT'S LOW...
AH... UM...
IDIO...
THAT'S NOT WHAT I MEANT!!
MOMIJI, YOU BETTER QUIT SAYIN' STUFF...

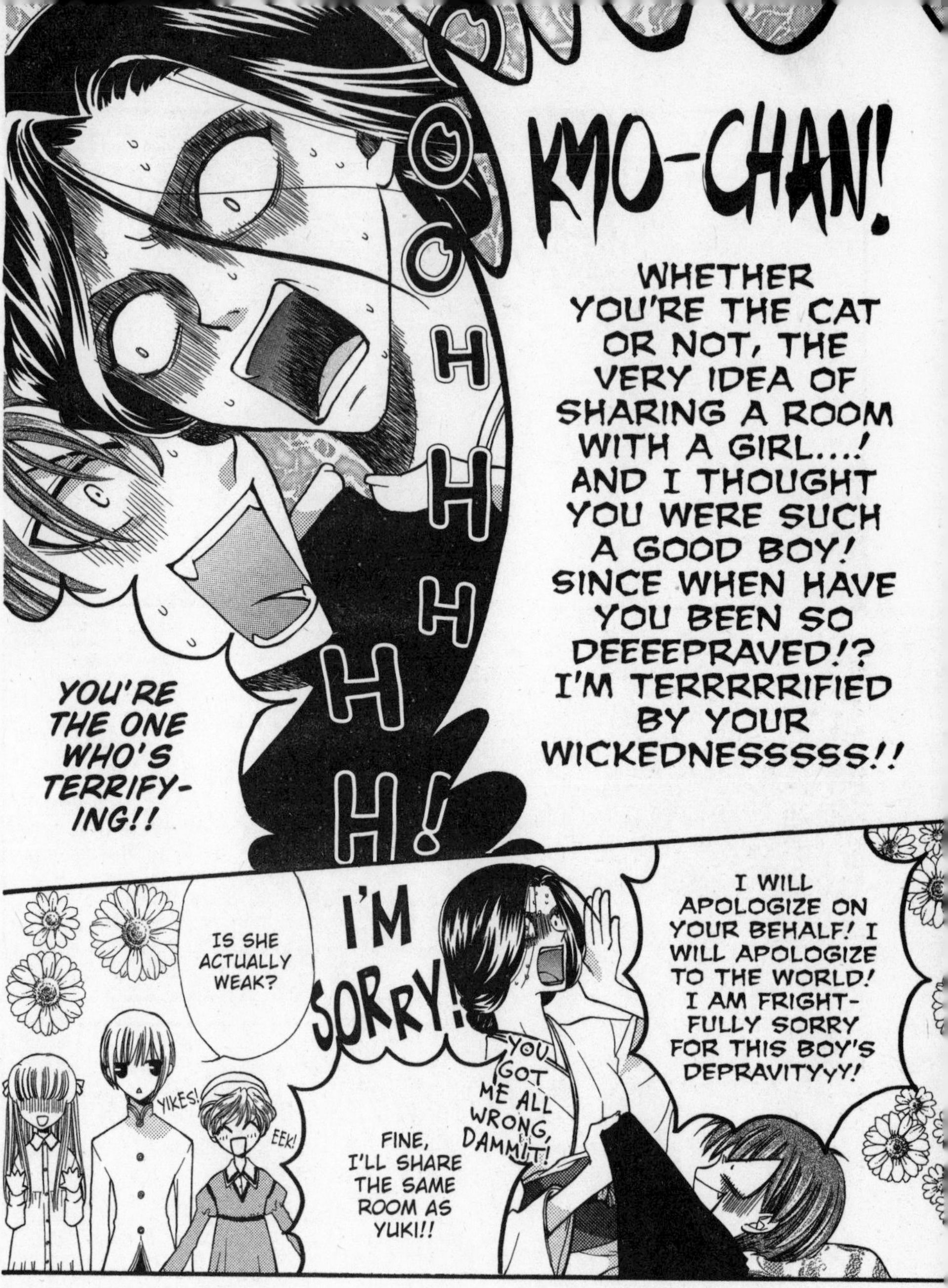
KYO-CHAN!
WHETHER YOU'RE THE CAT OR NOT, THE VERY IDEA OF SHARING A ROOM WITH A GIRL...! AND I THOUGHT YOU WERE SUCH A GOOD BOY! SINCE WHEN HAVE YOU BEEN SO DEEEEPRAVED!? I'M TERRRRRIFIED BY YOUR WICKEDNESSSSS!!
OOHHHHH!
YOU'RE THE ONE WHO'S TERRIFY-ING!!
I WILL APOLOGIZE ON YOUR BEHALF! I WILL APOLOGIZE TO THE WORLD! I AM FRIGHT-FULLY SORRY FOR THIS BOY'S DEPRAVITYyY!
I'M SORRY!
YOU GOT ME ALL WRONG, DAMMIT!
IS SHE ACTUALLY WEAK?
FINE, I'LL SHARE THE SAME ROOM AS YUKI!!
YIKES!
EEK!

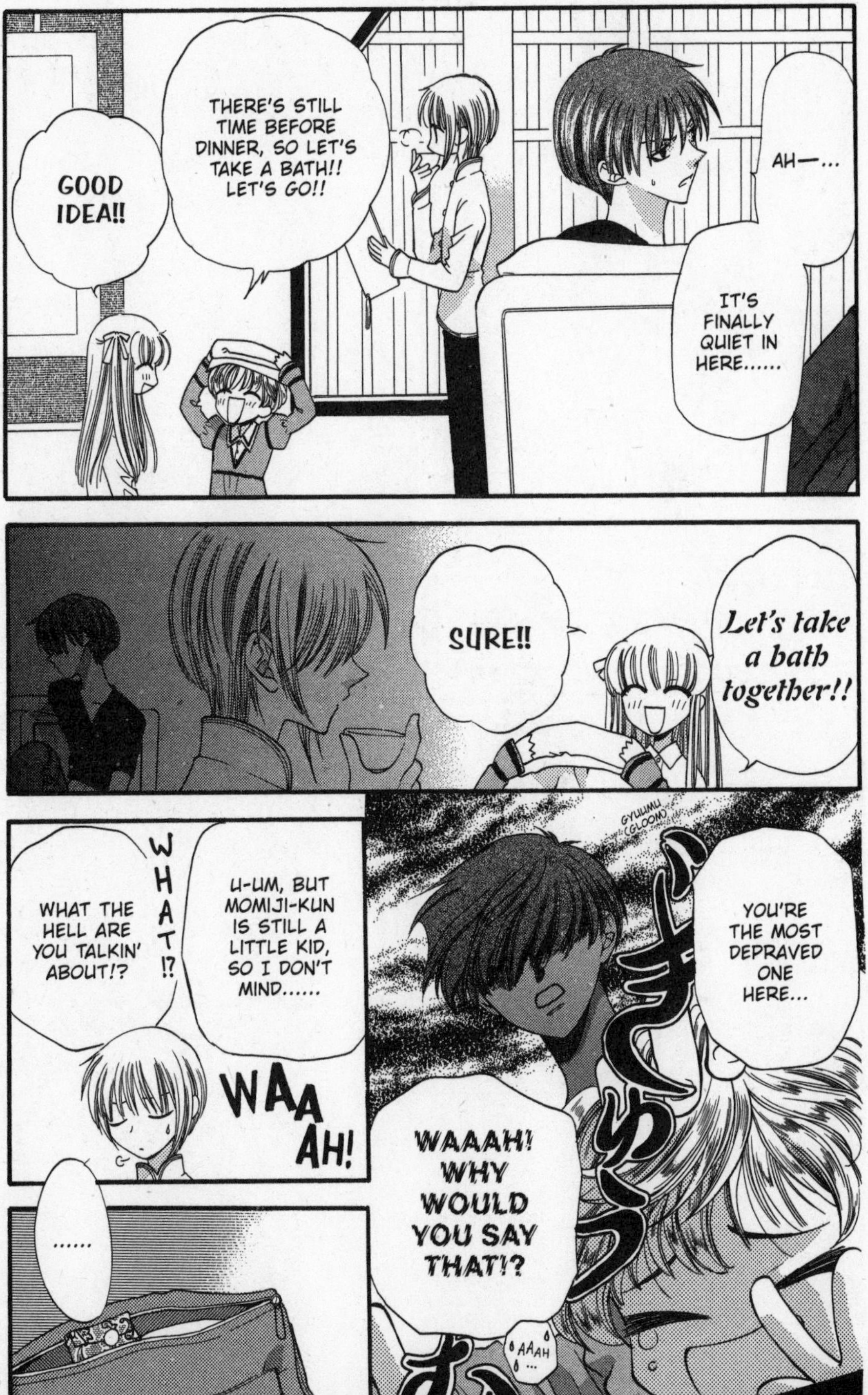
AH—...
IT'S FINALLY QUIET IN HERE......
THERE'S STILL TIME BEFORE DINNER, SO LET'S TAKE A BATH!! LET'S GO!!
GOOD IDEA!!
Let's take a bath together!!
SURE!!
GYUUMU (GLOOM)
YOU'RE THE MOST DEPRAVED ONE HERE...
WAAAH! WHY WOULD YOU SAY THAT!?
AAAH...
U-UM, BUT MOMIJI-KUN IS STILL A LITTLE KID, SO I DON'T MIND......
WHAT!?
WHAT THE HELL ARE YOU TALKIN' ABOUT!?
WAAAH!
......

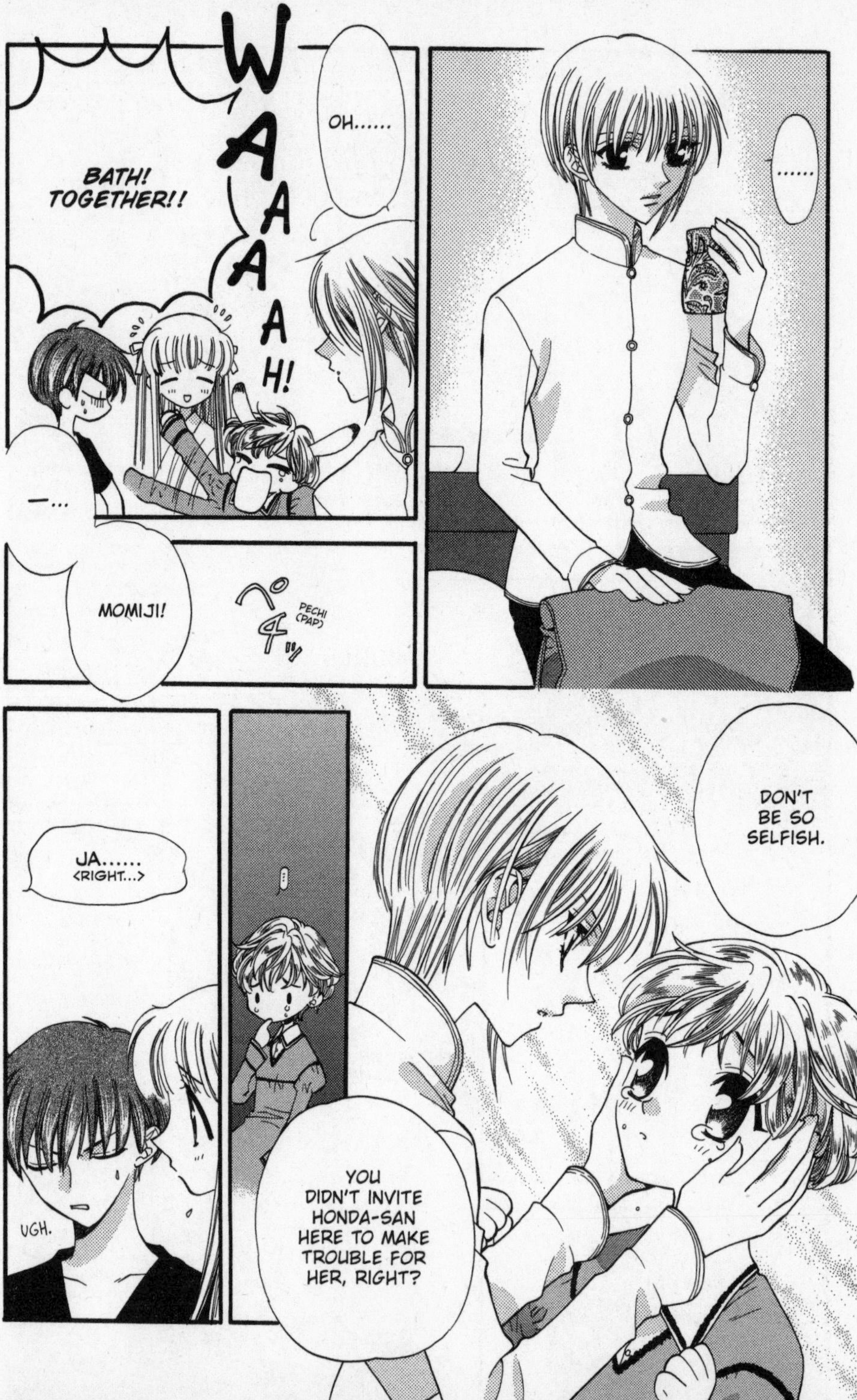
......
OH......
WAAAAH!
BATH! TOGETHER!!
—...
MOMIJI!
ぺち
PECHI (PAP)
DON'T BE SO SELFISH.
YOU DIDN'T INVITE HONDA-SAN HERE TO MAKE TROUBLE FOR HER, RIGHT?
...
JA...... <RIGHT...>
UGH.

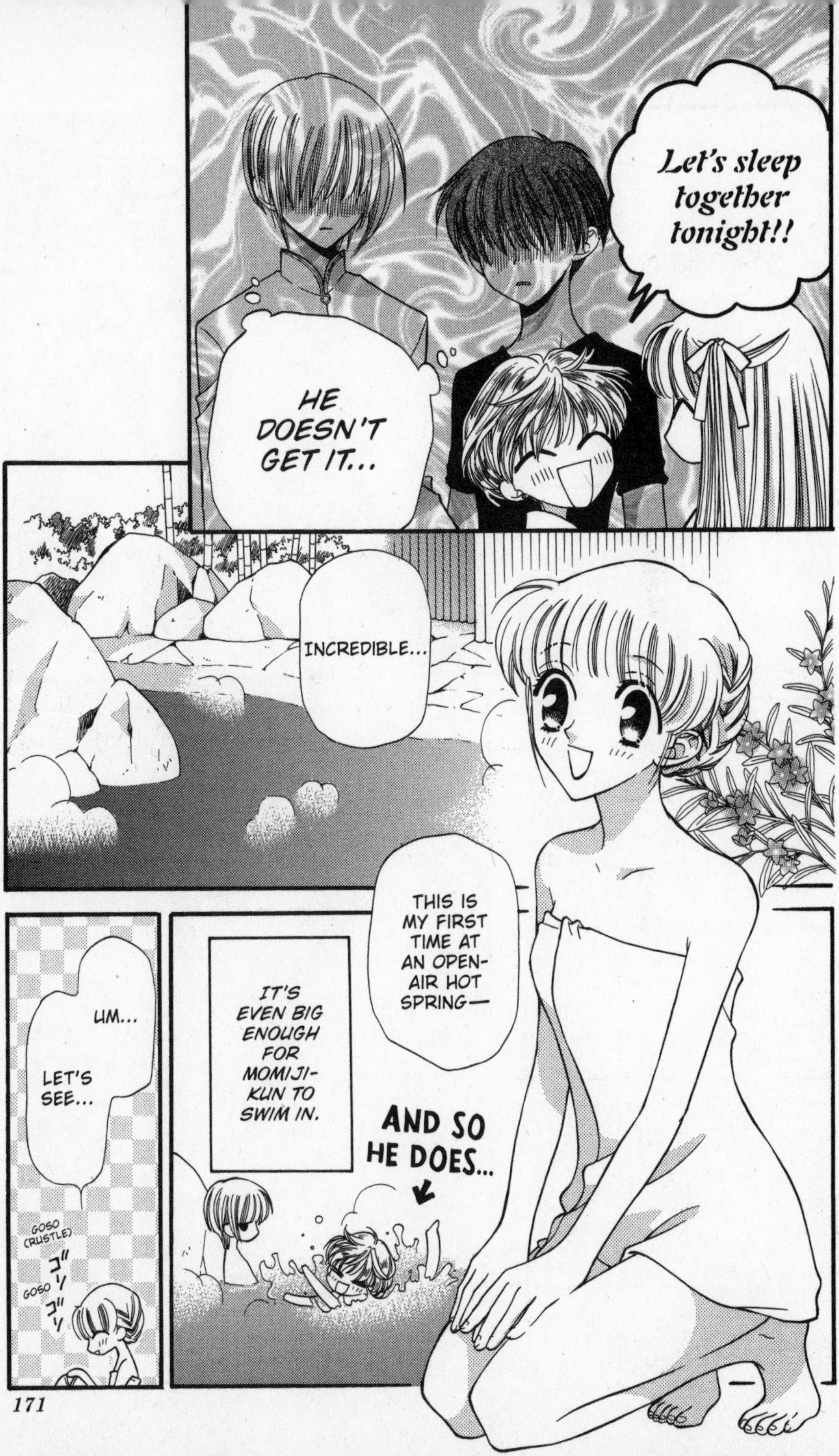
Let's sleep together tonight!!
HE DOESN'T GET IT...
INCREDIBLE...
THIS IS MY FIRST TIME AT AN OPEN-AIR HOT SPRING—
IT'S EVEN BIG ENOUGH FOR MOMIJI-KUN TO SWIM IN.
AND SO HE DOES...
UM...
LET'S SEE...
GOSO (RUSTLE)
ゴソ
GOSO
ゴソ

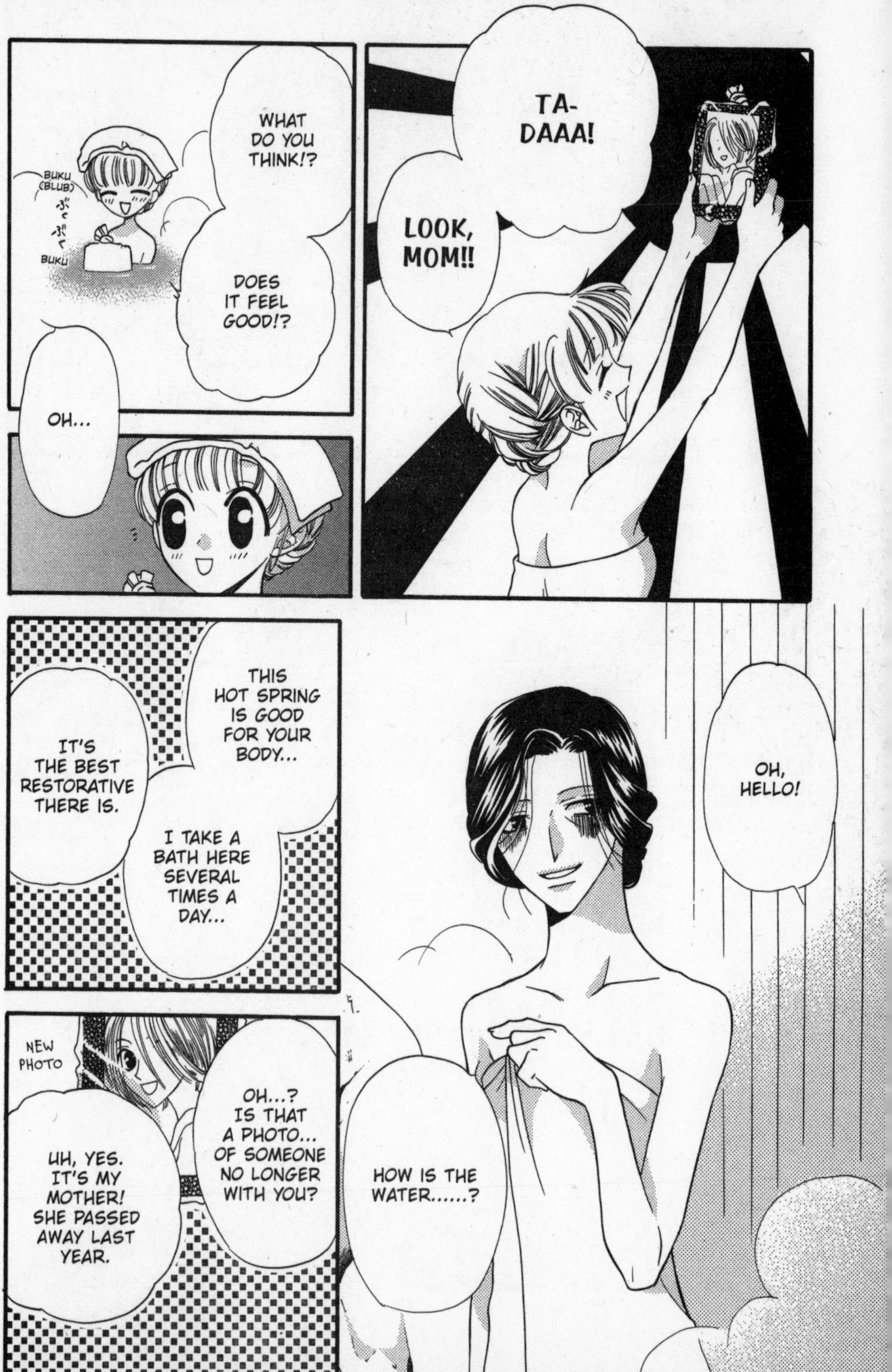
TA-DAAA!
LOOK, MOM!!
BUKU (BLUB)
ぶく
ぶく
BUKU
WHAT DO YOU THINK!?
DOES IT FEEL GOOD!?
OH...
OH, HELLO!
HOW IS THE WATER......?
THIS HOT SPRING IS GOOD FOR YOUR BODY...
IT'S THE BEST RESTORATIVE THERE IS.
I TAKE A BATH HERE SEVERAL TIMES A DAY...
OH...? IS THAT A PHOTO... OF SOMEONE NO LONGER WITH YOU?
NEW PHOTO
UH, YES. IT'S MY MOTHER! SHE PASSED AWAY LAST YEAR.

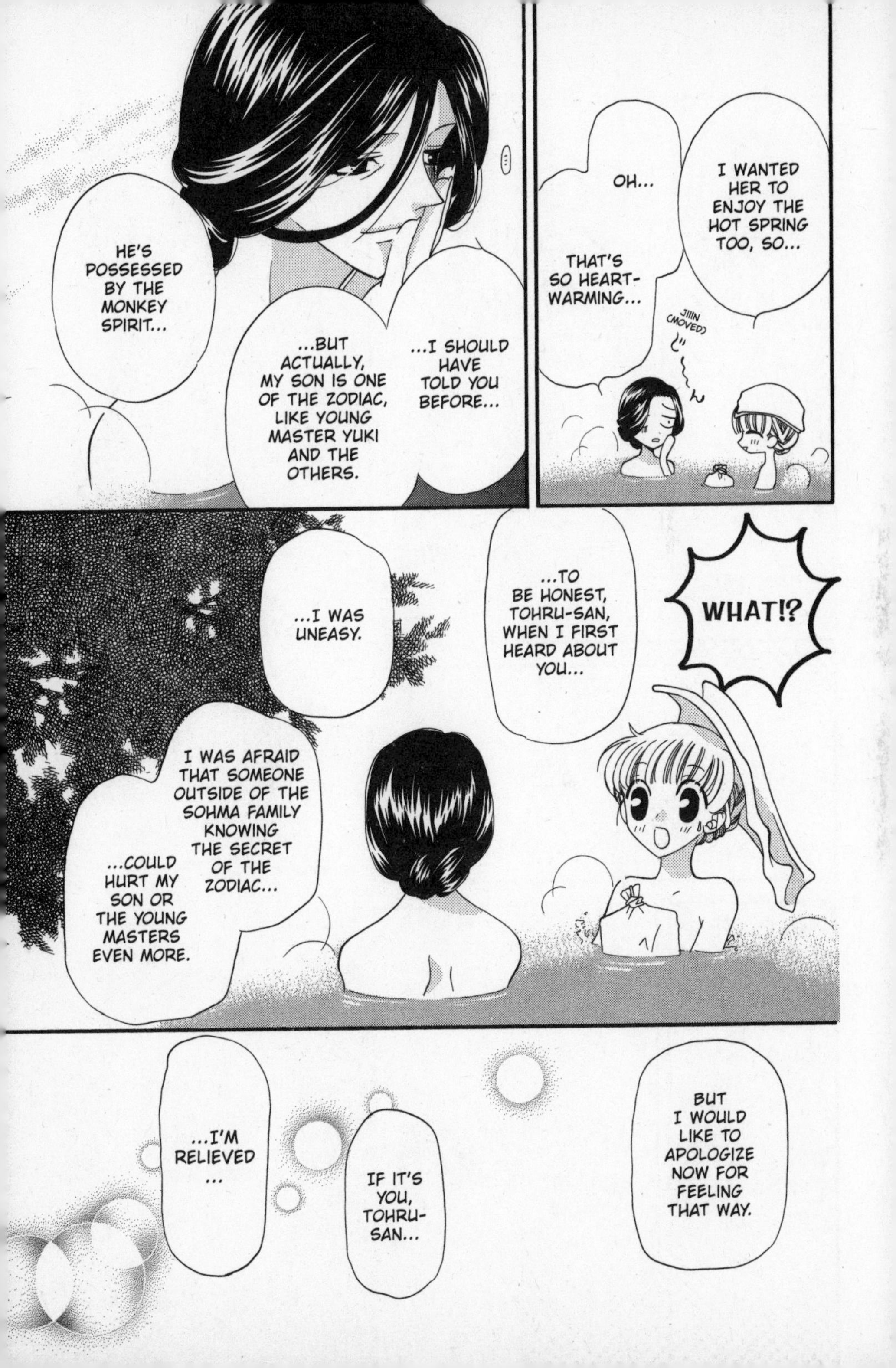
I WANTED HER TO ENJOY THE HOT SPRING TOO, SO...
OH...
THAT'S SO HEART-WARMING...
JIIIN (MOVED)
...
...I SHOULD HAVE TOLD YOU BEFORE...
...BUT ACTUALLY, MY SON IS ONE OF THE ZODIAC, LIKE YOUNG MASTER YUKI AND THE OTHERS.
HE'S POSSESSED BY THE MONKEY SPIRIT...
WHAT!?
...TO BE HONEST, TOHRU-SAN, WHEN I FIRST HEARD ABOUT YOU...
...I WAS UNEASY.
I WAS AFRAID THAT SOMEONE OUTSIDE OF THE SOHMA FAMILY KNOWING THE SECRET OF THE ZODIAC...
...COULD HURT MY SON OR THE YOUNG MASTERS EVEN MORE.
BUT I WOULD LIKE TO APOLOGIZE NOW FOR FEELING THAT WAY.
IF IT'S YOU, TOHRU-SAN...
...I'M RELIEVED...

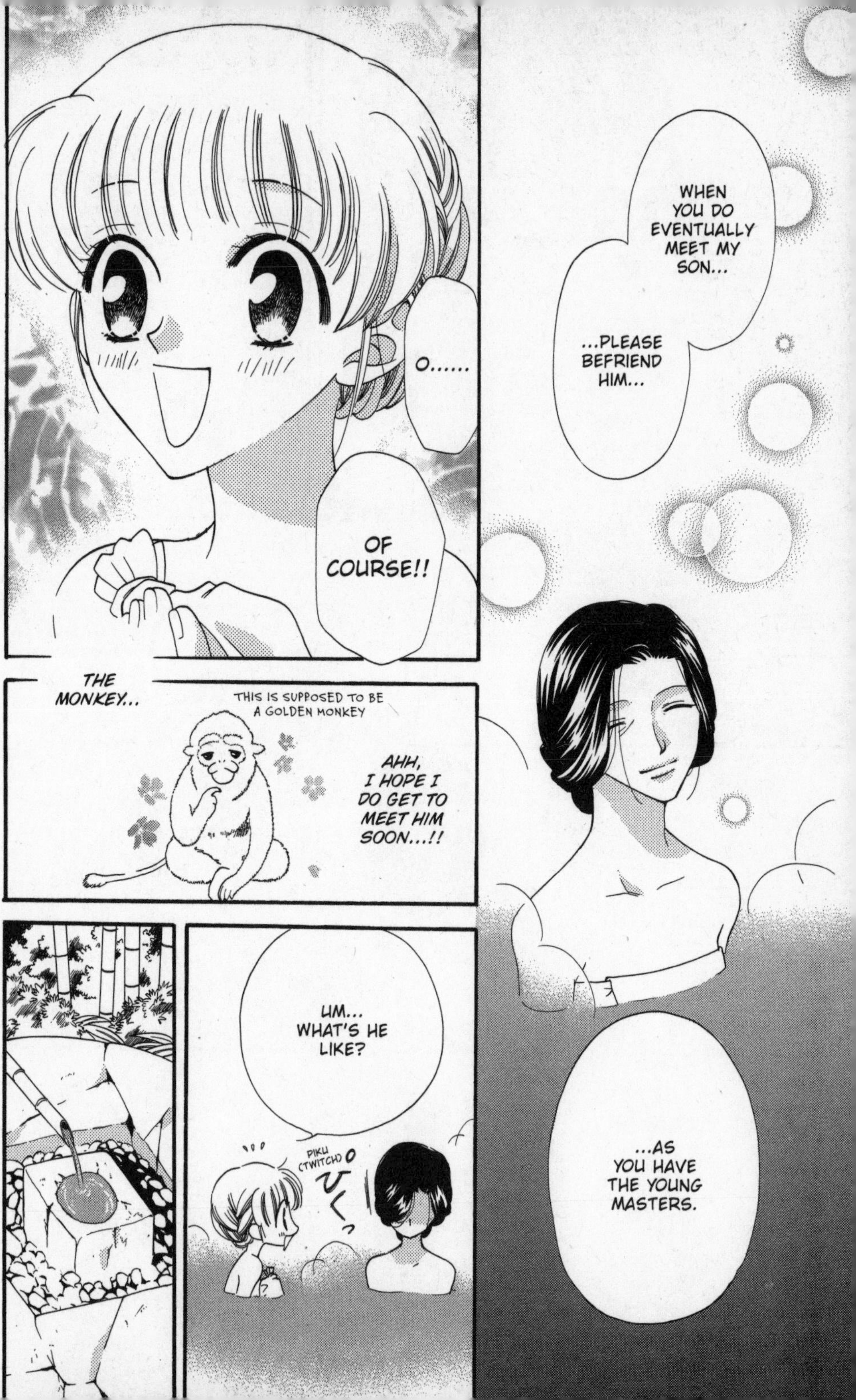
WHEN YOU DO EVENTUALLY MEET MY SON...
...PLEASE BEFRIEND HIM...
...AS YOU HAVE THE YOUNG MASTERS.
O......
OF COURSE!!
THE MONKEY...
THIS IS SUPPOSED TO BE A GOLDEN MONKEY
AHH, I HOPE I DO GET TO MEET HIM SOON...!!
UM... WHAT'S HE LIKE?
PIKU (TWITCH)

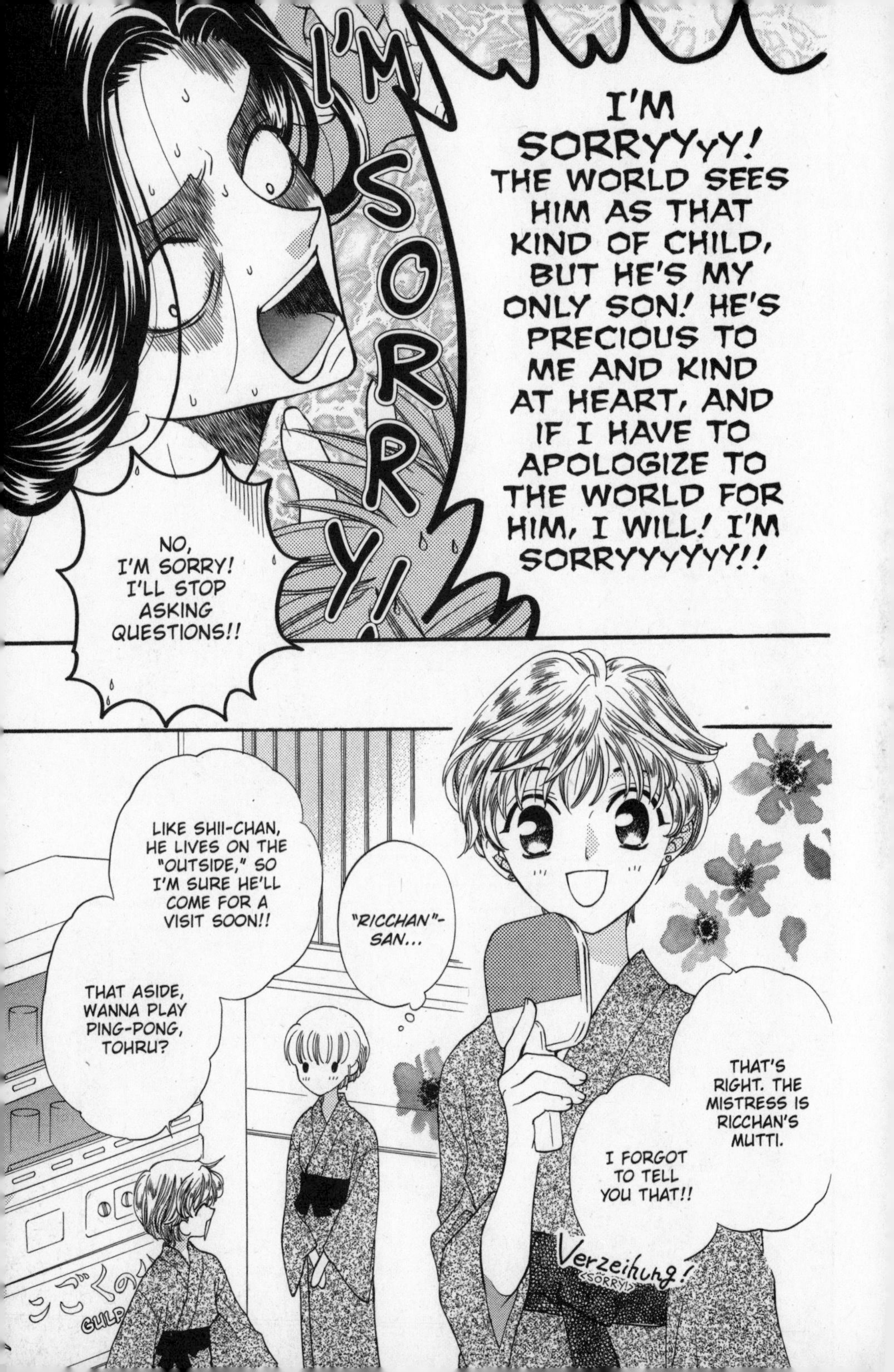
I'M SORRYYyY! THE WORLD SEES HIM AS THAT KIND OF CHILD, BUT HE'S MY ONLY SON! HE'S PRECIOUS TO ME AND KIND AT HEART, AND IF I HAVE TO APOLOGIZE TO THE WORLD FOR HIM, I WILL! I'M SORRYYYYYY!!
I'M SORRY!
NO, I'M SORRY! I'LL STOP ASKING QUESTIONS!!
THAT'S RIGHT. THE MISTRESS IS RICCHAN'S MUTTI.
I FORGOT TO TELL YOU THAT!!
Verzeihung!
<SORRY!>
"RICCHAN"-SAN...
LIKE SHII-CHAN, HE LIVES ON THE "OUTSIDE," SO I'M SURE HE'LL COME FOR A VISIT SOON!!
THAT ASIDE, WANNA PLAY PING-PONG, TOHRU?
GULP

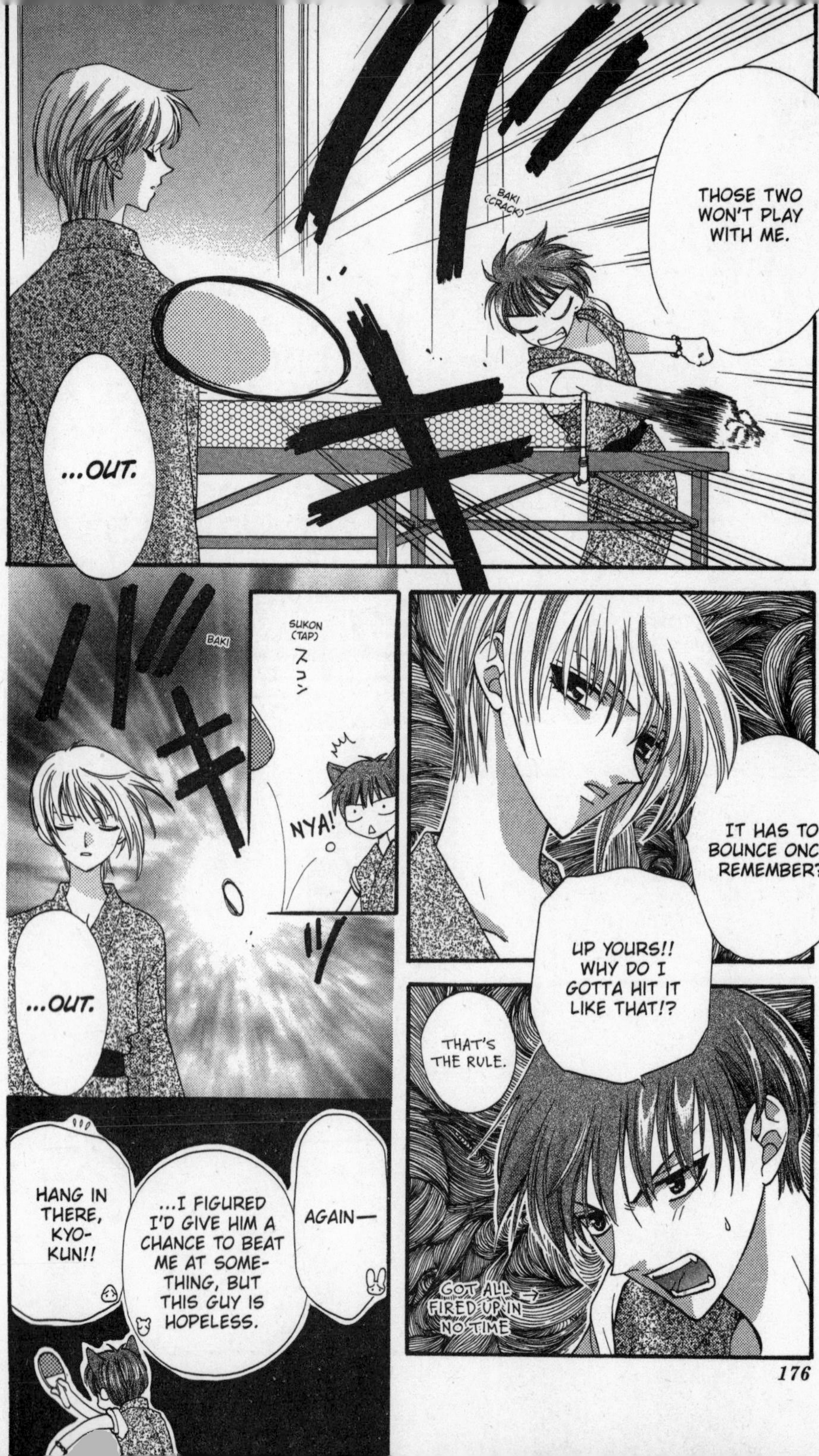

THOSE TWO WON'T PLAY WITH ME.
BAKI (CRACK)
...OUT.
IT HAS TO BOUNCE ONCE, REMEMBER?
SUKON (TAP)
NYA!
BAKI
...OUT.
UP YOURS!! WHY DO I GOTTA HIT IT LIKE THAT!?
THAT'S THE RULE.
GOT ALL FIRED UP IN NO TIME →
AGAIN—
...I FIGURED I'D GIVE HIM A CHANCE TO BEAT ME AT SOME-THING, BUT THIS GUY IS HOPELESS.
HANG IN THERE, KYO-KUN!!

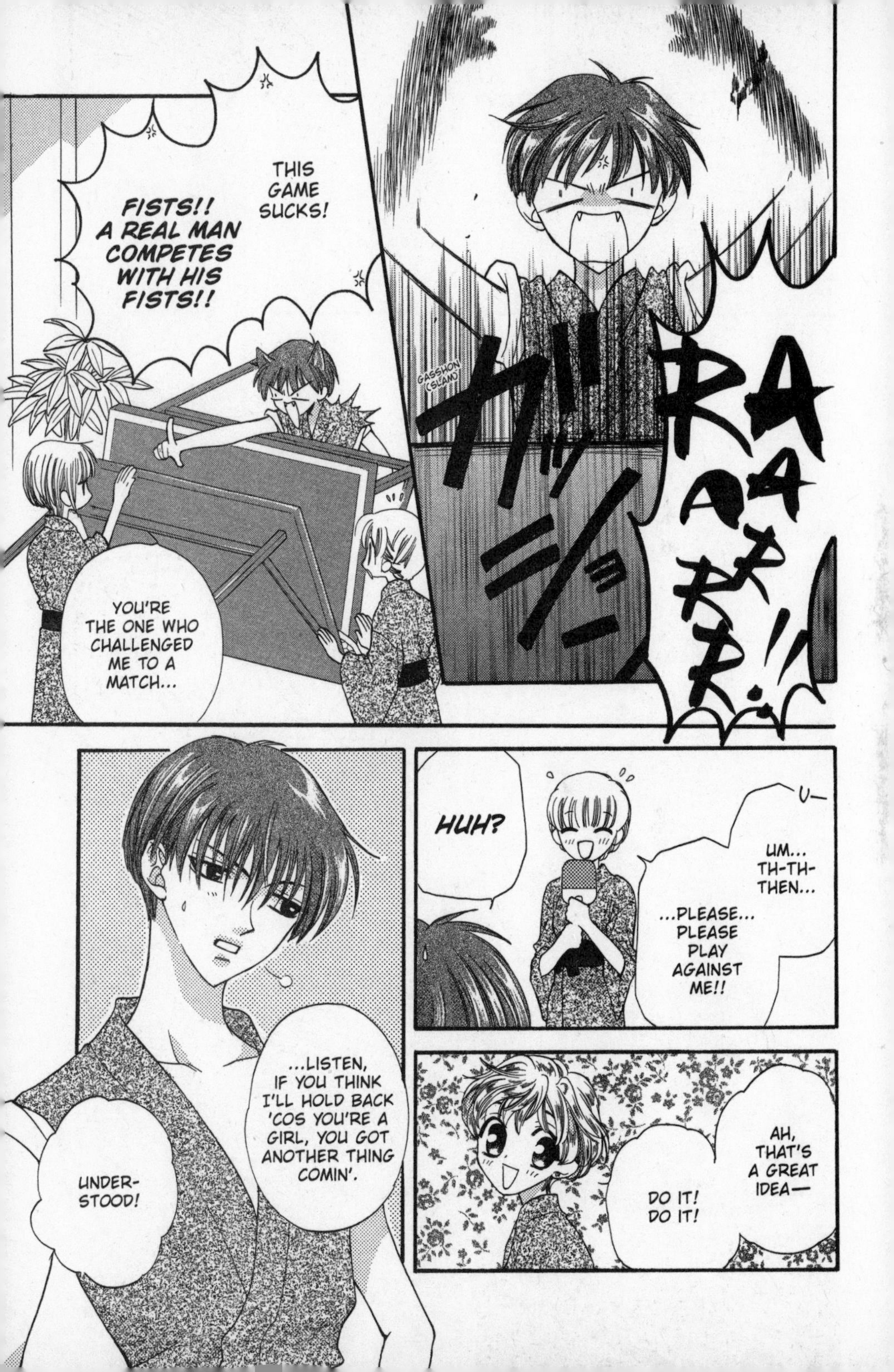
RAAARRR!!
ガッション
GASSHON (SLAM)
THIS GAME SUCKS!
FISTS!! A REAL MAN COMPETES WITH HIS FISTS!!
YOU'RE THE ONE WHO CHALLENGED ME TO A MATCH...
U—
UM... TH-TH-THEN...
...PLEASE... PLEASE PLAY AGAINST ME!!
HUH?
AH, THAT'S A GREAT IDEA—
DO IT! DO IT!
...LISTEN, IF YOU THINK I'LL HOLD BACK 'COS YOU'RE A GIRL, YOU GOT ANOTHER THING COMIN'.
UNDER-STOOD!

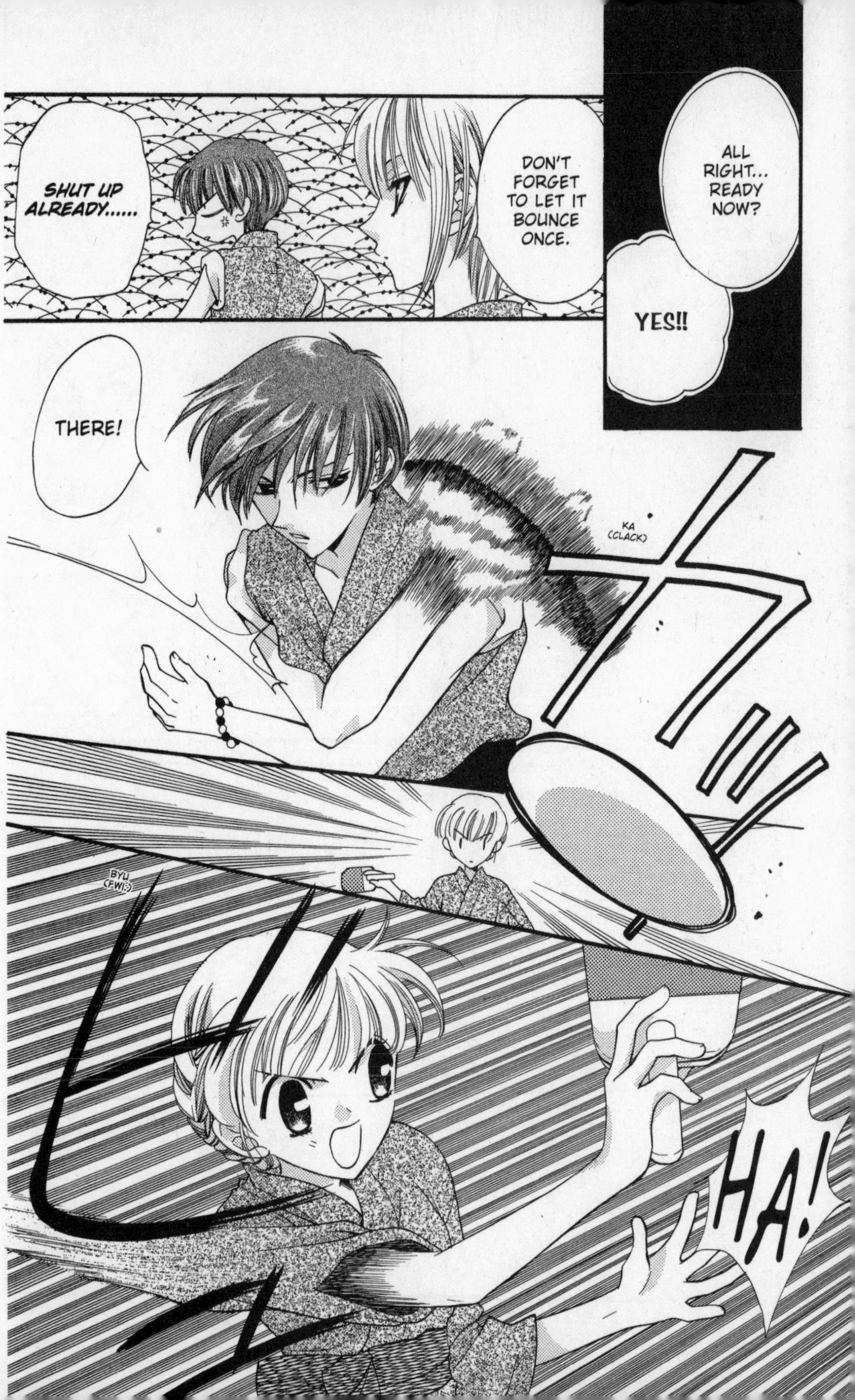
ALL RIGHT... READY NOW?
YES!!
DON'T FORGET TO LET IT BOUNCE ONCE.
SHUT UP ALREADY......
THERE!
KA (CLACK)
BYU (FWI:)
HA!

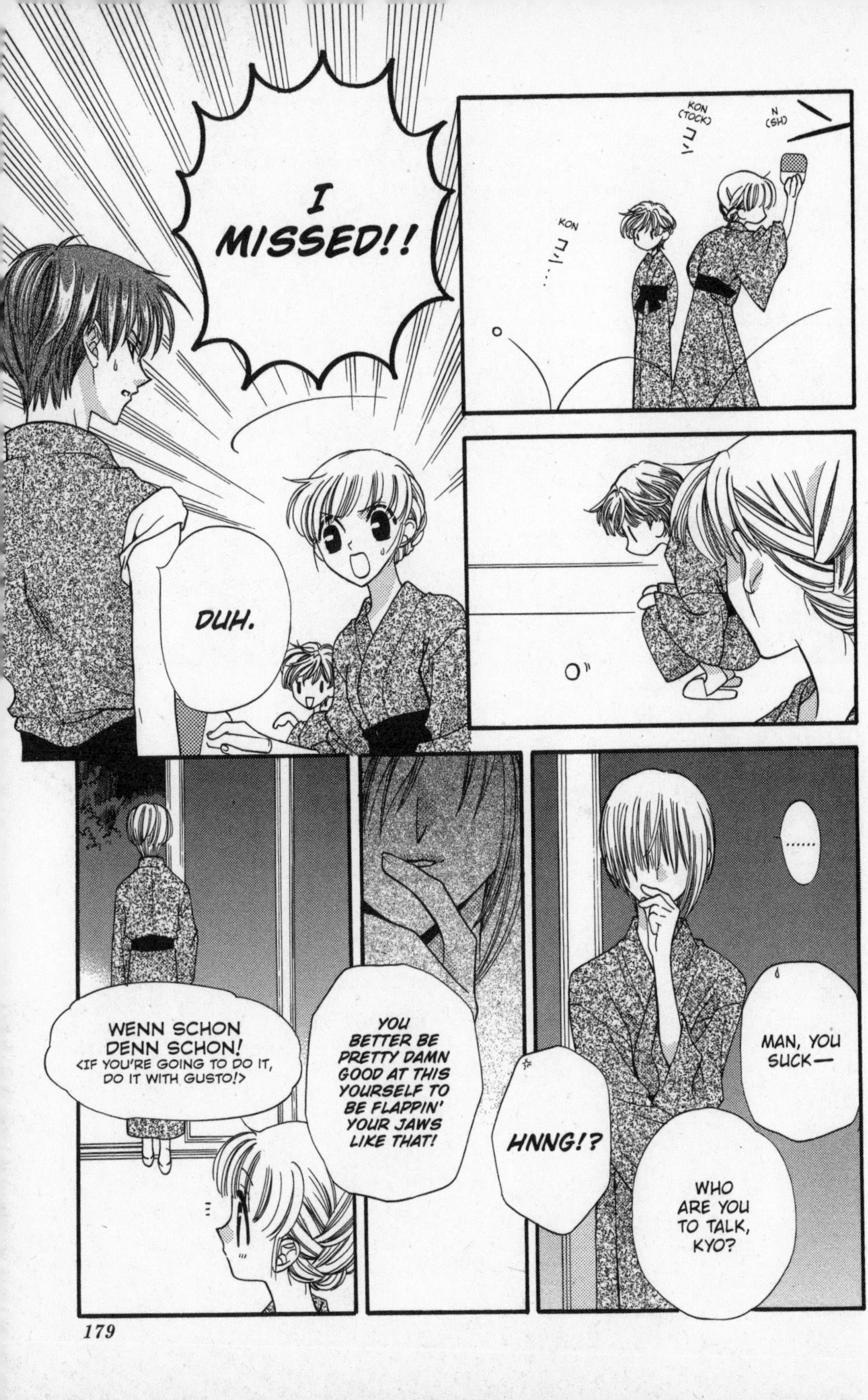
KON (TOCK)
N (SH)
KON
I MISSED!!
DUH.
......
MAN, YOU SUCK—
WHO ARE YOU TO TALK, KYO?
HNNG!?
YOU BETTER BE PRETTY DAMN GOOD AT THIS YOURSELF TO BE FLAPPIN' YOUR JAWS LIKE THAT!
WENN SCHON DENN SCHON! <IF YOU'RE GOING TO DO IT, DO IT WITH GUSTO!>

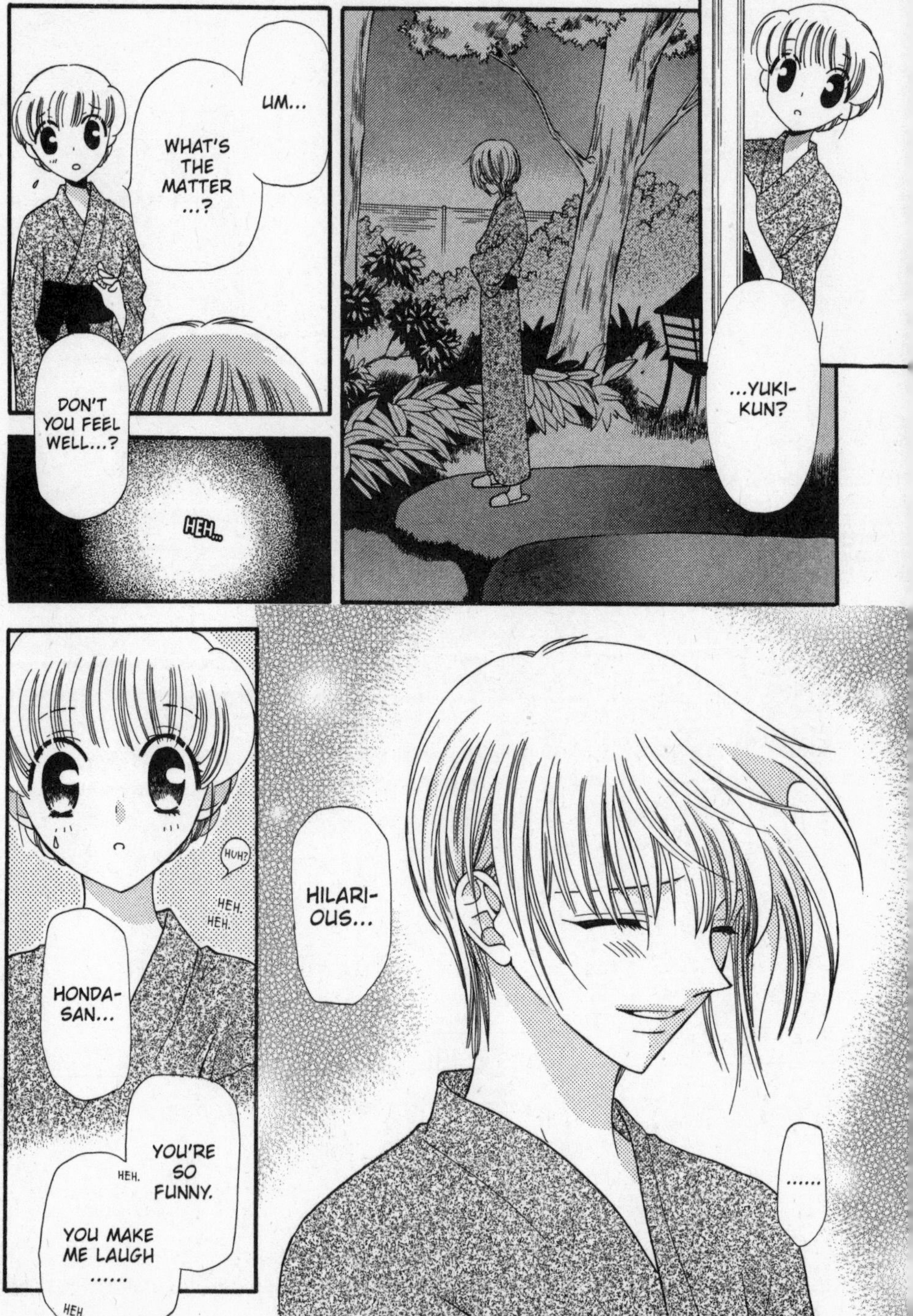
...YUKI-KUN?
UM...
WHAT'S THE MATTER ...?
DON'T YOU FEEL WELL...?
HEH...
HILARI-OUS...
......
HUH?
HEH. HEH.
HONDA-SAN...
YOU'RE SO FUNNY.
HEH.
YOU MAKE ME LAUGH ......
HEH.
HEH.

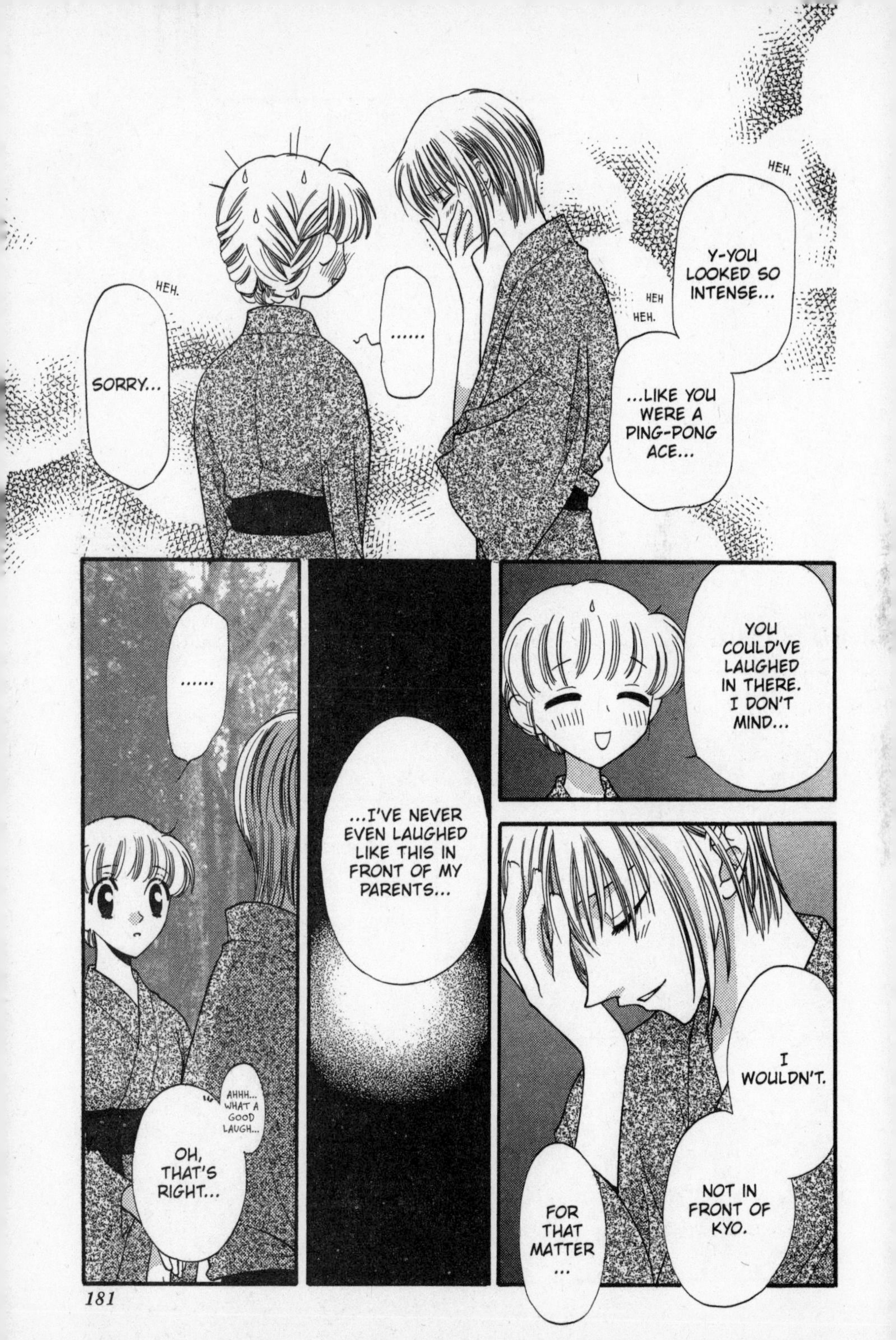
HEH.
Y-YOU LOOKED SO INTENSE...
HEH HEH.
...LIKE YOU WERE A PING-PONG ACE...
......
HEH.
SORRY...
YOU COULD'VE LAUGHED IN THERE. I DON'T MIND...
I WOULDN'T.
NOT IN FRONT OF KYO.
FOR THAT MATTER...
...I'VE NEVER EVEN LAUGHED LIKE THIS IN FRONT OF MY PARENTS...
......
AHHH... WHAT A GOOD LAUGH...
OH, THAT'S RIGHT...

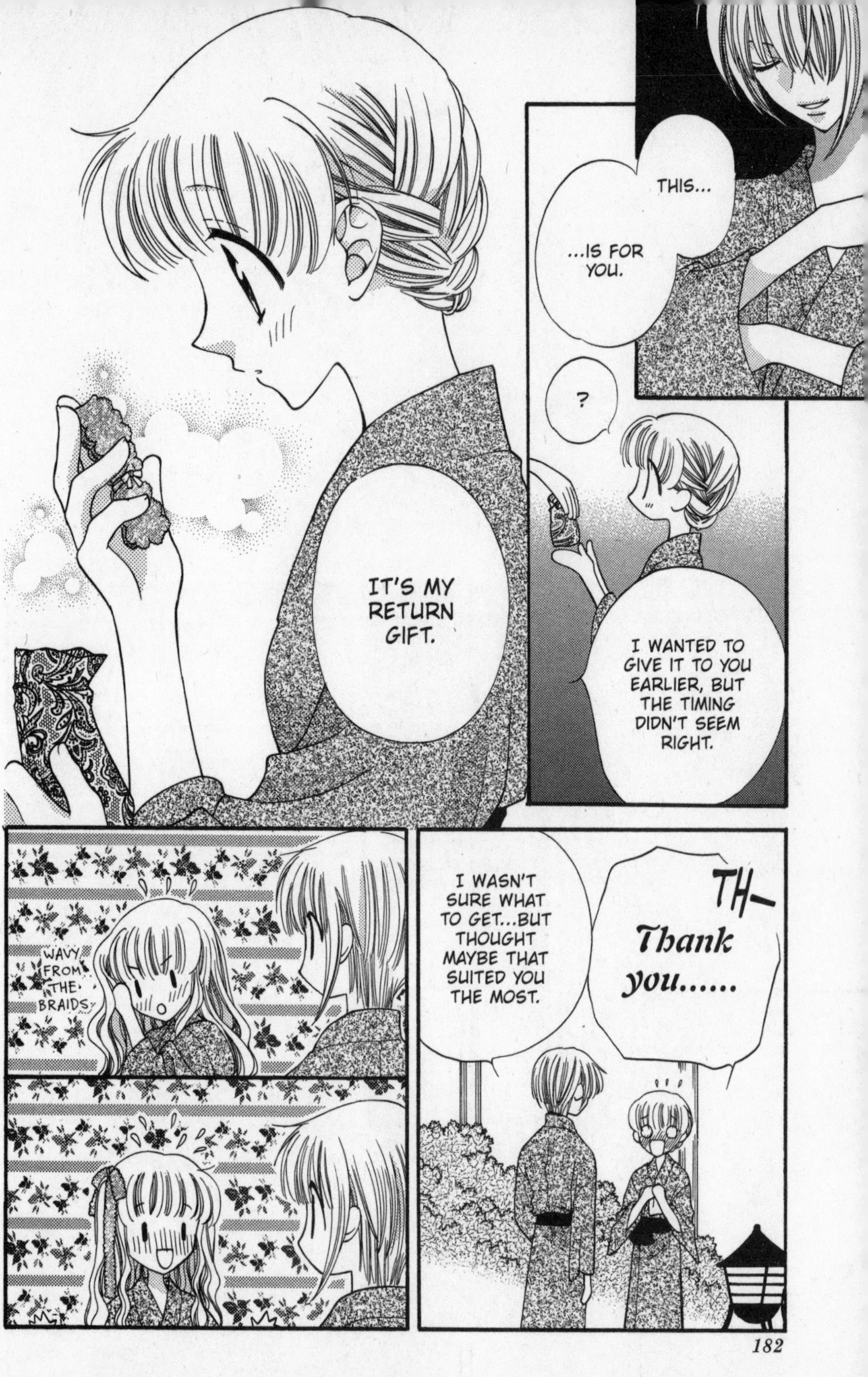
THIS...
...IS FOR YOU.
?
I WANTED TO GIVE IT TO YOU EARLIER, BUT THE TIMING DIDN'T SEEM RIGHT.
IT'S MY RETURN GIFT.
I WASN'T SURE WHAT TO GET...BUT THOUGHT MAYBE THAT SUITED YOU THE MOST.
TH-
Thank you......
WAVY FROM THE BRAIDS

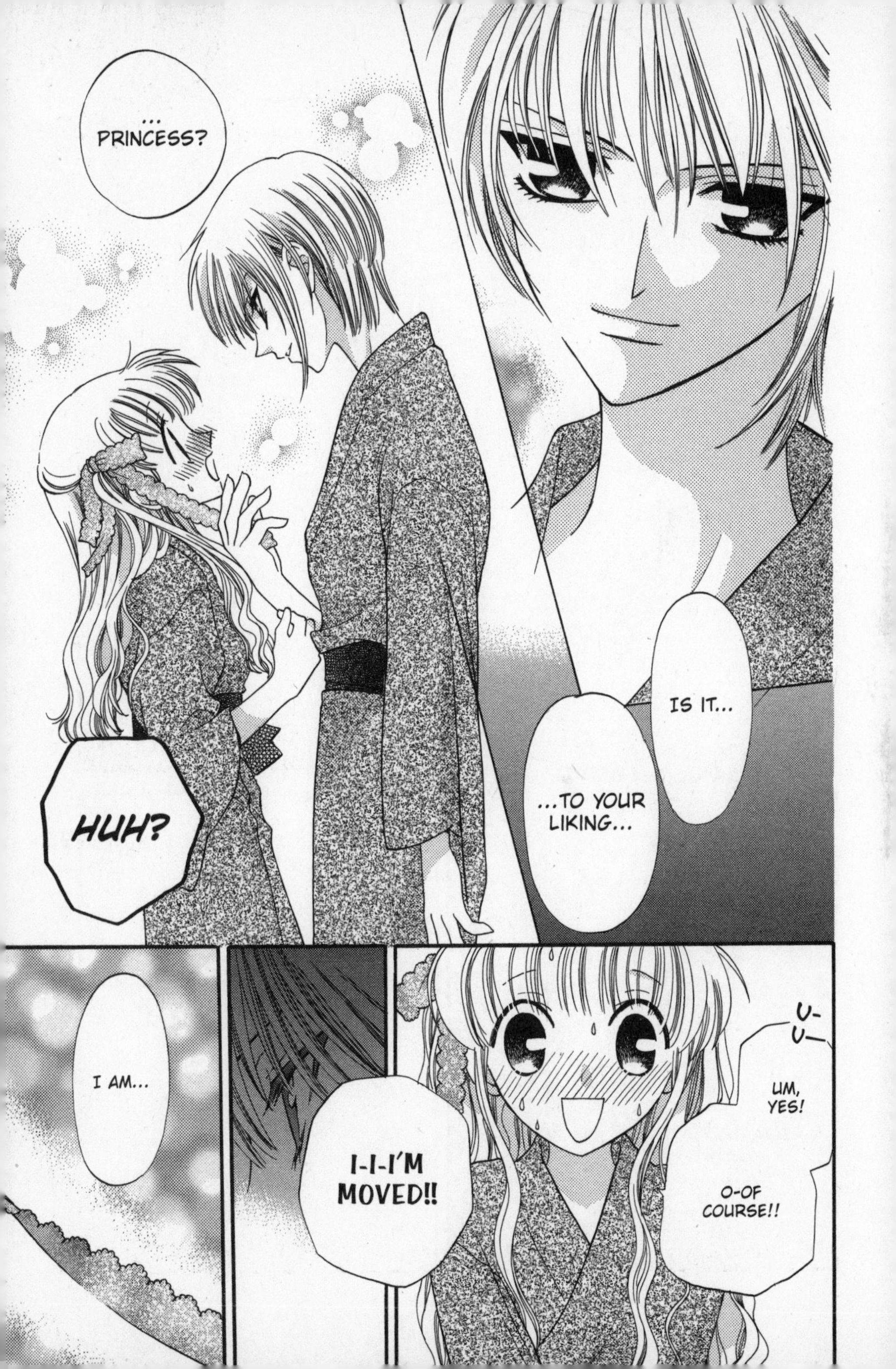
IS IT...
...TO YOUR LIKING...
...PRINCESS?
HUH?
U-U-
UM, YES!
O-OF COURSE!!
I-I-I'M MOVED!!
I AM...

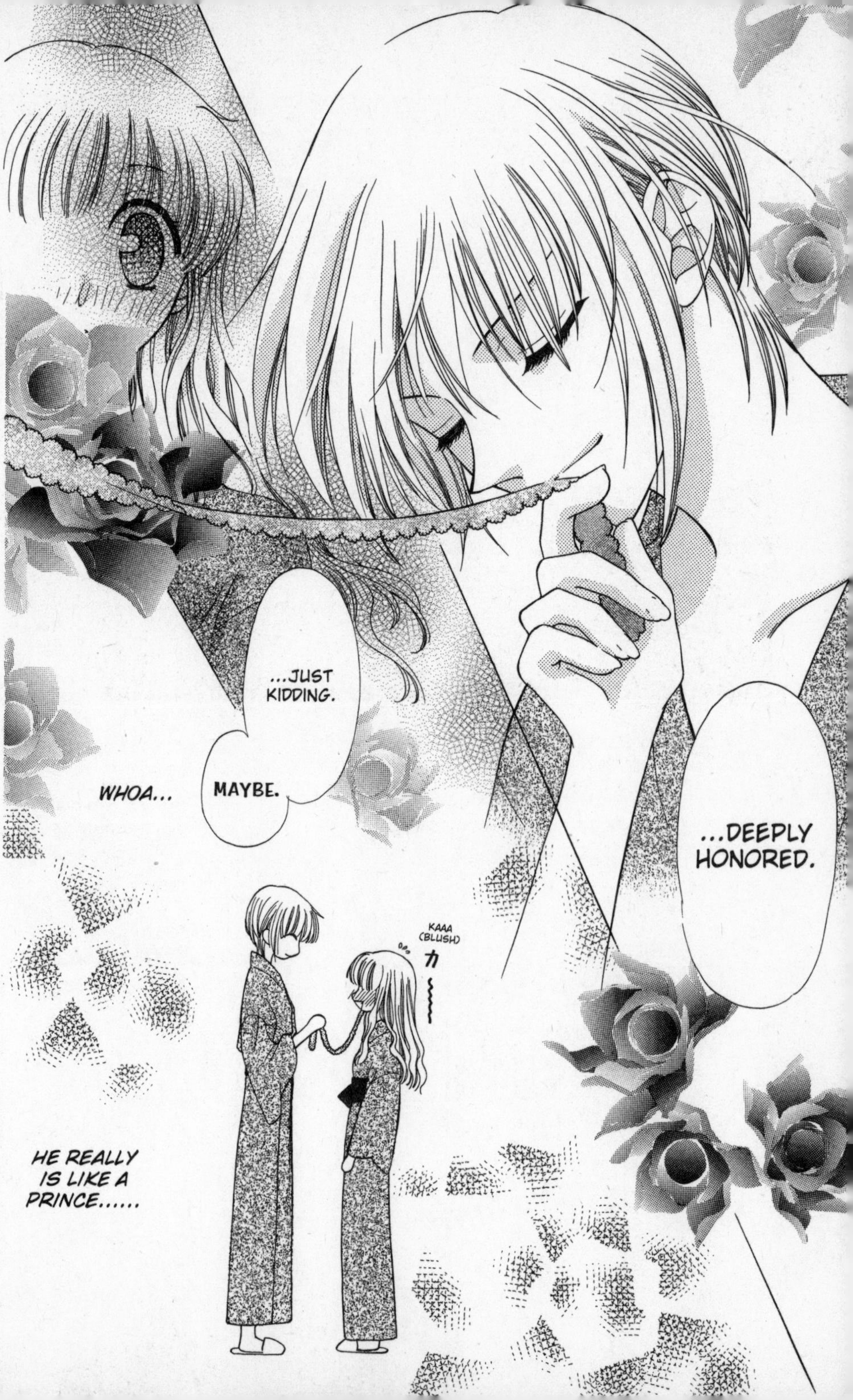
...DEEPLY HONORED.
...JUST KIDDING.
MAYBE.
WHOA...
KAAA (BLUSH)
カ
HE REALLY IS LIKE A PRINCE......

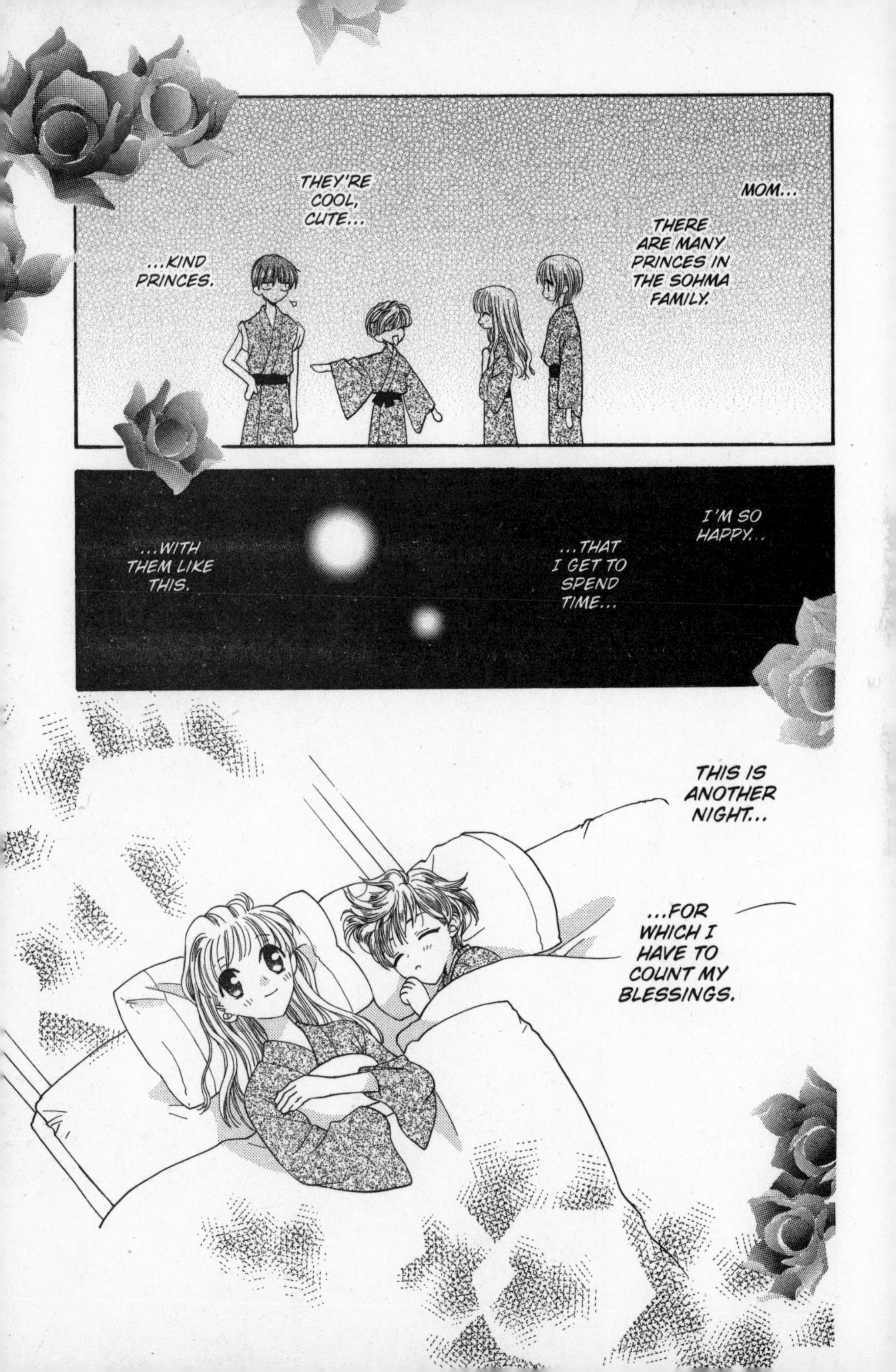
MOM...
THERE ARE MANY PRINCES IN THE SOHMA FAMILY.
THEY'RE COOL, CUTE...
...KIND PRINCES.
I'M SO HAPPY...
...THAT I GET TO SPEND TIME...
...WITH THEM LIKE THIS.
THIS IS ANOTHER NIGHT...
...FOR WHICH I HAVE TO COUNT MY BLESSINGS.

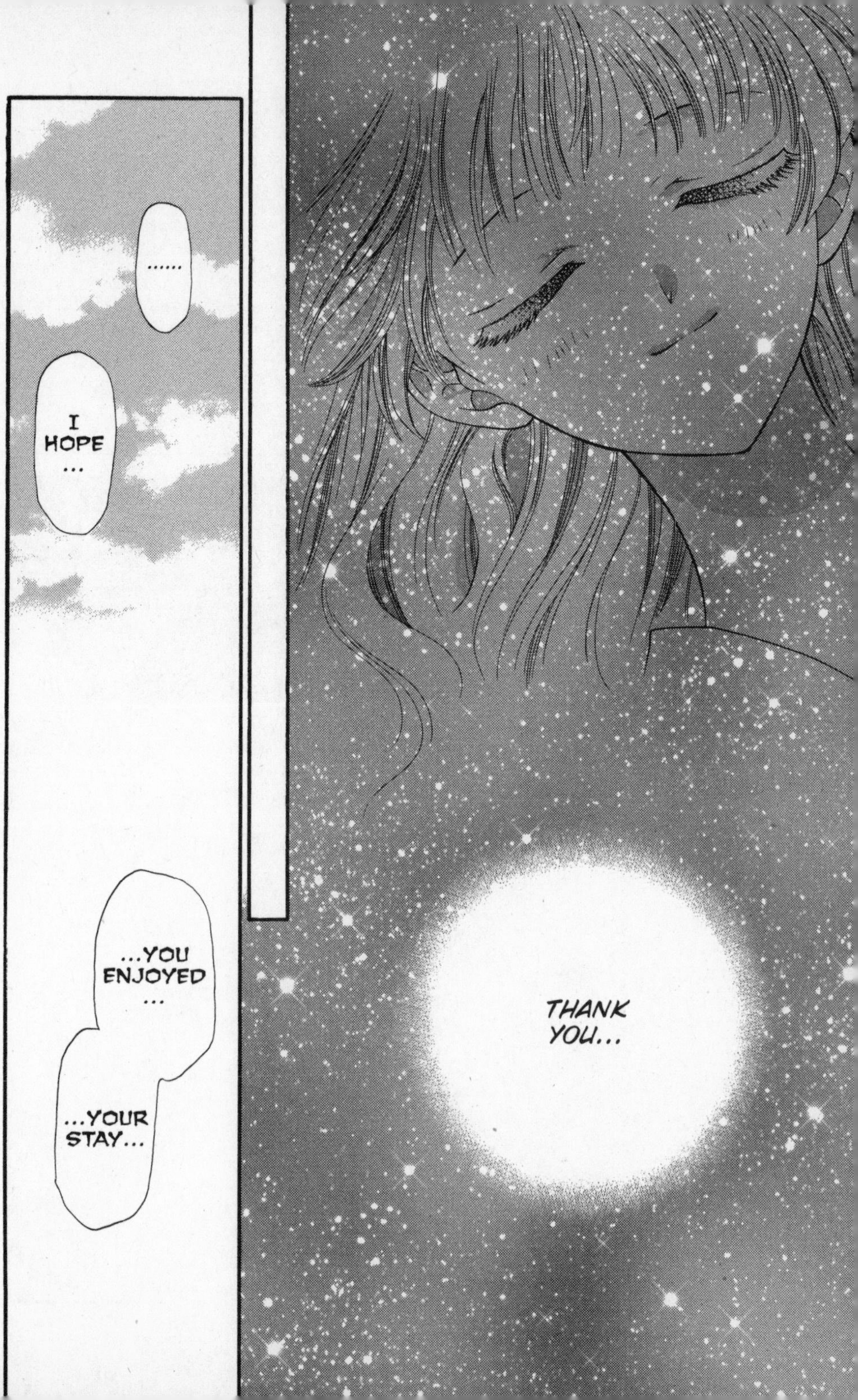
THANK YOU...
......
I HOPE...
...YOU ENJOYED...
...YOUR STAY...

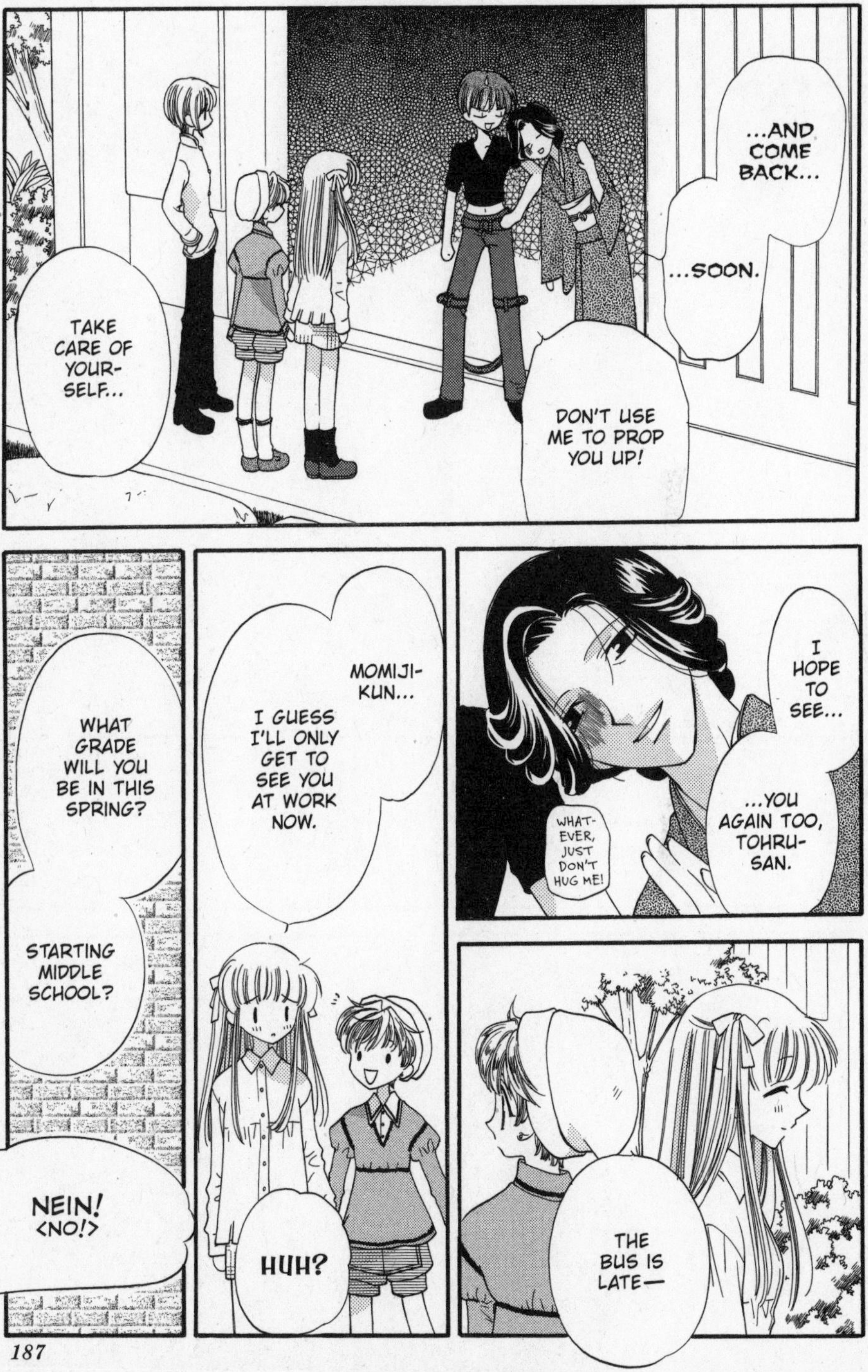
TAKE CARE OF YOUR-SELF...
...AND COME BACK...
...SOON.
DON'T USE ME TO PROP YOU UP!
I HOPE TO SEE...
...YOU AGAIN TOO, TOHRU-SAN.
WHAT-EVER, JUST DON'T HUG ME!
THE BUS IS LATE—
MOMIJI-KUN...
I GUESS I'LL ONLY GET TO SEE YOU AT WORK NOW.
HUH?
WHAT GRADE WILL YOU BE IN THIS SPRING?
STARTING MIDDLE SCHOOL?
NEIN! <NO!>

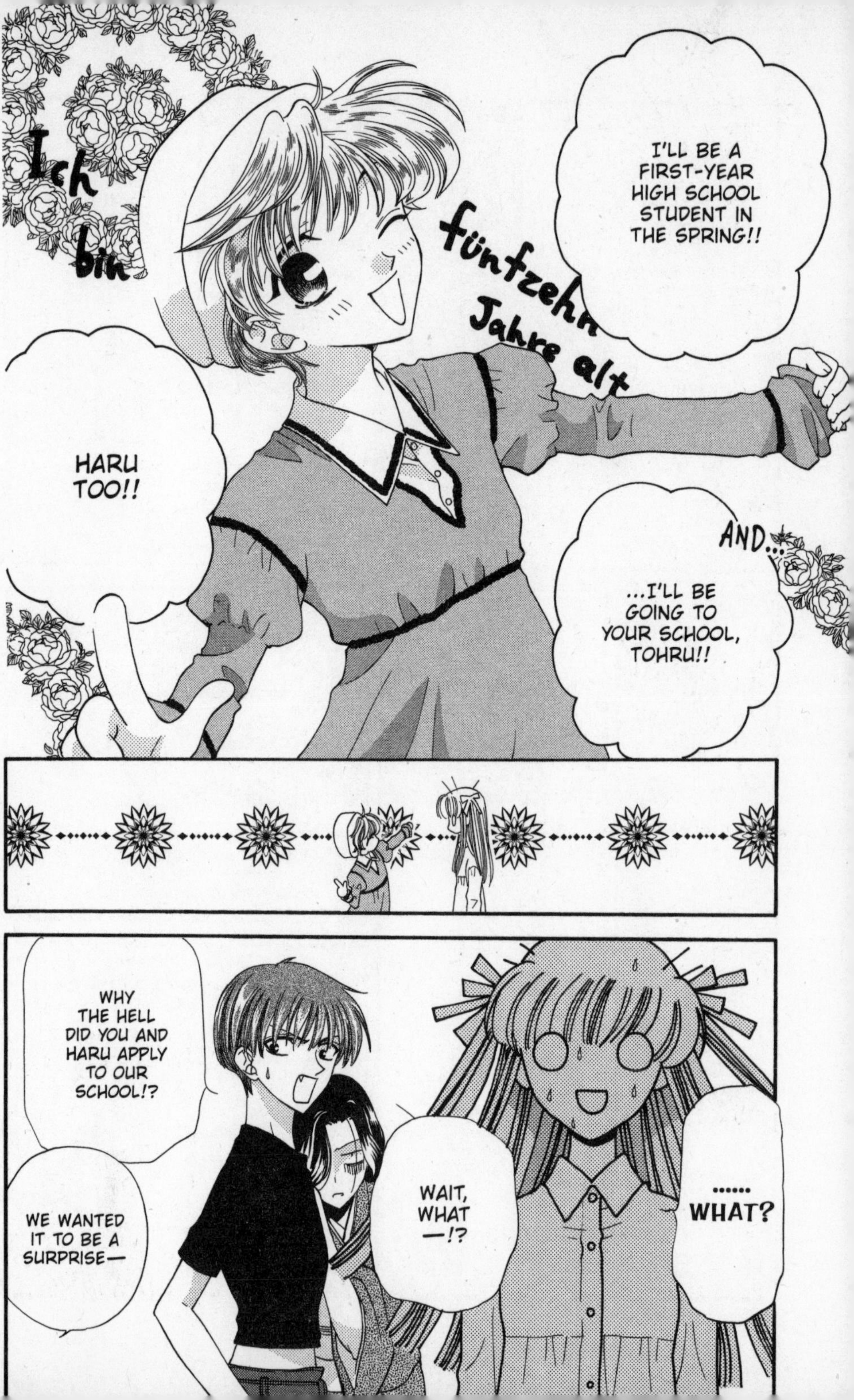
I'LL BE A FIRST-YEAR HIGH SCHOOL STUDENT IN THE SPRING!!
Ich bin fünfzehn Jahre alt
AND...
...I'LL BE GOING TO YOUR SCHOOL, TOHRU!!
HARU TOO!!
......WHAT?
WAIT, WHAT—!?
WHY THE HELL DID YOU AND HARU APPLY TO OUR SCHOOL!?
WE WANTED IT TO BE A SURPRISE—

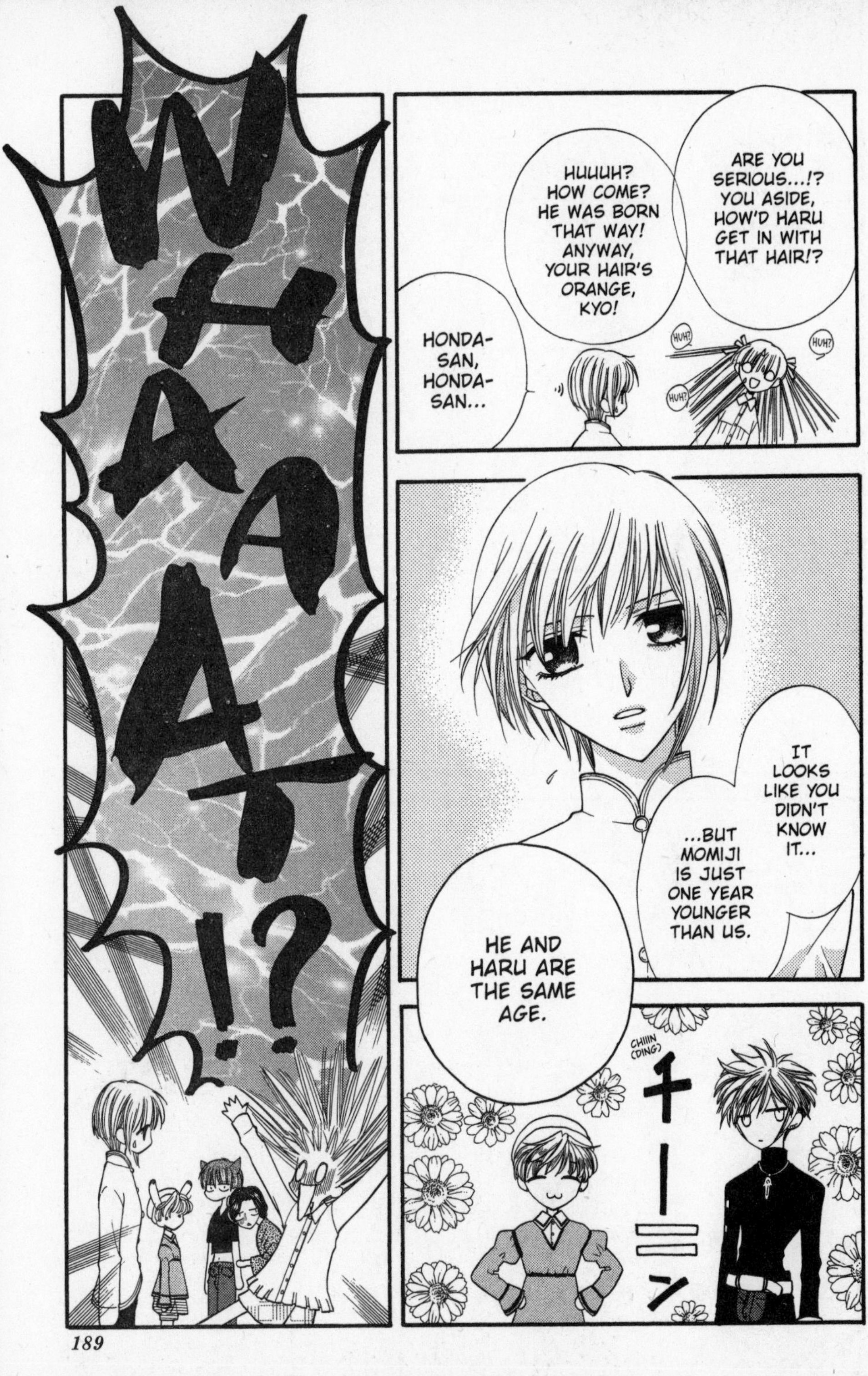
ARE YOU SERIOUS...!? YOU ASIDE, HOW'D HARU GET IN WITH THAT HAIR!?
HUUUH? HOW COME? HE WAS BORN THAT WAY! ANYWAY, YOUR HAIR'S ORANGE, KYO!
HUH?
HUH?
HUH?
HONDA-SAN, HONDA-SAN...
IT LOOKS LIKE YOU DIDN'T KNOW IT...
...BUT MOMIJI IS JUST ONE YEAR YOUNGER THAN US.
HE AND HARU ARE THE SAME AGE.
CHIIN (DING)
チーン
WHAAAT!?

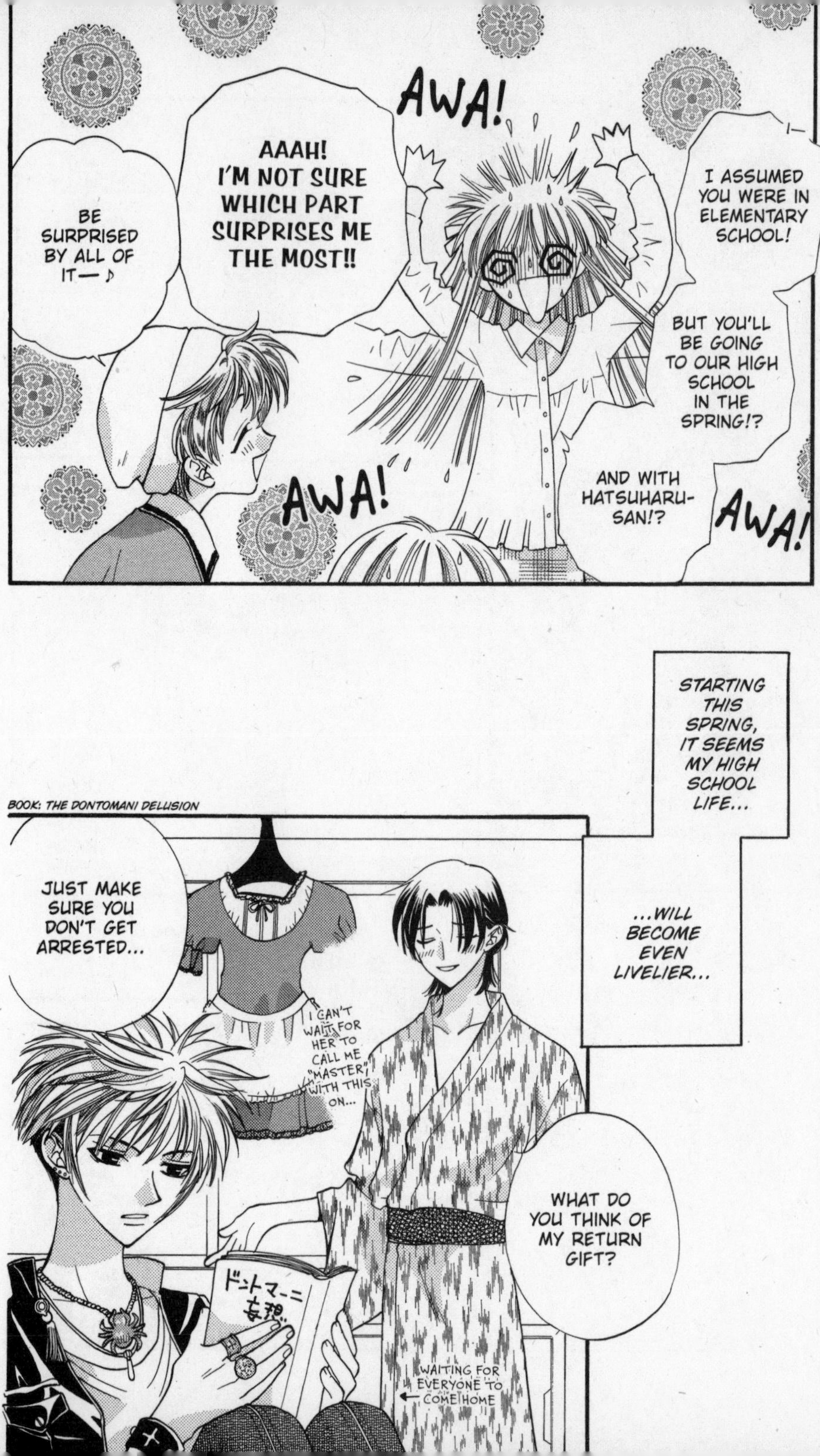
I—
I ASSUMED YOU WERE IN ELEMENTARY SCHOOL!
AWA!
BUT YOU'LL BE GOING TO OUR HIGH SCHOOL IN THE SPRING!?
AWA!
AND WITH HATSUHARU-SAN!?
AWA!
AAAH! I'M NOT SURE WHICH PART SURPRISES ME THE MOST!!
BE SURPRISED BY ALL OF IT—♪
STARTING THIS SPRING, IT SEEMS MY HIGH SCHOOL LIFE...
...WILL BECOME EVEN LIVELIER...
BOOK: THE DONTOMANI DELUSION
WHAT DO YOU THINK OF MY RETURN GIFT?
I CAN'T WAIT FOR HER TO CALL ME "MASTER" WITH THIS ON...
JUST MAKE SURE YOU DON'T GET ARRESTED...
ドントマーニ妄想
WAITING FOR EVERYONE TO COME HOME

COLLECTOR'S EDITION

Fruits Basket

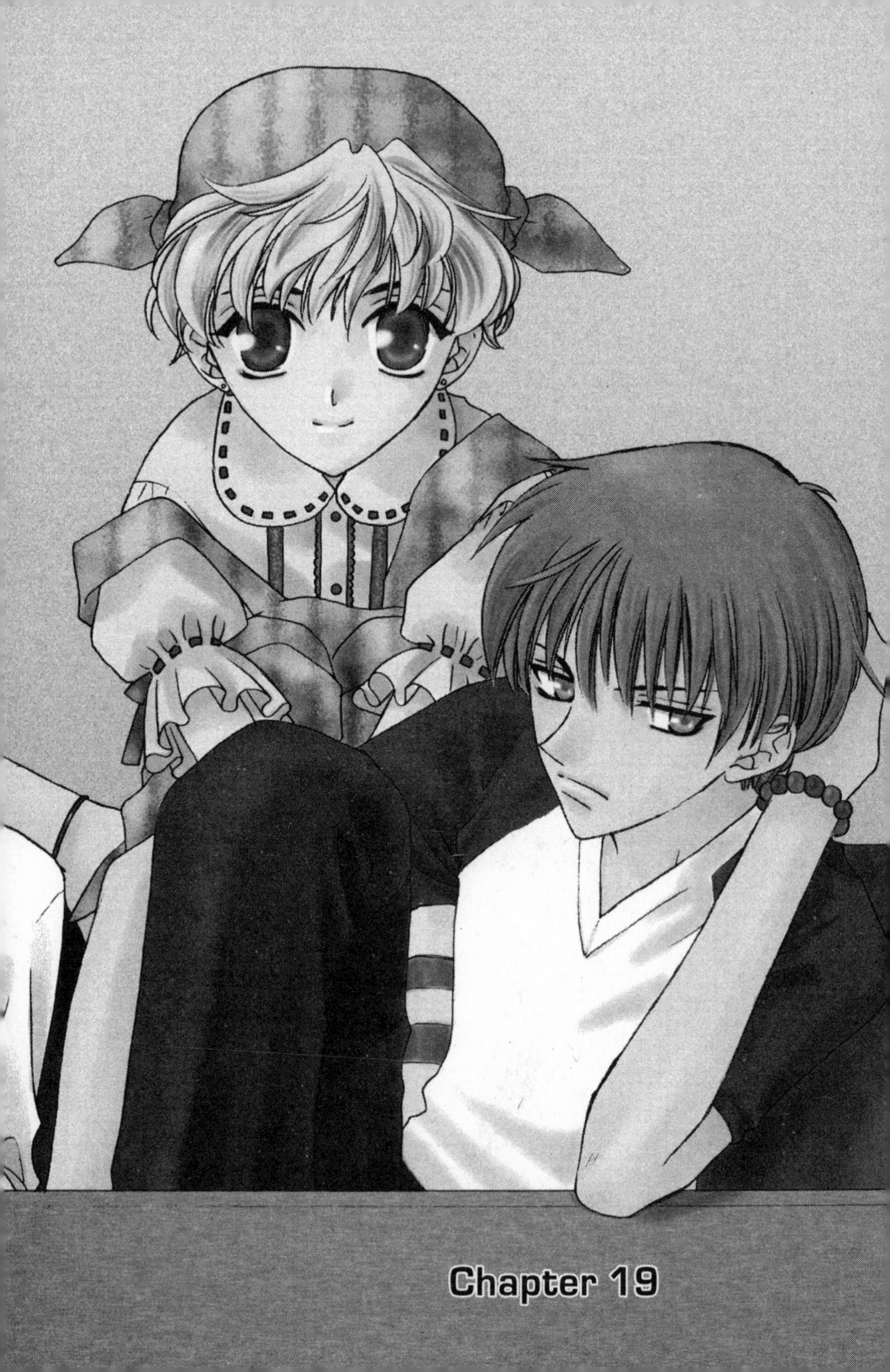

Chapter 19

Fruits Basket

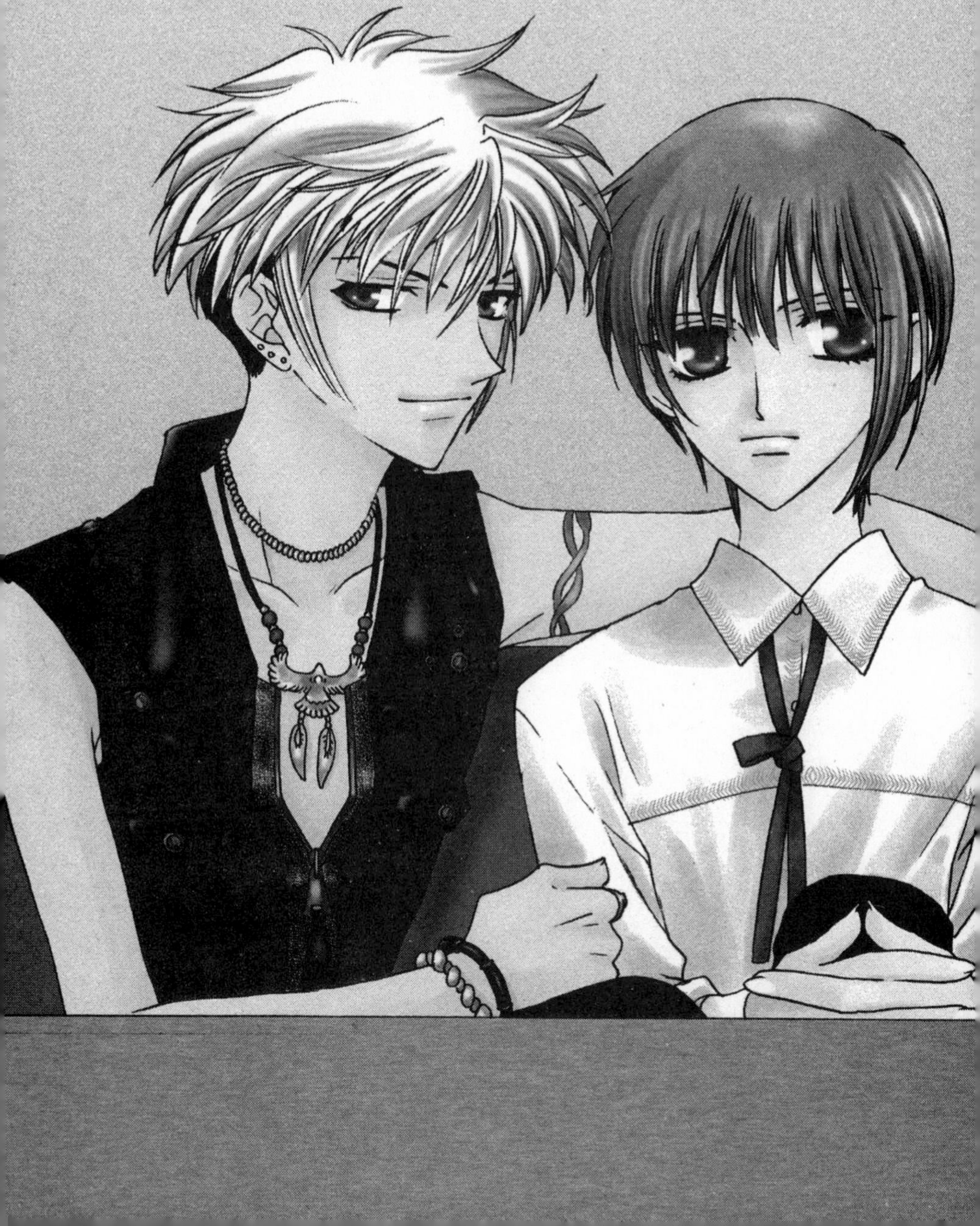

JUST BETWEEN YOU AND ME...

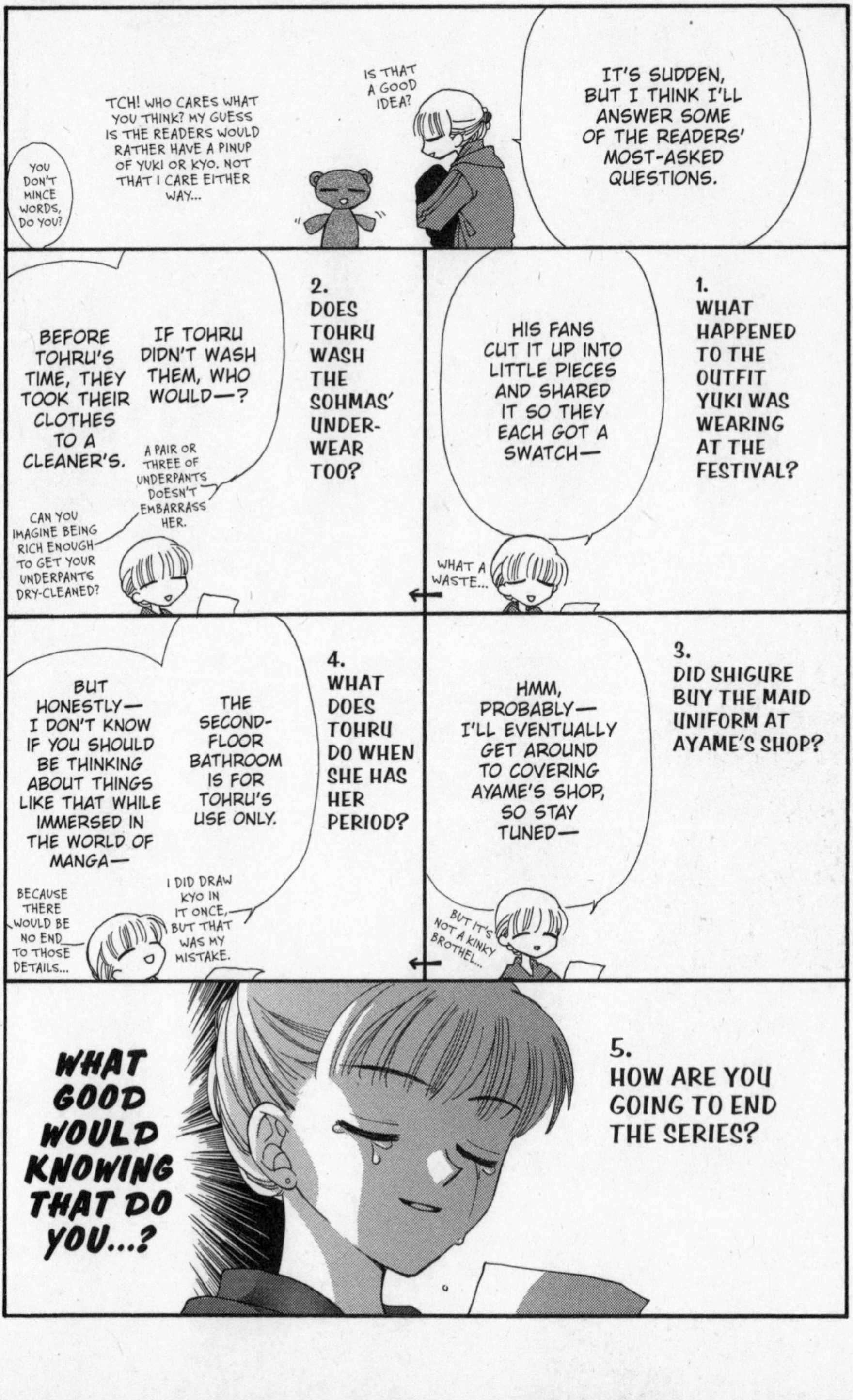

IT'S SUDDEN, BUT I THINK I'LL ANSWER SOME OF THE READERS' MOST-ASKED QUESTIONS.
IS THAT A GOOD IDEA?
TCH! WHO CARES WHAT YOU THINK? MY GUESS IS THE READERS WOULD RATHER HAVE A PINUP OF YUKI OR KYO. NOT THAT I CARE EITHER WAY...
YOU DON'T MINCE WORDS, DO YOU?
1. WHAT HAPPENED TO THE OUTFIT YUKI WAS WEARING AT THE FESTIVAL?
HIS FANS CUT IT UP INTO LITTLE PIECES AND SHARED IT SO THEY EACH GOT A SWATCH—
WHAT A WASTE...
2. DOES TOHRU WASH THE SOHMAS' UNDER-WEAR TOO?
IF TOHRU DIDN'T WASH THEM, WHO WOULD—?
BEFORE TOHRU'S TIME, THEY TOOK THEIR CLOTHES TO A CLEANER'S.
A PAIR OR THREE OF UNDERPANTS DOESN'T EMBARRASS HER.
CAN YOU IMAGINE BEING RICH ENOUGH TO GET YOUR UNDERPANTS DRY-CLEANED?
3. DID SHIGURE BUY THE MAID UNIFORM AT AYAME'S SHOP?
HMM, PROBABLY— I'LL EVENTUALLY GET AROUND TO COVERING AYAME'S SHOP, SO STAY TUNED—
BUT IT'S NOT A KINKY BROTHEL...
4. WHAT DOES TOHRU DO WHEN SHE HAS HER PERIOD?
THE SECOND-FLOOR BATHROOM IS FOR TOHRU'S USE ONLY.
BUT HONESTLY— I DON'T KNOW IF YOU SHOULD BE THINKING ABOUT THINGS LIKE THAT WHILE IMMERSED IN THE WORLD OF MANGA—
I DID DRAW KYO IN IT ONCE, BUT THAT WAS MY MISTAKE.
BECAUSE THERE WOULD BE NO END TO THOSE DETAILS...
5. HOW ARE YOU GOING TO END THE SERIES?
WHAT GOOD WOULD KNOWING THAT DO YOU...?

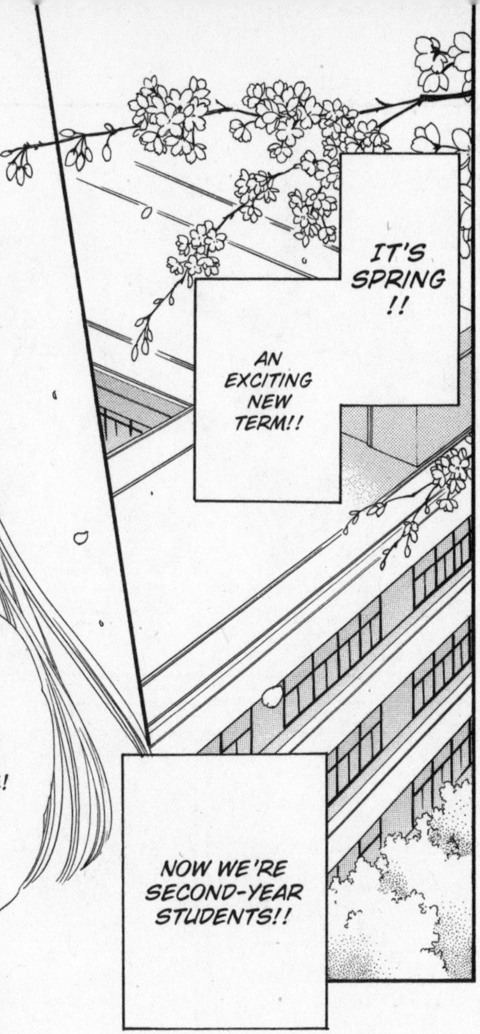
IT'S SPRING !!
AN EXCITING NEW TERM!!
NOW WE'RE SECOND-YEAR STUDENTS!!

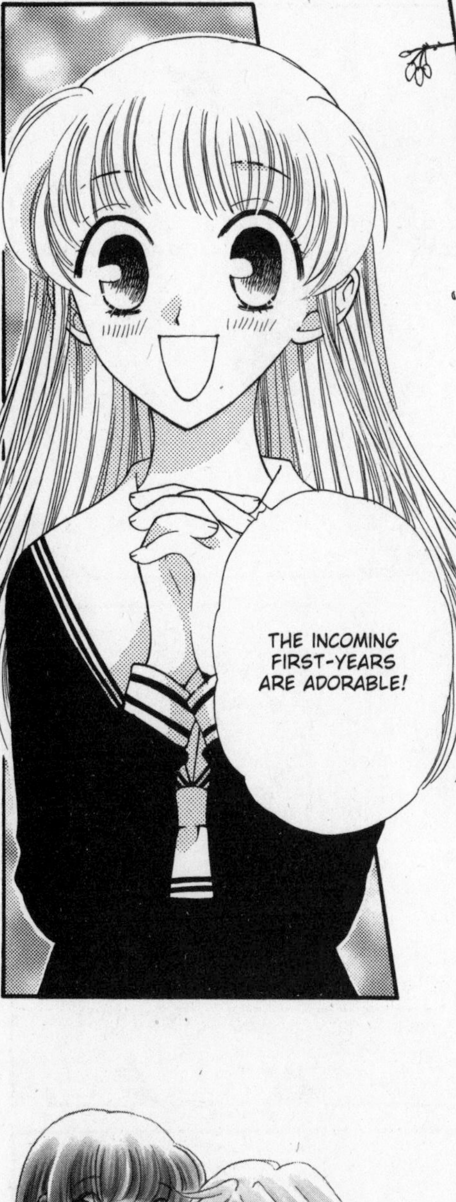
THE INCOMING FIRST-YEARS ARE ADORABLE!

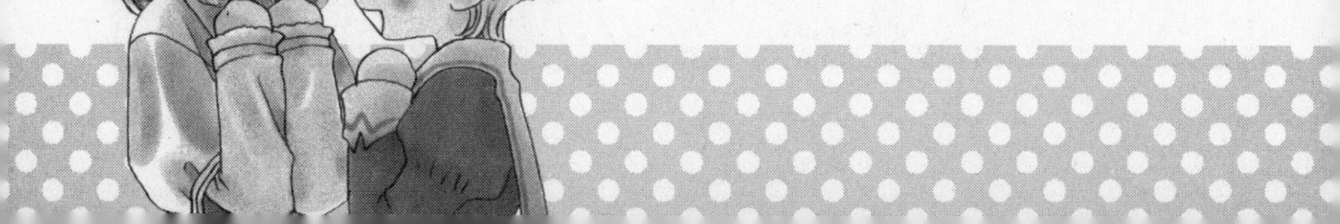

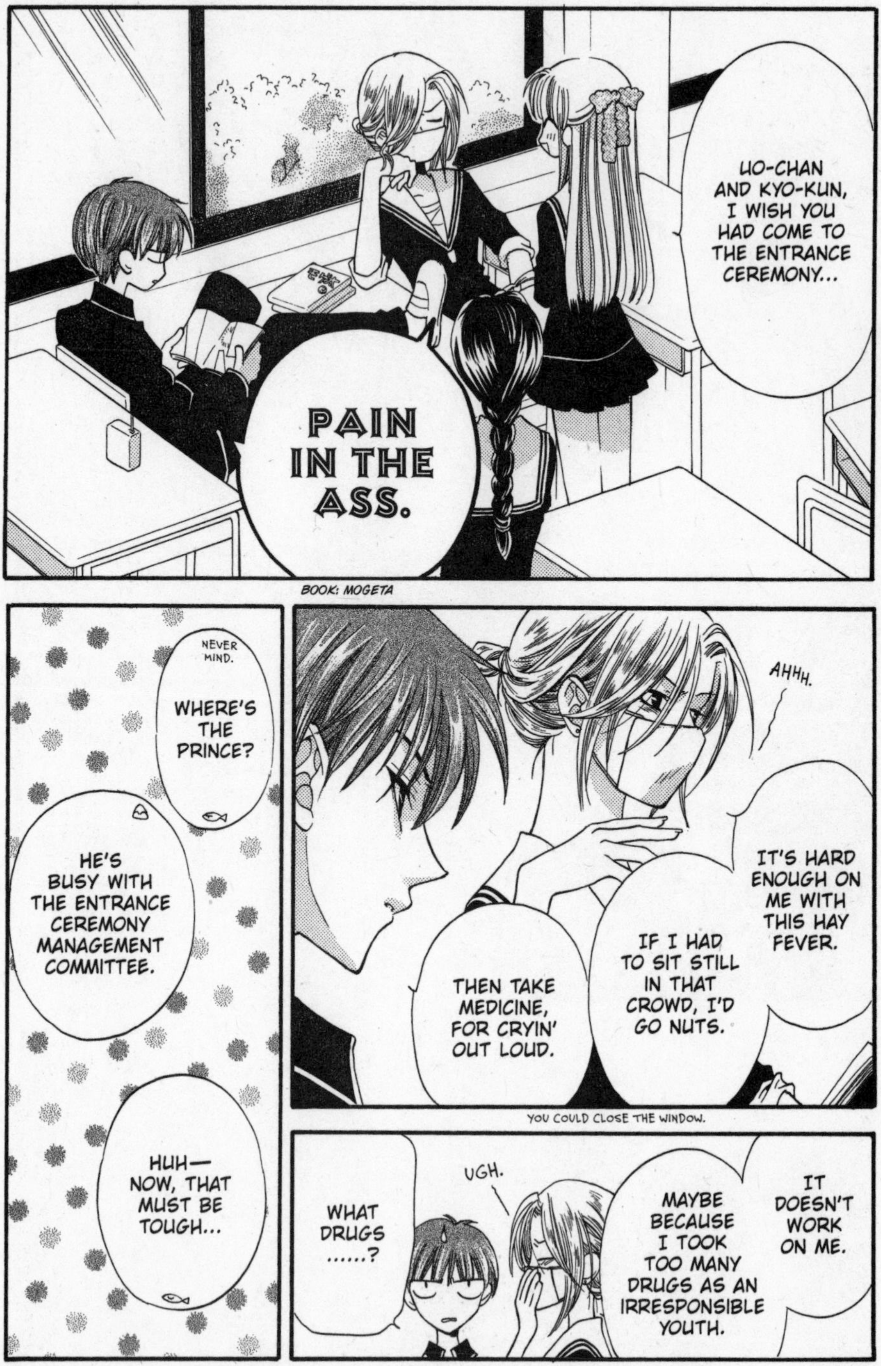
UO-CHAN AND KYO-KUN, I WISH YOU HAD COME TO THE ENTRANCE CEREMONY...
PAIN IN THE ASS.
BOOK: MOGETA
AHHH.
IT'S HARD ENOUGH ON ME WITH THIS HAY FEVER.
IF I HAD TO SIT STILL IN THAT CROWD, I'D GO NUTS.
THEN TAKE MEDICINE, FOR CRYIN' OUT LOUD.
YOU COULD CLOSE THE WINDOW.
IT DOESN'T WORK ON ME.
MAYBE BECAUSE I TOOK TOO MANY DRUGS AS AN IRRESPONSIBLE YOUTH.
UGH.
WHAT DRUGS ......?
NEVER MIND.
WHERE'S THE PRINCE?
HE'S BUSY WITH THE ENTRANCE CEREMONY MANAGEMENT COMMITTEE.
HUH— NOW, THAT MUST BE TOUGH...

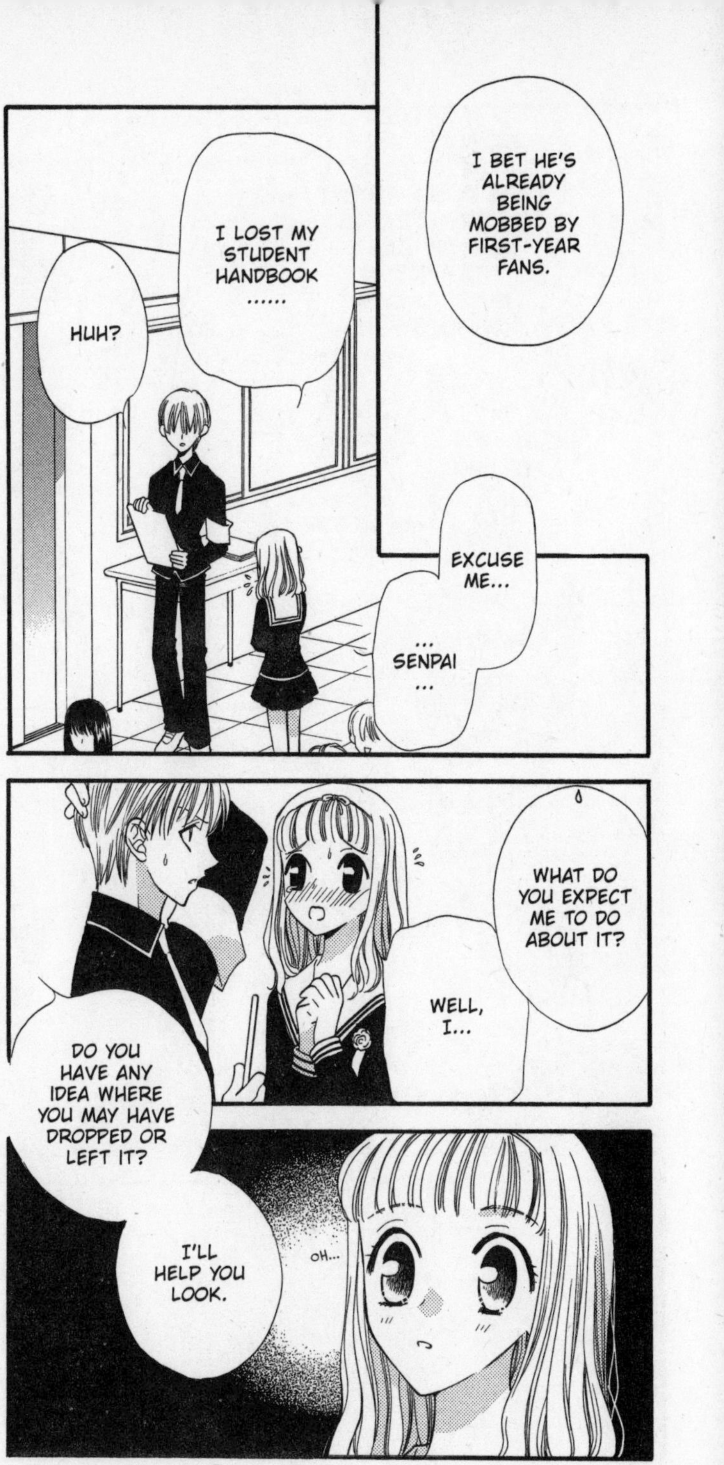
I BET HE'S ALREADY BEING MOBBED BY FIRST-YEAR FANS.
EXCUSE ME...
... SENPAI ...
I LOST MY STUDENT HANDBOOK ......
HUH?
WHAT DO YOU EXPECT ME TO DO ABOUT IT?
WELL, I...
DO YOU HAVE ANY IDEA WHERE YOU MAY HAVE DROPPED OR LEFT IT?
I'LL HELP YOU LOOK.
OH...
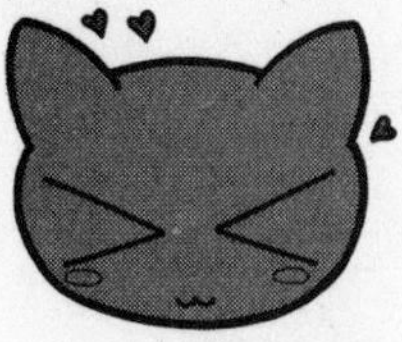

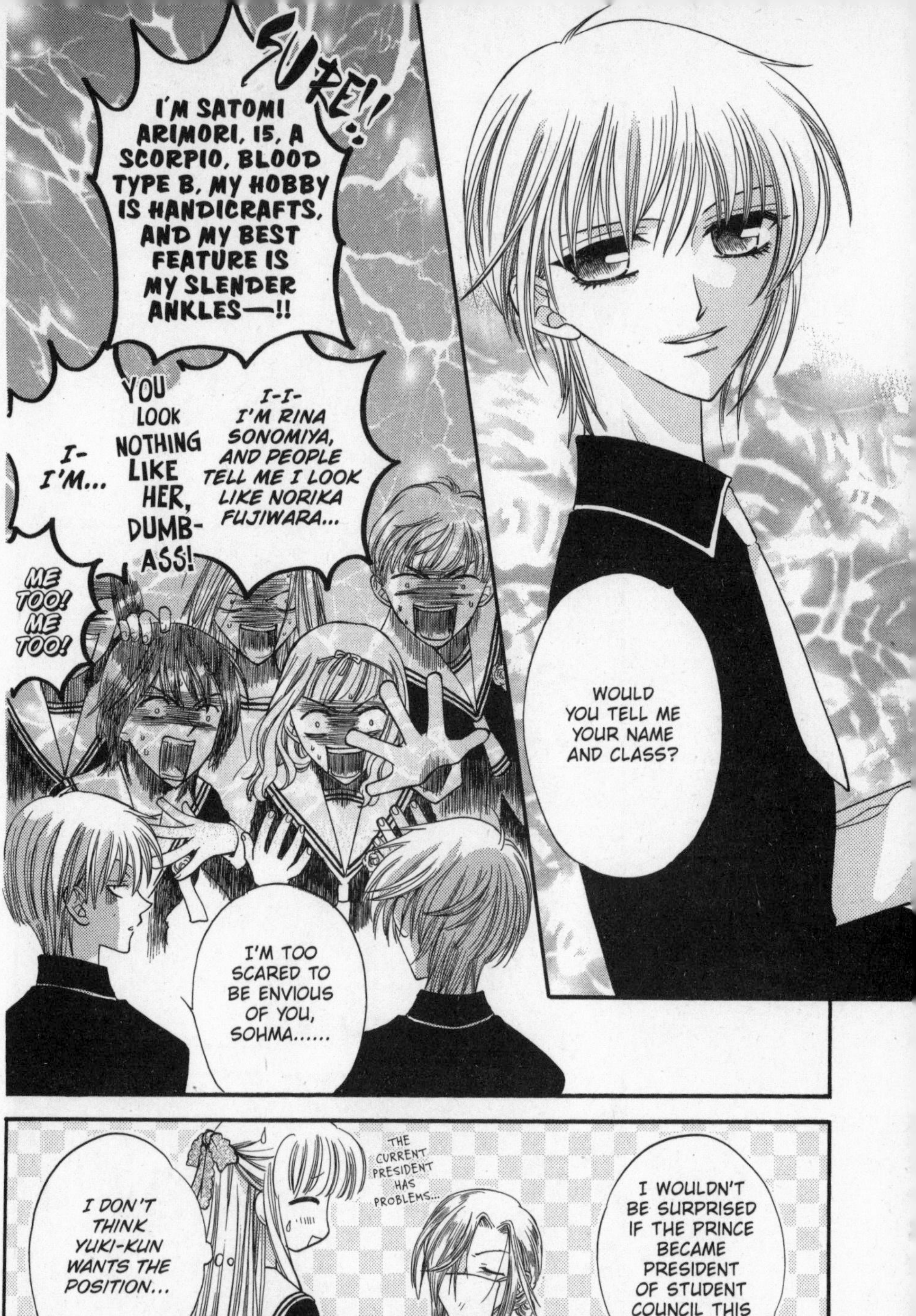
WOULD YOU TELL ME YOUR NAME AND CLASS?
SURE!!
I'M SATOMI ARIMORI, 15, A SCORPIO, BLOOD TYPE B, MY HOBBY IS HANDICRAFTS, AND MY BEST FEATURE IS MY SLENDER ANKLES—!!
I-I-I'M RINA SONOMIYA, AND PEOPLE TELL ME I LOOK LIKE NORIKA FUJIWARA...
YOU LOOK NOTHING LIKE HER, DUMB-ASS!
I-I'M...
ME TOO! ME TOO!
I'M TOO SCARED TO BE ENVIOUS OF YOU, SOHMA......
I WOULDN'T BE SURPRISED IF THE PRINCE BECAME PRESIDENT OF STUDENT COUNCIL THIS YEAR.
THE CURRENT PRESIDENT HAS PROBLEMS...
I DON'T THINK YUKI-KUN WANTS THE POSITION...

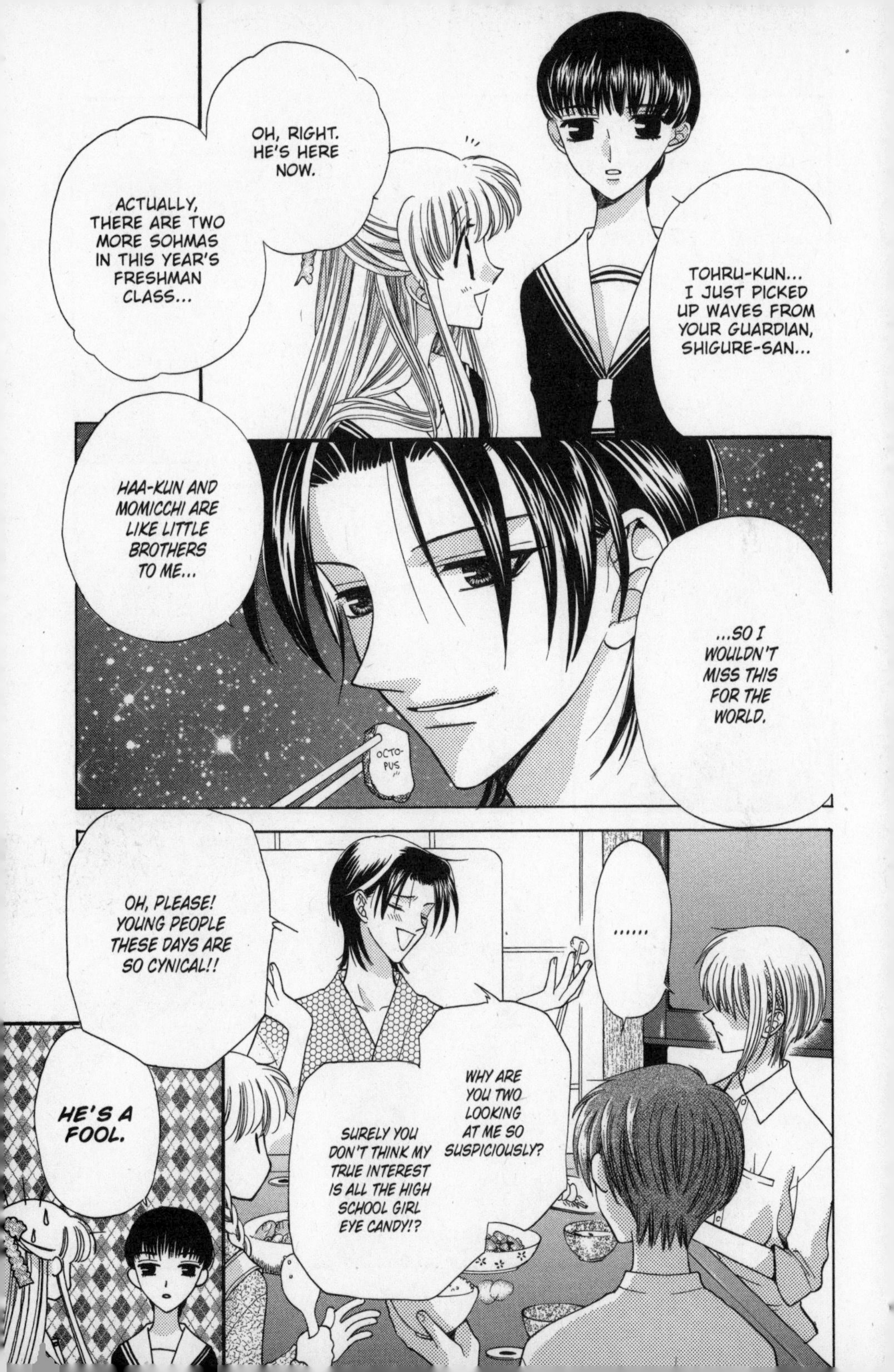

TOHRU-KUN... I JUST PICKED UP WAVES FROM YOUR GUARDIAN, SHIGURE-SAN...
OH, RIGHT. HE'S HERE NOW.
ACTUALLY, THERE ARE TWO MORE SOHMAS IN THIS YEAR'S FRESHMAN CLASS...
HAA-KUN AND MOMICCHI ARE LIKE LITTLE BROTHERS TO ME...
...SO I WOULDN'T MISS THIS FOR THE WORLD.
OCTO-PUS
......
WHY ARE YOU TWO LOOKING AT ME SO SUSPICIOUSLY?
SURELY YOU DON'T THINK MY TRUE INTEREST IS ALL THE HIGH SCHOOL GIRL EYE CANDY!?
OH, PLEASE! YOUNG PEOPLE THESE DAYS ARE SO CYNICAL!!
HE'S A FOOL.

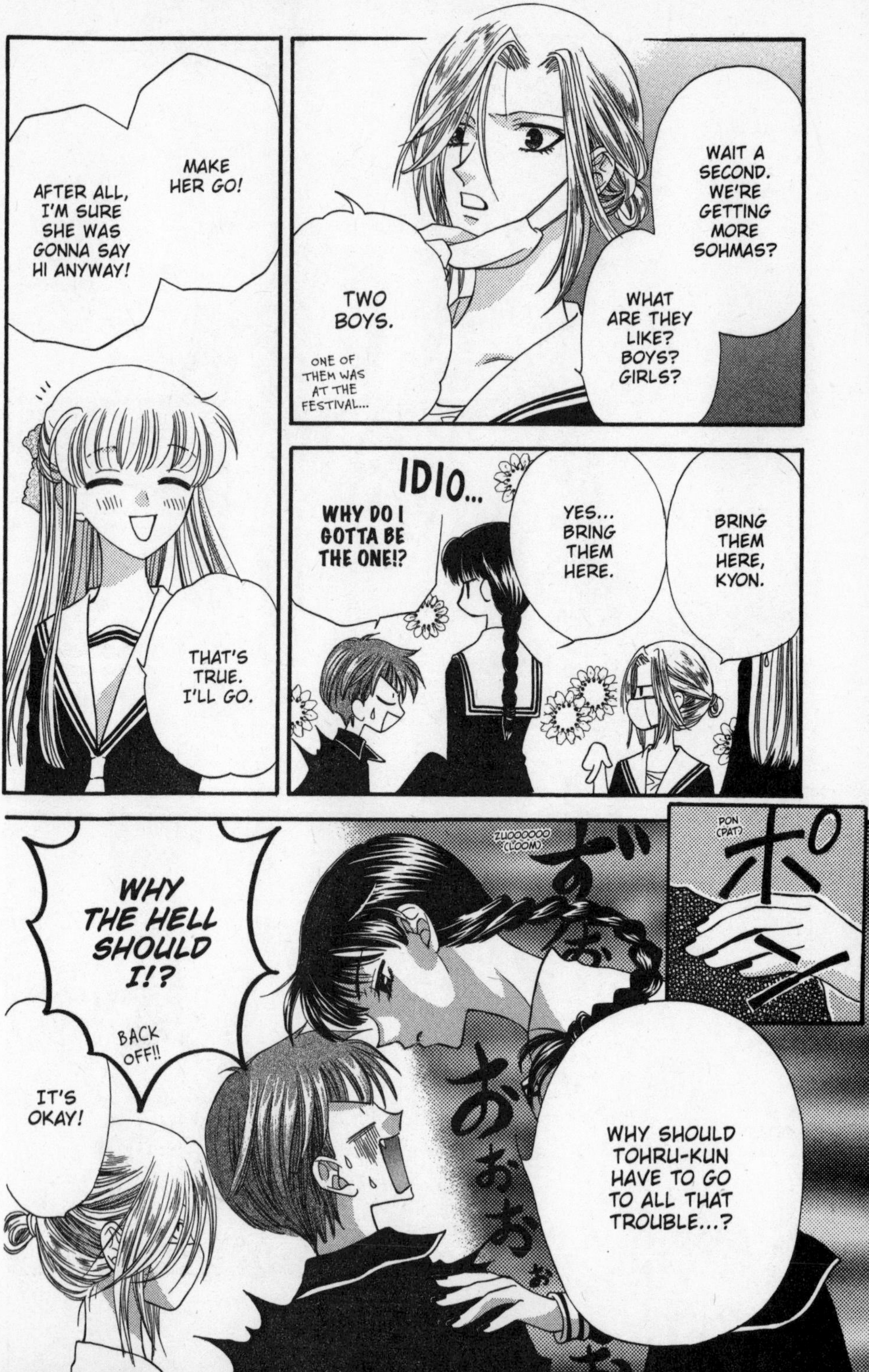
WAIT A SECOND. WE'RE GETTING MORE SOHMAS?
WHAT ARE THEY LIKE? BOYS? GIRLS?
TWO BOYS.
ONE OF THEM WAS AT THE FESTIVAL...
BRING THEM HERE, KYON.
YES... BRING THEM HERE.
IDIO...
WHY DO I GOTTA BE THE ONE!?
MAKE HER GO!
AFTER ALL, I'M SURE SHE WAS GONNA SAY HI ANYWAY!
THAT'S TRUE. I'LL GO.
PON (PAT)
ZUOOOOOO (LOOM)
WHY SHOULD TOHRU-KUN HAVE TO GO TO ALL THAT TROUBLE...?
WHY THE HELL SHOULD I!?
BACK OFF!!
IT'S OKAY!

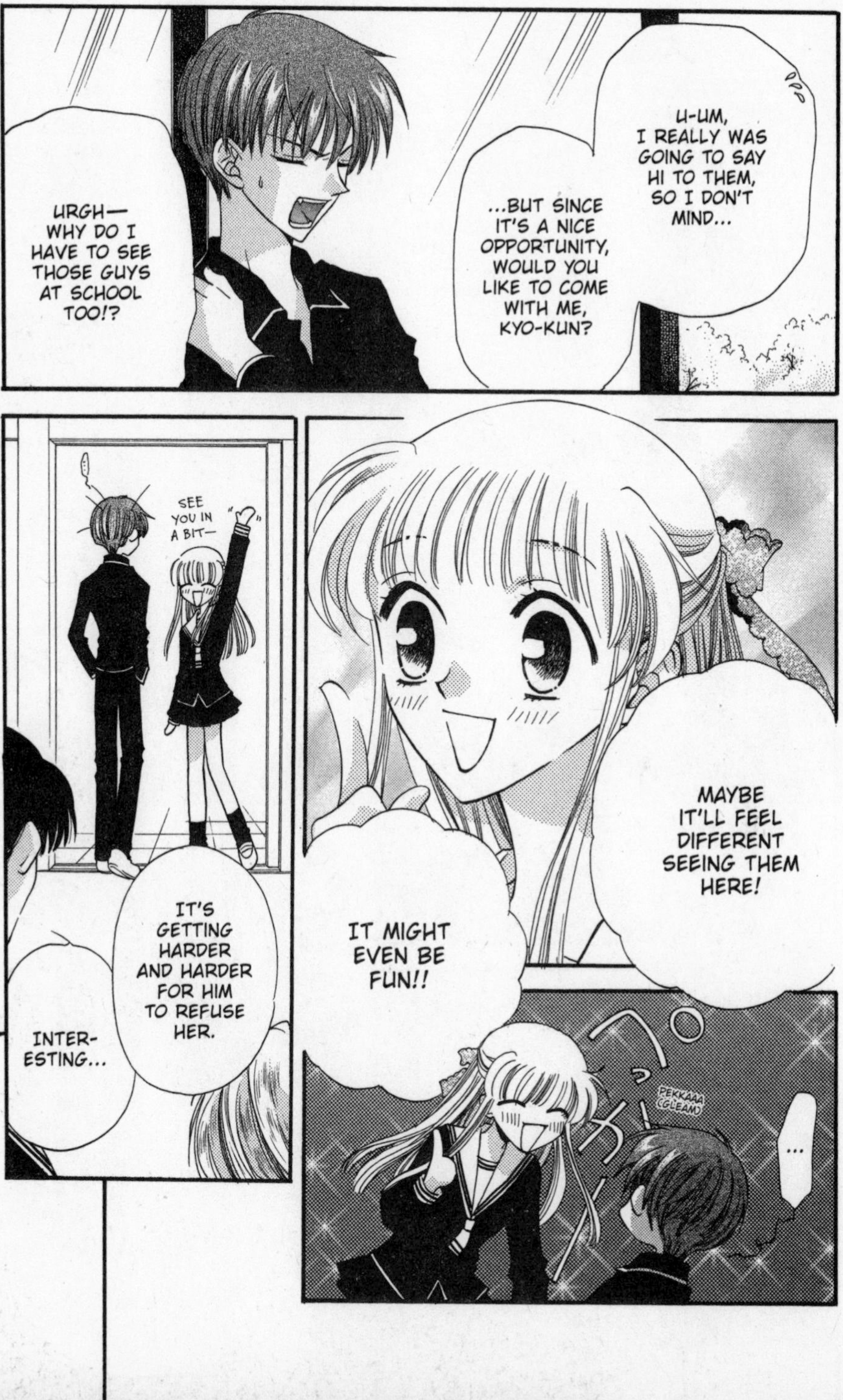
U-UM, I REALLY WAS GOING TO SAY HI TO THEM, SO I DON'T MIND...
...BUT SINCE IT'S A NICE OPPORTUNITY, WOULD YOU LIKE TO COME WITH ME, KYO-KUN?
URGH— WHY DO I HAVE TO SEE THOSE GUYS AT SCHOOL TOO!?
MAYBE IT'LL FEEL DIFFERENT SEEING THEM HERE!
IT MIGHT EVEN BE FUN!!
PEKKAAA (GLEAM)
...
!
SEE YOU IN A BIT—
IT'S GETTING HARDER AND HARDER FOR HIM TO REFUSE HER.
INTER-ESTING...

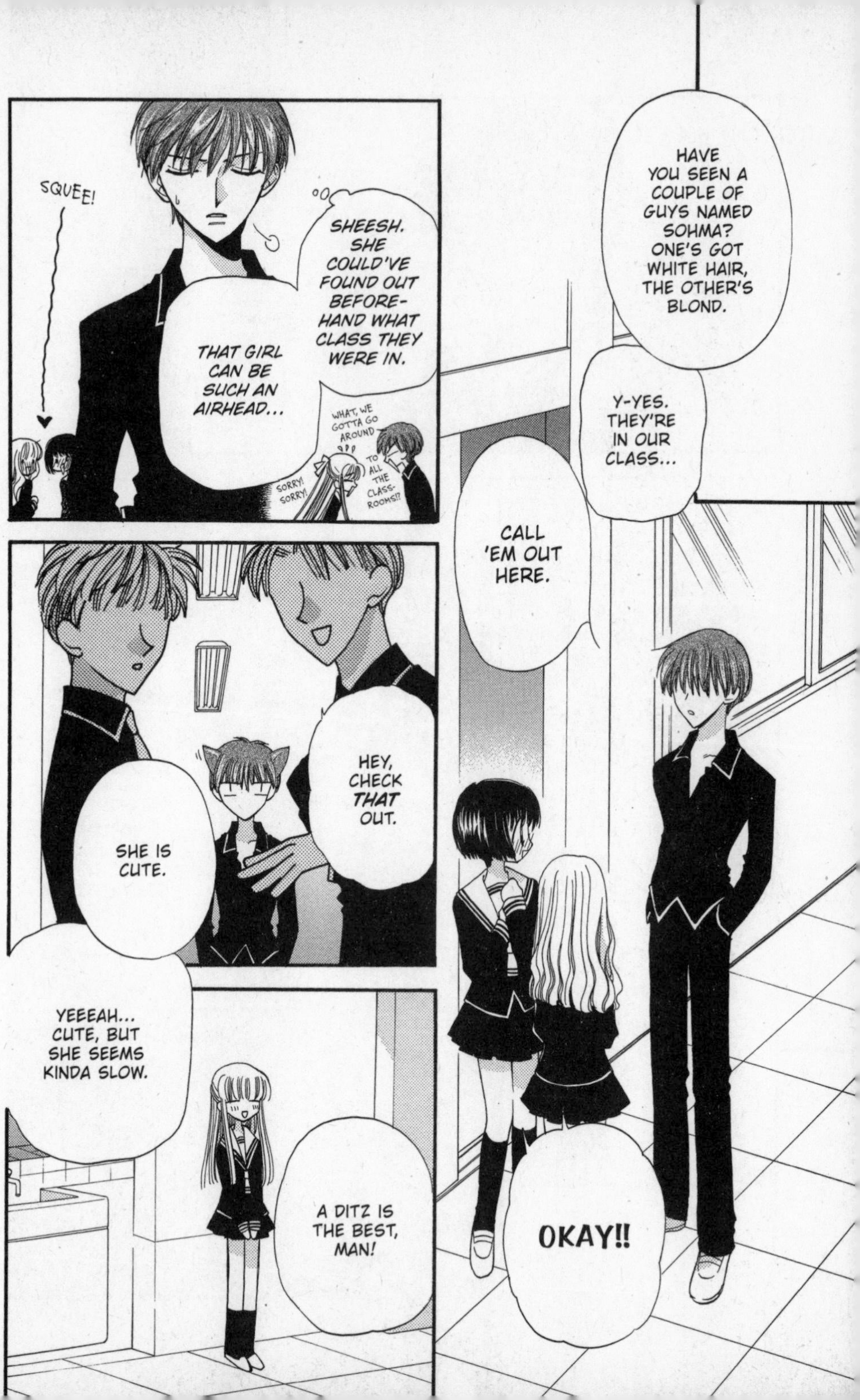

HAVE YOU SEEN A COUPLE OF GUYS NAMED SOHMA? ONE'S GOT WHITE HAIR, THE OTHER'S BLOND.
Y-YES. THEY'RE IN OUR CLASS...
CALL 'EM OUT HERE.
OKAY!!
SHEESH. SHE COULD'VE FOUND OUT BEFORE-HAND WHAT CLASS THEY WERE IN.
THAT GIRL CAN BE SUCH AN AIRHEAD...
SQUEE!
WHAT, WE GOTTA GO AROUND TO ALL THE CLASS-ROOMS!?
SORRY! SORRY!
HEY, CHECK THAT OUT.
SHE IS CUTE.
YEEEAH... CUTE, BUT SHE SEEMS KINDA SLOW.
A DITZ IS THE BEST, MAN!

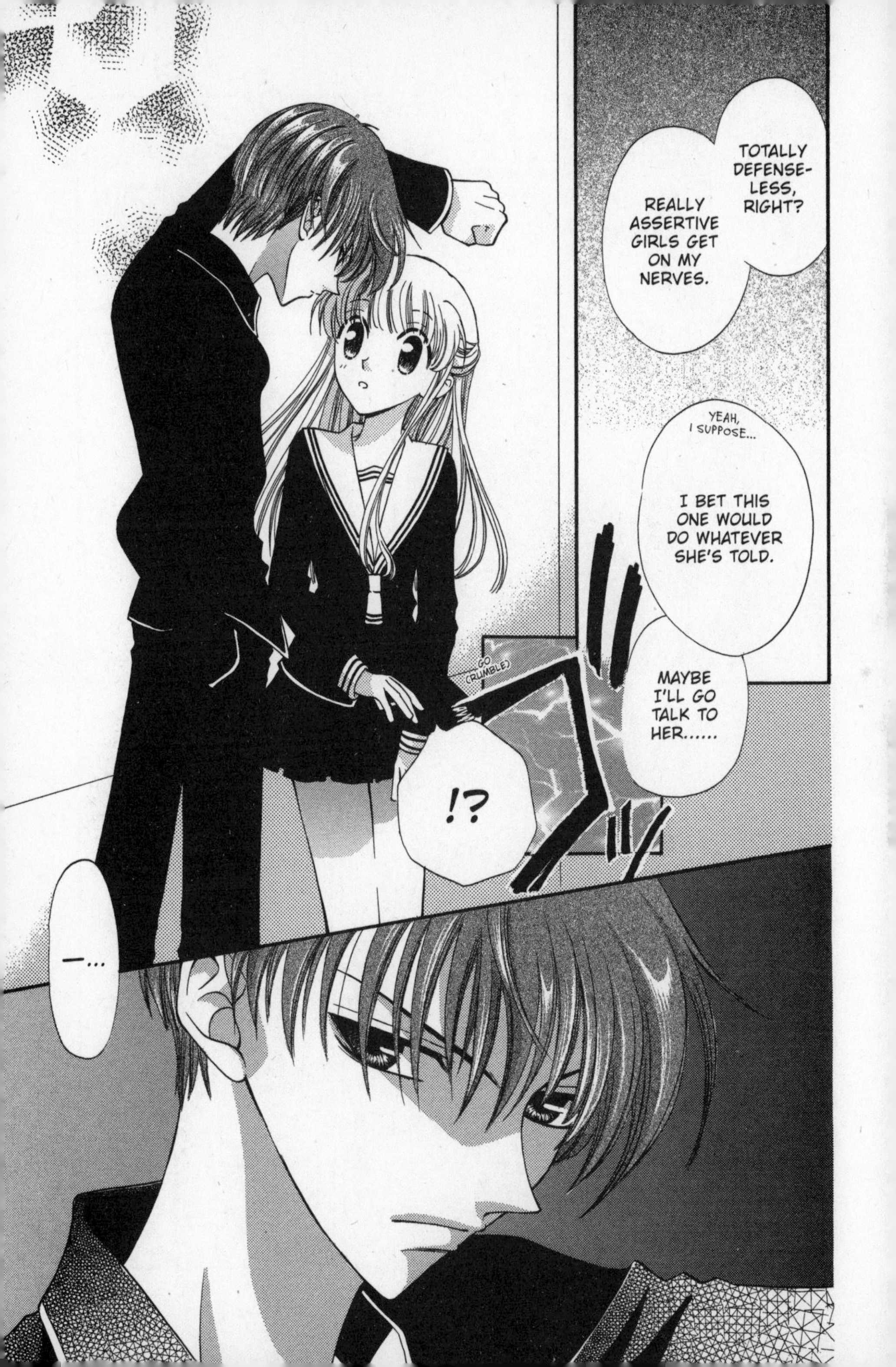
TOTALLY DEFENSE-LESS, RIGHT?
REALLY ASSERTIVE GIRLS GET ON MY NERVES.
YEAH, I SUPPOSE...
I BET THIS ONE WOULD DO WHATEVER SHE'S TOLD.
MAYBE I'LL GO TALK TO HER......
GO (RUMBLE)
!?
—...

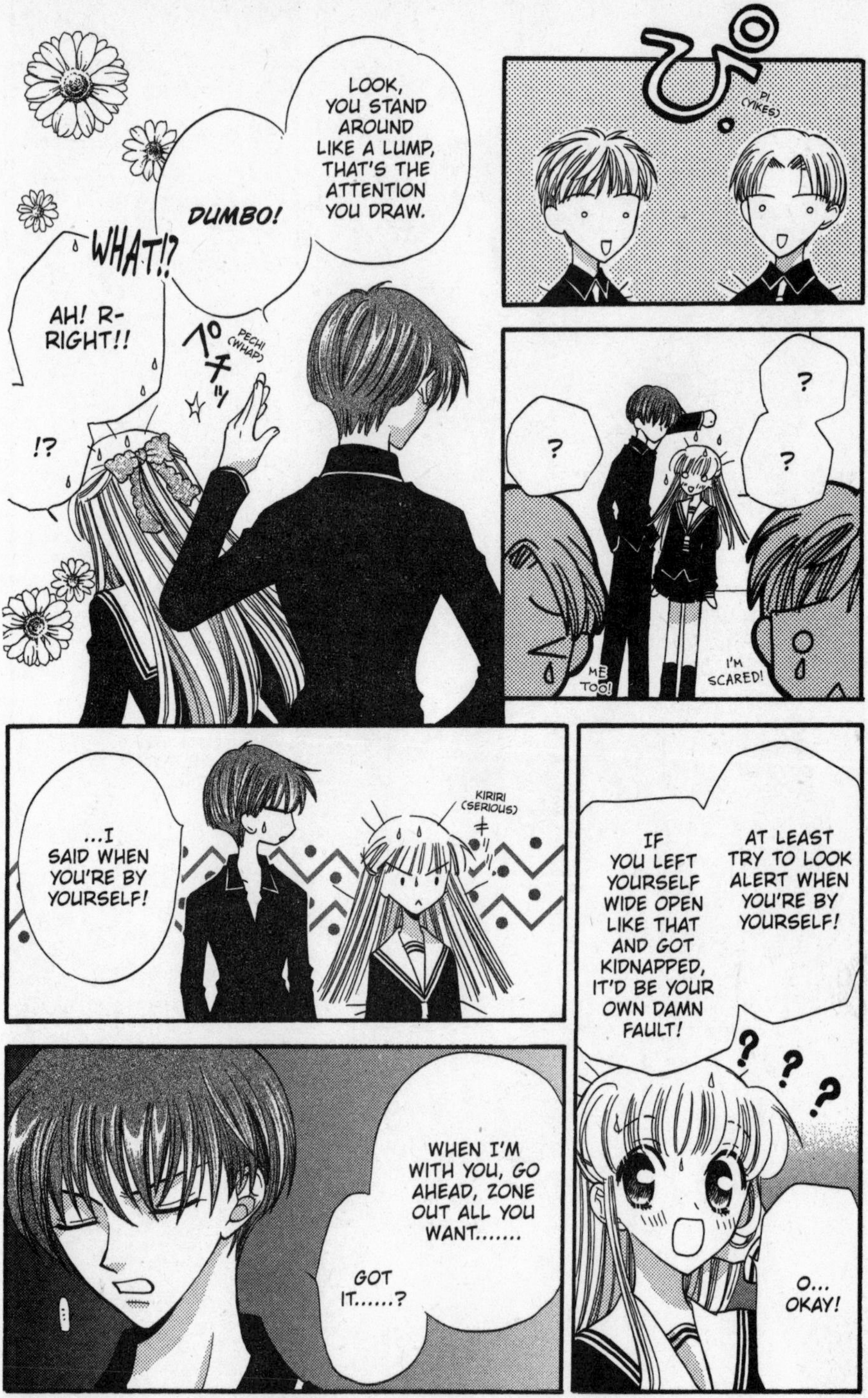
PI (YIKES)
?
?
?
ME TOO!
I'M SCARED!
LOOK, YOU STAND AROUND LIKE A LUMP, THAT'S THE ATTENTION YOU DRAW.
DUMBO!
WHAT!?
AH! R-RIGHT!!
PECHI (WHAP)
!?
AT LEAST TRY TO LOOK ALERT WHEN YOU'RE BY YOURSELF!
IF YOU LEFT YOURSELF WIDE OPEN LIKE THAT AND GOT KIDNAPPED, IT'D BE YOUR OWN DAMN FAULT!
O... OKAY!
KIRIRI (SERIOUS)
...I SAID WHEN YOU'RE BY YOURSELF!
WHEN I'M WITH YOU, GO AHEAD, ZONE OUT ALL YOU WANT.......
GOT IT......?
...

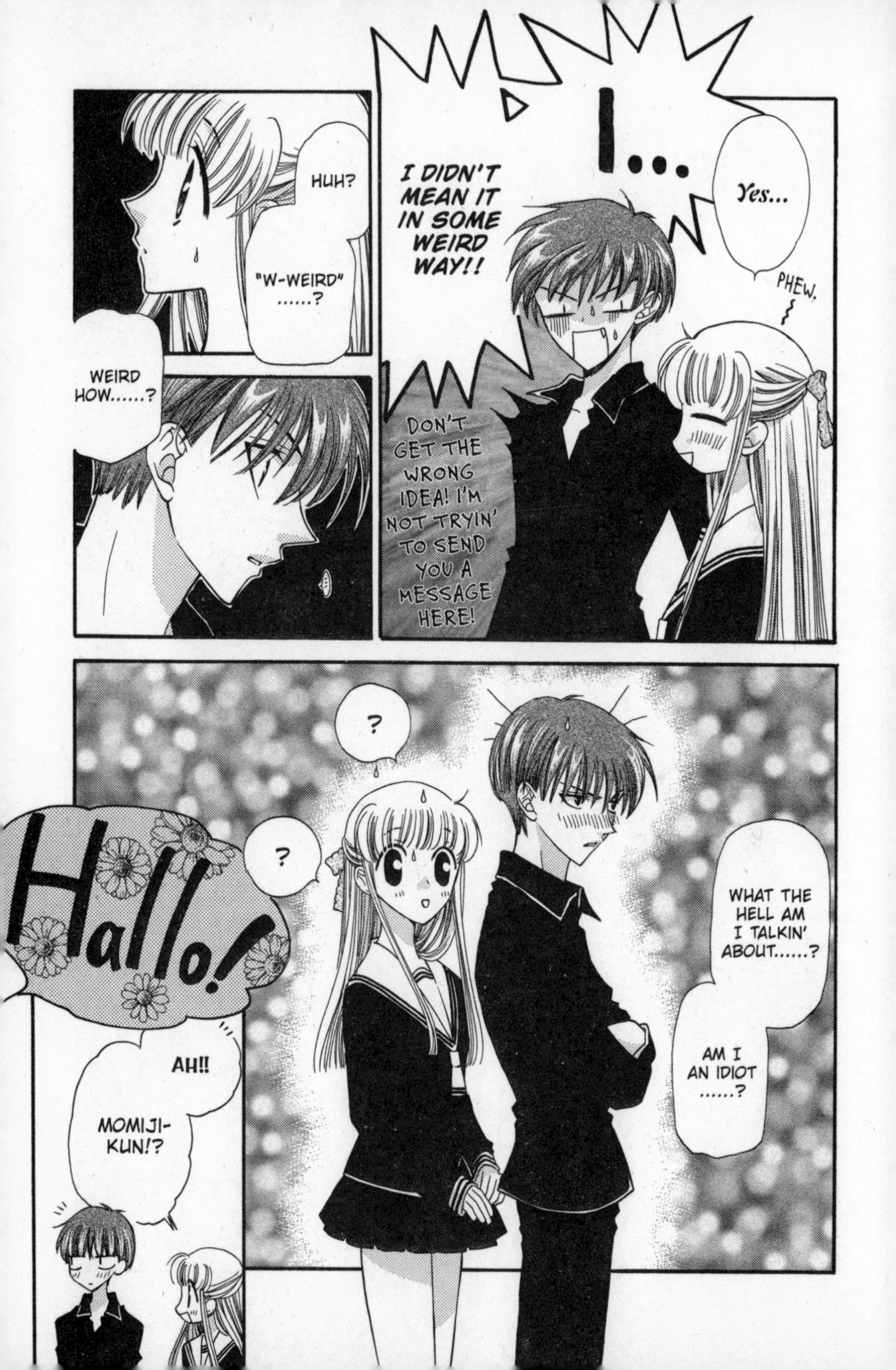
I...
Yes...
I DIDN'T MEAN IT IN SOME WEIRD WAY!!
PHEW.
DON'T GET THE WRONG IDEA! I'M NOT TRYIN' TO SEND YOU A MESSAGE HERE!
HUH?
"W-WEIRD" ......?
WEIRD HOW......?
?
?
WHAT THE HELL AM I TALKIN' ABOUT......?
AM I AN IDIOT ......?
Hallo!
AH!!
MOMIJI-KUN!?

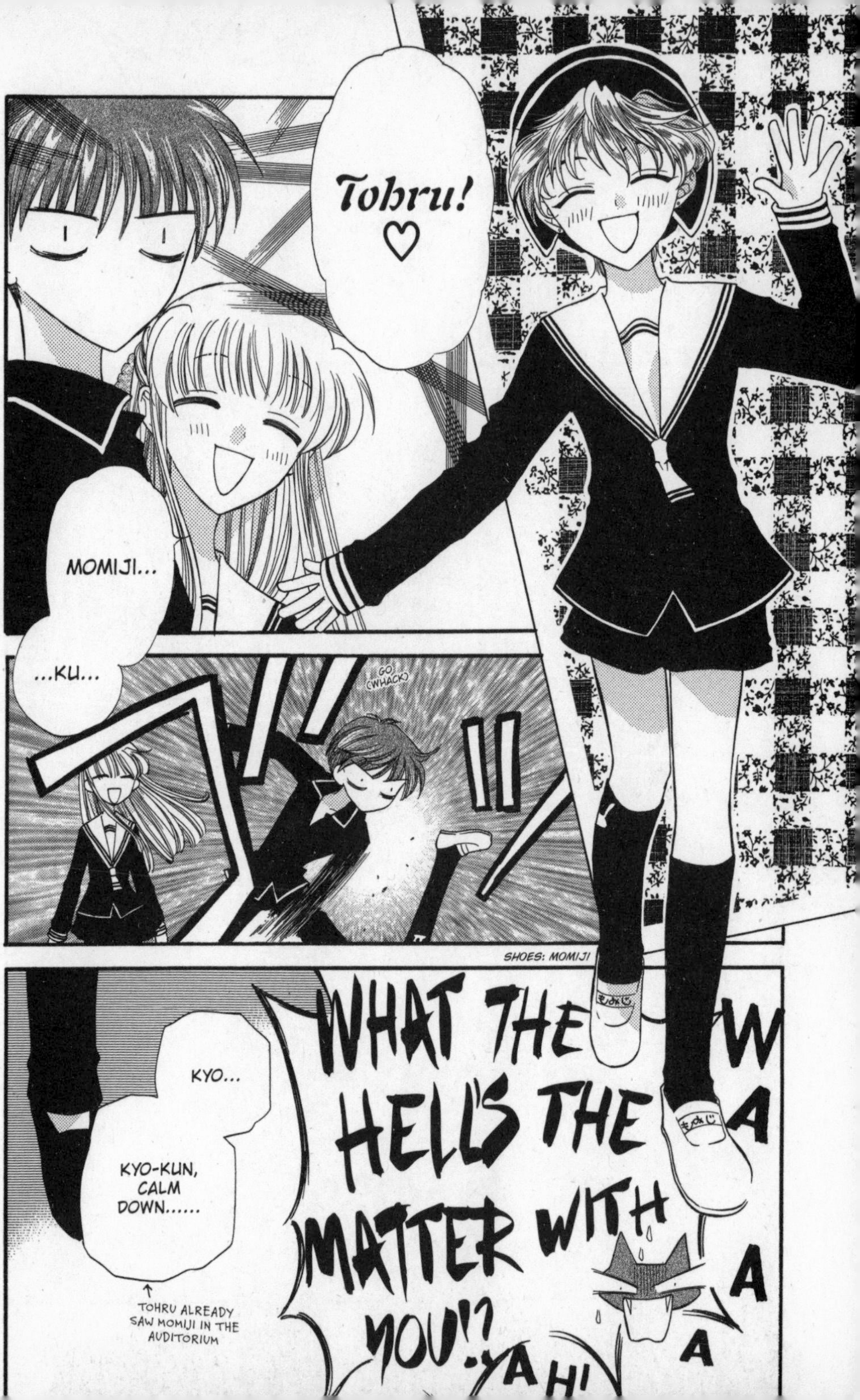

Tohru! ♡
MOMIJI...
...KU...
GO (WHACK)
SHOES: MOMIJI
WHAT THE HELL'S THE MATTER WITH YOU!?
WAAAAAH!
KYO...
KYO-KUN, CALM DOWN......
TOHRU ALREADY SAW MOMIJI IN THE AUDITORIUM

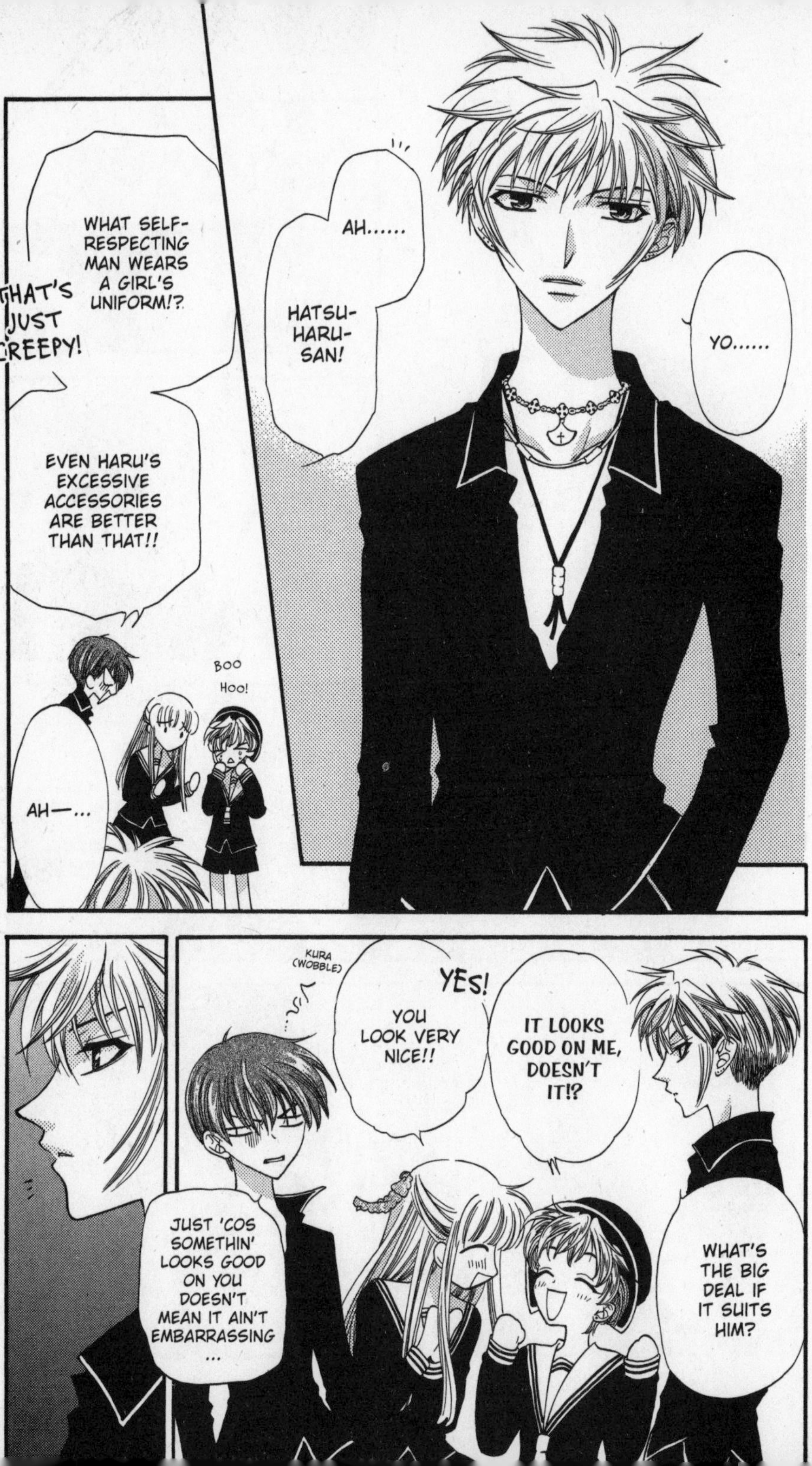
YO......
AH......
HATSU-HARU-SAN!
WHAT SELF-RESPECTING MAN WEARS A GIRL'S UNIFORM!?
THAT'S JUST CREEPY!
EVEN HARU'S EXCESSIVE ACCESSORIES ARE BETTER THAN THAT!!
BOO HOO!
AH—...
IT LOOKS GOOD ON ME, DOESN'T IT!?
YES!
YOU LOOK VERY NICE!!
KURA (WOBBLE)
WHAT'S THE BIG DEAL IF IT SUITS HIM?
JUST 'COS SOMETHIN' LOOKS GOOD ON YOU DOESN'T MEAN IT AIN'T EMBARRASSING ...

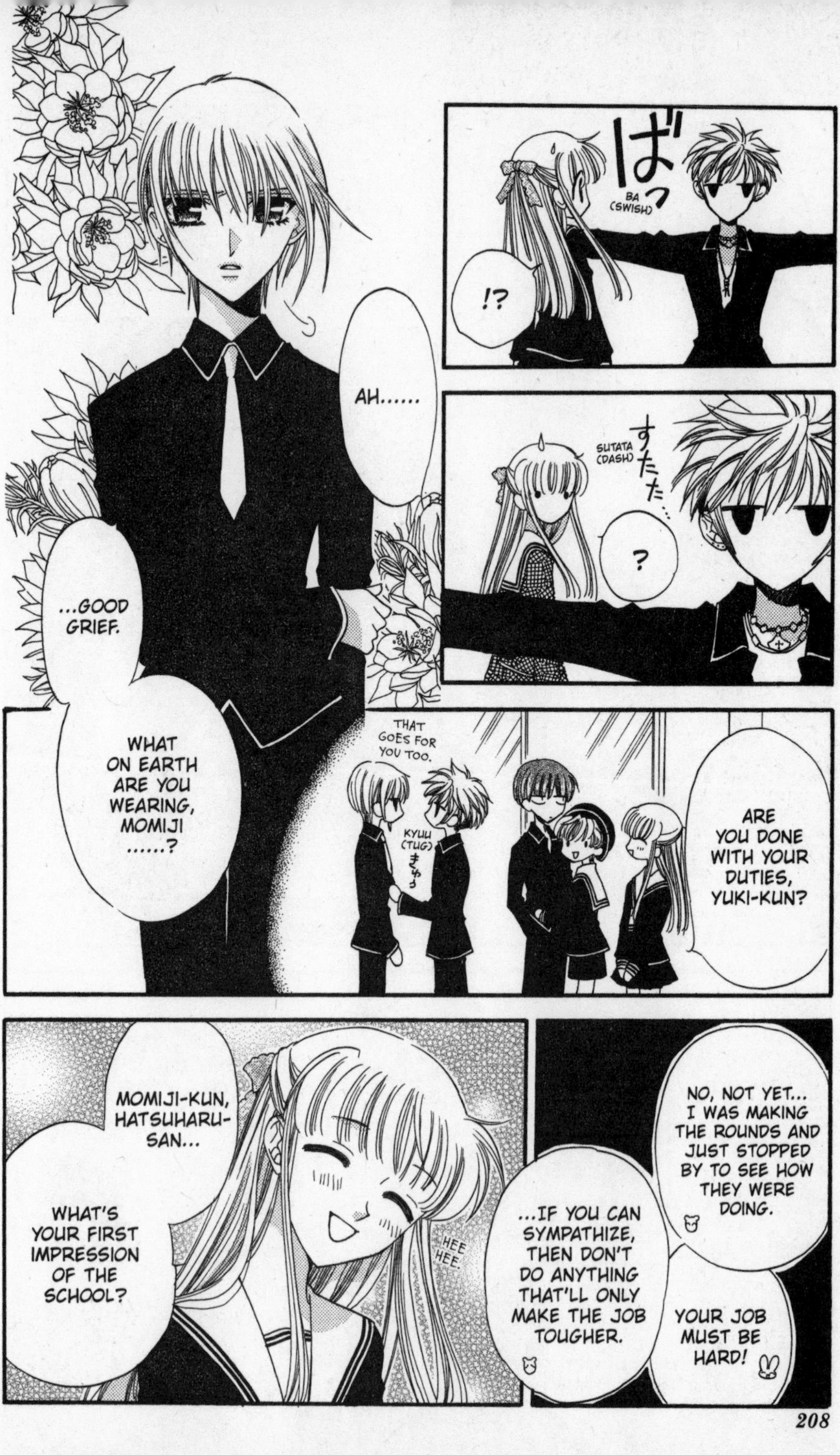
ばっ
BA (SWISH)
!?
すたた…
SUTATA (DASH)
?
AH......
...GOOD GRIEF.
WHAT ON EARTH ARE YOU WEARING, MOMIJI ......?
ARE YOU DONE WITH YOUR DUTIES, YUKI-KUN?
THAT GOES FOR YOU TOO.
きゅっ
KYUU (TUG)
NO, NOT YET... I WAS MAKING THE ROUNDS AND JUST STOPPED BY TO SEE HOW THEY WERE DOING.
YOUR JOB MUST BE HARD!
...IF YOU CAN SYMPATHIZE, THEN DON'T DO ANYTHING THAT'LL ONLY MAKE THE JOB TOUGHER.
MOMIJI-KUN, HATSUHARU-SAN...
WHAT'S YOUR FIRST IMPRESSION OF THE SCHOOL?
HEE HEE.

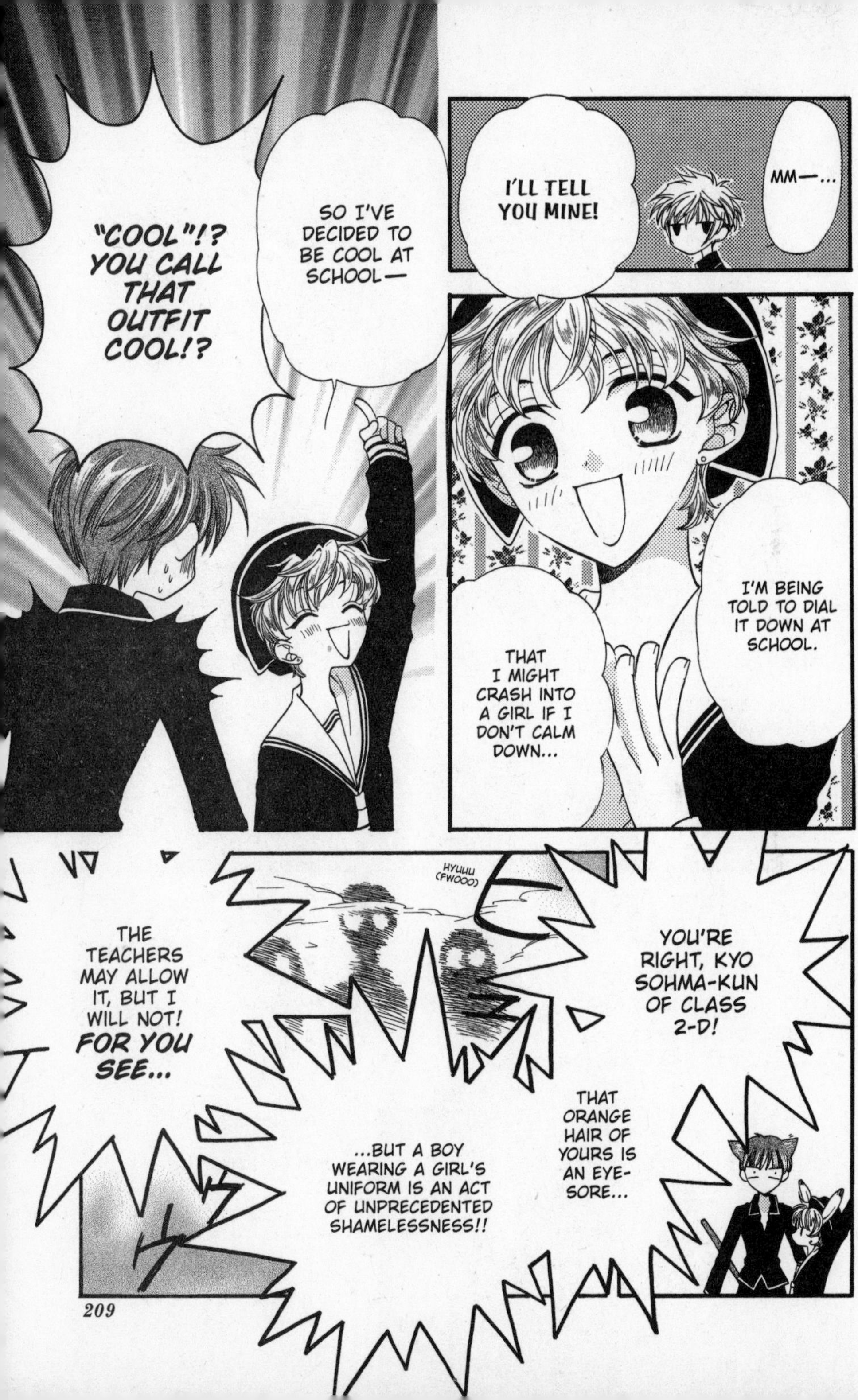
MM—...
I'LL TELL YOU MINE!
I'M BEING TOLD TO DIAL IT DOWN AT SCHOOL.
THAT I MIGHT CRASH INTO A GIRL IF I DON'T CALM DOWN...
SO I'VE DECIDED TO BE COOL AT SCHOOL—
"COOL"!? YOU CALL THAT OUTFIT COOL!?
HYUUU (FWOOO)
YOU'RE RIGHT, KYO SOHMA-KUN OF CLASS 2-D!
THAT ORANGE HAIR OF YOURS IS AN EYE-SORE...
THE TEACHERS MAY ALLOW IT, BUT I WILL NOT! FOR YOU SEE...
...BUT A BOY WEARING A GIRL'S UNIFORM IS AN ACT OF UNPRECEDENTED SHAMELESSNESS!!

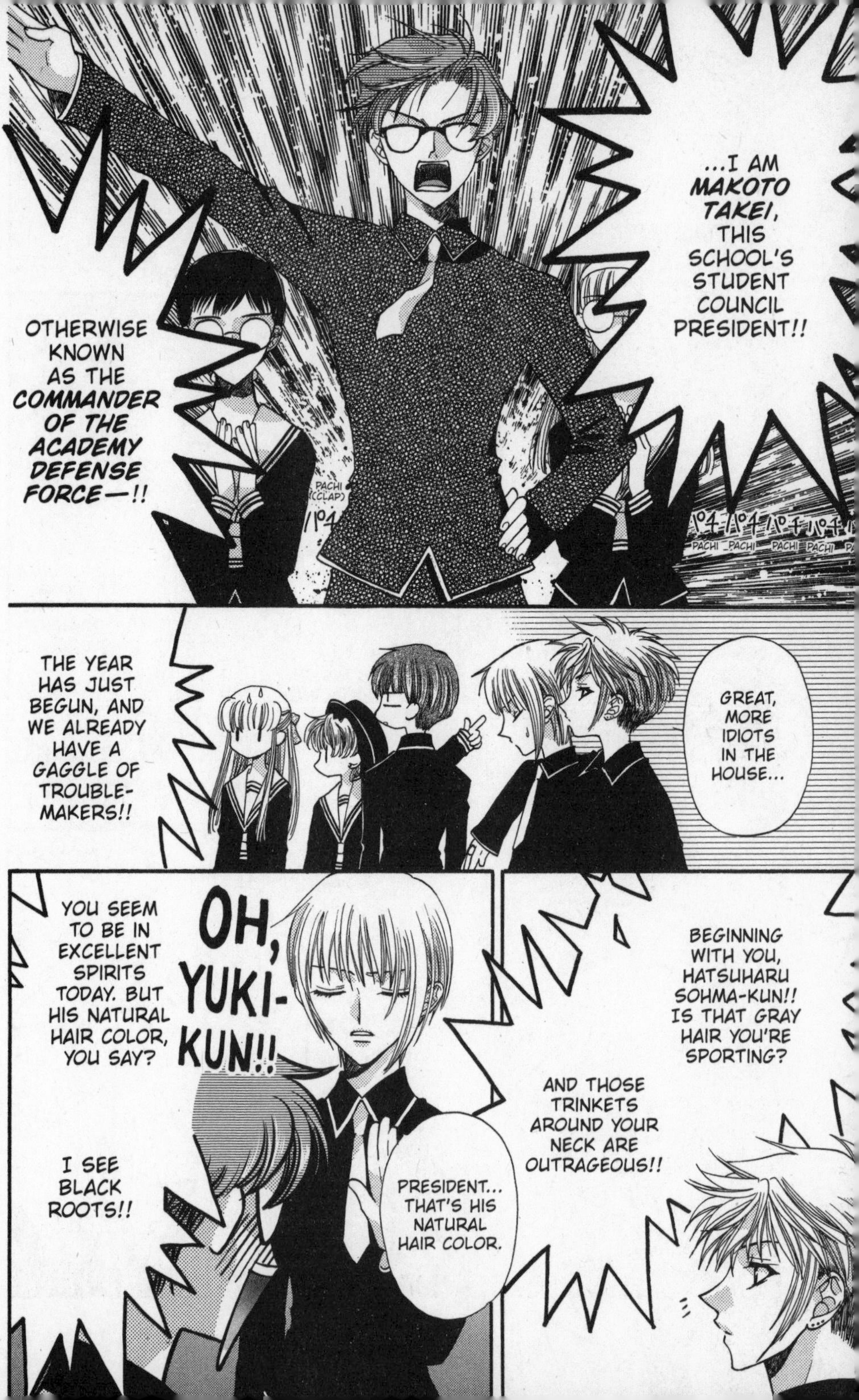
...I AM MAKOTO TAKEI, THIS SCHOOL'S STUDENT COUNCIL PRESIDENT!!
OTHERWISE KNOWN AS THE COMMANDER OF THE ACADEMY DEFENSE FORCE—!!
PACHI (CLAP)
PACHI PACHI PACHI PACHI
GREAT, MORE IDIOTS IN THE HOUSE...
THE YEAR HAS JUST BEGUN, AND WE ALREADY HAVE A GAGGLE OF TROUBLE-MAKERS!!
BEGINNING WITH YOU, HATSUHARU SOHMA-KUN!! IS THAT GRAY HAIR YOU'RE SPORTING?
AND THOSE TRINKETS AROUND YOUR NECK ARE OUTRAGEOUS!!
PRESIDENT... THAT'S HIS NATURAL HAIR COLOR.
OH, YUKI-KUN!!
YOU SEEM TO BE IN EXCELLENT SPIRITS TODAY. BUT HIS NATURAL HAIR COLOR, YOU SAY?
I SEE BLACK ROOTS!!

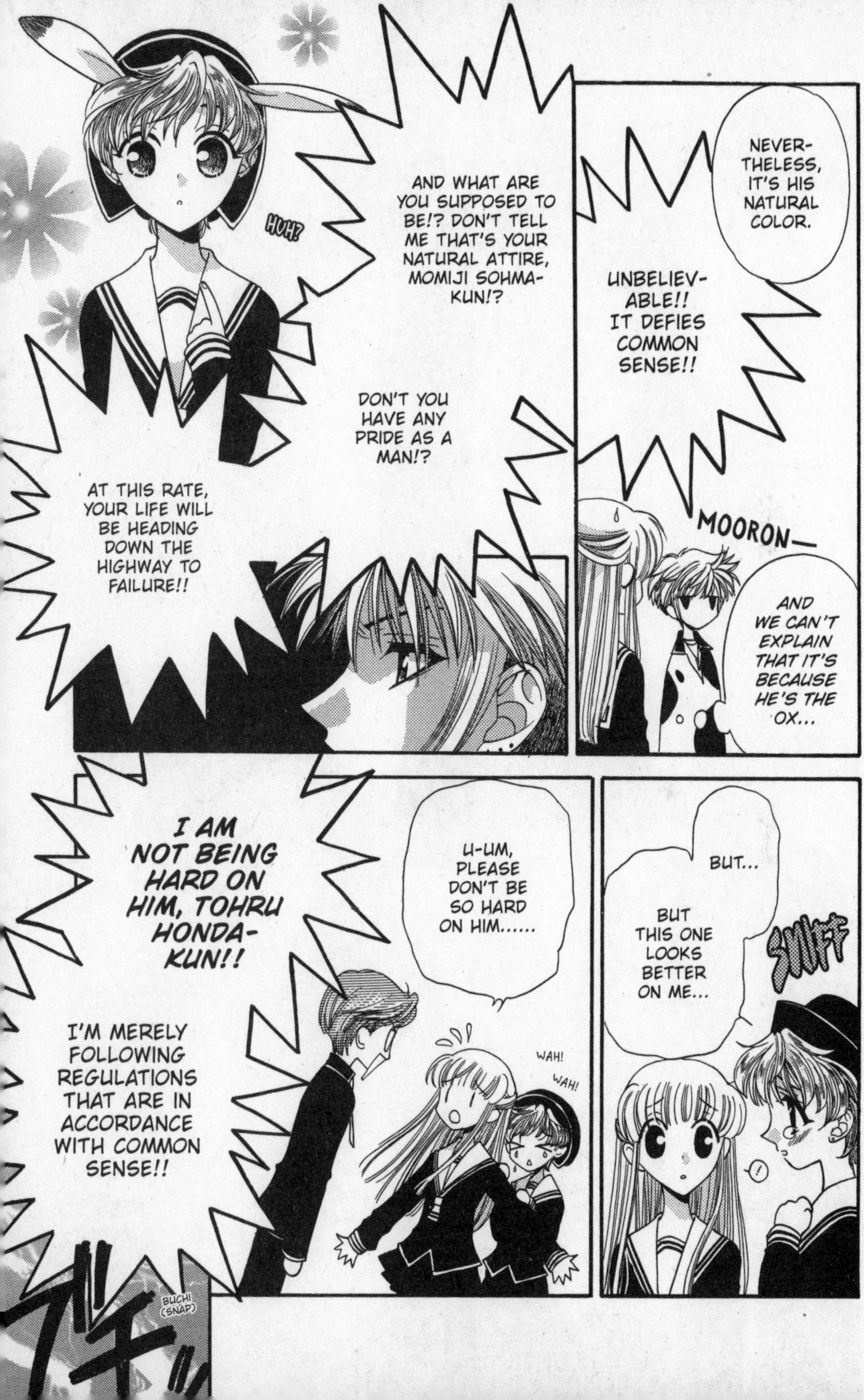
NEVER-THELESS, IT'S HIS NATURAL COLOR.
UNBELIEVABLE!! IT DEFIES COMMON SENSE!!
MOORON—
AND WE CAN'T EXPLAIN THAT IT'S BECAUSE HE'S THE OX...
HUH?
AND WHAT ARE YOU SUPPOSED TO BE!? DON'T TELL ME THAT'S YOUR NATURAL ATTIRE, MOMIJI SOHMA-KUN!?
DON'T YOU HAVE ANY PRIDE AS A MAN!?
AT THIS RATE, YOUR LIFE WILL BE HEADING DOWN THE HIGHWAY TO FAILURE!!
BUT...
BUT THIS ONE LOOKS BETTER ON ME...
SNIFF
!
U-UM, PLEASE DON'T BE SO HARD ON HIM......
WAH!
WAH!
I AM NOT BEING HARD ON HIM, TOHRU HONDA-KUN!!
I'M MERELY FOLLOWING REGULATIONS THAT ARE IN ACCORDANCE WITH COMMON SENSE!!
BUCHI (SNAP)

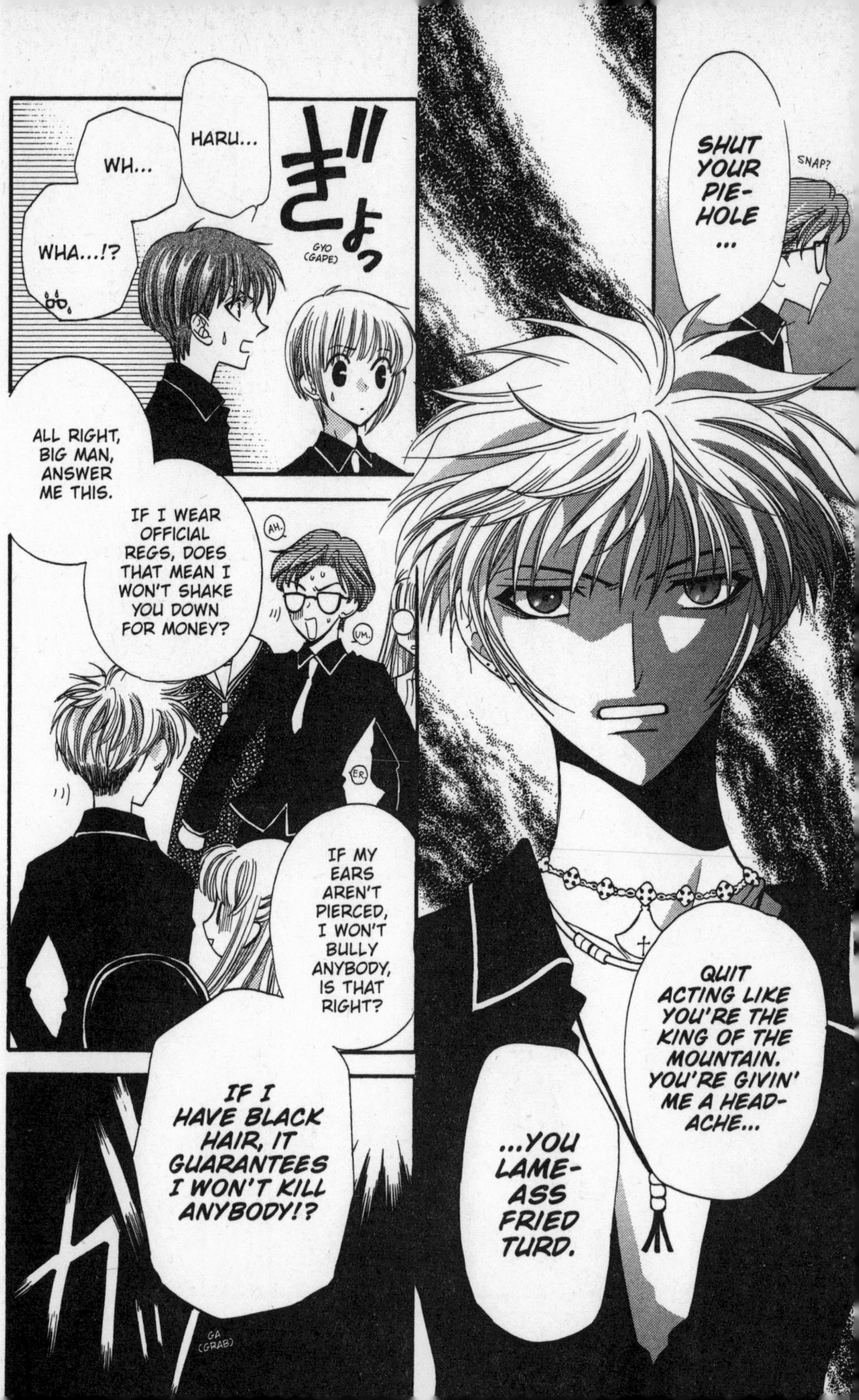
SHUT YOUR PIE-HOLE...
SNAP?
HARU...
WH...
WHA...!?
ぎょっ
GYO (GAPE)
ALL RIGHT, BIG MAN, ANSWER ME THIS.
IF I WEAR OFFICIAL REGS, DOES THAT MEAN I WON'T SHAKE YOU DOWN FOR MONEY?
AH.
UM.
ER.
IF MY EARS AREN'T PIERCED, I WON'T BULLY ANYBODY, IS THAT RIGHT?
IF I HAVE BLACK HAIR, IT GUARANTEES I WON'T KILL ANYBODY!?
GA (GRAB)
QUIT ACTING LIKE YOU'RE THE KING OF THE MOUNTAIN. YOU'RE GIVIN' ME A HEAD-ACHE...
...YOU LAME-ASS FRIED TURD.

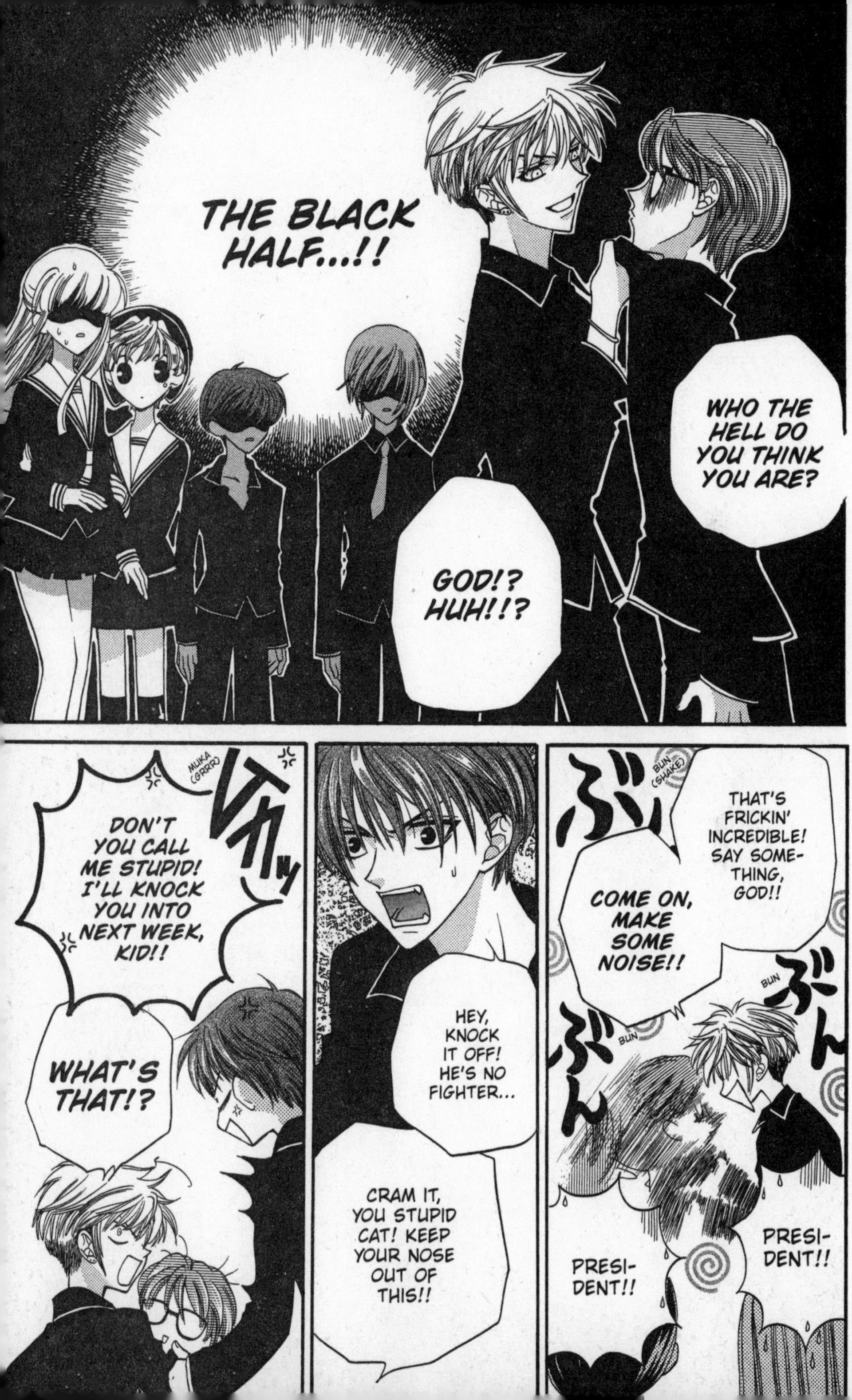
THE BLACK HALF...!!
WHO THE HELL DO YOU THINK YOU ARE?
GOD!? HUH!!?
ぶん
BUN (SHAKE)
THAT'S FRICKIN' INCREDIBLE! SAY SOME-THING, GOD!!
COME ON, MAKE SOME NOISE!!
ぶん
BUN
ぶん
BUN
PRESI-DENT!!
PRESI-DENT!!
HEY, KNOCK IT OFF! HE'S NO FIGHTER...
CRAM IT, YOU STUPID CAT! KEEP YOUR NOSE OUT OF THIS!!
ムカッ
MUKA (GRRR)
DON'T YOU CALL ME STUPID! I'LL KNOCK YOU INTO NEXT WEEK, KID!!
WHAT'S THAT!?

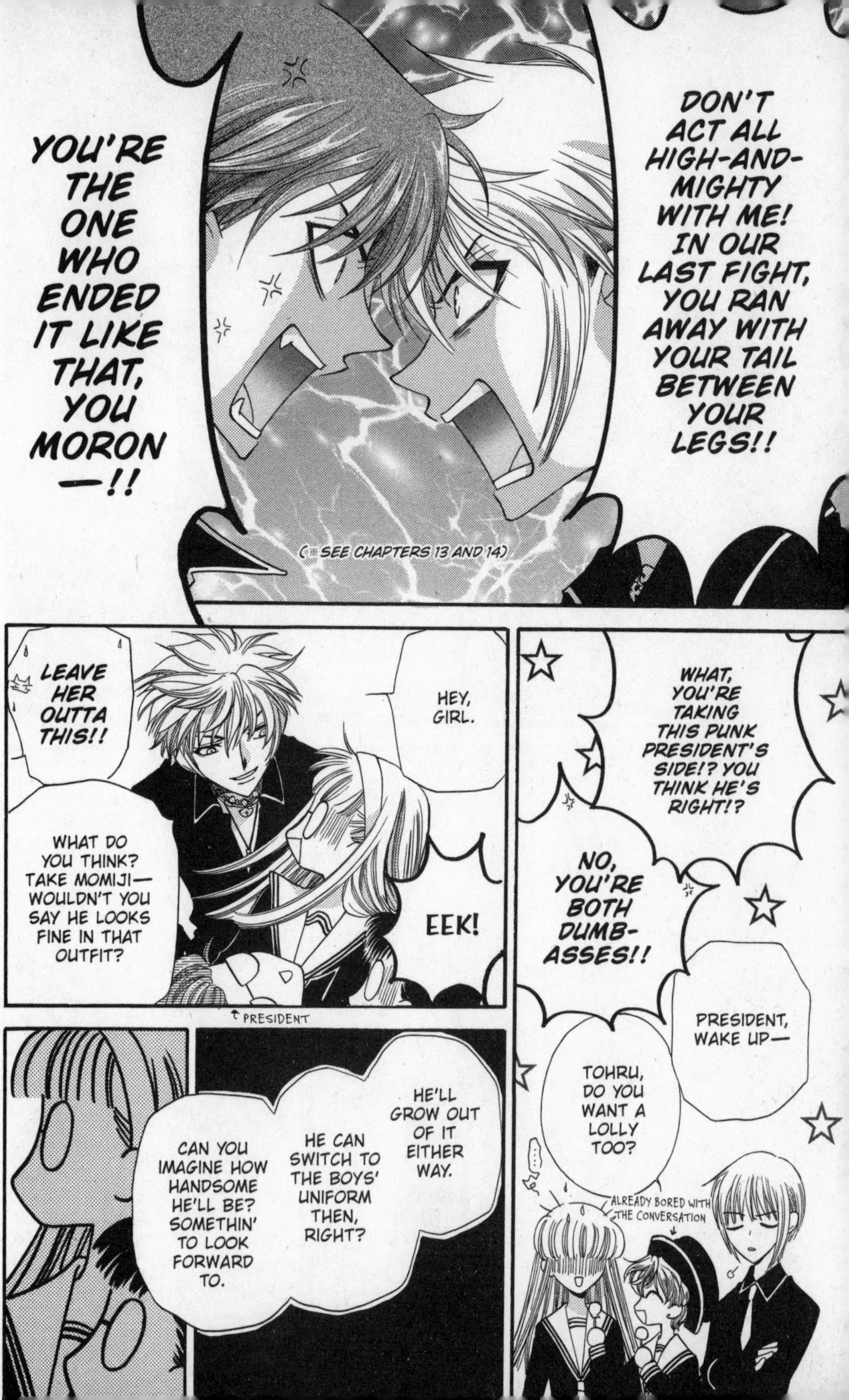
DON'T ACT ALL HIGH-AND-MIGHTY WITH ME! IN OUR LAST FIGHT, YOU RAN AWAY WITH YOUR TAIL BETWEEN YOUR LEGS!!
YOU'RE THE ONE WHO ENDED IT LIKE THAT, YOU MORON—!!
(※SEE CHAPTERS 13 AND 14)
WHAT, YOU'RE TAKING THIS PUNK PRESIDENT'S SIDE!? YOU THINK HE'S RIGHT!?
NO, YOU'RE BOTH DUMB-ASSES!!
PRESIDENT, WAKE UP—
TOHRU, DO YOU WANT A LOLLY TOO?
...
ALREADY BORED WITH THE CONVERSATION
HEY, GIRL.
LEAVE HER OUTTA THIS!!
EEK!
WHAT DO YOU THINK? TAKE MOMIJI—WOULDN'T YOU SAY HE LOOKS FINE IN THAT OUTFIT?
PRESIDENT
HE'LL GROW OUT OF IT EITHER WAY.
HE CAN SWITCH TO THE BOYS' UNIFORM THEN, RIGHT?
CAN YOU IMAGINE HOW HANDSOME HE'LL BE? SOMETHIN' TO LOOK FORWARD TO.

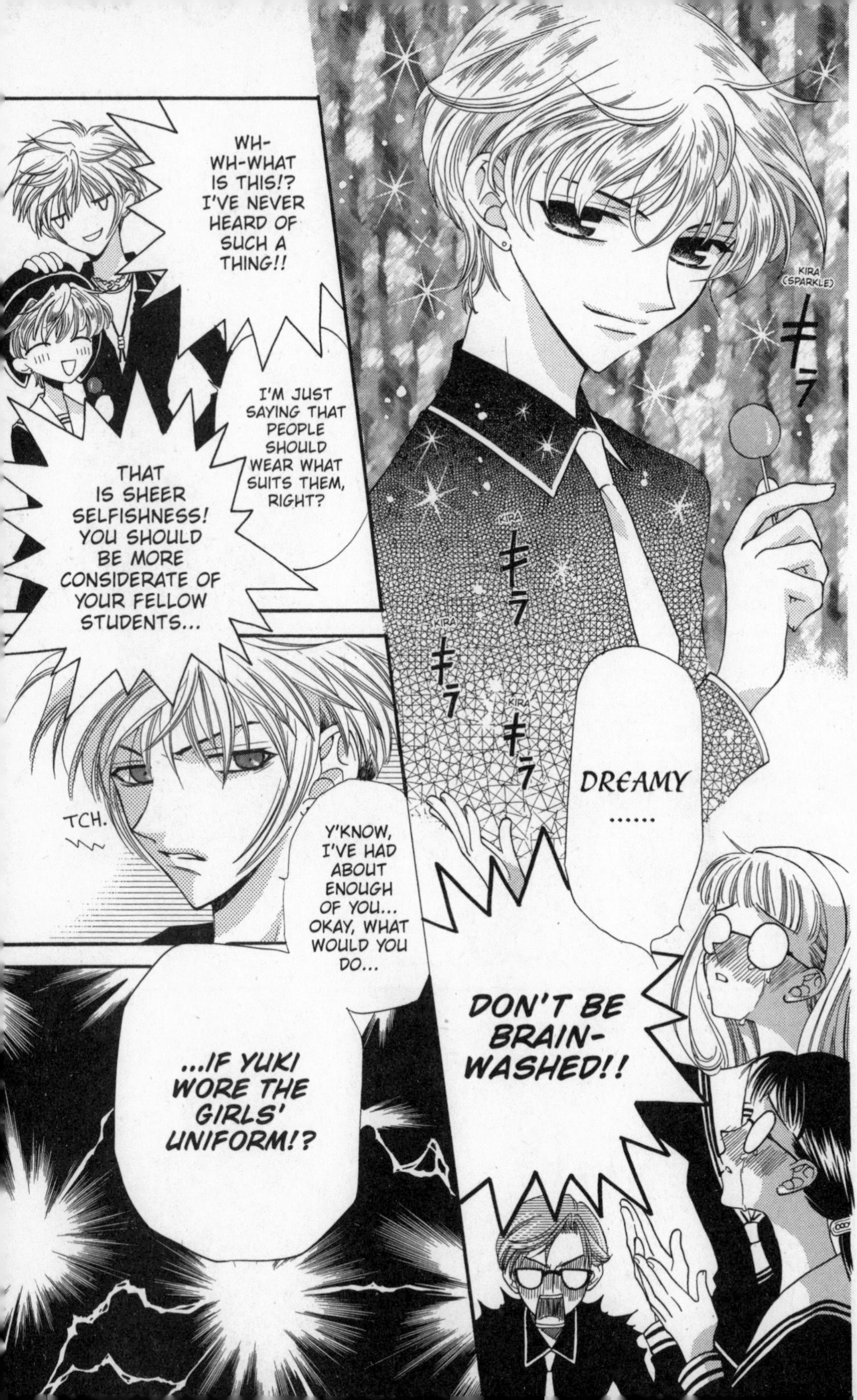

WH-WH-WHAT IS THIS!? I'VE NEVER HEARD OF SUCH A THING!!
I'M JUST SAYING THAT PEOPLE SHOULD WEAR WHAT SUITS THEM, RIGHT?
THAT IS SHEER SELFISHNESS! YOU SHOULD BE MORE CONSIDERATE OF YOUR FELLOW STUDENTS...
TCH.
Y'KNOW, I'VE HAD ABOUT ENOUGH OF YOU... OKAY, WHAT WOULD YOU DO...
...IF YUKI WORE THE GIRLS' UNIFORM!?
KIRA (SPARKLE)
KIRA
KIRA
KIRA
DREAMY ......
DON'T BE BRAIN-WASHED!!

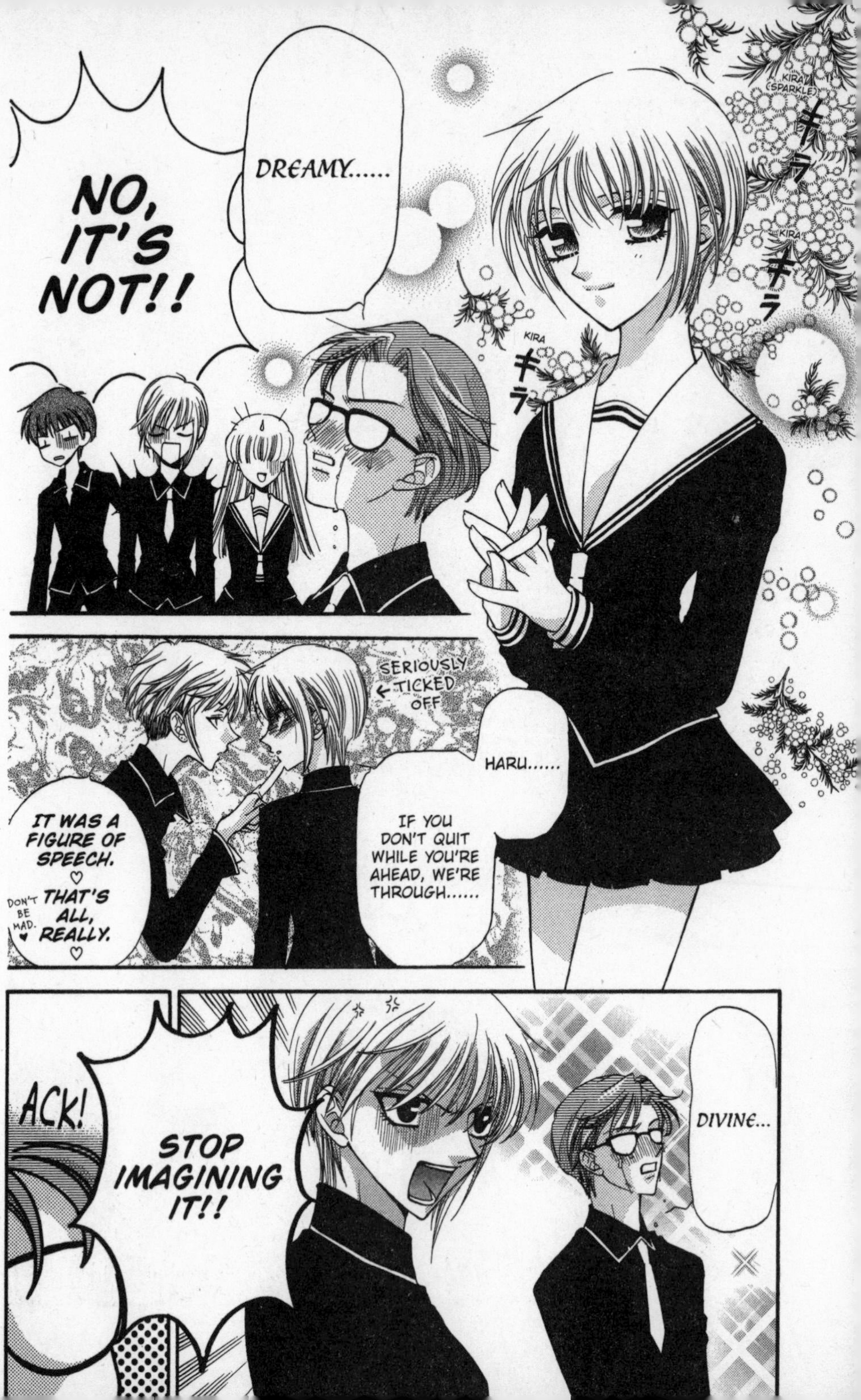

KIRA (SPARKLE)
キラ
KIRA
キラ
KIRA
キラ
DREAMY......
NO, IT'S NOT!!
HARU......
IF YOU DON'T QUIT WHILE YOU'RE AHEAD, WE'RE THROUGH......
SERIOUSLY ← TICKED OFF
IT WAS A FIGURE OF SPEECH. ♡ THAT'S ALL, REALLY. ♡
DON'T BE MAD. ♥
DIVINE...
STOP IMAGINING IT!!
ACK!

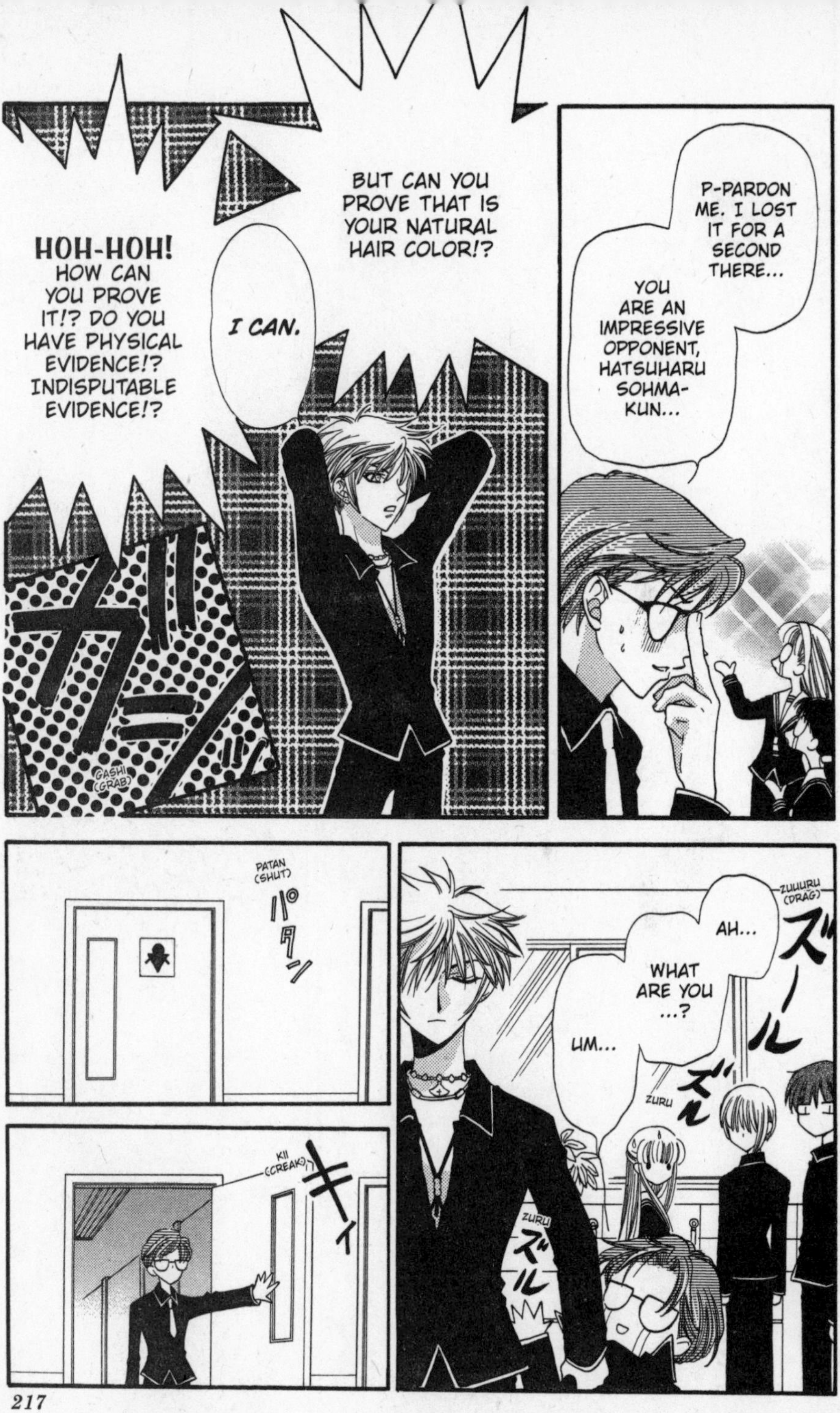
P-PARDON ME. I LOST IT FOR A SECOND THERE...
YOU ARE AN IMPRESSIVE OPPONENT, HATSUHARU SOHMA-KUN...
BUT CAN YOU PROVE THAT IS YOUR NATURAL HAIR COLOR!?
HOH-HOH! HOW CAN YOU PROVE IT!? DO YOU HAVE PHYSICAL EVIDENCE!? INDISPUTABLE EVIDENCE!?
I CAN.
GASHI (GRAB)
ZUUURU (DRAG)
AH...
WHAT ARE YOU ...?
UM...
ZURU
ZURU
PATAN (SHUT)
KII (CREAK)

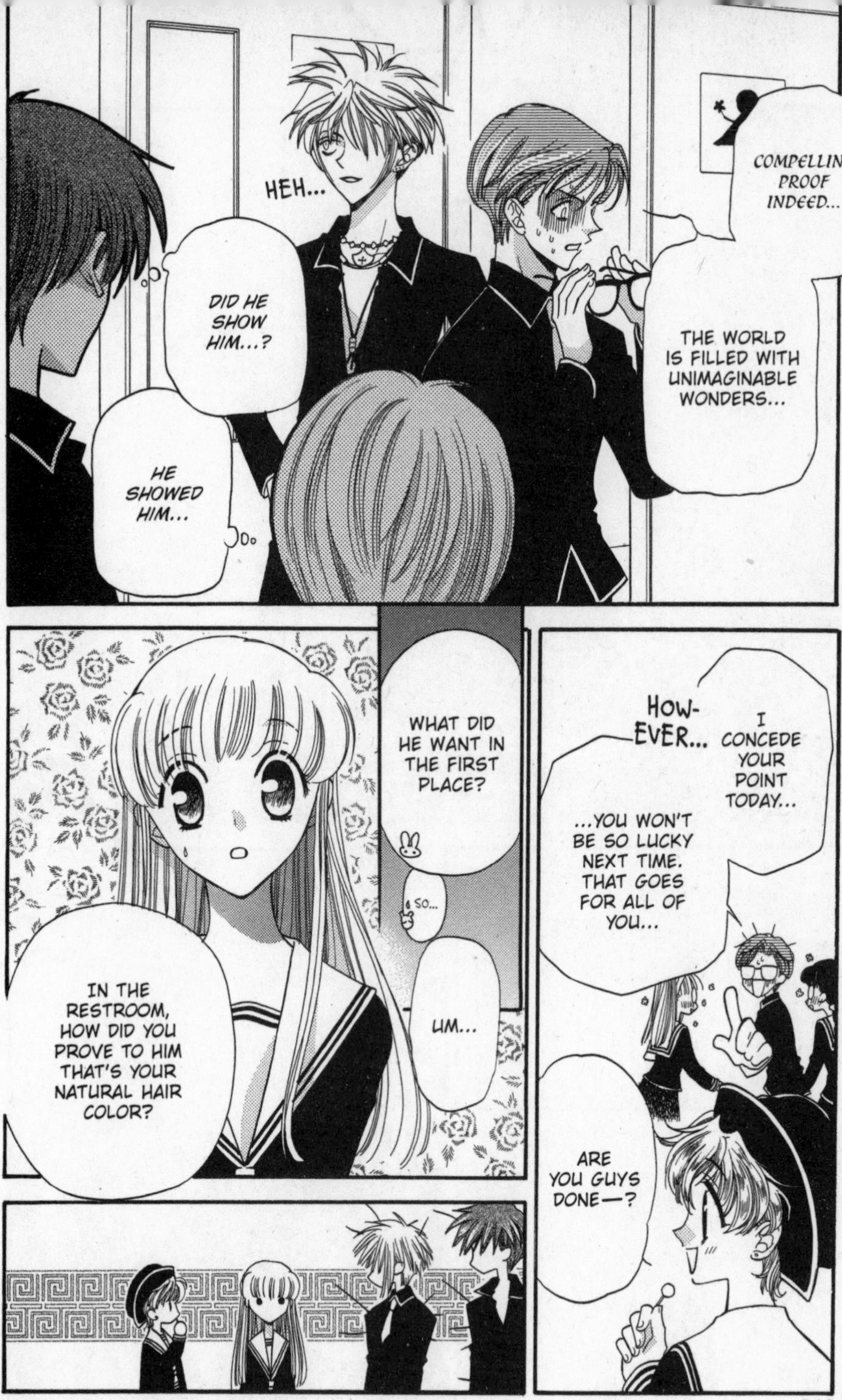

COMPELLING PROOF INDEED...
THE WORLD IS FILLED WITH UNIMAGINABLE WONDERS...
HEH...
DID HE SHOW HIM...?
HE SHOWED HIM...
I CONCEDE YOUR POINT TODAY...
HOW-EVER...
...YOU WON'T BE SO LUCKY NEXT TIME. THAT GOES FOR ALL OF YOU...
ARE YOU GUYS DONE—?
WHAT DID HE WANT IN THE FIRST PLACE?
SO...
UM...
IN THE RESTROOM, HOW DID YOU PROVE TO HIM THAT'S YOUR NATURAL HAIR COLOR?

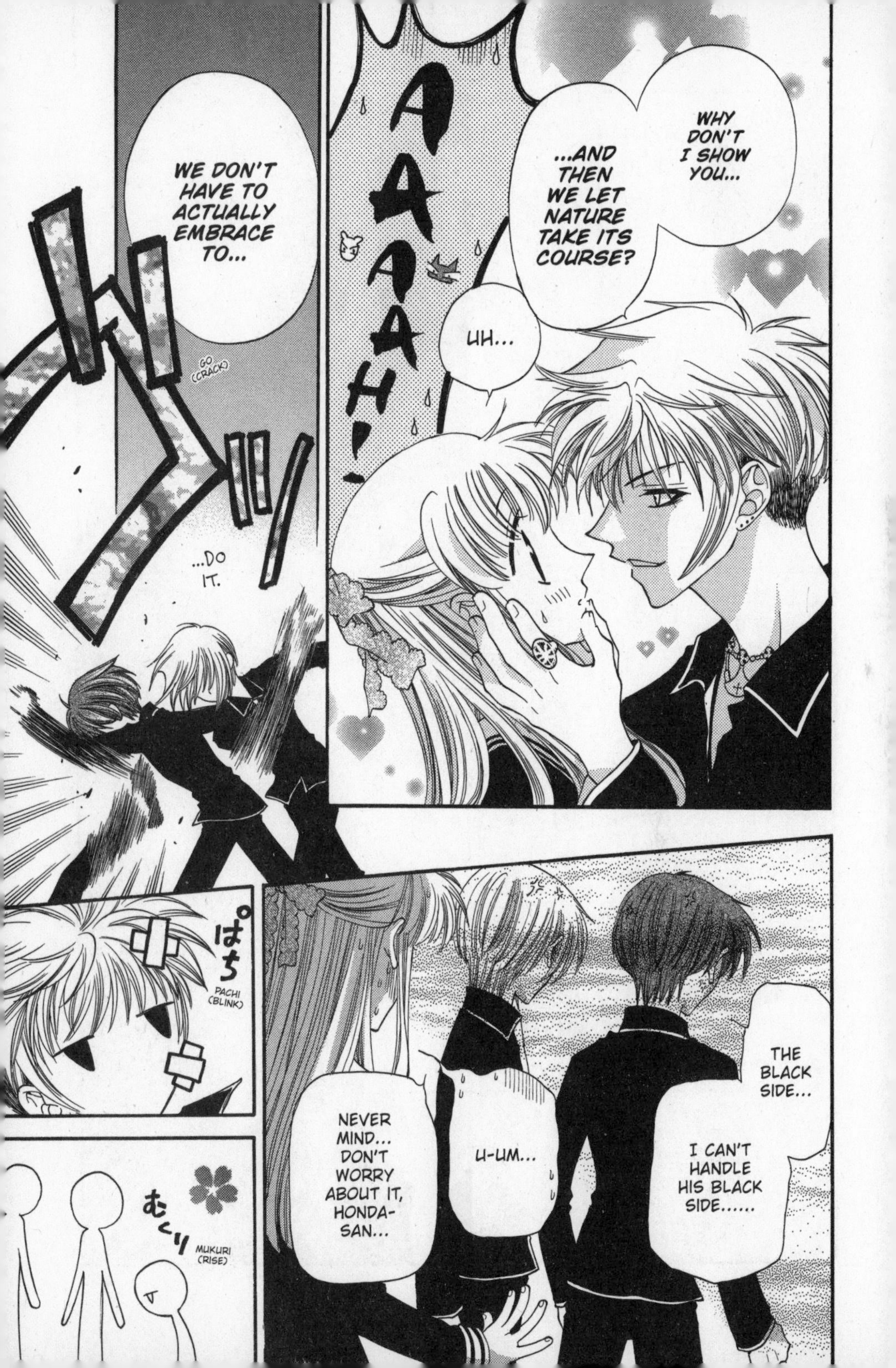

WHY DON'T I SHOW YOU...
...AND THEN WE LET NATURE TAKE ITS COURSE?
AAAAH!!
UH...
WE DON'T HAVE TO ACTUALLY EMBRACE TO...
GO (CRACK)
...DO IT.
THE BLACK SIDE...
I CAN'T HANDLE HIS BLACK SIDE......
U-UM...
NEVER MIND... DON'T WORRY ABOUT IT, HONDA-SAN...
ぱち
PACHI (BLINK)
むくり
MUKURI (RISE)

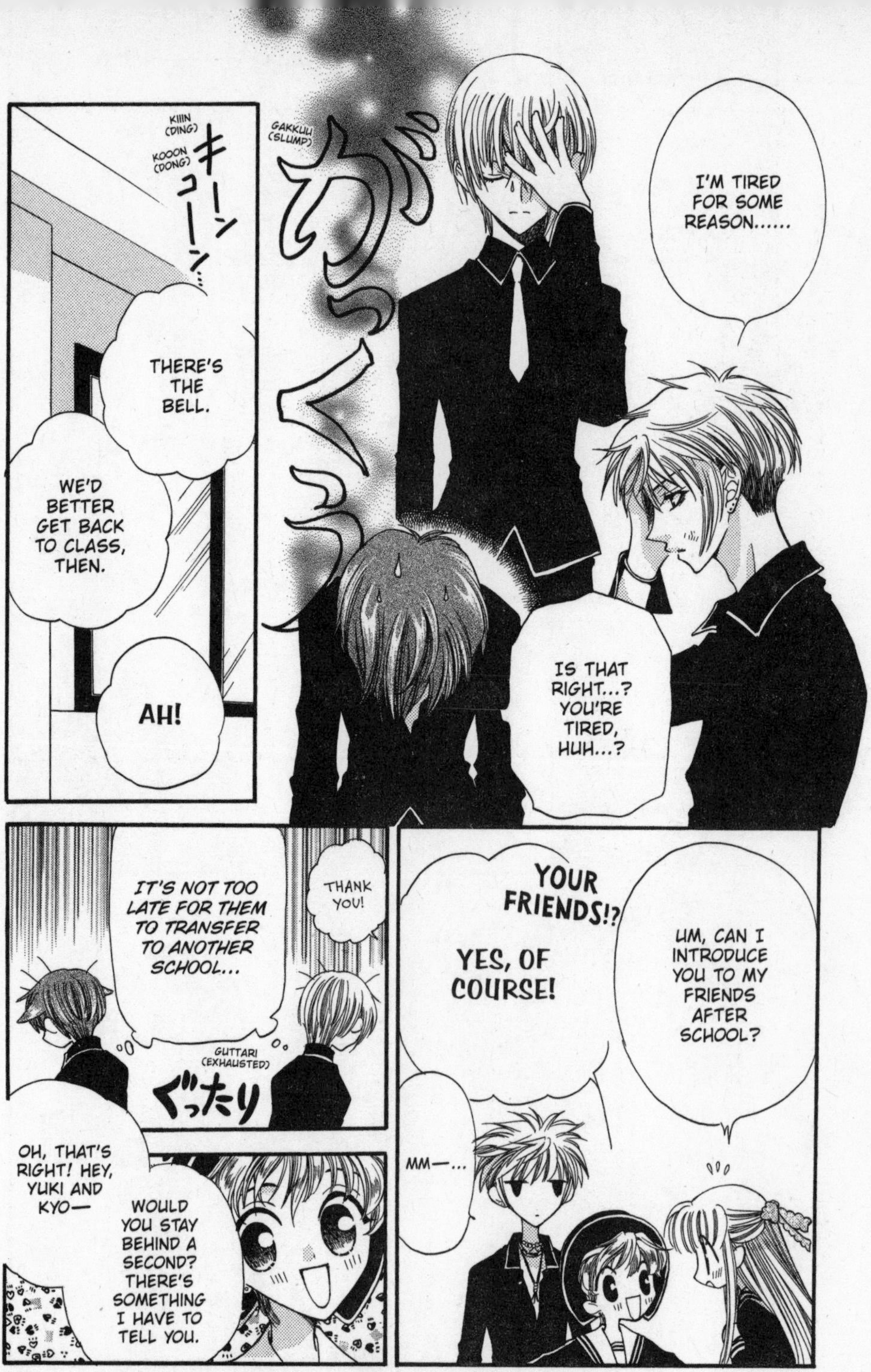
GAKKUU (SLUMP)
I'M TIRED FOR SOME REASON......
IS THAT RIGHT...? YOU'RE TIRED, HUH...?
KIIN (DING) KOOON (DONG)
キーンコーン
THERE'S THE BELL.
WE'D BETTER GET BACK TO CLASS, THEN.
AH!
UM, CAN I INTRODUCE YOU TO MY FRIENDS AFTER SCHOOL?
YOUR FRIENDS!?
YES, OF COURSE!
MM—...
THANK YOU!
IT'S NOT TOO LATE FOR THEM TO TRANSFER TO ANOTHER SCHOOL...
GUTTARI (EXHAUSTED)
ぐったり
OH, THAT'S RIGHT! HEY, YUKI AND KYO—
WOULD YOU STAY BEHIND A SECOND? THERE'S SOMETHING I HAVE TO TELL YOU.

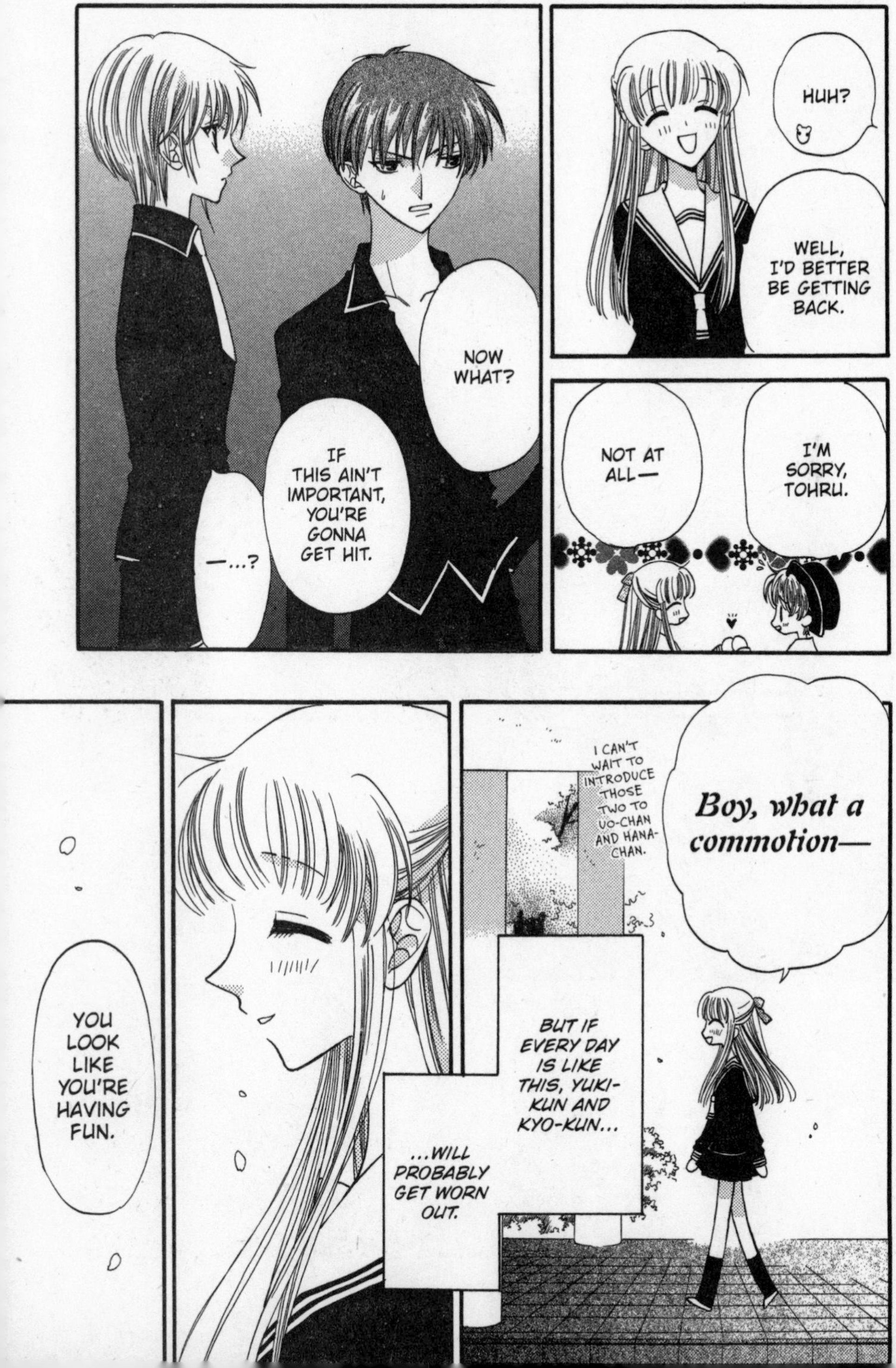
HUH?
WELL, I'D BETTER BE GETTING BACK.
I'M SORRY, TOHRU.
NOT AT ALL—
NOW WHAT?
IF THIS AIN'T IMPORTANT, YOU'RE GONNA GET HIT.
—...?
Boy, what a commotion—
I CAN'T WAIT TO INTRODUCE THOSE TWO TO UO-CHAN AND HANA-CHAN.
BUT IF EVERY DAY IS LIKE THIS, YUKI-KUN AND KYO-KUN...
...WILL PROBABLY GET WORN OUT.
YOU LOOK LIKE YOU'RE HAVING FUN.

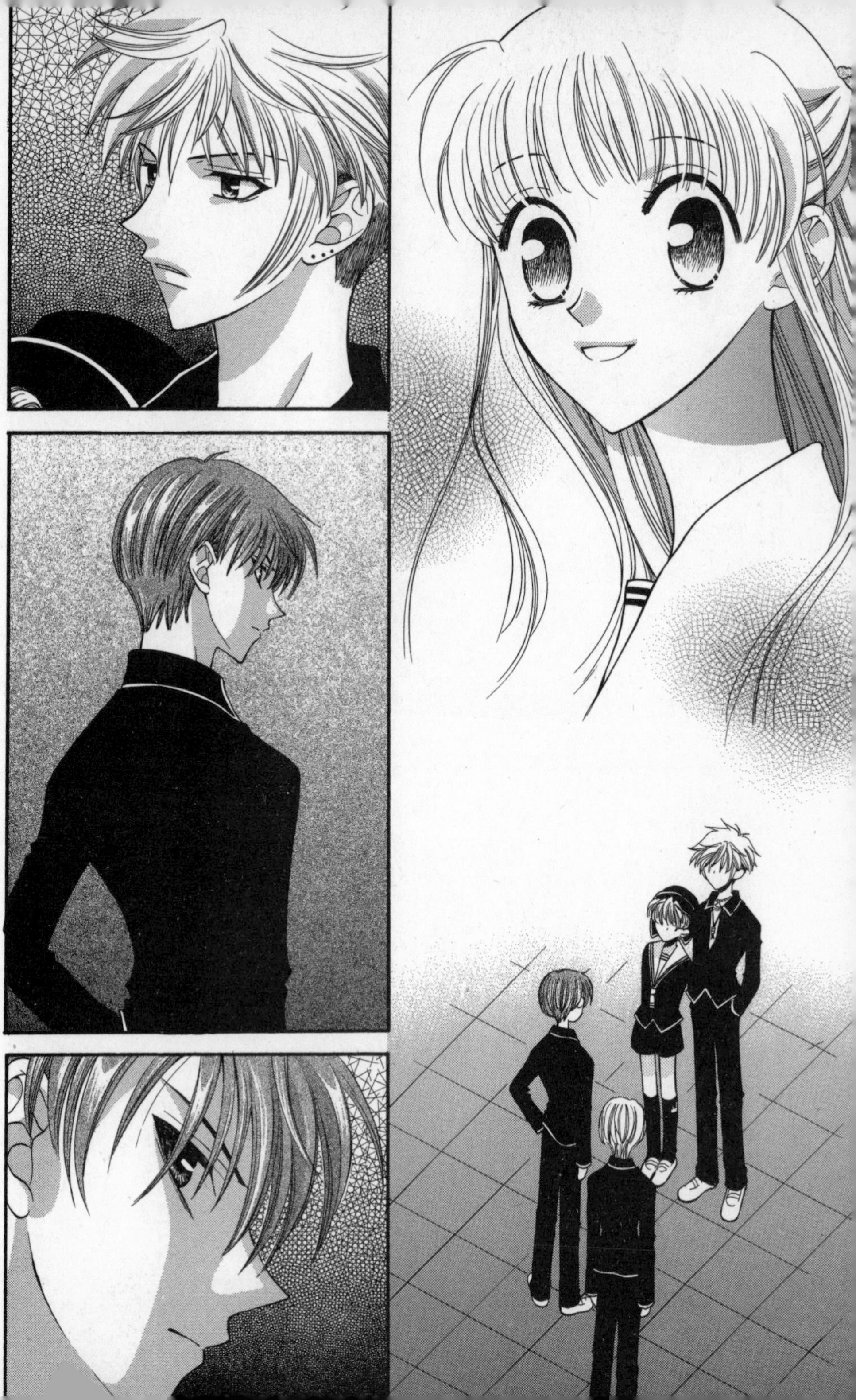

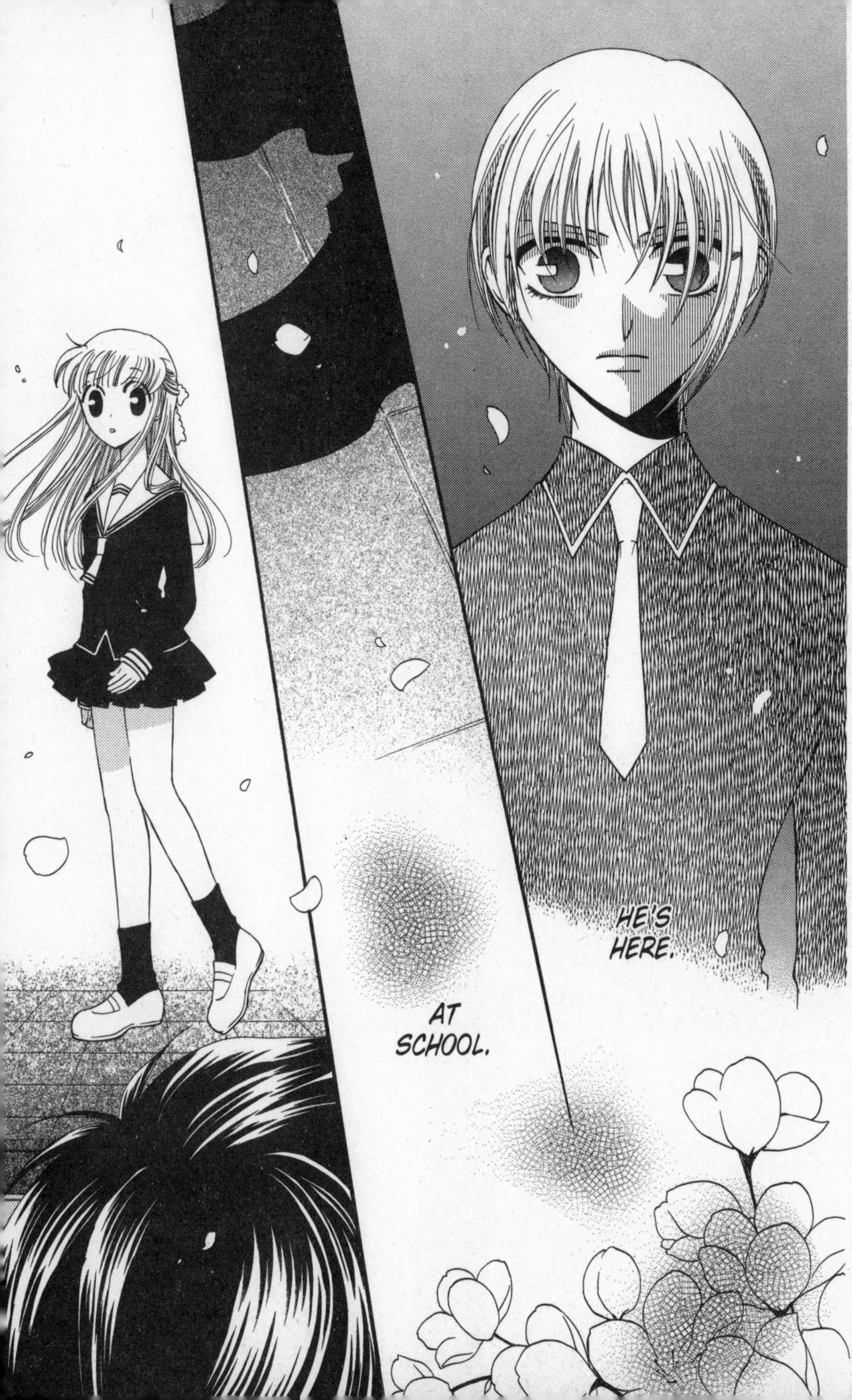
HE'S HERE.
AT SCHOOL.

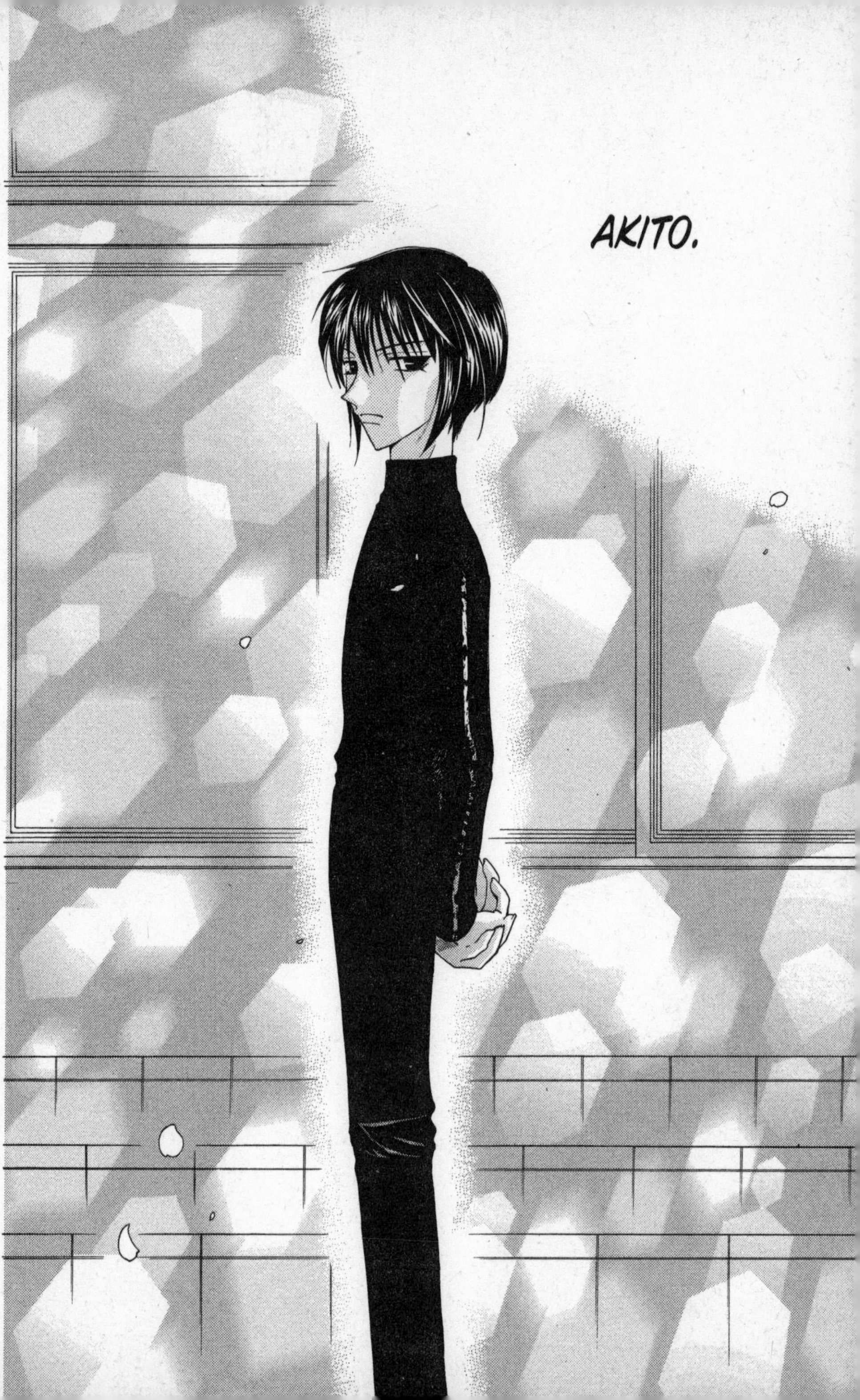
AKITO.

Chapter 20

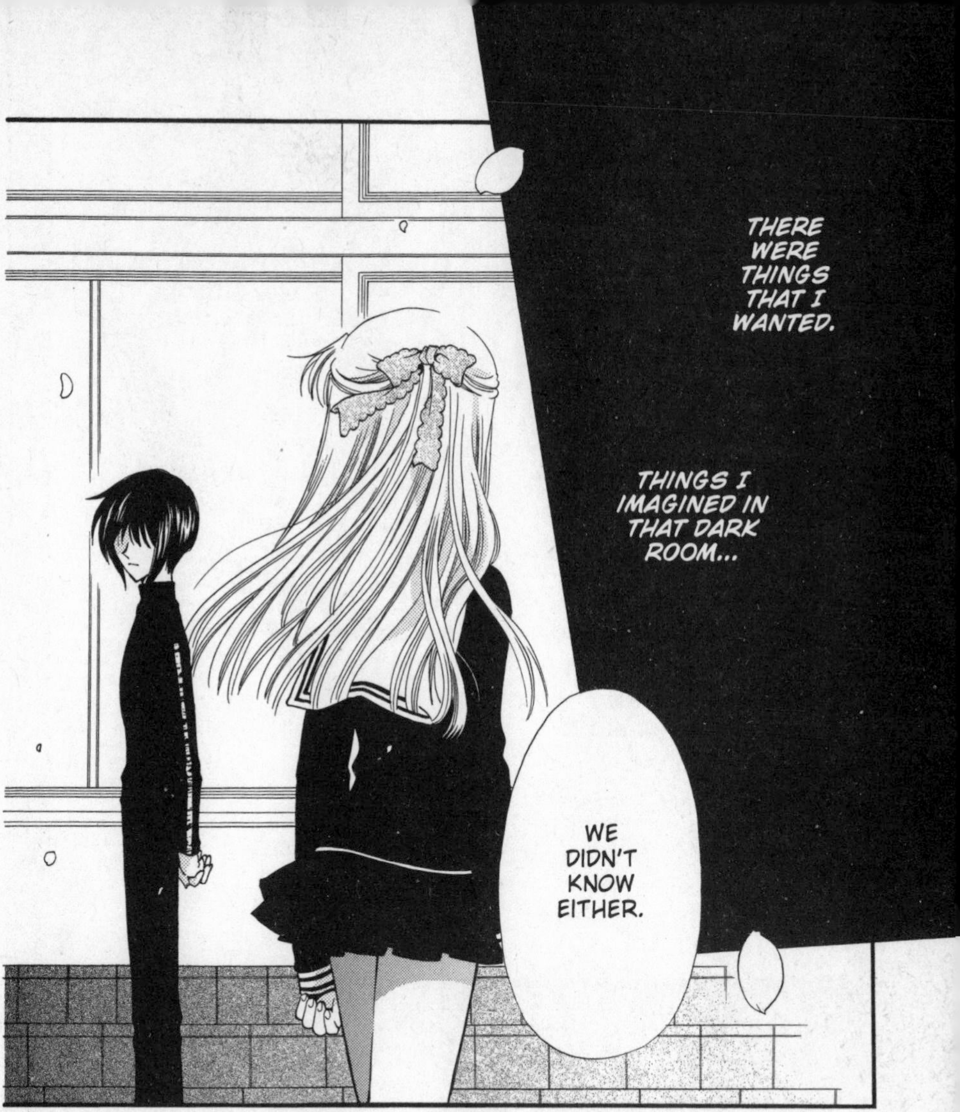
THERE WERE THINGS THAT I WANTED.
THINGS I IMAGINED IN THAT DARK ROOM...
WE DIDN'T KNOW EITHER.

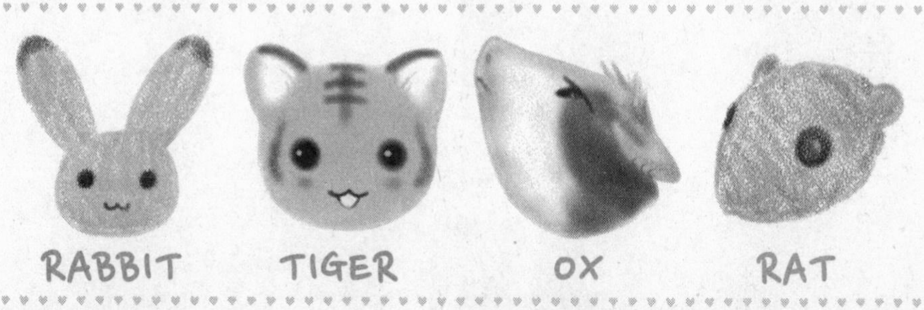
RAT
OX
TIGER
RABBIT

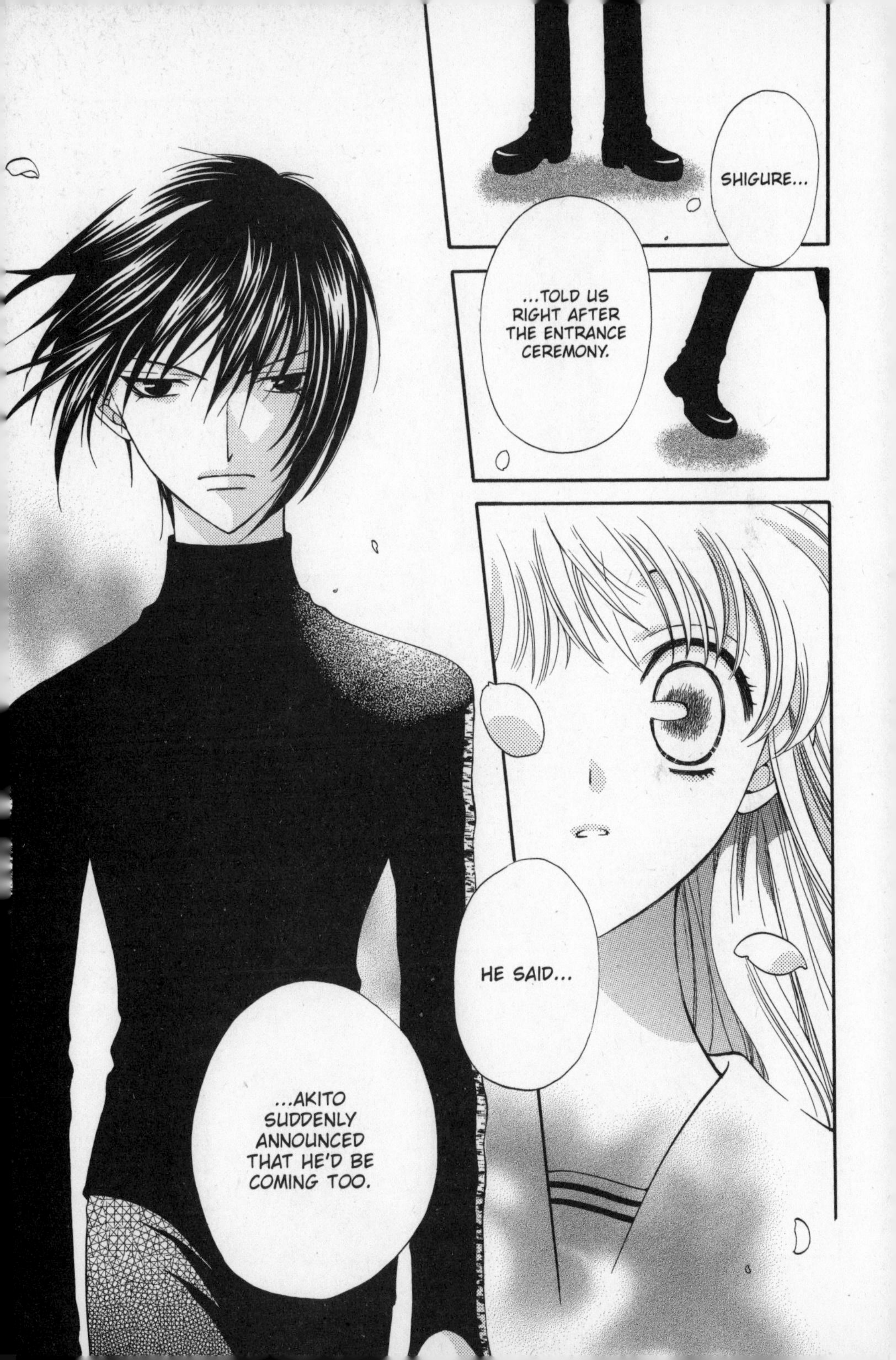
SHIGURE...
...TOLD US RIGHT AFTER THE ENTRANCE CEREMONY.
HE SAID...
...AKITO SUDDENLY ANNOUNCED THAT HE'D BE COMING TOO.

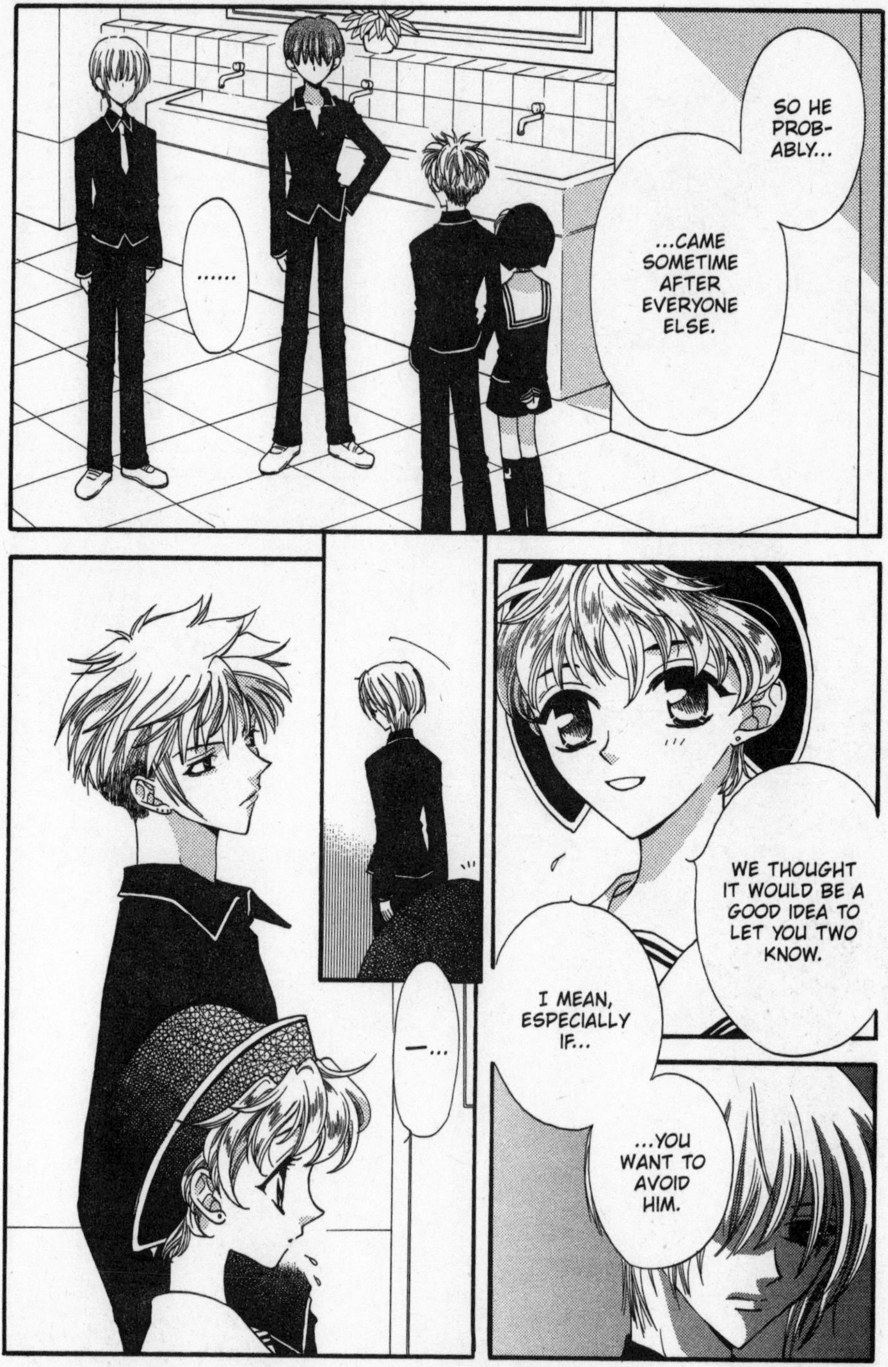
SO HE PROBABLY...
...CAME SOMETIME AFTER EVERYONE ELSE.
......
WE THOUGHT IT WOULD BE A GOOD IDEA TO LET YOU TWO KNOW.
I MEAN, ESPECIALLY IF...
...YOU WANT TO AVOID HIM.
—...

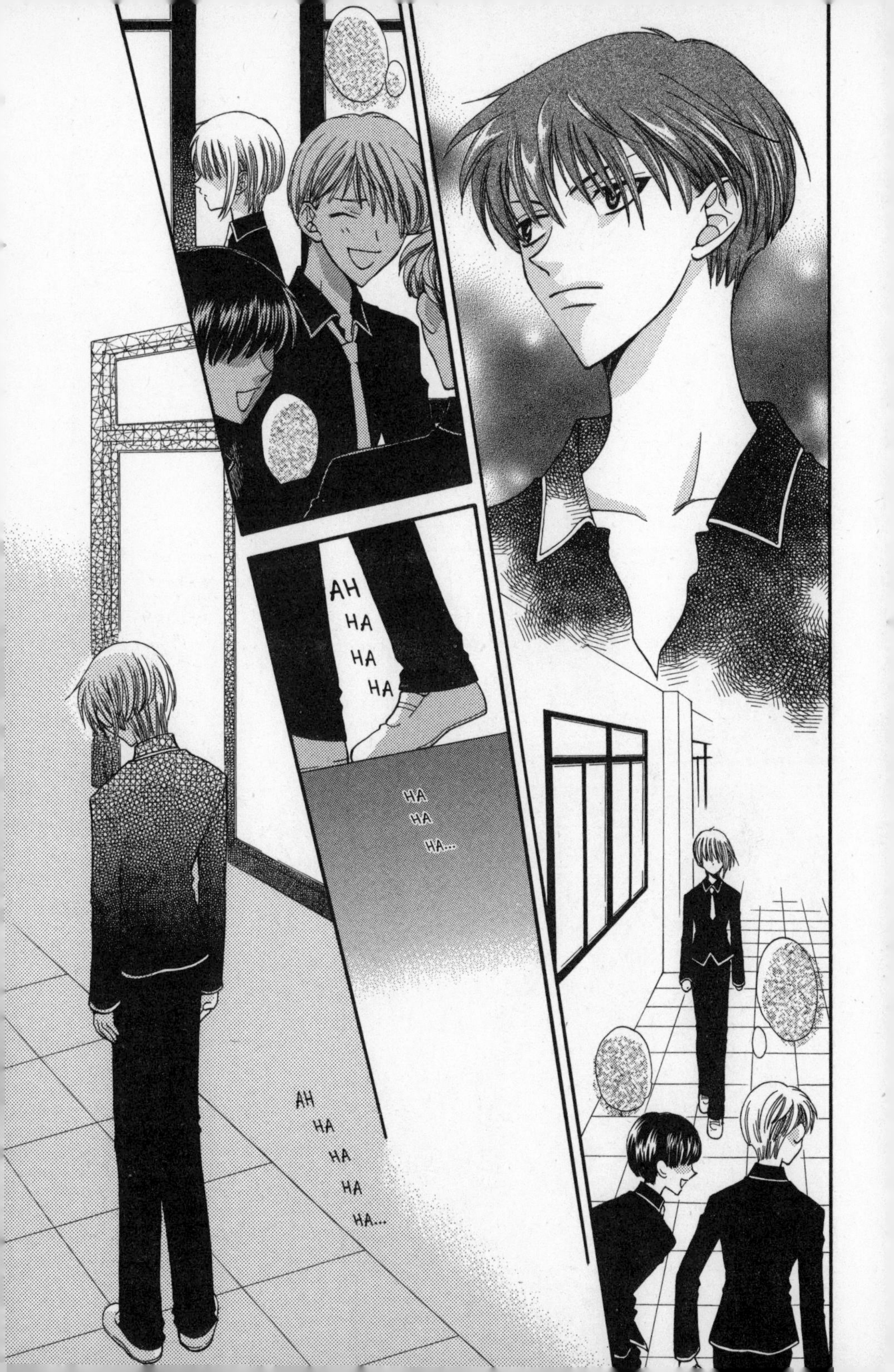
AH HA HA HA
HA HA HA...
AH HA HA HA HA...

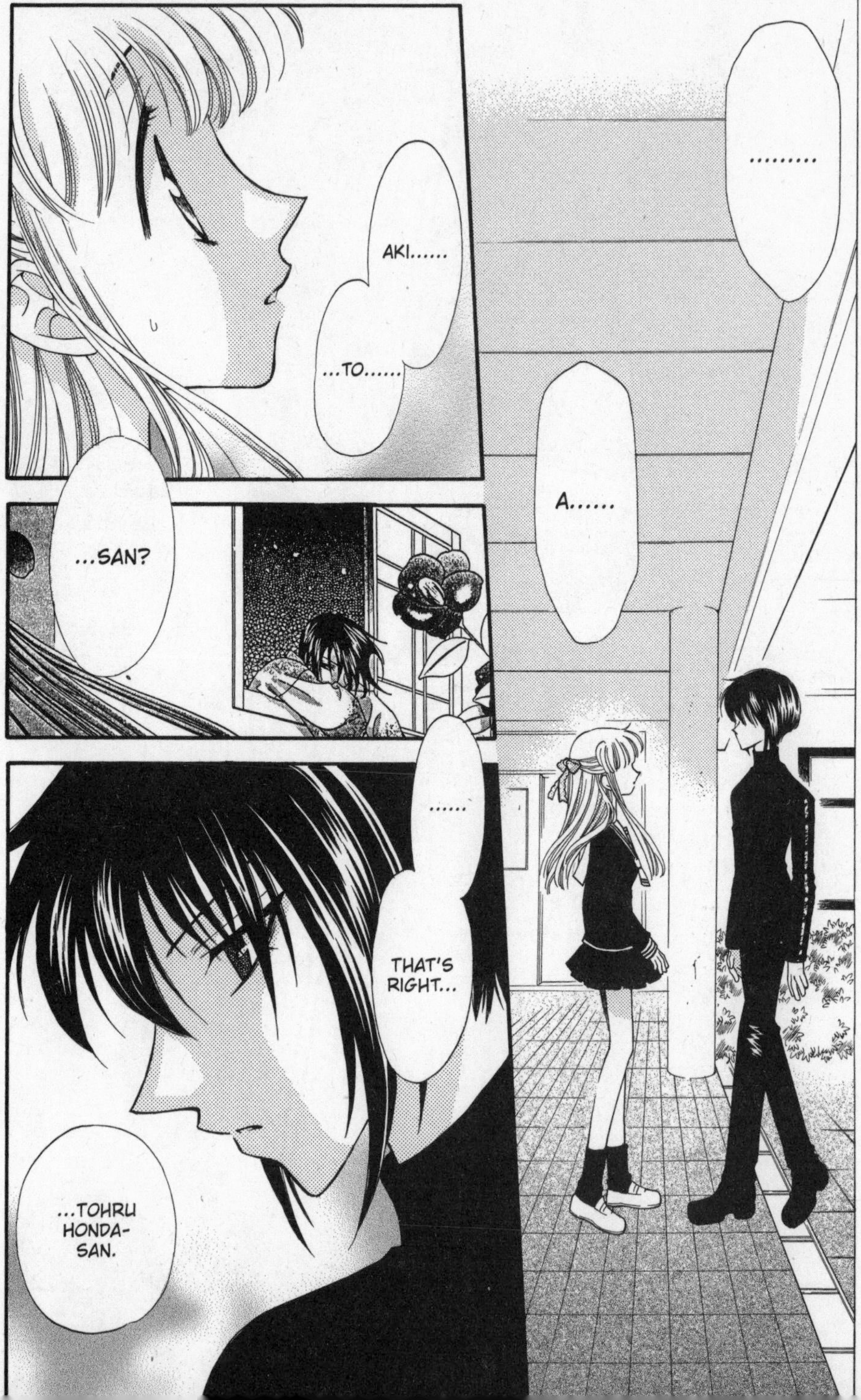
....
A......
AKI......
...TO......
...SAN?
......
THAT'S RIGHT...
...TOHRU HONDA-SAN.

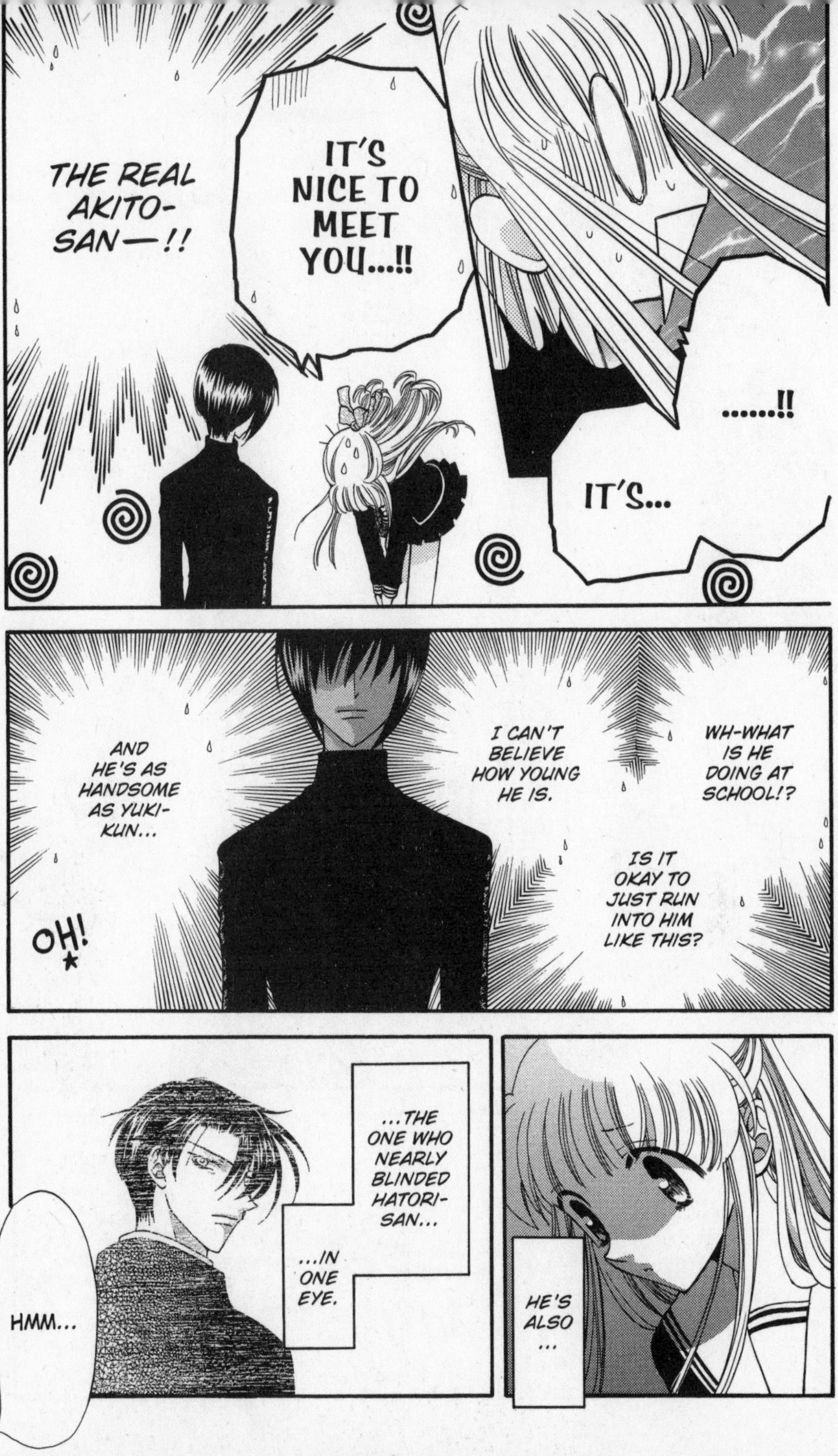
......!!
IT'S...
IT'S NICE TO MEET YOU...!!
THE REAL AKITO-SAN—!!
WH-WHAT IS HE DOING AT SCHOOL!?
IS IT OKAY TO JUST RUN INTO HIM LIKE THIS?
I CAN'T BELIEVE HOW YOUNG HE IS.
AND HE'S AS HANDSOME AS YUKI-KUN...
OH!
HE'S ALSO ...
...THE ONE WHO NEARLY BLINDED HATORI-SAN...
...IN ONE EYE.
HMM...

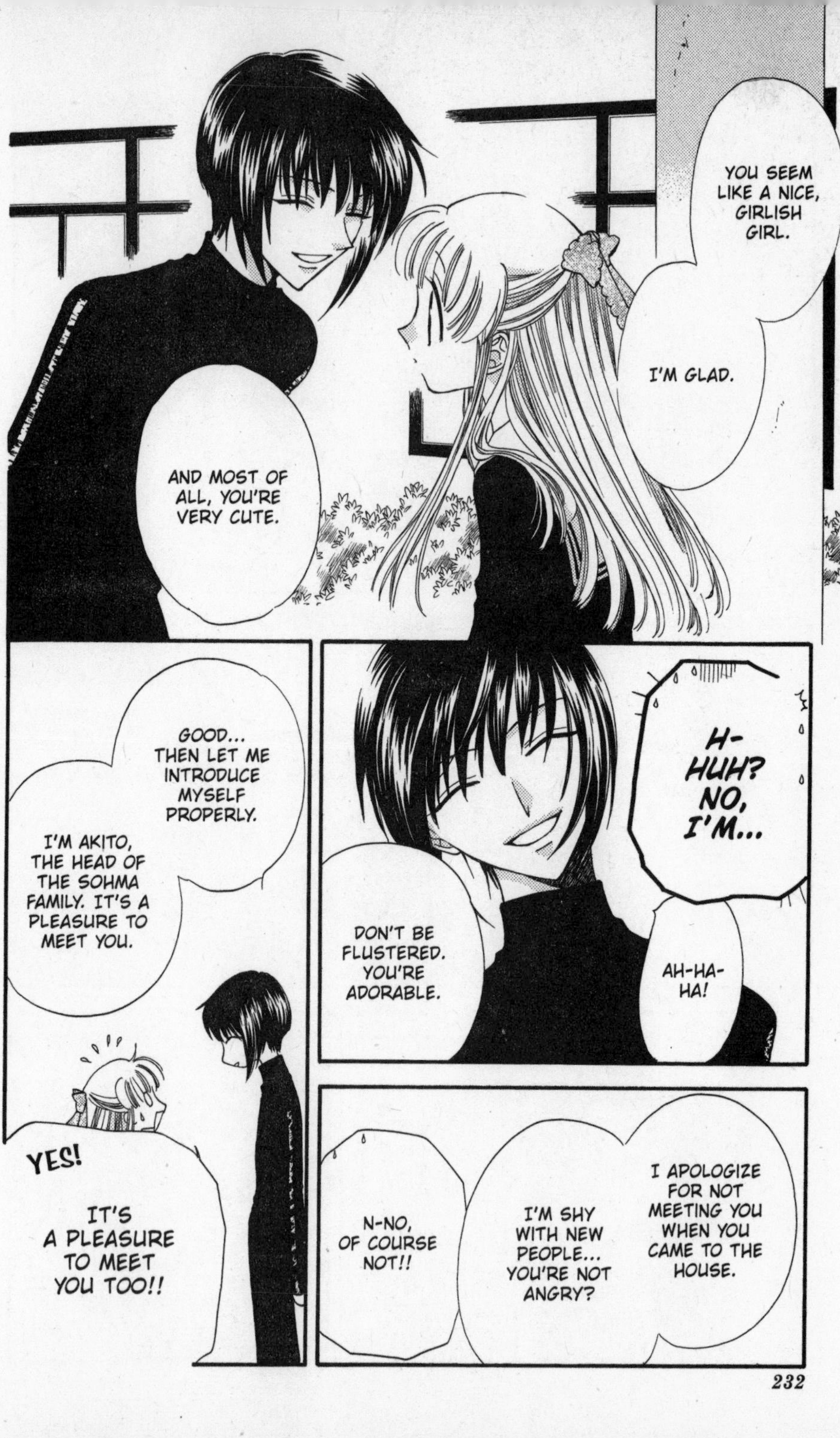
YOU SEEM LIKE A NICE, GIRLISH GIRL.
I'M GLAD.
AND MOST OF ALL, YOU'RE VERY CUTE.
H-HUH? NO, I'M...
AH-HA-HA!
DON'T BE FLUSTERED. YOU'RE ADORABLE.
I APOLOGIZE FOR NOT MEETING YOU WHEN YOU CAME TO THE HOUSE.
I'M SHY WITH NEW PEOPLE... YOU'RE NOT ANGRY?
N-NO, OF COURSE NOT!!
GOOD... THEN LET ME INTRODUCE MYSELF PROPERLY.
I'M AKITO, THE HEAD OF THE SOHMA FAMILY. IT'S A PLEASURE TO MEET YOU.
YES!
IT'S A PLEASURE TO MEET YOU TOO!!

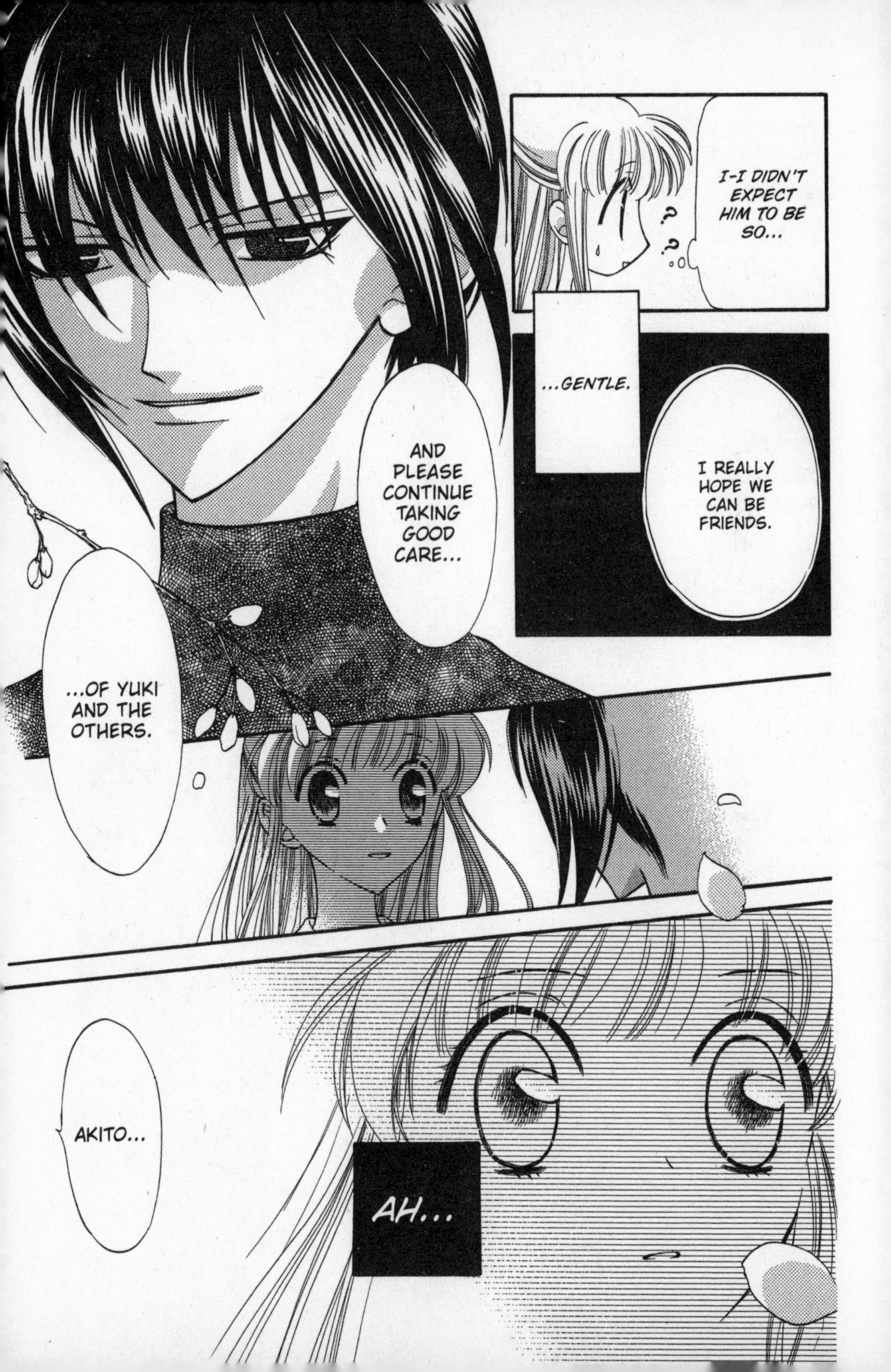
I-I DIDN'T EXPECT HIM TO BE SO...
...GENTLE.
I REALLY HOPE WE CAN BE FRIENDS.
AND PLEASE CONTINUE TAKING GOOD CARE...
...OF YUKI AND THE OTHERS.
AKITO...
AH...

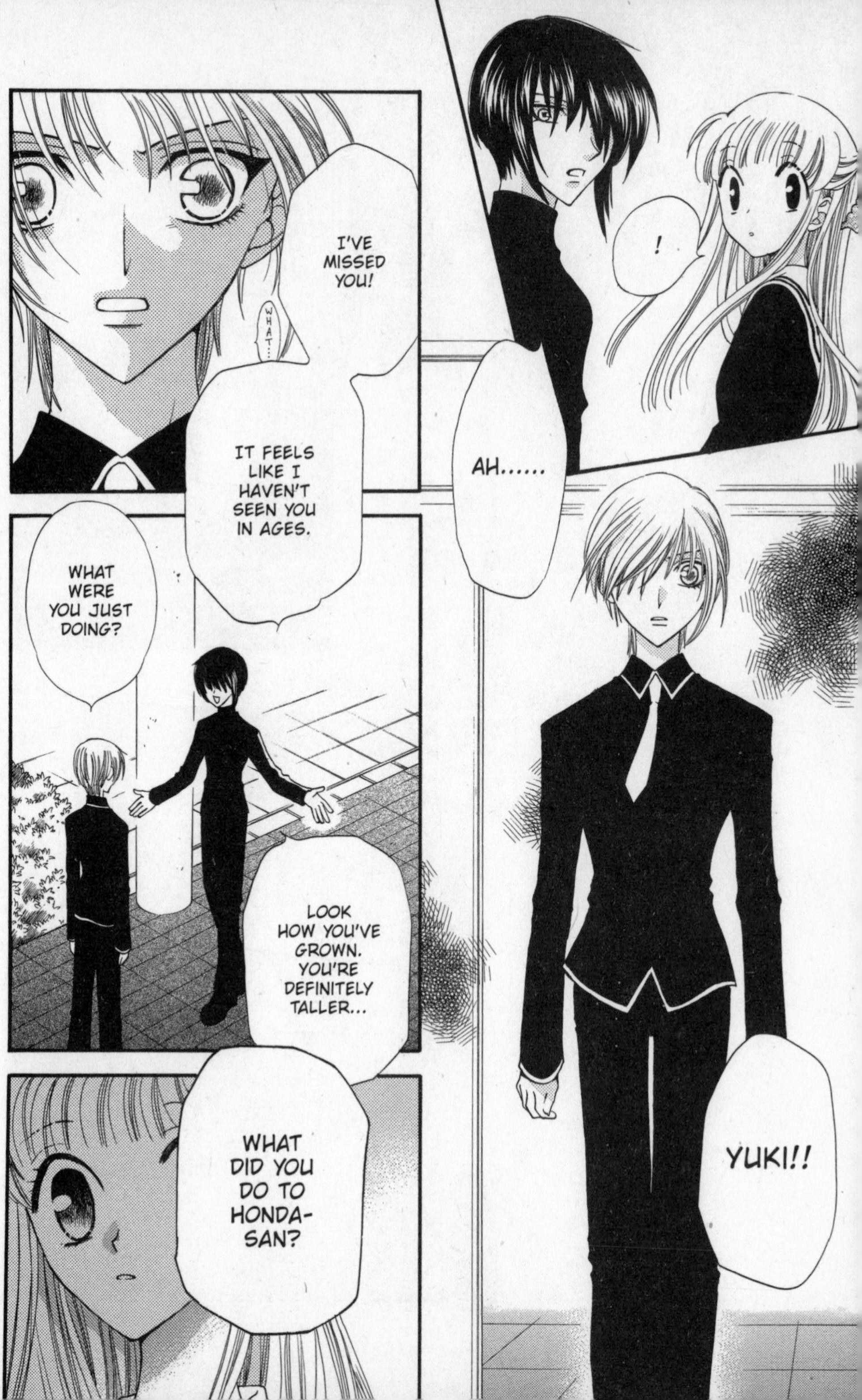
!
AH......
YUKI!!
WHAT...
I'VE MISSED YOU!
IT FEELS LIKE I HAVEN'T SEEN YOU IN AGES.
WHAT WERE YOU JUST DOING?
LOOK HOW YOU'VE GROWN. YOU'RE DEFINITELY TALLER...
WHAT DID YOU DO TO HONDA-SAN?

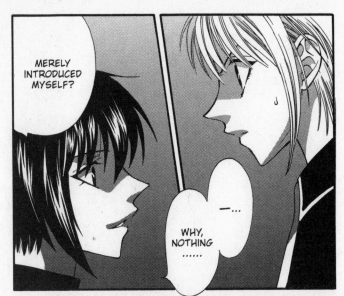

MERELY INTRODUCED MYSELF?

—...

WHY, NOTHING ......

HUH?

UH, YES!

RIGHT, TOHRU-SAN?

DIDN'T I JUST INTRODUCE MYSELF?

BUT YUKI, THAT ASIDE...

...THERE'S SOMETHING I WANT TO ASK YOU.

......

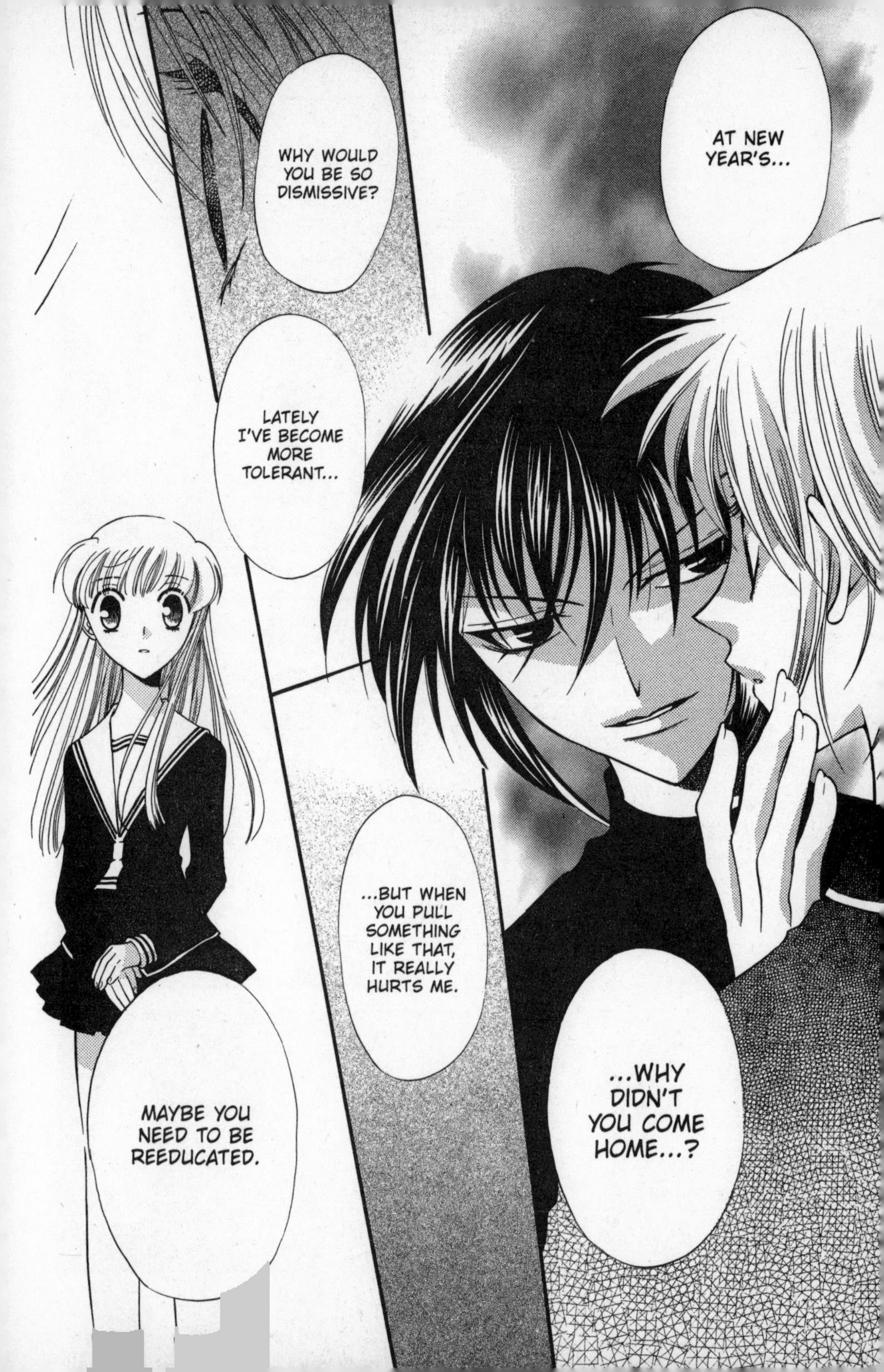
AT NEW YEAR'S...
...WHY DIDN'T YOU COME HOME...?
WHY WOULD YOU BE SO DISMISSIVE?
LATELY I'VE BECOME MORE TOLERANT...
...BUT WHEN YOU PULL SOMETHING LIKE THAT, IT REALLY HURTS ME.
MAYBE YOU NEED TO BE REEDUCATED.

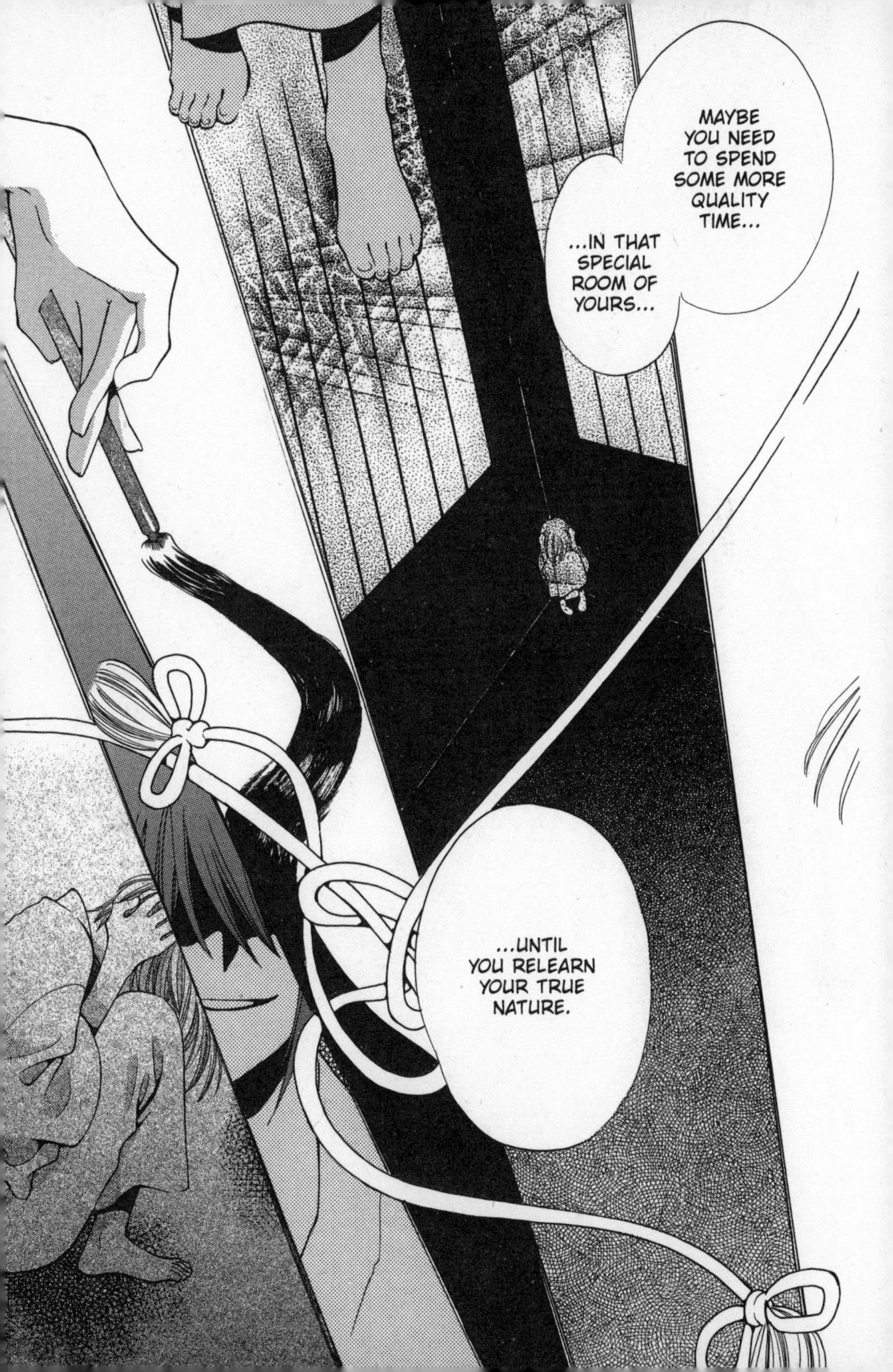
MAYBE YOU NEED TO SPEND SOME MORE QUALITY TIME...
...IN THAT SPECIAL ROOM OF YOURS...
...UNTIL YOU RELEARN YOUR TRUE NATURE.

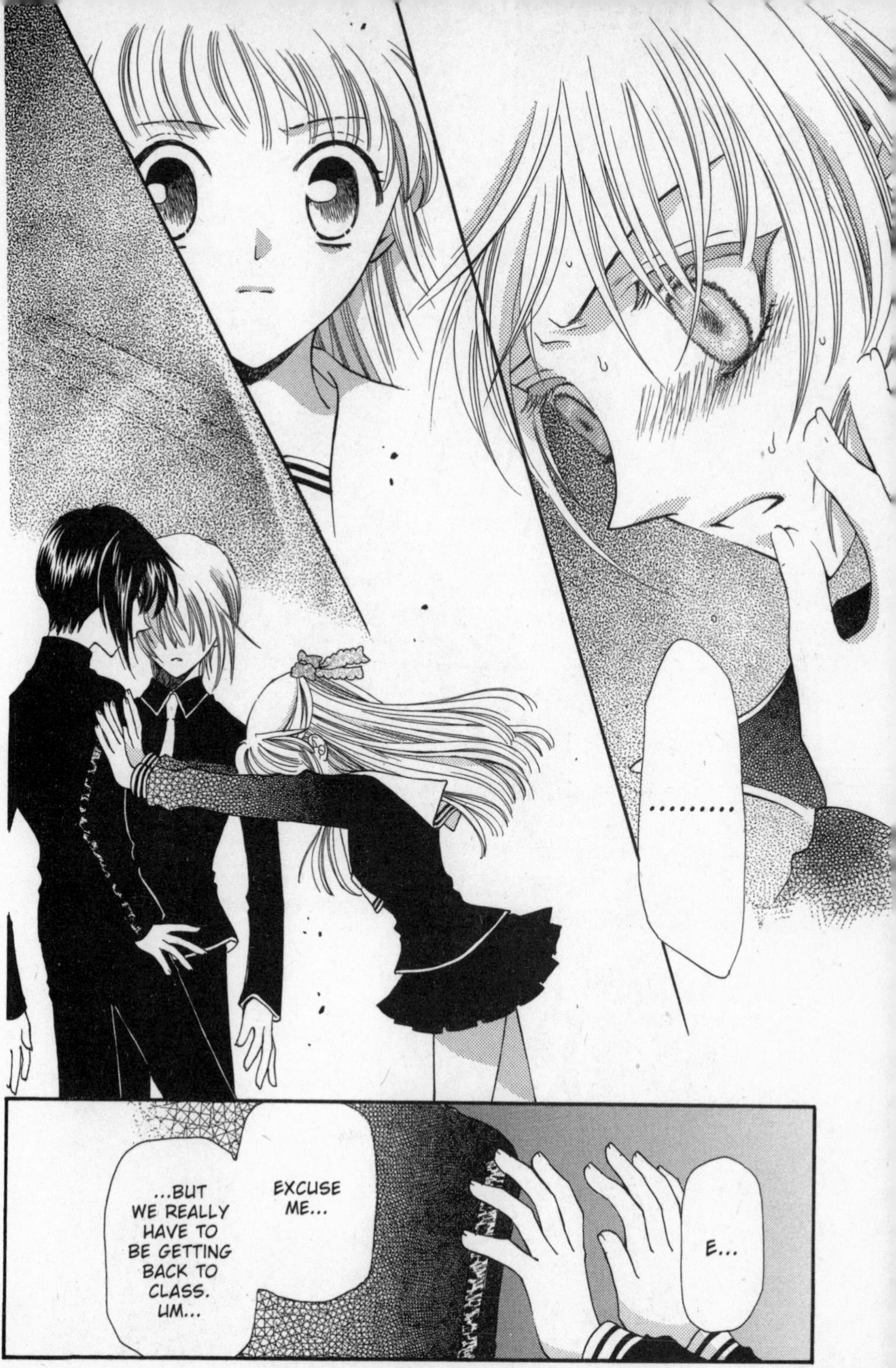
....
E...
EXCUSE ME...
...BUT WE REALLY HAVE TO BE GETTING BACK TO CLASS. UM...

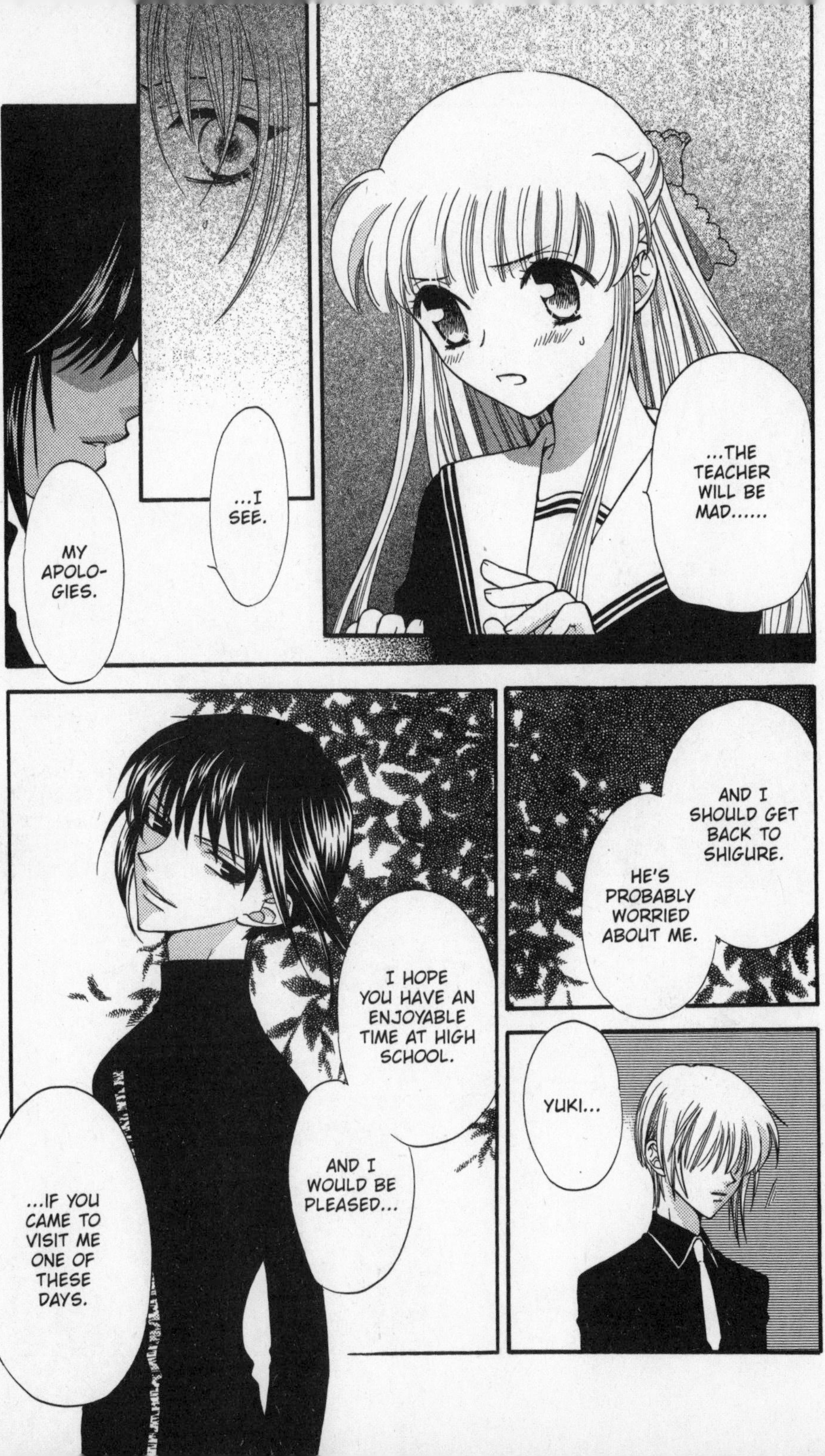
...THE TEACHER WILL BE MAD......
...I SEE.
MY APOLO-GIES.
AND I SHOULD GET BACK TO SHIGURE.
HE'S PROBABLY WORRIED ABOUT ME.
YUKI...
I HOPE YOU HAVE AN ENJOYABLE TIME AT HIGH SCHOOL.
AND I WOULD BE PLEASED...
...IF YOU CAME TO VISIT ME ONE OF THESE DAYS.

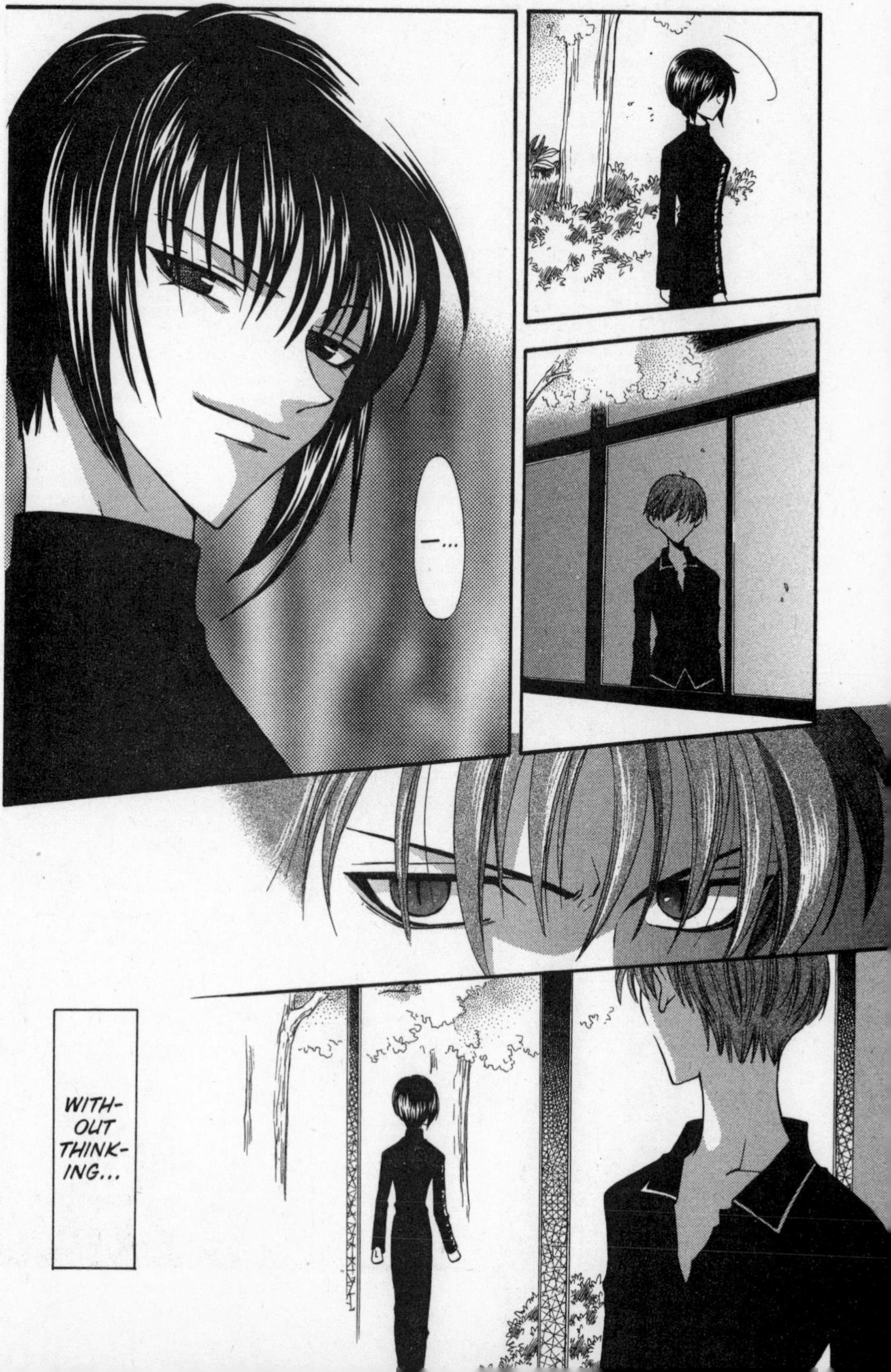
—...
WITH-OUT THINK-ING...

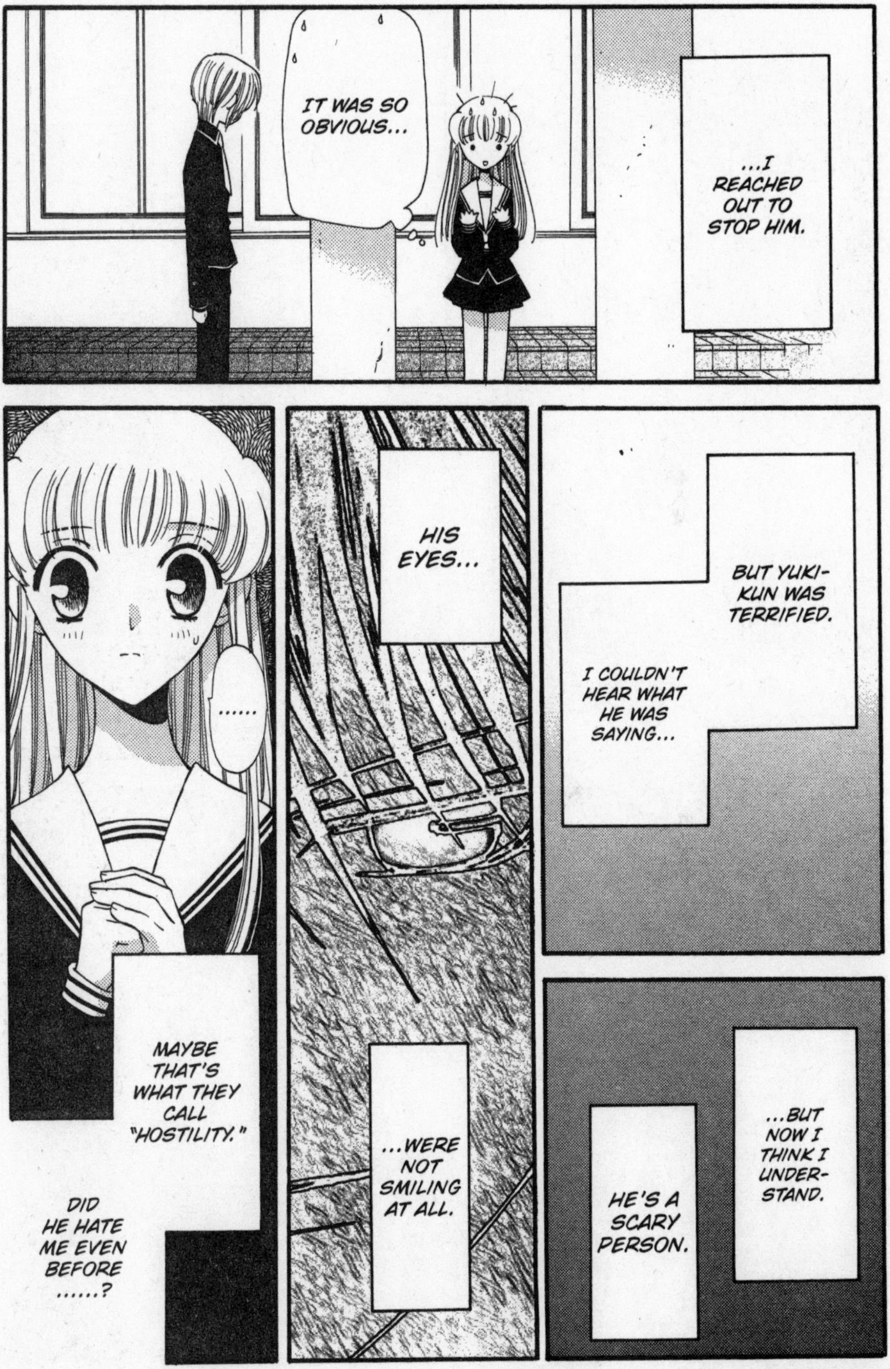
...I REACHED OUT TO STOP HIM.
IT WAS SO OBVIOUS...
BUT YUKI-KUN WAS TERRIFIED.
I COULDN'T HEAR WHAT HE WAS SAYING...
...BUT NOW I THINK I UNDERSTAND.
HE'S A SCARY PERSON.
HIS EYES...
...WERE NOT SMILING AT ALL.
......
MAYBE THAT'S WHAT THEY CALL "HOSTILITY."
DID HE HATE ME EVEN BEFORE ......?

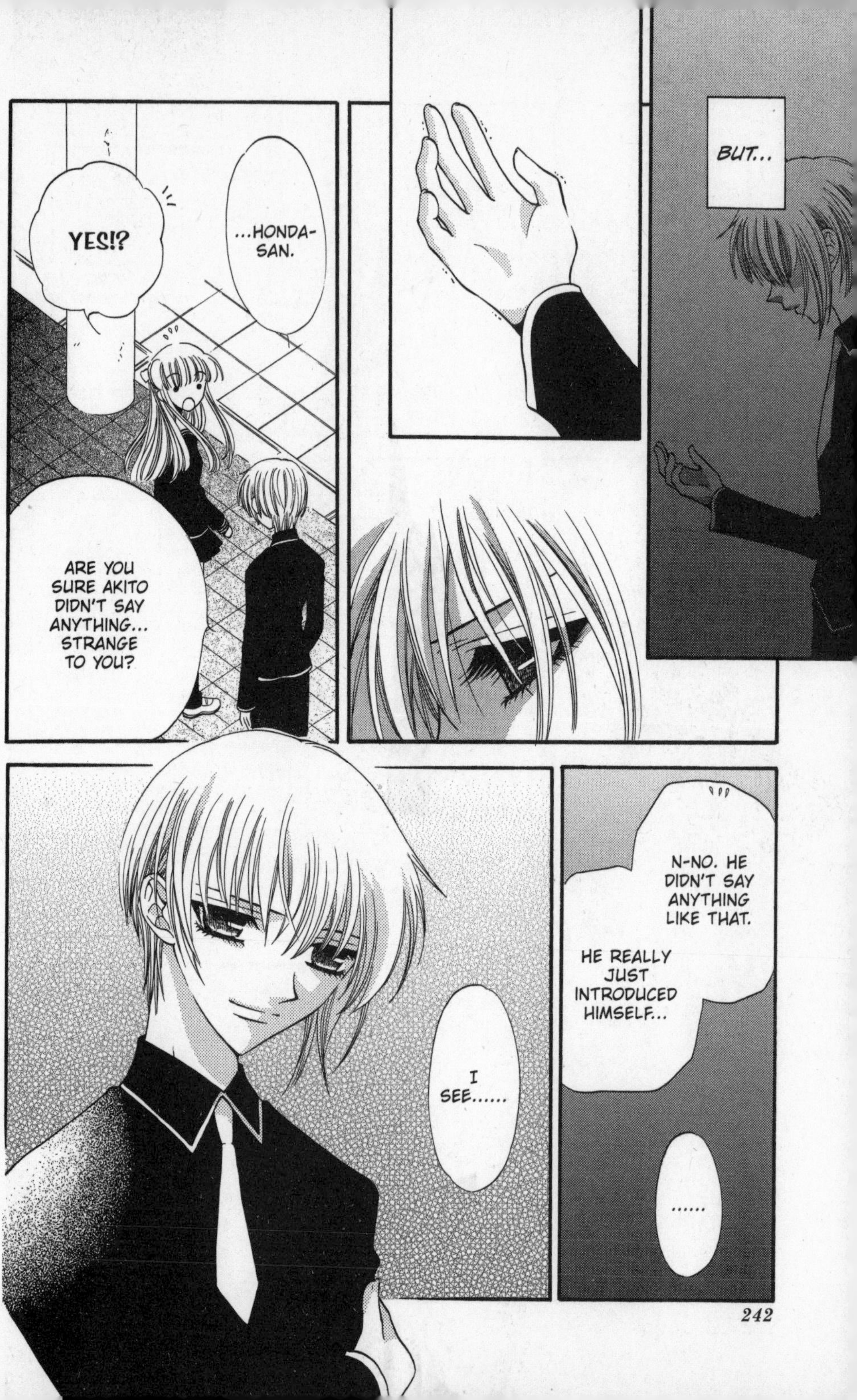
BUT...
...HONDA-SAN.
YES!?
ARE YOU SURE AKITO DIDN'T SAY ANYTHING... STRANGE TO YOU?
N-NO. HE DIDN'T SAY ANYTHING LIKE THAT.
HE REALLY JUST INTRODUCED HIMSELF...
......
I SEE......

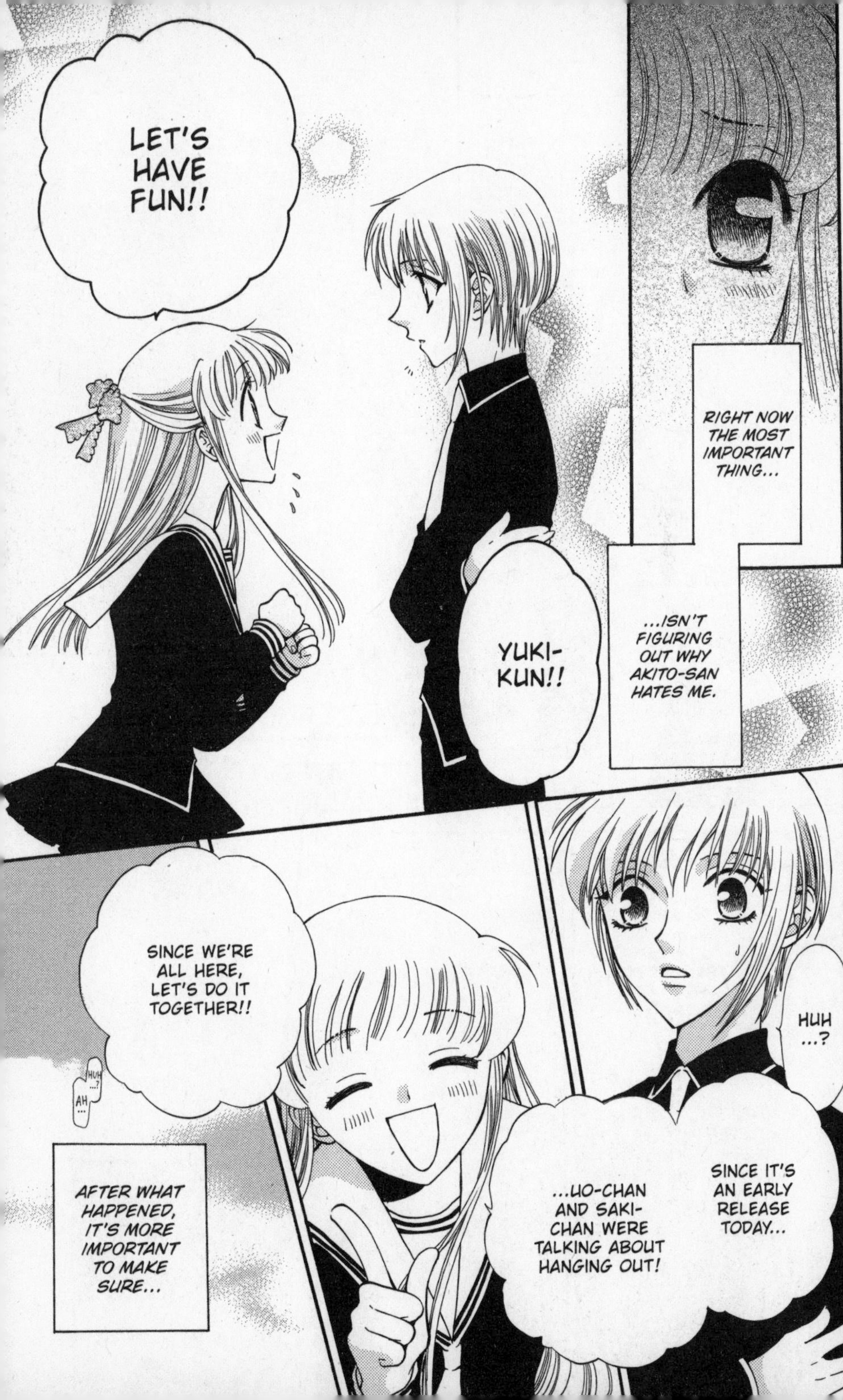
RIGHT NOW THE MOST IMPORTANT THING...
...ISN'T FIGURING OUT WHY AKITO-SAN HATES ME.
YUKI-KUN!!
LET'S HAVE FUN!!
HUH ...?
SINCE IT'S AN EARLY RELEASE TODAY...
...UO-CHAN AND SAKI-CHAN WERE TALKING ABOUT HANGING OUT!
SINCE WE'RE ALL HERE, LET'S DO IT TOGETHER!!
HUH ...?
AH ...
AFTER WHAT HAPPENED, IT'S MORE IMPORTANT TO MAKE SURE...

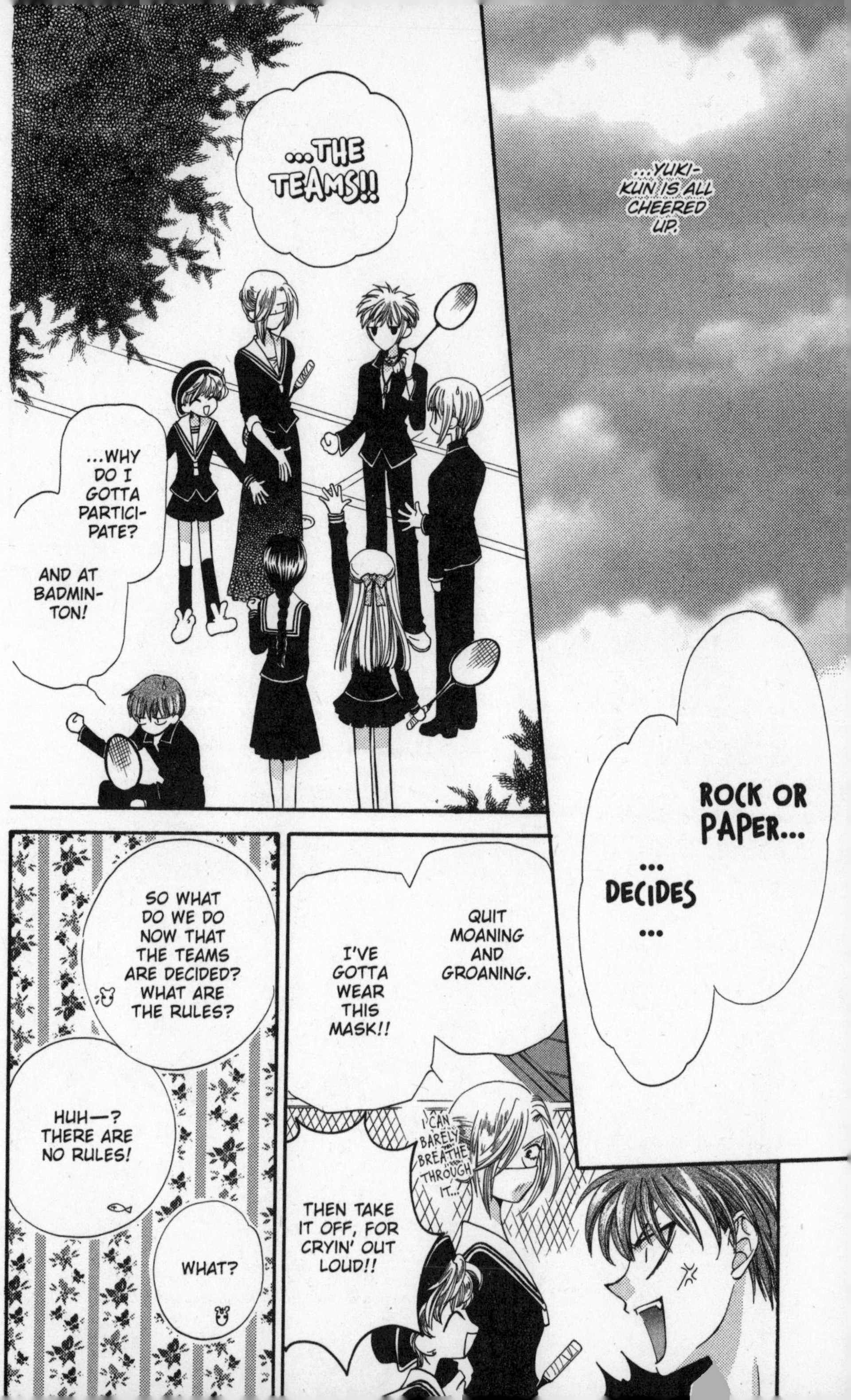

...YUKI-KUN IS ALL CHEERED UP.
ROCK OR PAPER...
...DECIDES...
...THE TEAMS!!
...WHY DO I GOTTA PARTICIPATE?
AND AT BADMINTON!
QUIT MOANING AND GROANING.
I'VE GOTTA WEAR THIS MASK!!
I CAN BARELY BREATHE THROUGH IT...
THEN TAKE IT OFF, FOR CRYIN' OUT LOUD!!
SO WHAT DO WE DO NOW THAT THE TEAMS ARE DECIDED? WHAT ARE THE RULES?
HUH—? THERE ARE NO RULES!
WHAT?

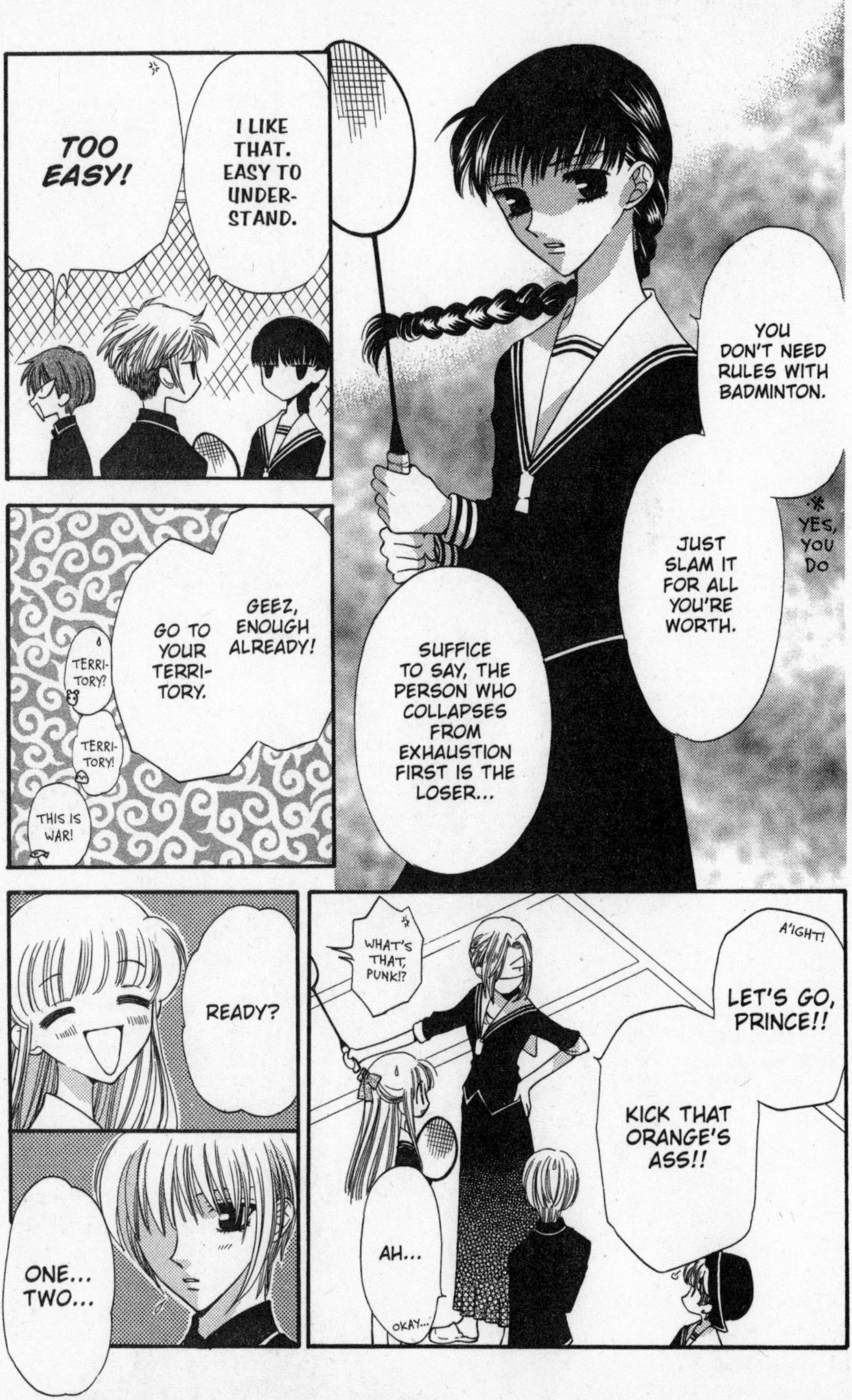
YOU DON'T NEED RULES WITH BADMINTON.
*YES, YOU DO
JUST SLAM IT FOR ALL YOU'RE WORTH.
SUFFICE TO SAY, THE PERSON WHO COLLAPSES FROM EXHAUSTION FIRST IS THE LOSER...
I LIKE THAT. EASY TO UNDERSTAND.
TOO EASY!
GEEZ, ENOUGH ALREADY!
GO TO YOUR TERRITORY.
TERRITORY?
TERRITORY!
THIS IS WAR!
A'IGHT!
LET'S GO, PRINCE!!
KICK THAT ORANGE'S ASS!!
WHAT'S THAT, PUNK!?
AH...
OKAY...
READY?
ONE... TWO...

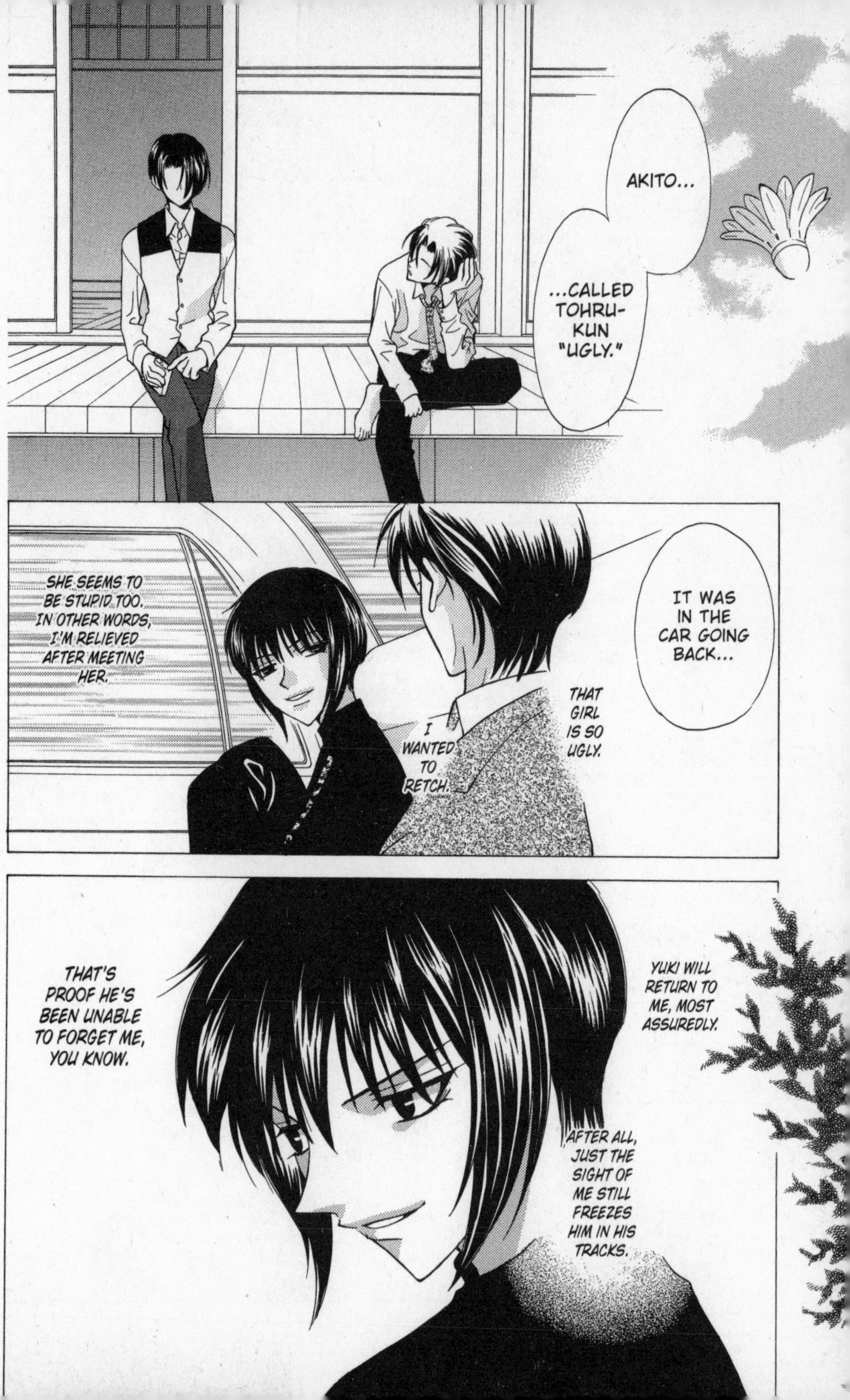
AKITO...
...CALLED TOHRU-KUN "UGLY."
IT WAS IN THE CAR GOING BACK...
THAT GIRL IS SO UGLY.
I WANTED TO RETCH.
SHE SEEMS TO BE STUPID TOO. IN OTHER WORDS, I'M RELIEVED AFTER MEETING HER.
YUKI WILL RETURN TO ME, MOST ASSUREDLY.
AFTER ALL, JUST THE SIGHT OF ME STILL FREEZES HIM IN HIS TRACKS.
THAT'S PROOF HE'S BEEN UNABLE TO FORGET ME, YOU KNOW.

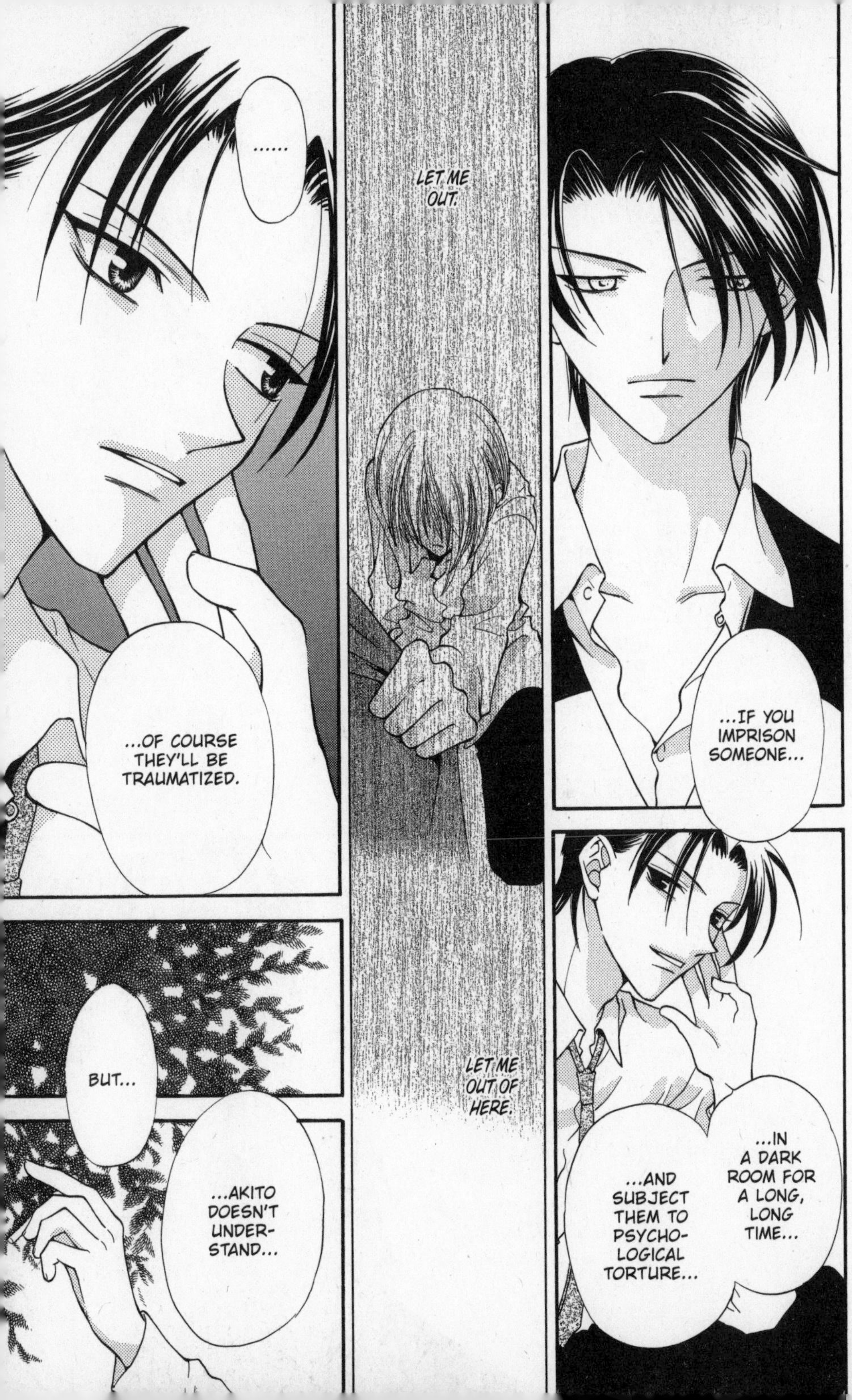
...IF YOU IMPRISON SOMEONE...
...IN A DARK ROOM FOR A LONG, LONG TIME...
...AND SUBJECT THEM TO PSYCHO-LOGICAL TORTURE...
LET ME OUT.
LET ME OUT OF HERE.
......
...OF COURSE THEY'LL BE TRAUMATIZED.
BUT...
...AKITO DOESN'T UNDER-STAND...

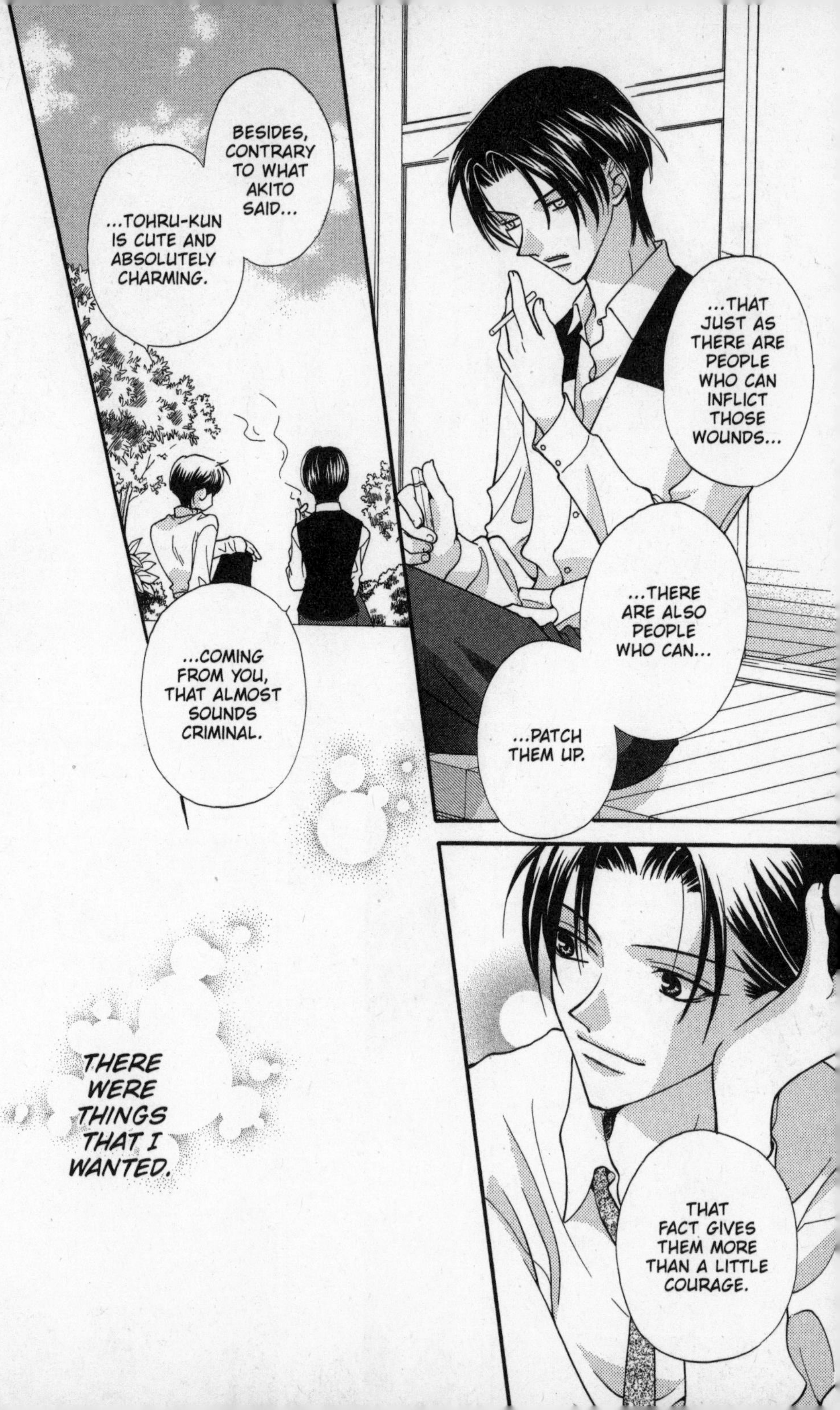
...THAT JUST AS THERE ARE PEOPLE WHO CAN INFLICT THOSE WOUNDS...
...THERE ARE ALSO PEOPLE WHO CAN...
...PATCH THEM UP.
THAT FACT GIVES THEM MORE THAN A LITTLE COURAGE.
BESIDES, CONTRARY TO WHAT AKITO SAID...
...TOHRU-KUN IS CUTE AND ABSOLUTELY CHARMING.
...COMING FROM YOU, THAT ALMOST SOUNDS CRIMINAL.
THERE WERE THINGS THAT I WANTED.

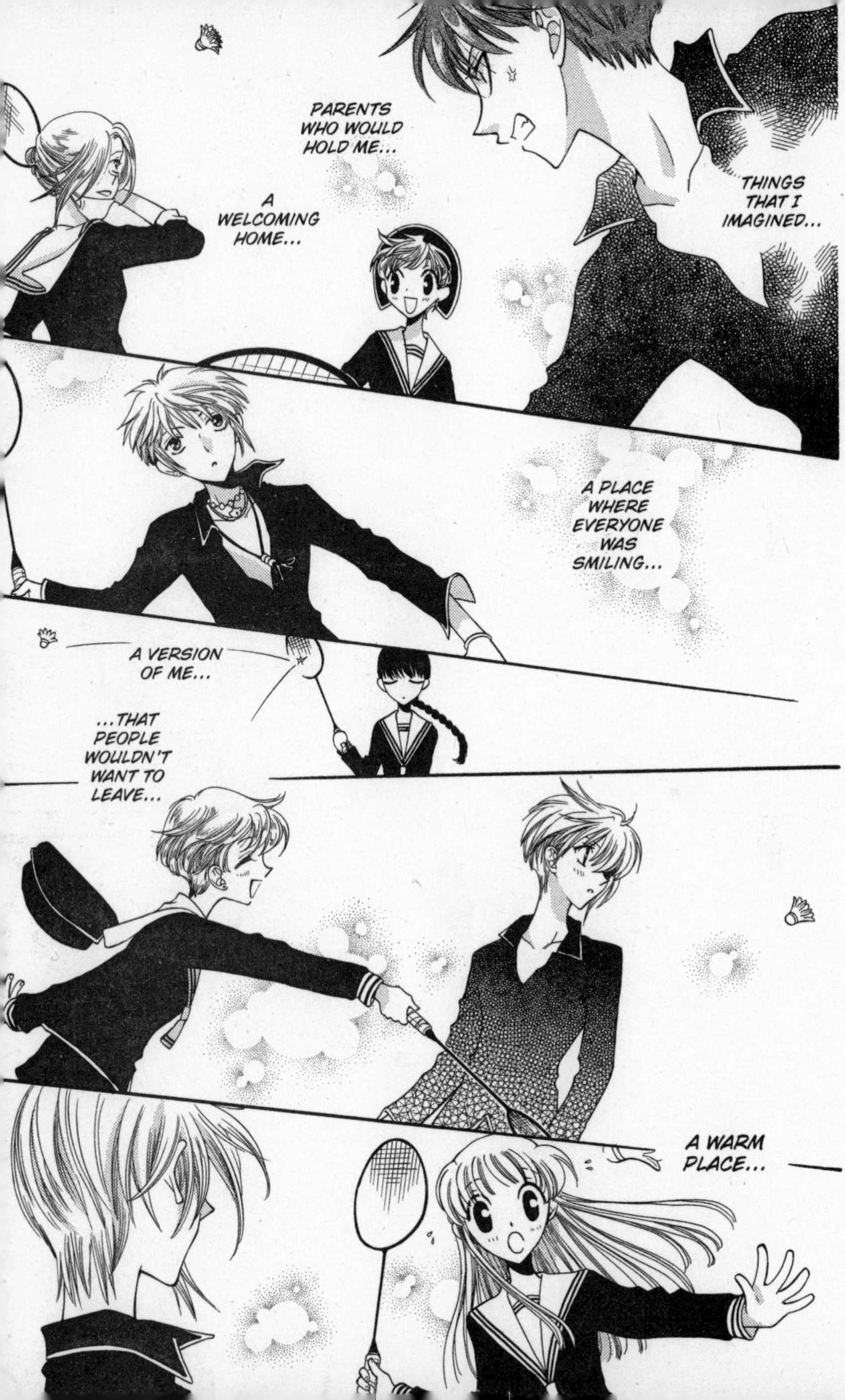
THINGS THAT I IMAGINED...
PARENTS WHO WOULD HOLD ME...
A WELCOMING HOME...
A PLACE WHERE EVERYONE WAS SMILING...
A VERSION OF ME...
...THAT PEOPLE WOULDN'T WANT TO LEAVE...
A WARM PLACE...

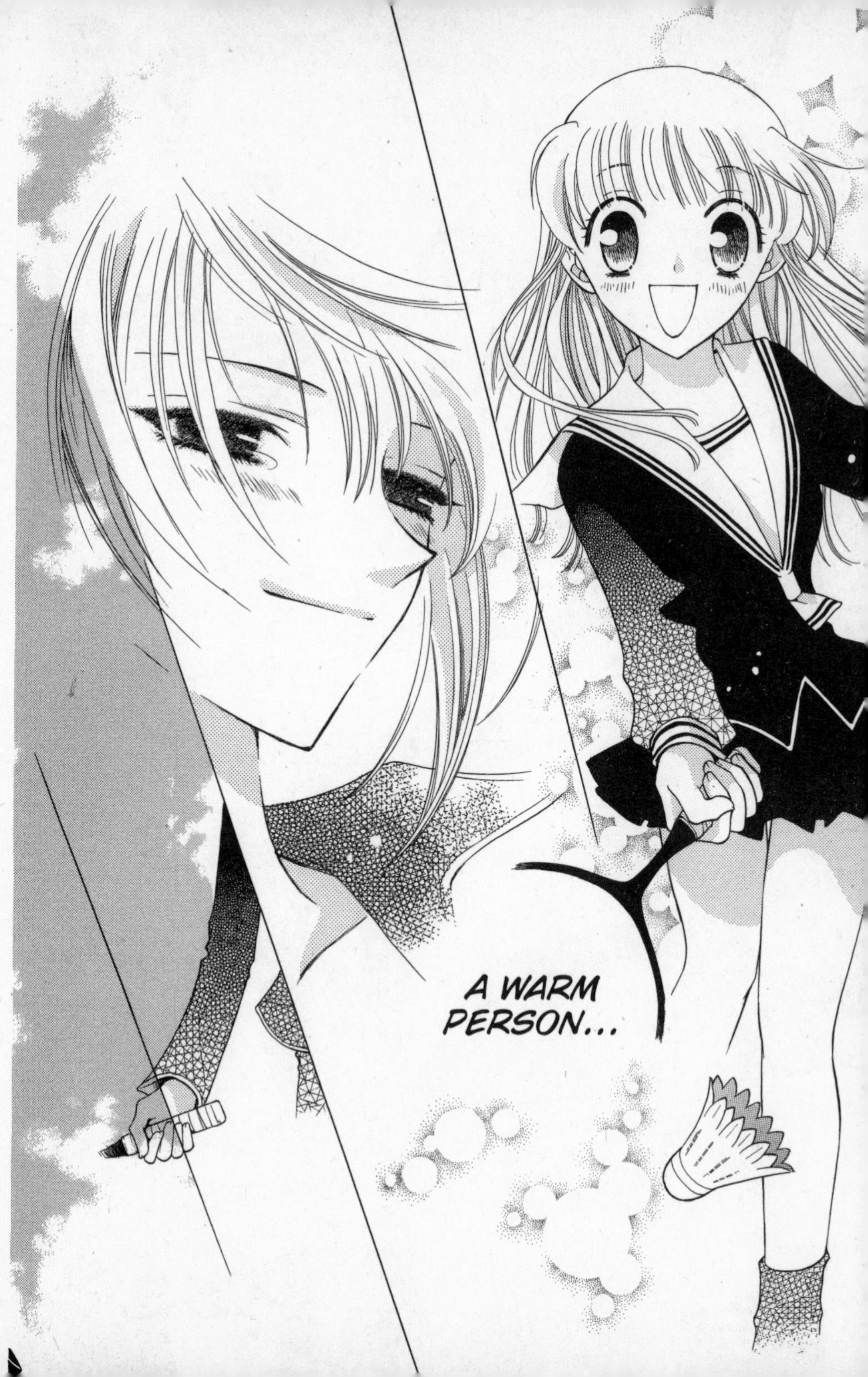
A WARM
PERSON...

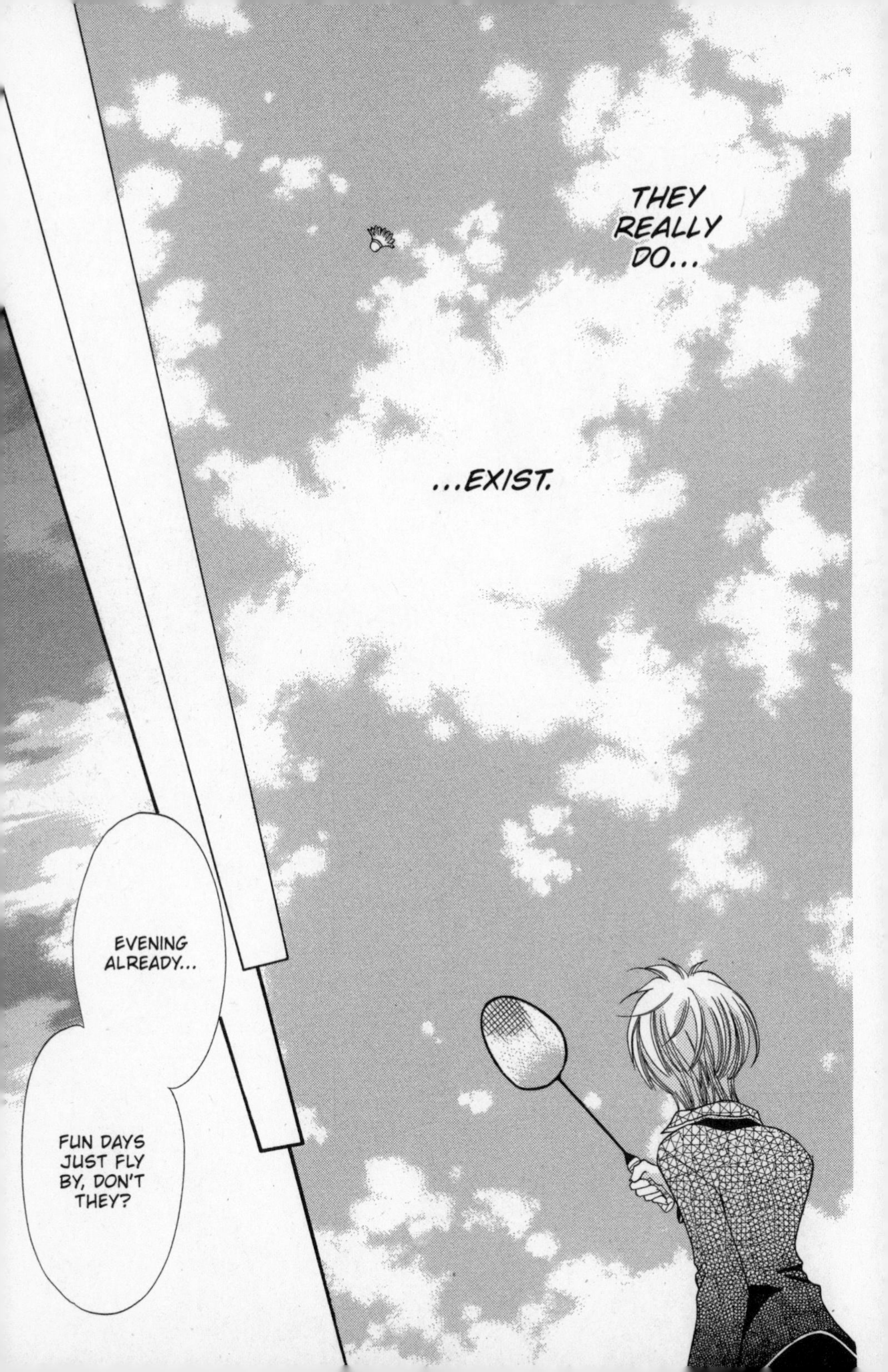
THEY REALLY DO...
...EXIST.
EVENING ALREADY...
FUN DAYS JUST FLY BY, DON'T THEY?

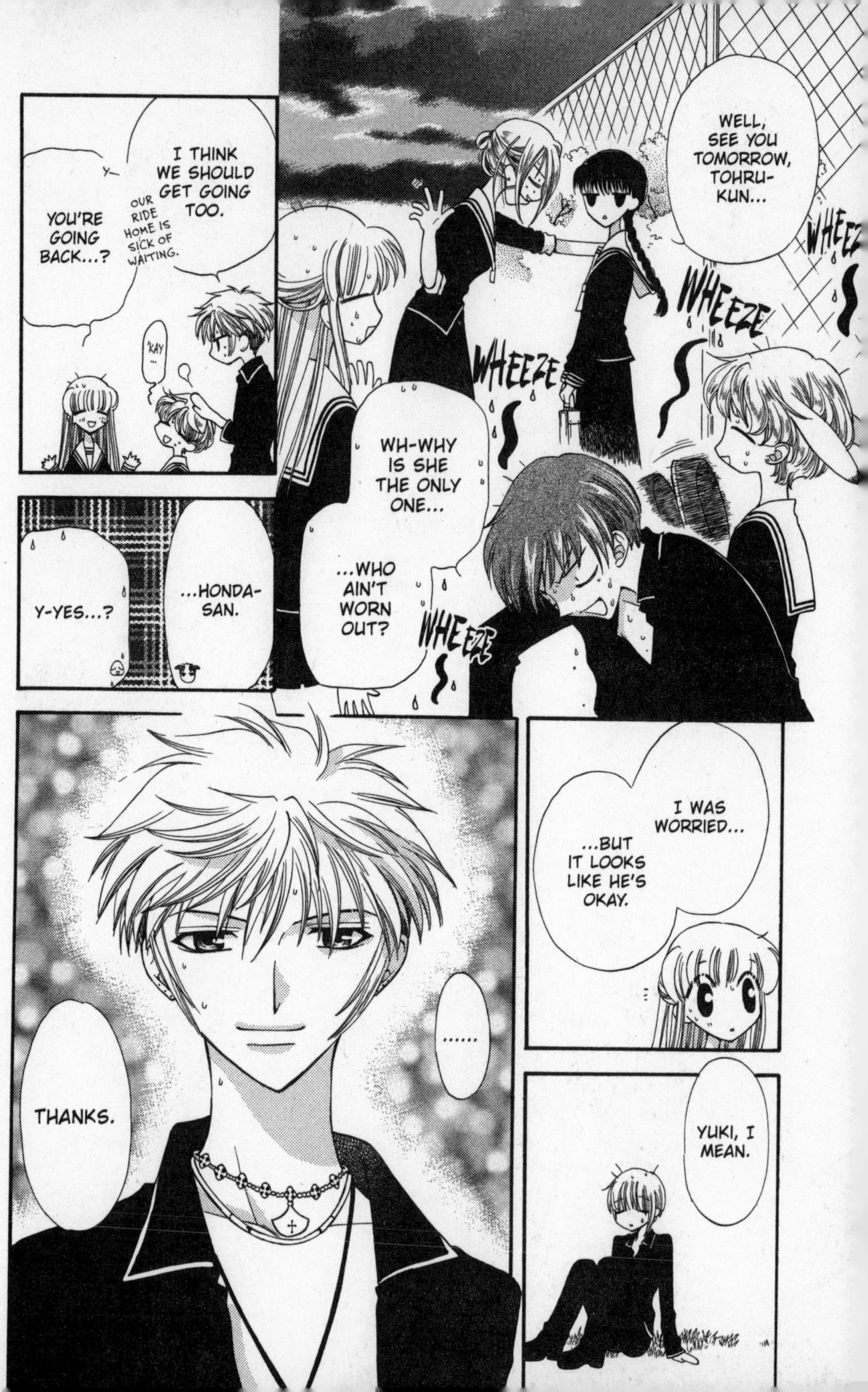
WELL, SEE YOU TOMORROW, TOHRU-KUN...
WHEEZE
WHEEZE
WHEEZE
WH-WHY IS SHE THE ONLY ONE...
...WHO AIN'T WORN OUT?
WHEEZE
I THINK WE SHOULD GET GOING TOO.
OUR RIDE HOME IS SICK OF WAITING.
Y—
YOU'RE GOING BACK...?
'KAY...
...HONDA-SAN.
Y-YES...?
I WAS WORRIED...
...BUT IT LOOKS LIKE HE'S OKAY.
YUKI, I MEAN.
......
THANKS.

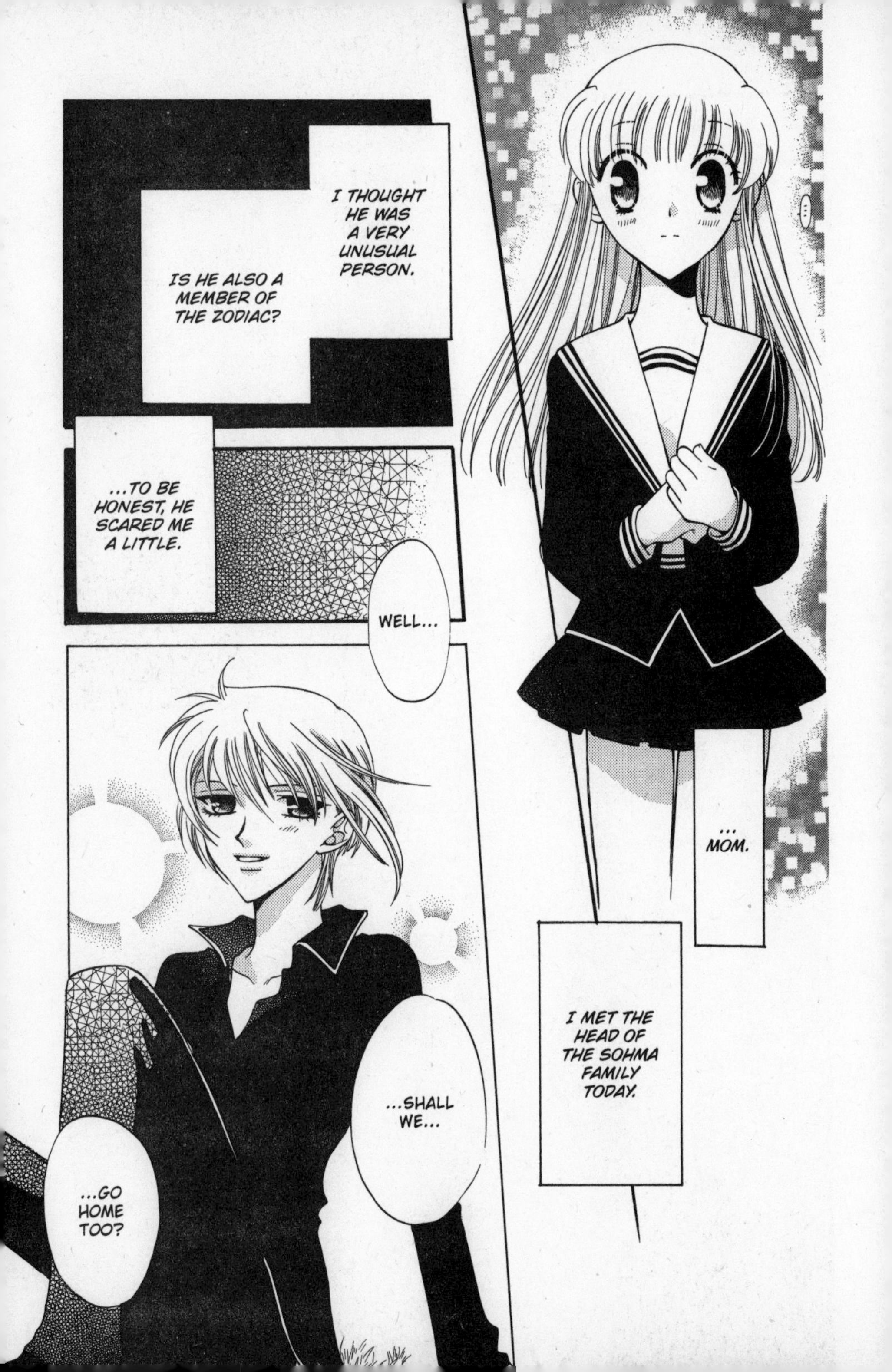
...
... MOM.
I MET THE HEAD OF THE SOHMA FAMILY TODAY.
I THOUGHT HE WAS A VERY UNUSUAL PERSON.
IS HE ALSO A MEMBER OF THE ZODIAC?
...TO BE HONEST, HE SCARED ME A LITTLE.
WELL...
...SHALL WE...
...GO HOME TOO?

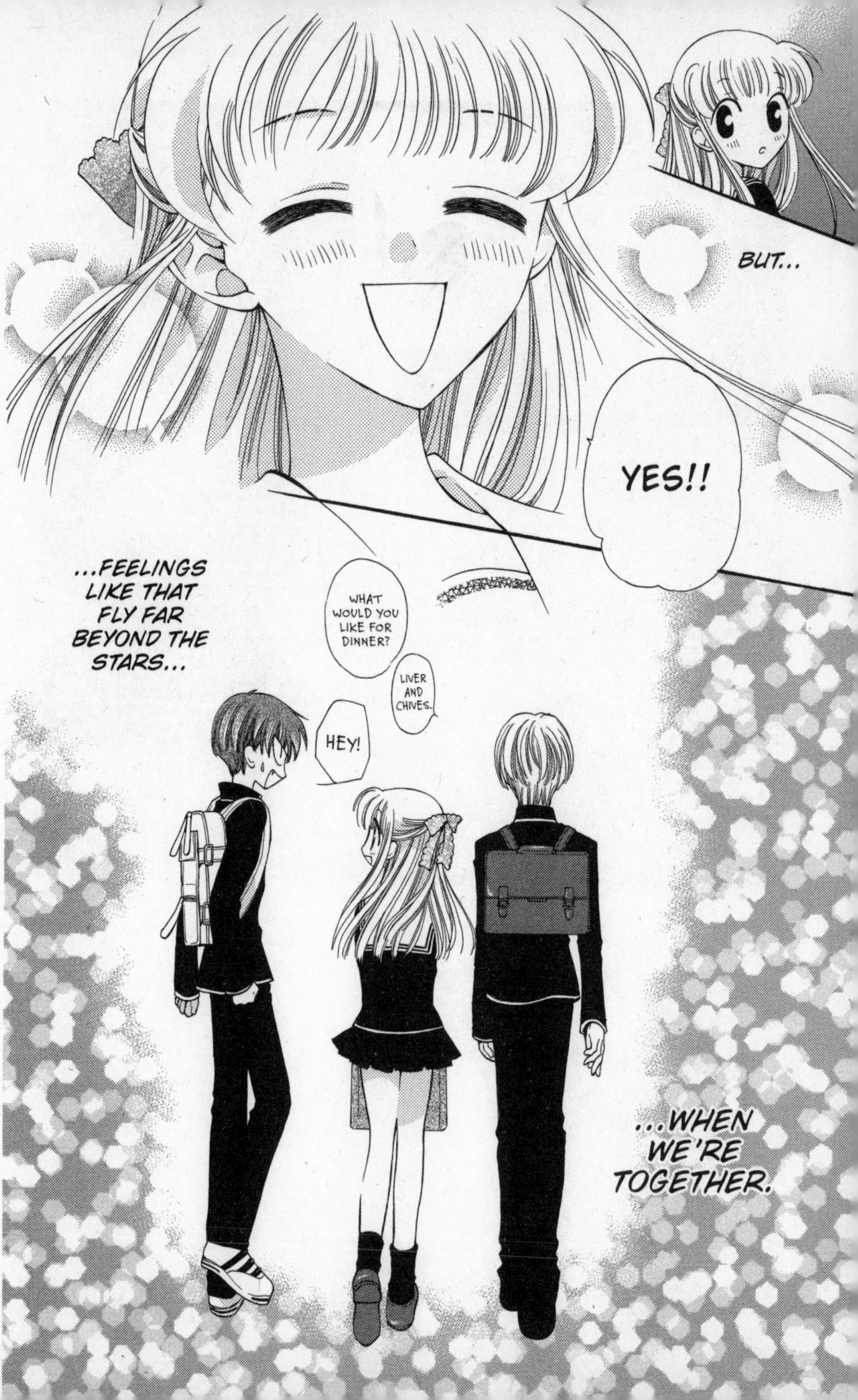
BUT...
YES!!
...FEELINGS LIKE THAT FLY FAR BEYOND THE STARS...
WHAT WOULD YOU LIKE FOR DINNER?
LIVER AND CHIVES.
HEY!
...WHEN WE'RE TOGETHER.

Chapter 21

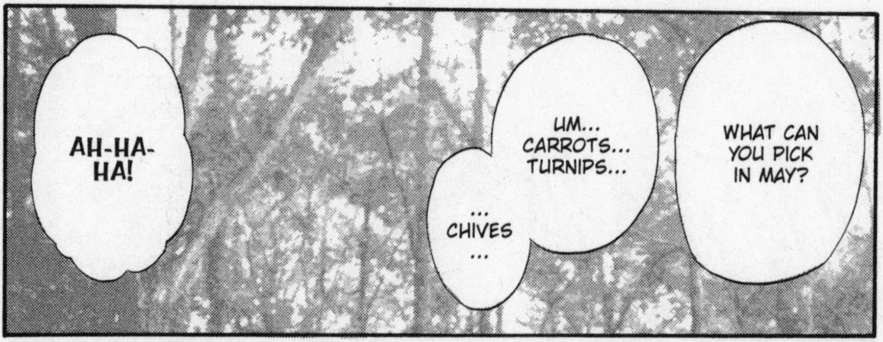
WHAT CAN YOU PICK IN MAY?
UM... CARROTS... TURNIPS...
... CHIVES ...
AH-HA-HA!
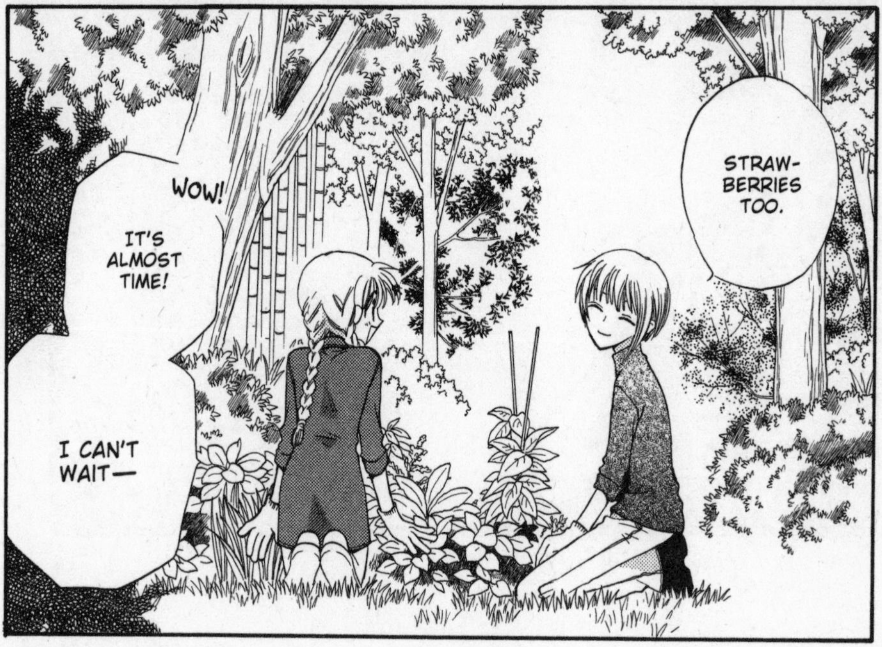
STRAW-BERRIES TOO.
WOW!
IT'S ALMOST TIME!
I CAN'T WAIT—
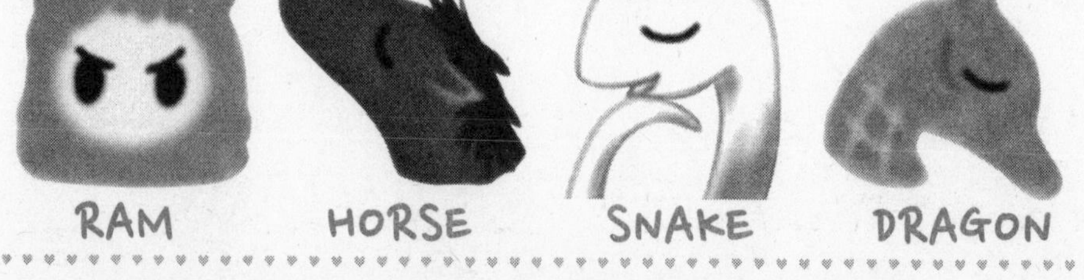
DRAGON
SNAKE
HORSE
RAM

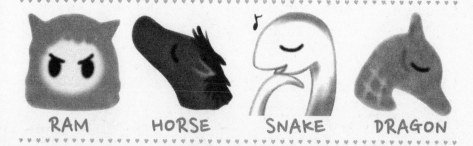

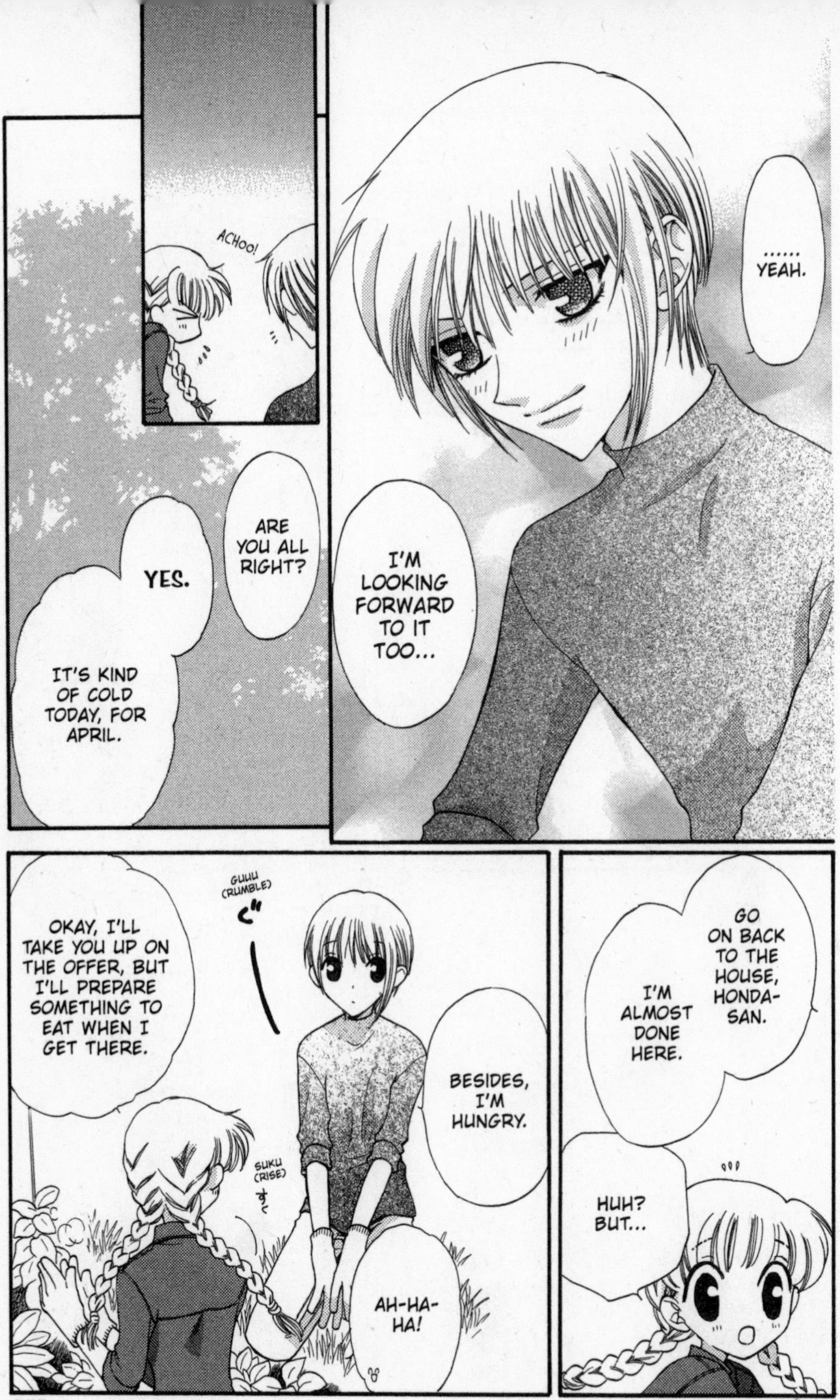
......YEAH.
I'M LOOKING FORWARD TO IT TOO...
ACHOO!
ARE YOU ALL RIGHT?
YES.
IT'S KIND OF COLD TODAY, FOR APRIL.
GO ON BACK TO THE HOUSE, HONDA-SAN.
I'M ALMOST DONE HERE.
HUH? BUT...
BESIDES, I'M HUNGRY.
GUUU (RUMBLE)
OKAY, I'LL TAKE YOU UP ON THE OFFER, BUT I'LL PREPARE SOMETHING TO EAT WHEN I GET THERE.
SUKU (RISE)
AH-HA-HA!

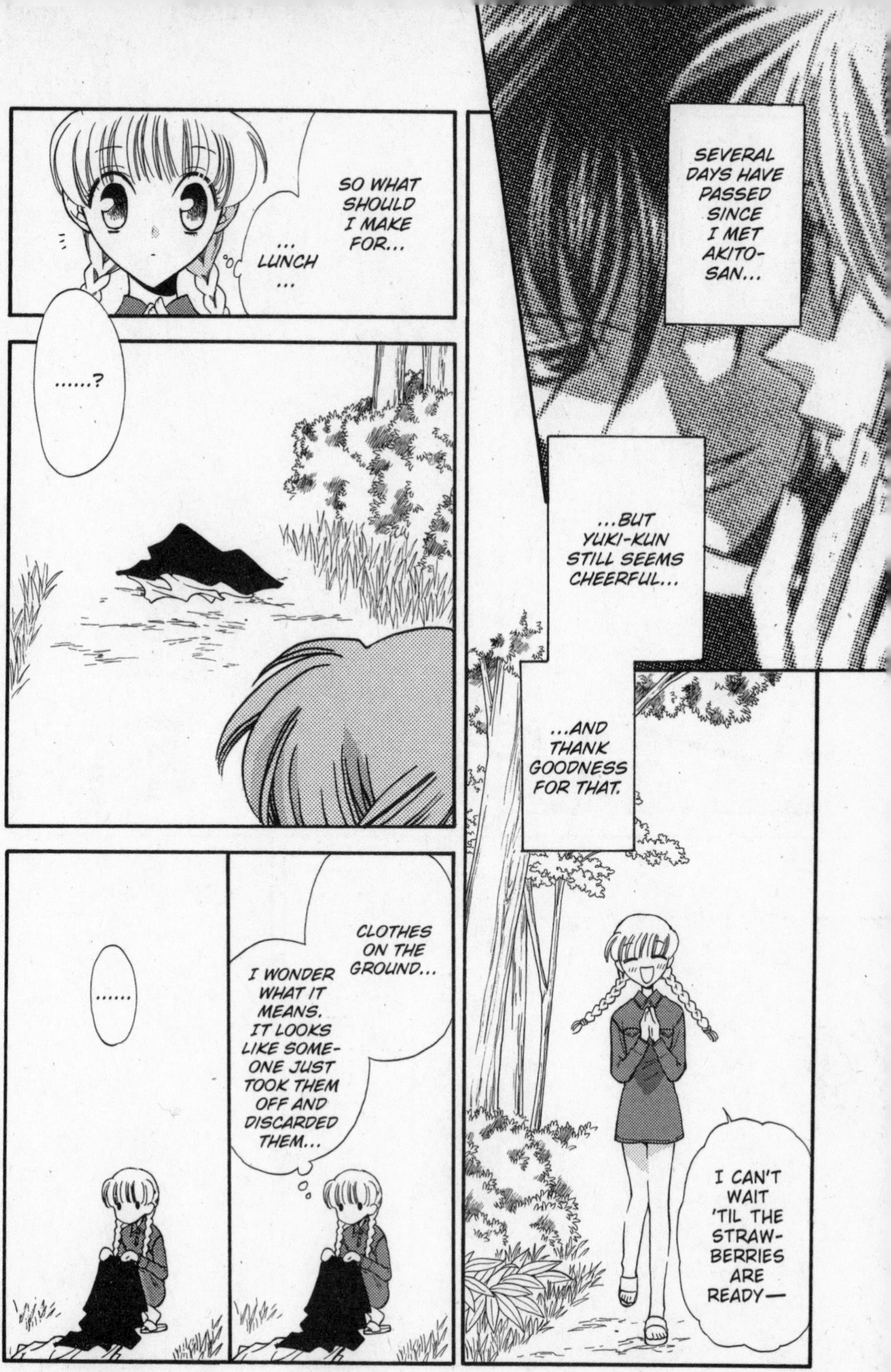
SEVERAL DAYS HAVE PASSED SINCE I MET AKITO-SAN...
...BUT YUKI-KUN STILL SEEMS CHEERFUL...
...AND THANK GOODNESS FOR THAT.
I CAN'T WAIT 'TIL THE STRAWBERRIES ARE READY—
SO WHAT SHOULD I MAKE FOR...
...LUNCH...
......?
CLOTHES ON THE GROUND...
I WONDER WHAT IT MEANS. IT LOOKS LIKE SOMEONE JUST TOOK THEM OFF AND DISCARDED THEM...
......

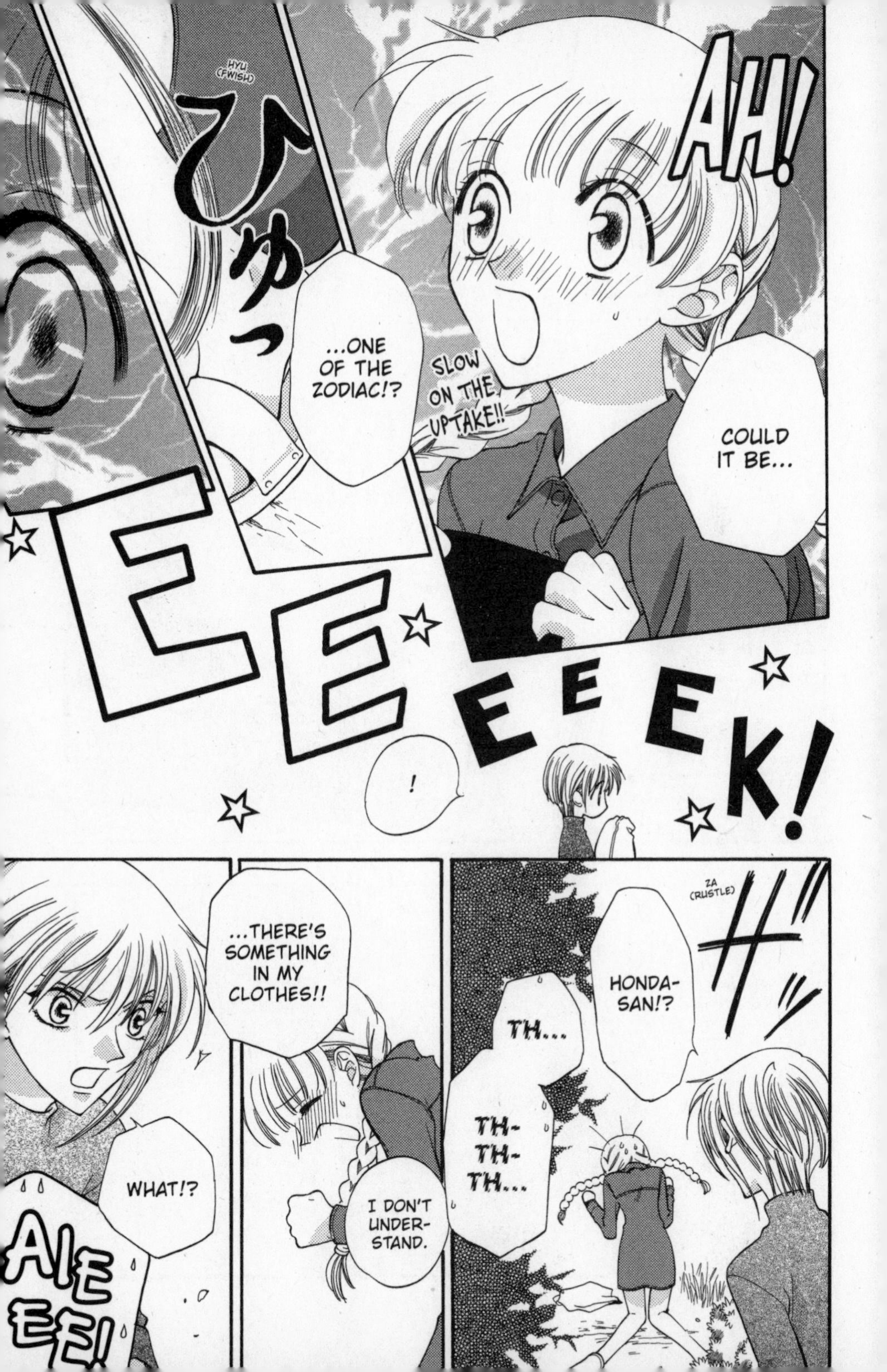
AH!
COULD IT BE...
SLOW ON THE UPTAKE!!
...ONE OF THE ZODIAC!?
HYU (FWISH)
ひゅっ
EEEEEEK!
!
ZA (RUSTLE)
HONDA-SAN!?
TH...
TH-TH-TH...
...THERE'S SOMETHING IN MY CLOTHES!!
I DON'T UNDER-STAND.
WHAT!?
AIEEE!

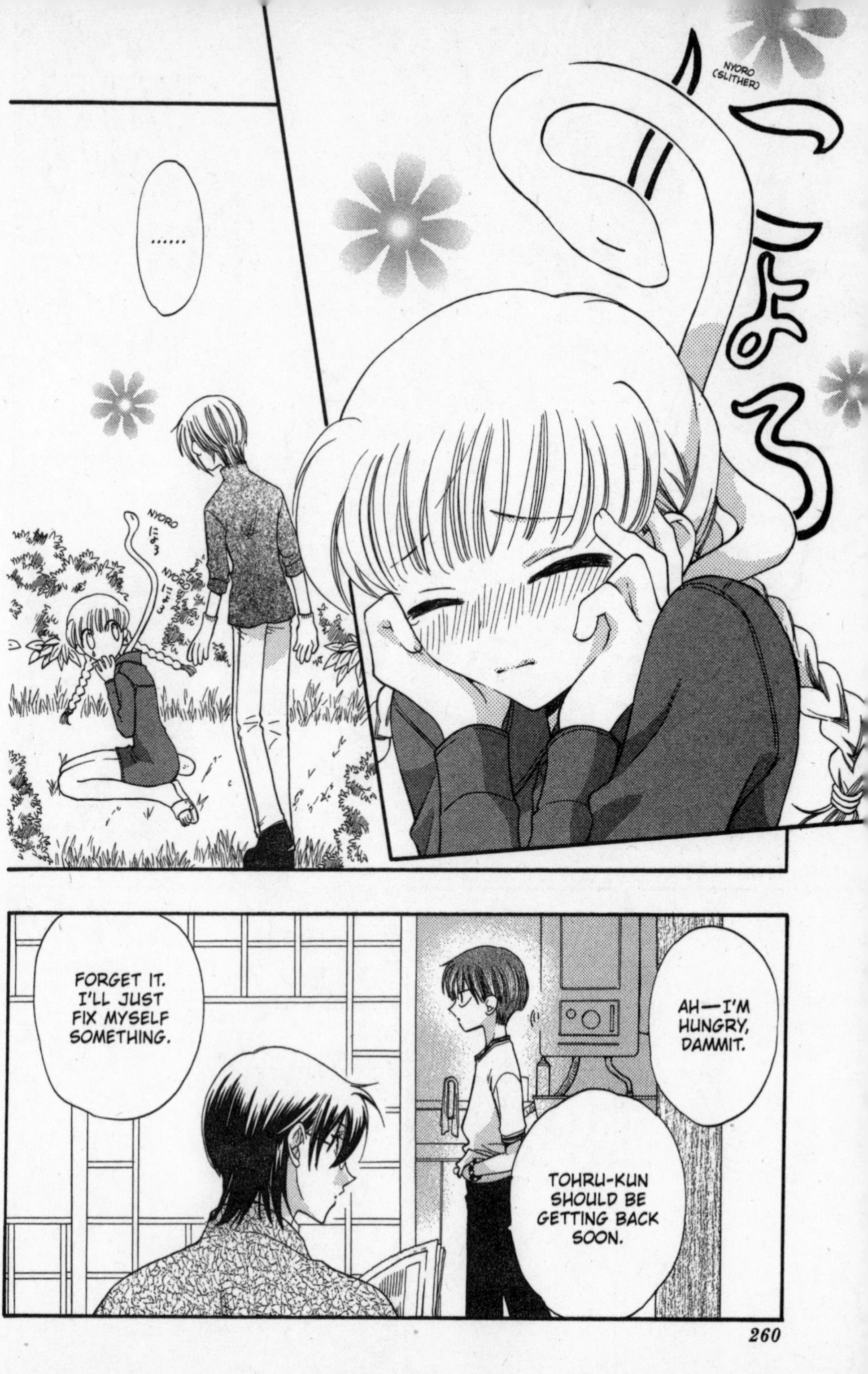
NYORO (SLITHER)
にょろ
......
NYORO
にょろ
NYORO
にょろ
AH—I'M HUNGRY, DAMMIT.
TOHRU-KUN SHOULD BE GETTING BACK SOON.
FORGET IT. I'LL JUST FIX MYSELF SOMETHING.

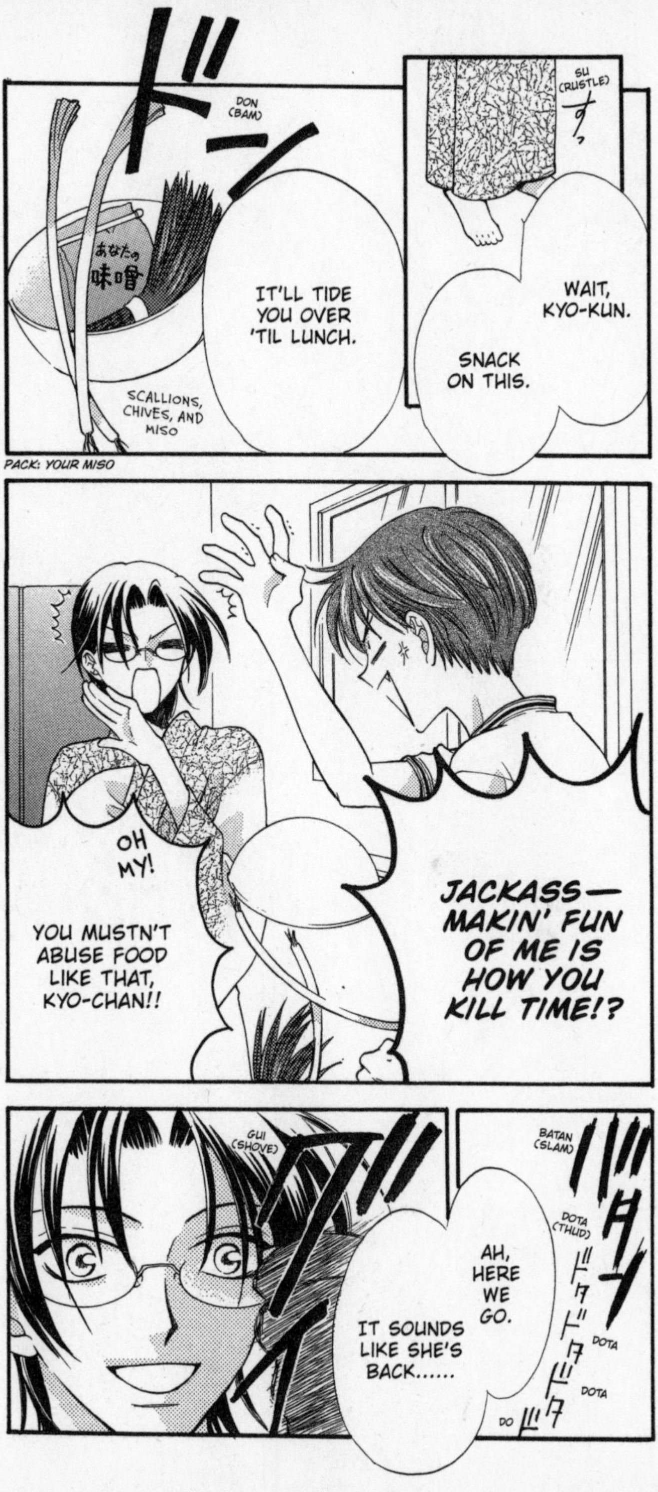
SU (RUSTLE)
すっ
WAIT, KYO-KUN.
SNACK ON THIS.
DON (BAM)
ドーン
IT'LL TIDE YOU OVER 'TIL LUNCH.
あなたの味噌
SCALLIONS, CHIVES, AND MISO
PACK: YOUR MISO
JACKASS— MAKIN' FUN OF ME IS HOW YOU KILL TIME!?
OH MY!
YOU MUSTN'T ABUSE FOOD LIKE THAT, KYO-CHAN!!
BATAN (SLAM)
DOTA (THUD)
DOTA
DOTA
DO
GUI (SHOVE)
AH, HERE WE GO.
IT SOUNDS LIKE SHE'S BACK......

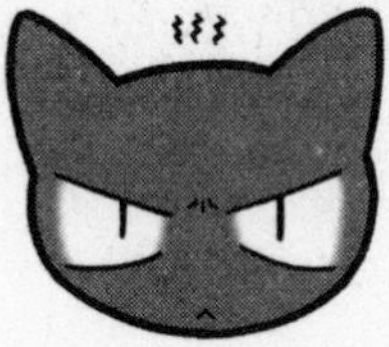

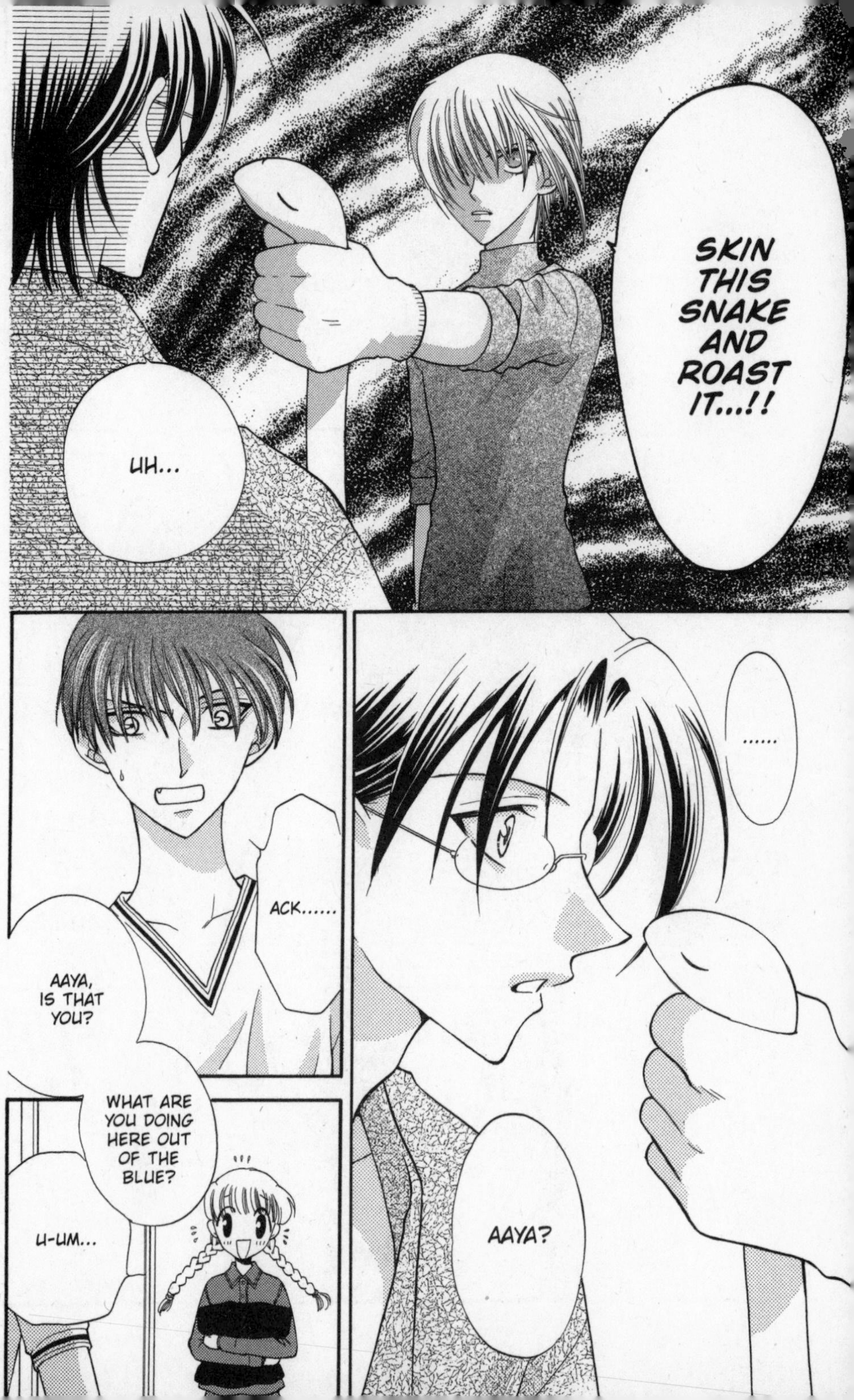
SKIN THIS SNAKE AND ROAST IT...!!
UH...
......
AAYA?
ACK......
AAYA, IS THAT YOU?
WHAT ARE YOU DOING HERE OUT OF THE BLUE?
U-UM...

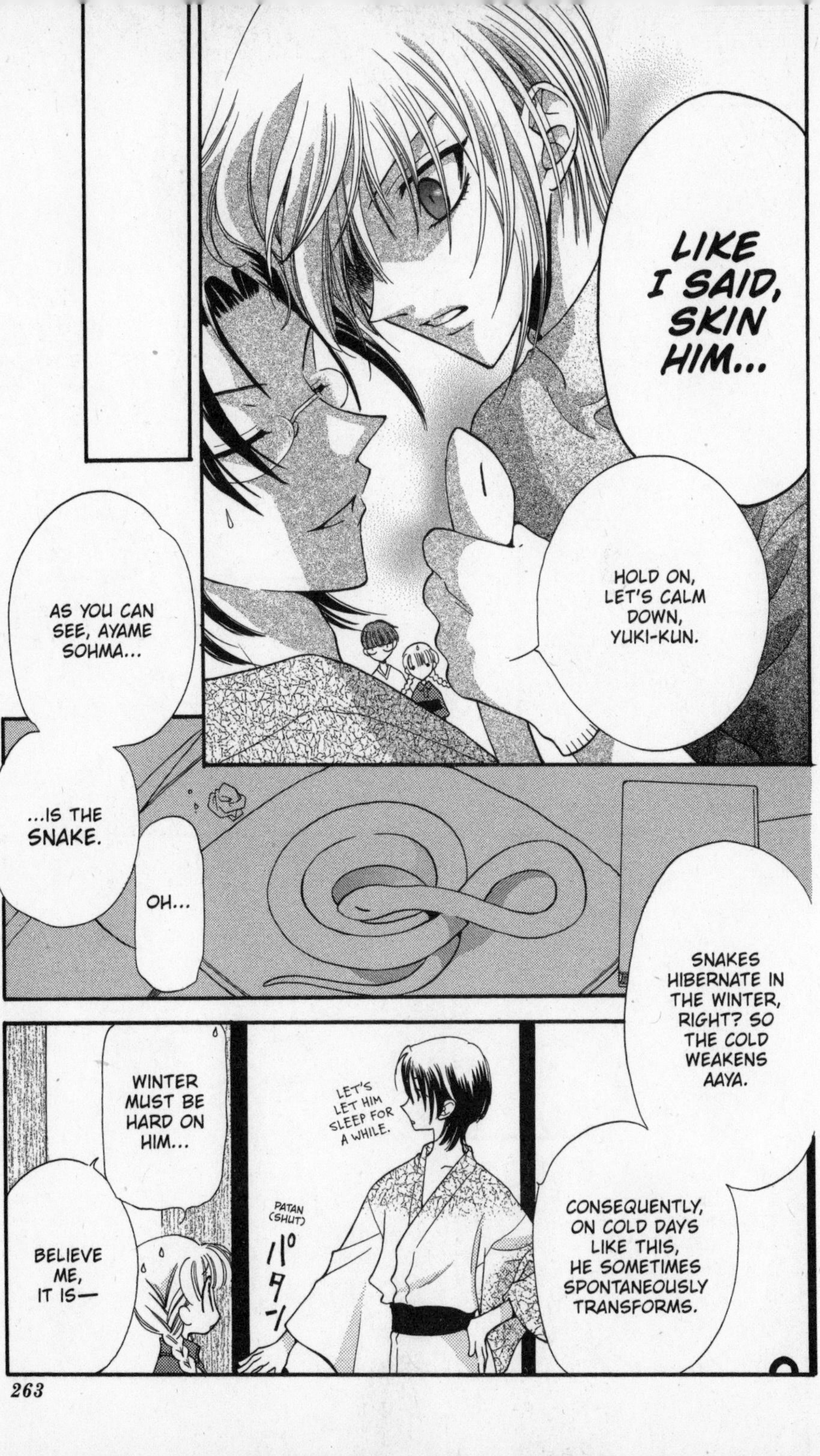
LIKE I SAID, SKIN HIM...
HOLD ON, LET'S CALM DOWN, YUKI-KUN.
AS YOU CAN SEE, AYAME SOHMA...
...IS THE SNAKE.
OH...
SNAKES HIBERNATE IN THE WINTER, RIGHT? SO THE COLD WEAKENS AAYA.
CONSEQUENTLY, ON COLD DAYS LIKE THIS, HE SOMETIMES SPONTANEOUSLY TRANSFORMS.
LET'S LET HIM SLEEP FOR A WHILE.
PATAN (SHUT)
パタン
WINTER MUST BE HARD ON HIM...
BELIEVE ME, IT IS—

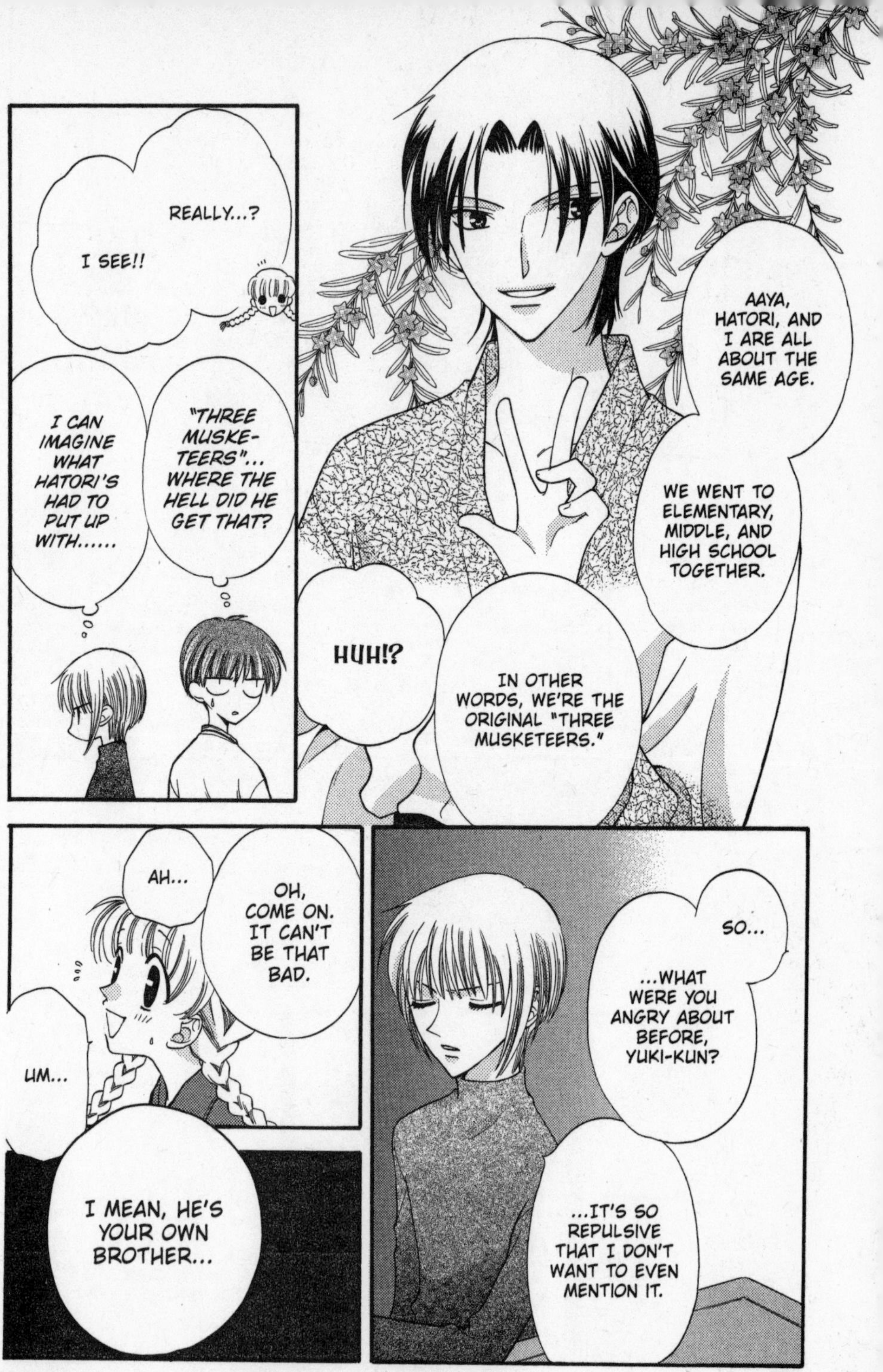
AAYA, HATORI, AND I ARE ALL ABOUT THE SAME AGE.
WE WENT TO ELEMENTARY, MIDDLE, AND HIGH SCHOOL TOGETHER.
IN OTHER WORDS, WE'RE THE ORIGINAL "THREE MUSKETEERS."
HUH!?
REALLY...?
I SEE!!
"THREE MUSKETEERS"... WHERE THE HELL DID HE GET THAT?
I CAN IMAGINE WHAT HATORI'S HAD TO PUT UP WITH......
SO...
...WHAT WERE YOU ANGRY ABOUT BEFORE, YUKI-KUN?
...IT'S SO REPULSIVE THAT I DON'T WANT TO EVEN MENTION IT.
OH, COME ON. IT CAN'T BE THAT BAD.
AH...
UM...
I MEAN, HE'S YOUR OWN BROTHER...

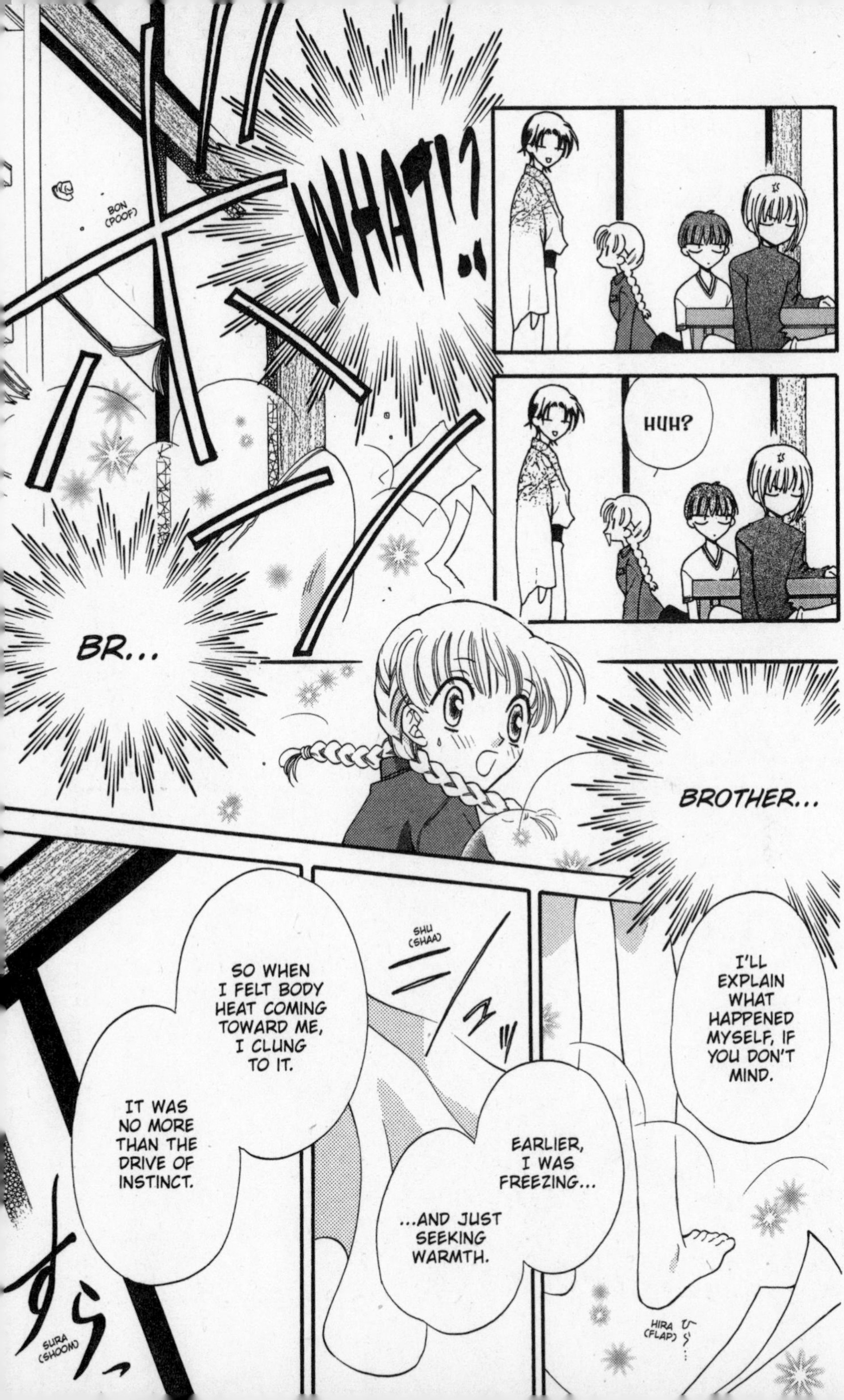
HUH?
BR...
BROTHER...
BON (POOF)
WHAT!?
I'LL EXPLAIN WHAT HAPPENED MYSELF, IF YOU DON'T MIND.
HIRA (FLAP)
SHU (SHAA)
EARLIER, I WAS FREEZING...
...AND JUST SEEKING WARMTH.
SO WHEN I FELT BODY HEAT COMING TOWARD ME, I CLUNG TO IT.
IT WAS NO MORE THAN THE DRIVE OF INSTINCT.
SURA (SHOOM)

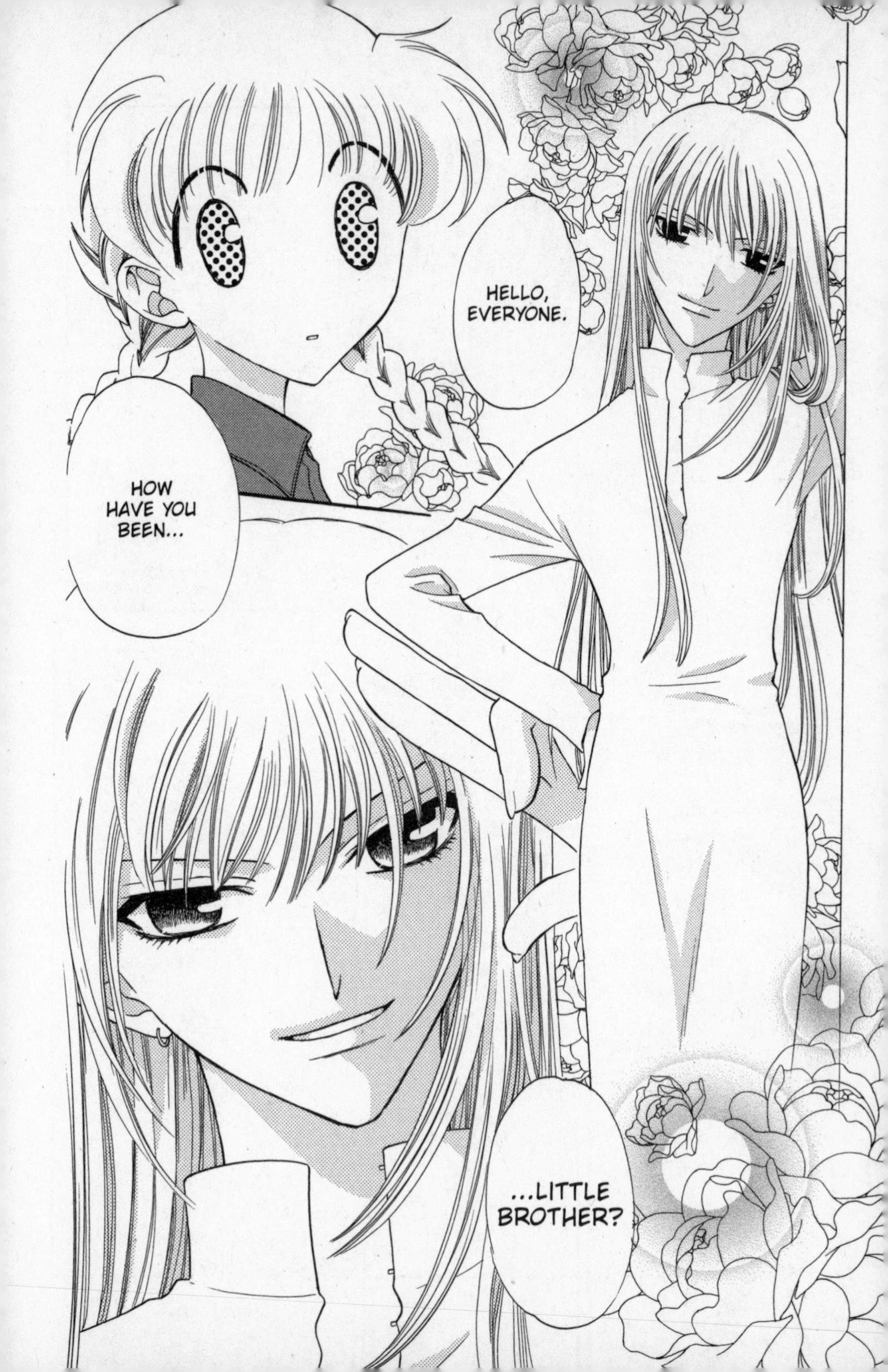
HELLO, EVERYONE.
HOW HAVE YOU BEEN...
...LITTLE BROTHER?

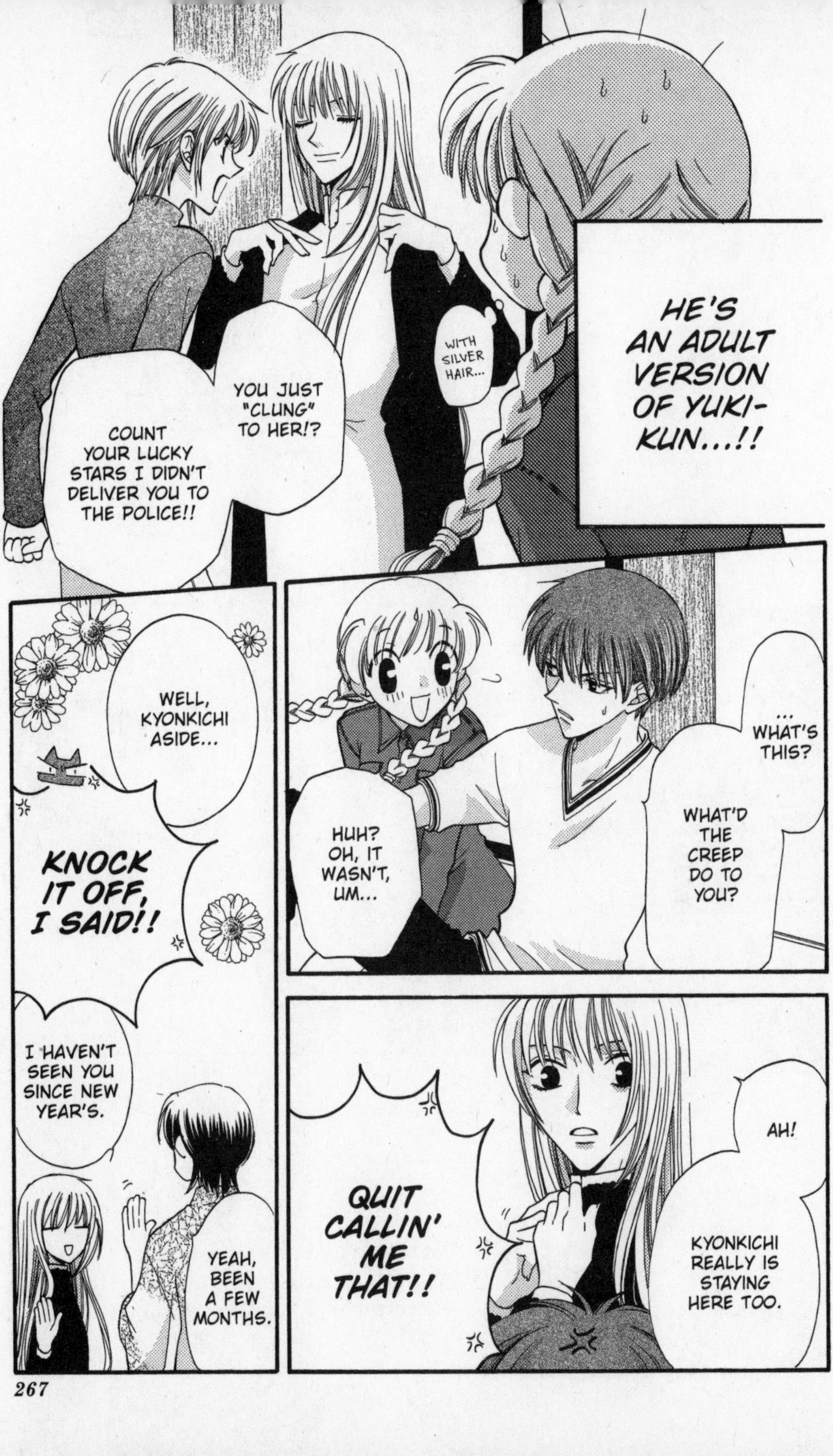
HE'S AN ADULT VERSION OF YUKI-KUN...!!
WITH SILVER HAIR...
YOU JUST "CLUNG" TO HER!?
COUNT YOUR LUCKY STARS I DIDN'T DELIVER YOU TO THE POLICE!!
... WHAT'S THIS?
WHAT'D THE CREEP DO TO YOU?
HUH? OH, IT WASN'T, UM...
AH!
KYONKICHI REALLY IS STAYING HERE TOO.
QUIT CALLIN' ME THAT!!
WELL, KYONKICHI ASIDE...
KNOCK IT OFF, I SAID!!
I HAVEN'T SEEN YOU SINCE NEW YEAR'S.
YEAH, BEEN A FEW MONTHS.

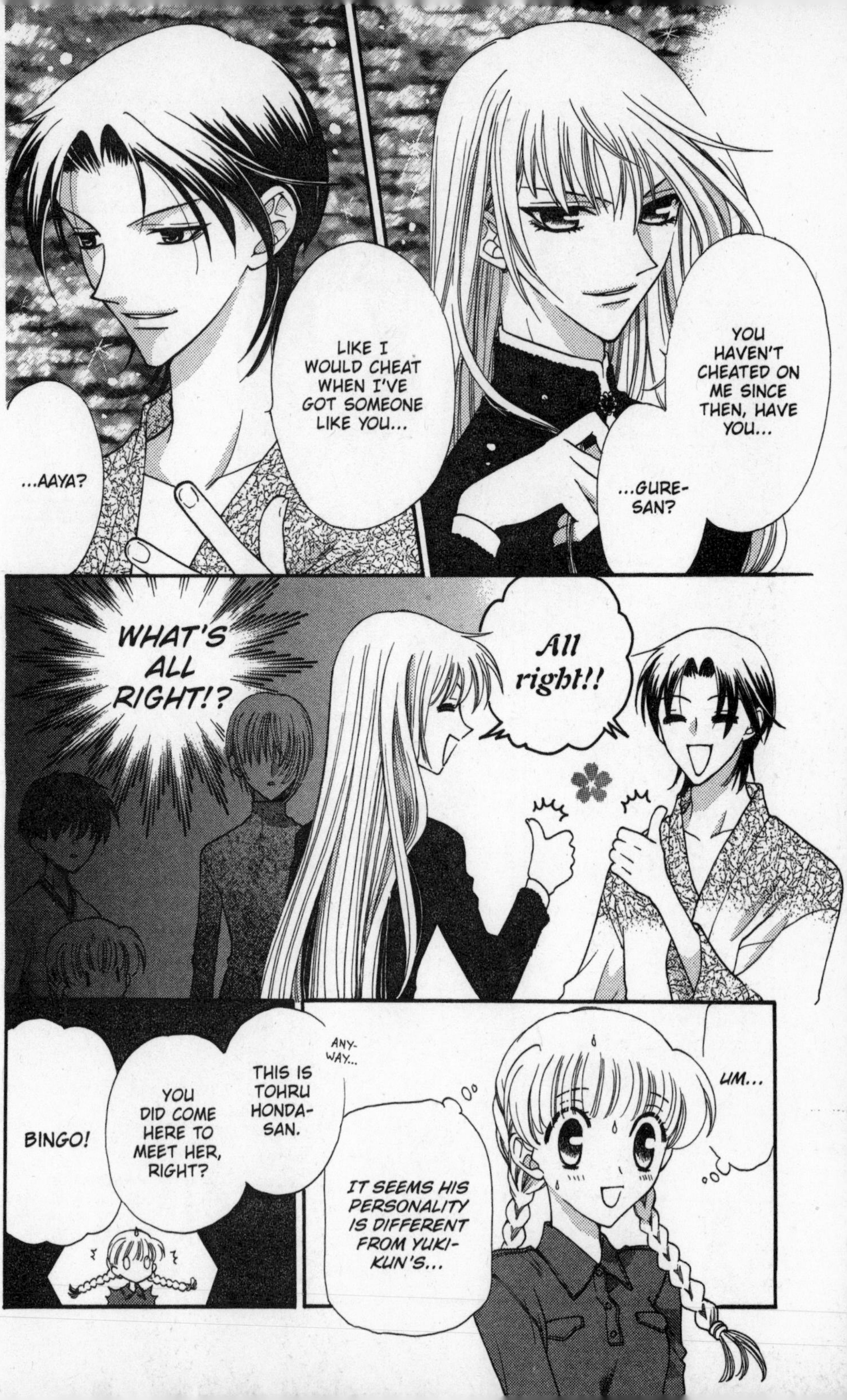
YOU HAVEN'T CHEATED ON ME SINCE THEN, HAVE YOU...
...GURE-SAN?
LIKE I WOULD CHEAT WHEN I'VE GOT SOMEONE LIKE YOU...
...AAYA?
All right!!
WHAT'S ALL RIGHT!?
UM...
IT SEEMS HIS PERSONALITY IS DIFFERENT FROM YUKI-KUN'S...
ANYWAY...
THIS IS TOHRU HONDA-SAN.
YOU DID COME HERE TO MEET HER, RIGHT?
BINGO!

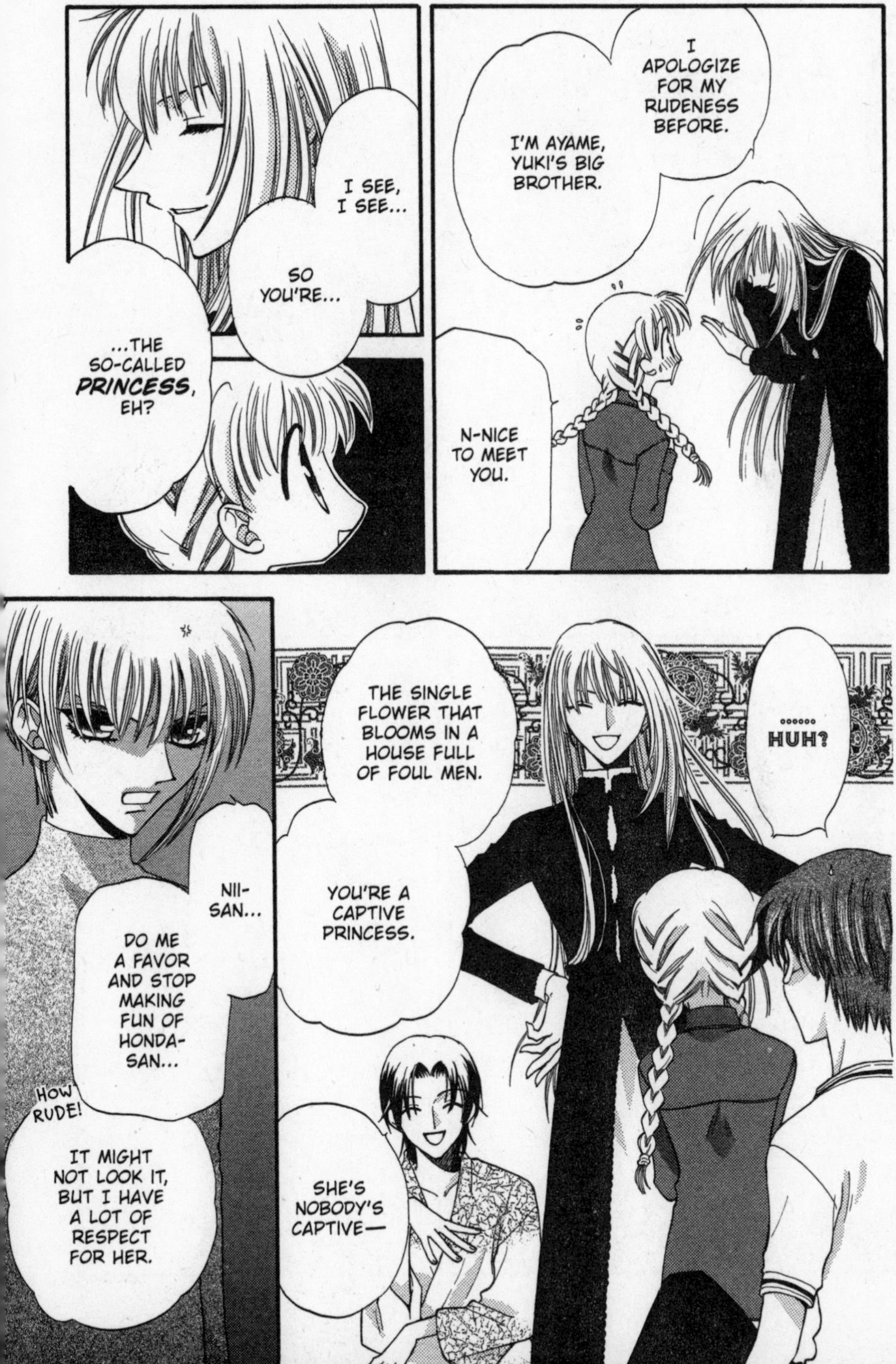
I APOLOGIZE FOR MY RUDENESS BEFORE.
I'M AYAME, YUKI'S BIG BROTHER.
N-NICE TO MEET YOU.
I SEE, I SEE...
SO YOU'RE...
...THE SO-CALLED **PRINCESS**, EH?
......HUH?
THE SINGLE FLOWER THAT BLOOMS IN A HOUSE FULL OF FOUL MEN.
YOU'RE A CAPTIVE PRINCESS.
SHE'S NOBODY'S CAPTIVE—
NII-SAN...
DO ME A FAVOR AND STOP MAKING FUN OF HONDA-SAN...
HOW RUDE!
IT MIGHT NOT LOOK IT, BUT I HAVE A LOT OF RESPECT FOR HER.

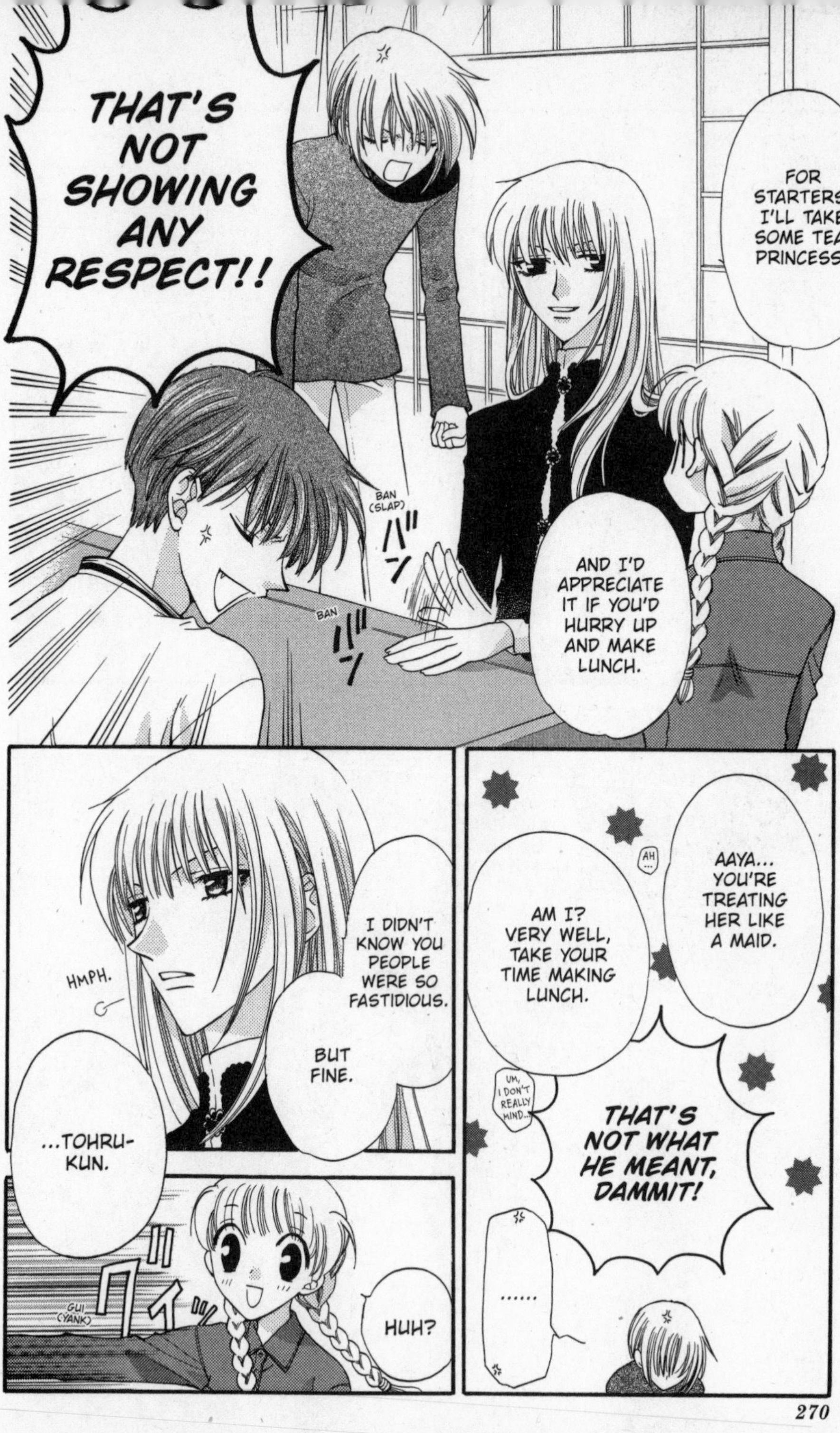
FOR STARTERS, I'LL TAKE SOME TEA, PRINCESS.
AND I'D APPRECIATE IT IF YOU'D HURRY UP AND MAKE LUNCH.
BAN (SLAP)
BAN
THAT'S NOT SHOWING ANY RESPECT!!
AAYA... YOU'RE TREATING HER LIKE A MAID.
AH...
AM I? VERY WELL, TAKE YOUR TIME MAKING LUNCH.
UM, I DON'T REALLY MIND...
THAT'S NOT WHAT HE MEANT, DAMMIT!
......
I DIDN'T KNOW YOU PEOPLE WERE SO FASTIDIOUS.
BUT FINE.
HMPH.
...TOHRU-KUN.
HUH?
GUI (YANK)

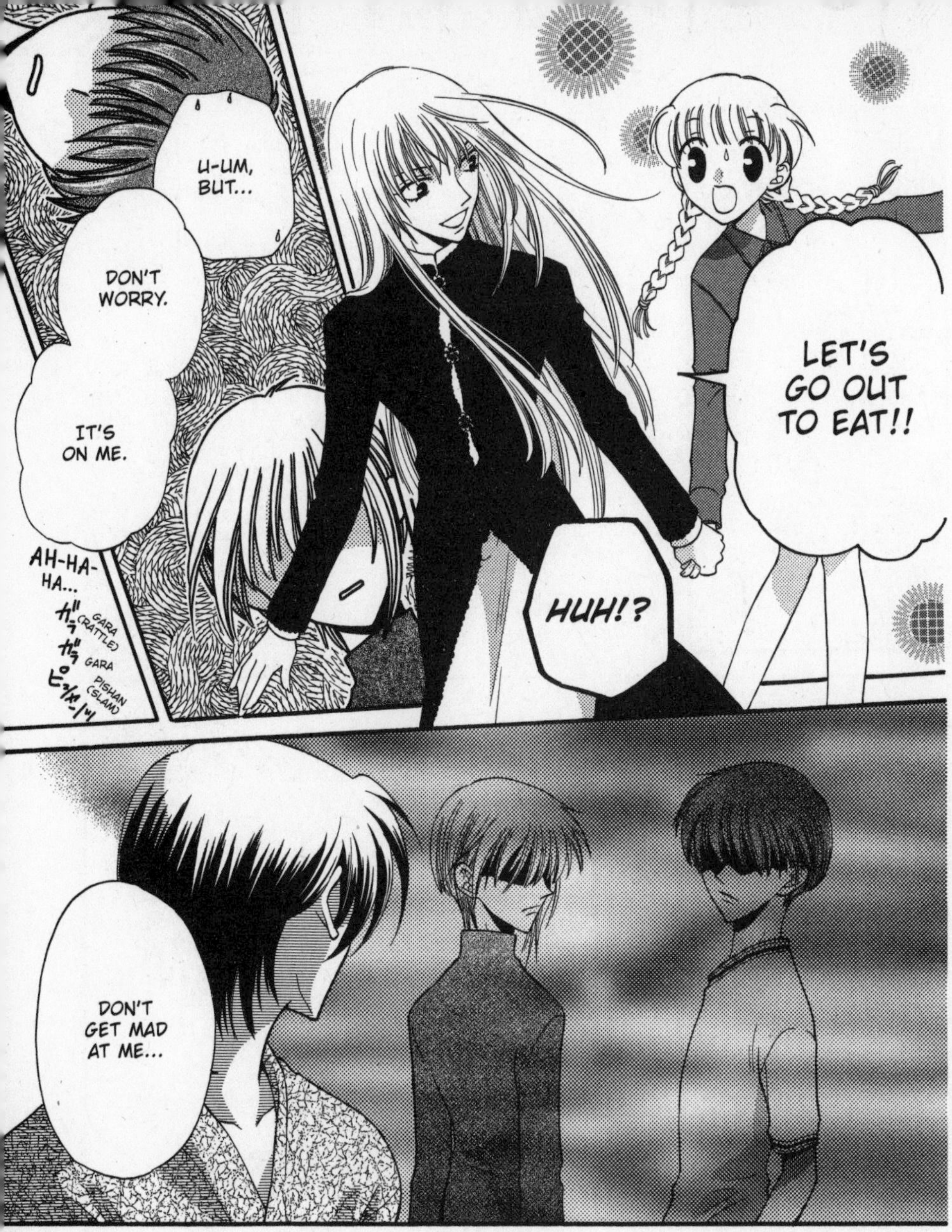
LET'S GO OUT TO EAT!!
HUH!?
U-UM, BUT...
DON'T WORRY.
IT'S ON ME.
AH-HA-HA...
ガラ GARA (RATTLE)
ガラ GARA
ピシャーン!! PISHAN (SLAM)
DON'T GET MAD AT ME...

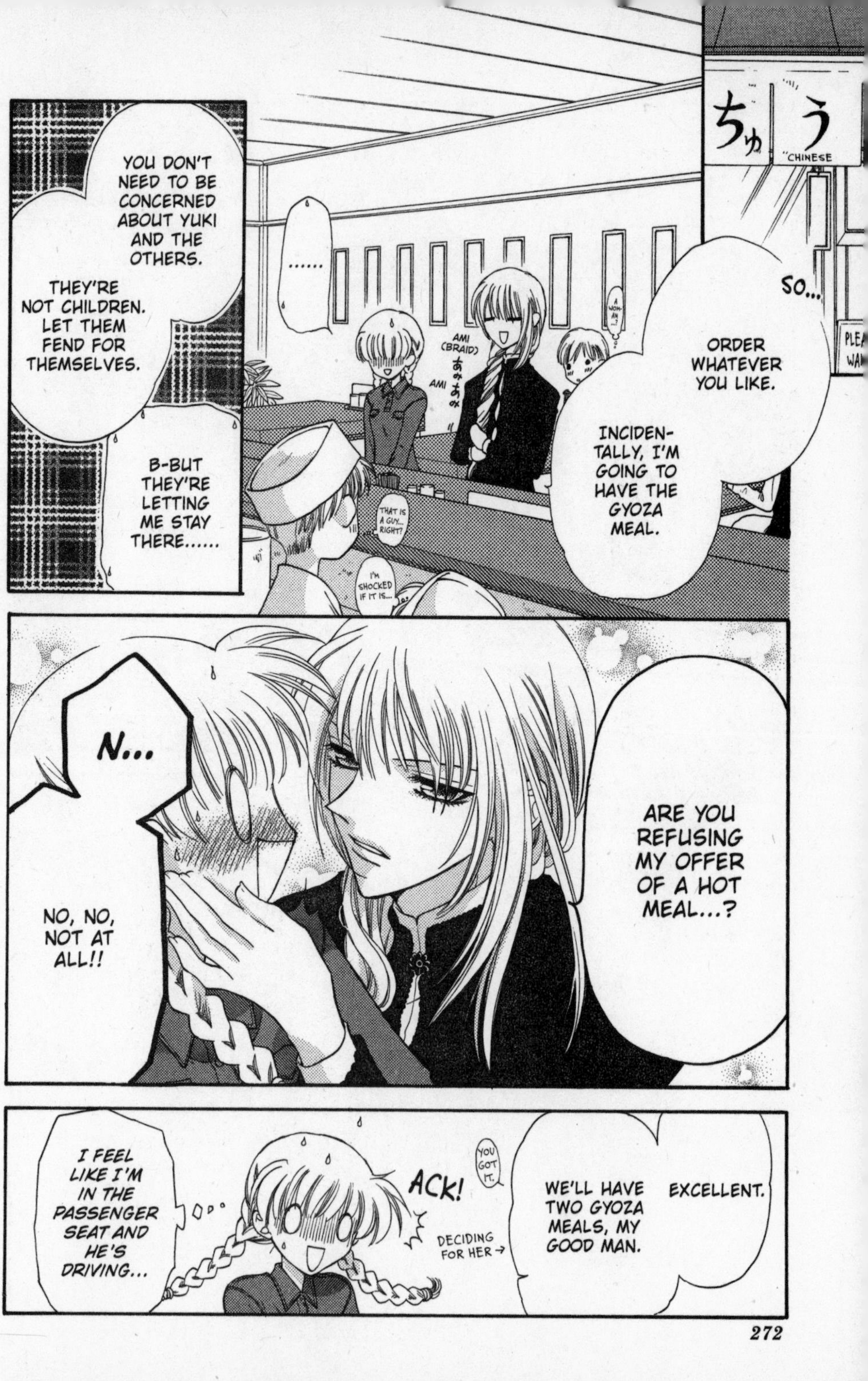
ちゅう
"CHINESE
SO...
ORDER WHATEVER YOU LIKE.
INCIDENTALLY, I'M GOING TO HAVE THE GYOZA MEAL.
A WOMAN...?
AMI (BRAID)
あみあみ
AMI
......
THAT IS A GUY... RIGHT?
I'M SHOCKED IF IT IS...
YOU DON'T NEED TO BE CONCERNED ABOUT YUKI AND THE OTHERS.
THEY'RE NOT CHILDREN. LET THEM FEND FOR THEMSELVES.
B-BUT THEY'RE LETTING ME STAY THERE......
ARE YOU REFUSING MY OFFER OF A HOT MEAL...?
N...
NO, NO, NOT AT ALL!!
EXCELLENT.
WE'LL HAVE TWO GYOZA MEALS, MY GOOD MAN.
YOU GOT IT.
ACK!
DECIDING FOR HER →
I FEEL LIKE I'M IN THE PASSENGER SEAT AND HE'S DRIVING...

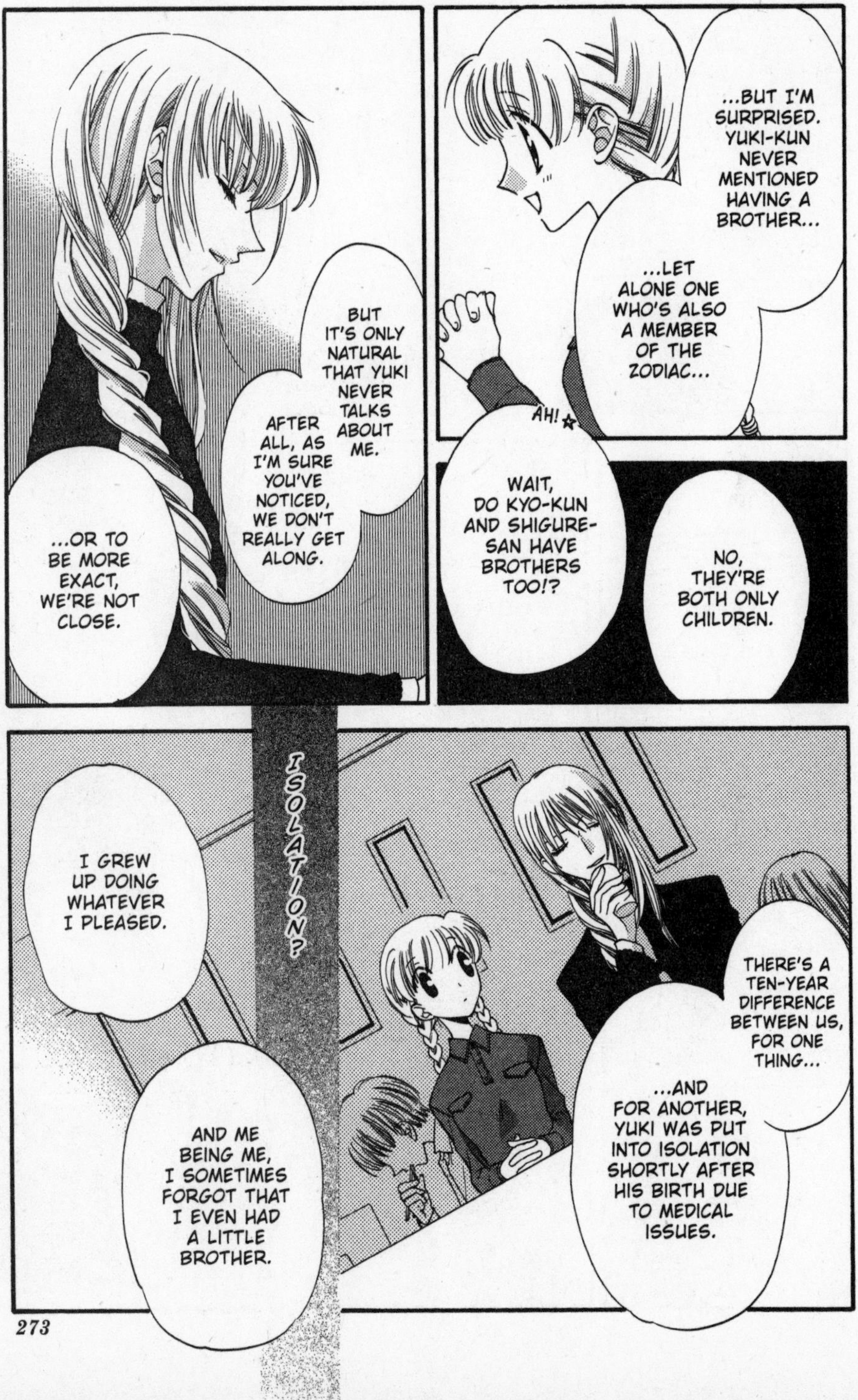
...BUT I'M SURPRISED. YUKI-KUN NEVER MENTIONED HAVING A BROTHER...
...LET ALONE ONE WHO'S ALSO A MEMBER OF THE ZODIAC...
AH! ☆
WAIT, DO KYO-KUN AND SHIGURE-SAN HAVE BROTHERS TOO!?
NO, THEY'RE BOTH ONLY CHILDREN.
BUT IT'S ONLY NATURAL THAT YUKI NEVER TALKS ABOUT ME.
AFTER ALL, AS I'M SURE YOU'VE NOTICED, WE DON'T REALLY GET ALONG.
...OR TO BE MORE EXACT, WE'RE NOT CLOSE.
THERE'S A TEN-YEAR DIFFERENCE BETWEEN US, FOR ONE THING...
...AND FOR ANOTHER, YUKI WAS PUT INTO ISOLATION SHORTLY AFTER HIS BIRTH DUE TO MEDICAL ISSUES.
ISOLATION?
I GREW UP DOING WHATEVER I PLEASED.
AND ME BEING ME, I SOMETIMES FORGOT THAT I EVEN HAD A LITTLE BROTHER.

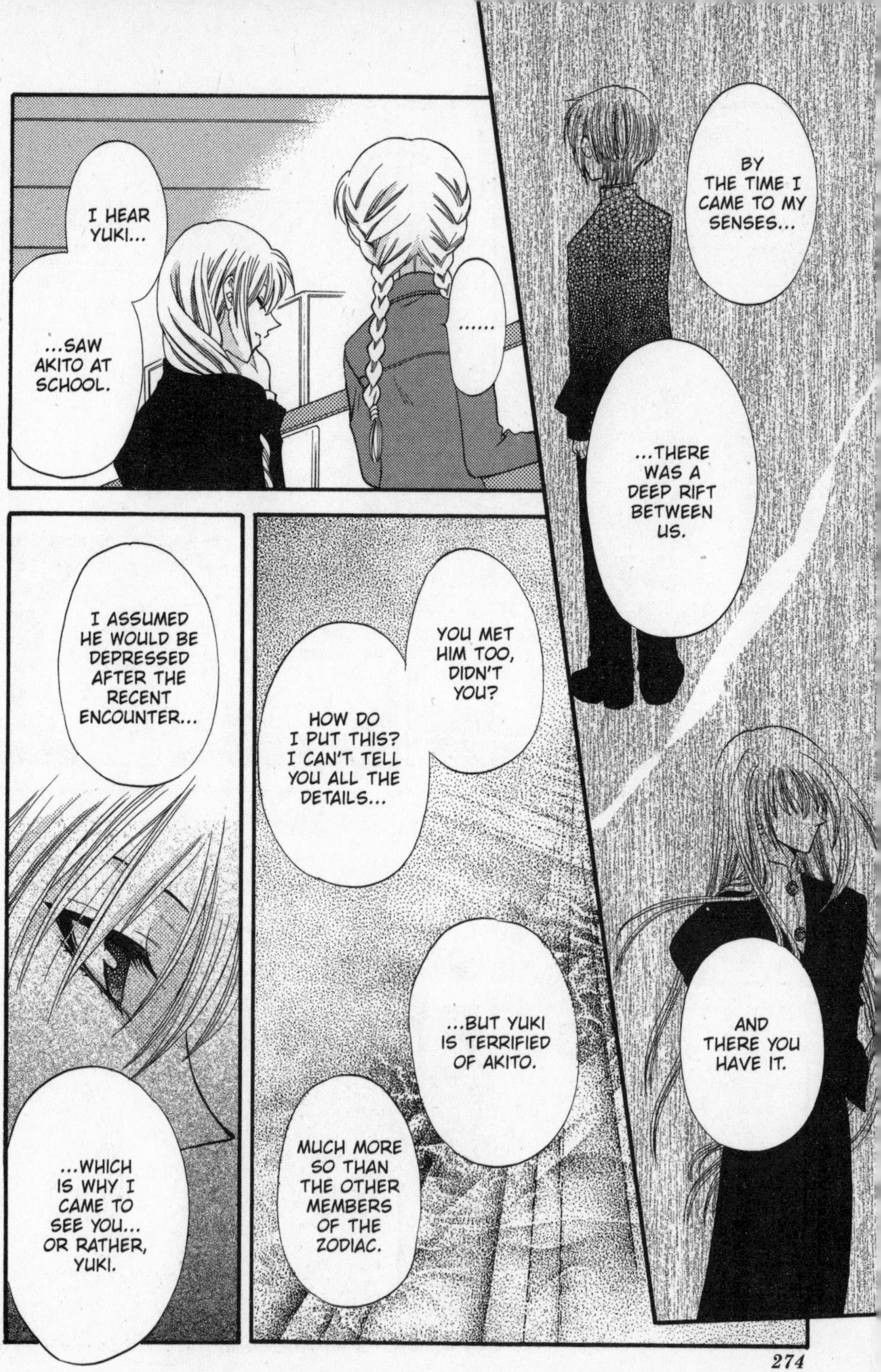
BY THE TIME I CAME TO MY SENSES...
...THERE WAS A DEEP RIFT BETWEEN US.
AND THERE YOU HAVE IT.
I HEAR YUKI...
...SAW AKITO AT SCHOOL.
......
YOU MET HIM TOO, DIDN'T YOU?
HOW DO I PUT THIS? I CAN'T TELL YOU ALL THE DETAILS...
...BUT YUKI IS TERRIFIED OF AKITO.
MUCH MORE SO THAN THE OTHER MEMBERS OF THE ZODIAC.
I ASSUMED HE WOULD BE DEPRESSED AFTER THE RECENT ENCOUNTER...
...WHICH IS WHY I CAME TO SEE YOU... OR RATHER, YUKI.

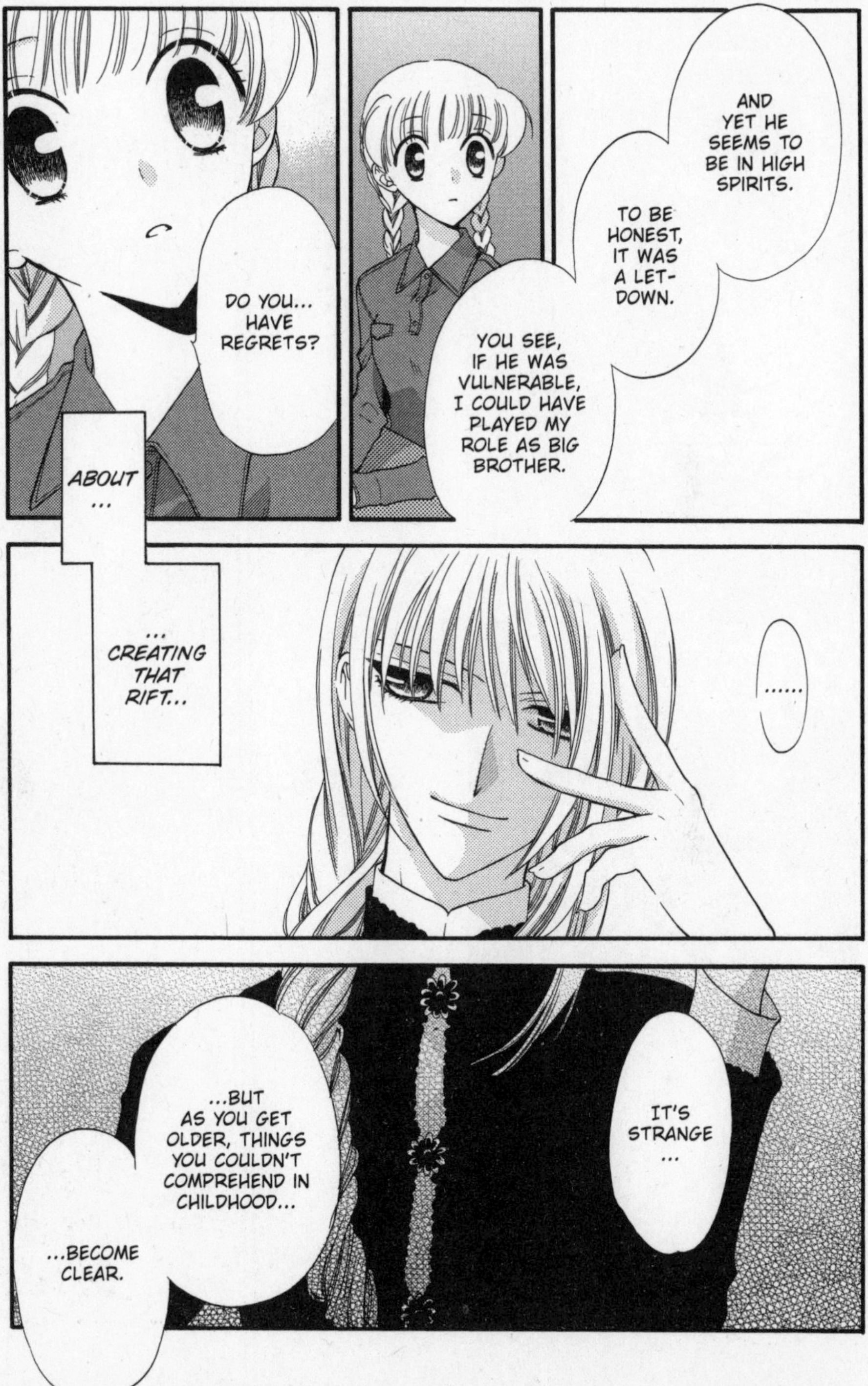
AND YET HE SEEMS TO BE IN HIGH SPIRITS.
TO BE HONEST, IT WAS A LET-DOWN.
YOU SEE, IF HE WAS VULNERABLE, I COULD HAVE PLAYED MY ROLE AS BIG BROTHER.
DO YOU... HAVE REGRETS?
ABOUT ...
... CREATING THAT RIFT...
......
IT'S STRANGE ...
...BUT AS YOU GET OLDER, THINGS YOU COULDN'T COMPREHEND IN CHILDHOOD...
...BECOME CLEAR.

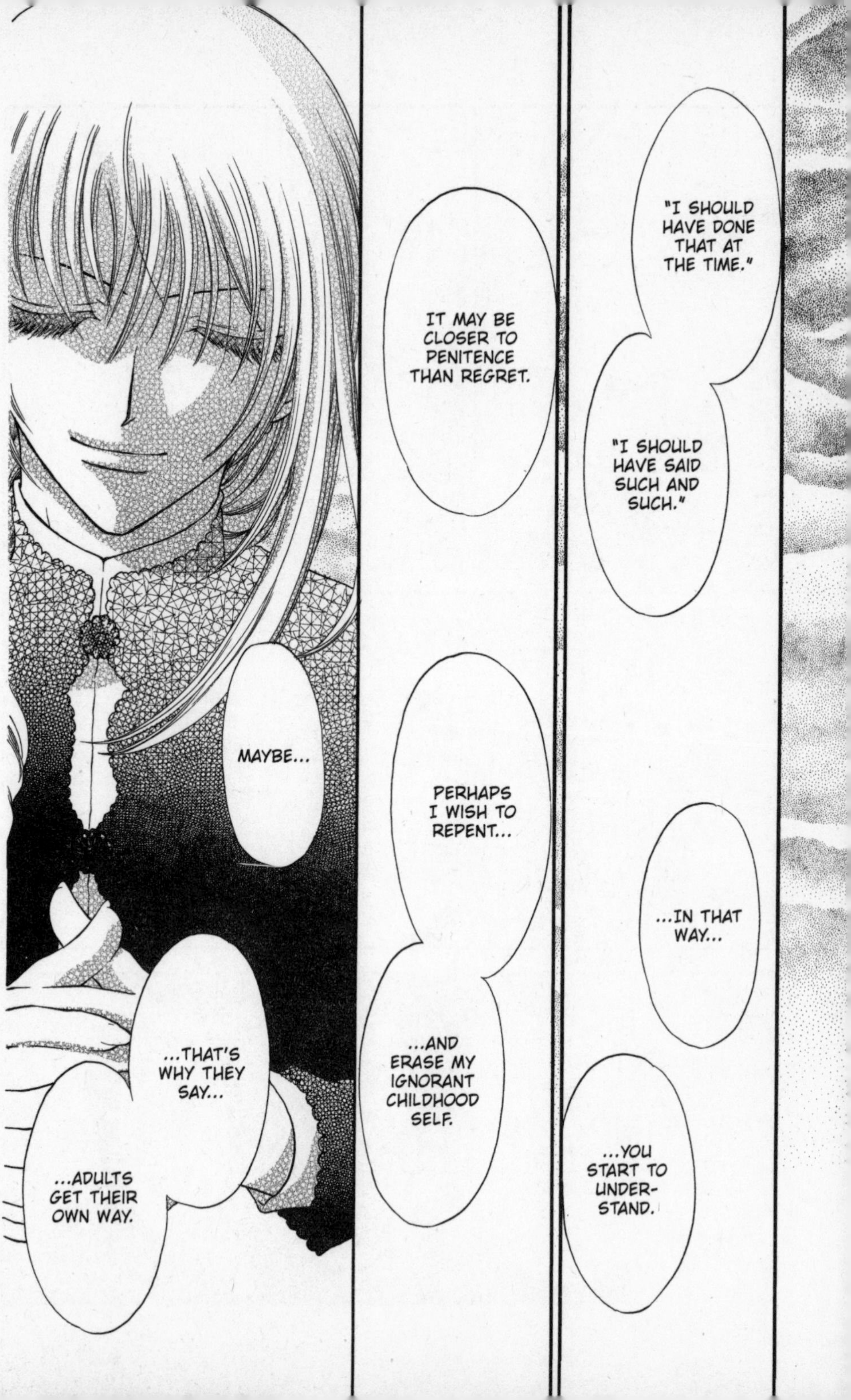
"I SHOULD HAVE DONE THAT AT THE TIME."
"I SHOULD HAVE SAID SUCH AND SUCH."
...IN THAT WAY...
...YOU START TO UNDERSTAND.
IT MAY BE CLOSER TO PENITENCE THAN REGRET.
PERHAPS I WISH TO REPENT...
...AND ERASE MY IGNORANT CHILDHOOD SELF.
MAYBE...
...THAT'S WHY THEY SAY...
...ADULTS GET THEIR OWN WAY.

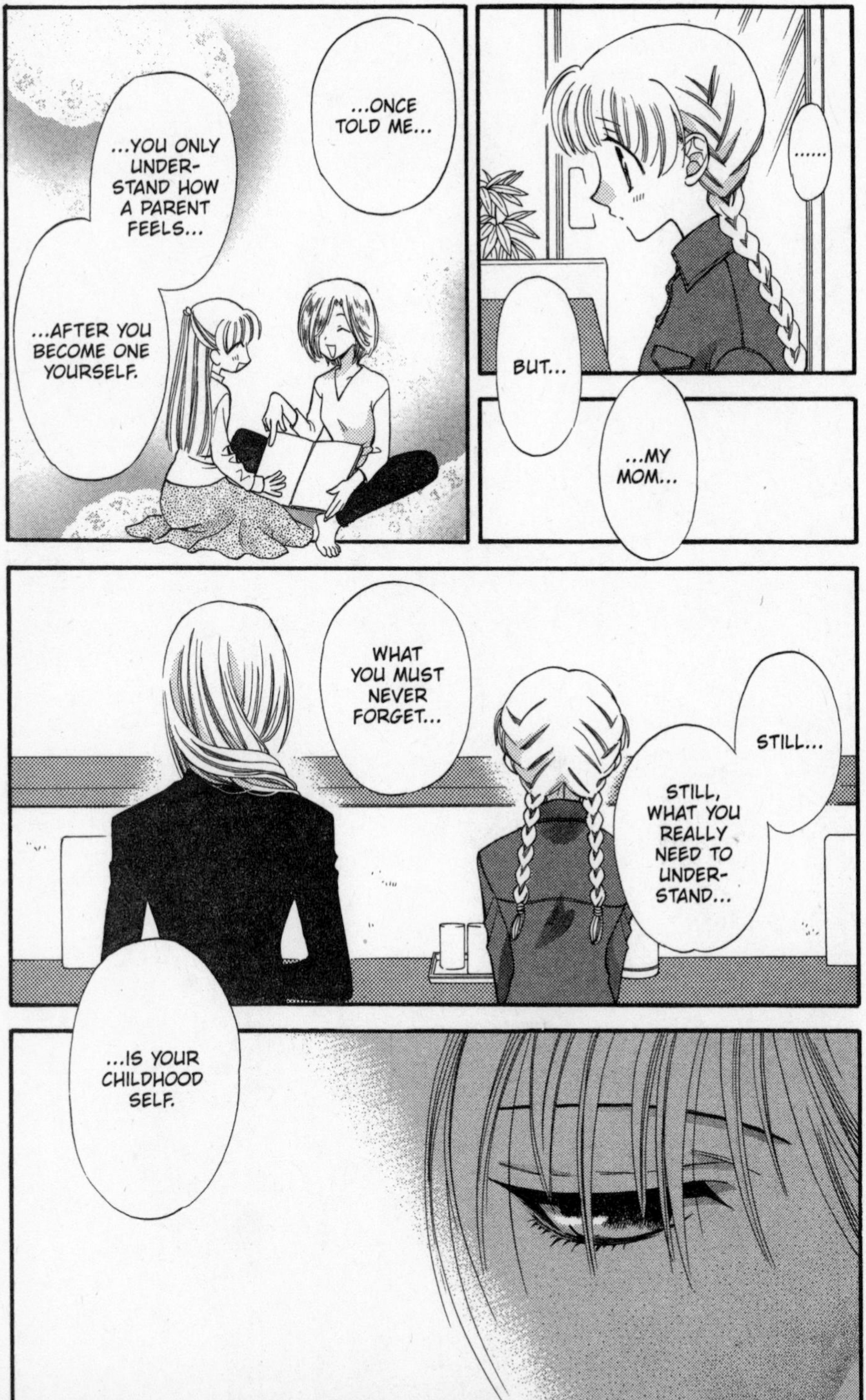
......
BUT...
...MY MOM...
...ONCE TOLD ME...
...YOU ONLY UNDER-STAND HOW A PARENT FEELS...
...AFTER YOU BECOME ONE YOURSELF.
STILL...
STILL, WHAT YOU REALLY NEED TO UNDER-STAND...
WHAT YOU MUST NEVER FORGET...
...IS YOUR CHILDHOOD SELF.

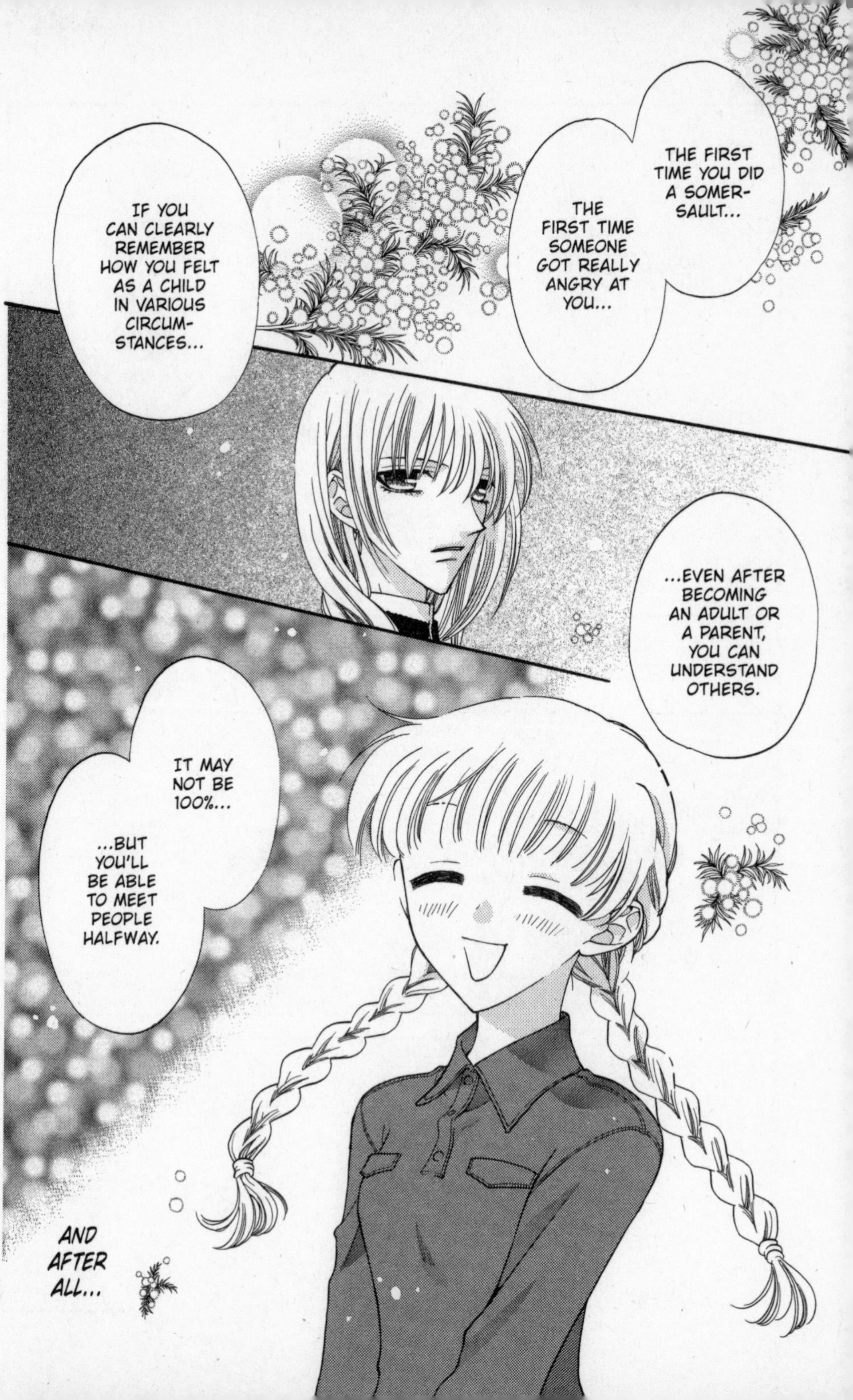
THE FIRST TIME YOU DID A SOMER-SAULT...
THE FIRST TIME SOMEONE GOT REALLY ANGRY AT YOU...
IF YOU CAN CLEARLY REMEMBER HOW YOU FELT AS A CHILD IN VARIOUS CIRCUM-STANCES...
...EVEN AFTER BECOMING AN ADULT OR A PARENT, YOU CAN UNDERSTAND OTHERS.
IT MAY NOT BE 100%...
...BUT YOU'LL BE ABLE TO MEET PEOPLE HALFWAY.
AND AFTER ALL...

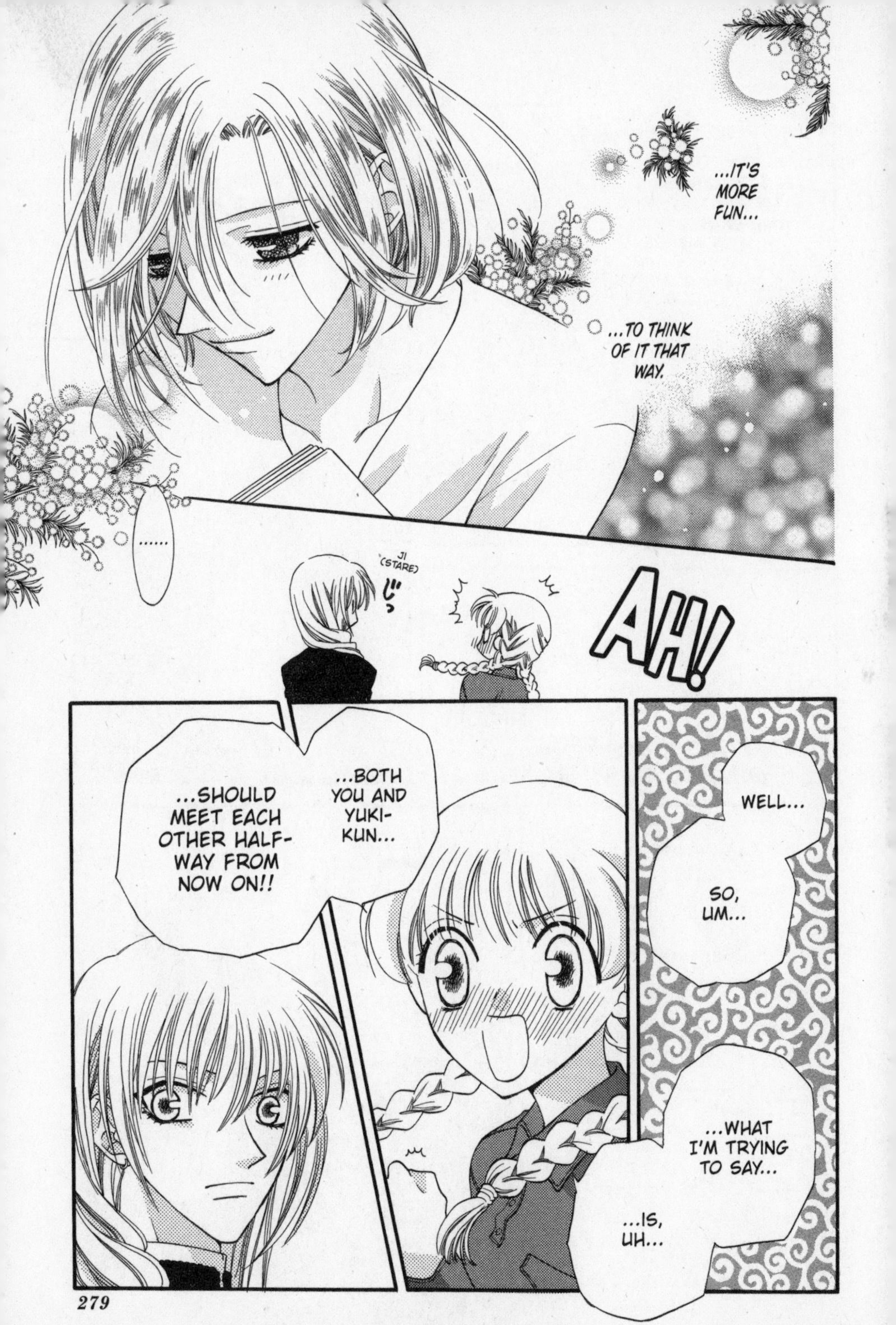
...IT'S MORE FUN...
...TO THINK OF IT THAT WAY.
......
JI (STARE)
じっ
AH!
WELL...
SO, UM...
...WHAT I'M TRYING TO SAY...
...IS, UH...
...BOTH YOU AND YUKI-KUN...
...SHOULD MEET EACH OTHER HALF-WAY FROM NOW ON!!

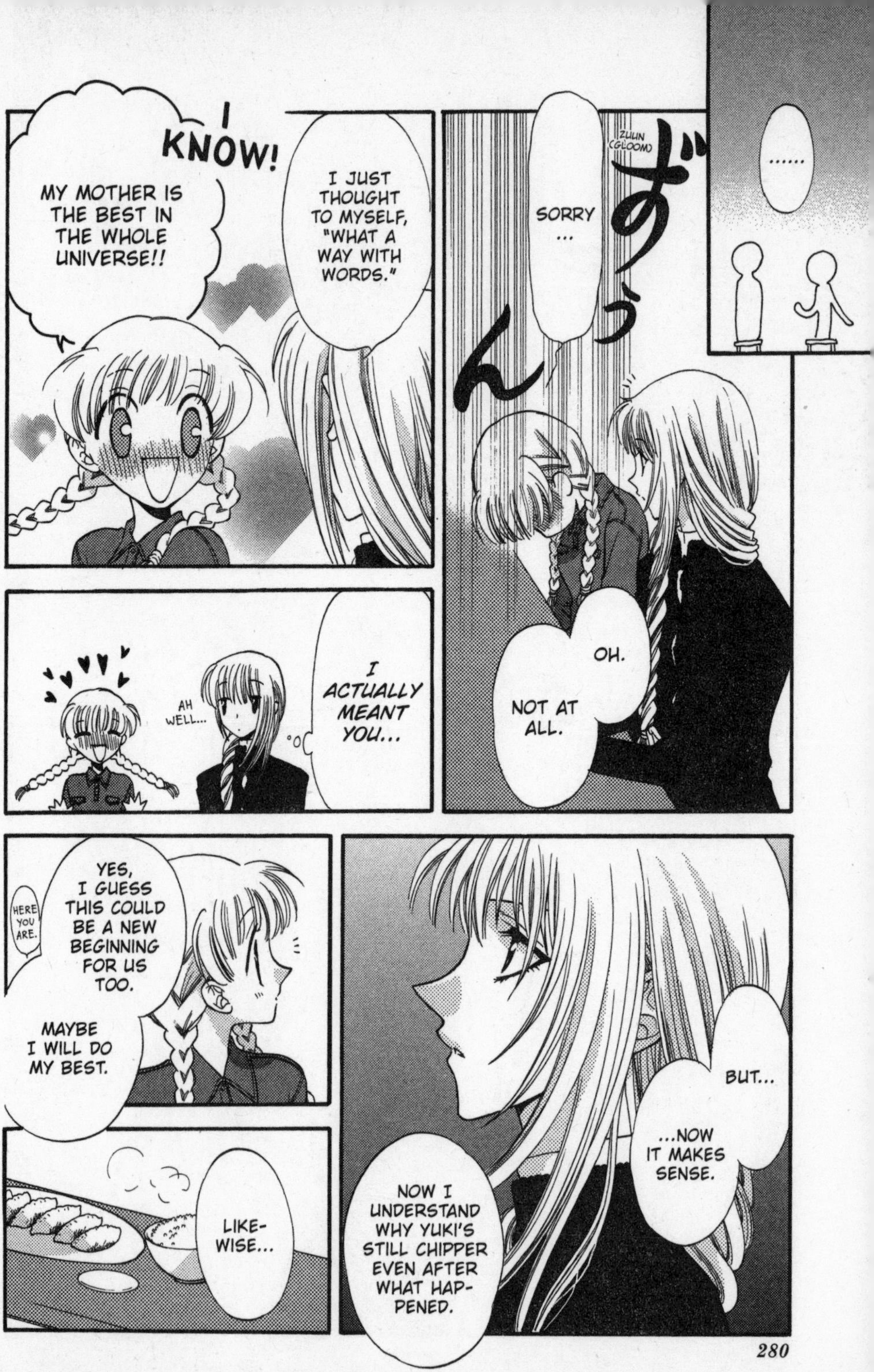
......
SORRY ...
ZUUN (GLOOM)
ずううん
OH.
NOT AT ALL.
I JUST THOUGHT TO MYSELF, "WHAT A WAY WITH WORDS."
I KNOW!
MY MOTHER IS THE BEST IN THE WHOLE UNIVERSE!!
I ACTUALLY MEANT YOU...
AH WELL...
BUT...
...NOW IT MAKES SENSE.
NOW I UNDERSTAND WHY YUKI'S STILL CHIPPER EVEN AFTER WHAT HAP-PENED.
YES, I GUESS THIS COULD BE A NEW BEGINNING FOR US TOO.
HERE YOU ARE.
MAYBE I WILL DO MY BEST.
LIKE-WISE...

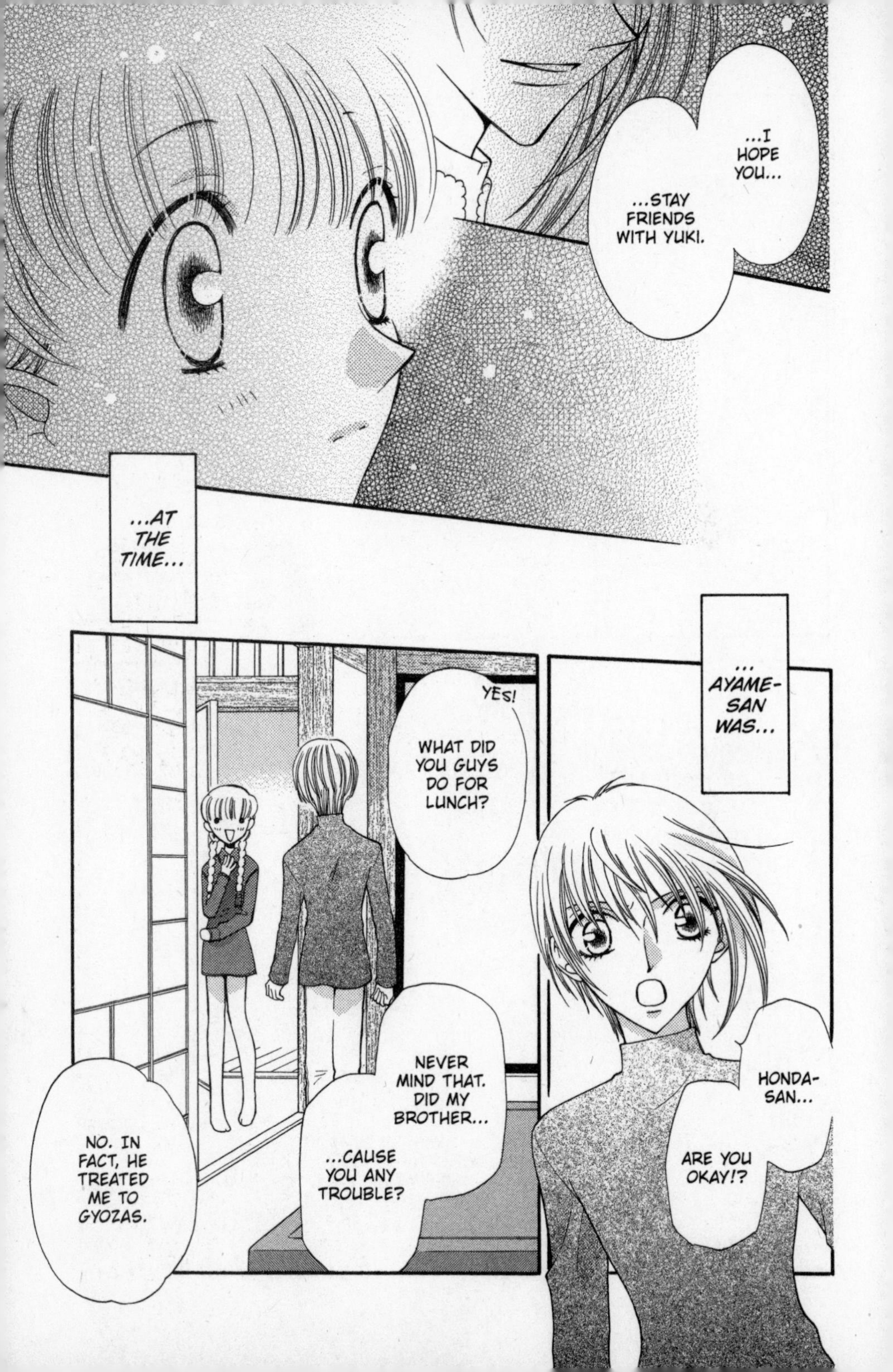
...I HOPE YOU...
...STAY FRIENDS WITH YUKI.
...AT THE TIME...
...AYAME-SAN WAS...
HONDA-SAN...
ARE YOU OKAY!?
YES!
WHAT DID YOU GUYS DO FOR LUNCH?
NEVER MIND THAT. DID MY BROTHER...
...CAUSE YOU ANY TROUBLE?
NO. IN FACT, HE TREATED ME TO GYOZAS.

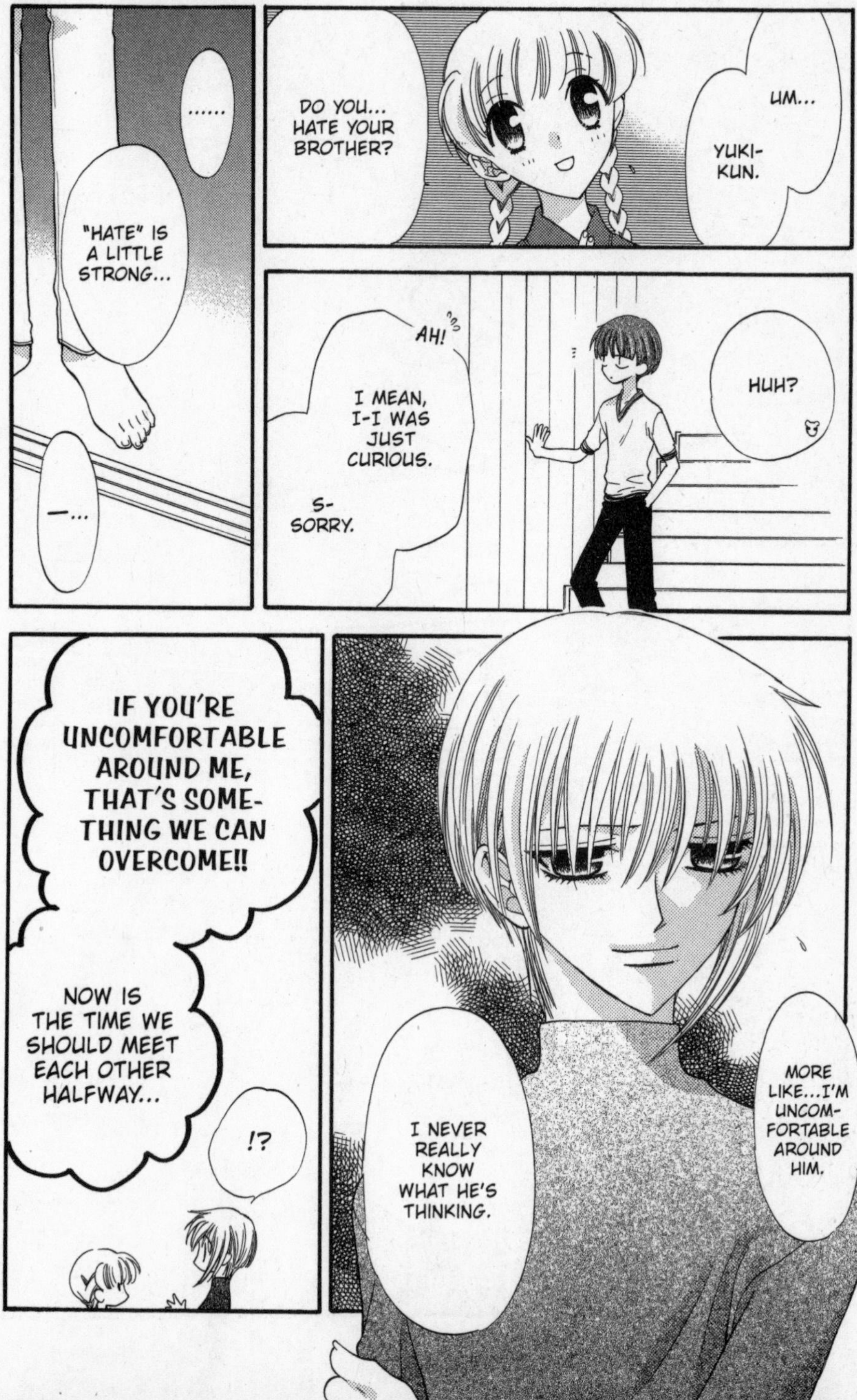
UM... YUKI-KUN.
DO YOU... HATE YOUR BROTHER?
HUH?
AH! I MEAN, I-I WAS JUST CURIOUS.
S-SORRY.
......
"HATE" IS A LITTLE STRONG...
—...
MORE LIKE...I'M UNCOMFORTABLE AROUND HIM.
I NEVER REALLY KNOW WHAT HE'S THINKING.
IF YOU'RE UNCOMFORTABLE AROUND ME, THAT'S SOMETHING WE CAN OVERCOME!!
NOW IS THE TIME WE SHOULD MEET EACH OTHER HALFWAY...
!?

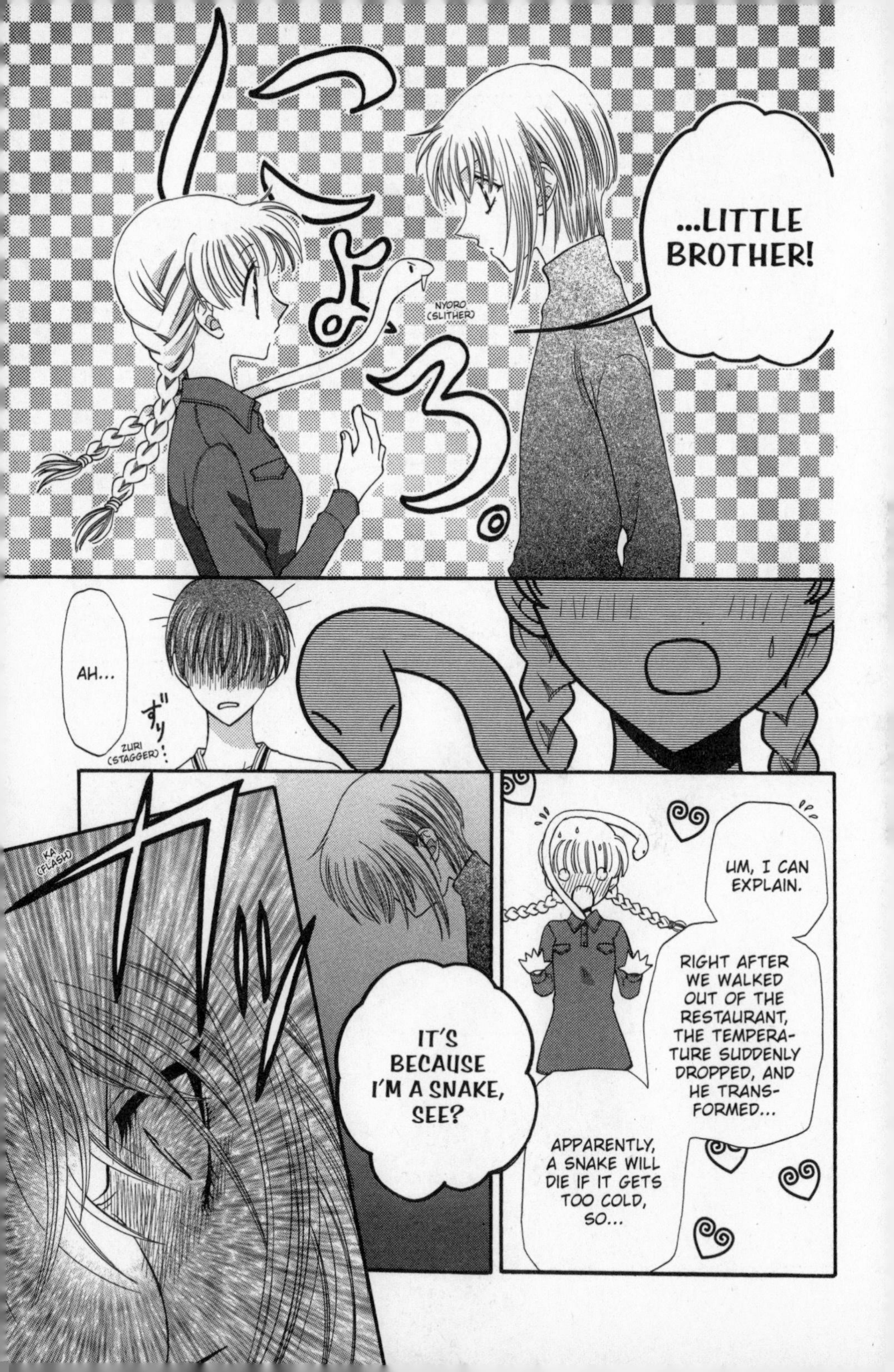
...LITTLE BROTHER!
NYORO (SLITHER)
AH...
ZURI (STAGGER)
UM, I CAN EXPLAIN.
RIGHT AFTER WE WALKED OUT OF THE RESTAURANT, THE TEMPERA-TURE SUDDENLY DROPPED, AND HE TRANS-FORMED...
APPARENTLY, A SNAKE WILL DIE IF IT GETS TOO COLD, SO...
KA (FLASH)
IT'S BECAUSE I'M A SNAKE, SEE?

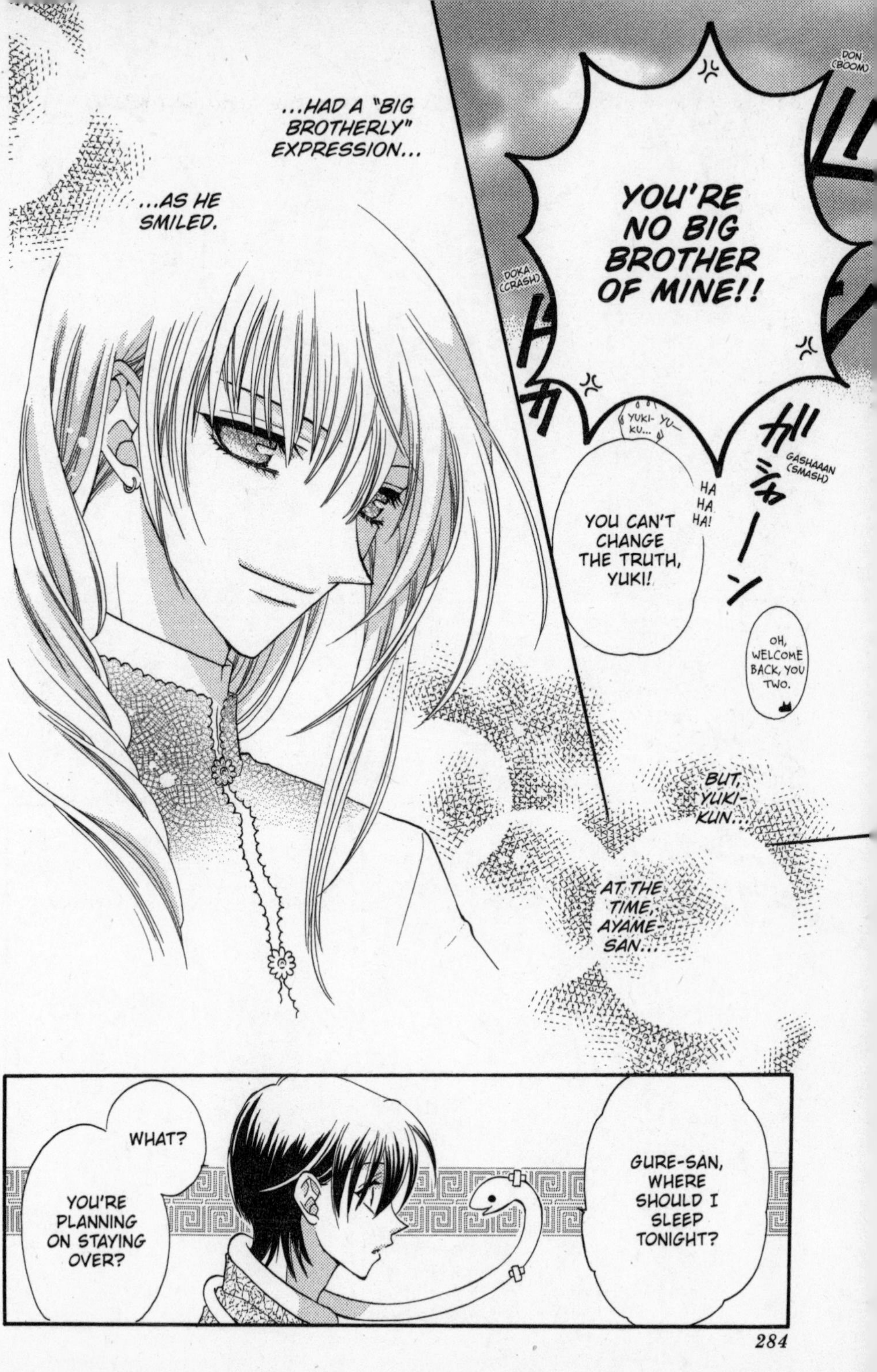
DON (BOOM)
YOU'RE NO BIG BROTHER OF MINE!!
DOKA (CRASH)
YUKI-KU... YU-
GASHAAAN (SMASH)
HA HA HA!
YOU CAN'T CHANGE THE TRUTH, YUKI!
OH, WELCOME BACK, YOU TWO.
BUT, YUKI-KUN...
AT THE TIME, AYAME-SAN...
...HAD A "BIG BROTHERLY" EXPRESSION...
...AS HE SMILED.
GURE-SAN, WHERE SHOULD I SLEEP TONIGHT?
WHAT?
YOU'RE PLANNING ON STAYING OVER?

Chapter 22

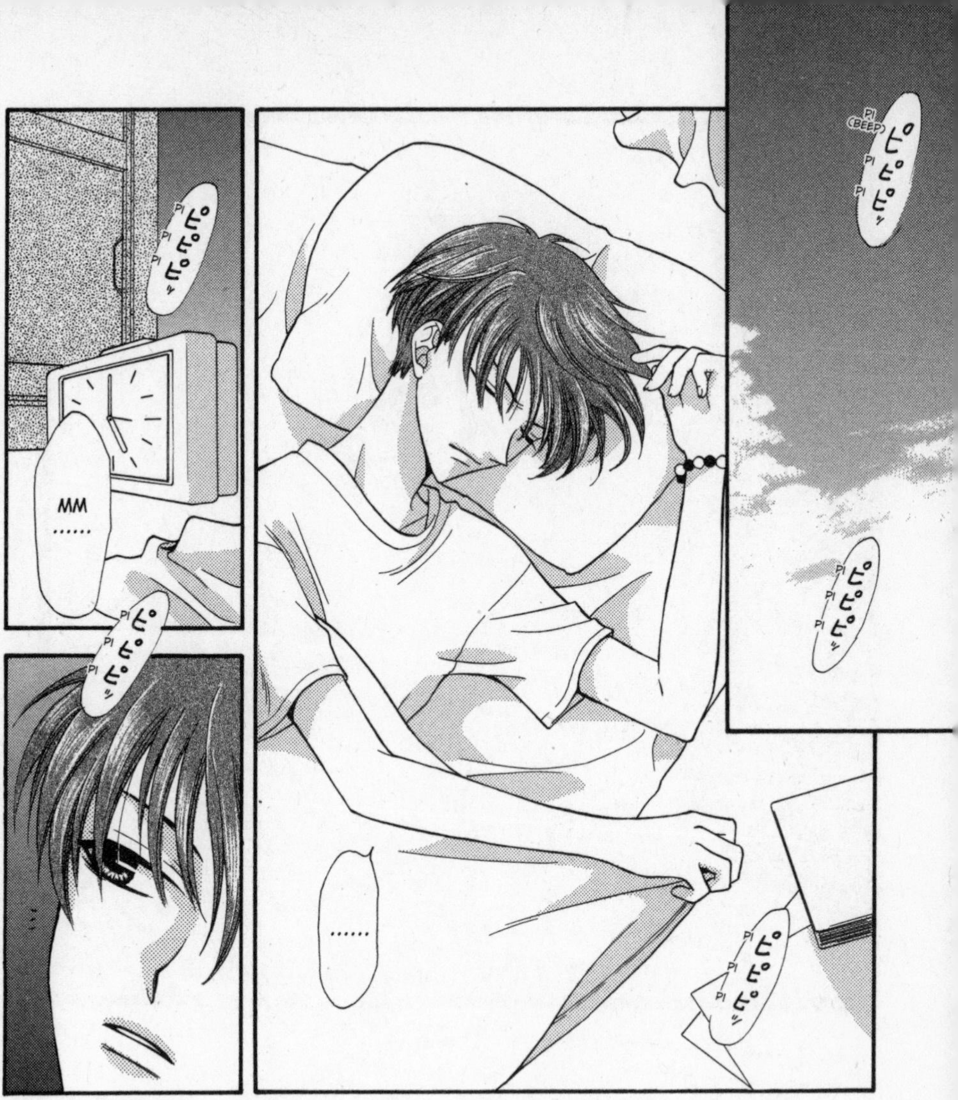
PI (BEEP) PI PI ピピピッ
PI PI PI ピピピッ
......
PI PI PI ピピピッ
PI PI PI ピピピッ
MM ......
PI PI PI ピピピッ

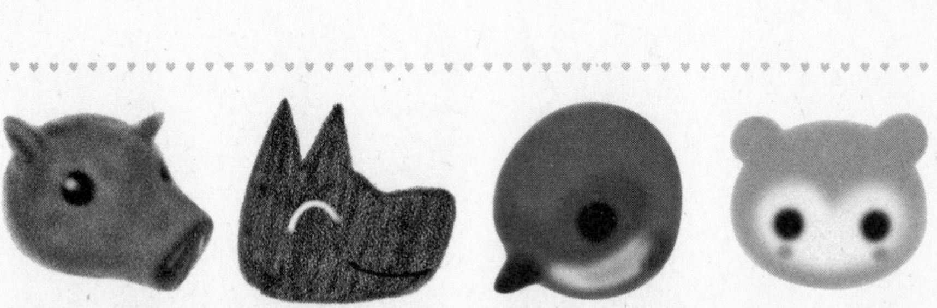

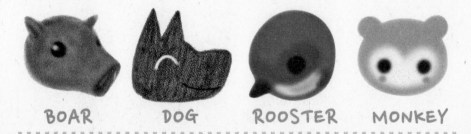

BOAR DOG ROOSTER MONKEY

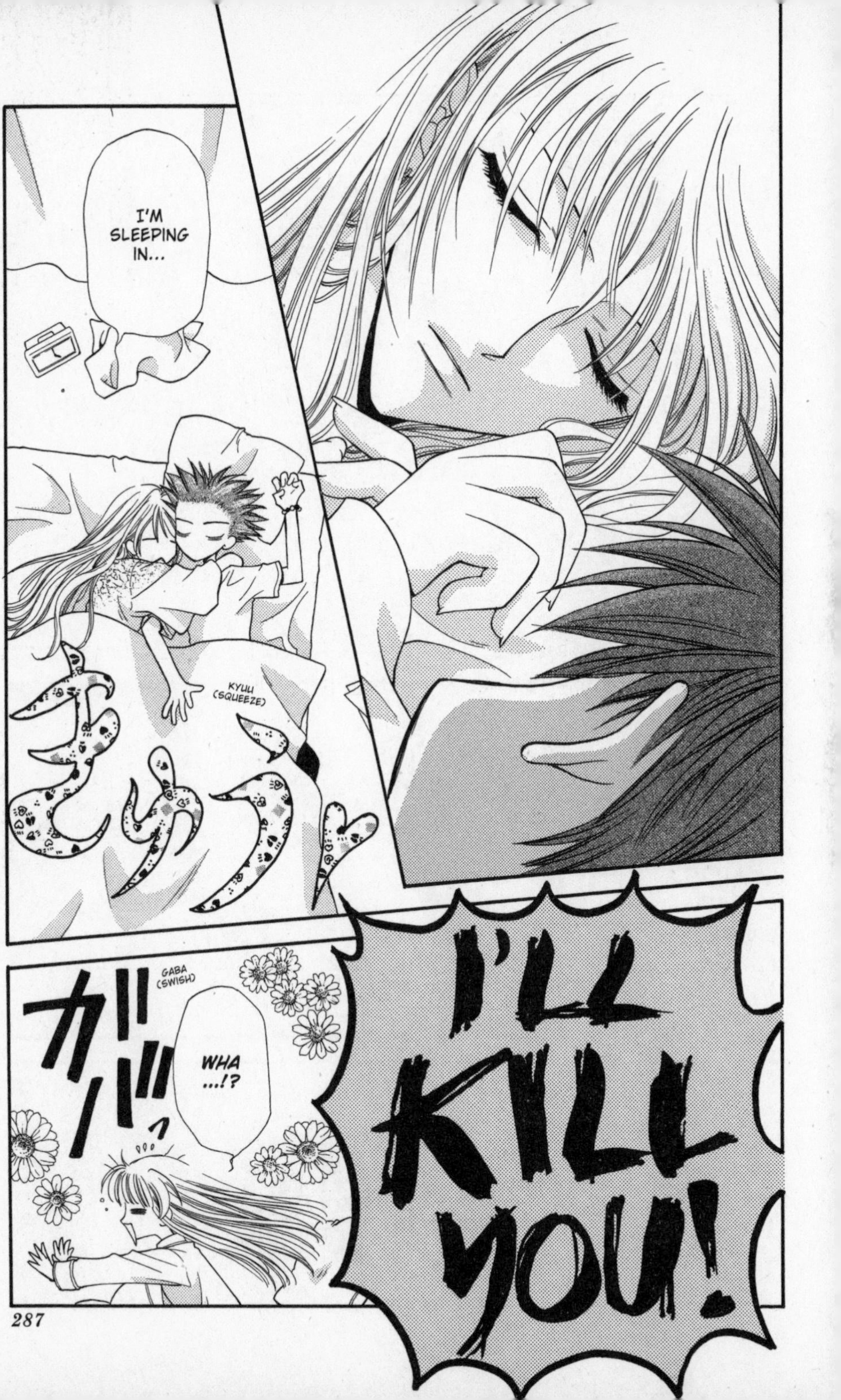
I'M SLEEPING IN...
KYUU (SQUEEZE)
I'LL KILL YOU!
GABA (SWISH)
WHA ...!?

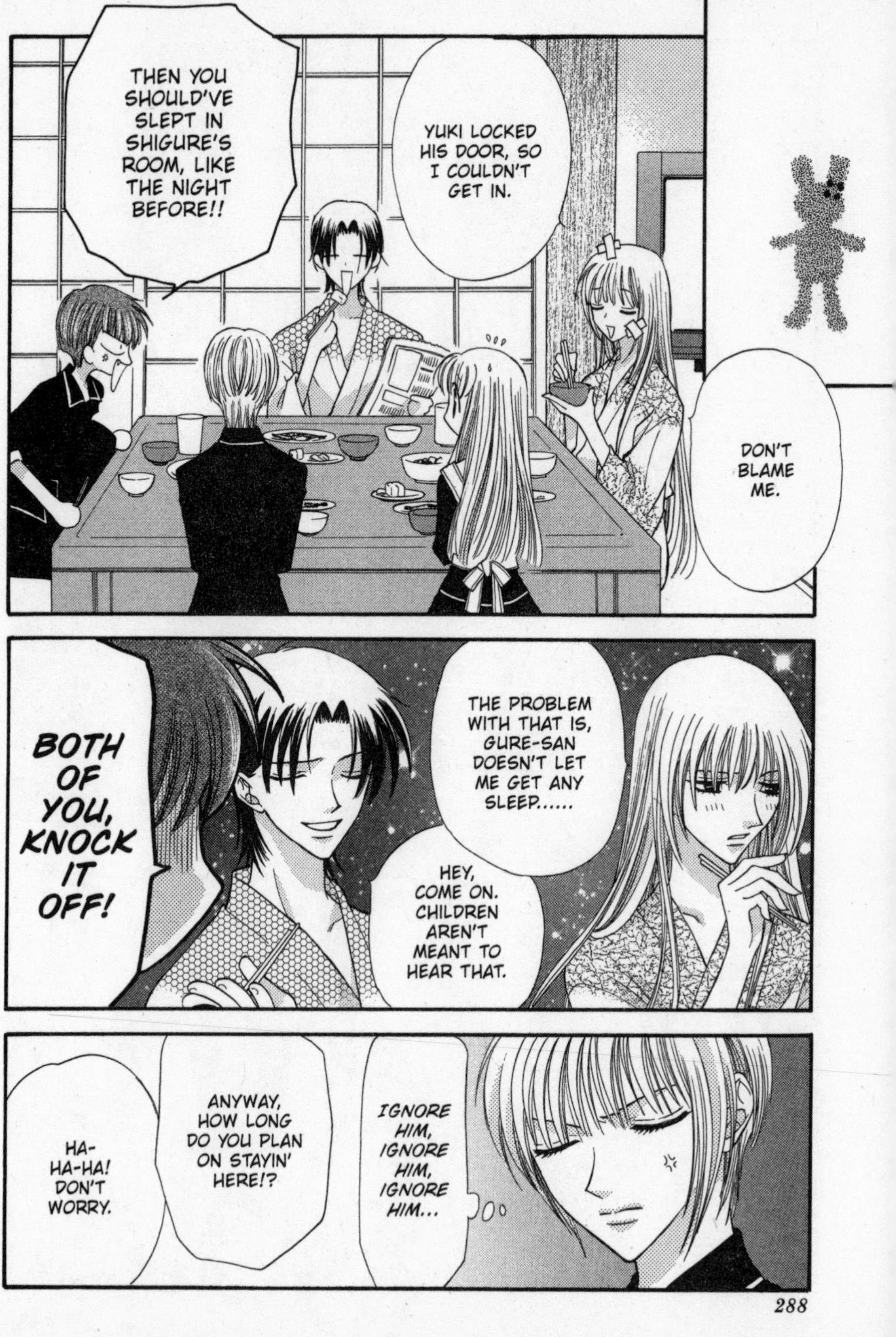
YUKI LOCKED HIS DOOR, SO I COULDN'T GET IN.
THEN YOU SHOULD'VE SLEPT IN SHIGURE'S ROOM, LIKE THE NIGHT BEFORE!!
DON'T BLAME ME.
THE PROBLEM WITH THAT IS, GURE-SAN DOESN'T LET ME GET ANY SLEEP......
HEY, COME ON. CHILDREN AREN'T MEANT TO HEAR THAT.
BOTH OF YOU, KNOCK IT OFF!
IGNORE HIM, IGNORE HIM, IGNORE HIM...
ANYWAY, HOW LONG DO YOU PLAN ON STAYIN' HERE!?
HA-HA-HA! DON'T WORRY.

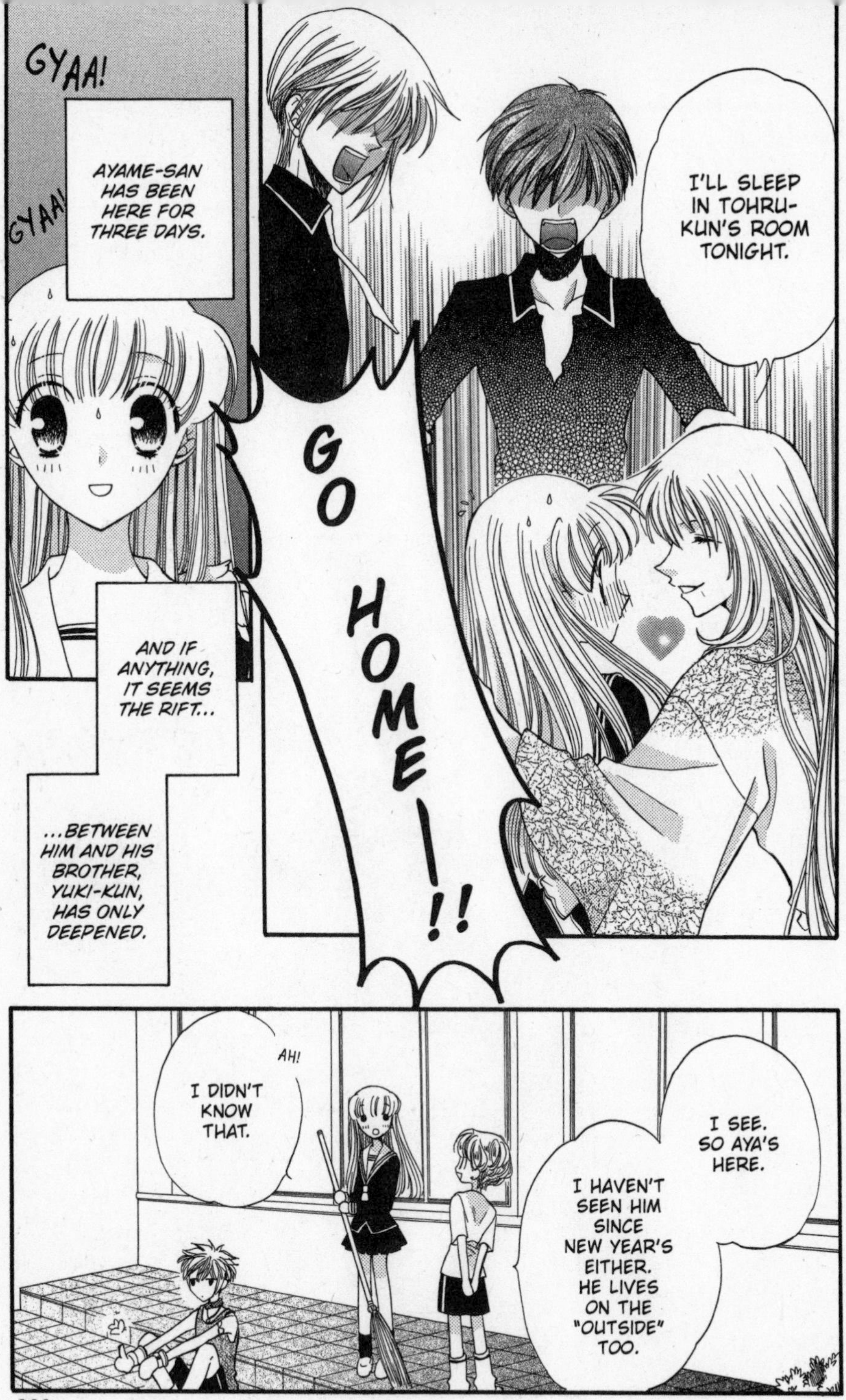
I'LL SLEEP IN TOHRU-KUN'S ROOM TONIGHT.
GO HOME—!!
GYAA!
GYAA!
AYAME-SAN HAS BEEN HERE FOR THREE DAYS.
AND IF ANYTHING, IT SEEMS THE RIFT...
...BETWEEN HIM AND HIS BROTHER, YUKI-KUN, HAS ONLY DEEPENED.
I SEE. SO AYA'S HERE.
I HAVEN'T SEEN HIM SINCE NEW YEAR'S EITHER. HE LIVES ON THE "OUTSIDE" TOO.
AH!
I DIDN'T KNOW THAT.

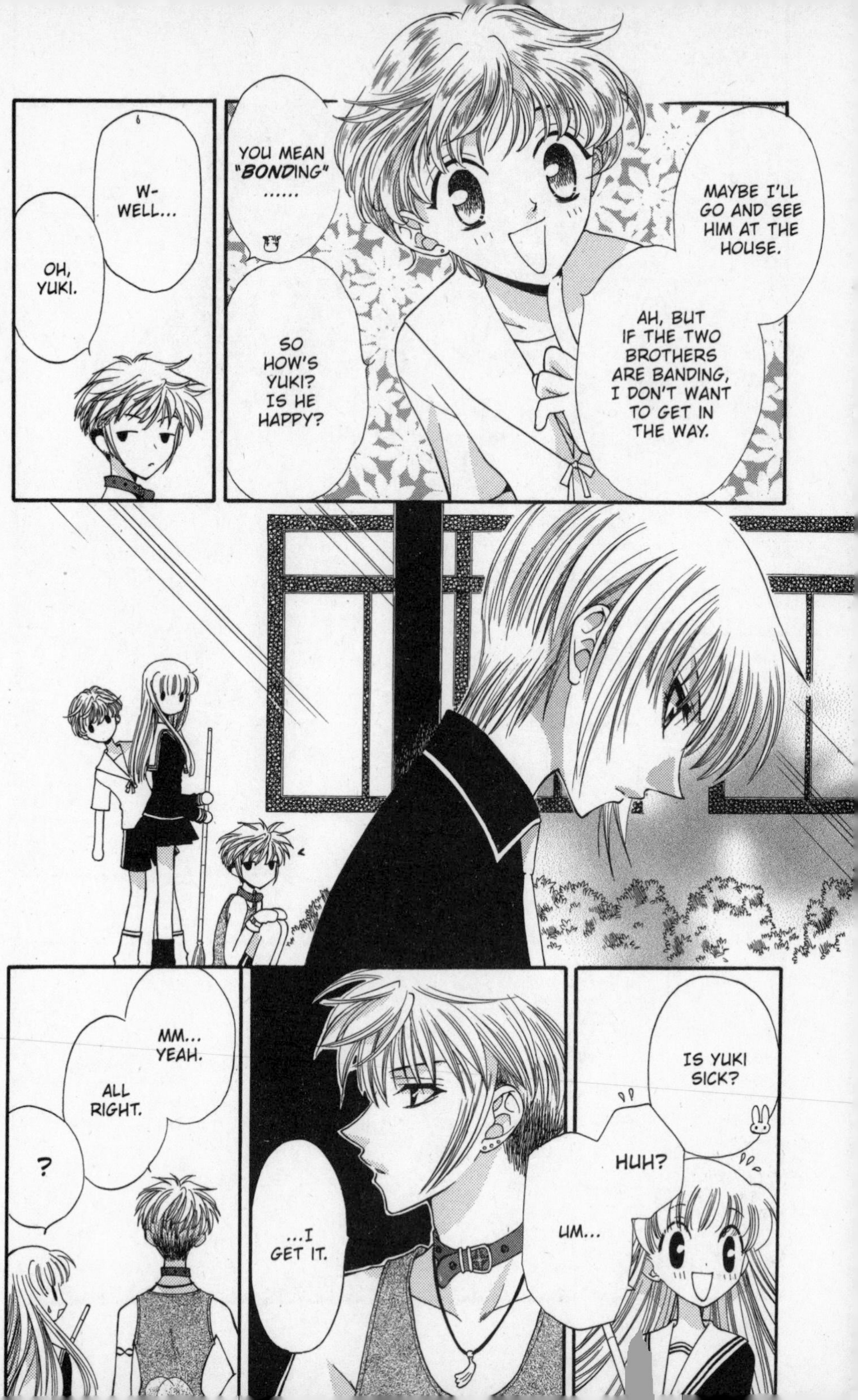

MAYBE I'LL GO AND SEE HIM AT THE HOUSE.
AH, BUT IF THE TWO BROTHERS ARE BANDING, I DON'T WANT TO GET IN THE WAY.
YOU MEAN "BONDING" ......
SO HOW'S YUKI? IS HE HAPPY?
W-WELL...
OH, YUKI.
IS YUKI SICK?
HUH?
UM...
...I GET IT.
MM... YEAH.
ALL RIGHT.
?

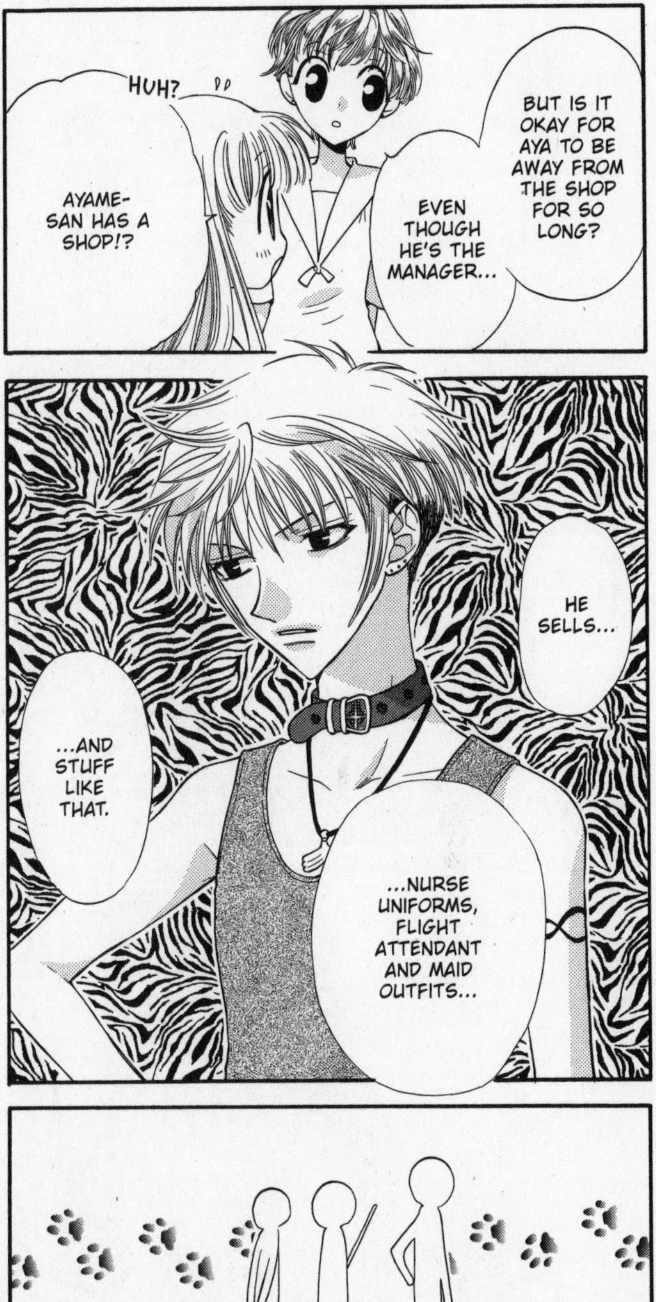
BUT IS IT OKAY FOR AYA TO BE AWAY FROM THE SHOP FOR SO LONG?
EVEN THOUGH HE'S THE MANAGER...
HUH?
AYAME-SAN HAS A SHOP!?
HE SELLS...
...NURSE UNIFORMS, FLIGHT ATTENDANT AND MAID OUTFITS...
...AND STUFF LIKE THAT.
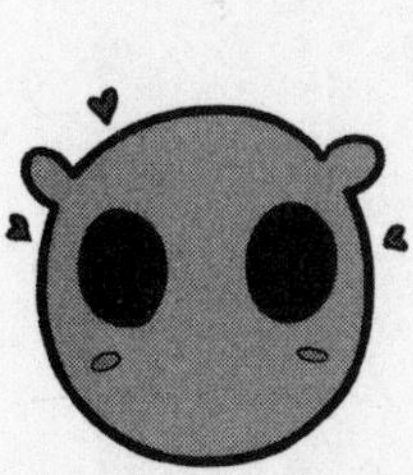

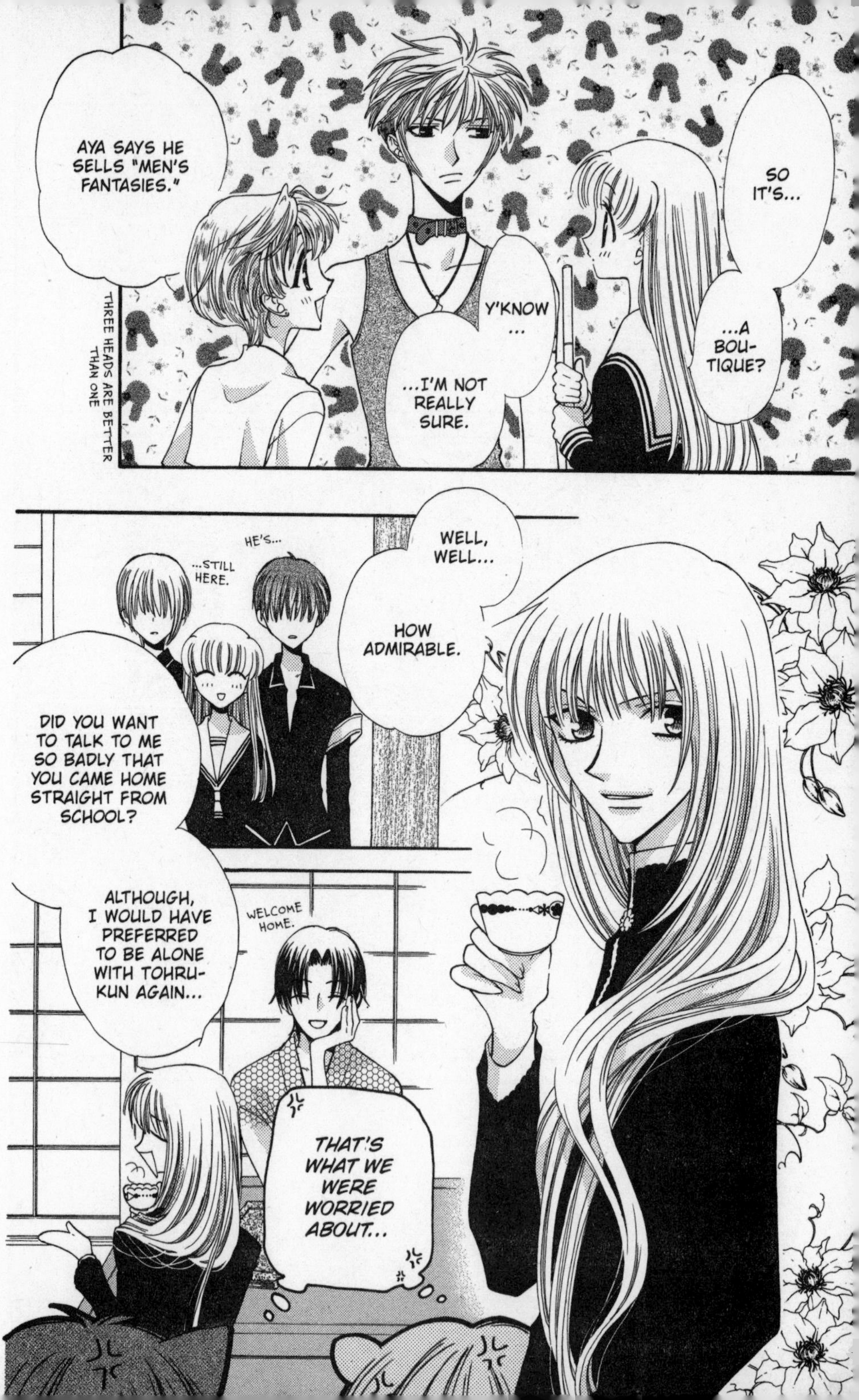
SO IT'S...
...A BOUTIQUE?
Y'KNOW...
...I'M NOT REALLY SURE.
AYA SAYS HE SELLS "MEN'S FANTASIES."
THREE HEADS ARE BETTER THAN ONE
WELL, WELL...
HOW ADMIRABLE.
HE'S...
...STILL HERE.
DID YOU WANT TO TALK TO ME SO BADLY THAT YOU CAME HOME STRAIGHT FROM SCHOOL?
ALTHOUGH, I WOULD HAVE PREFERRED TO BE ALONE WITH TOHRU-KUN AGAIN...
WELCOME HOME.
THAT'S WHAT WE WERE WORRIED ABOUT...

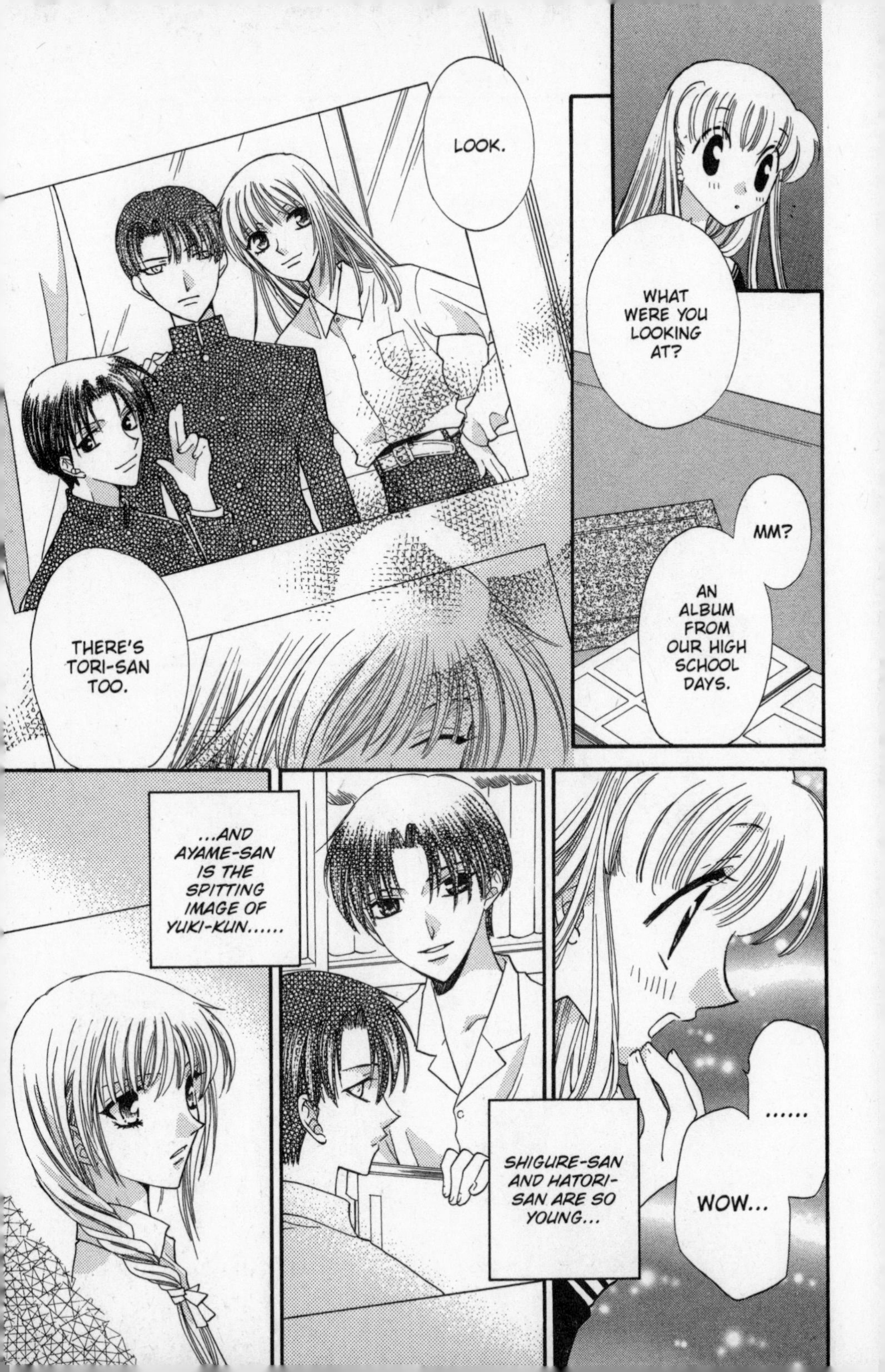
WHAT WERE YOU LOOKING AT?
MM?
AN ALBUM FROM OUR HIGH SCHOOL DAYS.
LOOK.
THERE'S TORI-SAN TOO.
......
WOW...
SHIGURE-SAN AND HATORI-SAN ARE SO YOUNG...
...AND AYAME-SAN IS THE SPITTING IMAGE OF YUKI-KUN......

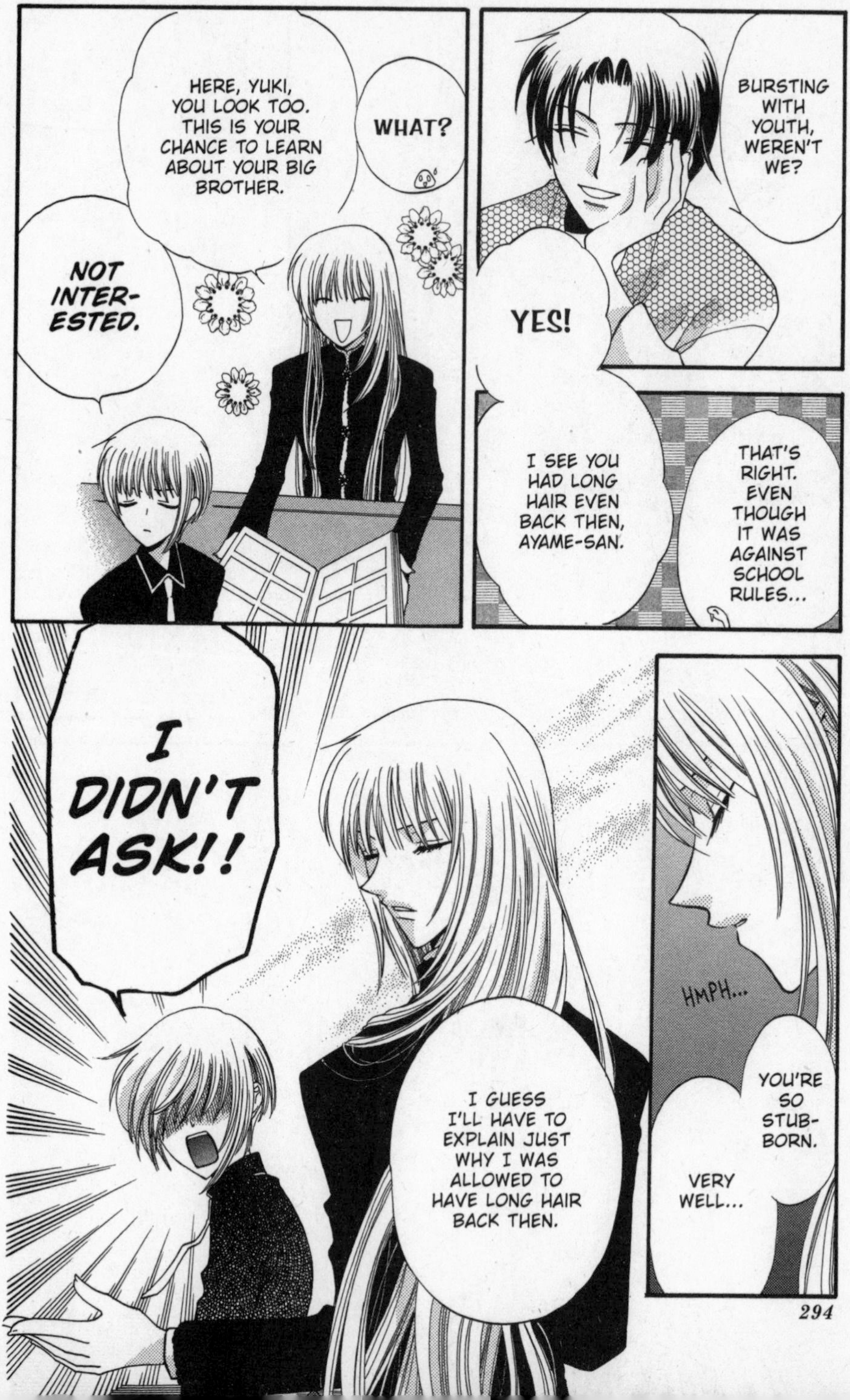
BURSTING WITH YOUTH, WEREN'T WE?
YES!
I SEE YOU HAD LONG HAIR EVEN BACK THEN, AYAME-SAN.
THAT'S RIGHT. EVEN THOUGH IT WAS AGAINST SCHOOL RULES...
WHAT?
HERE, YUKI, YOU LOOK TOO. THIS IS YOUR CHANCE TO LEARN ABOUT YOUR BIG BROTHER.
NOT INTER-ESTED.
HMPH...
YOU'RE SO STUB-BORN.
VERY WELL...
I GUESS I'LL HAVE TO EXPLAIN JUST WHY I WAS ALLOWED TO HAVE LONG HAIR BACK THEN.
I DIDN'T ASK!!

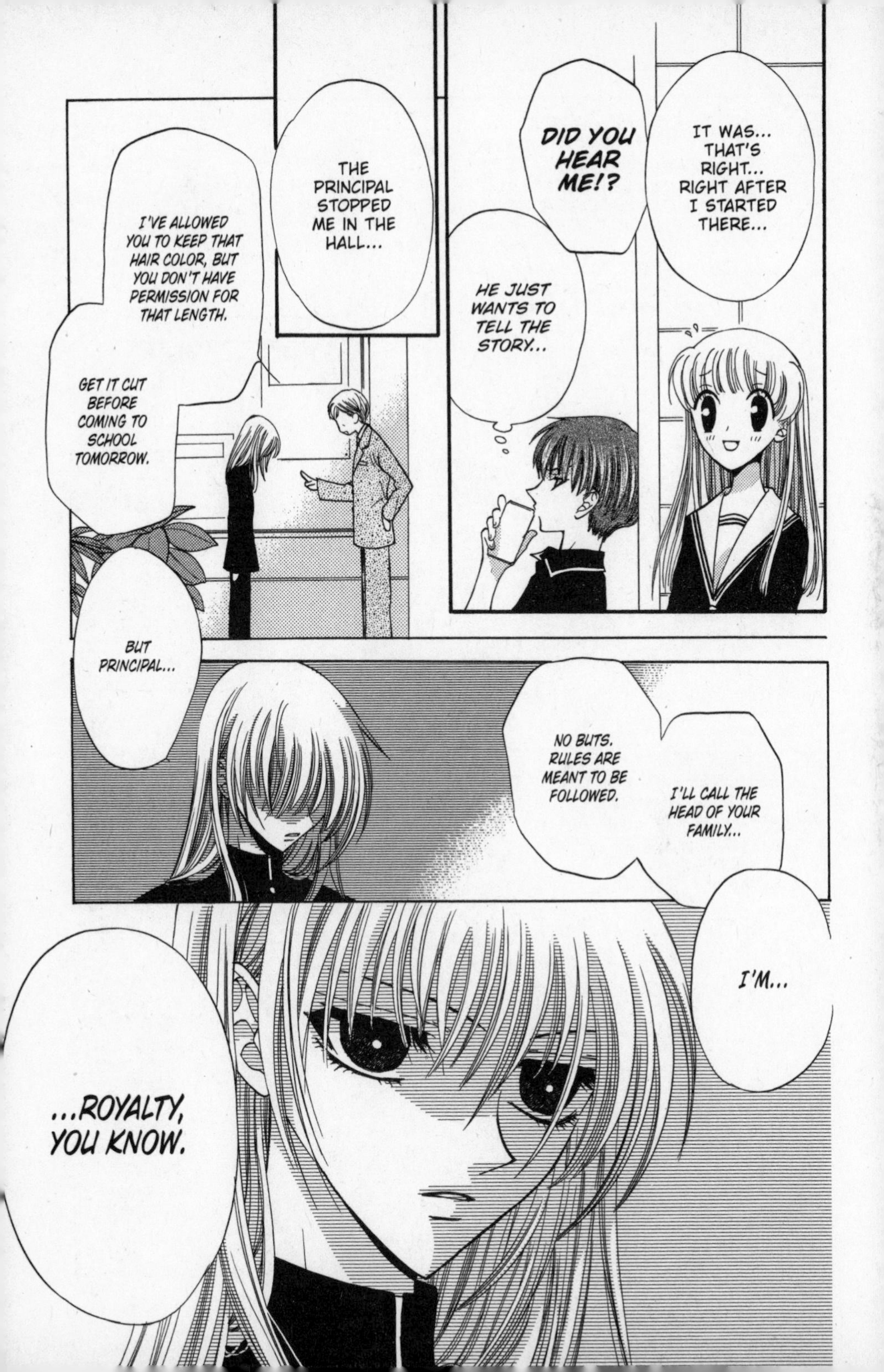

IT WAS... THAT'S RIGHT... RIGHT AFTER I STARTED THERE...
DID YOU HEAR ME!?
HE JUST WANTS TO TELL THE STORY...
THE PRINCIPAL STOPPED ME IN THE HALL...
I'VE ALLOWED YOU TO KEEP THAT HAIR COLOR, BUT YOU DON'T HAVE PERMISSION FOR THAT LENGTH.
GET IT CUT BEFORE COMING TO SCHOOL TOMORROW.
BUT PRINCIPAL...
NO BUTS. RULES ARE MEANT TO BE FOLLOWED.
I'LL CALL THE HEAD OF YOUR FAMILY...
I'M...
...ROYALTY, YOU KNOW.

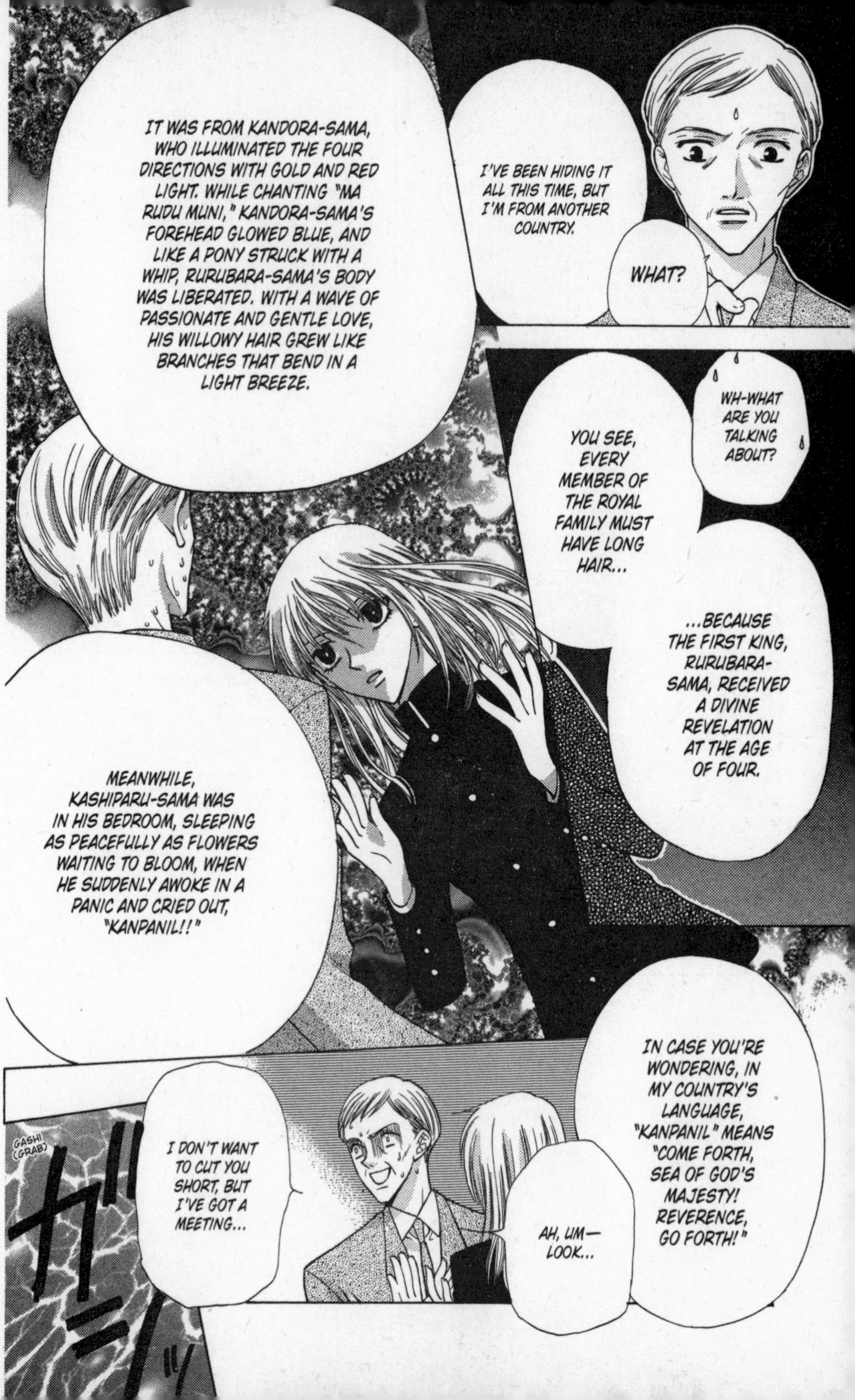

I'VE BEEN HIDING IT ALL THIS TIME, BUT I'M FROM ANOTHER COUNTRY.
WHAT?
WH-WHAT ARE YOU TALKING ABOUT?
YOU SEE, EVERY MEMBER OF THE ROYAL FAMILY MUST HAVE LONG HAIR...
...BECAUSE THE FIRST KING, RURUBARA-SAMA, RECEIVED A DIVINE REVELATION AT THE AGE OF FOUR.
IT WAS FROM KANDORA-SAMA, WHO ILLUMINATED THE FOUR DIRECTIONS WITH GOLD AND RED LIGHT. WHILE CHANTING "MA RUDU MUNI," KANDORA-SAMA'S FOREHEAD GLOWED BLUE, AND LIKE A PONY STRUCK WITH A WHIP, RURUBARA-SAMA'S BODY WAS LIBERATED. WITH A WAVE OF PASSIONATE AND GENTLE LOVE, HIS WILLOWY HAIR GREW LIKE BRANCHES THAT BEND IN A LIGHT BREEZE.
MEANWHILE, KASHIPARU-SAMA WAS IN HIS BEDROOM, SLEEPING AS PEACEFULLY AS FLOWERS WAITING TO BLOOM, WHEN HE SUDDENLY AWOKE IN A PANIC AND CRIED OUT, "KANPANIL!!"
IN CASE YOU'RE WONDERING, IN MY COUNTRY'S LANGUAGE, "KANPANIL" MEANS "COME FORTH, SEA OF GOD'S MAJESTY! REVERENCE, GO FORTH!"
AH, UM— LOOK...
I DON'T WANT TO CUT YOU SHORT, BUT I'VE GOT A MEETING...
GASHI (GRAB)

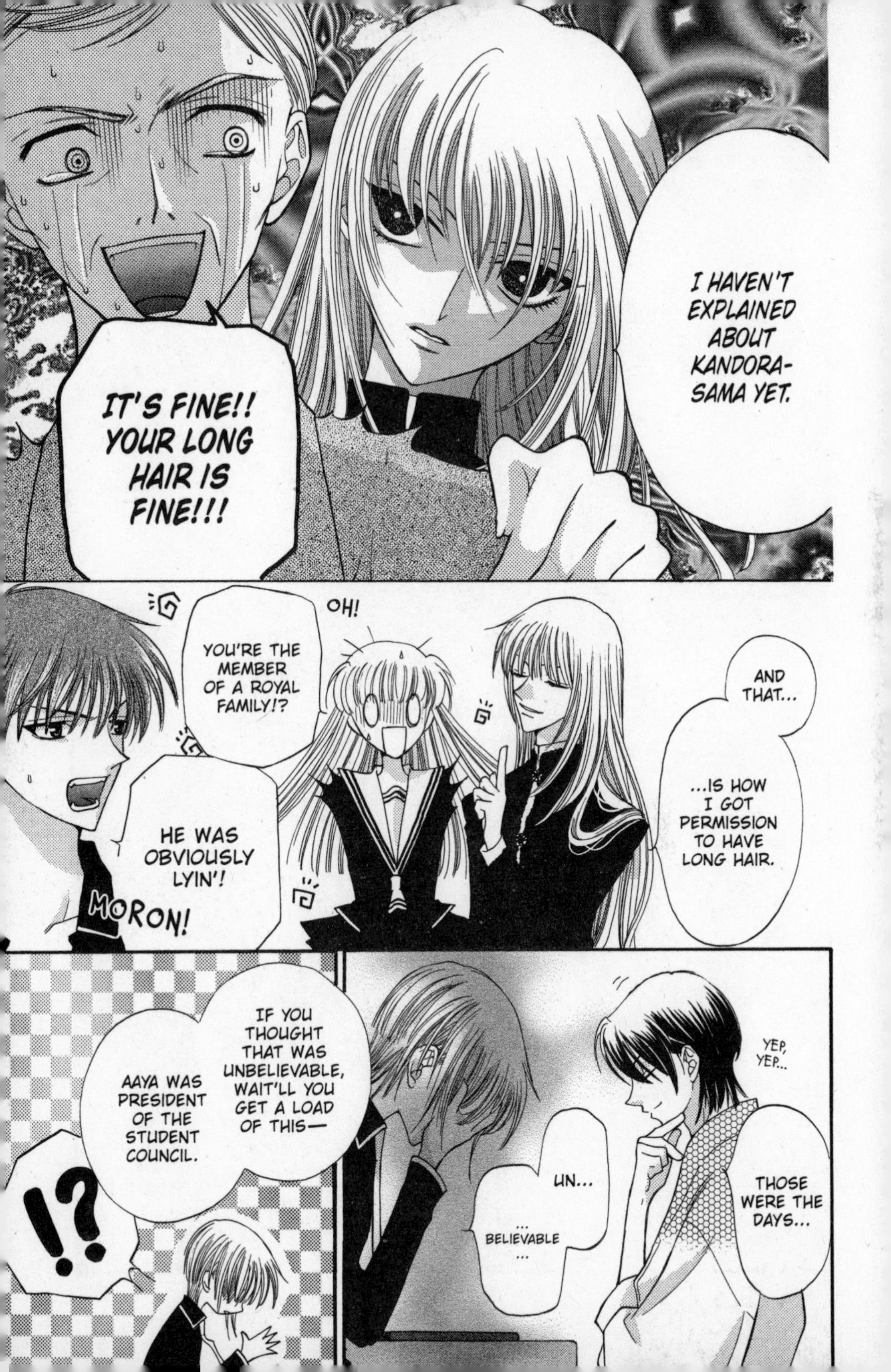
I HAVEN'T EXPLAINED ABOUT KANDORA-SAMA YET.
IT'S FINE!! YOUR LONG HAIR IS FINE!!!
AND THAT...
...IS HOW I GOT PERMISSION TO HAVE LONG HAIR.
OH!
YOU'RE THE MEMBER OF A ROYAL FAMILY!?
HE WAS OBVIOUSLY LYIN'!
MORON!
YEP, YEP...
THOSE WERE THE DAYS...
UN...
...BELIEVABLE...
IF YOU THOUGHT THAT WAS UNBELIEVABLE, WAIT'LL YOU GET A LOAD OF THIS—
AAYA WAS PRESIDENT OF THE STUDENT COUNCIL.
!?

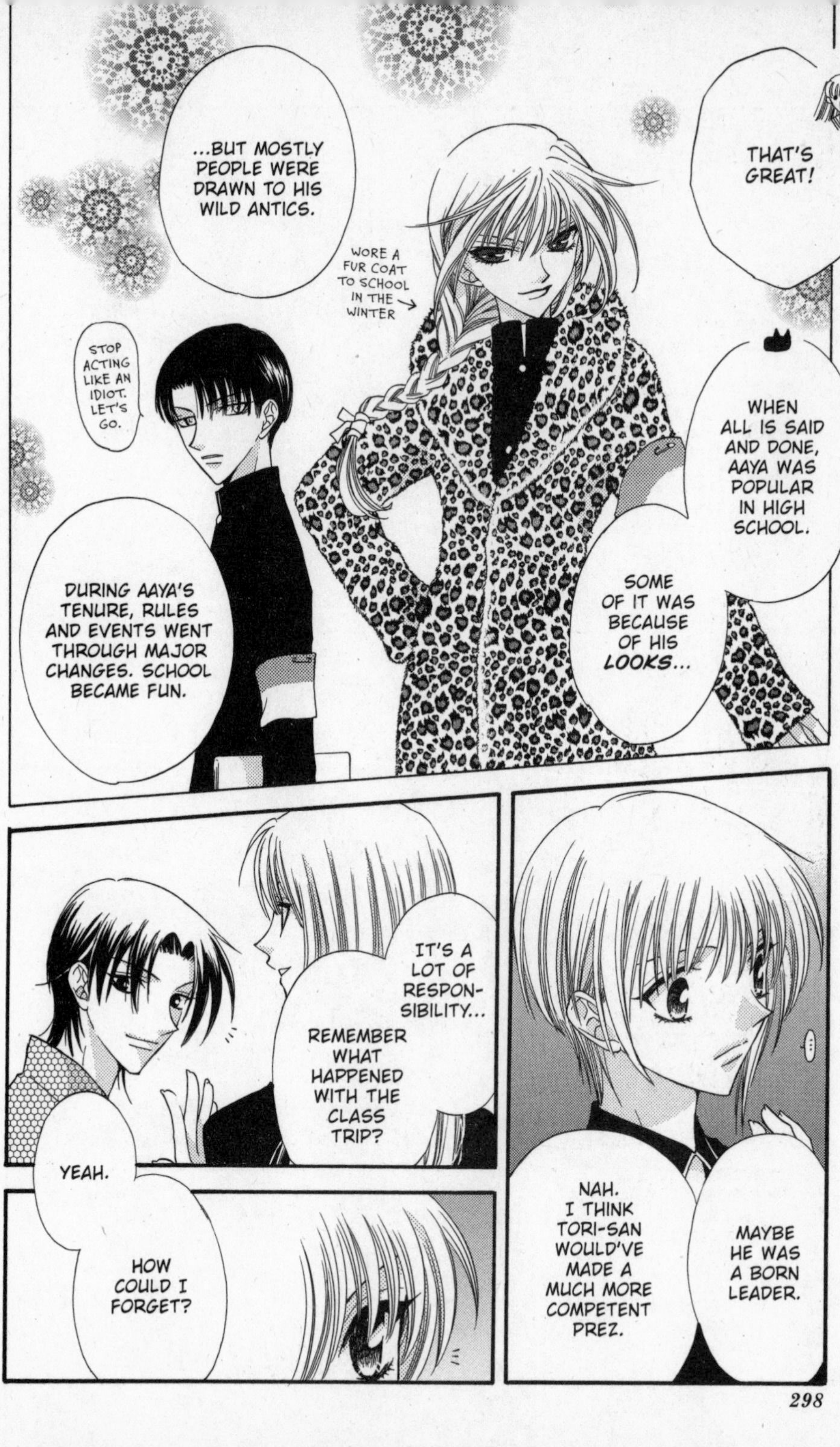
THAT'S GREAT!
WHEN ALL IS SAID AND DONE, AAYA WAS POPULAR IN HIGH SCHOOL.
SOME OF IT WAS BECAUSE OF HIS *LOOKS*...
...BUT MOSTLY PEOPLE WERE DRAWN TO HIS WILD ANTICS.
WORE A FUR COAT TO SCHOOL IN THE WINTER
STOP ACTING LIKE AN IDIOT. LET'S GO.
DURING AAYA'S TENURE, RULES AND EVENTS WENT THROUGH MAJOR CHANGES. SCHOOL BECAME FUN.
MAYBE HE WAS A BORN LEADER.
NAH. I THINK TORI-SAN WOULD'VE MADE A MUCH MORE COMPETENT PREZ.
...
IT'S A LOT OF RESPONSIBILITY...
REMEMBER WHAT HAPPENED WITH THE CLASS TRIP?
YEAH.
HOW COULD I FORGET?

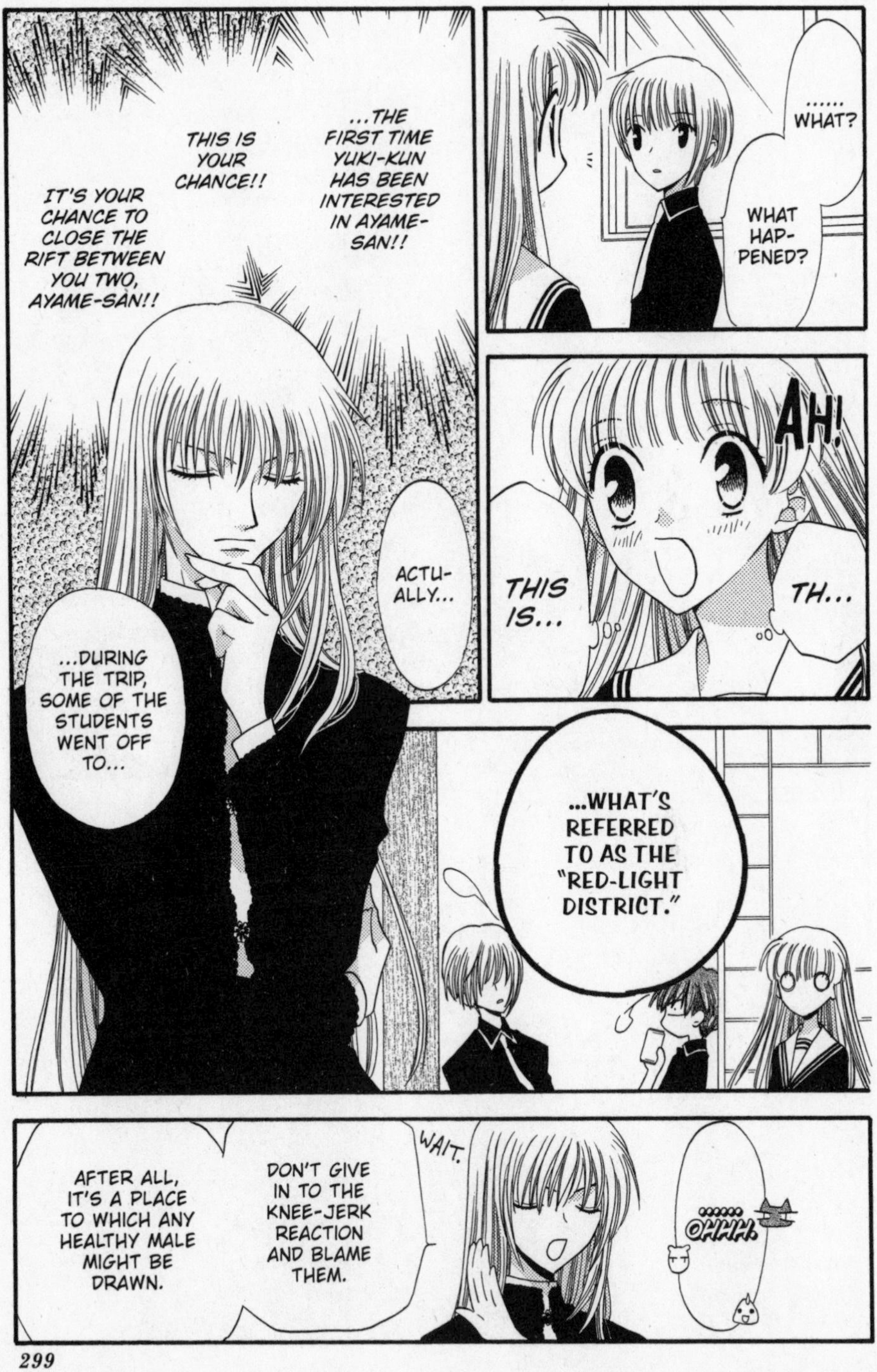

......WHAT?
WHAT HAP-PENED?
AH!
TH...
THIS IS...
...THE FIRST TIME YUKI-KUN HAS BEEN INTERESTED IN AYAME-SAN!!
THIS IS YOUR CHANCE!!
IT'S YOUR CHANCE TO CLOSE THE RIFT BETWEEN YOU TWO, AYAME-SAN!!
ACTU-ALLY...
...DURING THE TRIP, SOME OF THE STUDENTS WENT OFF TO...
...WHAT'S REFERRED TO AS THE "RED-LIGHT DISTRICT."
......OHHH.
WAIT.
DON'T GIVE IN TO THE KNEE-JERK REACTION AND BLAME THEM.
AFTER ALL, IT'S A PLACE TO WHICH ANY HEALTHY MALE MIGHT BE DRAWN.

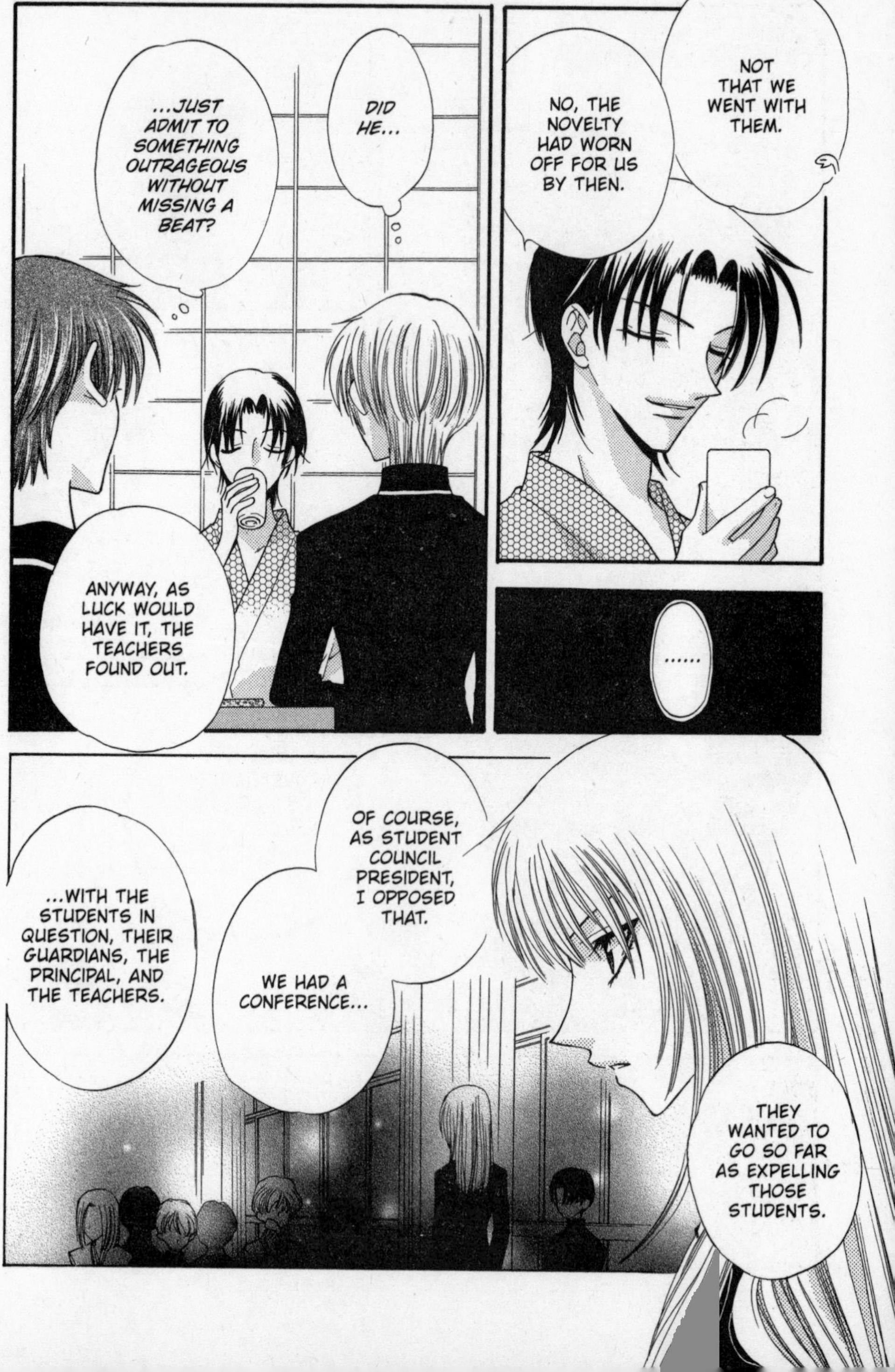
NOT THAT WE WENT WITH THEM.
NO, THE NOVELTY HAD WORN OFF FOR US BY THEN.
......
DID HE...
...JUST ADMIT TO SOMETHING OUTRAGEOUS WITHOUT MISSING A BEAT?
ANYWAY, AS LUCK WOULD HAVE IT, THE TEACHERS FOUND OUT.
THEY WANTED TO GO SO FAR AS EXPELLING THOSE STUDENTS.
OF COURSE, AS STUDENT COUNCIL PRESIDENT, I OPPOSED THAT.
WE HAD A CONFERENCE...
...WITH THE STUDENTS IN QUESTION, THEIR GUARDIANS, THE PRINCIPAL, AND THE TEACHERS.

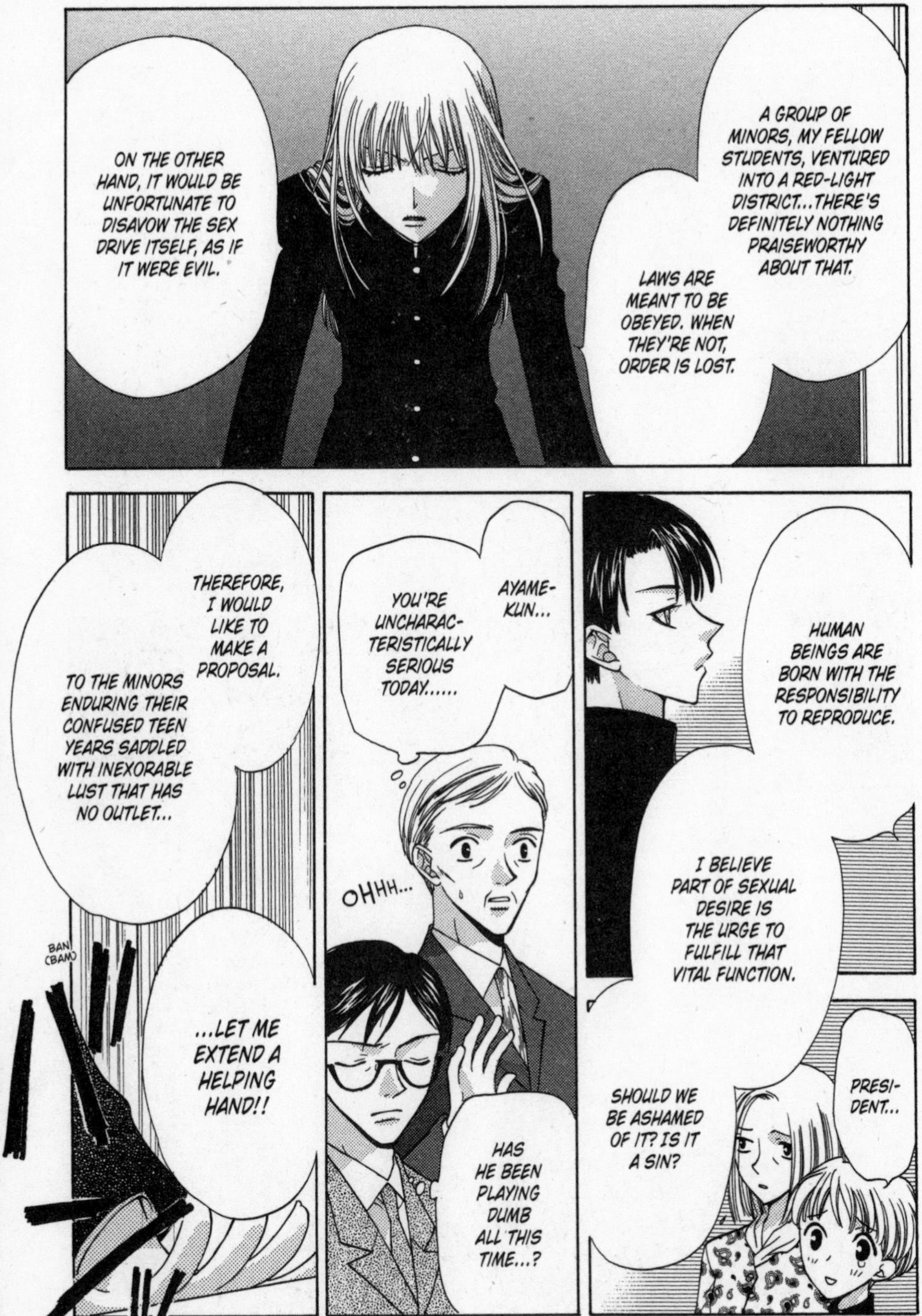
A GROUP OF MINORS, MY FELLOW STUDENTS, VENTURED INTO A RED-LIGHT DISTRICT...THERE'S DEFINITELY NOTHING PRAISEWORTHY ABOUT THAT.
LAWS ARE MEANT TO BE OBEYED. WHEN THEY'RE NOT, ORDER IS LOST.
ON THE OTHER HAND, IT WOULD BE UNFORTUNATE TO DISAVOW THE SEX DRIVE ITSELF, AS IF IT WERE EVIL.
HUMAN BEINGS ARE BORN WITH THE RESPONSIBILITY TO REPRODUCE.
I BELIEVE PART OF SEXUAL DESIRE IS THE URGE TO FULFILL THAT VITAL FUNCTION.
SHOULD WE BE ASHAMED OF IT? IS IT A SIN?
PRESI-DENT...
AYAME-KUN...
YOU'RE UNCHARAC-TERISTICALLY SERIOUS TODAY......
OHHH...
HAS HE BEEN PLAYING DUMB ALL THIS TIME...?
THEREFORE, I WOULD LIKE TO MAKE A PROPOSAL.
TO THE MINORS ENDURING THEIR CONFUSED TEEN YEARS SADDLED WITH INEXORABLE LUST THAT HAS NO OUTLET...
BAN (BAM)
...LET ME EXTEND A HELPING HAND!!

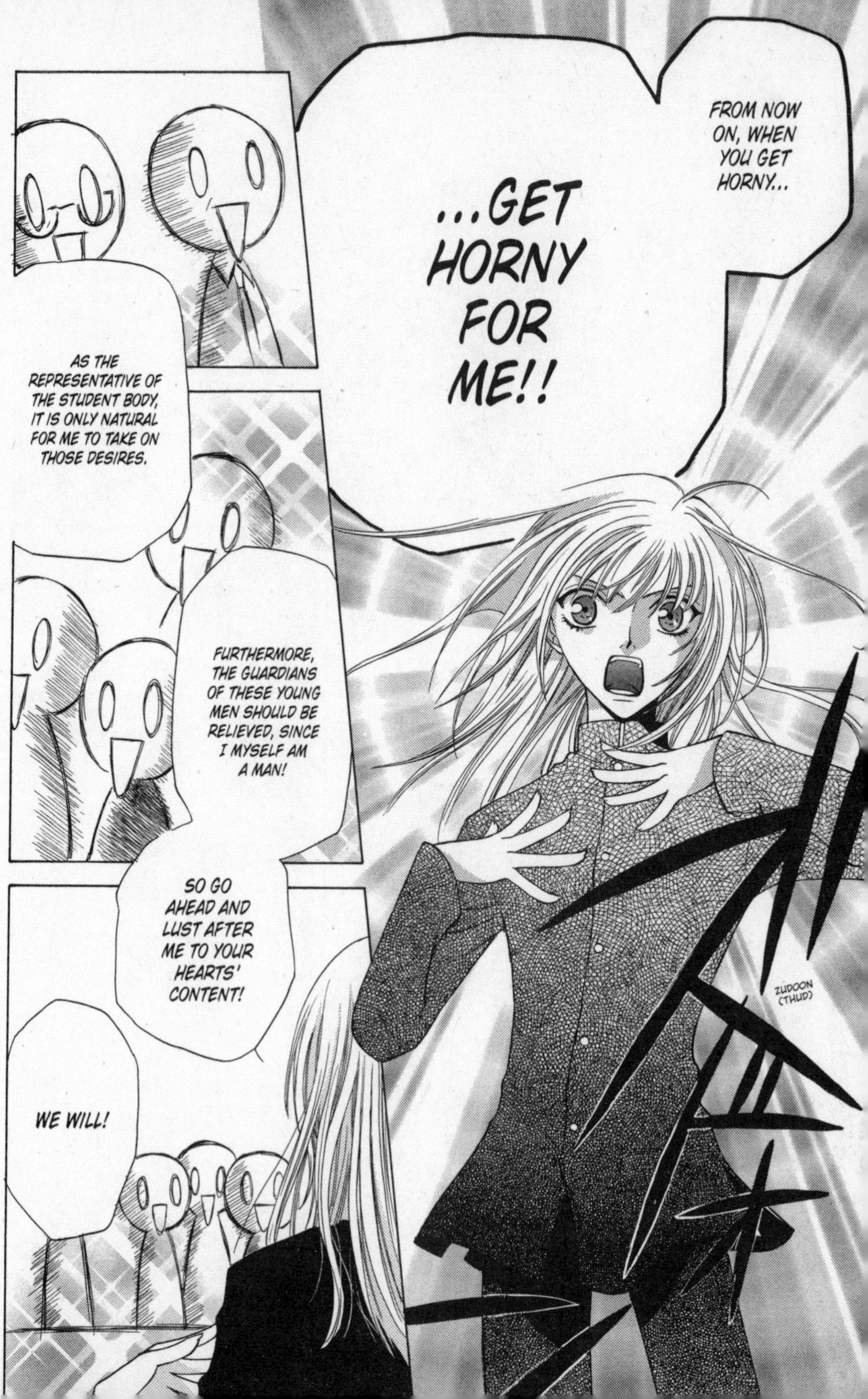
FROM NOW ON, WHEN YOU GET HORNY...
...GET HORNY FOR ME!!
ZUDOON (THUD)
AS THE REPRESENTATIVE OF THE STUDENT BODY, IT IS ONLY NATURAL FOR ME TO TAKE ON THOSE DESIRES.
FURTHERMORE, THE GUARDIANS OF THESE YOUNG MEN SHOULD BE RELIEVED, SINCE I MYSELF AM A MAN!
SO GO AHEAD AND LUST AFTER ME TO YOUR HEARTS' CONTENT!
WE WILL!

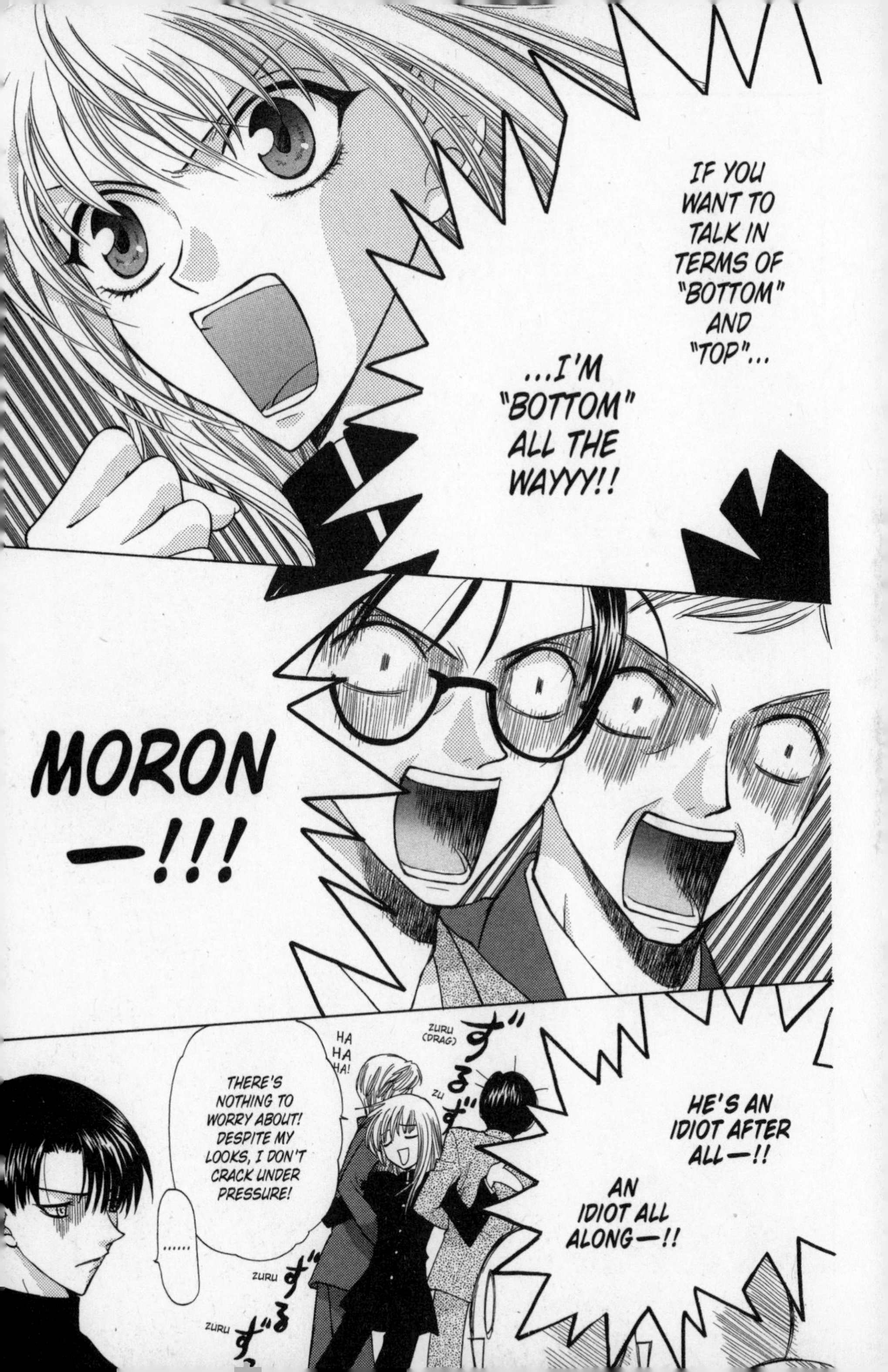
IF YOU WANT TO TALK IN TERMS OF "BOTTOM" AND "TOP"...
...I'M "BOTTOM" ALL THE WAYYY!!
MORON—!!!
HE'S AN IDIOT AFTER ALL—!!
AN IDIOT ALL ALONG—!!
ZURU (DRAG)
ずるずる
ZU
HA HA HA!
THERE'S NOTHING TO WORRY ABOUT! DESPITE MY LOOKS, I DON'T CRACK UNDER PRESSURE!
......
ZURU
ずる
ZURU

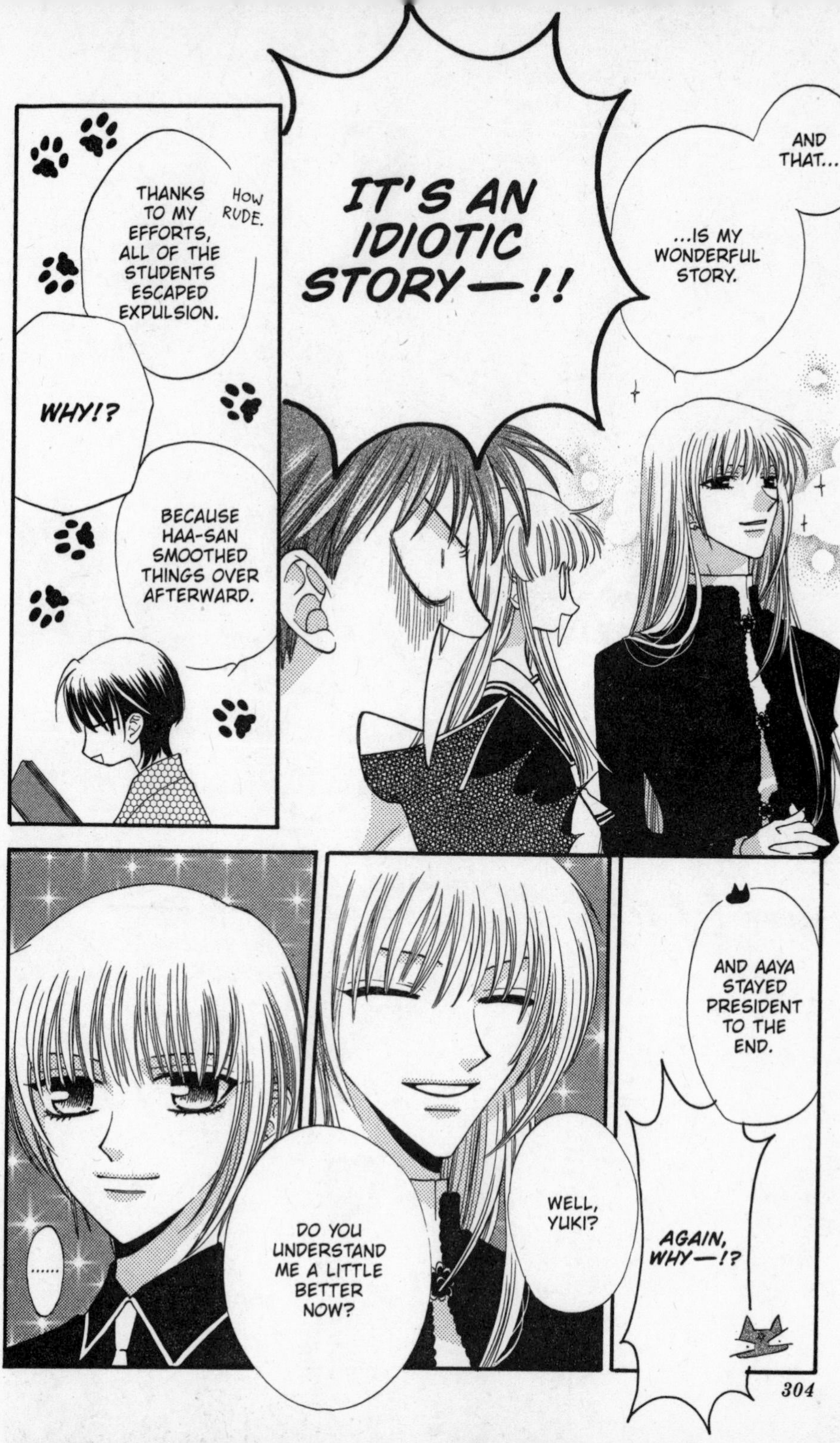
AND THAT...
...IS MY WONDERFUL STORY.
IT'S AN IDIOTIC STORY—!!
THANKS TO MY EFFORTS, ALL OF THE STUDENTS ESCAPED EXPULSION.
HOW RUDE.
WHY!?
BECAUSE HAA-SAN SMOOTHED THINGS OVER AFTERWARD.
AND AAYA STAYED PRESIDENT TO THE END.
AGAIN, WHY—!?
WELL, YUKI?
DO YOU UNDERSTAND ME A LITTLE BETTER NOW?
......

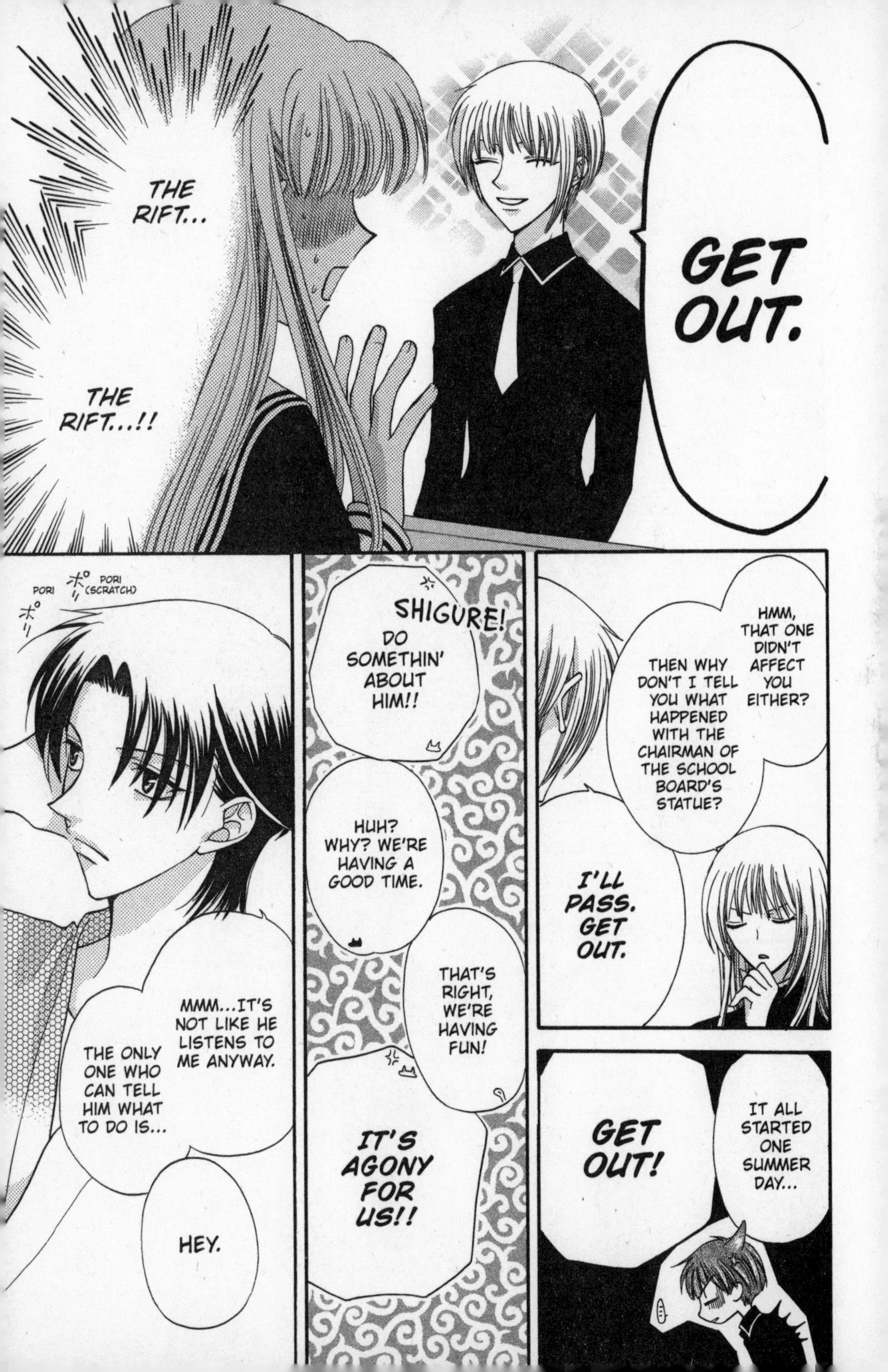
GET OUT.
THE RIFT...
THE RIFT...!!
HMM, THAT ONE DIDN'T AFFECT YOU EITHER?
THEN WHY DON'T I TELL YOU WHAT HAPPENED WITH THE CHAIRMAN OF THE SCHOOL BOARD'S STATUE?
I'LL PASS. GET OUT.
IT ALL STARTED ONE SUMMER DAY...
GET OUT!
SHIGURE! DO SOMETHIN' ABOUT HIM!!
HUH? WHY? WE'RE HAVING A GOOD TIME.
THAT'S RIGHT, WE'RE HAVING FUN!
IT'S AGONY FOR US!!
PORI PORI (SCRATCH)
MMM...IT'S NOT LIKE HE LISTENS TO ME ANYWAY.
THE ONLY ONE WHO CAN TELL HIM WHAT TO DO IS...
HEY.

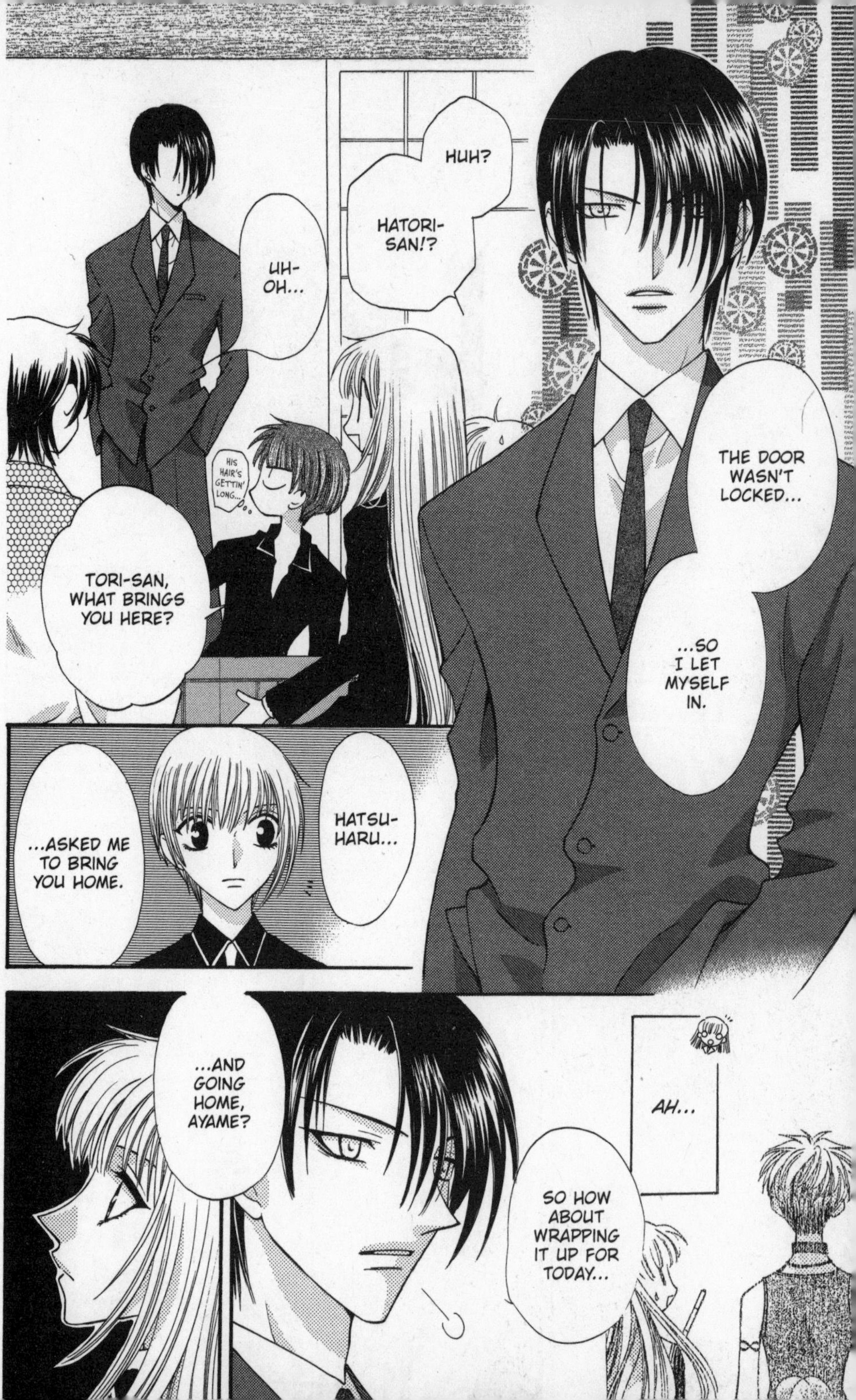
THE DOOR WASN'T LOCKED...
...SO I LET MYSELF IN.
HUH?
HATORI-SAN!?
UH-OH...
HIS HAIR'S GETTIN' LONG...
TORI-SAN, WHAT BRINGS YOU HERE?
HATSU-HARU...
...ASKED ME TO BRING YOU HOME.
AH...
SO HOW ABOUT WRAPPING IT UP FOR TODAY...
...AND GOING HOME, AYAME?

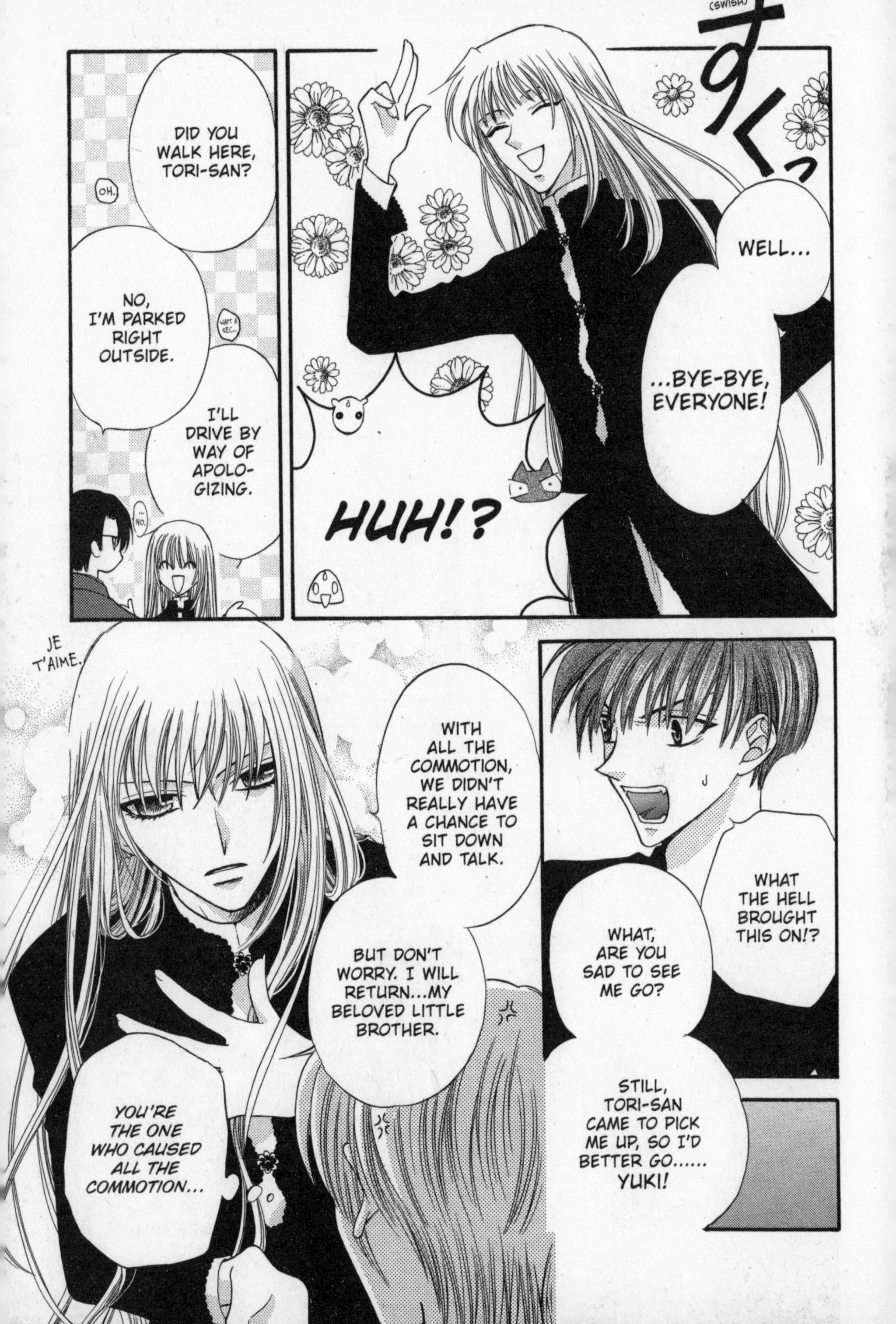

SUKU (SWISH)
すくっ
WELL...
...BYE-BYE, EVERYONE!
HUH!?
DID YOU WALK HERE, TORI-SAN?
OH.
NO, I'M PARKED RIGHT OUTSIDE.
WAIT A SEC...
I'LL DRIVE BY WAY OF APOLOGIZING.
...NO.
WHAT THE HELL BROUGHT THIS ON!?
WHAT, ARE YOU SAD TO SEE ME GO?
STILL, TORI-SAN CAME TO PICK ME UP, SO I'D BETTER GO...... YUKI!
JE T'AIME.
WITH ALL THE COMMOTION, WE DIDN'T REALLY HAVE A CHANCE TO SIT DOWN AND TALK.
BUT DON'T WORRY. I WILL RETURN...MY BELOVED LITTLE BROTHER.
YOU'RE THE ONE WHO CAUSED ALL THE COMMOTION...

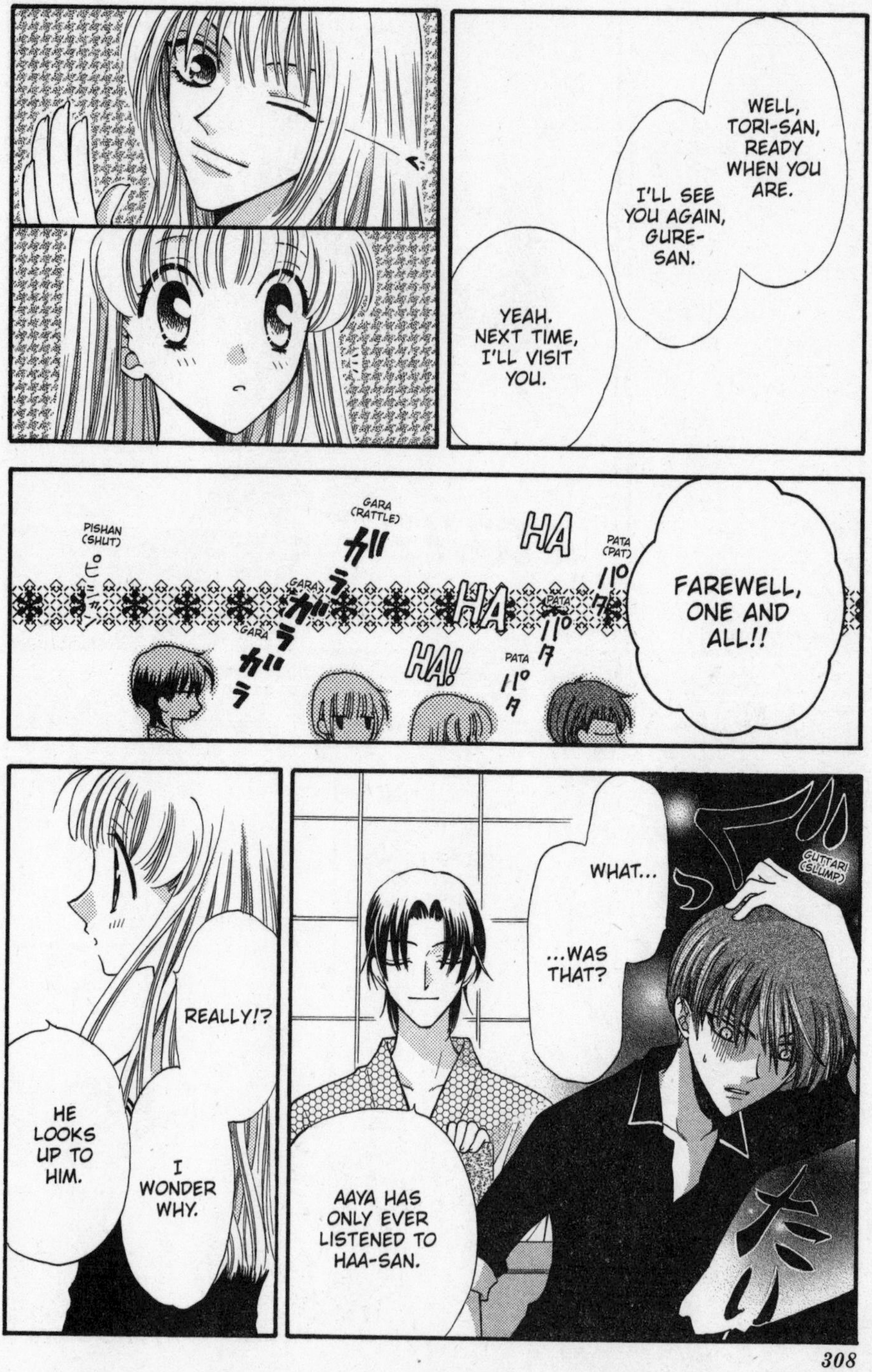
WELL, TORI-SAN, READY WHEN YOU ARE.
I'LL SEE YOU AGAIN, GURE-SAN.
YEAH. NEXT TIME, I'LL VISIT YOU.
FAREWELL, ONE AND ALL!!
PATA (PAT) パタ
HA
HA
HA!
PATA パタ
PATA パタ
GARA (RATTLE) ガラ
GARA ガラ
GARA ガラ
PISHAN (SHUT) ピシャン
GUTTARI (SLUMP)
WHAT...
...WAS THAT?
AAYA HAS ONLY EVER LISTENED TO HAA-SAN.
REALLY!?
I WONDER WHY.
HE LOOKS UP TO HIM.

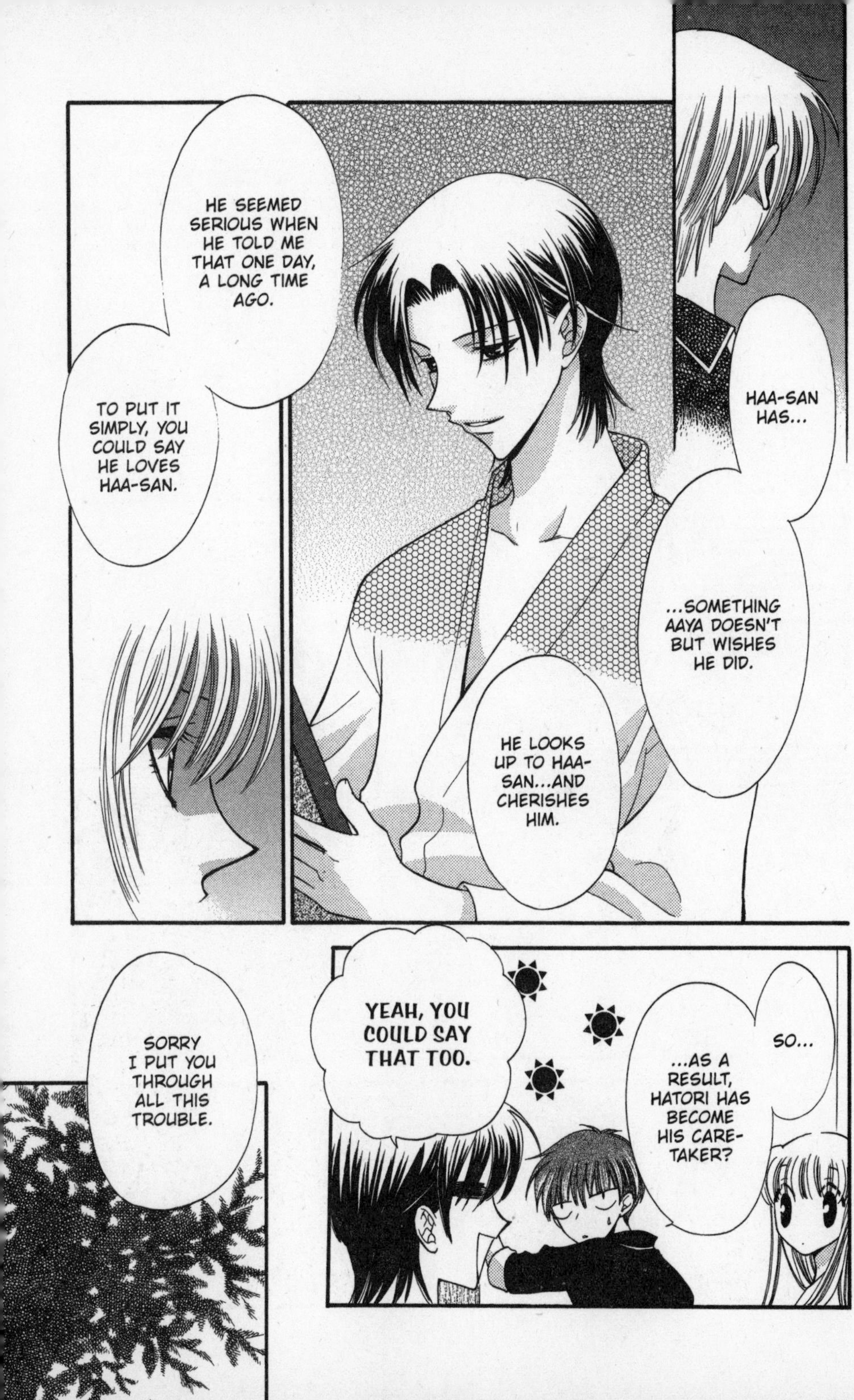
HAA-SAN HAS...
...SOMETHING AAYA DOESN'T BUT WISHES HE DID.
HE LOOKS UP TO HAA-SAN...AND CHERISHES HIM.
HE SEEMED SERIOUS WHEN HE TOLD ME THAT ONE DAY, A LONG TIME AGO.
TO PUT IT SIMPLY, YOU COULD SAY HE LOVES HAA-SAN.
SO...
...AS A RESULT, HATORI HAS BECOME HIS CARE-TAKER?
YEAH, YOU COULD SAY THAT TOO.
SORRY I PUT YOU THROUGH ALL THIS TROUBLE.

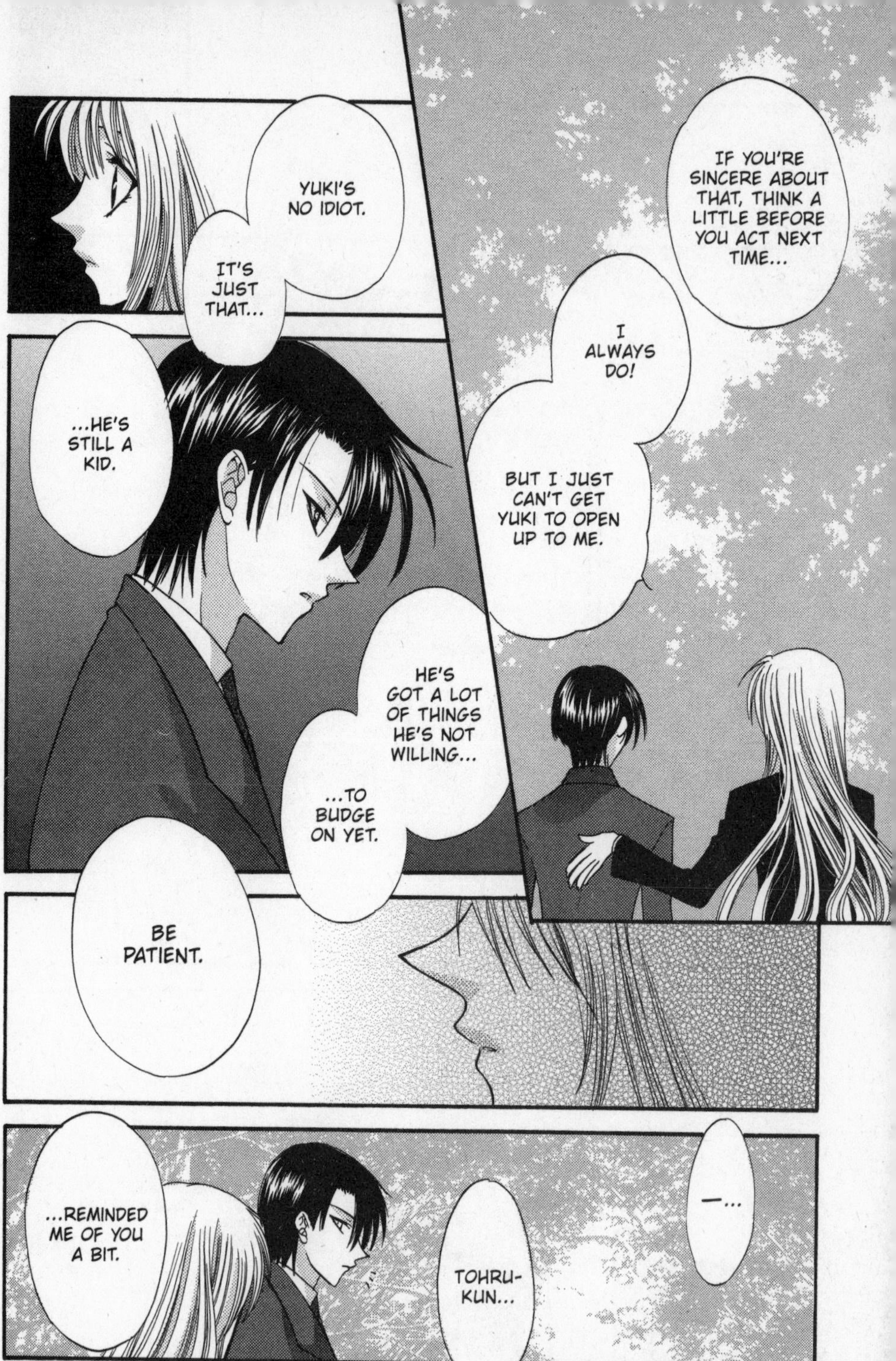
IF YOU'RE SINCERE ABOUT THAT, THINK A LITTLE BEFORE YOU ACT NEXT TIME...
I ALWAYS DO!
BUT I JUST CAN'T GET YUKI TO OPEN UP TO ME.
YUKI'S NO IDIOT.
IT'S JUST THAT...
...HE'S STILL A KID.
HE'S GOT A LOT OF THINGS HE'S NOT WILLING...
...TO BUDGE ON YET.
BE PATIENT.
—...
TOHRU-KUN...
...REMINDED ME OF YOU A BIT.

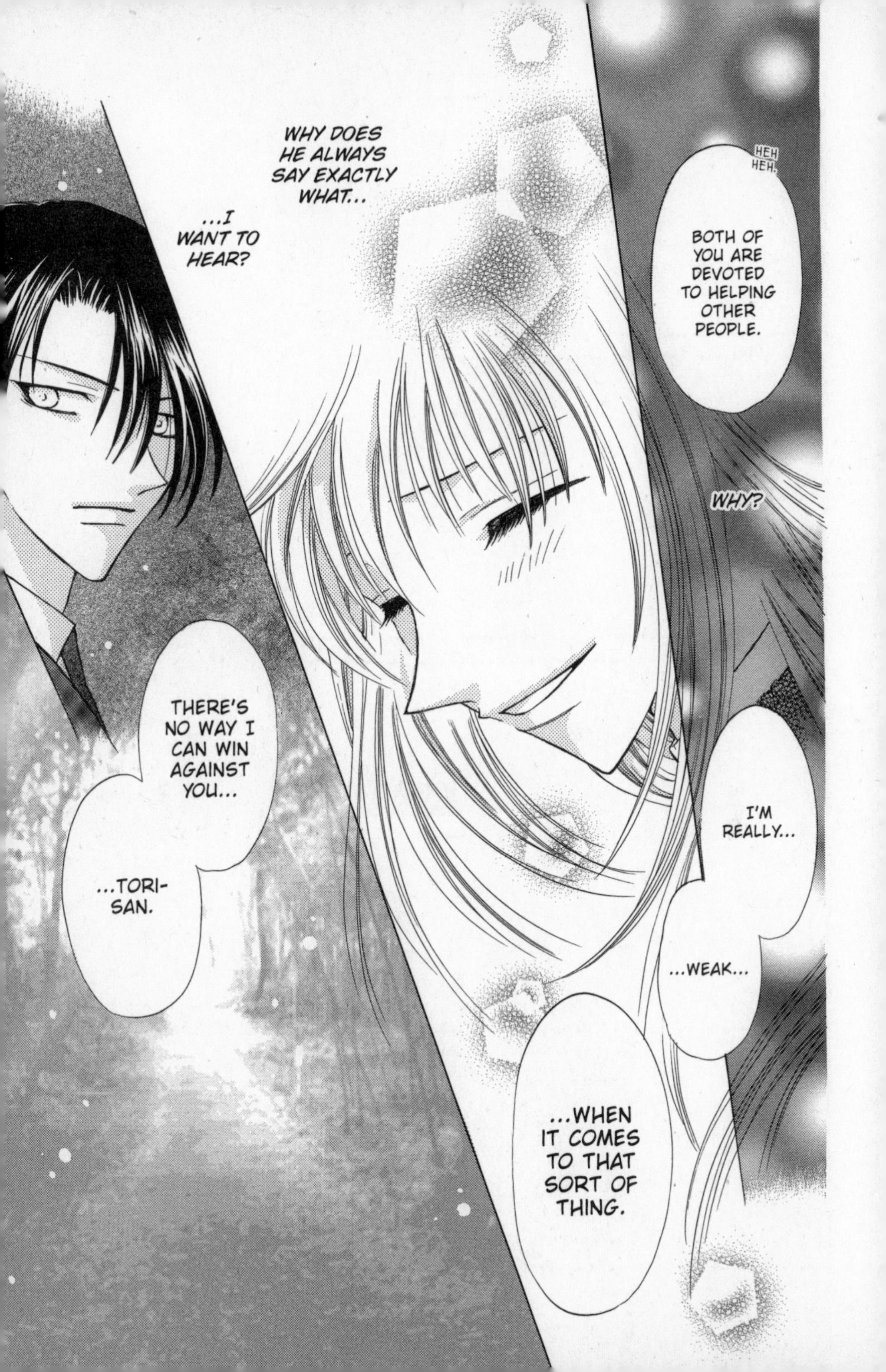
HEH HEH.
BOTH OF YOU ARE DEVOTED TO HELPING OTHER PEOPLE.
WHY?
I'M REALLY...
...WEAK...
...WHEN IT COMES TO THAT SORT OF THING.
WHY DOES HE ALWAYS SAY EXACTLY WHAT...
...I WANT TO HEAR?
THERE'S NO WAY I CAN WIN AGAINST YOU...
...TORI-SAN.

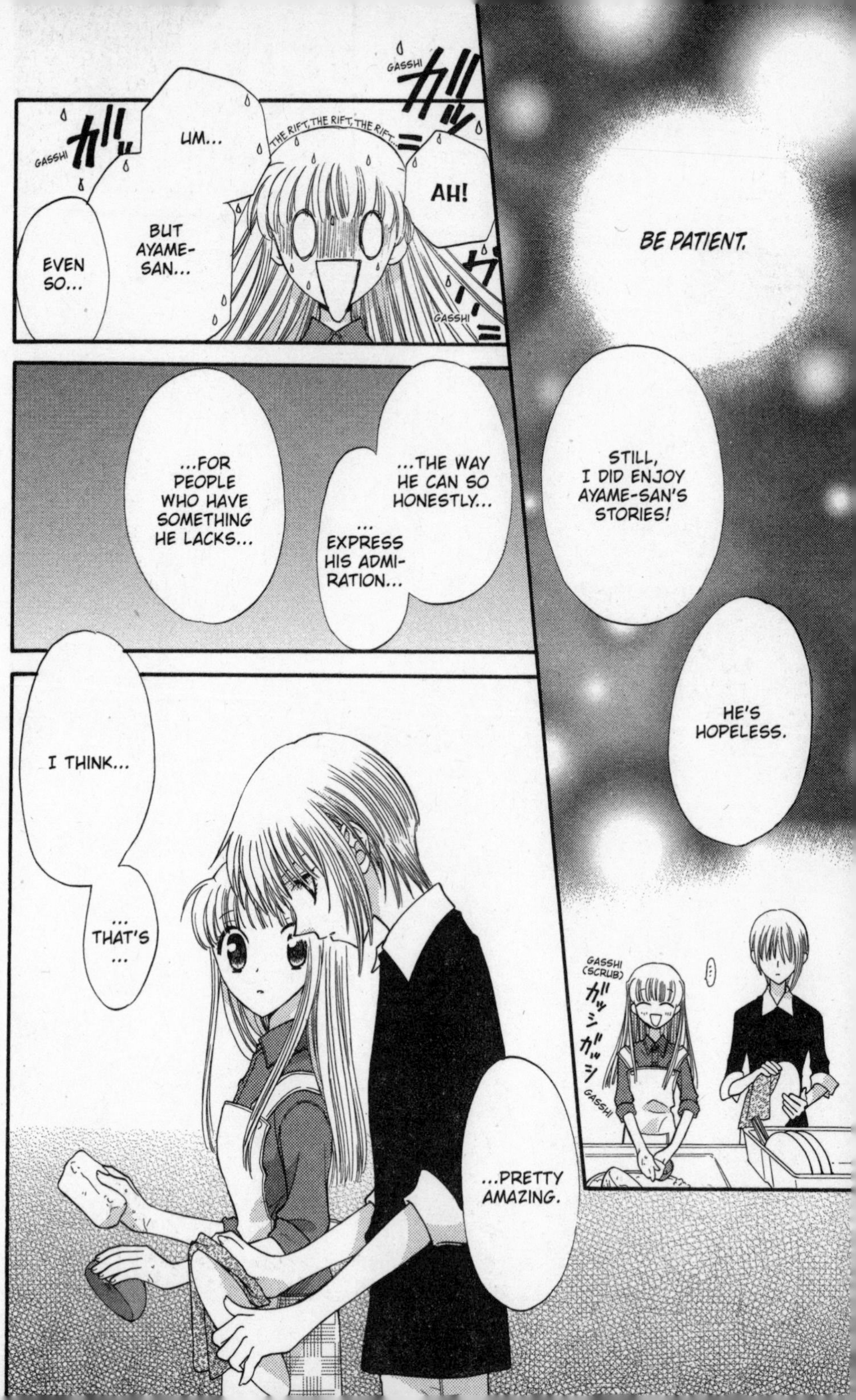
BE PATIENT.
STILL, I DID ENJOY AYAME-SAN'S STORIES!
HE'S HOPELESS.
GASSHI (SCRUB)
ガッシガッシ
GASSHI
...
GASSHI
GASSHI
AH!
THE RIFT, THE RIFT, THE RIFT...
UM...
BUT AYAME-SAN...
EVEN SO...
GASSHI
...THE WAY HE CAN SO HONESTLY...
...EXPRESS HIS ADMIRATION...
...FOR PEOPLE WHO HAVE SOMETHING HE LACKS...
I THINK...
...THAT'S...
...PRETTY AMAZING.

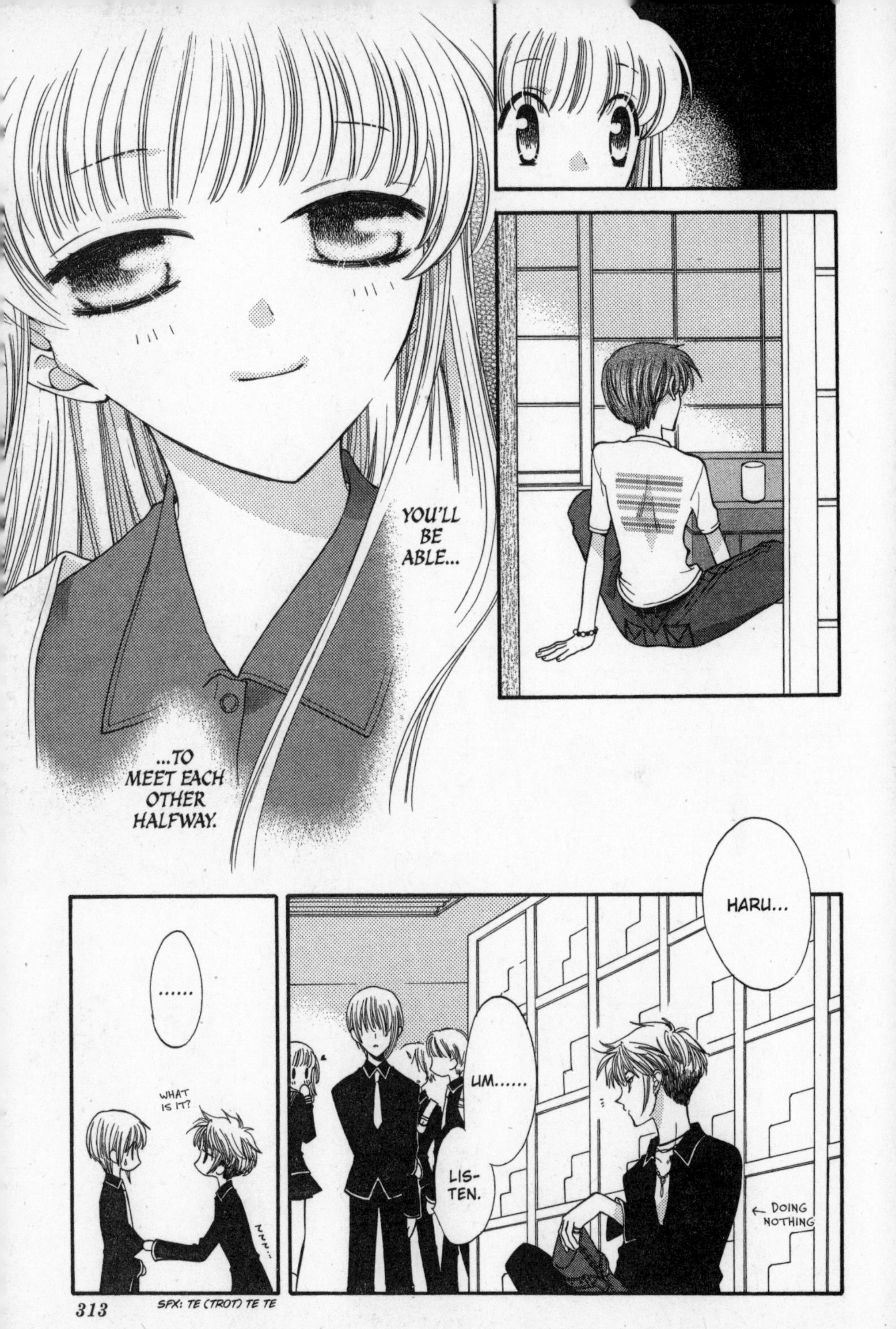
YOU'LL BE ABLE...
...TO MEET EACH OTHER HALFWAY.
HARU...
UM......
LIS-TEN.
← DOING NOTHING
......
WHAT IS IT?

SFX: TE (TROT) TE TE

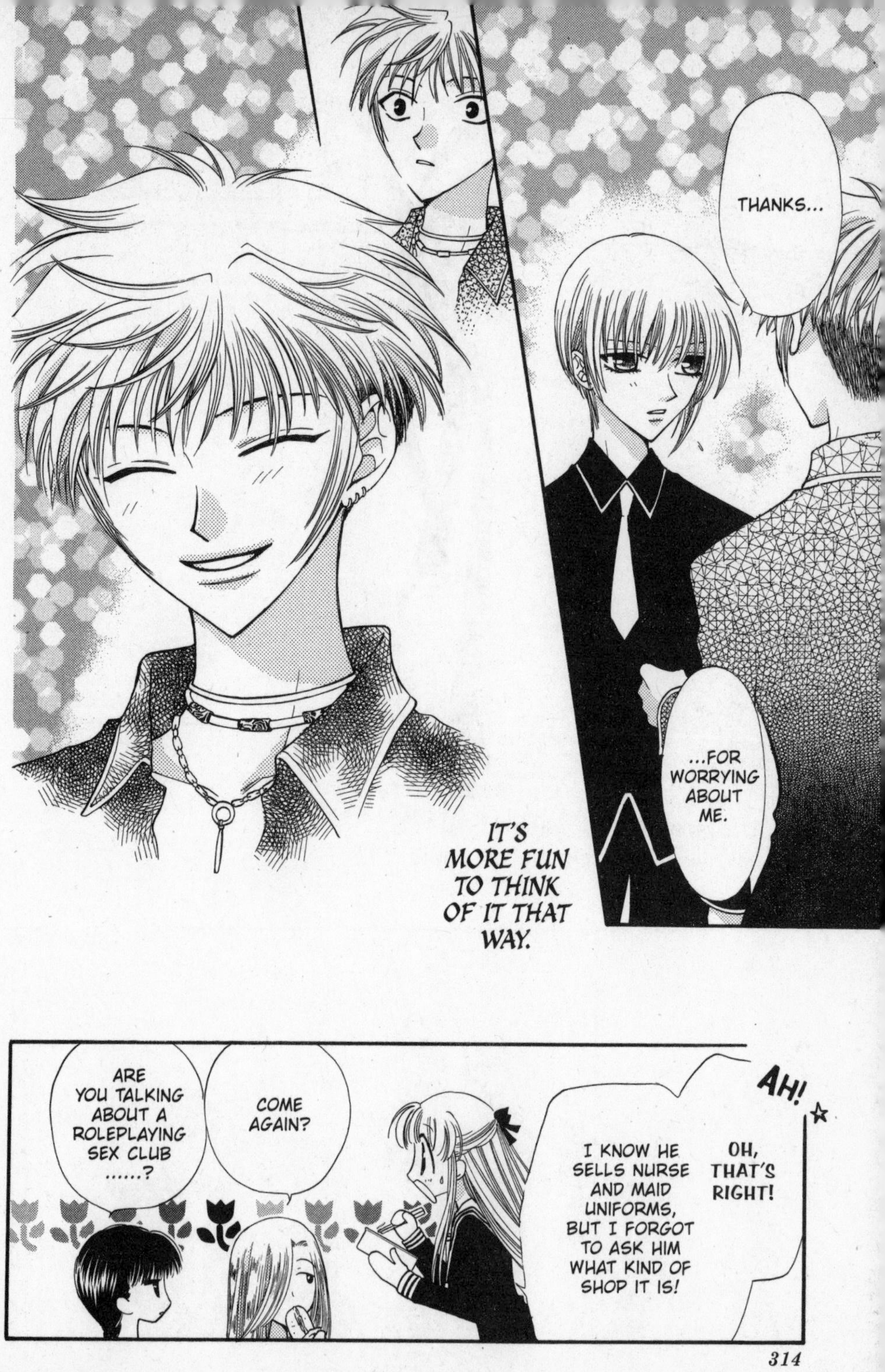
THANKS...
...FOR WORRYING ABOUT ME.
IT'S MORE FUN TO THINK OF IT THAT WAY.
AH! ☆
OH, THAT'S RIGHT!
I KNOW HE SELLS NURSE AND MAID UNIFORMS, BUT I FORGOT TO ASK HIM WHAT KIND OF SHOP IT IS!
COME AGAIN?
ARE YOU TALKING ABOUT A ROLEPLAYING SEX CLUB ......?

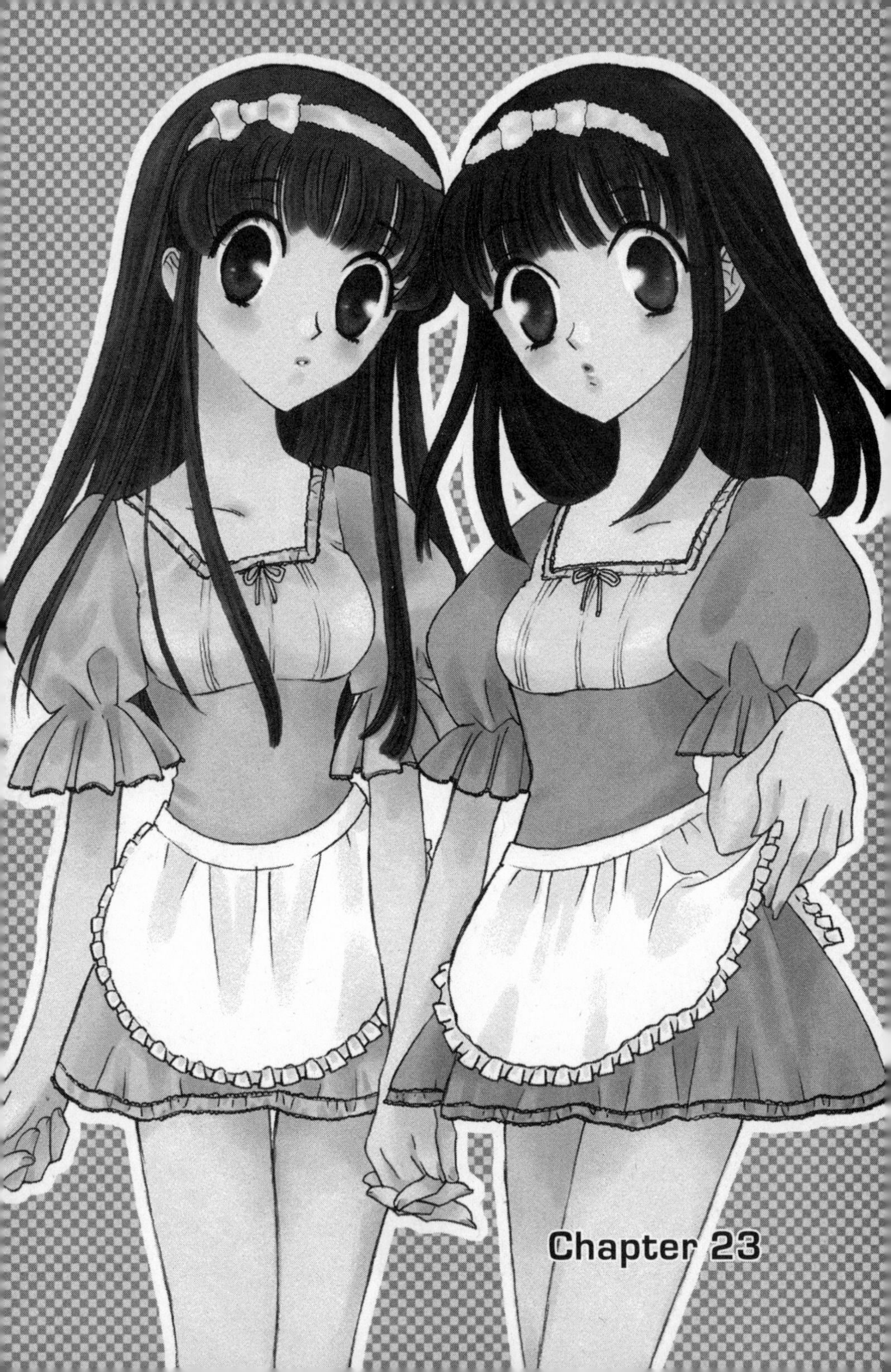
Chapter 23

COLLECTOR'S EDITION

Fruits Basket

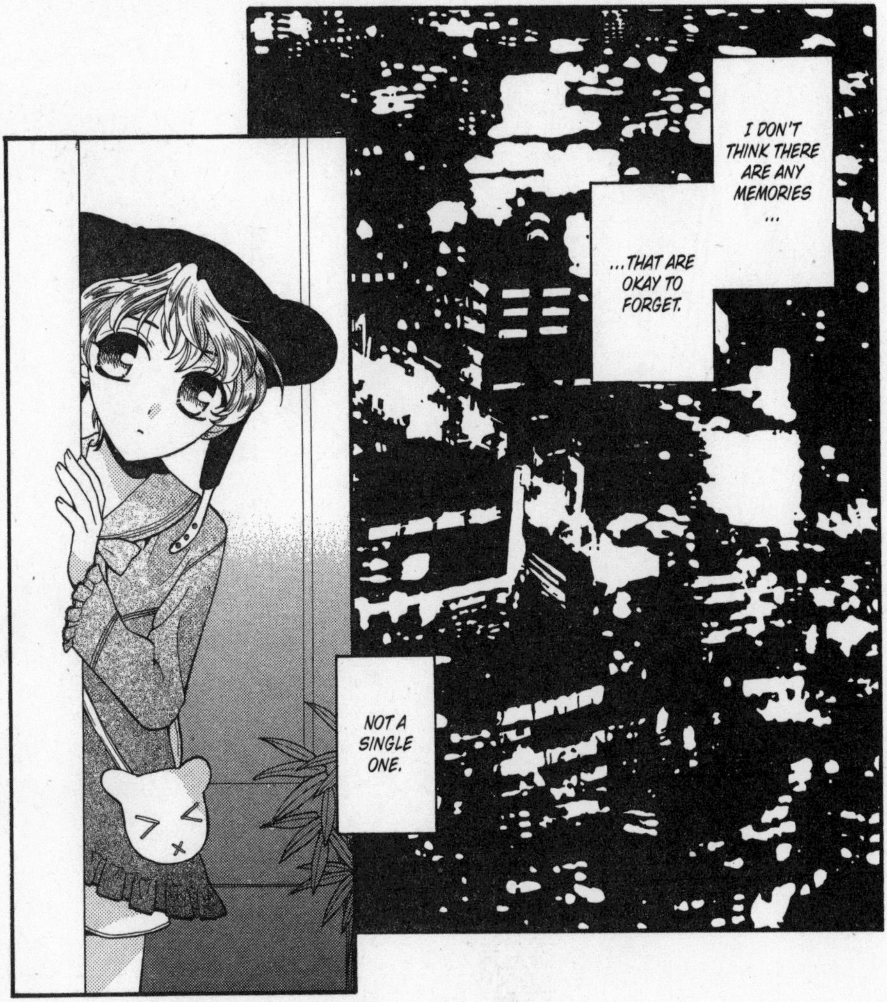
I DON'T THINK THERE ARE ANY MEMORIES ...
...THAT ARE OKAY TO FORGET.
NOT A SINGLE ONE.

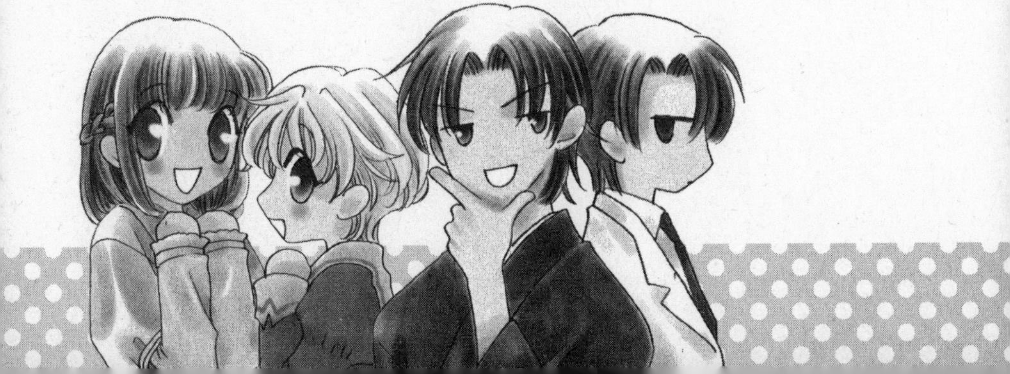

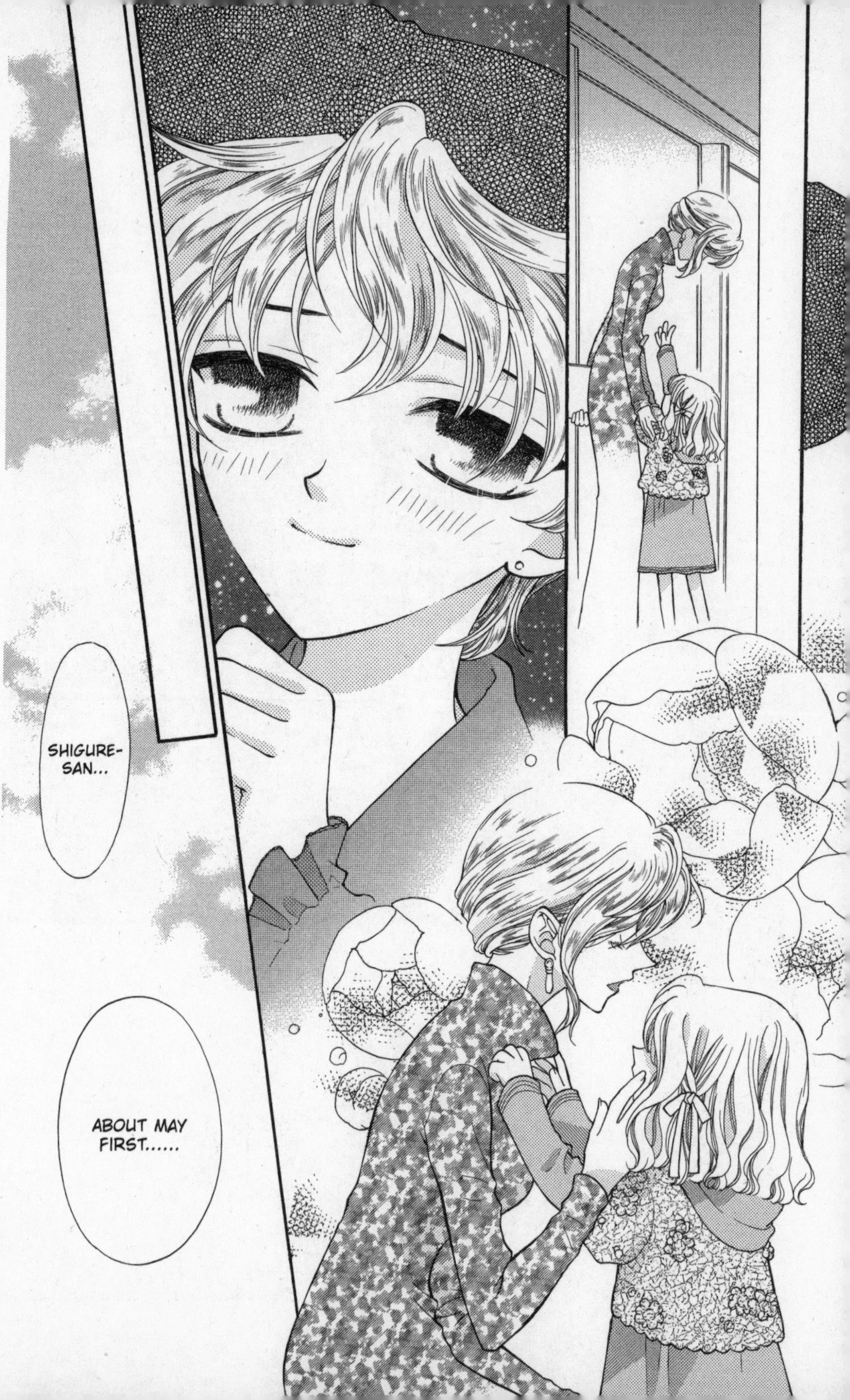
SHIGURE-SAN...
ABOUT MAY FIRST......

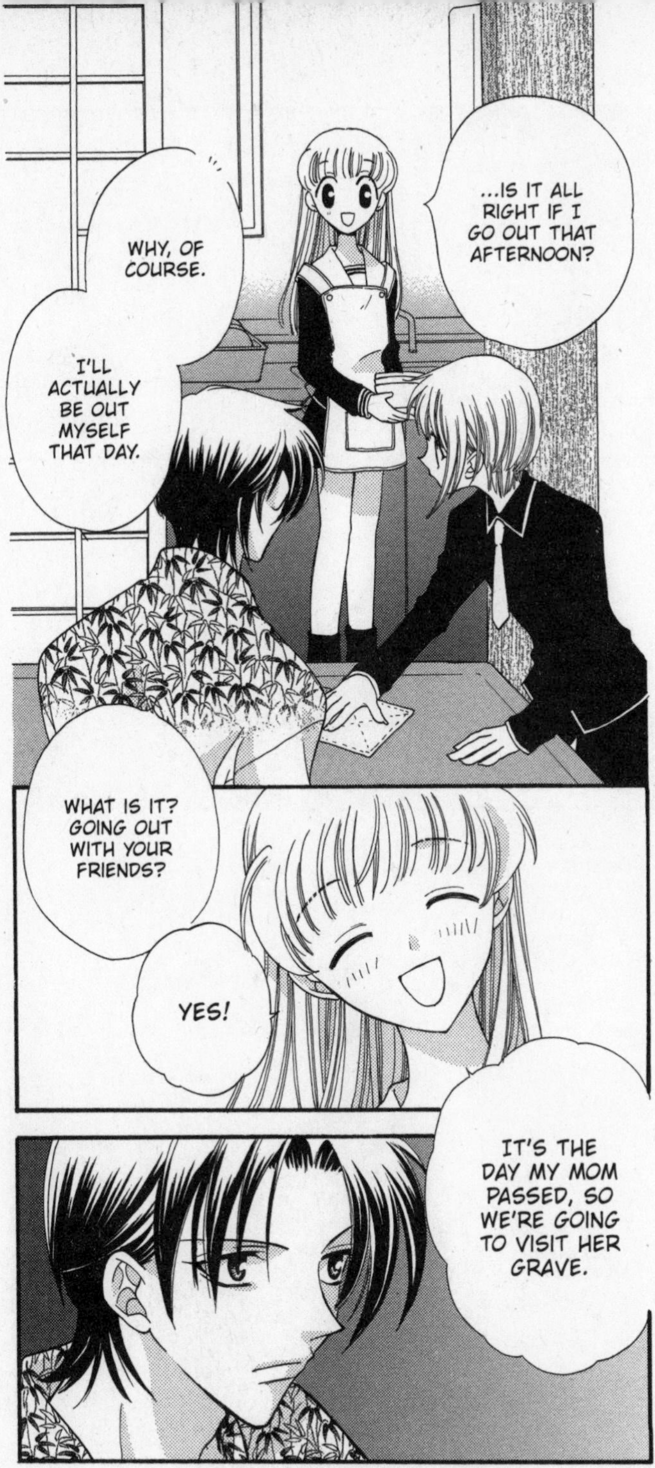
...IS IT ALL RIGHT IF I GO OUT THAT AFTERNOON?
WHY, OF COURSE.
I'LL ACTUALLY BE OUT MYSELF THAT DAY.
WHAT IS IT? GOING OUT WITH YOUR FRIENDS?
YES!
IT'S THE DAY MY MOM PASSED, SO WE'RE GOING TO VISIT HER GRAVE.

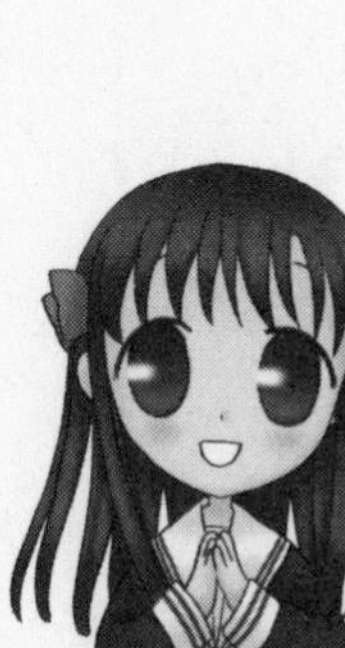

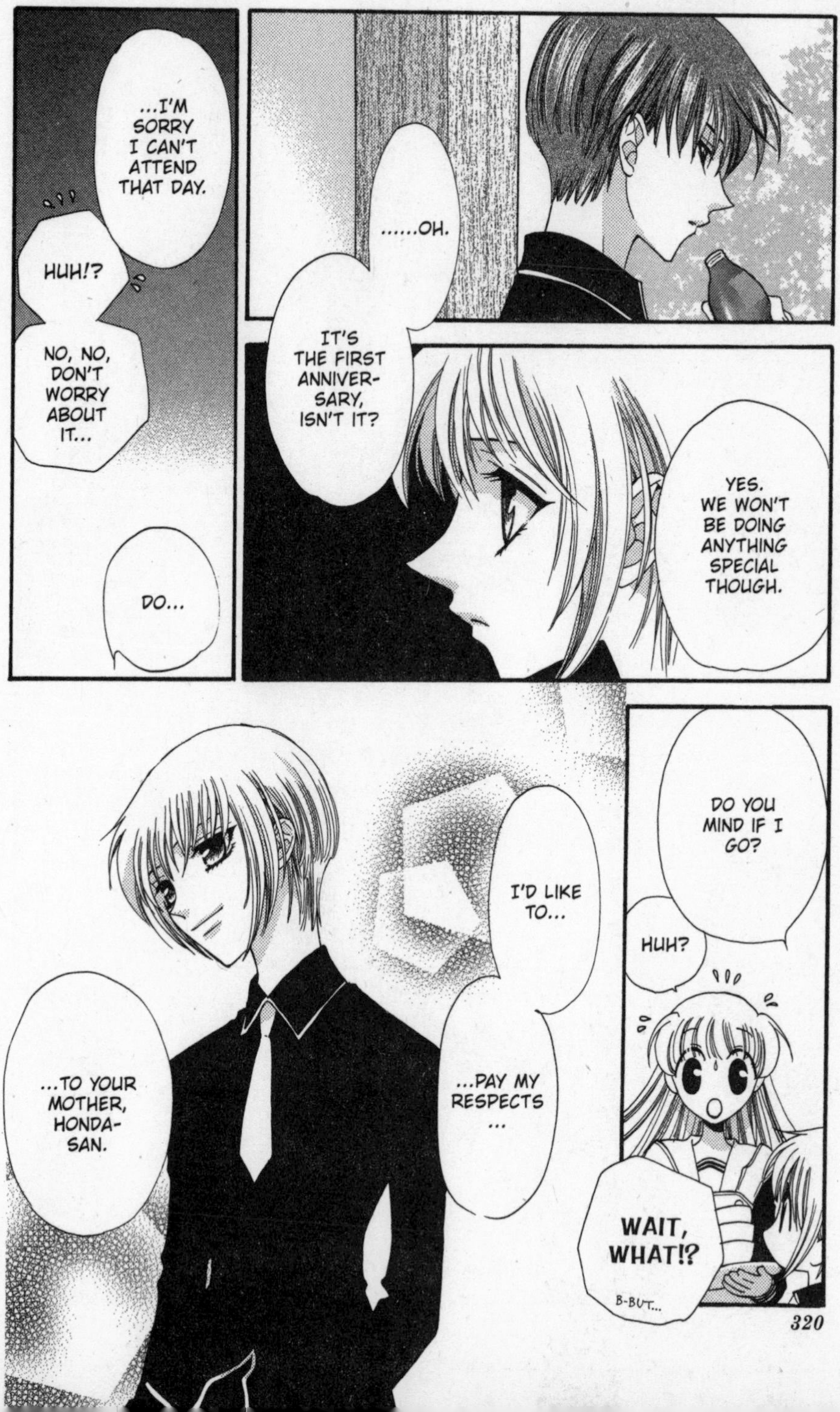
......OH.
IT'S THE FIRST ANNIVER-SARY, ISN'T IT?
YES. WE WON'T BE DOING ANYTHING SPECIAL THOUGH.
...I'M SORRY I CAN'T ATTEND THAT DAY.
HUH!?
NO, NO, DON'T WORRY ABOUT IT...
DO...
DO YOU MIND IF I GO?
HUH?
WAIT, WHAT!?
B-BUT...
I'D LIKE TO...
...PAY MY RESPECTS ...
...TO YOUR MOTHER, HONDA-SAN.

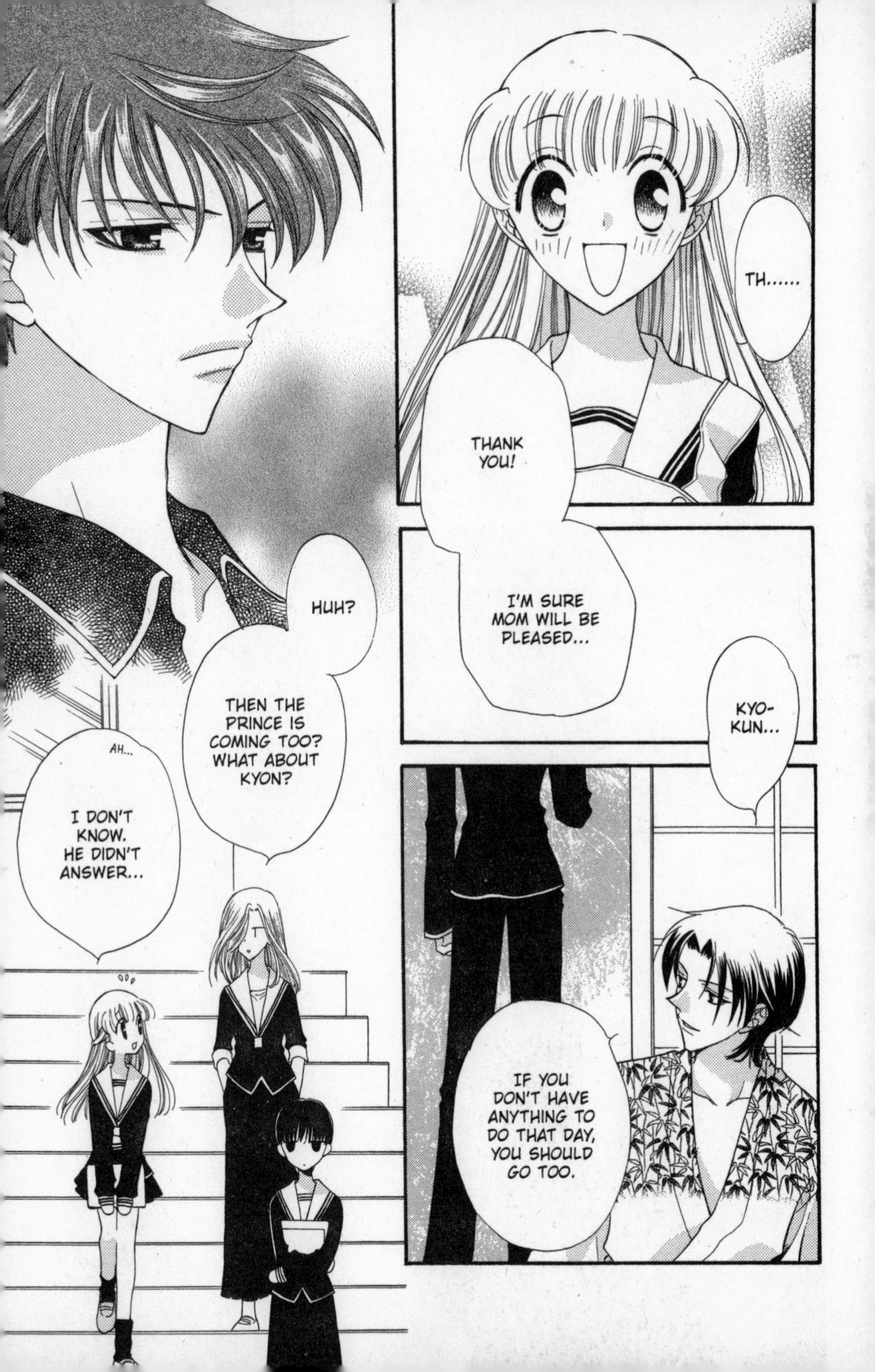
TH......
THANK YOU!
I'M SURE MOM WILL BE PLEASED...
KYO-KUN...
IF YOU DON'T HAVE ANYTHING TO DO THAT DAY, YOU SHOULD GO TOO.
HUH?
THEN THE PRINCE IS COMING TOO? WHAT ABOUT KYON?
AH...
I DON'T KNOW. HE DIDN'T ANSWER...

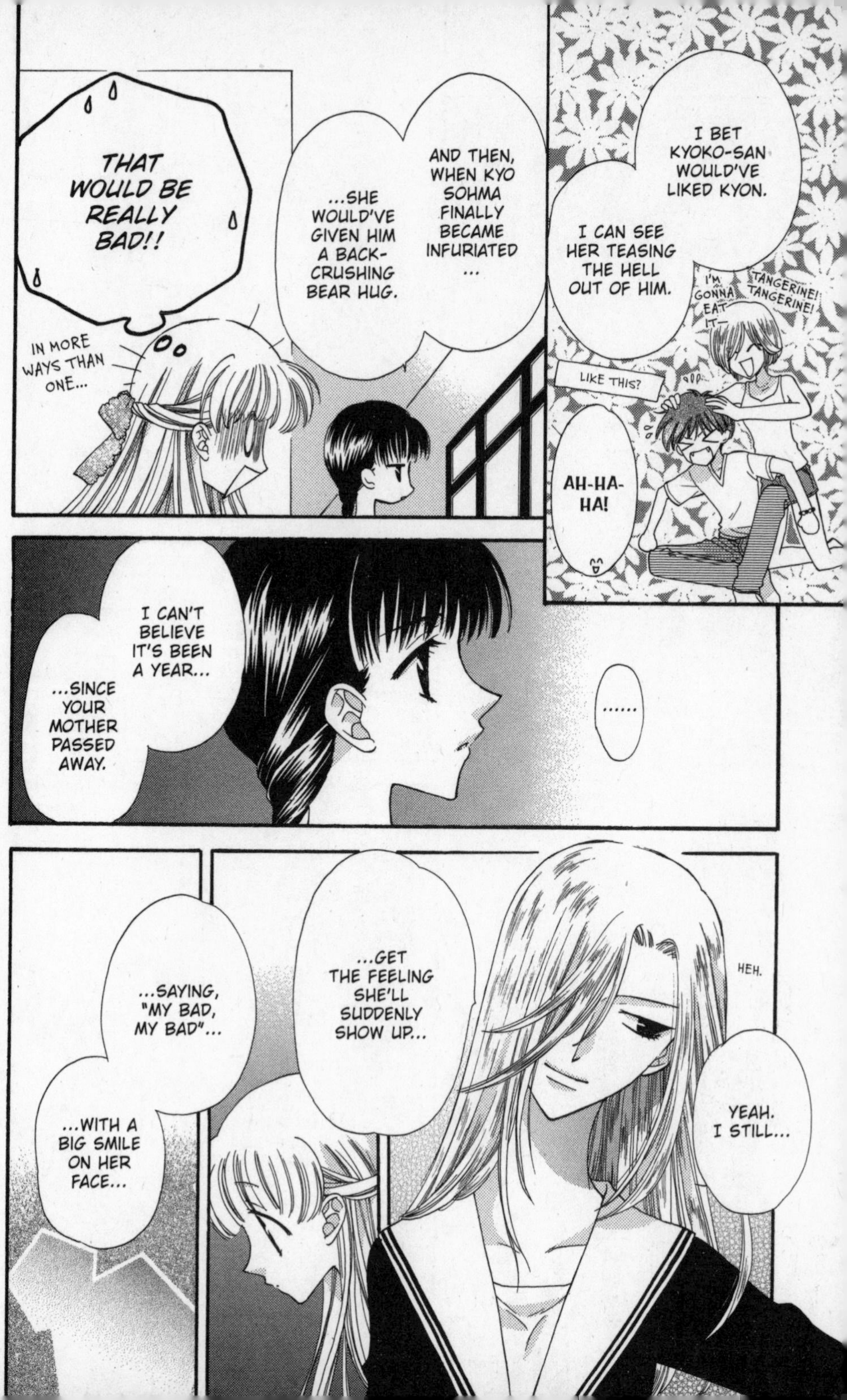
I BET KYOKO-SAN WOULD'VE LIKED KYON.
I CAN SEE HER TEASING THE HELL OUT OF HIM.
TANGERINE! TANGERINE!
I'M GONNA EAT IT—
LIKE THIS?
AH-HA-HA!
AND THEN, WHEN KYO SOHMA FINALLY BECAME INFURIATED ...
...SHE WOULD'VE GIVEN HIM A BACK-CRUSHING BEAR HUG.
THAT WOULD BE REALLY BAD!!
IN MORE WAYS THAN ONE...
......
I CAN'T BELIEVE IT'S BEEN A YEAR...
...SINCE YOUR MOTHER PASSED AWAY.
HEH.
YEAH. I STILL...
...GET THE FEELING SHE'LL SUDDENLY SHOW UP...
...SAYING, "MY BAD, MY BAD"...
...WITH A BIG SMILE ON HER FACE...

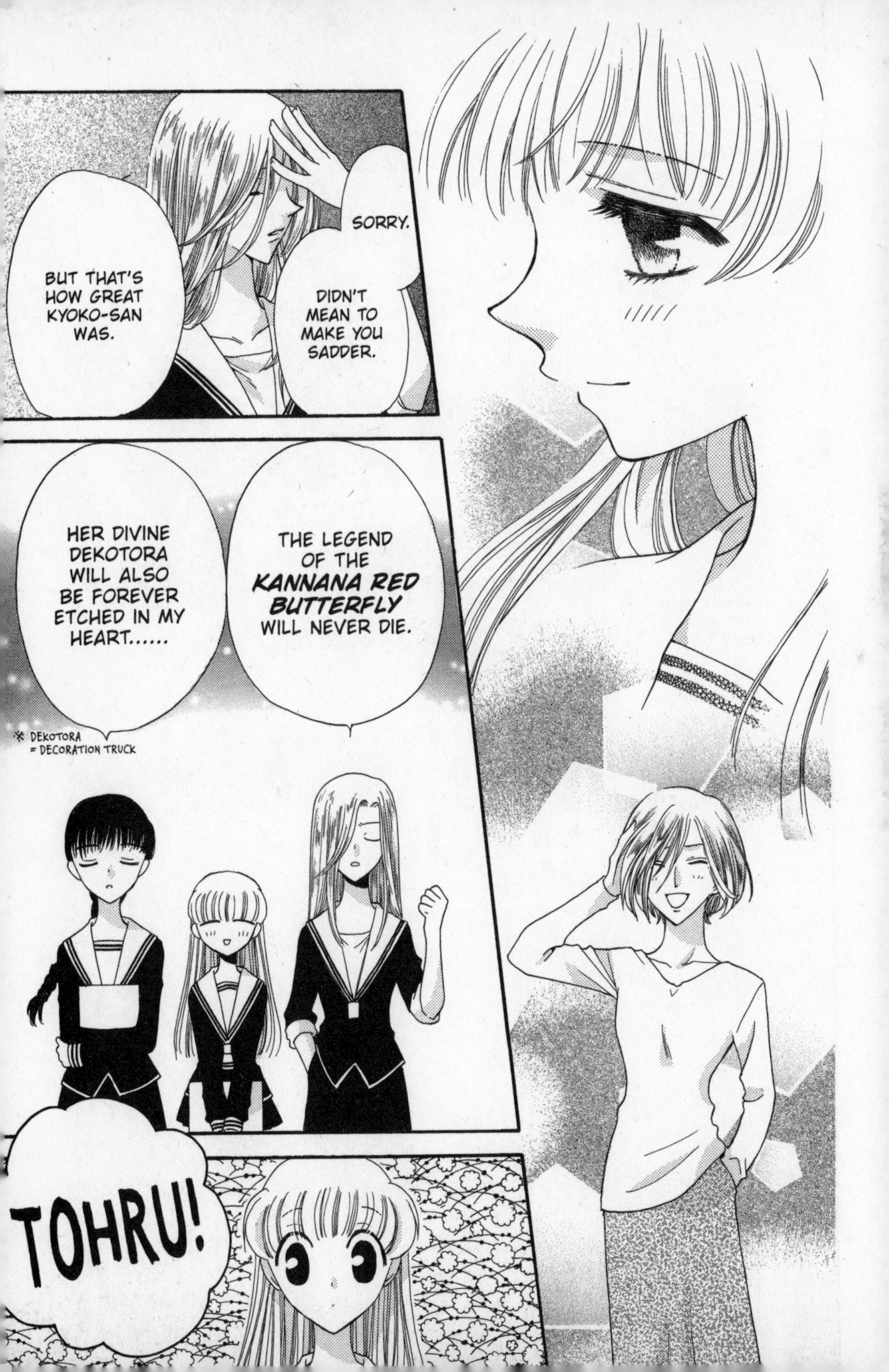
SORRY.
DIDN'T MEAN TO MAKE YOU SADDER.
BUT THAT'S HOW GREAT KYOKO-SAN WAS.
THE LEGEND OF THE *KANNANA RED BUTTERFLY* WILL NEVER DIE.
HER DIVINE DEKOTORA WILL ALSO BE FOREVER ETCHED IN MY HEART......
※ DEKOTORA = DECORATION TRUCK
TOHRU!

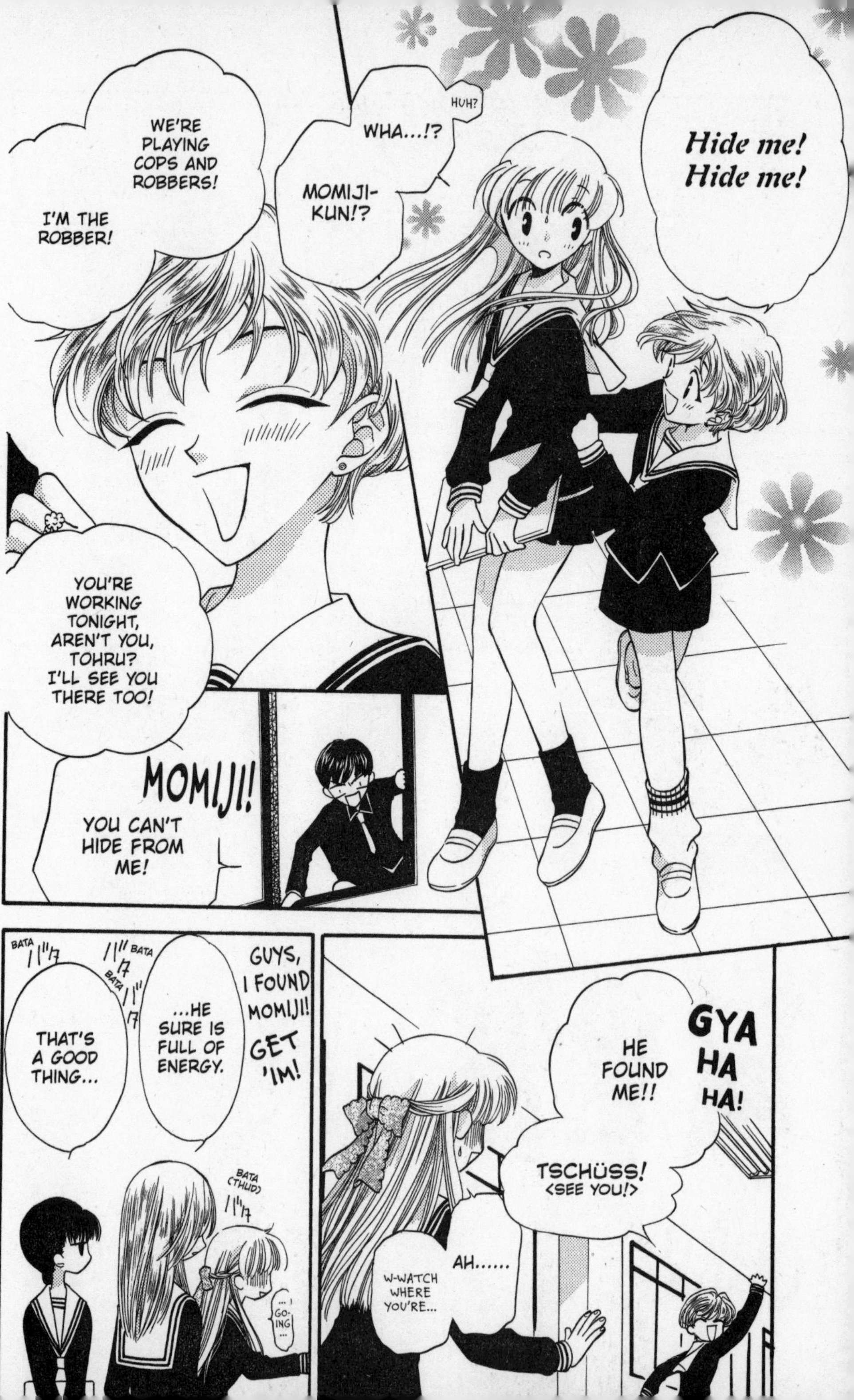
Hide me! Hide me!
WHA...!?
HUH?
MOMIJI-KUN!?
WE'RE PLAYING COPS AND ROBBERS!
I'M THE ROBBER!
YOU'RE WORKING TONIGHT, AREN'T YOU, TOHRU? I'LL SEE YOU THERE TOO!
MOMIJI!
YOU CAN'T HIDE FROM ME!
GYA HA HA!
HE FOUND ME!!
TSCHÜSS! <SEE YOU!>
AH......
W-WATCH WHERE YOU'RE...
GUYS, I FOUND MOMIJI!! GET 'IM!
BATA
BATA
BATA
...HE SURE IS FULL OF ENERGY.
THAT'S A GOOD THING...
BATA (THUD)
...I GO-ING...

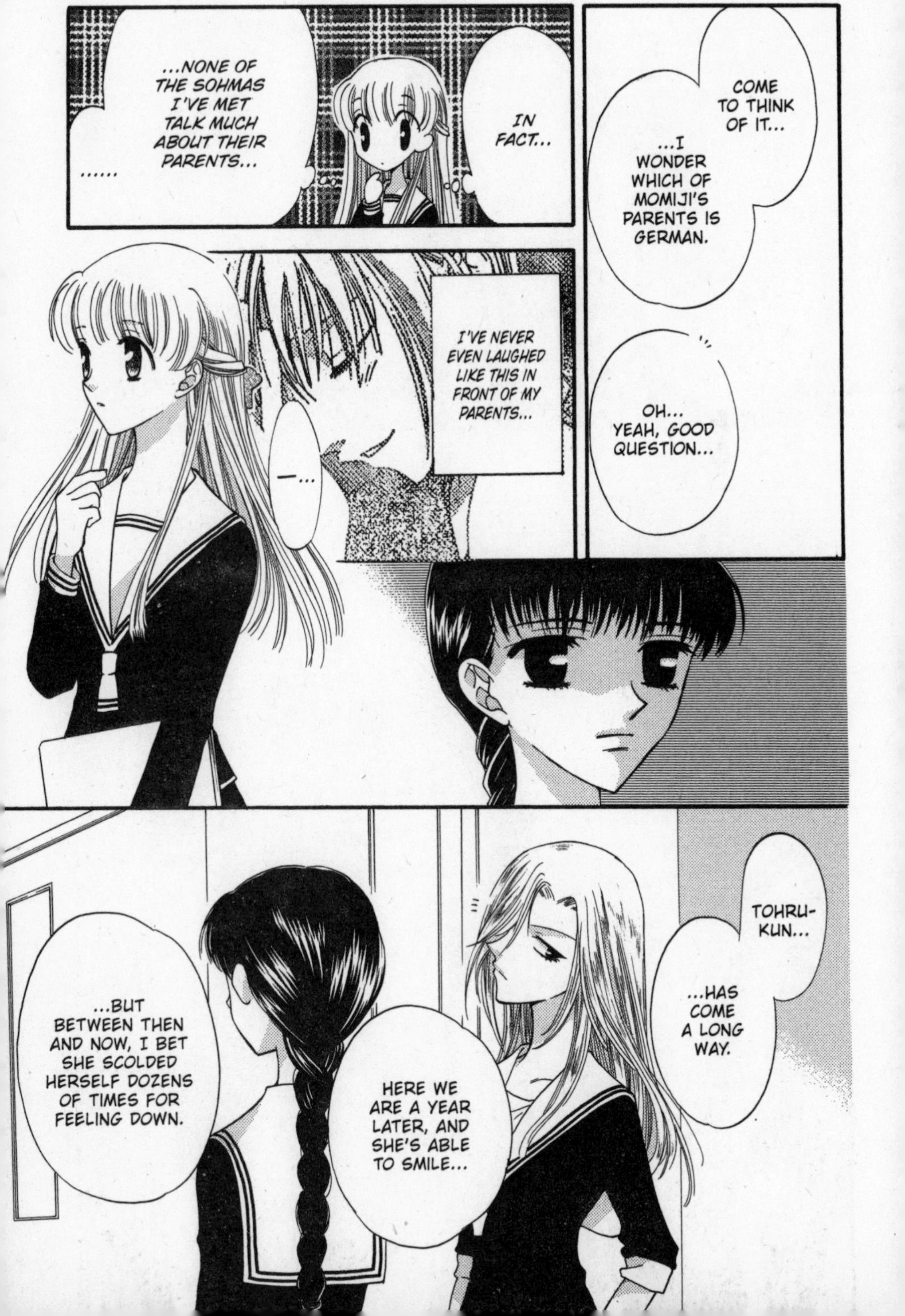
COME TO THINK OF IT...
...I WONDER WHICH OF MOMIJI'S PARENTS IS GERMAN.
OH... YEAH, GOOD QUESTION...
IN FACT...
...NONE OF THE SOHMAS I'VE MET TALK MUCH ABOUT THEIR PARENTS...
......
I'VE NEVER EVEN LAUGHED LIKE THIS IN FRONT OF MY PARENTS...
—...
TOHRU-KUN...
...HAS COME A LONG WAY.
HERE WE ARE A YEAR LATER, AND SHE'S ABLE TO SMILE...
...BUT BETWEEN THEN AND NOW, I BET SHE SCOLDED HERSELF DOZENS OF TIMES FOR FEELING DOWN.

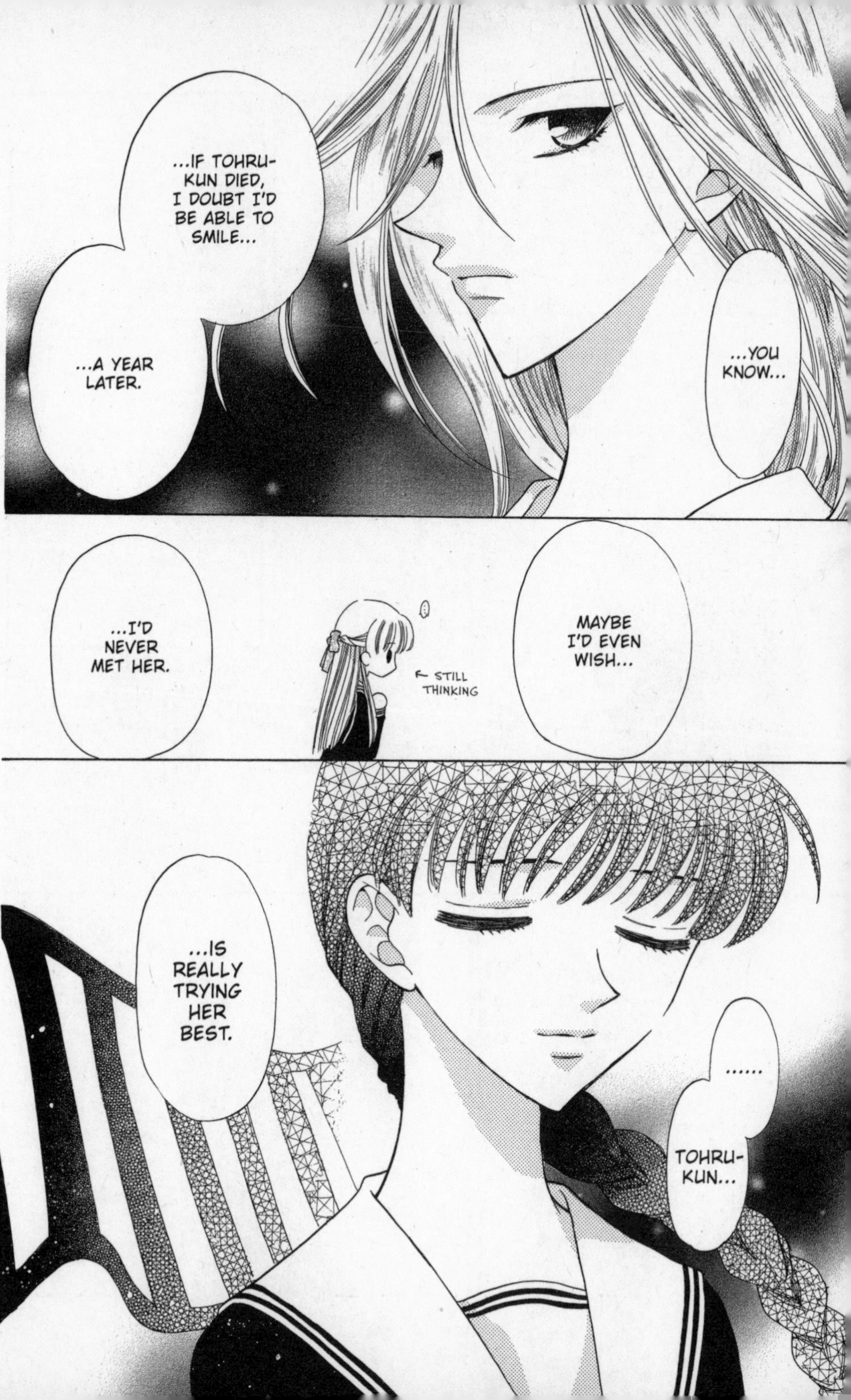
...YOU KNOW...
...IF TOHRU-KUN DIED, I DOUBT I'D BE ABLE TO SMILE...
...A YEAR LATER.
MAYBE I'D EVEN WISH...
← STILL THINKING
...I'D NEVER MET HER.
...... TOHRU-KUN...
...IS REALLY TRYING HER BEST.

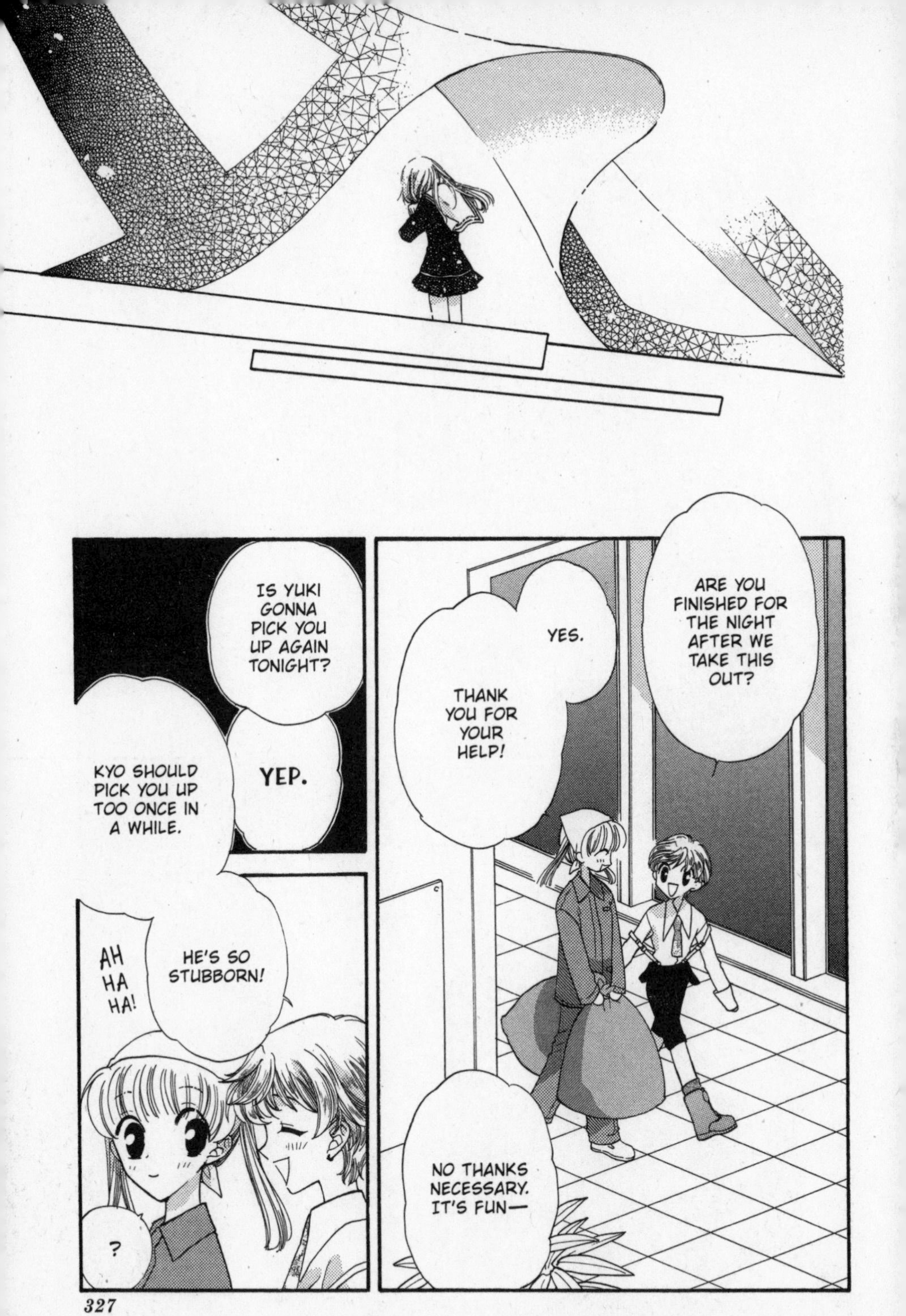
ARE YOU FINISHED FOR THE NIGHT AFTER WE TAKE THIS OUT?
YES.
THANK YOU FOR YOUR HELP!
NO THANKS NECESSARY. IT'S FUN—
IS YUKI GONNA PICK YOU UP AGAIN TONIGHT?
YEP.
KYO SHOULD PICK YOU UP TOO ONCE IN A WHILE.
HE'S SO STUBBORN!
AH HA HA!
?

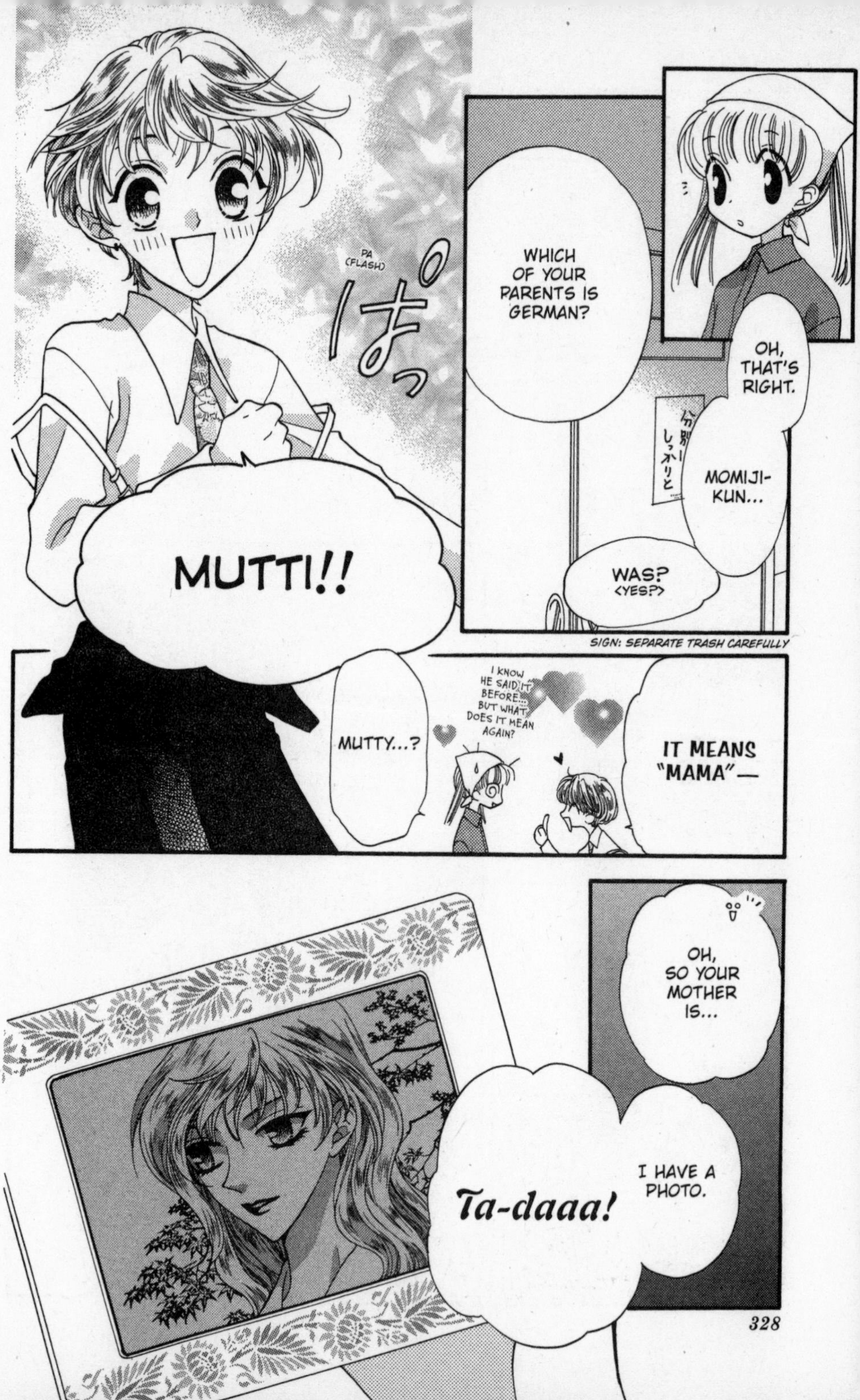
OH, THAT'S RIGHT.
MOMIJI-KUN...
WAS? <YES?>
WHICH OF YOUR PARENTS IS GERMAN?
分別しっかりと
SIGN: SEPARATE TRASH CAREFULLY
PA (FLASH)
ぱっ
MUTTI!!
IT MEANS "MAMA"—
I KNOW HE SAID IT BEFORE... BUT WHAT DOES IT MEAN AGAIN?
MUTTY...?
OH, SO YOUR MOTHER IS...
I HAVE A PHOTO.
Ta-daaa!

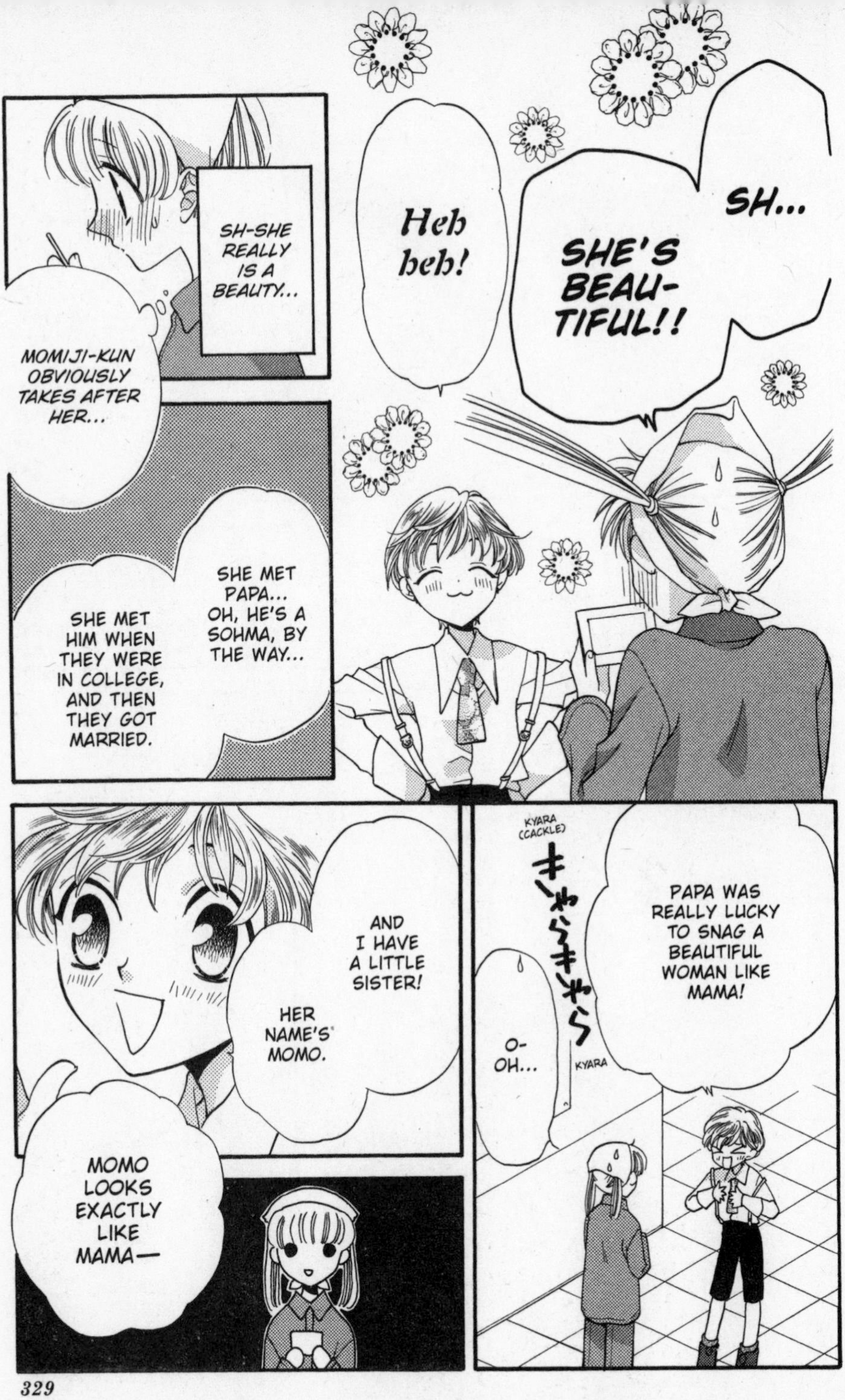
SH...
SHE'S BEAU-TIFUL!!
Heh heh!
SH-SHE REALLY IS A BEAUTY...
MOMIJI-KUN OBVIOUSLY TAKES AFTER HER...
SHE MET PAPA... OH, HE'S A SOHMA, BY THE WAY...
SHE MET HIM WHEN THEY WERE IN COLLEGE, AND THEN THEY GOT MARRIED.
PAPA WAS REALLY LUCKY TO SNAG A BEAUTIFUL WOMAN LIKE MAMA!
KYARA (CACKLE)
きゃらきゃら
KYARA
O-OH...
AND I HAVE A LITTLE SISTER!
HER NAME'S MOMO.
MOMO LOOKS EXACTLY LIKE MAMA—

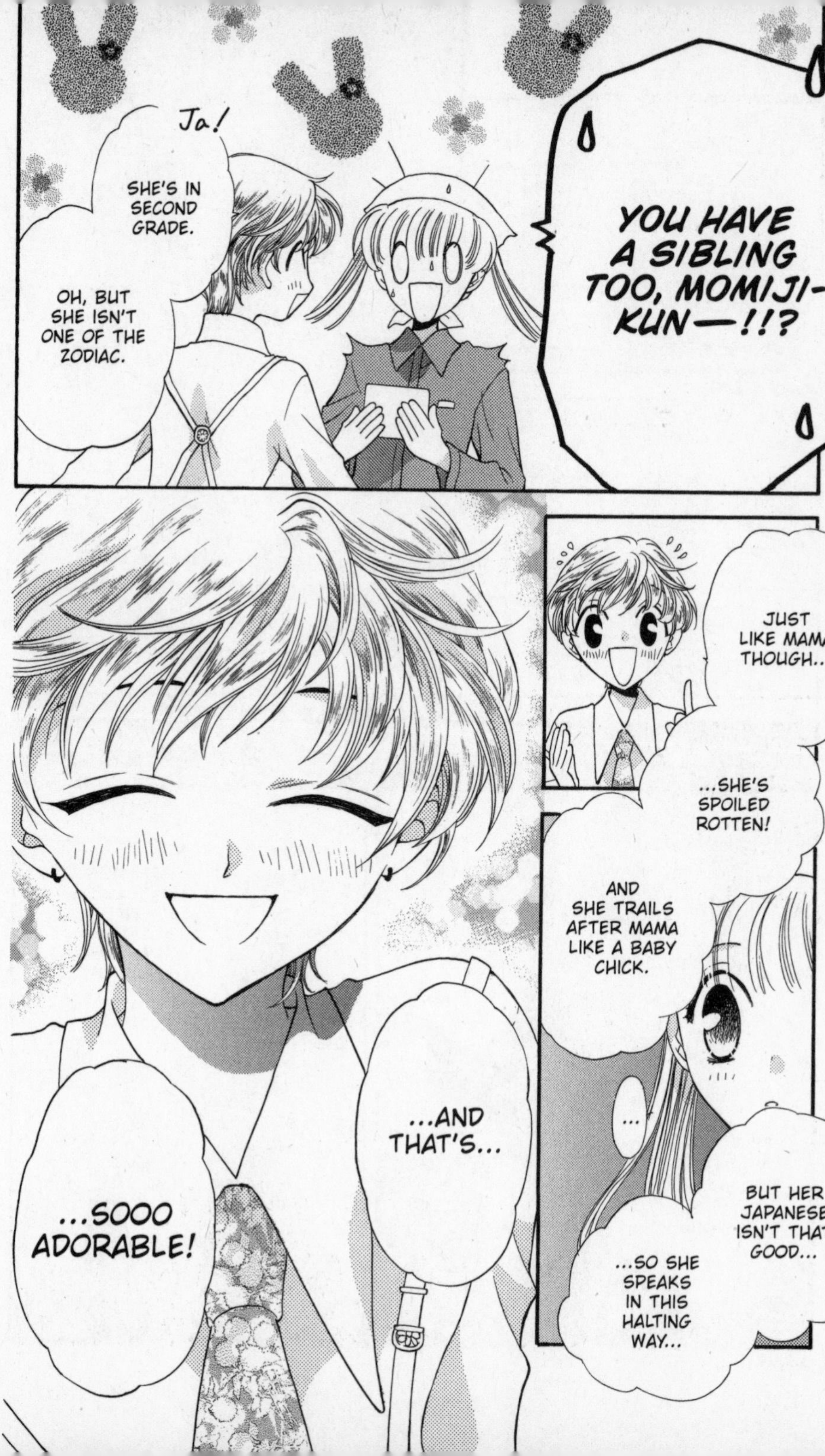
YOU HAVE A SIBLING TOO, MOMIJI-KUN—!!?
Ja!
SHE'S IN SECOND GRADE.
OH, BUT SHE ISN'T ONE OF THE ZODIAC.
JUST LIKE MAMA THOUGH...
...SHE'S SPOILED ROTTEN!
AND SHE TRAILS AFTER MAMA LIKE A BABY CHICK.
...
BUT HER JAPANESE ISN'T THAT GOOD...
...SO SHE SPEAKS IN THIS HALTING WAY...
...AND THAT'S...
...SOOO ADORABLE!

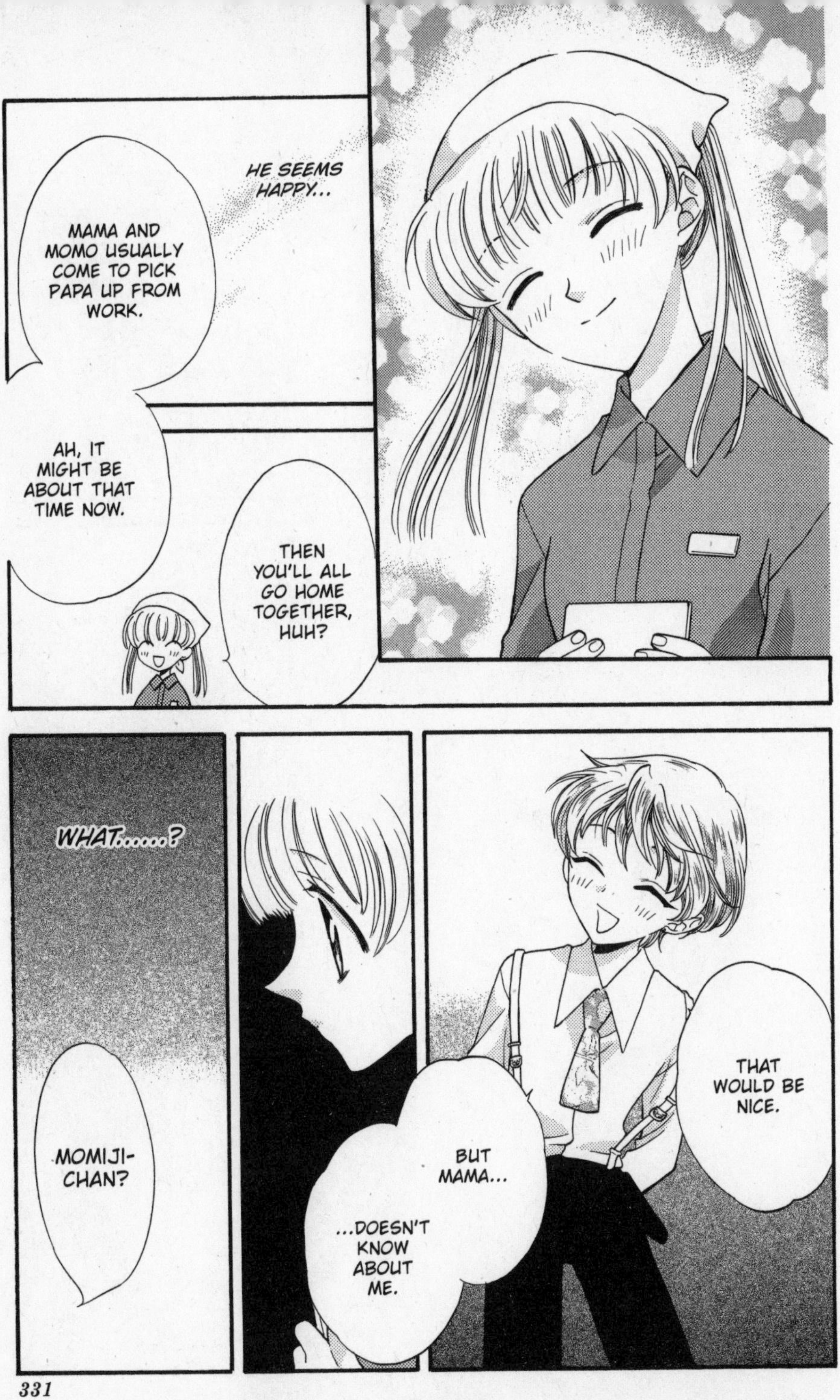
HE SEEMS HAPPY...
MAMA AND MOMO USUALLY COME TO PICK PAPA UP FROM WORK.
AH, IT MIGHT BE ABOUT THAT TIME NOW.
THEN YOU'LL ALL GO HOME TOGETHER, HUH?
THAT WOULD BE NICE.
BUT MAMA...
...DOESN'T KNOW ABOUT ME.
WHAT......?
MOMIJI-CHAN?

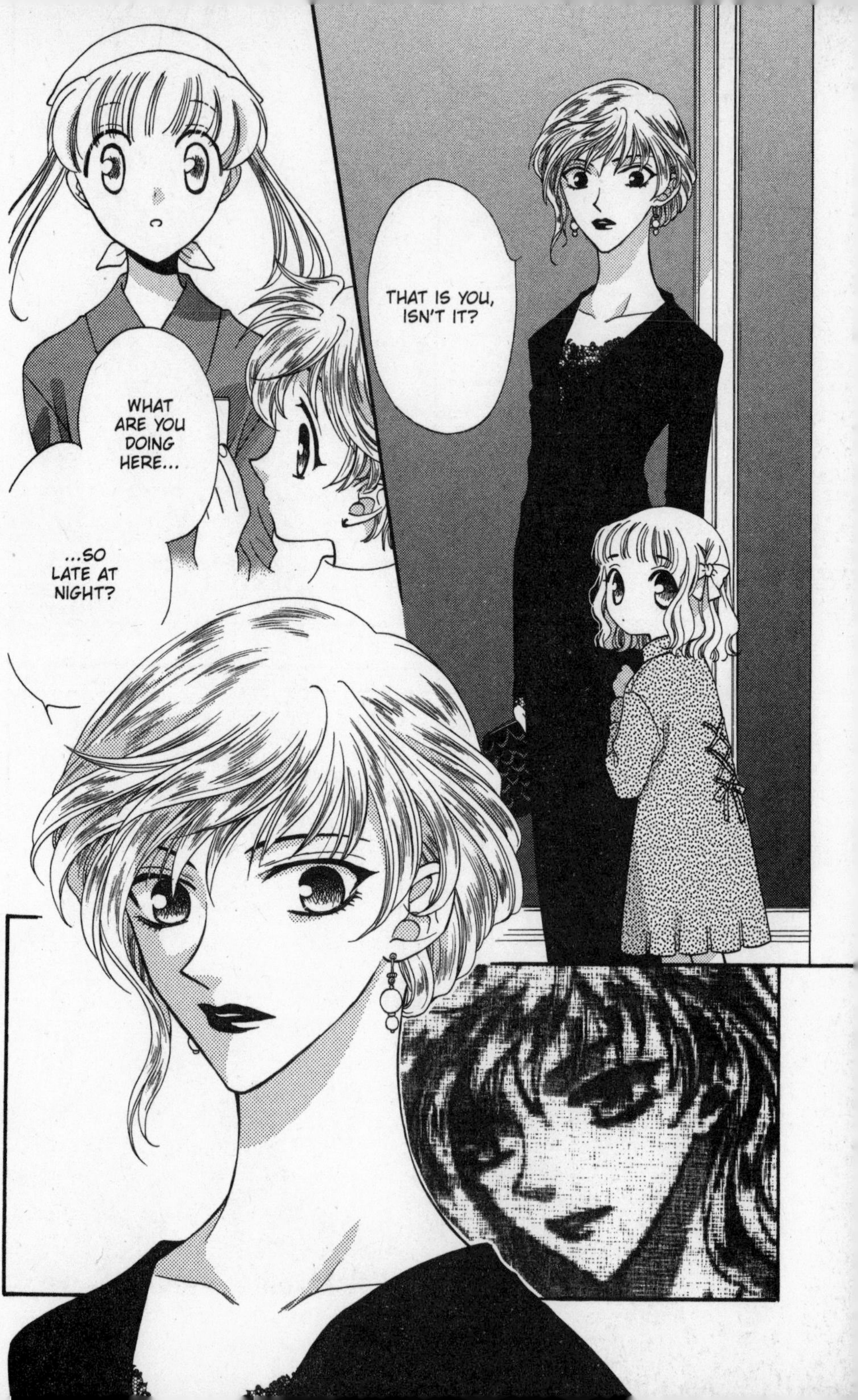
THAT IS YOU, ISN'T IT?
WHAT ARE YOU DOING HERE...
...SO LATE AT NIGHT?

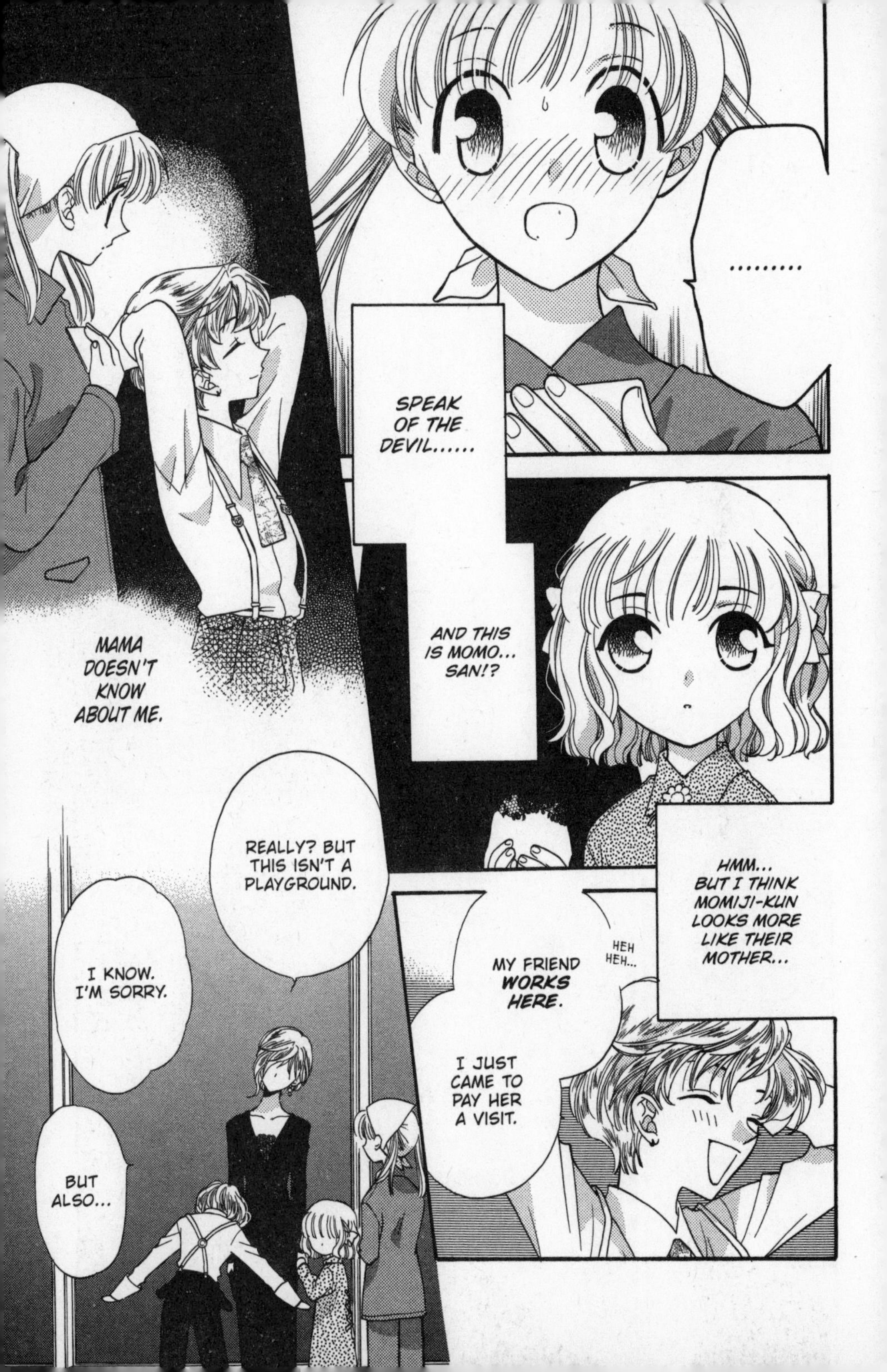
....
SPEAK OF THE DEVIL......
AND THIS IS MOMO... SAN!?
HMM... BUT I THINK MOMIJI-KUN LOOKS MORE LIKE THEIR MOTHER...
HEH HEH...
MY FRIEND **WORKS HERE**.
I JUST CAME TO PAY HER A VISIT.
MAMA DOESN'T KNOW ABOUT ME.
REALLY? BUT THIS ISN'T A PLAYGROUND.
I KNOW. I'M SORRY.
BUT ALSO...

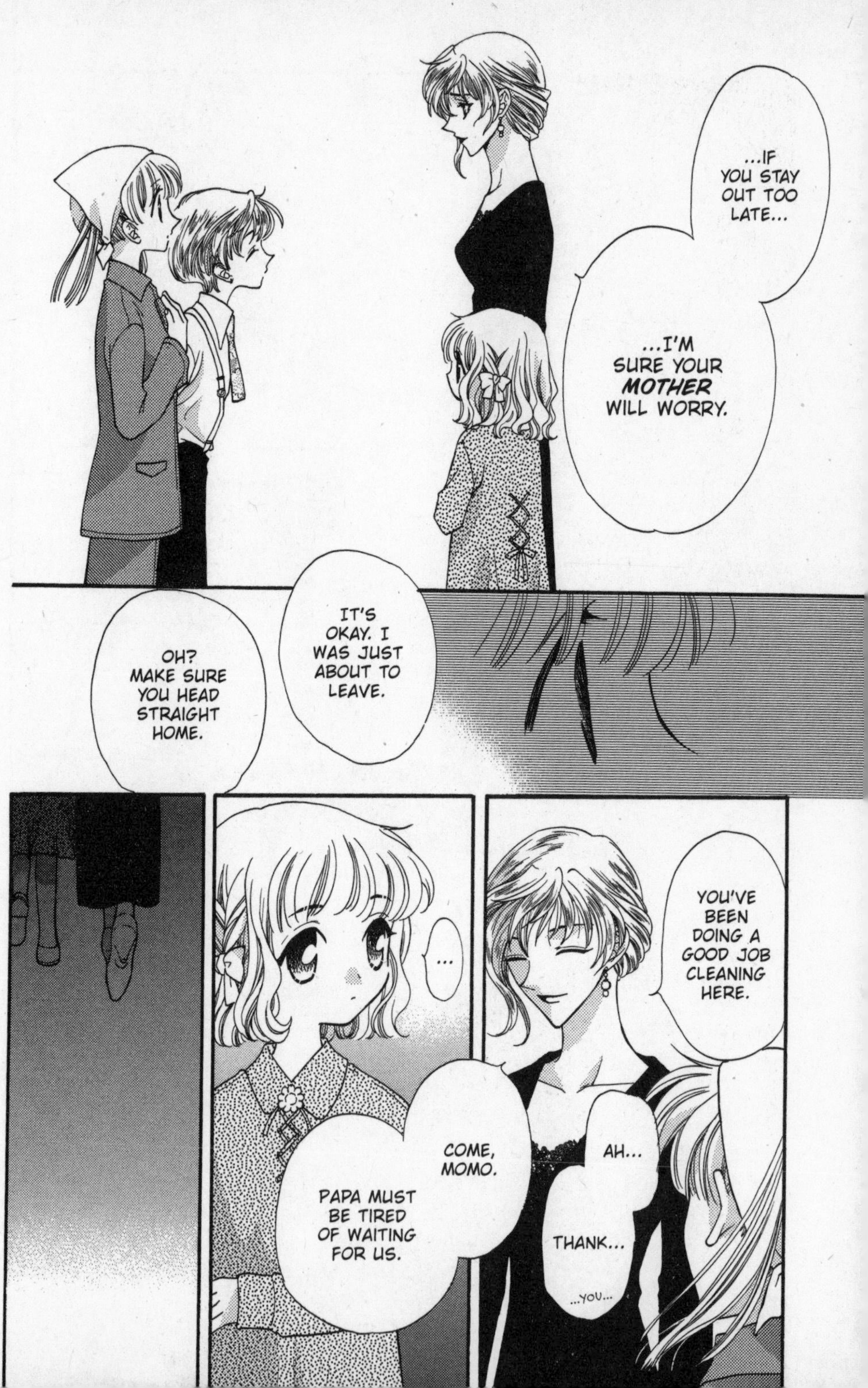
...IF YOU STAY OUT TOO LATE...
...I'M SURE YOUR *MOTHER* WILL WORRY.
IT'S OKAY. I WAS JUST ABOUT TO LEAVE.
OH? MAKE SURE YOU HEAD STRAIGHT HOME.
YOU'VE BEEN DOING A GOOD JOB CLEANING HERE.
AH...
THANK...
...YOU...
...
COME, MOMO.
PAPA MUST BE TIRED OF WAITING FOR US.

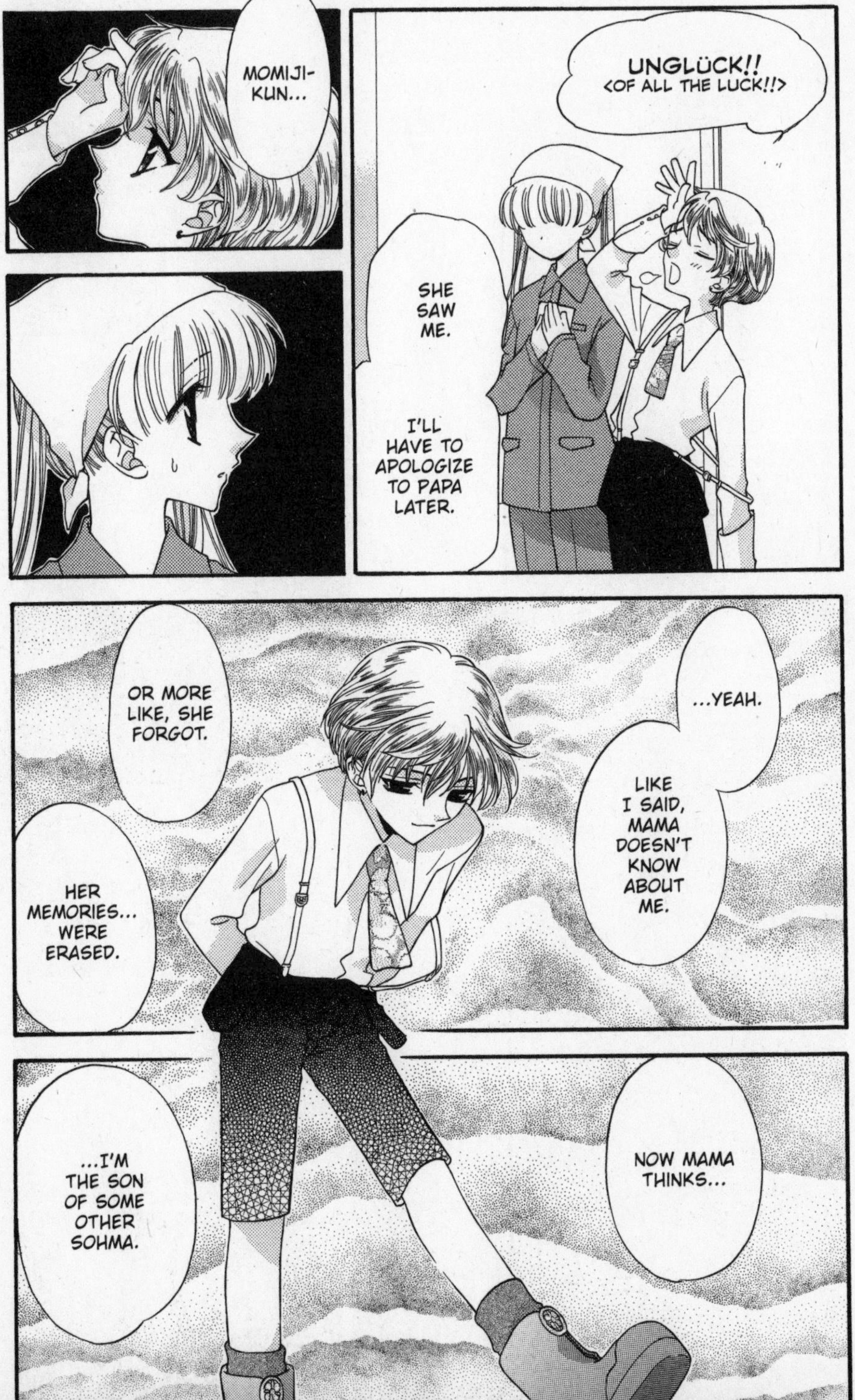
UNGLÜCK!!
<OF ALL THE LUCK!!>
SHE SAW ME.
I'LL HAVE TO APOLOGIZE TO PAPA LATER.
MOMIJI-KUN...
...YEAH.
LIKE I SAID, MAMA DOESN'T KNOW ABOUT ME.
OR MORE LIKE, SHE FORGOT.
HER MEMORIES... WERE ERASED.
NOW MAMA THINKS...
...I'M THE SON OF SOME OTHER SOHMA.

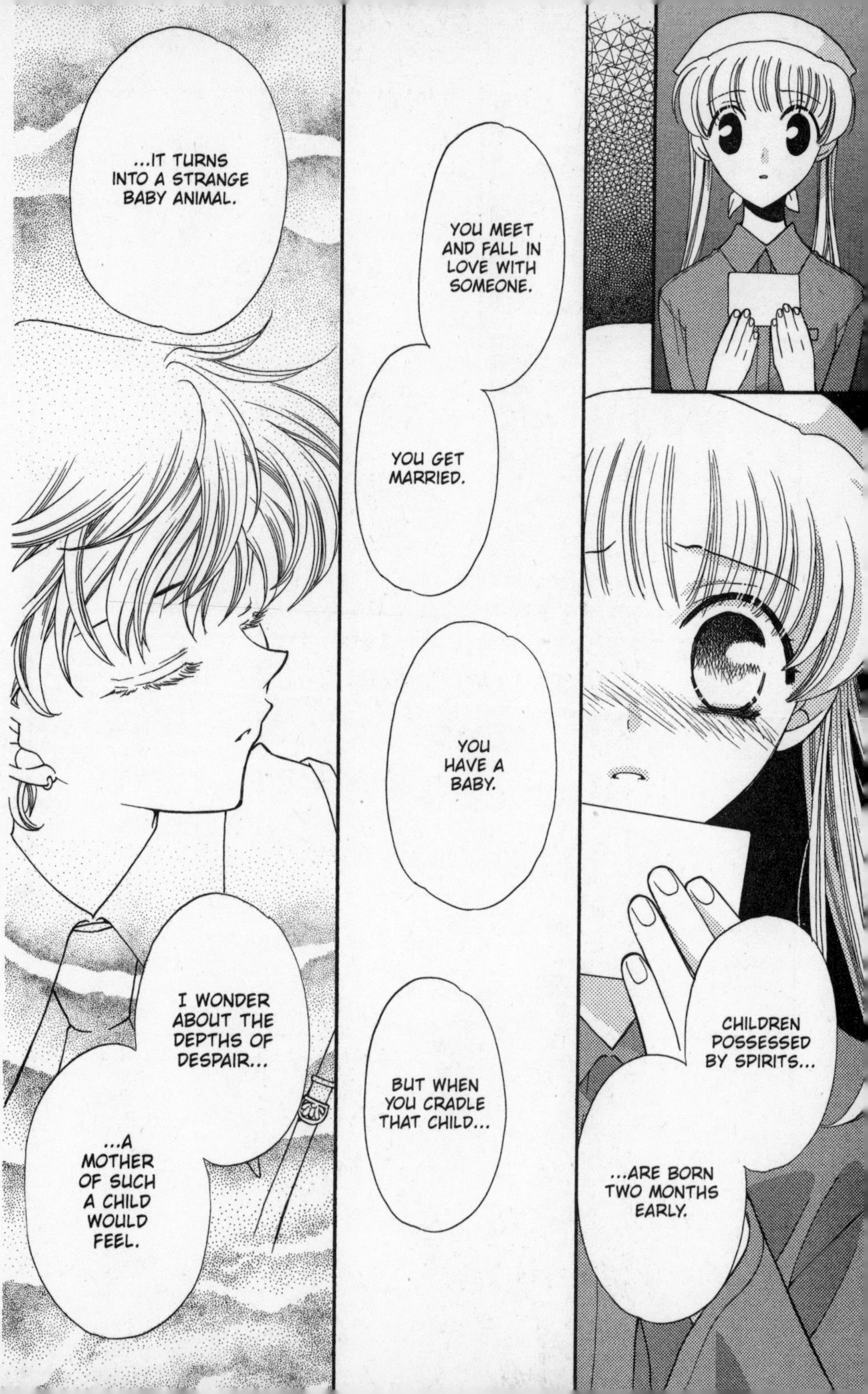
CHILDREN POSSESSED BY SPIRITS...
...ARE BORN TWO MONTHS EARLY.
YOU MEET AND FALL IN LOVE WITH SOMEONE.
YOU GET MARRIED.
YOU HAVE A BABY.
BUT WHEN YOU CRADLE THAT CHILD...
...IT TURNS INTO A STRANGE BABY ANIMAL.
I WONDER ABOUT THE DEPTHS OF DESPAIR...
...A MOTHER OF SUCH A CHILD WOULD FEEL.

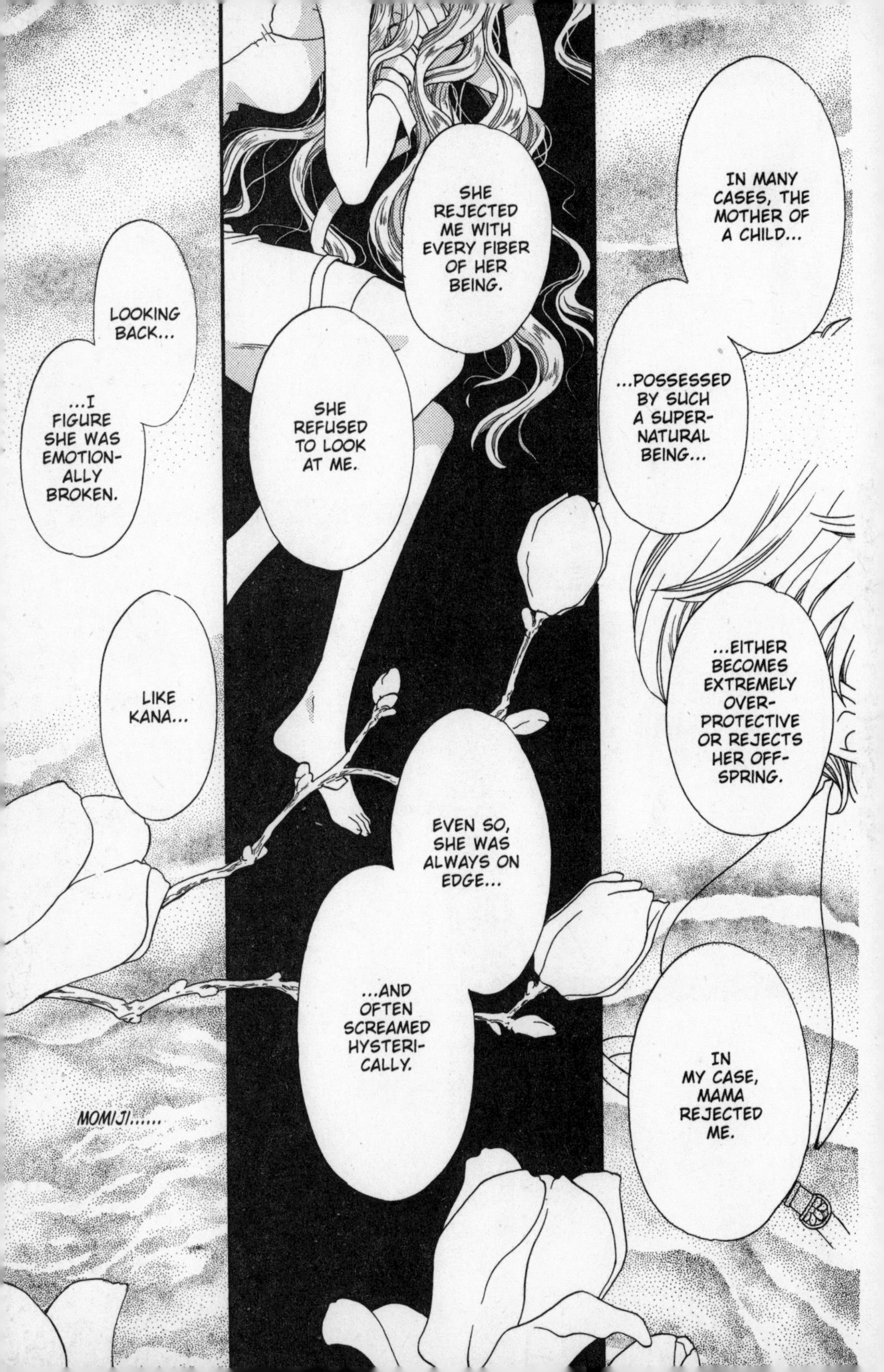
IN MANY CASES, THE MOTHER OF A CHILD...
...POSSESSED BY SUCH A SUPERNATURAL BEING...
...EITHER BECOMES EXTREMELY OVERPROTECTIVE OR REJECTS HER OFFSPRING.
IN MY CASE, MAMA REJECTED ME.
SHE REJECTED ME WITH EVERY FIBER OF HER BEING.
SHE REFUSED TO LOOK AT ME.
EVEN SO, SHE WAS ALWAYS ON EDGE...
...AND OFTEN SCREAMED HYSTERICALLY.
LOOKING BACK...
...I FIGURE SHE WAS EMOTIONALLY BROKEN.
LIKE KANA...
MOMIJI......

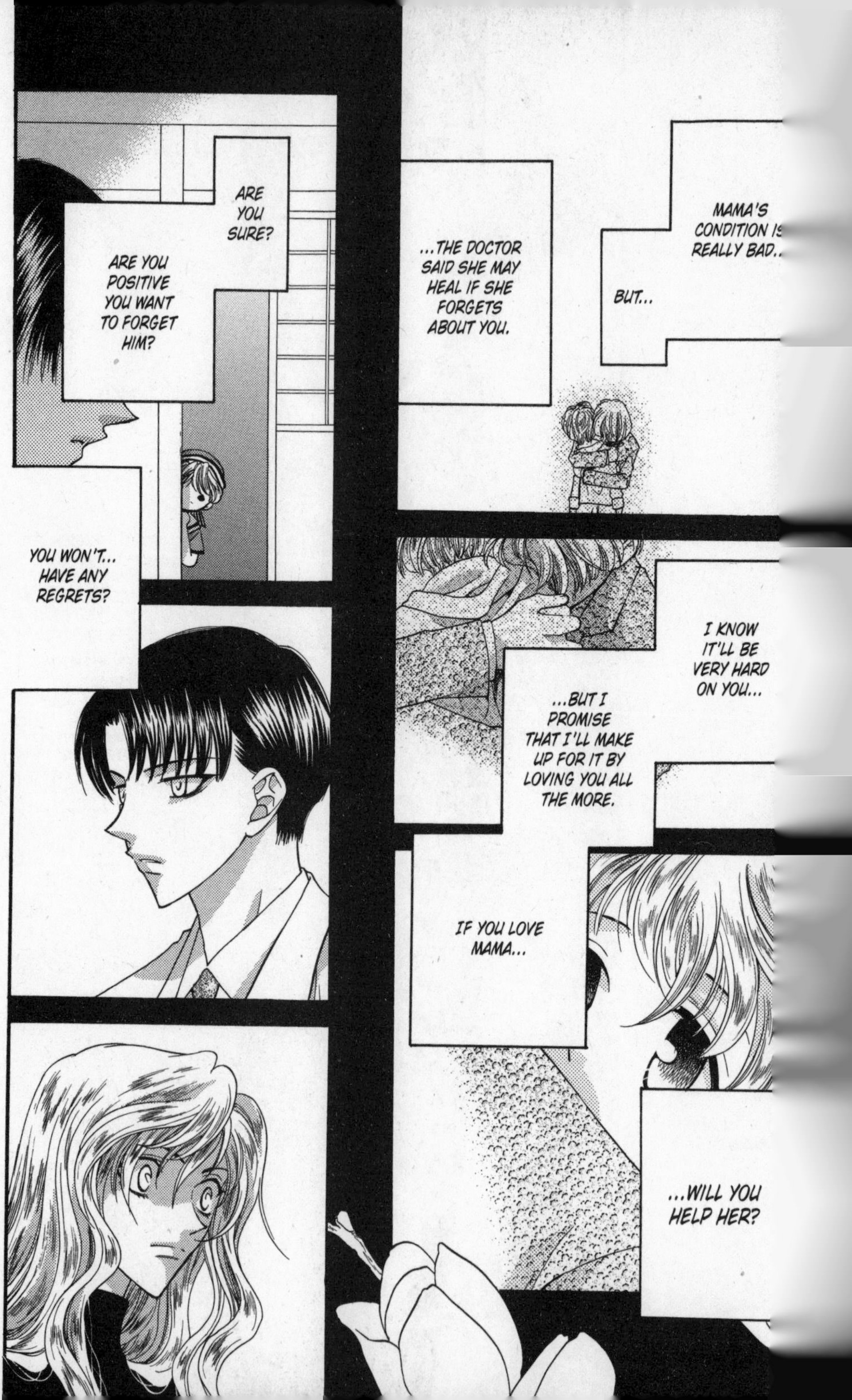
MAMA'S CONDITION IS REALLY BAD...
BUT...
...THE DOCTOR SAID SHE MAY HEAL IF SHE FORGETS ABOUT YOU.
I KNOW IT'LL BE VERY HARD ON YOU...
...BUT I PROMISE THAT I'LL MAKE UP FOR IT BY LOVING YOU ALL THE MORE.
IF YOU LOVE MAMA...
...WILL YOU HELP HER?
ARE YOU SURE?
ARE YOU POSITIVE YOU WANT TO FORGET HIM?
YOU WON'T... HAVE ANY REGRETS?

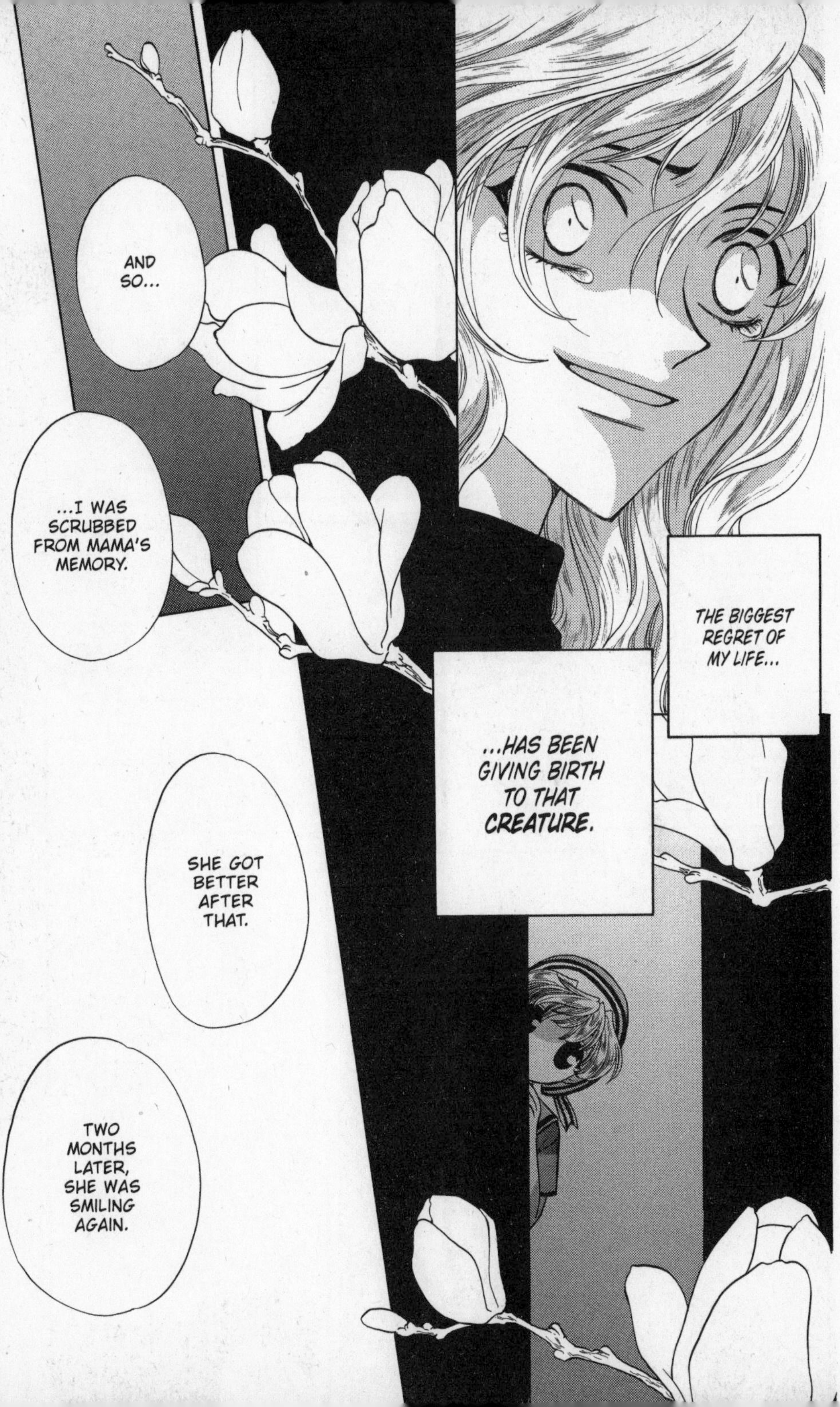
THE BIGGEST REGRET OF MY LIFE...
...HAS BEEN GIVING BIRTH TO THAT CREATURE.
AND SO...
...I WAS SCRUBBED FROM MAMA'S MEMORY.
SHE GOT BETTER AFTER THAT.
TWO MONTHS LATER, SHE WAS SMILING AGAIN.

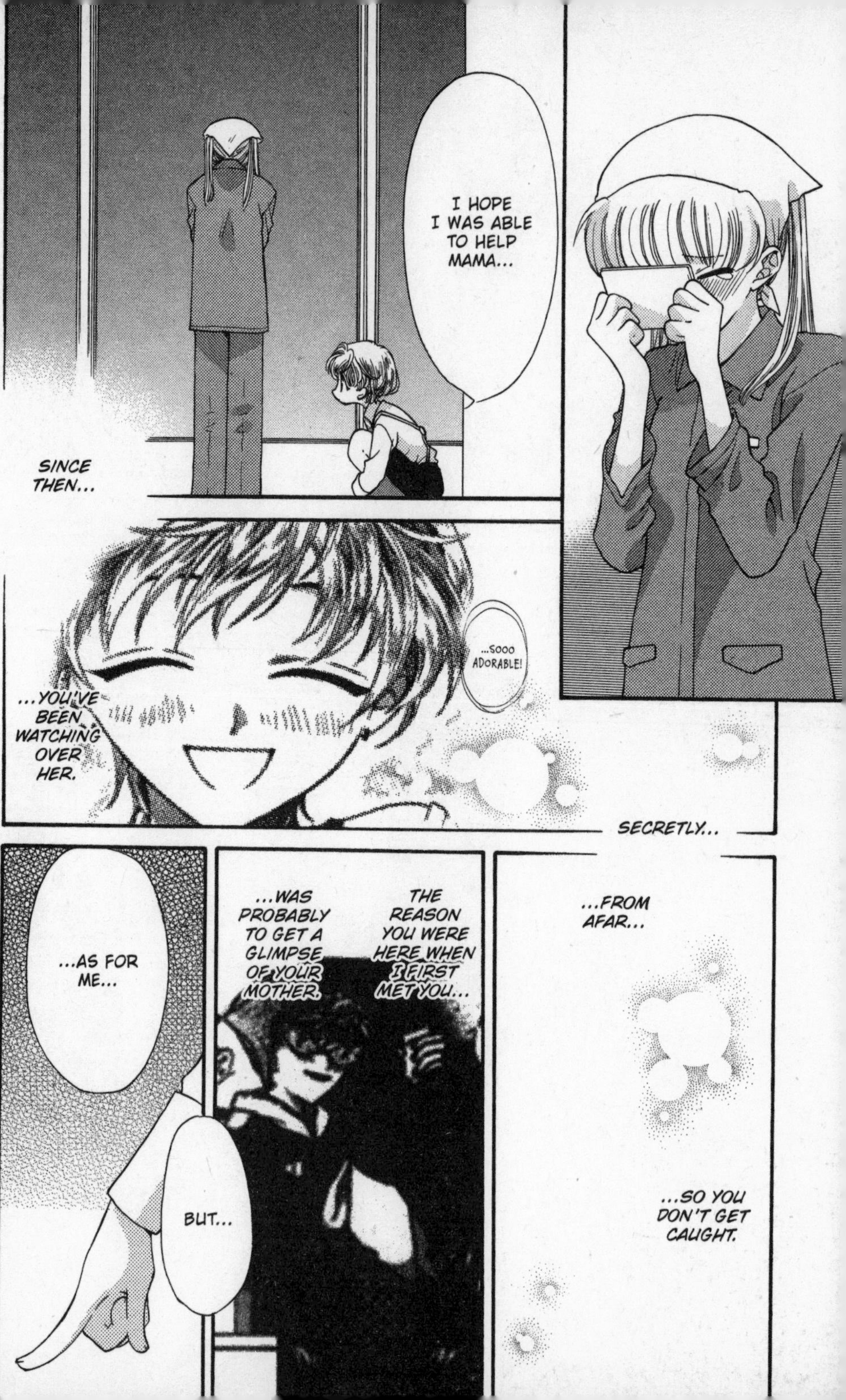
I HOPE I WAS ABLE TO HELP MAMA...
SINCE THEN...
...SOOO ADORABLE!
...YOU'VE BEEN WATCHING OVER HER.
SECRETLY...
...FROM AFAR...
...SO YOU DON'T GET CAUGHT.
THE REASON YOU WERE HERE WHEN I FIRST MET YOU...
...WAS PROBABLY TO GET A GLIMPSE OF YOUR MOTHER.
...AS FOR ME...
BUT...

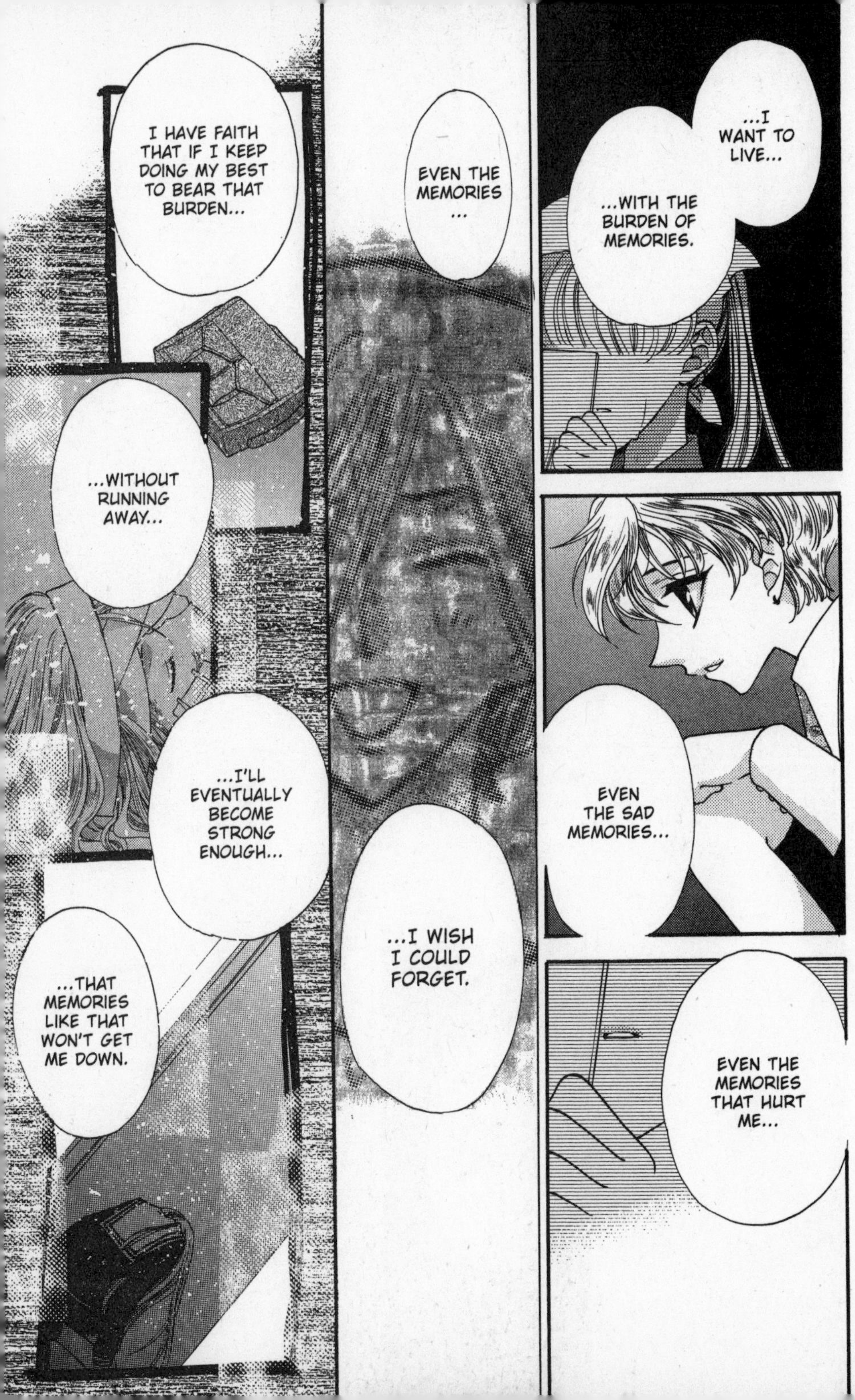
...I WANT TO LIVE...
...WITH THE BURDEN OF MEMORIES.
EVEN THE SAD MEMORIES...
EVEN THE MEMORIES THAT HURT ME...
EVEN THE MEMORIES ...
...I WISH I COULD FORGET.
I HAVE FAITH THAT IF I KEEP DOING MY BEST TO BEAR THAT BURDEN...
...WITHOUT RUNNING AWAY...
...I'LL EVENTUALLY BECOME STRONG ENOUGH...
...THAT MEMORIES LIKE THAT WON'T GET ME DOWN.

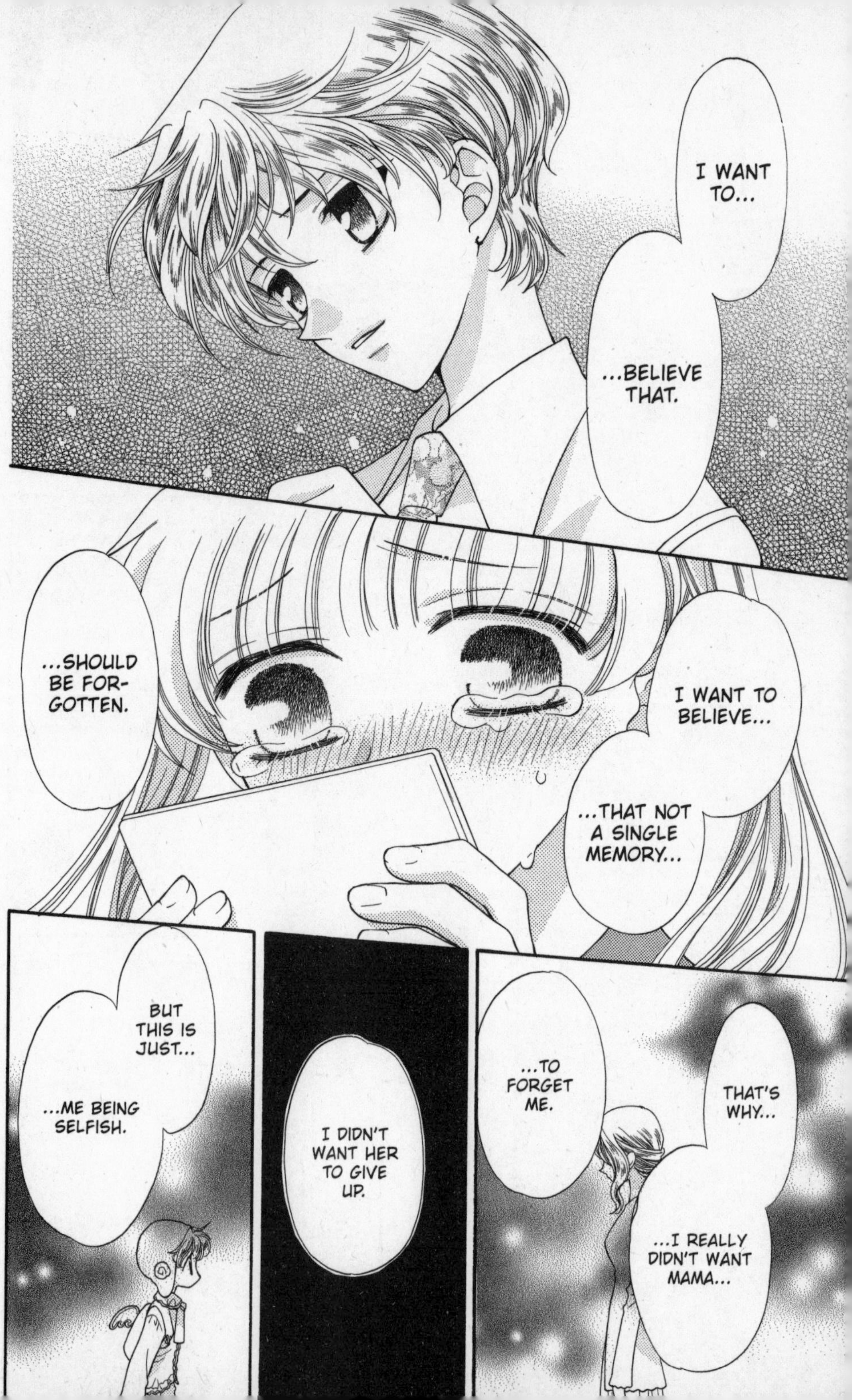
I WANT TO...
...BELIEVE THAT.
I WANT TO BELIEVE...
...THAT NOT A SINGLE MEMORY...
...SHOULD BE FORGOTTEN.
THAT'S WHY...
...I REALLY DIDN'T WANT MAMA...
...TO FORGET ME.
I DIDN'T WANT HER TO GIVE UP.
BUT THIS IS JUST...
...ME BEING SELFISH.

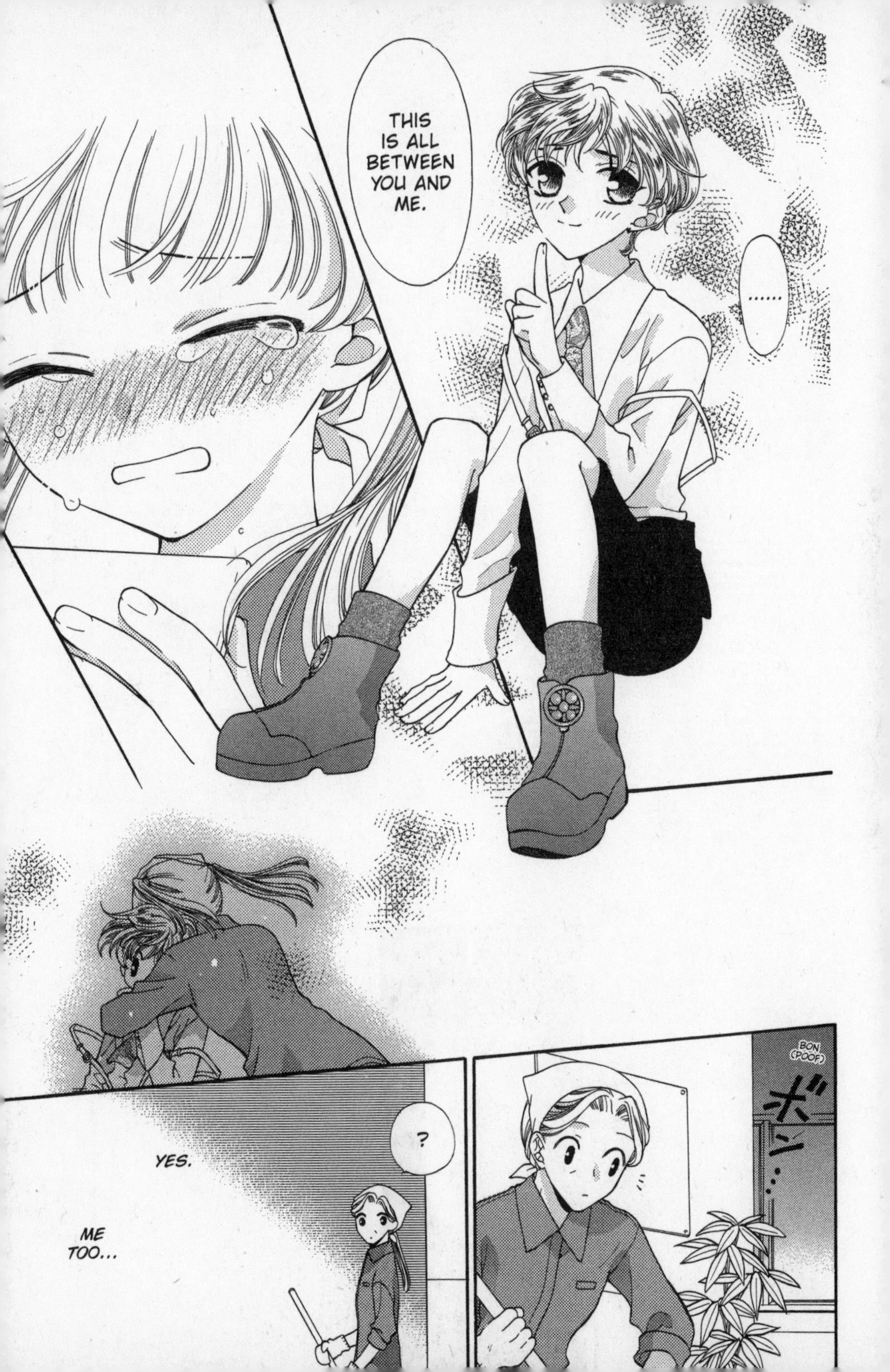

THIS IS ALL BETWEEN YOU AND ME.
......
BON (POOF)
ボン…
?
YES.
ME TOO...

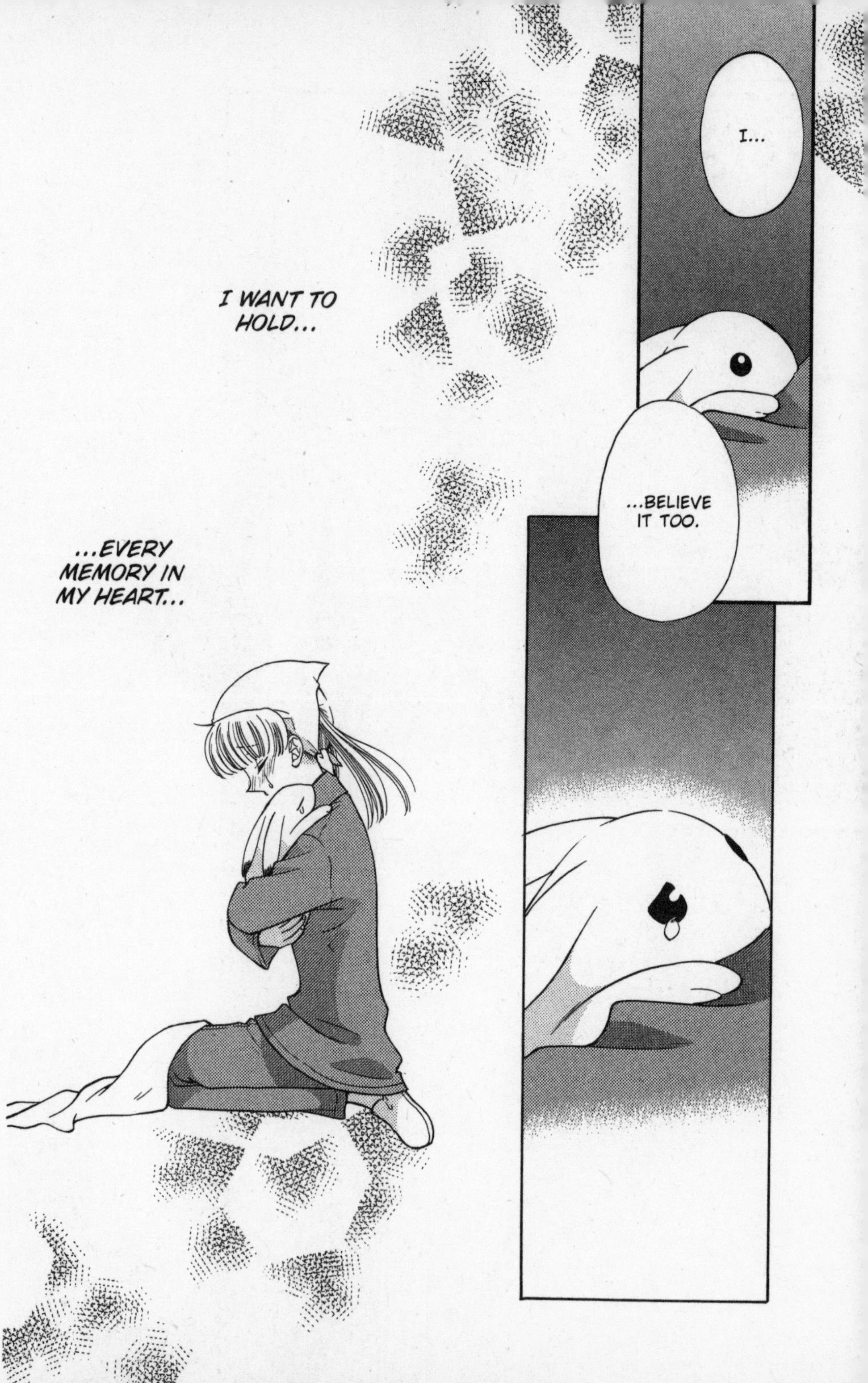
I...
...BELIEVE IT TOO.
I WANT TO HOLD...
...EVERY MEMORY IN MY HEART...

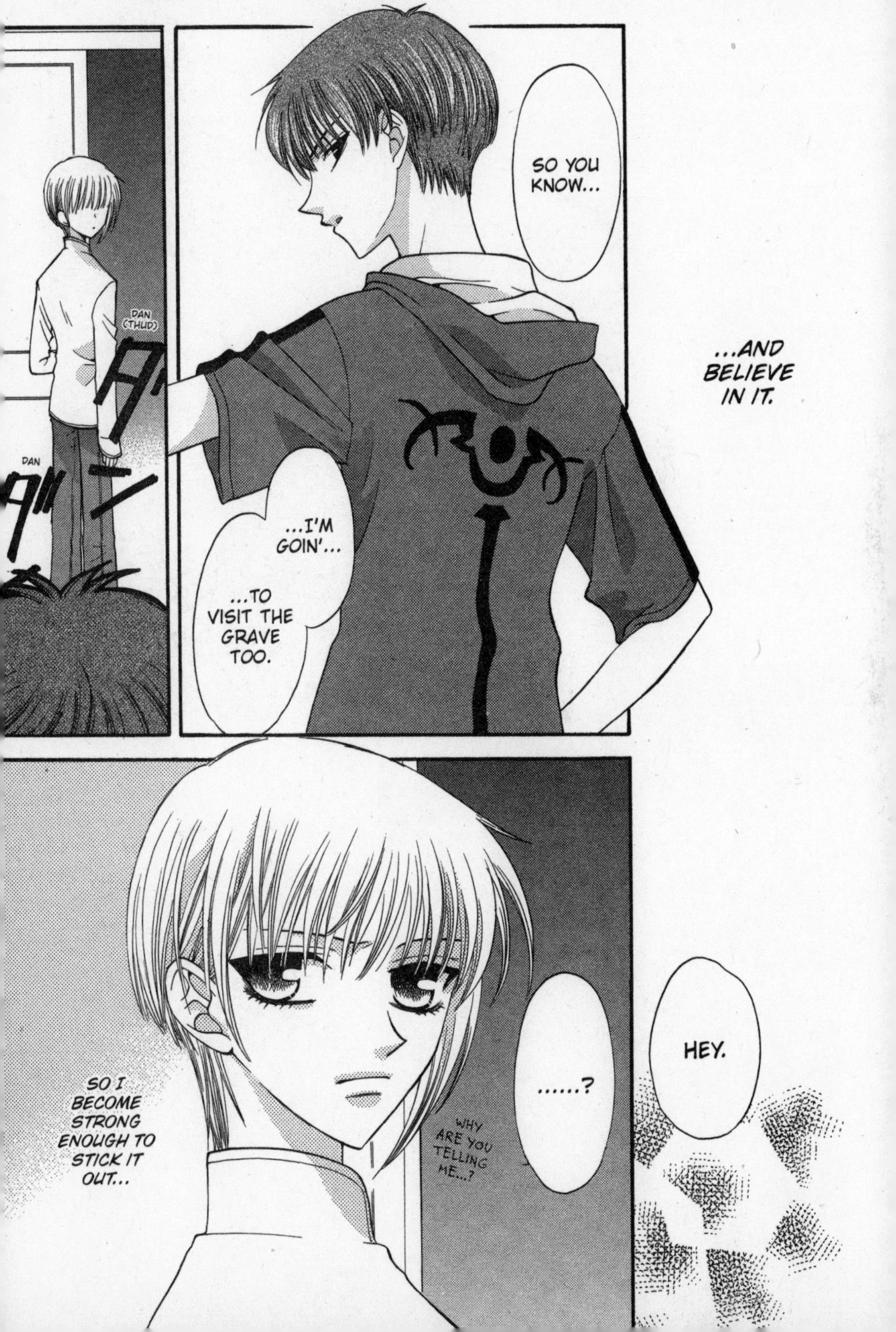
...AND BELIEVE IN IT.
SO YOU KNOW...
...I'M GOIN'...
...TO VISIT THE GRAVE TOO.
DAN (THUD)
DAN
HEY.
......?
WHY ARE YOU TELLING ME...?
SO I BECOME STRONG ENOUGH TO STICK IT OUT...

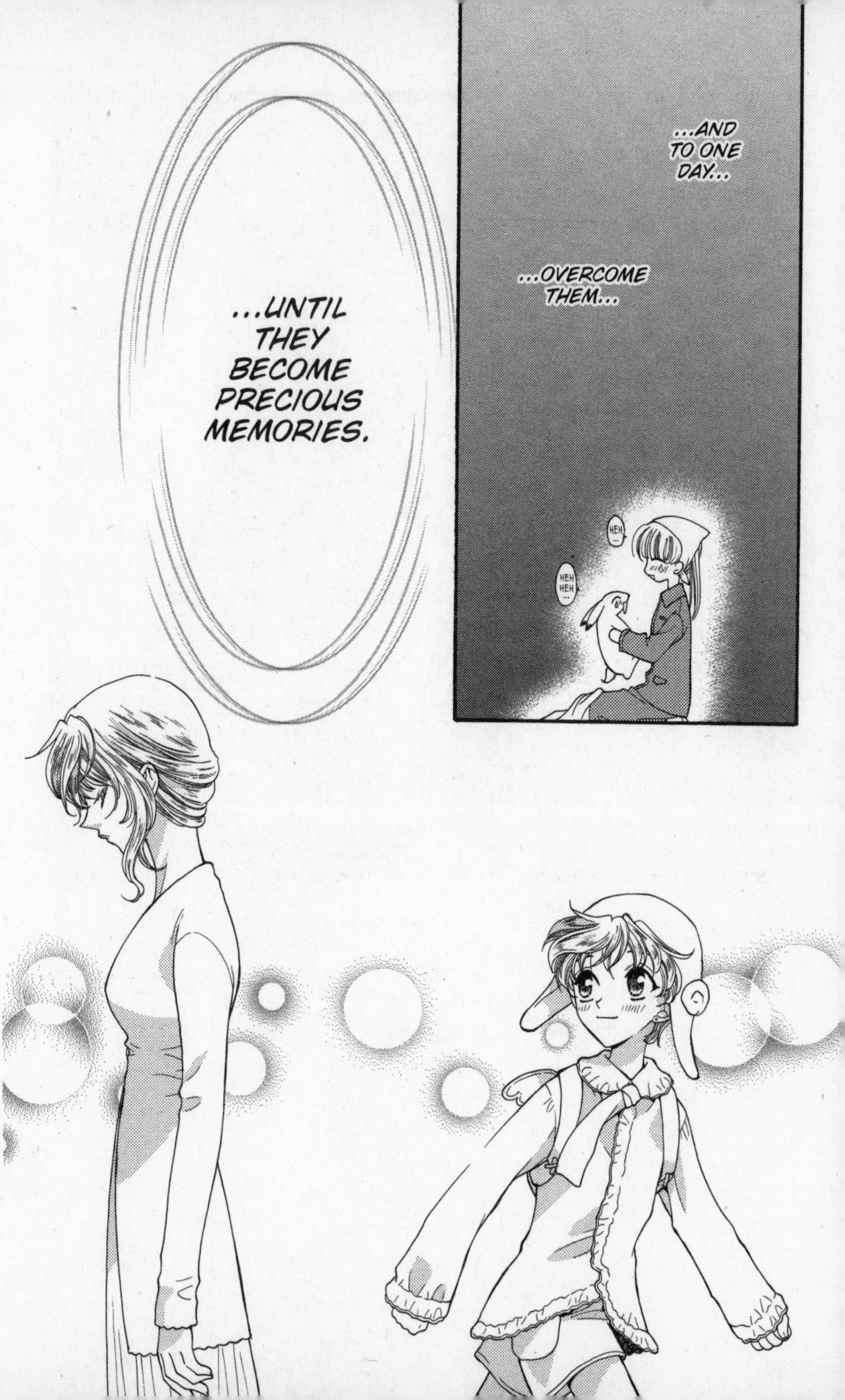
...AND TO ONE DAY...
...OVERCOME THEM...
HEH...
HEH HEH...
...UNTIL THEY BECOME PRECIOUS MEMORIES.

Chapter 24

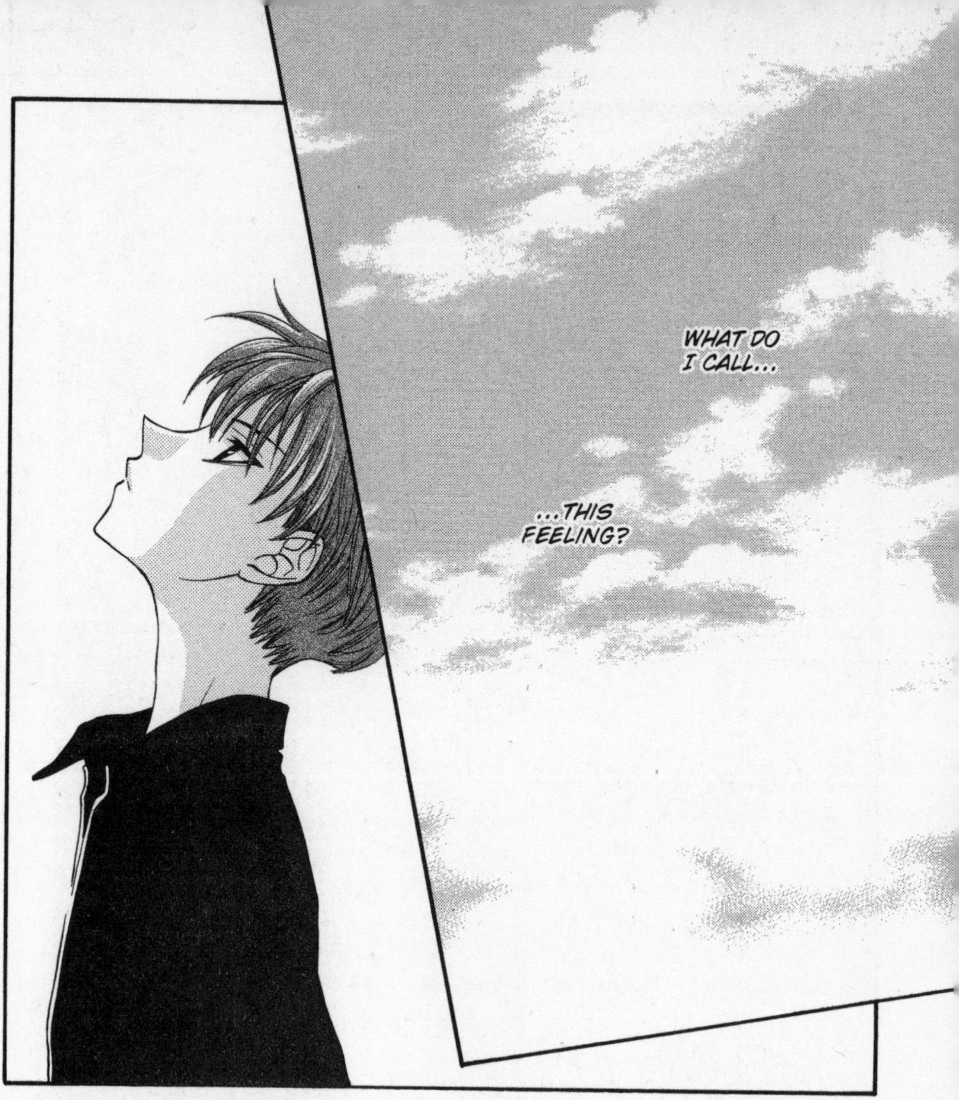
WHAT DO I CALL...
...THIS FEELING?

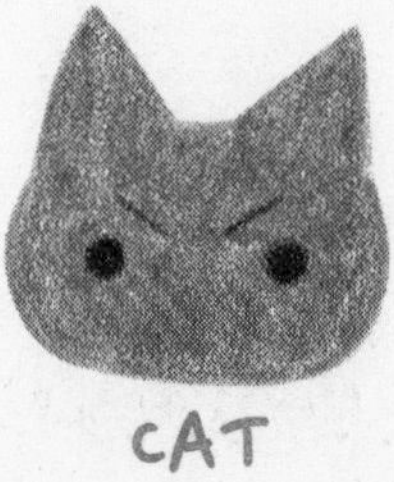

CAT

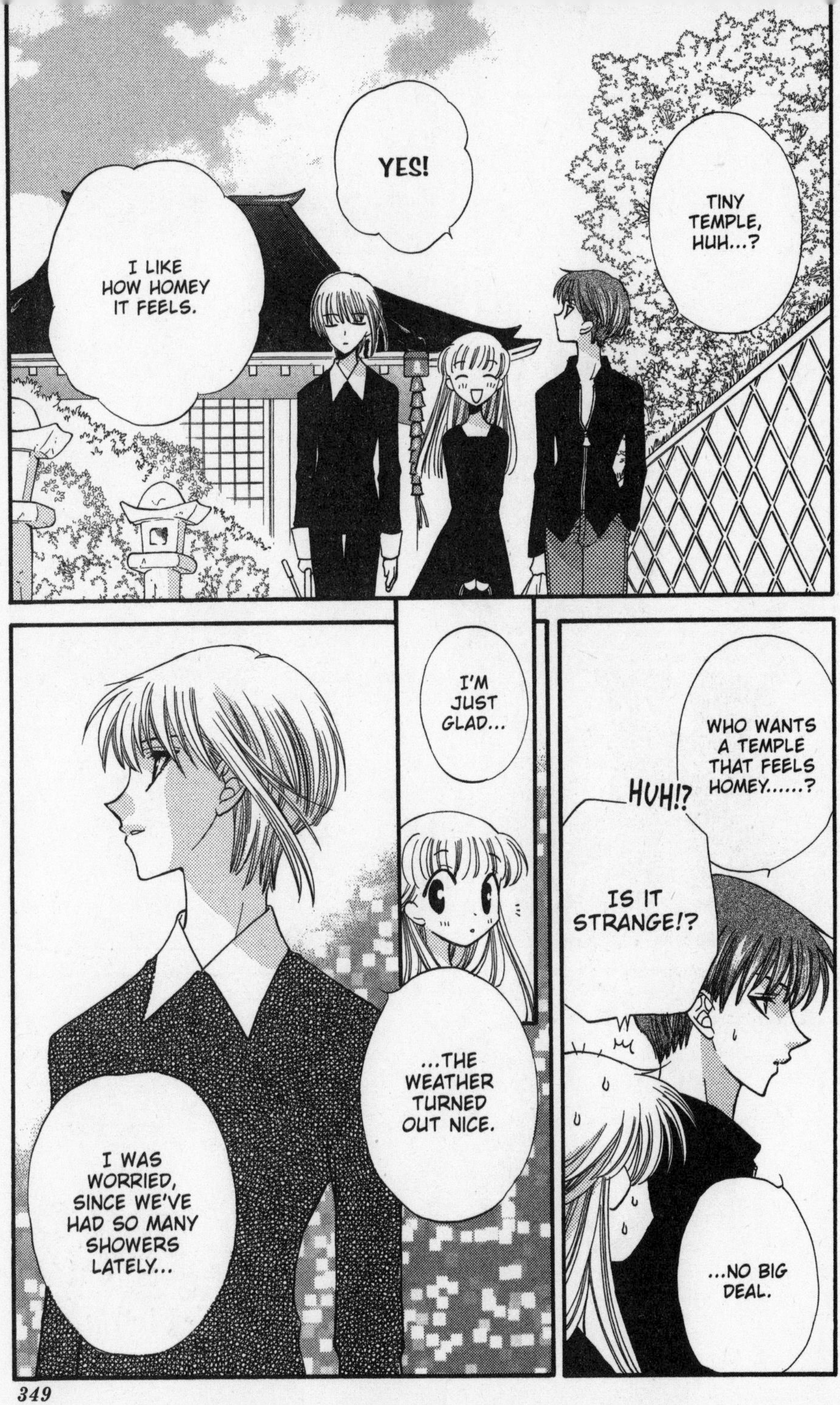
TINY TEMPLE, HUH...?
YES!
I LIKE HOW HOMEY IT FEELS.
WHO WANTS A TEMPLE THAT FEELS HOMEY......?
HUH!?
IS IT STRANGE!?
...NO BIG DEAL.
I'M JUST GLAD...
...THE WEATHER TURNED OUT NICE.
I WAS WORRIED, SINCE WE'VE HAD SO MANY SHOWERS LATELY...

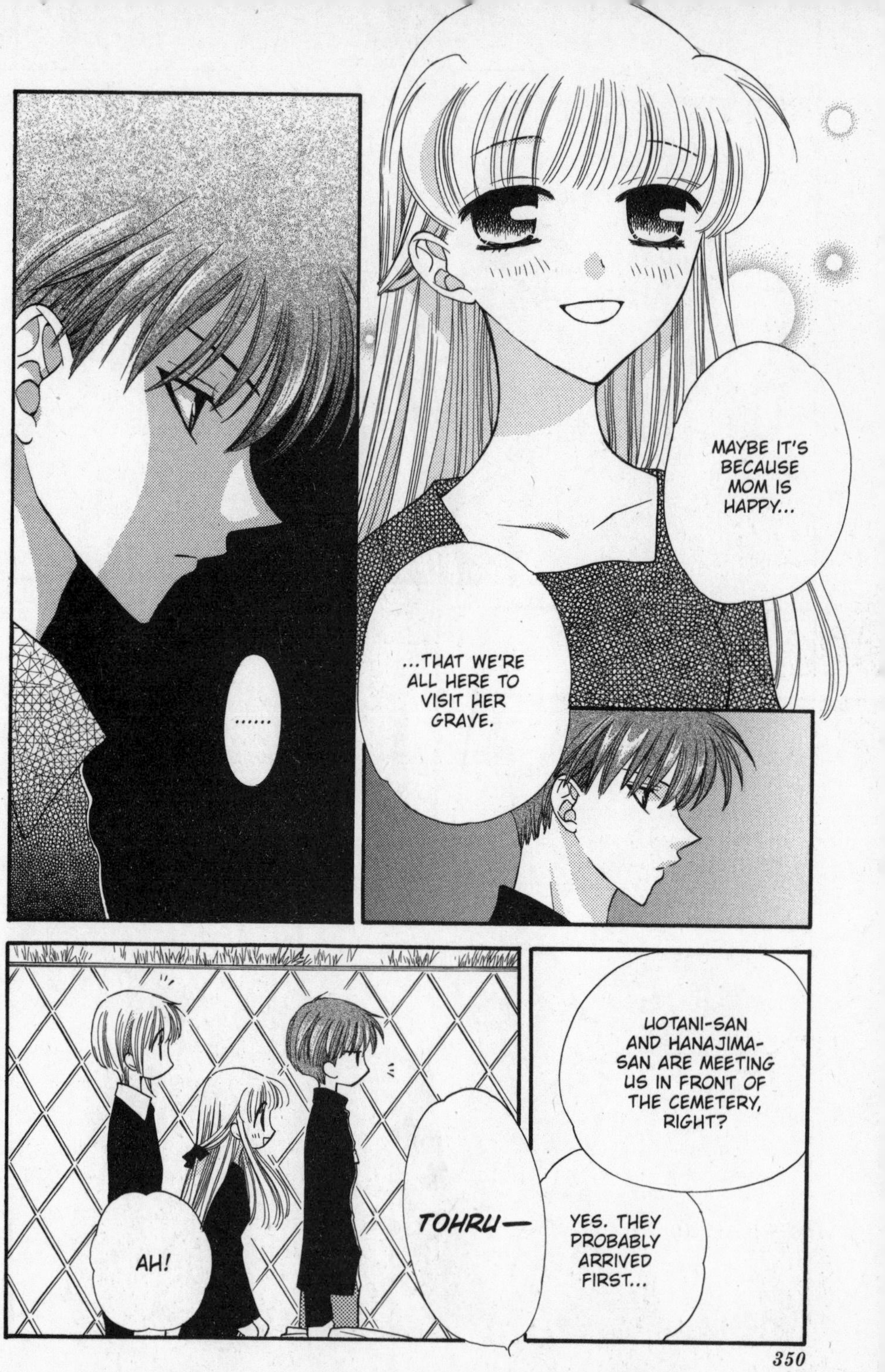
MAYBE IT'S BECAUSE MOM IS HAPPY...
...THAT WE'RE ALL HERE TO VISIT HER GRAVE.
......
UOTANI-SAN AND HANAJIMA-SAN ARE MEETING US IN FRONT OF THE CEMETERY, RIGHT?
YES. THEY PROBABLY ARRIVED FIRST...
TOHRU—
AH!

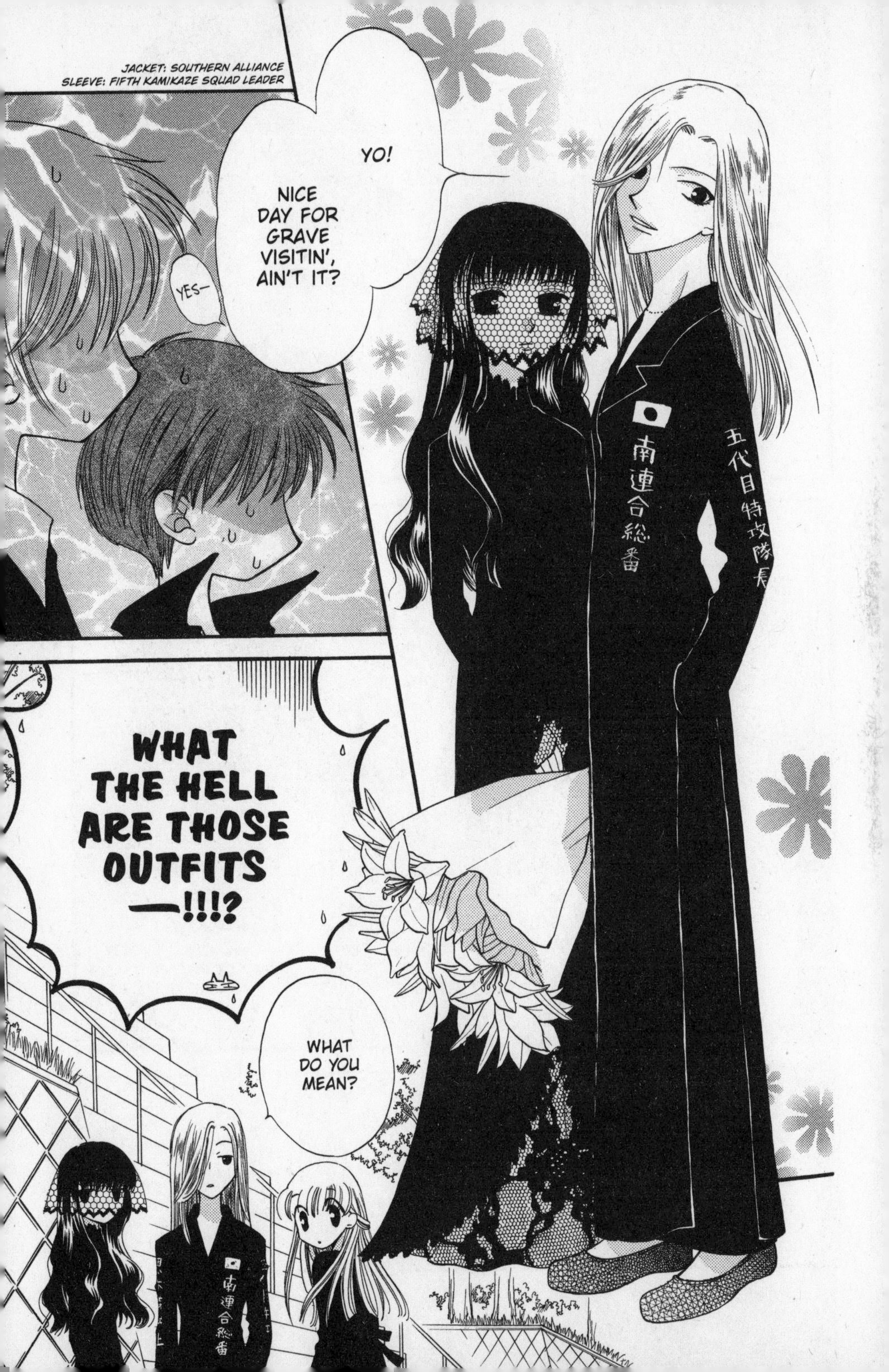
JACKET: SOUTHERN ALLIANCE
SLEEVE: FIFTH KAMIKAZE SQUAD LEADER
南連合総番
五代目特攻隊長
YO!
NICE DAY FOR GRAVE VISITIN', AIN'T IT?
YES—
WHAT THE HELL ARE THOSE OUTFITS—!!!?
WHAT DO YOU MEAN?

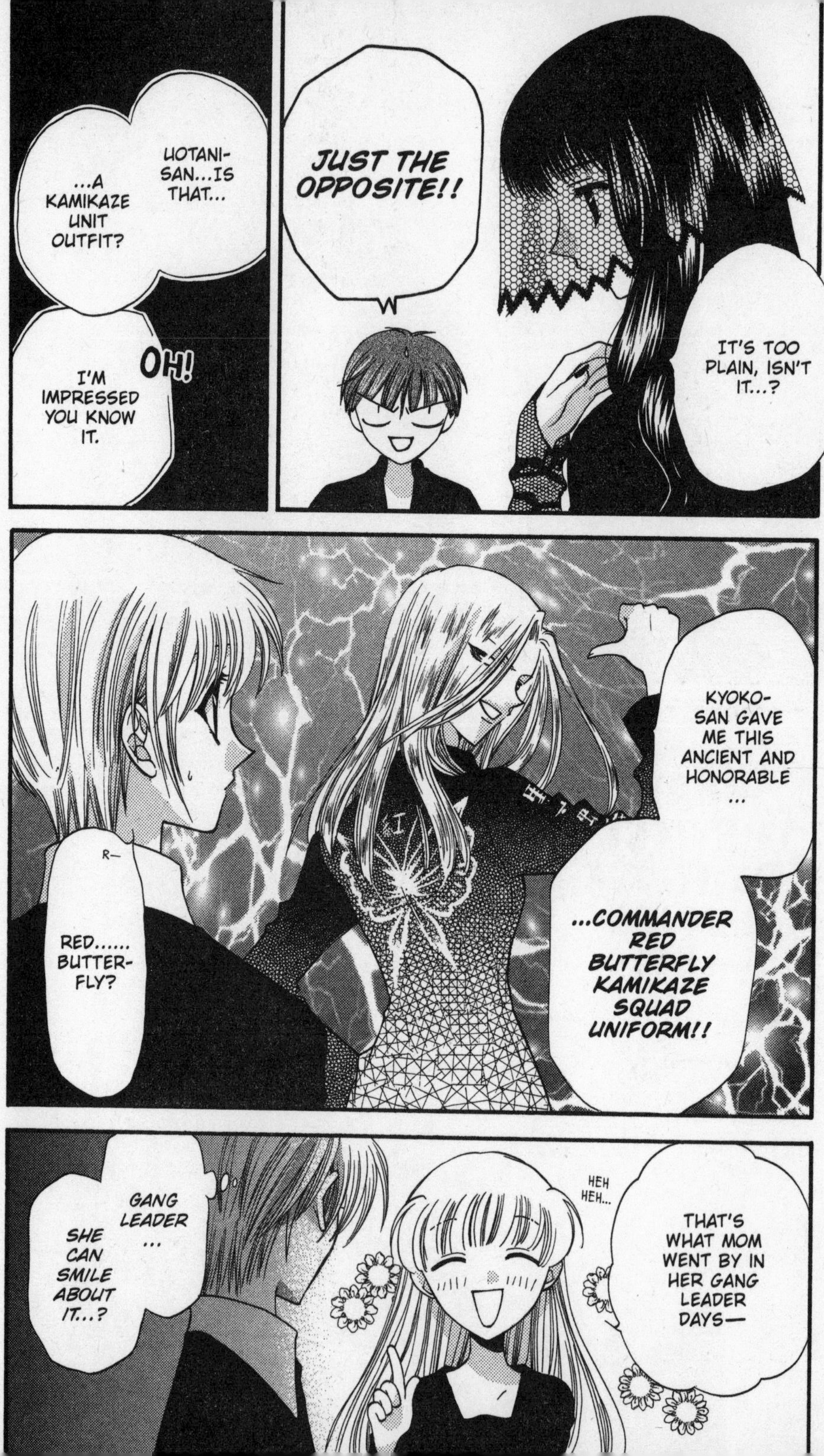
IT'S TOO PLAIN, ISN'T IT...?
JUST THE OPPOSITE!!
UOTANI-SAN...IS THAT...
...A KAMIKAZE UNIT OUTFIT?
OH!
I'M IMPRESSED YOU KNOW IT.
KYOKO-SAN GAVE ME THIS ANCIENT AND HONORABLE ...
...COMMANDER RED BUTTERFLY KAMIKAZE SQUAD UNIFORM!!
R—
RED...... BUTTER-FLY?
HEH HEH...
THAT'S WHAT MOM WENT BY IN HER GANG LEADER DAYS—
GANG LEADER ...
SHE CAN SMILE ABOUT IT...?

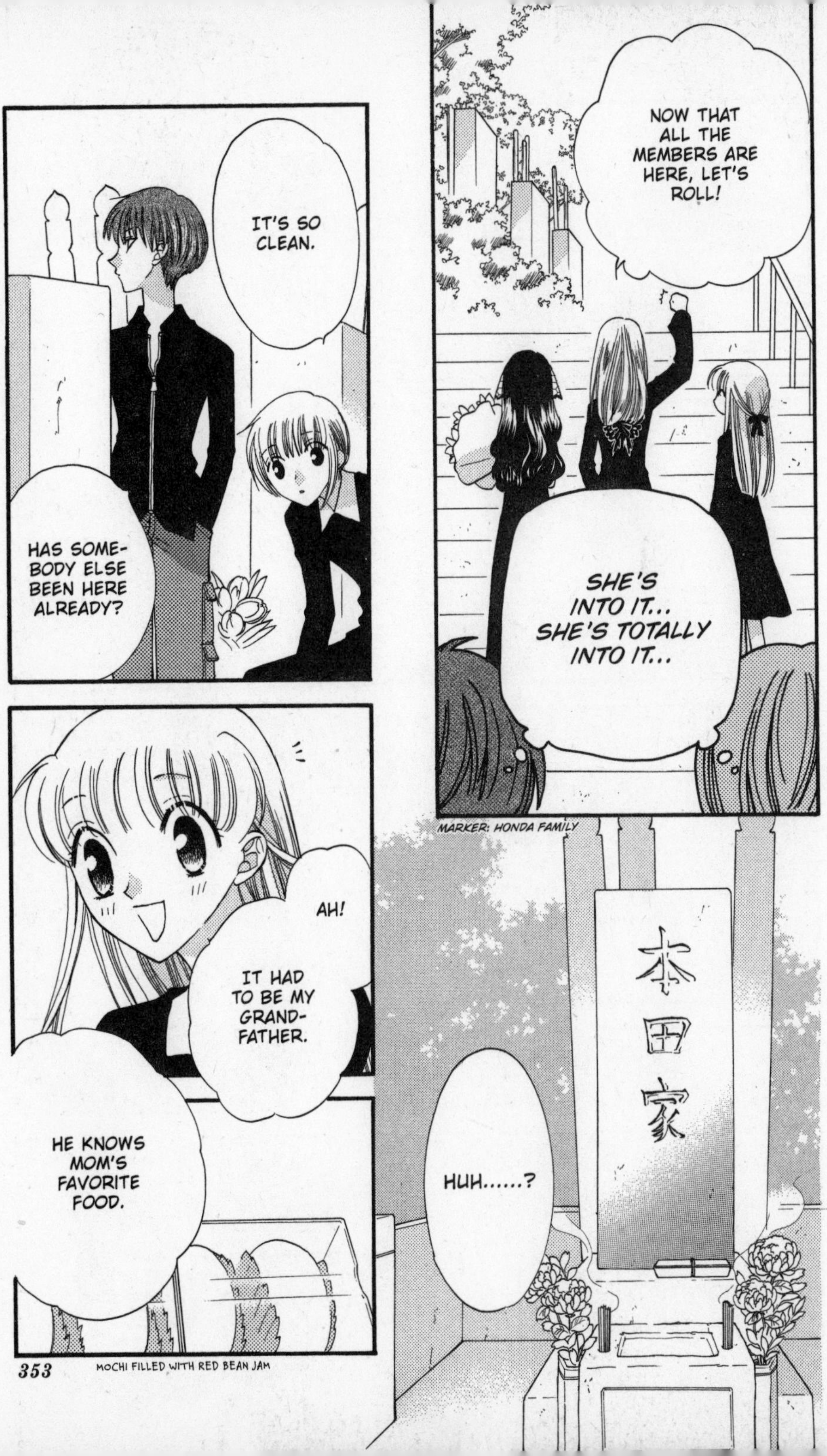
NOW THAT ALL THE MEMBERS ARE HERE, LET'S ROLL!
SHE'S INTO IT... SHE'S TOTALLY INTO IT...
IT'S SO CLEAN.
HAS SOMEBODY ELSE BEEN HERE ALREADY?
MARKER: HONDA FAMILY
本田家
HUH......?
AH!
IT HAD TO BE MY GRANDFATHER.
HE KNOWS MOM'S FAVORITE FOOD.
MOCHI FILLED WITH RED BEAN JAM

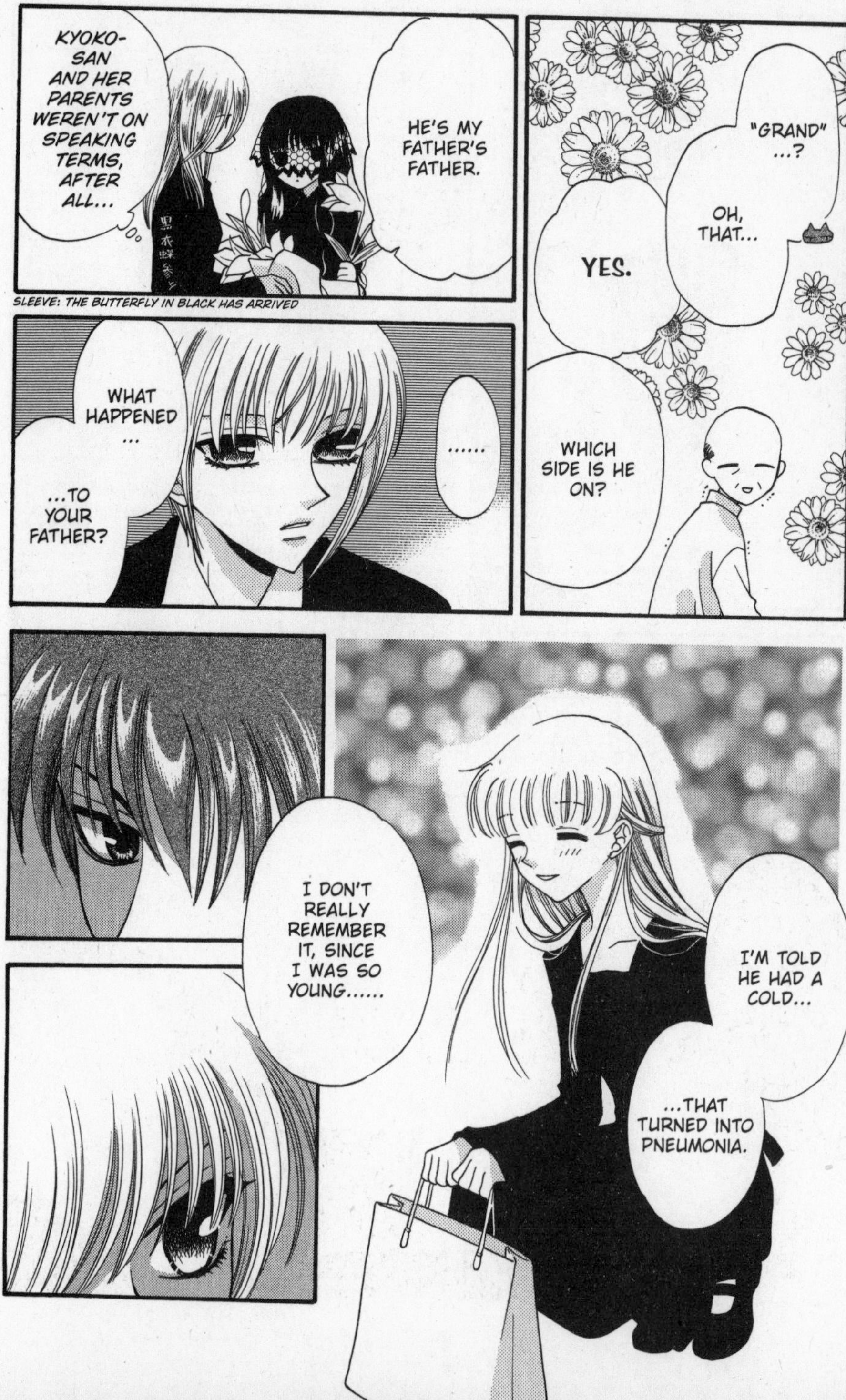
"GRAND" ...?
OH, THAT...
YES.
WHICH SIDE IS HE ON?
HE'S MY FATHER'S FATHER.
KYOKO-SAN AND HER PARENTS WEREN'T ON SPEAKING TERMS, AFTER ALL...
黒衣蝶参上
SLEEVE: THE BUTTERFLY IN BLACK HAS ARRIVED
......
WHAT HAPPENED ...
...TO YOUR FATHER?
I'M TOLD HE HAD A COLD...
...THAT TURNED INTO PNEUMONIA.
I DON'T REALLY REMEMBER IT, SINCE I WAS SO YOUNG......

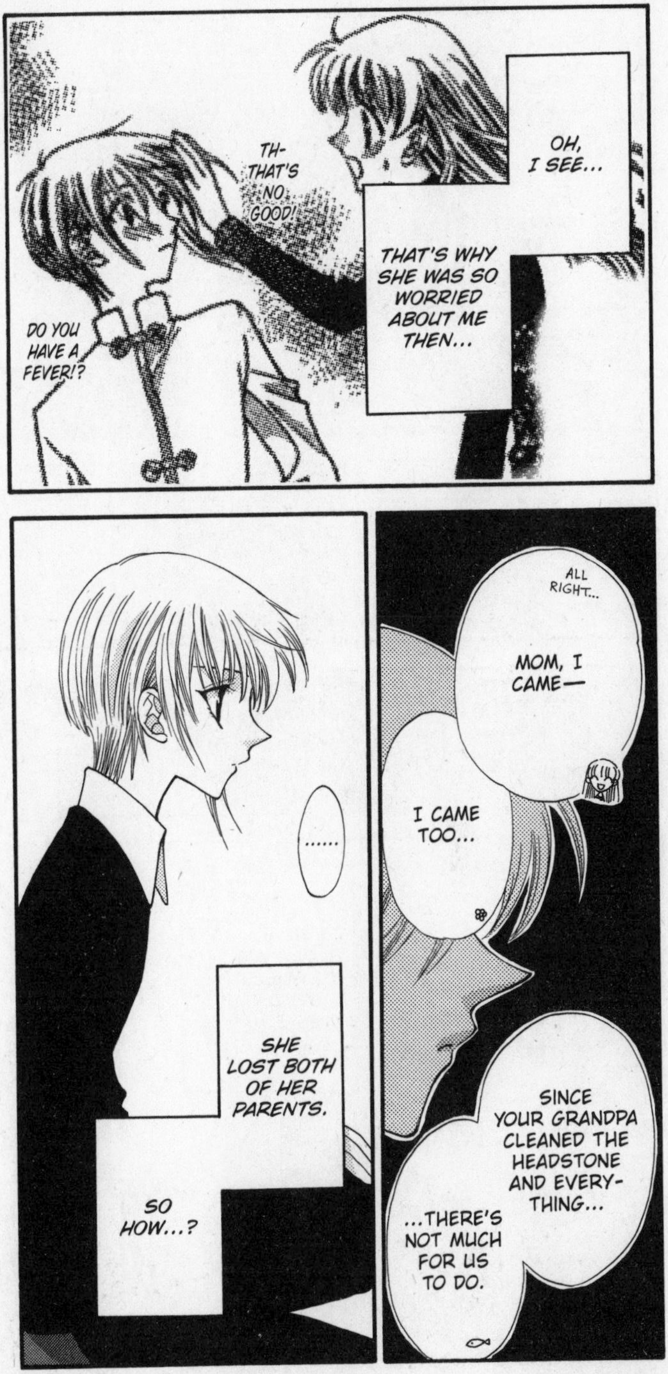
OH, I SEE...
THAT'S WHY SHE WAS SO WORRIED ABOUT ME THEN...
TH-THAT'S NO GOOD!
DO YOU HAVE A FEVER!?
ALL RIGHT...
MOM, I CAME—
I CAME TOO...
SINCE YOUR GRANDPA CLEANED THE HEADSTONE AND EVERY-THING...
...THERE'S NOT MUCH FOR US TO DO.
......
SHE LOST BOTH OF HER PARENTS.
SO HOW...?

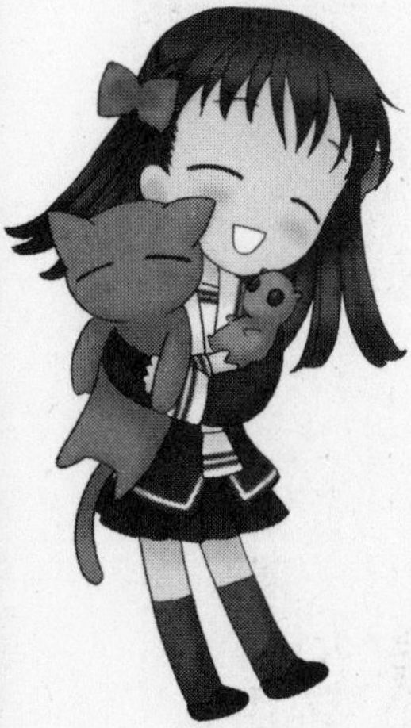

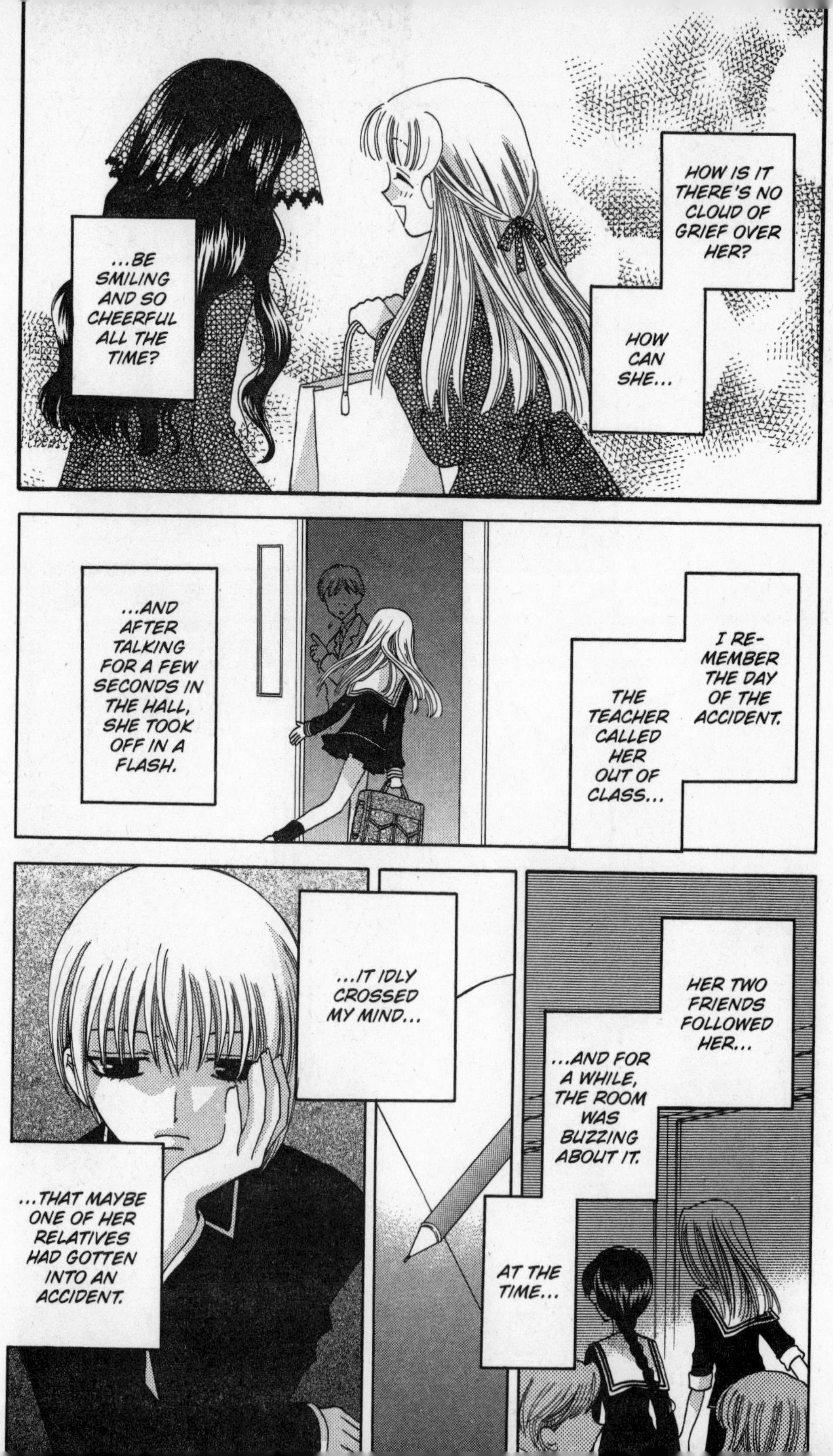
HOW IS IT THERE'S NO CLOUD OF GRIEF OVER HER?
HOW CAN SHE...
...BE SMILING AND SO CHEERFUL ALL THE TIME?
I RE-MEMBER THE DAY OF THE ACCIDENT.
THE TEACHER CALLED HER OUT OF CLASS...
...AND AFTER TALKING FOR A FEW SECONDS IN THE HALL, SHE TOOK OFF IN A FLASH.
HER TWO FRIENDS FOLLOWED HER...
...AND FOR A WHILE, THE ROOM WAS BUZZING ABOUT IT.
AT THE TIME...
...IT IDLY CROSSED MY MIND...
...THAT MAYBE ONE OF HER RELATIVES HAD GOTTEN INTO AN ACCIDENT.

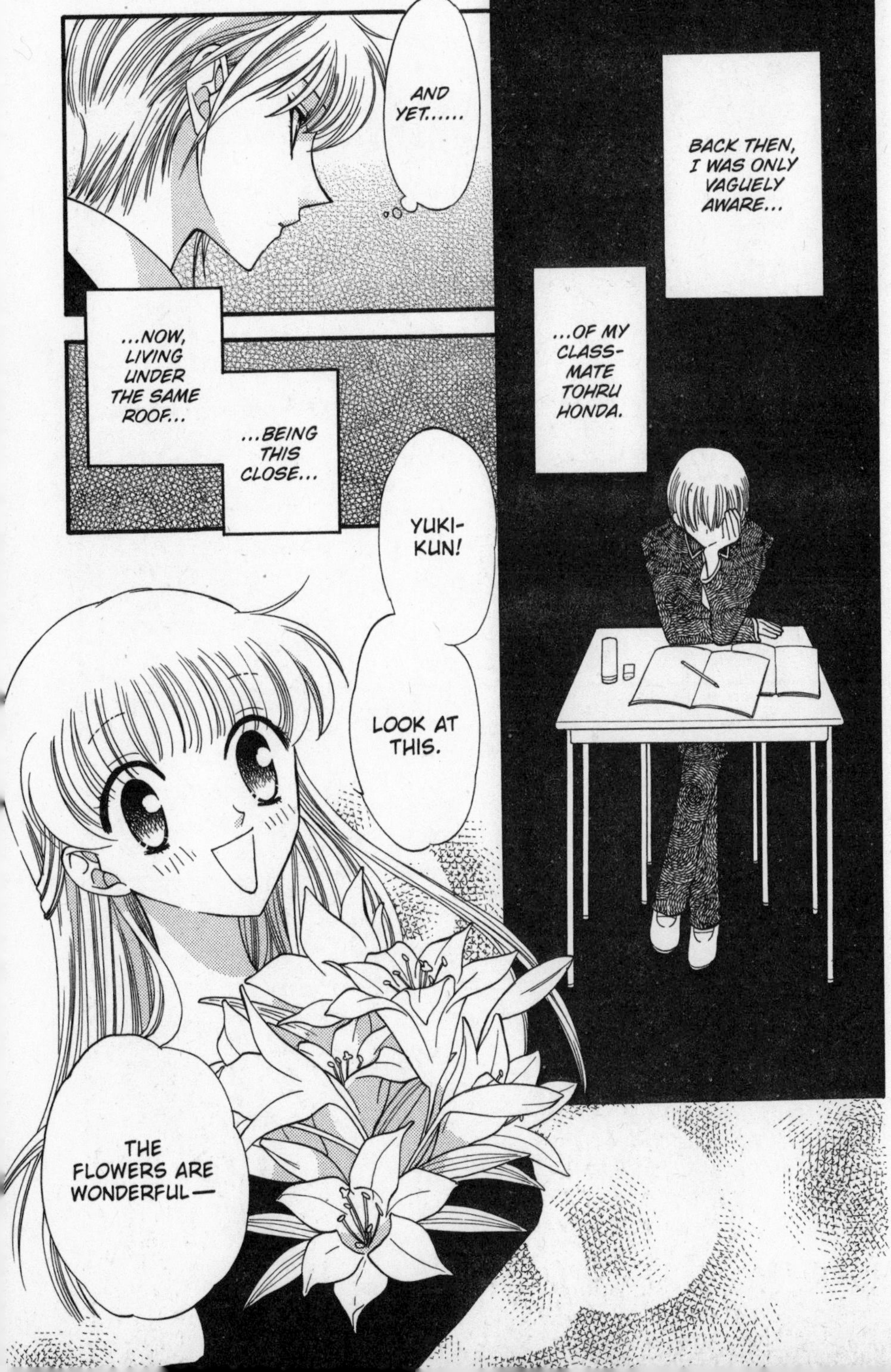
BACK THEN, I WAS ONLY VAGUELY AWARE...
...OF MY CLASS-MATE TOHRU HONDA.
AND YET......
...NOW, LIVING UNDER THE SAME ROOF...
...BEING THIS CLOSE...
YUKI-KUN!
LOOK AT THIS.
THE FLOWERS ARE WONDERFUL—

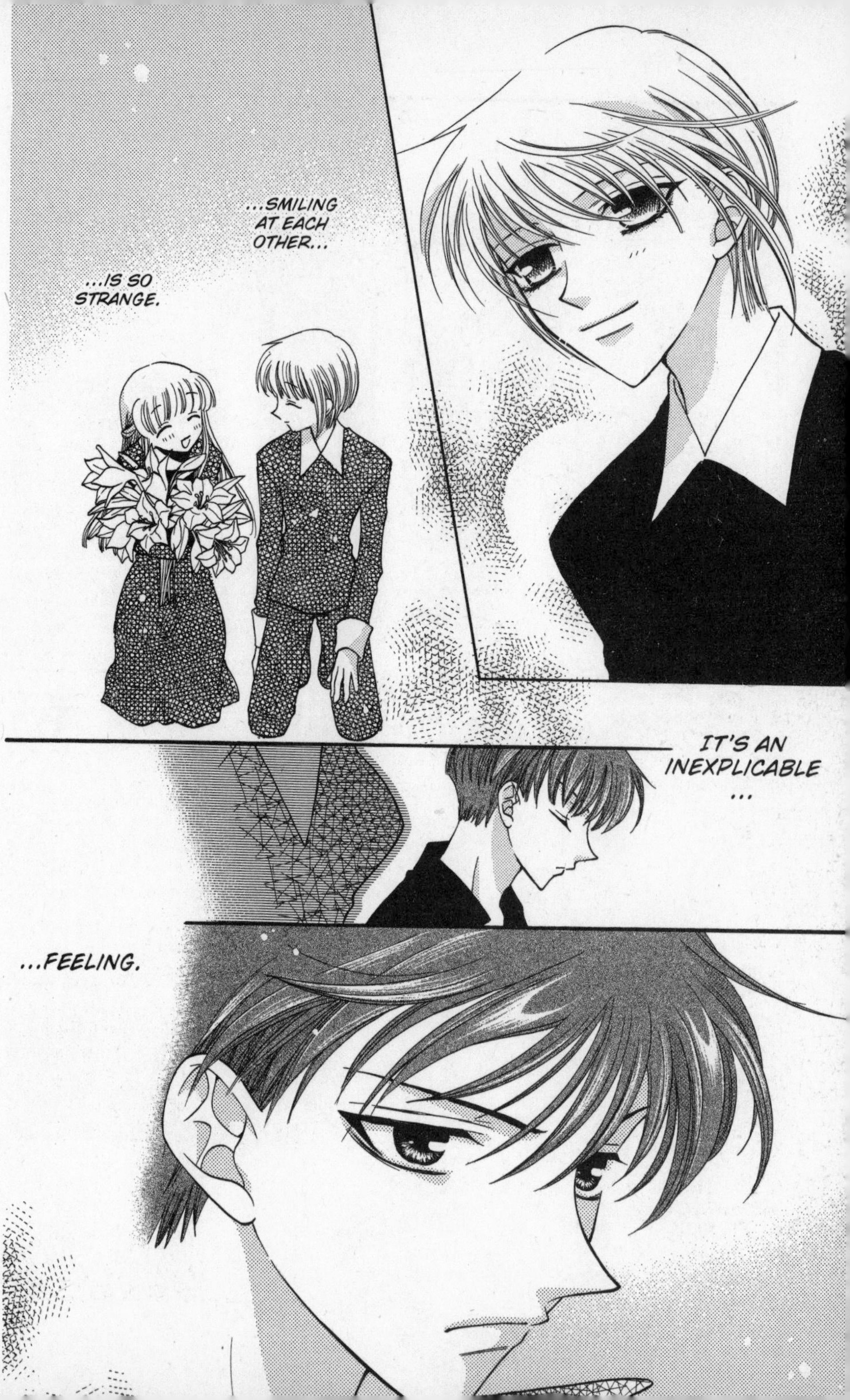
...SMILING AT EACH OTHER...
...IS SO STRANGE.
IT'S AN INEXPLICABLE ...
...FEELING.

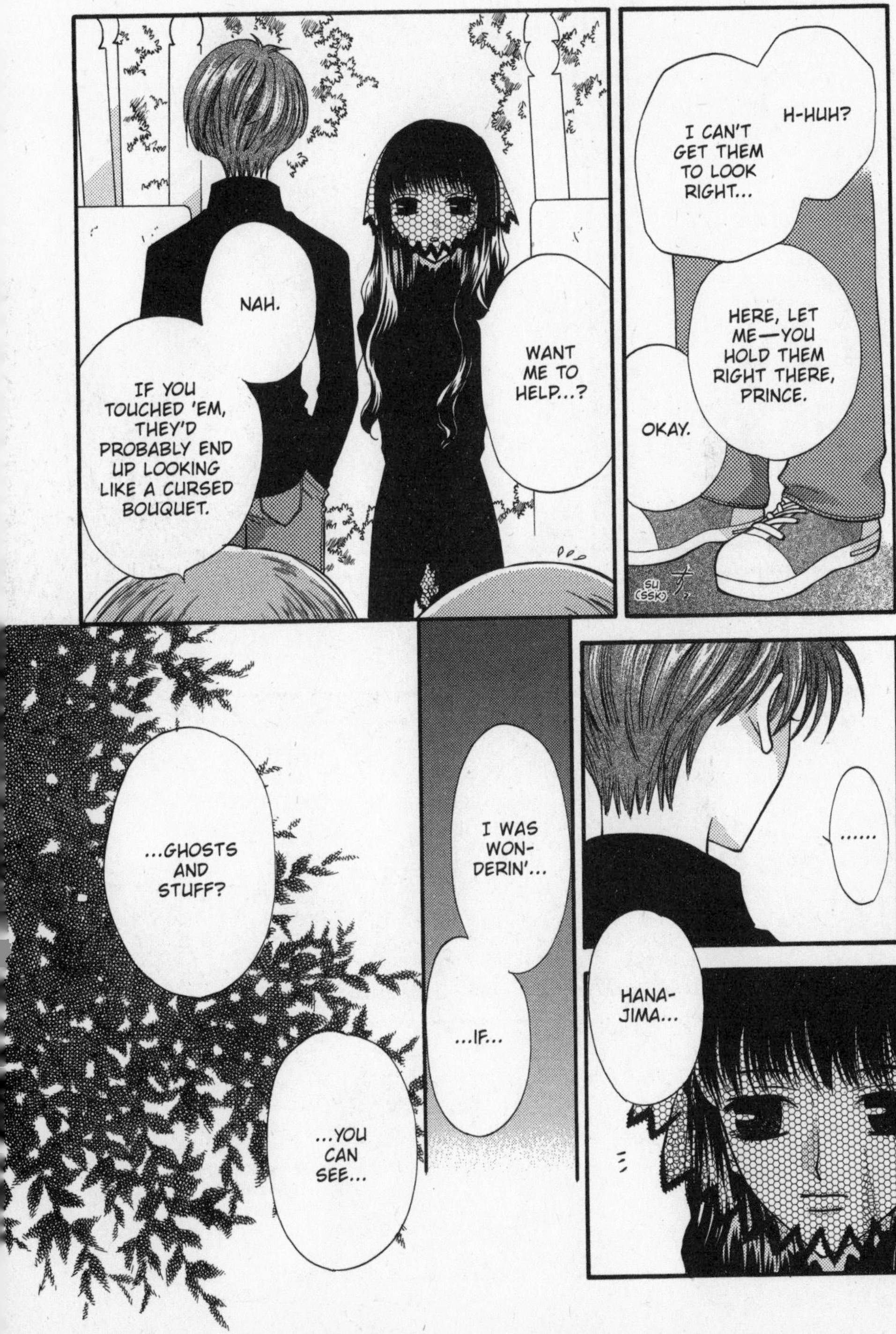
H-HUH?
I CAN'T GET THEM TO LOOK RIGHT...
HERE, LET ME—YOU HOLD THEM RIGHT THERE, PRINCE.
OKAY.
SU (SSK)
WANT ME TO HELP...?
NAH.
IF YOU TOUCHED 'EM, THEY'D PROBABLY END UP LOOKING LIKE A CURSED BOUQUET.
......
HANA-JIMA...
I WAS WON-DERIN'...
...IF...
...YOU CAN SEE...
...GHOSTS AND STUFF?

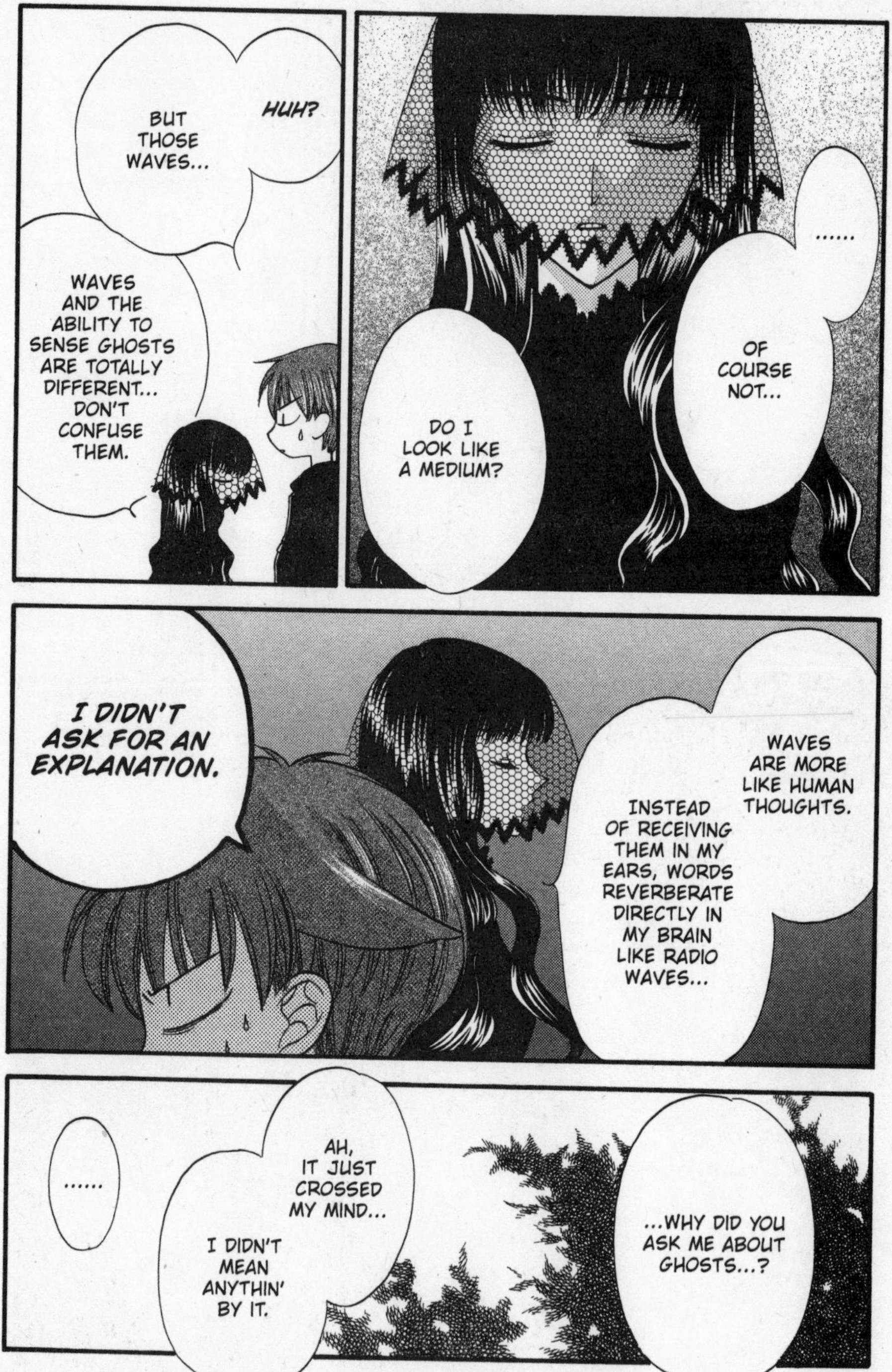
......
OF COURSE NOT...
DO I LOOK LIKE A MEDIUM?
HUH?
BUT THOSE WAVES...
WAVES AND THE ABILITY TO SENSE GHOSTS ARE TOTALLY DIFFERENT... DON'T CONFUSE THEM.
WAVES ARE MORE LIKE HUMAN THOUGHTS.
INSTEAD OF RECEIVING THEM IN MY EARS, WORDS REVERBERATE DIRECTLY IN MY BRAIN LIKE RADIO WAVES...
I DIDN'T ASK FOR AN EXPLANATION.
...WHY DID YOU ASK ME ABOUT GHOSTS...?
AH, IT JUST CROSSED MY MIND...
I DIDN'T MEAN ANYTHIN' BY IT.
......

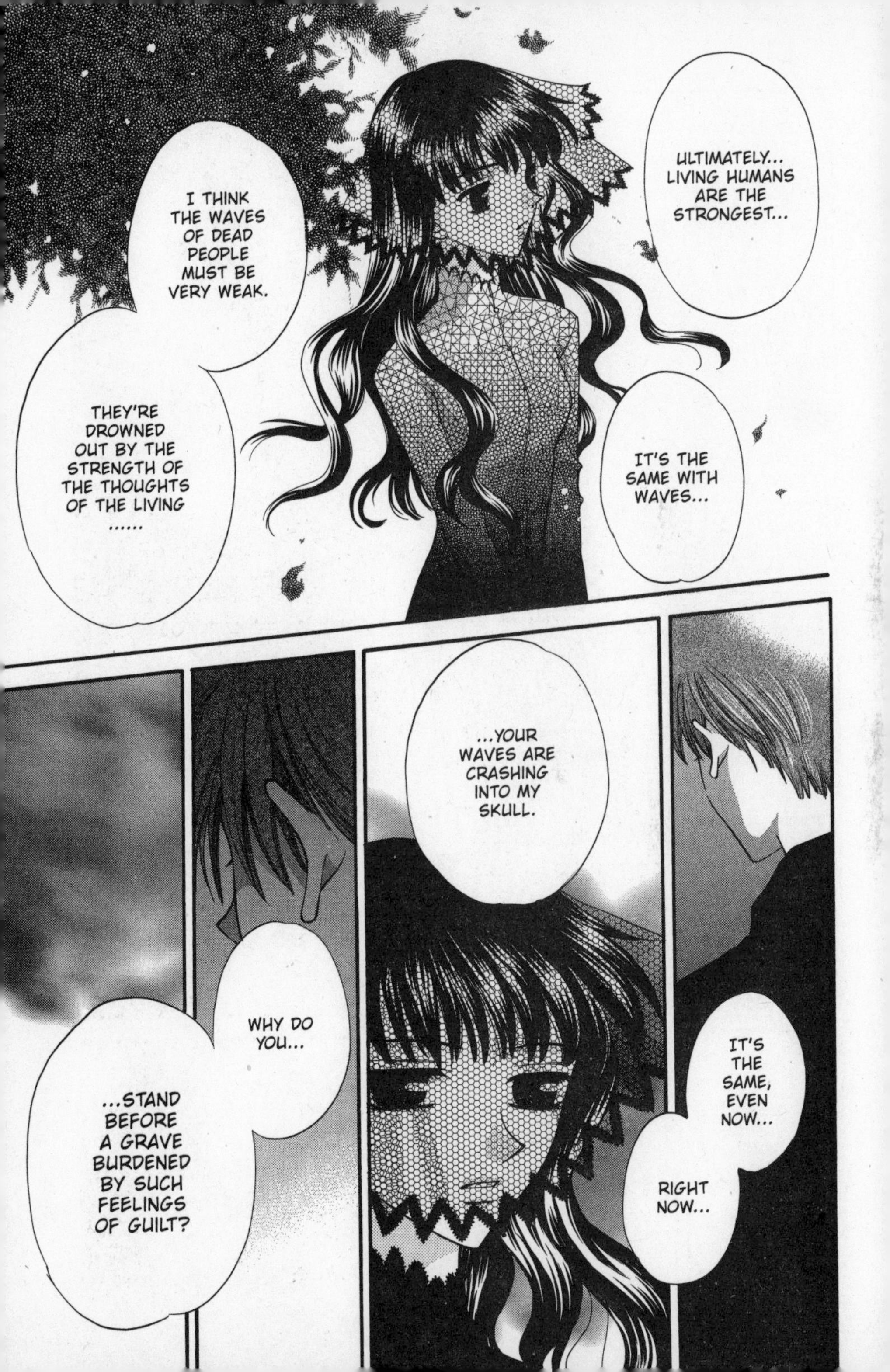
ULTIMATELY... LIVING HUMANS ARE THE STRONGEST...
IT'S THE SAME WITH WAVES...
I THINK THE WAVES OF DEAD PEOPLE MUST BE VERY WEAK.
THEY'RE DROWNED OUT BY THE STRENGTH OF THE THOUGHTS OF THE LIVING ......
...YOUR WAVES ARE CRASHING INTO MY SKULL.
IT'S THE SAME, EVEN NOW...
RIGHT NOW...
WHY DO YOU...
...STAND BEFORE A GRAVE BURDENED BY SUCH FEELINGS OF GUILT?

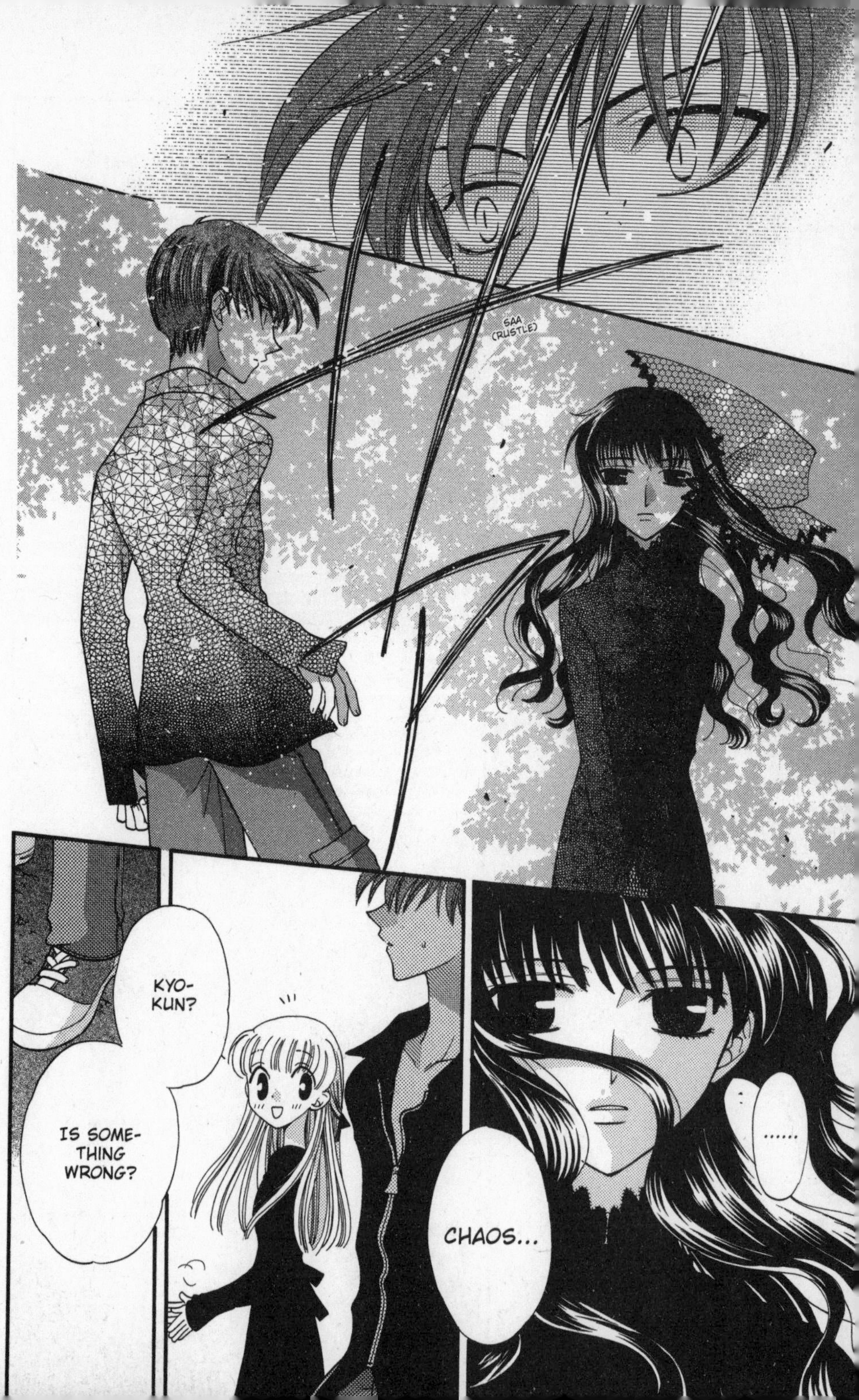
SAA (RUSTLE)
......
CHAOS...
KYO-KUN?
IS SOME-THING WRONG?

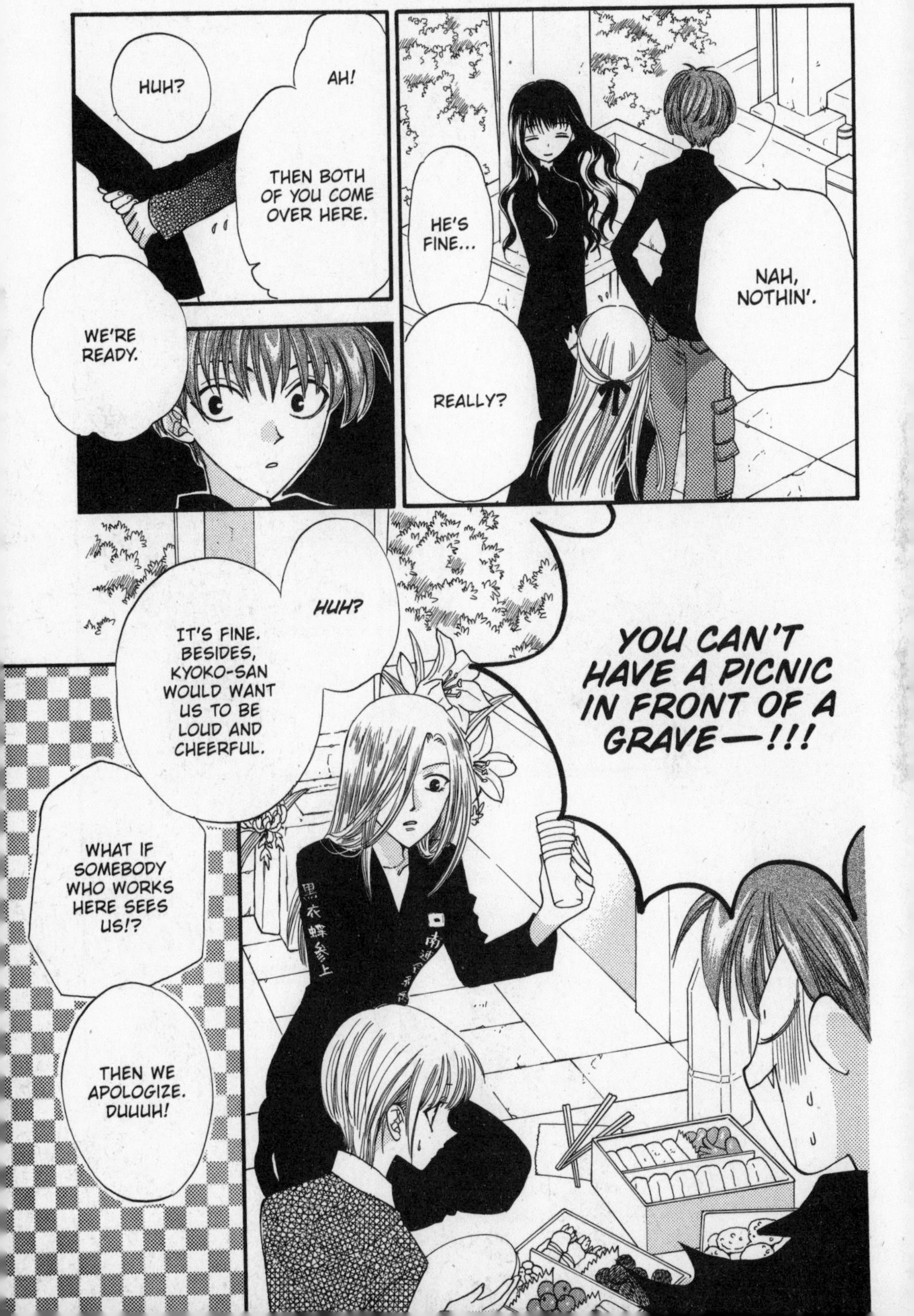
NAH, NOTHIN'.
HE'S FINE...
REALLY?
AH!
THEN BOTH OF YOU COME OVER HERE.
HUH?
WE'RE READY.
YOU CAN'T HAVE A PICNIC IN FRONT OF A GRAVE—!!!
HUH?
IT'S FINE. BESIDES, KYOKO-SAN WOULD WANT US TO BE LOUD AND CHEERFUL.
WHAT IF SOMEBODY WHO WORKS HERE SEES US!?
THEN WE APOLOGIZE. DUUUH!

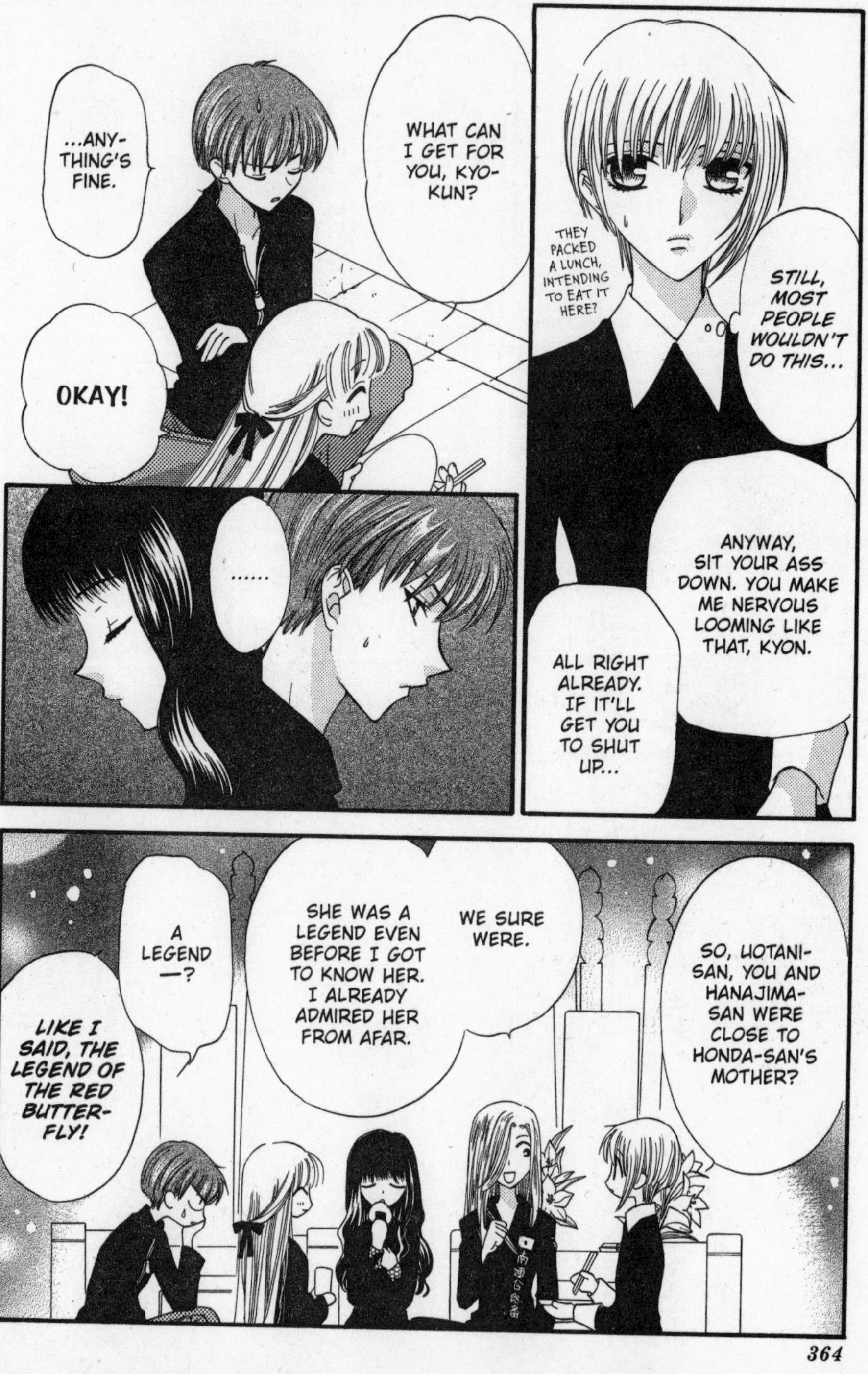
THEY PACKED A LUNCH, INTENDING TO EAT IT HERE?
STILL, MOST PEOPLE WOULDN'T DO THIS...
ANYWAY, SIT YOUR ASS DOWN. YOU MAKE ME NERVOUS LOOMING LIKE THAT, KYON.
ALL RIGHT ALREADY. IF IT'LL GET YOU TO SHUT UP...
WHAT CAN I GET FOR YOU, KYO-KUN?
...ANY-THING'S FINE.
OKAY!
......
SO, UOTANI-SAN, YOU AND HANAJIMA-SAN WERE CLOSE TO HONDA-SAN'S MOTHER?
WE SURE WERE.
SHE WAS A LEGEND EVEN BEFORE I GOT TO KNOW HER. I ALREADY ADMIRED HER FROM AFAR.
A LEGEND—?
LIKE I SAID, THE LEGEND OF THE RED BUTTER-FLY!

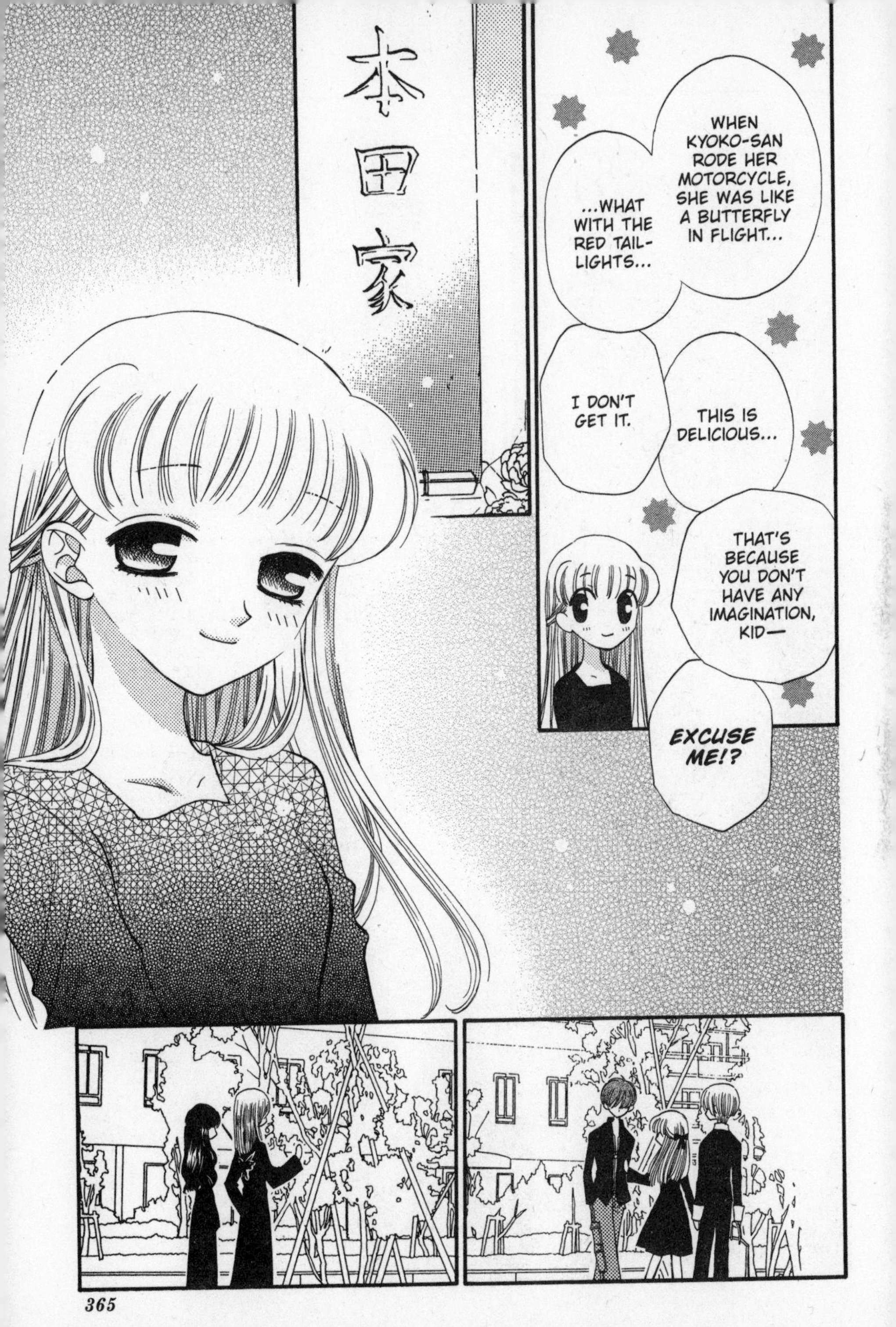

WHEN KYOKO-SAN RODE HER MOTORCYCLE, SHE WAS LIKE A BUTTERFLY IN FLIGHT...
...WHAT WITH THE RED TAIL-LIGHTS...
THIS IS DELICIOUS...
I DON'T GET IT.
THAT'S BECAUSE YOU DON'T HAVE ANY IMAGINATION, KID—
EXCUSE ME!?
本田家

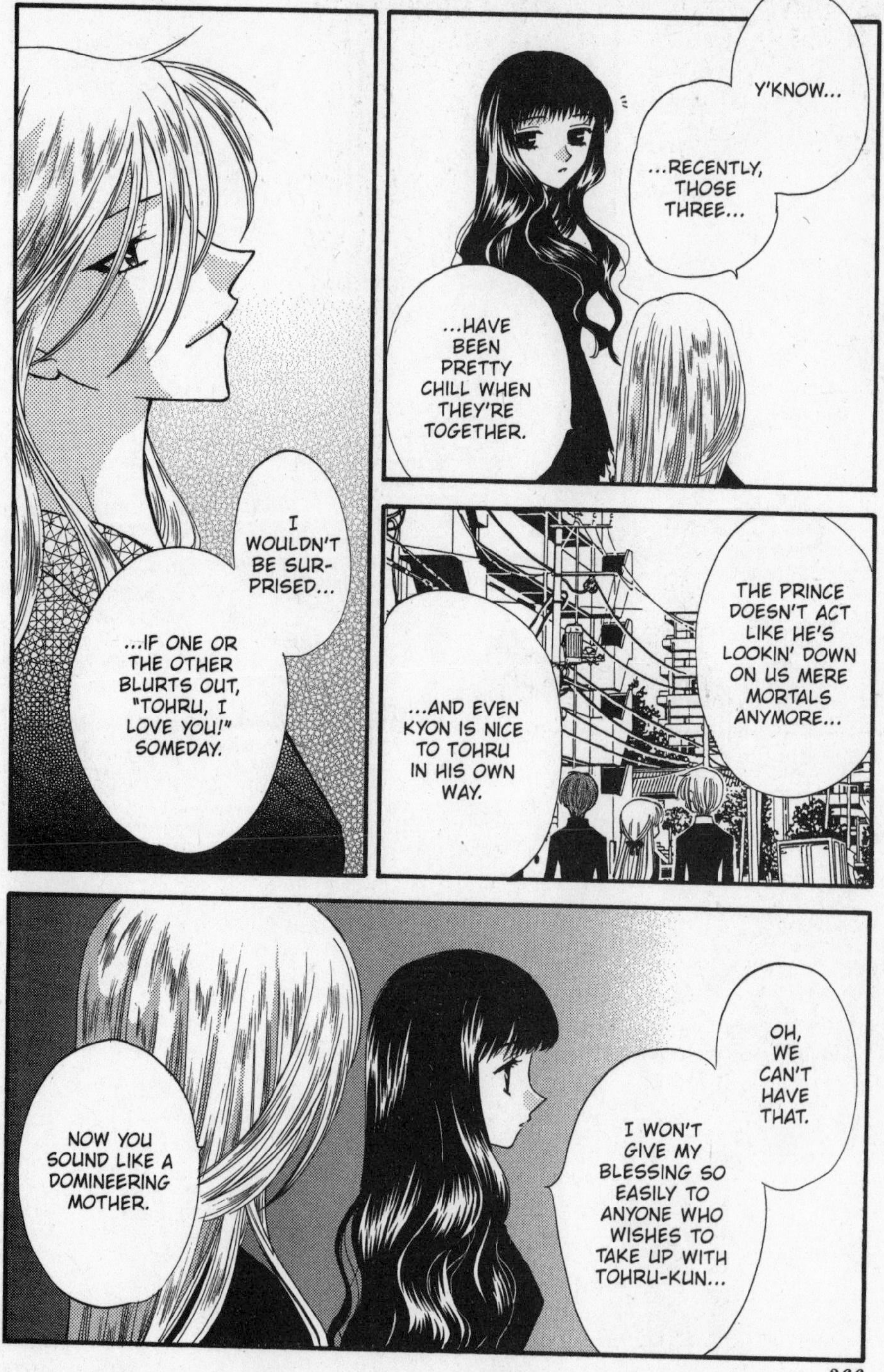
Y'KNOW...
...RECENTLY, THOSE THREE...
...HAVE BEEN PRETTY CHILL WHEN THEY'RE TOGETHER.
THE PRINCE DOESN'T ACT LIKE HE'S LOOKIN' DOWN ON US MERE MORTALS ANYMORE...
...AND EVEN KYON IS NICE TO TOHRU IN HIS OWN WAY.
I WOULDN'T BE SUR-PRISED...
...IF ONE OR THE OTHER BLURTS OUT, "TOHRU, I LOVE YOU!" SOMEDAY.
OH, WE CAN'T HAVE THAT.
I WON'T GIVE MY BLESSING SO EASILY TO ANYONE WHO WISHES TO TAKE UP WITH TOHRU-KUN...
NOW YOU SOUND LIKE A DOMINEERING MOTHER.

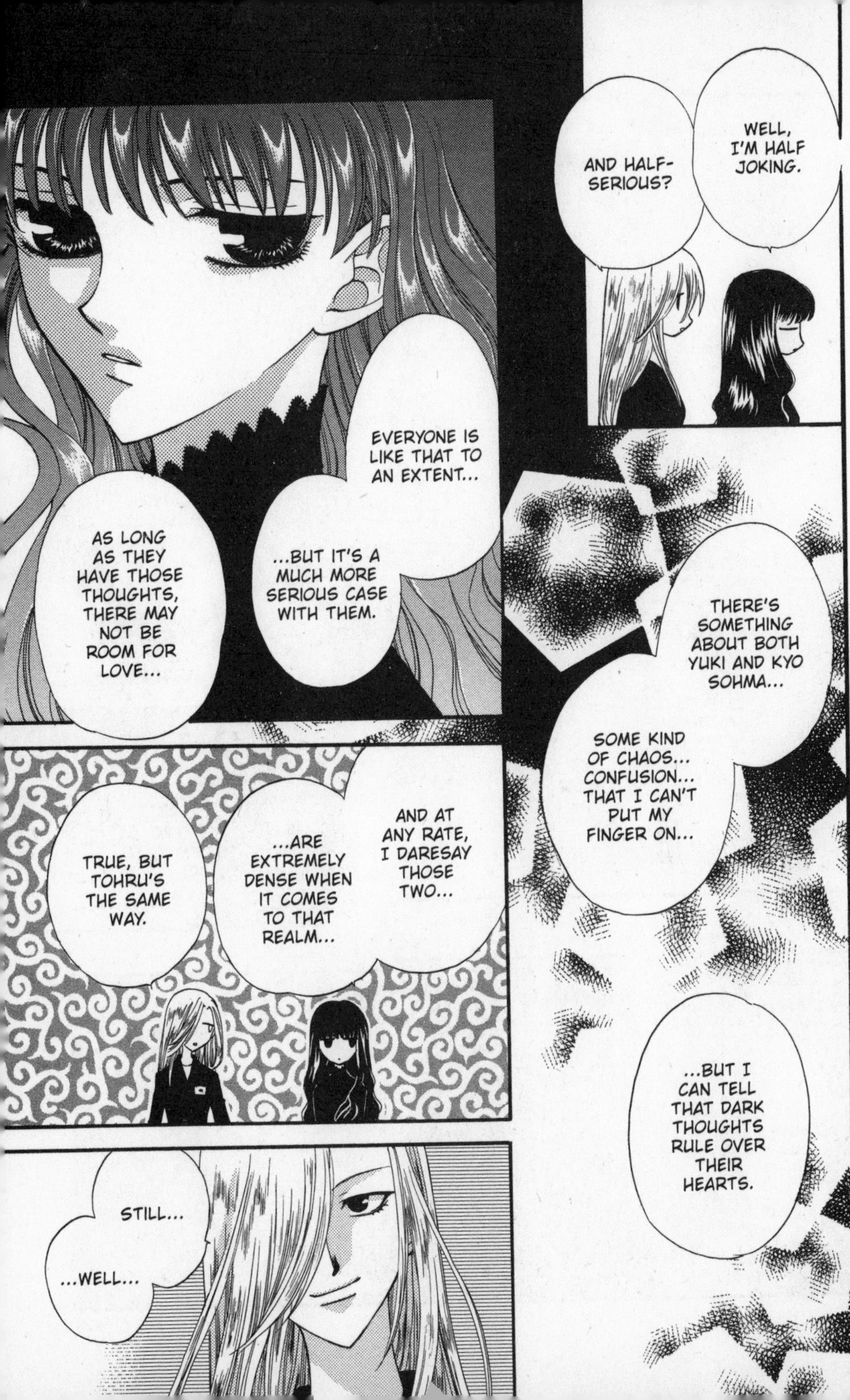
WELL, I'M HALF JOKING.
AND HALF-SERIOUS?
THERE'S SOMETHING ABOUT BOTH YUKI AND KYO SOHMA...
SOME KIND OF CHAOS... CONFUSION... THAT I CAN'T PUT MY FINGER ON...
...BUT I CAN TELL THAT DARK THOUGHTS RULE OVER THEIR HEARTS.
EVERYONE IS LIKE THAT TO AN EXTENT...
...BUT IT'S A MUCH MORE SERIOUS CASE WITH THEM.
AS LONG AS THEY HAVE THOSE THOUGHTS, THERE MAY NOT BE ROOM FOR LOVE...
AND AT ANY RATE, I DARESAY THOSE TWO...
...ARE EXTREMELY DENSE WHEN IT COMES TO THAT REALM...
TRUE, BUT TOHRU'S THE SAME WAY.
STILL...
...WELL...

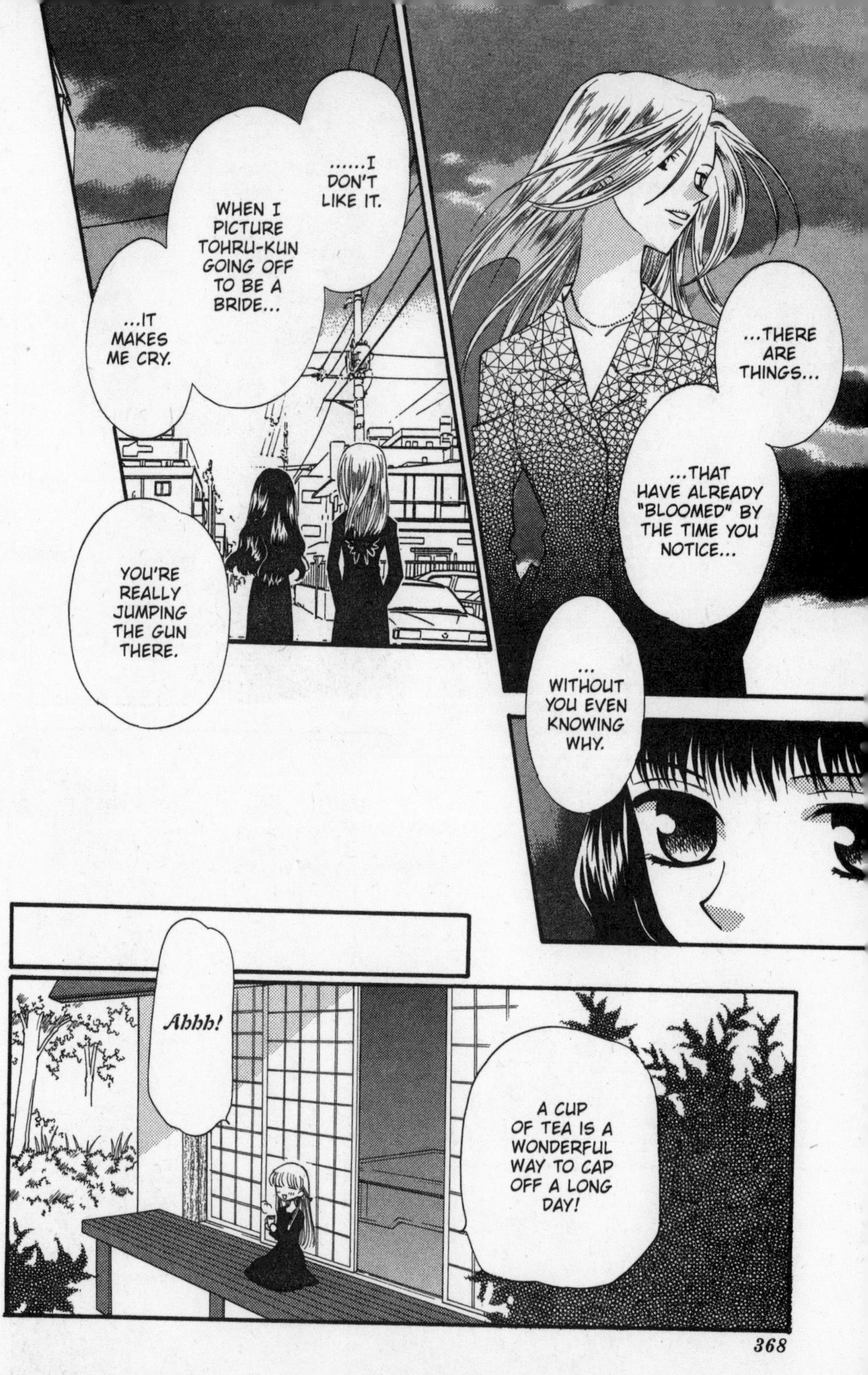
...THERE ARE THINGS...
...THAT HAVE ALREADY "BLOOMED" BY THE TIME YOU NOTICE...
...WITHOUT YOU EVEN KNOWING WHY.
......I DON'T LIKE IT.
WHEN I PICTURE TOHRU-KUN GOING OFF TO BE A BRIDE...
...IT MAKES ME CRY.
YOU'RE REALLY JUMPING THE GUN THERE.
Ahhh!
A CUP OF TEA IS A WONDERFUL WAY TO CAP OFF A LONG DAY!

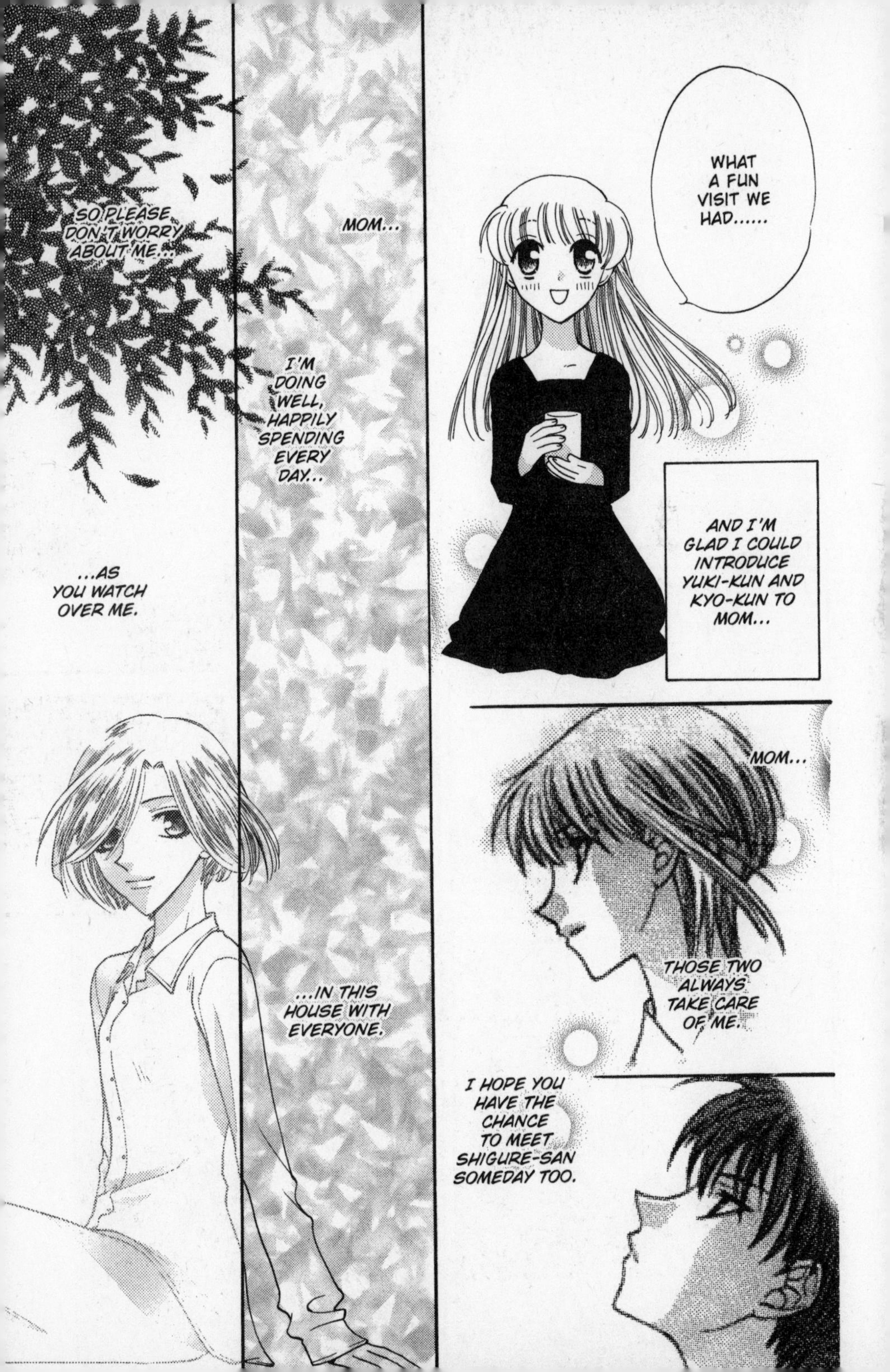
WHAT A FUN VISIT WE HAD......
AND I'M GLAD I COULD INTRODUCE YUKI-KUN AND KYO-KUN TO MOM...
MOM...
THOSE TWO ALWAYS TAKE CARE OF ME.
I HOPE YOU HAVE THE CHANCE TO MEET SHIGURE-SAN SOMEDAY TOO.
MOM...
I'M DOING WELL, HAPPILY SPENDING EVERY DAY...
...IN THIS HOUSE WITH EVERYONE.
SO PLEASE DON'T WORRY ABOUT ME...
...AS YOU WATCH OVER ME.

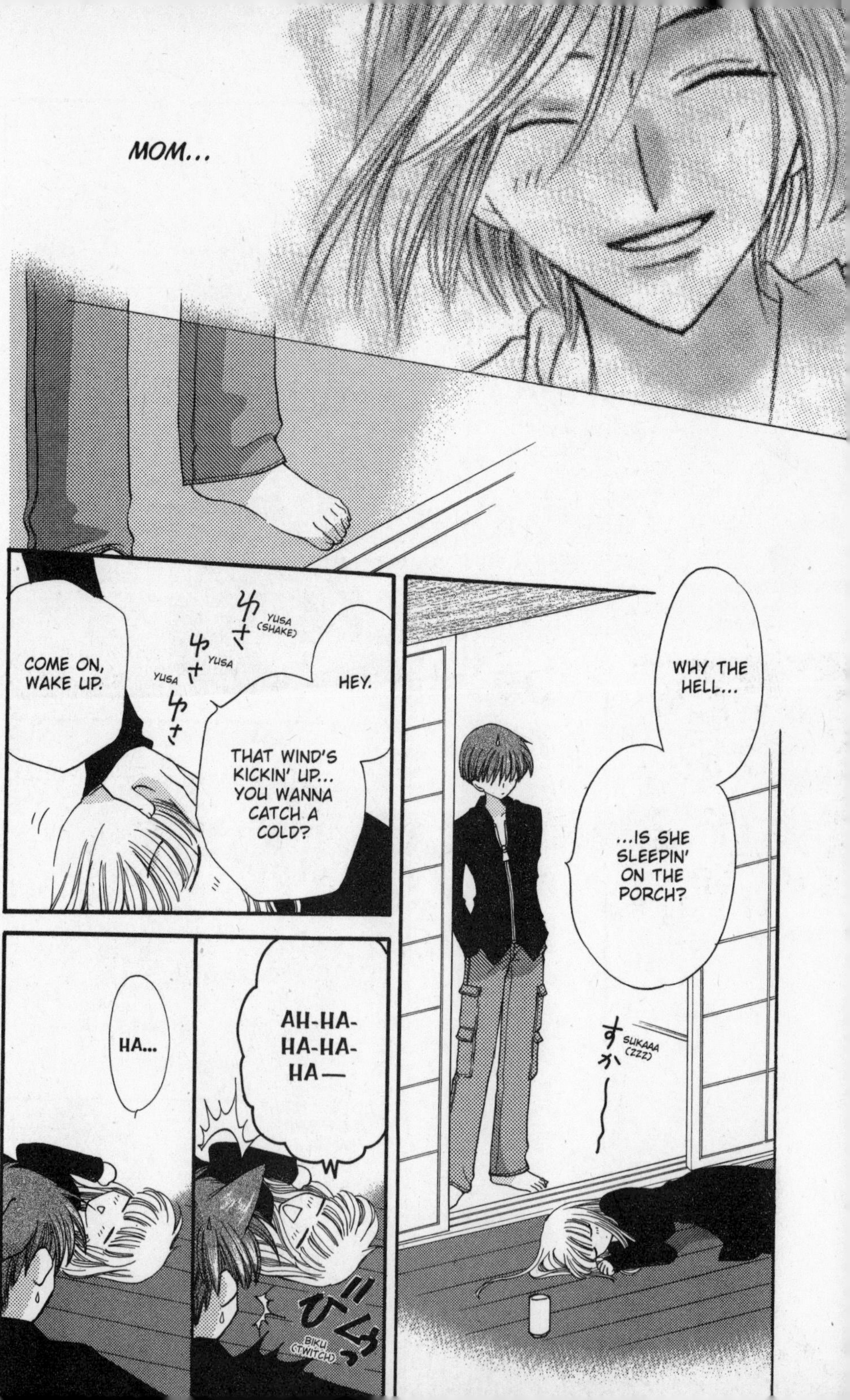
MOM...
WHY THE HELL...
...IS SHE SLEEPIN' ON THE PORCH?
すか～ SUKAAA (ZZZ)
HEY.
THAT WIND'S KICKIN' UP... YOU WANNA CATCH A COLD?
ゆさ YUSA (SHAKE)
ゆさ YUSA
ゆさ YUSA
COME ON, WAKE UP.
AH-HA-HA-HA-HA—
びくっ BIKU (TWITCH)
HA...

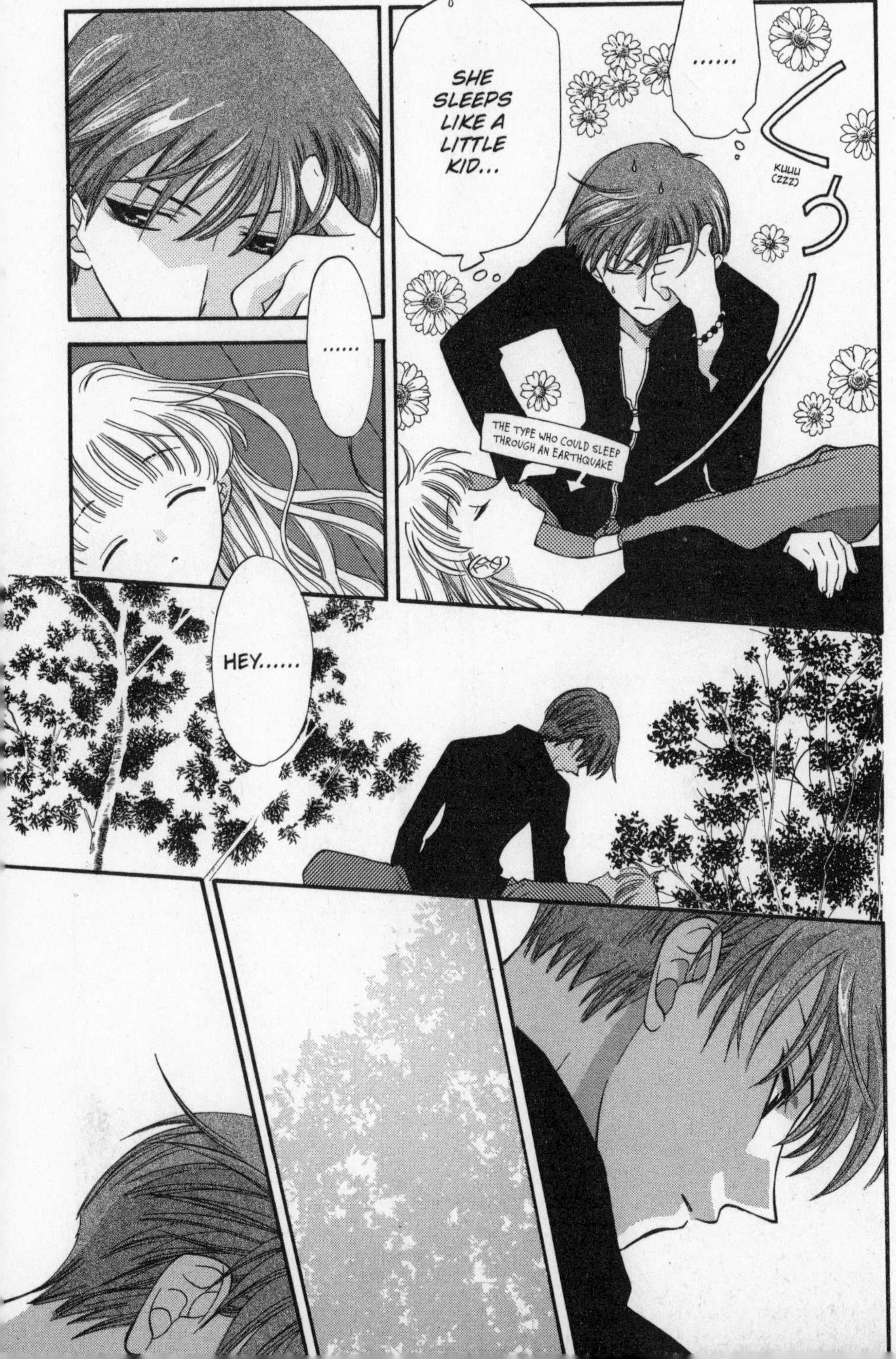
......
KUUU (ZZZ)
SHE SLEEPS LIKE A LITTLE KID...
THE TYPE WHO COULD SLEEP THROUGH AN EARTHQUAKE
......
HEY......

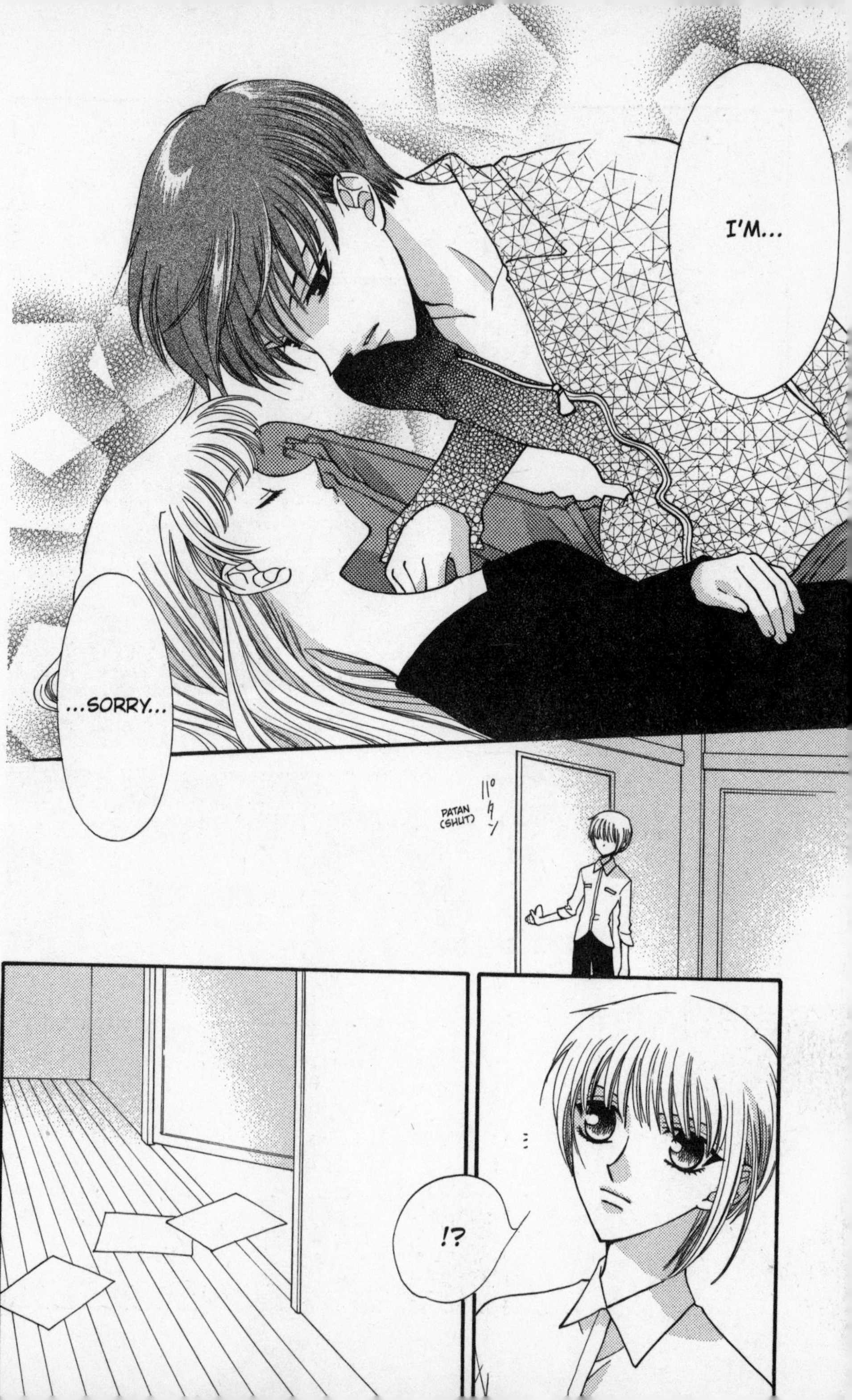
I'M...
...SORRY...
パタン
PATAN (SHUT)
!?

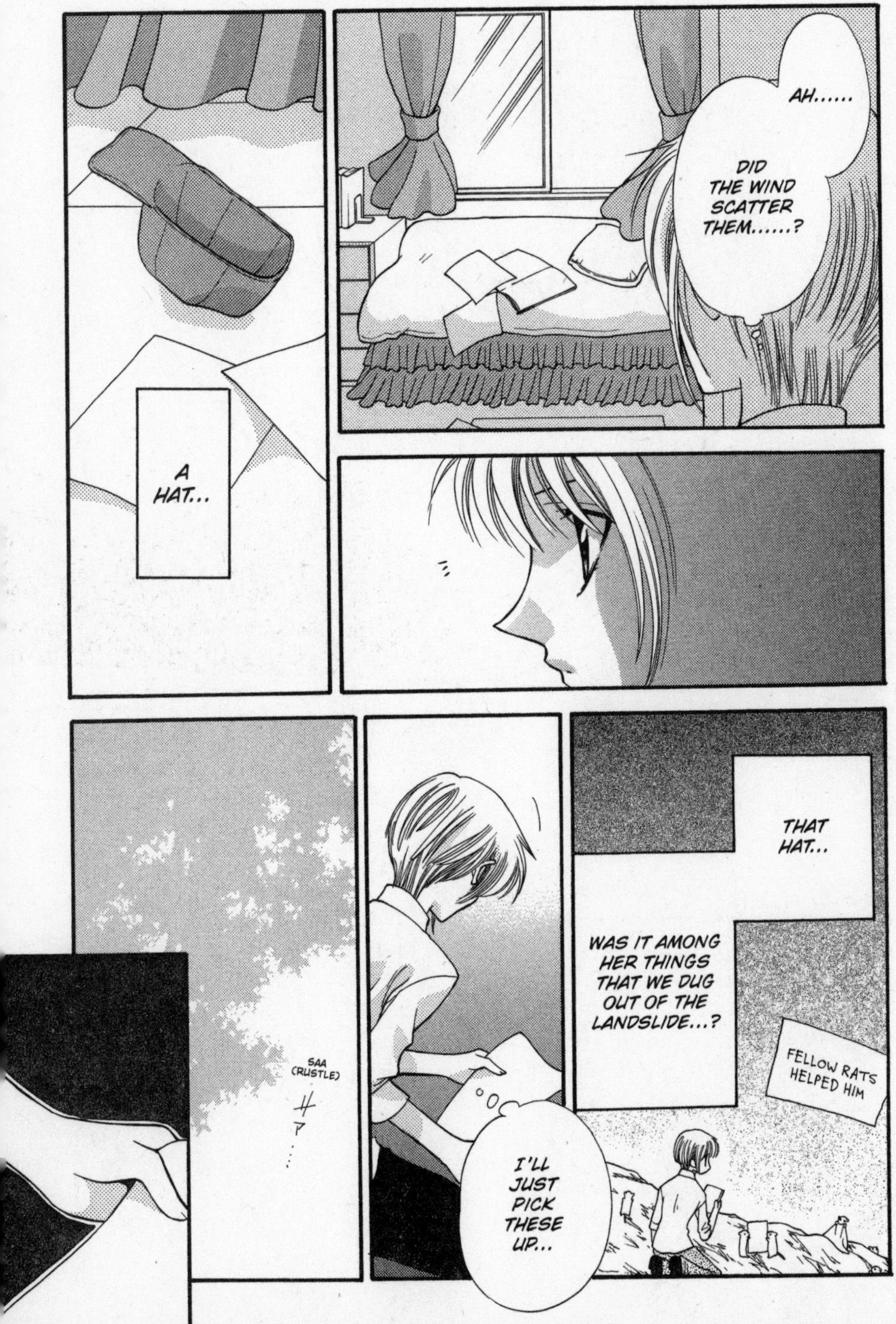
AH......
DID THE WIND SCATTER THEM......?
A HAT...
THAT HAT...
WAS IT AMONG HER THINGS THAT WE DUG OUT OF THE LANDSLIDE...?
FELLOW RATS HELPED HIM
I'LL JUST PICK THESE UP...
SAA (RUSTLE)
サァ…

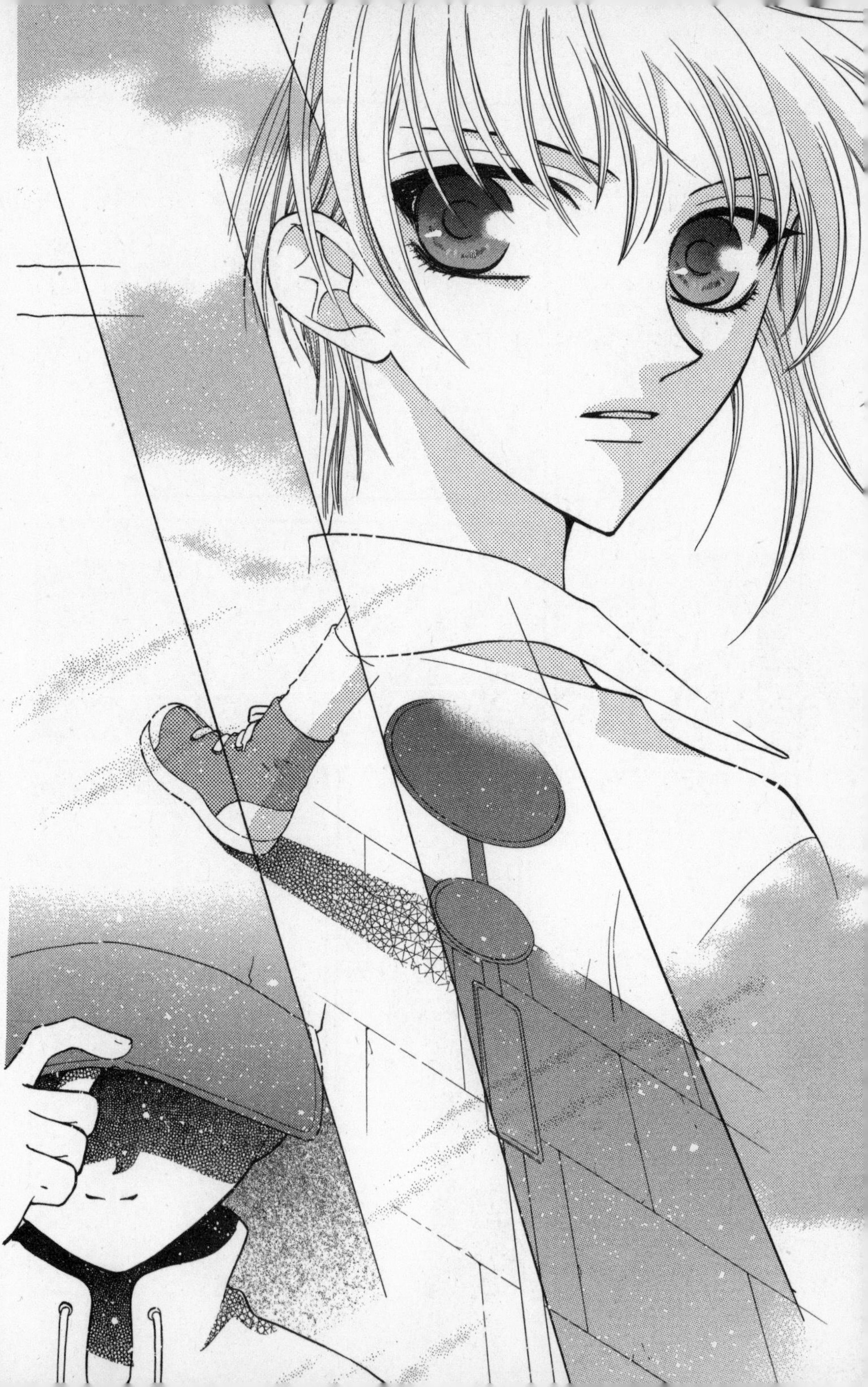

TRANSLATION NOTES

COMMON HONORIFICS

no honorific: Indicates familiarity or closeness; if used without permission or reason, addressing someone in this manner would constitute an insult.

-san: The Japanese equivalent of Mr./Mrs./Miss. If a situation calls for politeness, this is the fail-safe honorific.

-sama: Conveys great respect; may also indicate that the social status of the speaker is lower than that of the addressee.

-kun: Used most often when referring to boys, this indicates affection or familiarity. Occasionally used by older men among their peers, but it may also be used by anyone referring to a person of lower standing.

-chan: An affectionate honorific indicating familiarity used mostly in reference to girls; also used in reference to cute persons or animals of either gender.

-senpai: A suffix used to address upperclassmen or more experienced coworkers.

-kouhai: A suffix used to address underclassmen or less experienced coworkers.

-sensei: A respectful term for teachers, artists, or high-level professionals.

Page 70

Shoe lockers: Japanese students typically have a separate pair of shoes that they wear inside the school building, and these lockers are used to store their "outside" shoes. In manga, they are often multipurpose, used for passing notes, love letters, and Valentine's Day candy.

Page 139

After-test break: In Japan, this equivalent of spring break (usually about ten days) follows final exams, and then the new school year starts afterward.

Page 139

Vati: This is the German word for "father," used by Momiji here. He also uses *mutti*, German for "mother," later in the volume.

Page 142

White Day: In general, only females give chocolate to males on Valentine's Day in Japan, so March 14th, White Day, is the chance for boys and men to reciprocate by giving candy, white chocolate, or another gift to the initial givers.

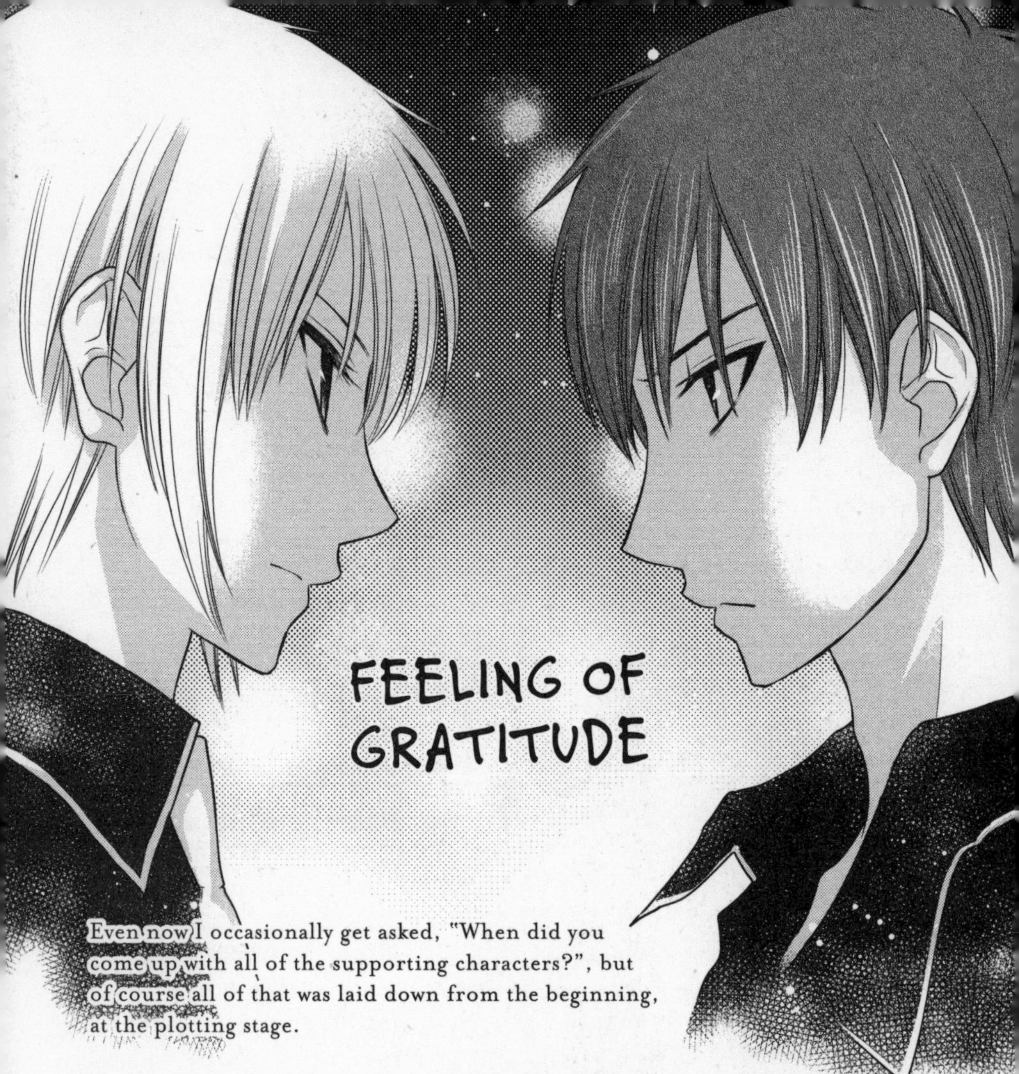

FEELING OF GRATITUDE

Even now I occasionally get asked, "When did you come up with all of the supporting characters?", but of course all of that was laid down from the beginning, at the plotting stage.

If you haven't decided beforehand the way things will go, you won't be able to move forward with the story. In fact, I don't think you would be able to create characters that way. Goals and objectives are part of the direction of the story, but more than that, it's about who likes and dislikes who. Who do the characters love the most? Who do they hate? Who do they treasure? In my works, at the end of the day, those things are the characters' goals and objectives, as well as their fundamental reason to live. Otherwise, I think my work would lack a certain meaning, for better or worse. That's what I think.

...I'm also often told, "The love you depict is heavy," but I'm aware of this. (LOL)

高屋奈月。

NATSUKI TAKAYA

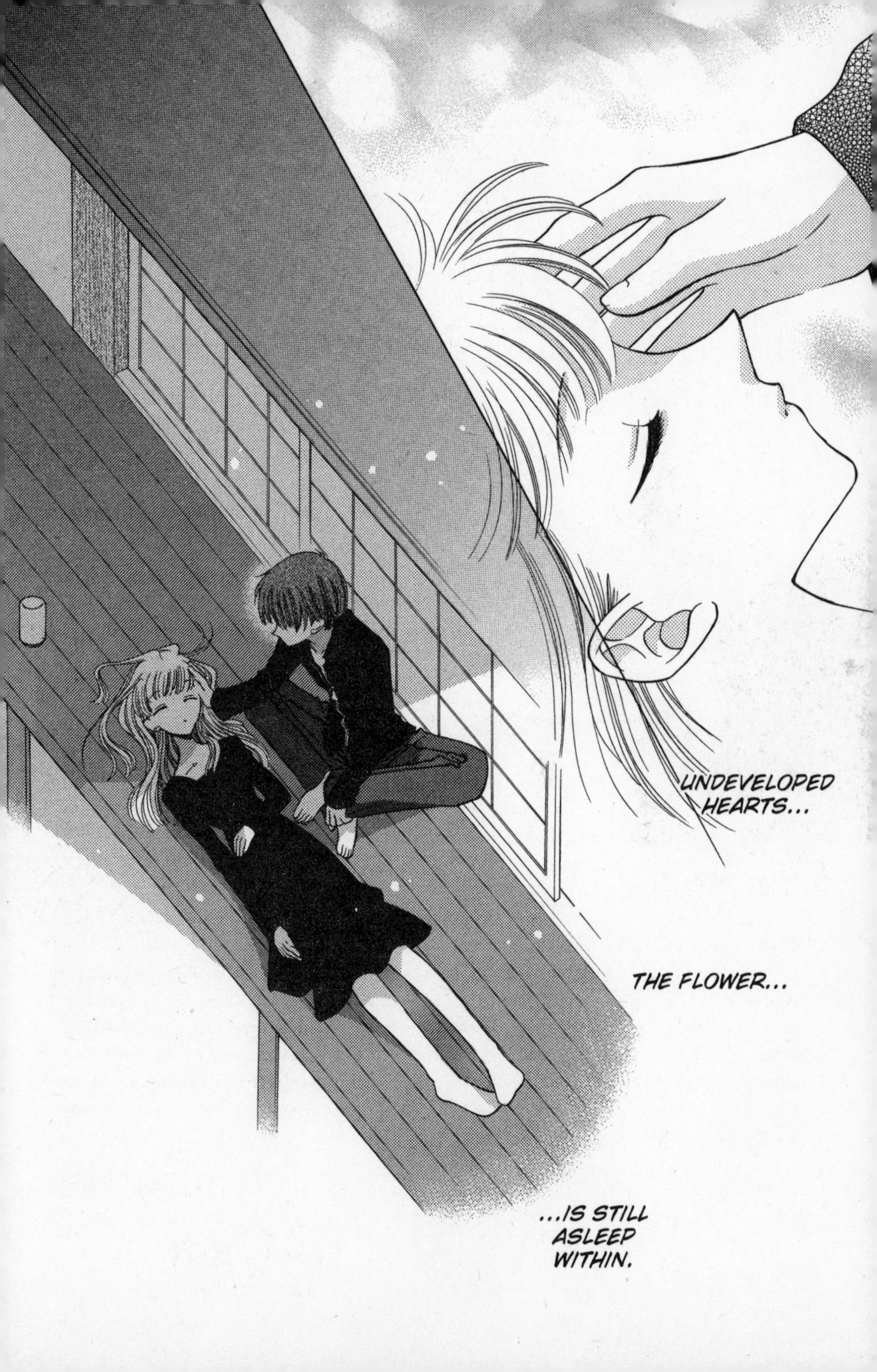
UNDEVELOPED HEARTS...
THE FLOWER...
...IS STILL ASLEEP WITHIN.

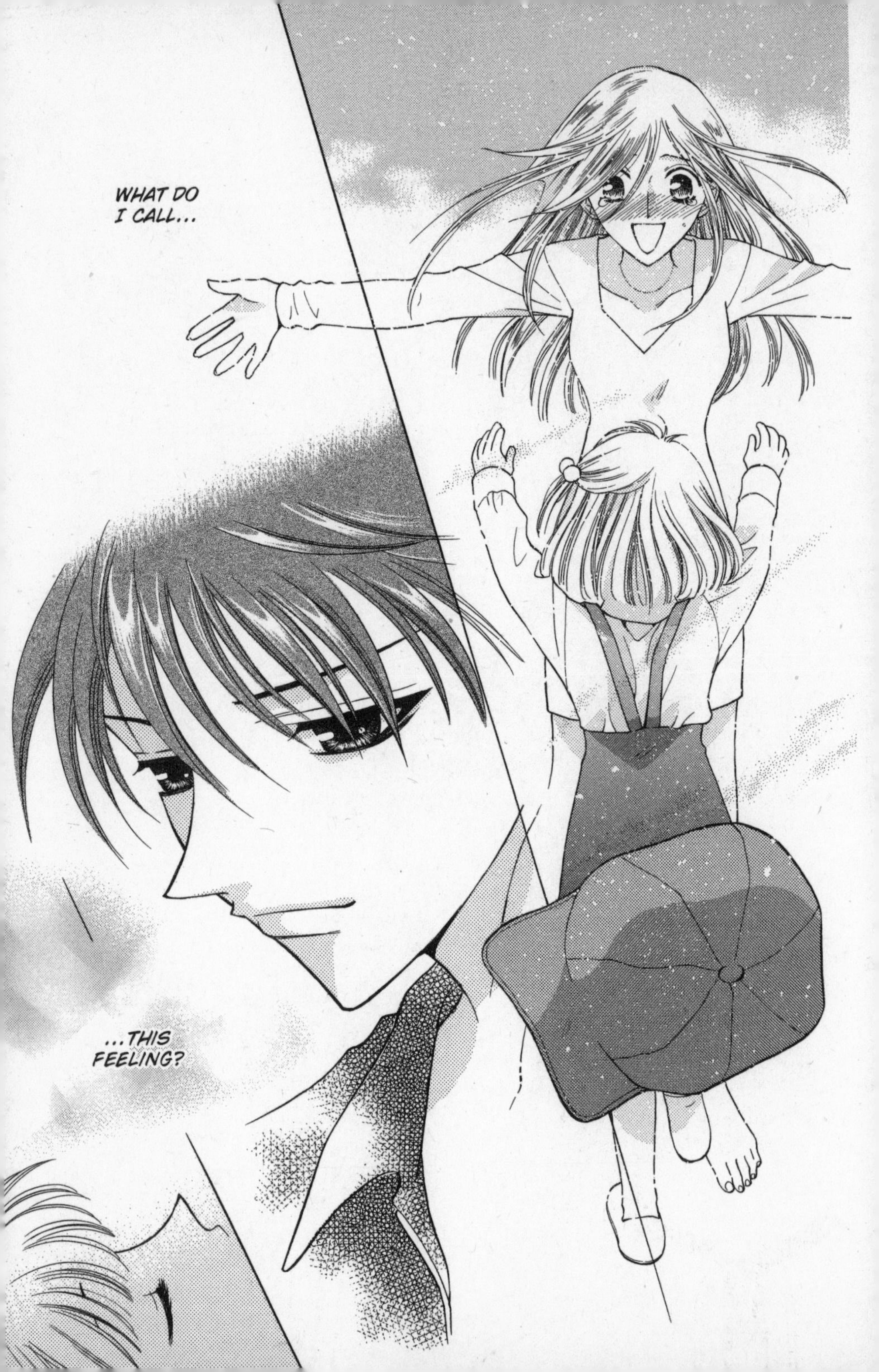
WHAT DO I CALL...
...THIS FEELING?

COLLECTOR'S EDITION

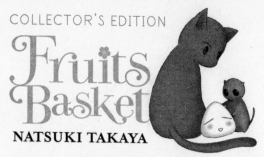

Fruits Basket

NATSUKI TAKAYA

Translation: Sheldon Drzka • Lettering: Lys Blakeslee

This book is a work of fiction. Names, characters, places, and incidents are the product of the author's imagination or are used fictitiously. Any resemblance to actual events, locales, or persons, living or dead, is coincidental.

Fruits Basket Collector's Edition, Vol. 2 by Natsuki Takaya
© Natsuki Takaya 2015
All rights reserved.
First published in Japan in 2015 by HAKUSENSHA, INC., Tokyo.
English language translation rights in U.S.A., Canada and U.K. arranged with
HAKUSENSHA, INC., Tokyo through Tuttle-Mori Agency, Inc., Tokyo.

English translation © 2016 by Yen Press, LLC

Yen Press
1290 Avenue of the Americas
New York, NY 10104

Visit us at yenpress.com
facebook.com/yenpress
twitter.com/yenpress
yenpress.tumblr.com
instagram.com/yenpress

First Yen Press Edition: June 2016

Yen Press is an imprint of Yen Press, LLC.
The Yen Press name and logo are trademarks of Yen Press, LLC.

The publisher is not responsible for websites (or their content) that are not owned by the publisher.

Library of Congress Control Number: 2016932692

ISBN: 978-0-316-36018-0

10 9 8 7 6 5 4

WOR

Printed in the United States of America

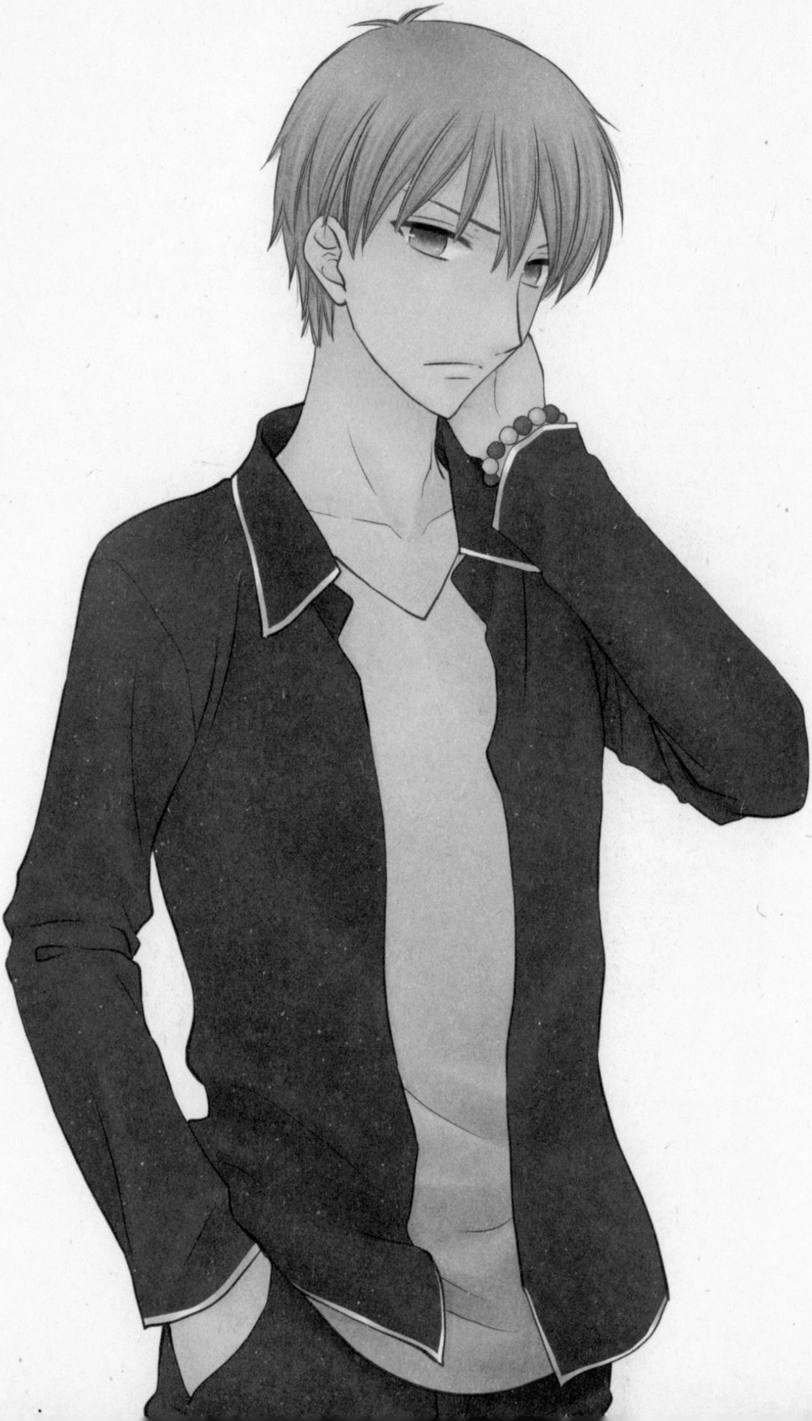

Page 349
Japanese cemetery: Almost all Japanese burials are cremations, and a family's ashes are typically housed together at a single stone monument with a place for offerings in front.

Fruits Basket

clothing. Accessories are often completely forbidden, and hair color, hairstyles, and even overall cleanliness are closely monitored.

Page 264
Three Musketeers: The Japanese term Shigure uses when talking about himself, Hatori, and Ayame is the *mabudachi torio*, which translates to "a trio of close friends."

Page 269
Nii-san: "Big brother" in Japanese, this is a respectful form of address for an older brother or a young man who is older than the speaker.

Page 272
Gyoza: Found on menus across Japan, this very popular dumpling originated in China and consists of ground meat and vegetables wrapped in thin dough.

Page 290
Banding vs. bonding: In Japanese, Momiji mistakenly speaks the Japanese phrase *kyoudai mizuirazu* ("letting the brothers have private time") as *kyoudai mizuirezu* ("without putting water in the brothers"), and Haru corrects him.

Page 299
Character symbols: Throughout this series, dialogue is often attributed to the character speaking by a symbol in a given balloon. Identifying the Sohmas is easy enough (they are depicted as their respective Zodiac animals), but it may be a little more difficult when it comes to (a rice ball for obvious reasons) Tohru's school friends. Uotani is a fish—the first kanji in her surname means "fish"—while Hanajima is a flower—the first kanji in her surname means "flower."

Page 314
Roleplaying sex club: In Japanese, Saki mentions *imekura*, or "image club," a type of Japanese establishment in which the female employees are paid to engage in adult-oriented services while wearing a variety of costumes.

Page 323
Kannana Red Butterfly: Kannana-*dori* is the name of a road circling the center of the Tokyo metropolis.

Page 323
Dekotora: This style of vehicle decoration heavy on insignia and inscriptions comes from the words "decorated truck," but the style can also apply to cars, video games, and clothing.

Page 330
Ja: Used by Momiji, this is German for "yes."

Page 145
Class trip: In Japan, class trips can be a major undertaking; they often involve taking an entire grade of students to a distant location for three days or more. As a result, the financial burden on the student can be quite high.

Page 164
Mistress vs. hostess: In Japanese, Momiji uses *meshou*, an antiquated word for "female proprietor of a traditional Japanese inn." Yuki corrects him with the modern Japanese word, *okami*.

Page 172
Memorial portrait: Like many people in Japan with deceased loved ones, Tohru has a memorial portrait of her mother. These are usually kept in a small home altar in remembrance of the deceased. Tohru, however, takes her mother's framed photo wherever she goes.

Page 175
Ricchan-san: Unfailingly polite, Tohru even uses the honorific *-san* at the end of Ritsu's nickname, creating the unusual "*-chan-san*" combination.

Page 188
Ich bin fünfzehn jahre alt!: Momiji is saying, "I'm fifteen years old!" in German.

Page 196
Face mask: Like Uo with her hay fever here, it is quite commonplace in Japan and other countries in Asia to wear a face mask in public when one is sick to prevent the spread of germs. Coincidentally, the face mask can also be considered a staple of a stereotypical Japanese girl gang member's uniform.

Page 198
Norika Fujiwara: Fujiwara is a beauty queen, model, and actress, born in 1971 and especially popular throughout the 1990s and 2000s.

Page 198
Blood type: In Japan and other East Asian countries, blood types are considered a window to someone's personality, and compatibility between types often factors into relationships. Type Bs like Satomi Arimori are said to be passionate and creative.

Page 205
Hallo: The German word for "Hello."

Page 210
Dress code: Most Japanese schools have strict dress codes that extend beyond